TOWARD THE ABYSS

ISRAEL AND THE PALESTINIANS

Dr. Alon Ben-Meir

WESTPHALIA PRESS
An imprint of the Policy Studies Organization

Washington, DC

Also from Westphalia Press

TOWARD THE ABYSS

ISRAEL AND THE PALESTINIANS

Westphalia Press
An imprint of Policy Studies Organization
1527 New Hampshire Ave., NW
Washington, D.C. 20036
info@ipsonet.org

ISBN-13: 978-1-63391-165-9
ISBN-10: 1633911659

Cover design by Taillefer Long at Illuminated Stories:
www.illuminatedstories.com

Daniel Gutierrez-Sandoval, Executive Director
PSO and Westphalia Press

Rahima Schwenkbeck, Director of Media and Marketing
PSO and Westphalia Press

Updated material and comments on this edition
can be found at the Westphalia Press website:
www.westphaliapress.org

CONTENTS

SETTLEMENTS AND OCCUPATION

REFUGEES

ISRAELI POLITICS

PSYCHOLOGICAL IMPEDIMENTS 557

CONCLUSION 603

APPENDIX 609

ACKNOWLEDGMENTS

This book represents nearly five years of tireless efforts to make sense of the increasingly intractable Israeli-Palestinian conflict. Although I have little to show for these efforts, I do not believe for a single moment that the time I spent was all in vain. I, like many others who are concerned about Israel's and the Palestinians' future, must never give up because if we do, only the enemies of peace will win.

I am grateful to my staff, especially Chris Wilson, whose dedication, resourcefulness, and superb research skills were of immense help, and to Kim Hurley, whose devotion to my work is surpassed only by her talent as an editor and coordinator.

I also want to thank my son, Sam Ben-Meir, whose nuanced contributions were invaluable. Finally, I am ever more grateful to my wife Deanna, who not only put up with me but supported my work every step of the way with passion and extraordinary care.

I want to particularly extend my deepest sense of gratitude to my dear friend Paul Rich, President of the Policy Studies Organization, who has always embraced my work with enthusiasm; to Daniel Gutierrez-Sandoval, Executive Director of the Policy Studies Organization, who facilitated the process; and to Rahima Schwenkbeck, Director of Media and Marketing at Westphalia Press, who was relentless in keeping the process moving on time.

Alon Ben-Meir

INTRODUCTION

As one who has spent much of his adult life observing, analyzing, and criticizing the Israeli-Palestinian conflict and advocating certain ideas to end it, I have often found myself at a loss—but not once have I given up in despair. Many of my friends and detractors have called me the ultimate optimist, but it is optimism that has helped me weather the storm and nurtured my perseverance and hope. Although every chapter in the history of the conflict is littered with blood, fear, and uncertainty, the reality of coexistence remains unshakable as if it were ordained by a higher authority, beyond the grasp of mortals.

The question for me, then, was not whether the two sides can coexist, but only the nature of that coexistence. In fact, both sides accept this stark reality, knowing that neither can dislodge the other, short of a self-inflicted catastrophe. Indeed, the conflict is about the leverage that either can exercise over the other and how that might translate territorially while still living in peace and security.

Surely there are extremists on both sides who seek to have it all and wish to subordinate the other to their whims and dictates. This position, however, is not attainable because it requires voluntary or forceful submission, either of which is unlikely because of historic and religious reasons, as well as their unmitigated national aspiration to be free and independent. The political leaders on both sides who continue to attempt to achieve this elusive goal of having it all have over time come to realize the impossibility of their blind ambition, as the whole world stands united against their wanton designs.

Every conflicting issue, including secure borders, the future of Jerusalem, the refugee problem, and the fate of the settlements, can and will be resolved because ultimately the people and only the people can determine their own destiny. A consistent majority of Israelis and Palestinians hope for and seek an end to the conflict; they have reached the point of exhaustion and wish to live a normal life with dignity.

This is the source—the people—that inspires me and nurtures my hope that the day will come when the people will rise—and rise they will—and no wicked leader can stand in the way of the mighty surge of the people.

This book is a collection of essays reflecting on the development of events between Israel and the Palestinians as they occurred. It is a journey in time that will hopefully allow the reader to experience the ups and downs of this endemic conflict and absorb the events as they unfolded along the long and winding road.

The time will come when Israelis and Palestinians sit together and listen with compassion and empathy to each other's concerns, fears, and grievances, and they will also listen to each other's hopes, dreams, and aspirations for the future.

In the end, both sides will emerge triumphant, because ultimately it is the human spirit that allows us to dream the impossible dream and still live to see it.

NATIONAL IDENTITY

ESCAPING THE ISRAEL GHETTO

JULY 17, 2011

While Prime Minister Benjamin Netanyahu insists that the Palestinians recognize the State of Israel as a Jewish state, his own policies are encouraging a mass exodus of Jewish Israelis from the country. Today, the notion of a Jewish refuge in the land of Israel is greatly at risk. Much has been made of what former Prime Minister Ehud Olmert once called a "demographic time bomb," with the Palestinian birthrate steadily increasing the number of Palestinians living between the Jordan River and the Mediterranean Sea, which will exceed that of Israelis. Yet Palestinian demographics aside, more Israelis are living abroad than ever, and many Israeli residents are eager to join them.

The lack of visionary leadership in Israel today has served to entrench the notion that the future of the state is at risk, that the conflict will only continue and intensify, and that opportunities for a prosperous, secure livelihood are better to be sought elsewhere. Netanyahu's Israel is one that is increasingly beholden to extremist religious and intolerant voices, exacerbating the outlook for the future. As a result, Israel is looking more like its avowed enemy, Iran, than its ally with whom it claims to have shared values, the United States. In effect, life in Netanyahu's "Jewish state" amounts to a new kind of Jewish ghetto, which many Israelis are increasingly opting to escape.

To be sure, calling Israel a "ghetto" may appear to be drastic

1

hyperbole, and of course in some ways it is. Today, however, Israel is in control of its own fate; it has the tools and resources to defend itself and the means to establish a nation-state with a bright future shaped by the vision of creative and bold leaders, empowered by a diverse, vibrant democracy. This is the vision of Israel that captured the imagination not only of world Jewry, but also of Israel's friends and allies across the world. The problem is that this vision that characterized Israel when it was created in 1948 is rapidly disappearing. Israel today is more isolated than ever before in the international arena, with friends and allies dwindling amid a growth of delegitimization efforts and rising anti-Semitism globally. The idea of creative and bold leadership that enhances diversity even within the Jewish community in Israel today has become, sadly, laughable. Rather than uphold democratic values in shaping a bright future for all its citizens, Israeli leaders are more apt to promote ideologically-charged legislation like the recently passed anti-boycott law and pending legislation to investigate the funding of left-wing NGOs. Meanwhile, despite repeated criticism of the prime minster by over a dozen ex-chiefs of the Shin Bet and Mossad, Netanyahu failed to advance a compelling peace initiative. He and his coalition partners remain obstinate and alarmingly clueless.

As a result, many Israelis feel trapped. They are caged in a small, increasingly isolated country, surrounded by enemies and led by leaders more interested in advancing warped ideologies than a secure and prosperous future for its citizenry. The economic conditions today may be bright, but the future looks uncertain and even bleak. It should be no surprise that many Israelis want out. The statistics are plentiful and worrying. Some already estimate the number of Israelis living abroad is nearly one million.[1] A study by the Menachem Begin Heritage Center in 2008 indicated more than 30 percent of Israelis had applied for a second passport or intended to do so, but some have put the number as high as 60 percent.[2] A 2007 study by Tel

---

1 Joseph Chamie and Barry Mirkin, "The Million Missing Israelis," *Foreign Policy*, July 5, 2011, http://mideastafrica.foreignpolicy.com/posts/2011/07/05/the_million_missing_israelis.

2 See Tobias Buck, "Israeli rush to secure dual nationality," *Financial Times*, June 5, 2011, http://www.ft.com/intl/cms/s/0/88b9e7d0-8f8e-

Hai Academic College showed that nearly half of teens 14–18 want to live elsewhere, with 68 percent citing Israel's condition as "not good."[3] Eighty-one percent of Israelis recently indicated that they would like Israel to become part of the European Union (EU), with 11 percent saying that if they had EU citizenship, they would move immediately.[4] Already, over 100,000 Israelis have German citizenship, with as many as 7,000 being given new passports each year.[5] Yet even more troubling is that current statistics confirm the same trend, and what is worse is who is in fact leaving. Recently, researchers Joseph Chamie and Barry Mirkin wrote in Foreign Policy that "The Israeli emigrants are deemed to be disproportionately secular, liberal, and cosmopolitan."[6] Nearly half of Israeli emigrants have a university degree, twice as many as that of average Israeli residents. Meanwhile, the Haredi population in Israel, which is highly dependent on government assistance, has more than tripled in size in just 20 years.

This is a recipe for an economic disaster and democratic atrophy, and secular Israelis in particular know it. Combine these ingredients with the ongoing conflict and the Netanyahu government's propensity to ratchet up tensions with Israel's neighbors rather than diffuse them, and it becomes quite understandable why moderate and educated Israelis cannot bear to continue raising their children in

---

11e0-954d-00144feab49a.html?siteedition=intl#axzz2roPXfXuP; and Yossi Alpher, "Proudly Israeli, Even With a Second Passport," *The Jewish Daily Forward*, June 5, 2008, http://forward.com/articles/13523/proudly-israeli-even-with-a-second-passport-/.

3   Tamar Trabelsi-Hadad, "Half of Israeli Teens Want to Live Abroad," *Y Net News*, July 20, 2007, http://www.ynetnews.com/articles/0,7340,L-3427762,00.html.

4   Ricky Kreitner, "81% Of Israelis Want To Join The European Union," *Business Insider*, July 12, 2011, http://www.businessinsider.com/81-of-israelis-want-to-join-the-european-union-2011-7; and Ronny Sofer, "Poll: 75 Percent of Israelis Want to be in EU," *Ynet News*, February 22, 2007, http://www.ynetnews.com/articles/0,7340,L-3368220,00.html.

5   Gideon Levy, "Fear is Driving Israelis to Obtain Foreign Passports," *Haaretz*, June 2, 2011, http://www.haaretz.com/print-edition/opinion/fear-is-driving-israelis-to-obtain-foreign-passports-1.365454.

6   Chamie and Mirkin, "The Million Missing Israelis."

such a state. Whereas the Israel Defense Forces (IDF) used to serve as a national symbol of solidarity, defending the Jewish homeland from terrorists and enemy states seeking Israel's destruction, today it is increasingly viewed with apprehension as an occupying force. At the present, less educated and secular Israelis are enlisting. Nearly half of military age Israelis no longer serve in the military. A 2010 study by Tel Aviv University Professor Camille Fuchs showed that 59 percent of Israeli teens did not want to serve in combat units.[7]

IDF statistics show within a generation, 30 percent of recruits will be Haredi, despite the fact that nearly 15 percent of military-age Haredi men receive a waiver for IDF service,[8] a testament to the substantial growth of the religious community in Israel. Research last year by the military journal Ma'arachot showed that in 1990, the percentage of combat officers who were religious was just 2.5 percent. Twenty years later, nearly one-third of IDF combat officers are religious.[9] Historically, in Israel the one institution that brought the citizenry together as a cohesive "unit," which was most admired and above the fray of politics, was the military. Sadly, today it is seen by the outside world and a growing number of Israelis as a tool of suppression, destroying the moral fabric of Israeli society.

Many Israelis witnessing these trends rightfully foresee the following: an Israel facing considerable economic challenges caused by brain drain, an exponential rise in religious families receiving government assistance, and continued increasing military expenditures to protect the settlers while maintaining a state of military readiness. Politically, the picture is equally bleak; Israel's future looks more right-wing, less democratic, and more isolated within the international arena.

So what is Prime Minister Benjamin Netanyahu doing about

---

7   Or Kashti, "Poll: Half of Israeli Teens Don't Want Arab Students in Their Class," *Haaretz*, September 6, 2010, http://www.haaretz.com/news/national/poll-half-of-israeli-teens-don-t-want-arab-students-in-their-class-1.312479.

8   Jonathan Rosenblum, "Nahal Haredi Comes of Age," *Jewish Action*, May 13, 2010, http://www.ou.org/jewish_action/05/2010/nahal_haredi_comes_of_age/.

9   Amos Harel, "Sharp Rise in Number of Religious IDF Officers," *Haaretz*, September 15, 2010, http://www.haaretz.com/print-edition/news/sharp-rise-in-number-of-religious-idf-officers-1.313861.

this? Although this dangerous trend began by his predecessors, he is making the situation considerably worse. On the one hand, he demands that the Palestinians recognize Israel as a Jewish state, while on the other he is adding fuel to the fire that is the exodus of the secular, educated Israelis from the country by advancing the politics of the hardened ideological and religious right. As a result, he is actually undermining Israel's Jewish future, not safeguarding it. In effect, his demand that the Palestinians recognize Israel as a Jewish state is nothing but a ploy to make up for his own bankrupt policies that are jeopardizing the country's future as a safe and secure haven for all Jewish people.

Indeed, the Jewish national identity of the state cannot be maintained by Palestinian recognition but only through a sustainable Jewish majority. Rather than establishing a vision for Israel's future that combats the disturbing trends outlined above, Netanyahu is exacerbating them. As a result, as his fellow citizens despair of perpetual conflict and look for any possible way to escape it, Netanyahu is using Israel's legitimate national security concerns to advance an ideological land grab in the West Bank which undermines rather than enhances Israel's national security prospects.

Thus, Netanyahu's policies are reinforcing the notion of the modern State of Israel as a ghetto. Israel is no longer about serving as the only secure refuge for the Jewish people. After all, today, as noted above, Israelis are ironically clamoring to return to Germany and other free countries. Of course the notion of a refuge was a leading argument for the need for a Jewish state, one that would be a "light unto the nations," and promote a vibrant democracy providing for all its citizens. Yet today that notion of a Jewish state is unfortunately not one of inclusion, but of exclusion. More than half of Jewish Israelis polled by the Israel Democracy Institute last year stated that the government should be encouraging Israeli Arabs to emigrate, with even more saying that Arab communities should receive fewer resources than Jewish ones.[10] No longer is the Jewish state about a

---

10   Lahav Harkov, "'53% of Israelis Say Arabs Should Be Encouraged to Leave'," *The Jerusalem Post*, November 30, 2010, http://www.jpost.com/National-News/53-percent-of-Israelis-say-Arabs-should-be-encouraged-to-leave.

3

safe, secure, and prosperous future for the Jewish people living in a diverse democracy. Gone is the notion of Israel as a nation with a pioneering, democratic spirit.

However, Israel should not be—and is not—resigned to this fate. A new leadership can still change the country's direction. The current government has already discredited itself as an inclusive democracy. Netanyahu is unlikely to change course and initiate efforts to usher in an Israeli future based on a vibrant, educated democracy utilizing the economic opportunities that would arise from genuine, lasting peace treaties with its neighbors. However, instead of opening the gates of the new ghetto that Israel has become, Netanyahu and his government are closing those gates. Under this misguided leadership, Israel is becoming a garrison state, locking itself into religious and ideological extremism, international isolation, and a future of perpetual conflict.

Israel could harness the spirit of the evolving region to create a vision for what President Shimon Peres used to call a "new Middle East." Such policies would offer the kind of future for which Israeli emigrants are searching, where they can expand their horizon and seek unlimited opportunities throughout the region while anchored in Israel, instead of leaving it behind.

"THE JEWISH STATE OF ISRAEL"

OCTOBER 21, 2013

As the Israelis and Palestinians are presently negotiating in an effort to end a nearly seven decades-old conflict, Prime Minister Netanyahu has made recognition of the Jewish right to a homeland in Israel "the most important key to solving the conflict."[11] The 1947 UN Partition Plan called for the establishment of a Jewish state and a Palestinian state, and this fact was not lost to the 160 countries that have since recognized Israel—but none were required to recognize it by name as **the Jewish state**. Why, then, is Netanyahu making this requirement *sine qua non* to resolving the conflict with the Palestinians?

There is no doubt that the Jewish right to a homeland in Israel is central to preserving the Jewish national identity of the state and providing a safe and secure haven for the Jews to ensure their survival.

The Jewish people have for millennia endured persecution, discrimination, and expulsions, culminating in the unimaginably horrific Nazi Holocaust. *Only when seen in the context of survival itself* is one able to grasp why the vast majority of Jews in and outside Israel are committed to the survival of the state and its Jewish identity.

That said, the irony is that current and previous Israeli governments have regularly embraced policies and taken measures that directly undermined any prospect of preserving Israel as the state for the Jewish people.

The problem here is *while a sustainable Jewish majority is central to permanently securing that objective*, there are many indicators that clearly demonstrate the diminishing Jewish majority in Israel, and little is being done by Netanyahu to reverse the trend.

---

11   Herb Keinon, "Netanyahu: For Peace, Palestinians Must Recognize Jewish Homeland," *Jerusalem Post*, October 6, 2013, http://www.jpost.com/Diplomacy-and-Politics/Netanyahu-Palestinian-recognition-of-Israel-as-a-Jewish-state-is-crucial-condition-for-peace-328038.

Instead, Netanyahu is demanding that the Palestinians recognize Israel as a Jewish state, as if such recognition will eternally guarantee the national identity of the state regardless of the changing demographic composition of Jews and Arabs in Israel.

Writing in *Commentary* magazine in May 2009, historian Michael B. Oren, who shortly thereafter became Israel's Ambassador to the United States, identified "the Arab demographic threat" as one of seven "existential threats" facing the existence of Israel.[12]

"Israel, the Jewish State, is predicated on a decisive and stable Jewish majority of at least 70 percent," wrote Oren. "Any lower than that and Israel will have to decide between being a Jewish state and a democratic state. If it chooses democracy, then Israel as a Jewish state will cease to exist."

Here are the startling demographic trends that if continued unchecked will reduce Israeli Jews to a minority and endanger the very purpose for which Israel was created.

First, the Arab citizens of Israel constituted 20.7% of the total population in 2012.[13] In 2011, the birth rate among Israeli Jews was 3.0 births per woman verses 4.38 per Palestinian woman.[14] Some reports state that the Israeli Arab population will

---

12   Michael B. Oren, "Seven Existential Threats," *Commentary*, May 2009, http://www.commentarymagazine.com/article/seven-existential-threats/.

13   See "Monthly Bulletin of Statistics," *Israel Central Bureau of Statistics*, December 2012, http://www.cbs.gov.il/www/yarhon/b1_e.htm; and Jodi Rudoren, "Service to Israel Tugs at Identity of Arab Citizens," *New York Times*, July 12, 2012, http://www.nytimes.com/2012/07/13/world/middleeast/service-to-israel-tugs-at-arab-citizens-identity.html?_r=1&.

14   See Shmuel Rosner, "Children of Israel," *New York Times*, August 28, 2013, http://latitude.blogs.nytimes.com/2013/08/28/children-of-israel/; "Israeli Jews now number 6 million, Palestinians will exceed Jews by 2020," *Global Post*, January 1, 2013, http://www.globalpost.com/dispatch/news/regions/middle-east/israel-and-palestine/130101/israeli-jews-now-number-6-million-pale; and "World Development Indicators," *World Bank*, cited in Google Public Data Explorer, accessed October 20, 2013, http://www.google.com/publicdata/explore?ds=d5bncppjof8f9_&met_y=sp_dyn_tfrt_in&hl=en&dl=en&idim=country:ISR:EGY:USA#!ctype=l&strail=false&bcs=d&nselm=h&

grow from the current number of 1.658 million to 2.4 million by the year 2030.[15] This could represent nearly one quarter of the Israeli population.

Ironically, in his speech in 2003 at the Interdisciplinary Center (IDC) in Herzliya, Netanyahu spoke of the demographic threat. "We have a demographic problem," he said, "but it lies not with the Palestinian Arabs, but with the Israeli Arabs [who will remain Israeli citizens]."

He continued to say, "If Israel's Arabs become well integrated and reach 35-45 percent of the population, *there will no longer be a Jewish state* [emphasis added]."[16] Therefore, a policy is needed that will balance the two. Paradoxically, Netanyahu's policy is in fact gradually realizing his own ominous prediction.

Second, there is an alarming number of Israelis who are emigrating from Israel. Statistics show that up to one million Israelis (13 percent of the population) are living abroad, and very few are planning to return to Israel.[17]

Many have left because they are seeking better job opportunities, others because they are weary of the continuing conflict with the Palestinians. Many have concerns about security, while others flatly admit that they want to shield their children from compulsory military service.

Third, immigration to Israel is barely balancing emigration from Israel. In the year 2012, 16,577 Jews immigrated to Israel verses

---

met_y=sp_dyn_tfrt_in&scale_y=lin&ind_y=false&rdim=region&idim=country:ISR:WBG&ifdim=region&hl=en_US&dl=en&ind=false.

15   Gabe Fisher, "On Eve of 2013, Israel's Population Stands at Cusp of 8 Million," *The Times of Israel*, December 30, 2012, http://www.timesofisrael.com/on-eve-of-2013-israels-population-stands-at-cusp-of-8-million/; and Yael Branovsky, "Forecast: Arabs to Comprise 25% of Population by 2030," *Y Net*, March 25, 2008, http://www.ynetnews.com/articles/0,7340,L-3523625,00.html.

16   "Sowing conflict and division," *Haaretz*, December 19, 2003, http://www.haaretz.com/print-edition/opinion/sowing-conflict-and-division-1.109215.

17   Chamie and Mirkin, "The Million Missing Israelis ."

16,000 who emigrated from Israel.[18] It is projected that by 2030, between 440,000 and 623,000 will immigrate to Israel[19] and perhaps as many will leave Israel if current trends continue.

The largest reservoir of Jews outside Israel is in the United States with 6–6.7 million,[20] followed by Europe with 1.4 million.[21] Given the continuing conflict with the Palestinians and the growing disenchantment of young American and European Jews with the Israeli occupation, the likelihood of a huge influx of newcomers from these two major Jewish centers is diminishing.

Many Israelis, led by a prime minister who warned of the coming demographic threat, are doing nothing to reverse this trend by taking the necessary measures to increase the Jewish population.

On the contrary, Netanyahu is making matters worse by his expansionist policies in the West Bank and his discriminatory treatment of Israeli Arabs, which can only further exacerbate the poor relations between them. Thus, *instead of becoming a positive component of the Israeli social fabric, they may well become a fifth column.*

What will it take then to ensure that Israel maintains its Jewish national identity while still preserving its democratic nature, given the gloomy demographic picture?

First, Israel must resolve the conflict with the Palestinians based on a two-state solution, which would remove Palestinians

---

18   Lior Dattel, "Israel's Emigration Rate Among Lowest in Developed World," *Haaretz*, October 2, 2013, http://www.haaretz.com/news/national/.premium-1.550127.

19   Sofia Phren and Nitzan Peri, "Prospective Immigration to Israel Through 2030: Methodological Issues and Challenges," United Nations Statistical Commission and Economic Commission for Europe (Lisbon, Portugal, April 28–30, 2010), http://www.unece.org/fileadmin/DAM/stats/documents/ece/ces/ge.11/2010/wp.21.e.pdf.

20   J.J. Goldberg, "How Many American Jews Are There?," *The Jewish Daily Forward*, February 18, 2013, http://forward.com/articles/171204/how-many-american-jews-are-there/?p=all.

21   "Inhospitable Europe," *The Jerusalem Post*, October 6, 2013, http://www.jpost.com/Opinion/Editorials/Inhospitable-Europe-328036.

in the West Bank and Gaza from the demographic equation that Israel faces today.

The continuing occupation and the expansion of settlements run contrary to the need to establish a Palestinian state in order to prevent the creation of a de facto one state, which will obliterate Israel's Jewish national identity. This would also enhance Israel's security and serve to make it a more attractive destination for Jews worldwide.

Former Prime Minister Ehud Olmert's warning in a 2007 interview with Haaretz remains as valid today as it was six years ago when he said, "If the day comes when the two-state solution collapses, and we face a South African-style struggle for equal voting rights (also for the Palestinians in the territories), then, as soon as that happens, the State of Israel is finished."

"The Jewish organizations," he continued, "which were our power base in America, will be the first to come out against us because they will say they cannot support a state that does not support democracy and equal voting rights for all its residents."[22] This will certainly dry up any prospect of immigration of American Jews in any significant number.

Second, Israel must discourage emigration of Israeli Jews to Western countries by providing job opportunities and better prospects for the future. It was inequality and rising prices that brought hundreds of thousands of Israelis to the streets in the summer of 2011.

Meanwhile, the government is spending hundreds of millions of dollars on building new and expanding current settlements at the expense of poor Israelis who are living hand-to-mouth, driving many from raising their families in Israel.

The answer to this dilemma is a new economic policy that diminishes the socioeconomic gaps in Israel while sparing no effort to establish a comprehensive peace with the Arab states. This would open up new markets on Israel's borders, enabling new business opportunities to flourish in what President Shimon Peres used to call "a new Middle East."

---

22   Barak Ravid, David Landau, Aluf Benn and Shmuel Rosner, "Olmert to Haaretz: Two-State Solution, or Israel is Done For," *Haaretz*, November 29, 2007, http://www.haaretz.com/news/olmert-to-haaretz-two-state-solution-or-israel-is-done-for-1.234201.

Third, although the pool of Jews who wish to immigrate to Israel is limited, cultural and religious ties are still a magnet that will bring Jews to reside in Israel. These potential immigrants will be encouraged to make the move provided that they believe Israel offers new and exciting opportunities for growth and serves the purpose that was intended by its founders: a secure and democratic Jewish state at peace with its neighbors.

Fourth, Israel should institute policies that encourage a greater birthrate among secular Jews by providing appropriate subsidies, especially affordable housing. The divide between Israel's religious and secular communities is often portrayed in the animosity driven by the significant subsidies offered to the rapidly-growing religious community.

A campaign to reach all Israelis and offer appropriate assistance for higher education and housing is essential if Israeli citizens are to have the *confidence that they can provide* for larger families.

Fifth, as beloved as Israel may be in the eyes of American and European Jews, they are weary of Israel's tarnished image resulting from its discriminatory policies toward the Palestinians through bending democratic principles and perpetuating the occupation, which is akin to apartheid.

Never before has Israeli democracy been so clearly under attack. Bills introduced in the Knesset in 2011 under Netanyahu's stewardship sought to limit free speech by cutting funding from left-wing nongovernmental organizations, curtailing the power of the judiciary, and explicitly declaring Israel as a Jewish state in a blatant measure to isolate its Arab citizens.

Even former Secretary of State Hillary Clinton reportedly likened Israel's undemocratic legislation with the mullahs of Iran in her 2011 address to the closed-door Saban Forum, hosted by the Brookings Institution in Washington, DC.[23]

Clinton's comments came days after former Defense Secretary Leon Panetta implored Israel to institute civil measures and American

---

23   Barak Ravid, "Clinton Warns of Israel's Eroding Democratic Values," *Haaretz*, December 5, 2011, http://www.haaretz.com/print-edition/news/clinton-warns-of-israel-s-eroding-democratic-values-1.399543.

Ambassador Dan Shapiro joined his European colleagues in conveying to Israeli officials the United States' concerns regarding the state of Israel's democracy.

Israel must decide what kind of nation it seeks to become: an undemocratic apartheid state or a democracy at peace with its neighbors that enjoy strong relations with allies in the West. *It has never been clearer that Israel cannot have it both ways.*

Recognizing Israel as a Jewish state by the Palestinians, as demanded by Netanyahu, is of no value or consequence, not any more than the four countries identified by their religious majority: the Islamic Republic of Afghanistan, the Islamic Republic of Iran, the Islamic Republic of Pakistan, and the Islamic Republic of Mauritania.

Perhaps Netanyahu should call for renaming Israel *"The Jewish State of Israel,"* but then he must remember *that only a sustainable Jewish majority will make it so.*

It is time for the Israelis to ask their prime minister where Israel will be in 15–20 years down the line should he pursue the same illusionary policy. I am prepared to venture that his answer will be, "I do not know."

The absurdity of linking peace with the Palestinians to their recognition of Israel as a Jewish state is glaringly clear because this will neither mitigate the challenging growth of the Israeli Arabs nor advance the peace process. Moreover, it will neither retain the democratic principles of the state nor will it ensure Israel's Jewish national identity.

Therein lies the danger to Israel's existence as a Jewish state, regardless of what name Israel is recognized by, and by whom.

FORFEITING ISRAEL'S REASON TO EXIST

APRIL 23, 2014

It is a given that every Jew in and outside Israel wants to see Israel as a vibrant country: an economic powerhouse with a thriving democracy, self-confident and secure, capable of defending itself and deterring any enemy far and near from challenging its right to exist, at peace with its neighbors, respected by the international community, excelling in its humanity and caring about others, a beacon and a light unto other nations.

Yes, Israel can be all that and some, I am sure. All Israeli leaders, regardless of their political leanings, believe in their heart of hearts that the country that has risen from the ashes of extinction to a glorious nation offers a refuge and a haven to every Jew, so that never again will any live at the whims and mercy of others. This is why Israel exists and what it is meant to be, and this is the only way Israel will realize its destiny.

Today Israel faces a fateful crossroads: either end the occupation, or continue the subjugation of the Palestinians and forfeit the one historic chance to become a truly free nation that can live up to the promise of its divine creation.

The imminent collapse of the Israeli-Palestinian peace negotiations raises the critical question: will the Israeli-Palestinian conflict ever be resolved? More than six decades of debilitating violent discord did little to usher in an agreement. The shifting reality on the ground made the prospect for a solution increasingly dimmer, more distant, and laden with ominous danger.

Continued occupation of Palestinian land slowly consumes Israel's moral standing and physical well-being, inching it ever closer to self-destruction. Though the Palestinians are not innocent bystanders, Israel alone must now bear the burden because it is the undisputed power that can change the course of events and prevent the looming disaster.

No one knows the history of the Jews better than the Jews themselves. Persecution, segregation, expulsion, and death unmatched in human history were their lot nearly everywhere. But such unspeakable historic misfortune offers no license to inflict pain, suffering, and indignity onto others.

Knowing the true meaning of dehumanization, degradation, and derision must give rise to the Jews' moral values and humanity by treating the Palestinians with compassion and sensitivity. With the inevitability of coexistence and fate intertwined, what hope will be in the offing for tomorrow if not harmony and peace?

A new disaster will be waiting in the wings, obliterating the Jews' dream to build a lasting free nation like many others, rather than live in isolation as a garrison state surrounded by fences and foes, caging itself in and drowning in an ocean of hostility and contempt.

Occupation must end not only because of its inherent injustice, as it demeans, debases, and degrades the Palestinians, but because of what the occupation does to the Israelis—it discredits and disgraces Jewish heritage and changes the once-oppressed Jews into merciless, heartless oppressors. No, this is not why Israel was created.

The Jews' historic victimhood proffers no license to victimize others. Israelis who take freedom for granted should never sleep easy knowing that millions of Palestinians retire at night deprived of pleasant dreams, wondering what tomorrow will bring, only to wake up still shackled and fused with anger and malice.

They want what you Israelis cherish. They want dignity, they want freedom, and they want the human rights that you so relish, but you want only to deny them the very values you uphold so high.

To the settlers and their supporters: as you build and expand settlements, usurping Palestinian land inch by inch, you deny them their aspiration for nationhood, as they witness daily the creeping annexation, dreading what will await them tomorrow—nothing but the fear of more land to be seized.

You feed the Palestinians with a daily dosage of hatred and fury, but then you blame them for hating you. As the settlements strike deeper roots, you strengthen their resolve to uproot you. This is how this tragic story goes; instead of building bridges of peace, you are erecting monuments of revulsion and hate.

The onus falls squarely on the Israeli government. Netanyahu, who genuinely seeks a strong, thriving, and prosperous Israel, pursues contrarian policies that deprive Israel of its potentially brilliant future. He is living in denial, never accepting, acceding, or assenting to a Palestinian state.

He is an ideological zealot, driven by biblical precepts that have long since lost any relevance to today's reality. He believes that he was divinely chosen to lead, but fails to understand that divinity placed the Palestinians inescapably and permanently side-by-side Israel.

He falsely links the country's national security to his insatiable thirst for more Palestinian land. He remains marred in illusions and grandiose dreams, blindly crawling through dark alleys, dragging Israel ever steadily to the abyss, foolishly misleading a county and a people he is entrusted to lead.

It is understandable that Jews anywhere have a unique affinity to the state of Israel; for the world's Jewry, Israel represents the last refuge, the sanctuary that offers a safe haven, independently determining its own fate. Hence, Israel must remain strong and powerful because they see their fate and fortune intertwined with Israel's strength, perseverance, and longevity.

But Diaspora Jewry must also understand that the occupation of Palestinian land destroys the very premise on which the state was created. Continued occupation in any form chips away the moral tenet of the country on which its very survival rests.

Yes, stand beside Israel they must, but supporting misguided policies like the blind leading the blind not only denies the Palestinians their human rights but imperils the very existence of the third commonwealth the Jews yearned for millennia, which they must never forget.

It is time for you, the Israelis, to wake up to the bitter reality you choose to ignore. The relative nonviolent atmosphere and the prosperity you enjoy today is nothing but a mirage. You buy into the rhetoric of misguided leaders who are unwittingly leading you astray.

Your complacency is your worst enemy; it is not that the Palestinians are innocent, it is that you have the power to force a change in direction, if you only will it. The alternative to the continuing debilitating conflict is not simply continuing much of the same. It will spell disaster for Israel as the world is tuned to the Palestinian plight and condemns Israel for its intransigence and gross human rights violations.

Israelis must remember that the entire global community vehemently opposes the occupation. Israel's national security concerns, though legitimate, have been excessively used like a smoke screen to obscure its expansionist policy, which any blind person can see through.

America remains the last beacon of hope to save Israel from traveling this suicidal path. As the United States deliberates its future plans about the peace process, this may well be Secretary Kerry's last ditch effort.

Israeli leaders will be wise to remember that once the United States decides that the prospect for a peace agreement remains elusive at best, it may well leave the Israelis and Palestinians to their own devices.

The Palestinians will play for time and grow stronger by sheer numbers and iron resolve, and Israel's self-consuming policies will make it steadily weaker. Its mighty military strength will pale in comparison to the Palestinians' inexhaustible human endurance, knowing full well that time is on their side.

History has shown that time and again.

RELIGION

GOD HAS ALREADY SPOKEN

AUGUST 30, 2010

As direct negotiations between Israel and the Palestinians are launched this week, it will be critical that the talks address the religious dimension of the conflict. This has been given only scant attention thus far, despite the fact that it has and will continue to have a tremendous impact on the ultimate outcome of the negotiations. Religious radicals—both Jewish and Muslim—seek to transform the Israeli-Palestinian dispute from a territorial and national conflict to a religious one, fueled by the conviction that God bequeathed the land exclusively to one faith. It is a view that prevents rational discourse between the two sides and leads to the conclusion that agreeing to a two-state solution to the conflict would be tantamount to defying God's will. However, it is time that leaders on both sides—with the assistance of the United States—begin to challenge those who purport to seek God's will to consider that Jews and Muslims may be intended to share the land after all.

Religious radicals on both sides have been guilty of fueling the conflict through violence and human rights violations perpetrated in the name of God. Guided by a blind belief that they are performing God's will, they do not pause to question: "Would an all-loving and merciful God really want us to continue killing each other and contaminate the land which is holy to us both?" Even more, those who believe that they have an exclusive right to the land should ask, "If

God wished to ordain the land in perpetuity to either the Israelis or the Palestinians, why then did God thrust them together in this same land?" After many years of bloodshed and destruction, one would think that the so-called believers would conclude that it is not a fluke that the great monotheistic religions—Judaism, Christianity, and Islam—happen to be anchored in the same land. It may very well be that they are intended to live alongside each other in peace, not to fight each other in perpetual self-destructive war and paradoxically do so in the name of God.

It would not be the first time that Jews and Muslims have lived side-by-side in peace. Jewish scholarship and culture reached a zenith under Islamic rule. It was the Islamic world that served as a refuge for those Jews who were persecuted and expelled from Christian-dominated Europe, most notably following the end of the Spanish Inquisition in 1492. Although a subordinated minority subjected to some forms of discrimination and confinements, Jews were free to openly practice and develop their religious practice under Islamic rule. In fact, in the Iberian Peninsula under Muslim rule, Jews were able to make great advances in mathematics, astronomy, philosophy, chemistry, and philology, in an era often referred to as the "Golden Age" of Jewish culture.

Instead of perpetuating conflict driven by religious fervor, Jews and Muslims should use their shared belief and affinity for the Holy Land as a source of commonality to create a new "Golden Age" in Jewish-Muslim relations. Rather than a source of tension, the holy sites in the region sacred to both peoples—such as the Cave of Machpelah (Me'arat ha-Machpela in Hebrew, Al-Haram al-Ibrahimi in Arabic), the burial place of Abraham and Sarah, Isaac and Rebekah, and Jacob and Leah—should be viewed as an indication of the need to safeguard the rights of both Jews and Muslims in the land they both cherish. Such sites, and the historic and psychological implications of their existence, cannot be subject to change short of catastrophic developments. Both sides must come to accept this simple, indisputable and unchallengeable fact: the "other" believes the land to be sacred and holy as well.

Unfortunately, religious extremists on both sides have shown no willingness to espouse such a view through three generations of bloodshed and wars. Instead, they distort interpretations of their respective holy texts in order to legitimize and foster their warped theological and political beliefs. While some argue that their interpretations of religious texts demand that there be no reconciliation between Jews and Muslims (and by extension Israelis and Palestinians), others claim that the pain and suffering caused by years of bloodshed was meant to test their tenacity and will, and has made such a rapprochement impossible. But if the Jewish state found a way to reconcile with Germany following the Holocaust, it must—and can—find a way to reconcile with Muslims—and Palestinians—today. The same, of course, applies to Palestinian extremists like Hamas and Islamic Jihad. Violently resisting Israel in the name of God has proven to be futile and will continue to be self-consuming and destructive if pursued further. They, as any true believer—whether Jewish or Muslim—must recognize that both faiths, Islam and Judaism, identify Abraham/Ibrahim as their shared patriarch. Just as it was God's will that these two peoples share an ancestry, both peoples must recognize that it too is God's will that they share a common future alongside one another in peace. Indeed, if the inhabitants of the land live in peace, harmony, and brotherhood, rather than acrimony and violence, the land can be as the Old Testament characterized it: the land of "milk and honey," rather than conflict and bloodshed that will consume its inhabitants.

The outrageous words expressed earlier this week by Rabbi OvadiaYosef, the spiritual leader of the ultra-orthodox Israeli political party, Shas, wishing that "Abu Mazen and all these evil people should perish from this world"[24] provides evidence that the leaders of faith are too often part of the problem, rather than part of the solution in the Middle East. Rabbi Ovadia's radical rhetoric and intolerance blinds him to the reality that should Abu Mazen pass, he would be replaced by thousands who share his national aspiration for statehood and are prepared to make the same demands and sacrifices to achieve it. The choice is therefore quite simple for those like Rabbi Ovadia, whose theology and political ideology are intertwined: prosperity

---

24 "Shas Spiritual Leader: Abbas and Palestinians Should Perish," *Haaretz*, August 29, 2010, http://www.haaretz.com/news/national/shas-spiritual-leader-abbas-and-palestinians-should-perish-1.310800.

or destruction? In this regard, the reality today is that coexistence between Israelis and Palestinians is not one of many choices, but the only choice and a solution to their religious conflict must be an integral part of that choice. To that single and indisputable end, as the Israelis and Palestinians begin to resolve their political and territorial differences, the Obama administration should insist that the two sides appoint a joint Israeli and Palestinian committee composed of distinguished religious scholars to immediately engage in an interfaith dialogue to begin addressing the theological aspects of the conflict. There may be no easy solution, but a solution must be found regarding such sensitive issues as managing the various holy sites of an agreement on the future of East Jerusalem.

Continuing the struggle against the reality that is their shared past and future should be viewed as nothing less than a defiance of God's intentions. As such, Muslims and Jews of faith should accept that they are destined—or doomed—to coexist. In this sense, God has already spoken.

"BLIND LEADING THE BLIND"

MARCH 12, 2011

It is difficult to be an American Jewish organization advocating support for Israel today. On the one hand, there is the staunch belief that Israel must be defended at all costs, and that any division will expose a weakness in the united Jewish front. On the other, American Jews traditionally advocate progressive policies in domestic and global affairs, which seemingly contradict their hardline stances in support of an Israeli government that is apt to reject such liberalism. At a time when Israel is led by a government that is steering it toward unending conflict, and whose actions are threatening Israel's Jewish and democratic nature, much of the American Jewish community today is merely echoing the Netanyahu government's talking points. While unity has kept the Jewish world strong throughout the Diaspora, if it is perpetuated through blind support of misguided policies, it could severely undermine Israel's national security in the name of a misplaced sense of unity.

The instinct to unify is one that is ingrained in Jews the world over. This heritage of unity goes back not only generations, but millennia. Divisions among the early Israelites are cited as key factors leading to the destruction of the First and Second Temples of ancient Jerusalem. The expulsion of the Hebrews from the Holy Land, and their dispersal throughout the Middle East and Europe, provided the impetus for the elevated importance of the Jewish community for centuries. Whether by choice or by force, Jewish communities banded together to survive the Spanish Inquisition, the pogroms of Eastern Europe, and, of course, the Holocaust and the eventual creation of the Yishuv in what would become the State of Israel. Jewish holidays like Hanukkah and Purim celebrate the success of the Jewish people being saved from the threat of destruction; others like Tisha B'av and Yom Ha'shoah commemorate those periods when Jews failed to do so.

The psyche of a people with a history under almost constant siege has served as the key unifying agent between Israel and the American Jewish community. The narrative of the Jewish people surrounded by hostile enemies, and needing the constant support and vigilance of its brethren to survive, is indeed a powerful one. Today, when faced with the threat of a nuclear Iran, Israeli and American Jewish leaders are often quick to compare the current period to 1939 in an effort to demonstrate the urgent need to safeguard a Jewish people under the threat of annihilation.

Of course, the State of Israel was supposed to change all this. The Zionist ideology was about Jews not cowering in fear of those who would threaten them, but rather about binding together in strength to create a great nation that would proactively serve to protect and defend the Jewish people. And build a great nation they did. Nearly 63 years after the creation of the modern Jewish state, Israel enjoys one of the world's greatest militaries, a strong economy despite the worldwide downturn, the most advanced technology, and an unprecedented partnership with the global superpower, the United States. In short, today the Jewish people may be more secure, and better off, than ever before.

But the sense of vulnerability within Israel, and among Jews worldwide, has become so deeply engrained that it is hard to recover. Even dissent against Israeli policies which threaten to upend its remarkable accomplishments is intolerable. Those that do so have often been shunted, sidelined, and all but completely discredited within their communities. Rather than face such "excommunication," many Jews choose therefore to be silent when it comes to Israel—but their silence is in turn interpreted as acquiescence and even support. This cycle has, at times, become so out-of-hand that Jewish advocates of Israel have surpassed even Israeli hardliners in their defense of the Jewish state and their support for misguided policies. In the past decade, American Jews have contributed over $200 million to West Bank settlements, whose more than 500,000 inhabitants—many with American passports—serve as central obstacles to a two-state solution that would secure Israel's democracy as a Jewish state. Prime Minister Yitzhak Rabin is known to have questioned whether he would obtain support from American Jewish leaders in launching the Oslo peace process in 1993. In the midst of pursuing a peace process with Palestinian

President Mahmoud Abbas in 2008, then-Prime Minister Ehud Olmert was met with a proposition by the World Jewish Congress demanding that any negotiations on Jerusalem be approved by the Jewish Diaspora community. And, while American Jews do have a measure of influence in Congress, advocates of the Jewish state vociferously deny the often-inflated extent of their influence, while at the same time using the specter of such power to advance their agenda.

This strategy is backfiring against Israel and the United States. Take the recent United States veto of the United Nations Security Council (UNSC) Resolution condemning Israeli settlement activity: Israel and the Jewish community have considered the veto a major victory for Israel and for the United States-Israel relationship. But in truth, it is a defeat. Had Prime Minster Netanyahu been truly committed to a two-state solution, he could have used the resolution as cover to press forward with a new peace agenda, with the support of the United States. Or, American Jews could have promoted the idea that the United States supports the resolution but ensure that it would serve to oversee its implementation as a step toward jumpstarting the dormant peace process. Instead, Israel—and the United States—is even more isolated than it was before, and the mediation and influence of the United States, Israel's most critical benefactor and ally, is being questioned as never before. Even more, as a result of the veto, the notions of Jewish power and conspiracy have again reached a fever pitch, providing fuel to anti-Israel and anti-Semitic sentiments.

In truth, the United States decided to veto the resolution for its own reasons. The Obama administration recognizes that an Israel on the defensive is one that is unlikely to take courageous steps toward peace. It is also true that the United States vetoed the resolution with an eye toward domestic politics. However, those who point to a supposedly all-powerful Jewish lobby as the key source of the administration's concerns are mistaken. In a recent Gallup poll, 63 percent of Americans indicted that they sympathized with Israel more than the Palestinians, the highest ratings of support for Israel since 1991.[25] American Jews makeup only 2.2 percent of the

---

25   Lydia Saad, "Support for Israel in U.S. at 63%, Near Record High," *Gallup*, February 24, 2010, http://www.gallup.com/poll/126155/support-israel-near-record-high.aspx.

United States—support for Israel is an American interest, certainly not strictly a Jewish one.

Even so, American Jews have an important voice, and they are failing to use it effectively. To be sure, while a united Jewish people is important, and even critical for the continued survival and growth of global Jewry and its relationship with Israel, this relationship should be based on a shared vision of the future, not on the vulnerability and fears that have characterized the past. American Jews should use their voice today to communicate a different path for the future of Israel's relations with the United States and the Diaspora—and there is no better time to start than now.

With the Arabs of the Middle East rising up against their corrupt dictators and demanding freedom and opportunity, the Arab world will be increasingly more confident and forward-looking than ever. Israel's neighbors clearly will continue to lag behind the Jewish state for the foreseeable future, but as they regain their footing, they will eventually look again to the continued conflict with Israel. That is why Israel, and its brethren in the Diaspora, should not be caught obsessively preparing for the challenges of the past when it could be grasping the opportunity being presented today by the changes occurring in its neighborhood.

American Jews must open their eyes—and help Israel to do the same—to witness the unpleasant realities of the region and the state, and to recognize that they will not disappear simply because they are wished away. Israel and world Jewry today are acting like a reckless gambler, unnecessarily risking the future even though Israel already has the chips it needs to realize all its dreams—if both sides could only open their eyes and grasp them.

JERUSALEM

JERUSALEM MUST EXEMPLIFY ISRAELI-PALESTINIAN COEXISTENCE

OCTOBER 27, 2011

The religious, demographic, physical, psychological, and political realities facing Israelis and Palestinians in Jerusalem today require that it be an undivided—yet shared—city serving as a microcosm exemplifying Israeli-Palestinian coexistence. Neither Israel nor the Palestinians can uproot the other from the city. Jerusalem not only represents the largest urban concentration of Israelis and Palestinians coexisting alongside one another, but it is also the epicenter of the conflict that divides them. Now is the time for respected scholars and religious leaders to take the lead in beginning a concerted dialogue on the future of peaceful coexistence in Jerusalem, which respects the sanctity with which each side holds this sacred city.

The demographic reality in East and West Jerusalem makes a division of the city impossible. While Palestinian residents are largely concentrated in East Jerusalem and Jewish residents in West Jerusalem, they are interspersed throughout the city. Over 40 percent of East Jerusalem residents today are Jews, and nearly 40 percent of the city's Israelis live east of the so-called "seam line" that once divided Jerusalem prior to the 1967 Six Day War. In addition to establishing this demographic mix, Israel has deliberately developed the city in a concerted manner that has united the eastern and western neighborhoods. Various municipal services, such as gas lines and electricity,

25

are shared across the city. Israel has understood that such structural ties make a future division of the city impossible. Indeed, today Palestinian leaders do not call for a physical division of the city, rather for sovereignty over a Palestinian capital in the eastern portion of the city. As such, any solution to Jerusalem must take into account the fact that the city is physically united in every way.

Furthermore, Jerusalem's religious significance makes it holy to the three largest monotheistic religions, Judaism, Islam, and Christianity, a fact which can never be changed short of a catastrophe. No faith can claim sovereignty over the holy places of another. Just as the guardians of the Dome of the Rock are and must remain Muslims, so should the caretakers of the Western Wall be Jews. The familiar Jewish call to return "next year in Jerusalem" has lasted millennia; Islam's veneration of Jerusalem also spans numerous centuries. Efforts to delegitimize Judaism's or Islam's affinity for the city as a holy place deny the unmitigated religious attachment of both peoples to the city.

However, the affinity for Jerusalem on both sides also transcends religion. Secular Israelis and Palestinians value Jerusalem as more than a place revered by the religious, but as the rightful capital of their respective nations. To dismiss the conflict over Jerusalem as simply one among the religious is to ignore the reality that both peoples in totality share psychological and emotional ties to the city as the epicenter of their national aspirations.

Recognizing these realities, it is a foregone conclusion across the Israeli spectrum that Jerusalem cannot and will not be divided. No Israeli politician could survive the political upheaval that would follow an attempt to structurally divide the city. If peace and security is assured, Israelis will support the removal of settlers from communities outside of the major settlement blocs. Yet they will never support the removal of Israelis from the Jerusalem environs. Similarly, Palestinian leaders will never relinquish their demand for the capital of the Palestinian state to be in East Jerusalem. Adding these political realities to the aforementioned facts, it becomes inconceivable that the city could be divided in any physical way. This consensus view requires one to consider an approach to ending the conflict by sharing the sovereignty of the city in order to exemplify Israeli-Palestinian coexistence and peace.

The solution to Jerusalem therefore requires an institutionalization of simple realities: Jewish neighborhoods should be under Jewish sovereignty, Palestinians neighborhoods under Palestinian sovereignty, and the holy shrines should be administered in an independent manner by the appropriate faiths. However, getting to such an agreement will require creative thinking that extends beyond the current political limitations imposed on Israeli and Palestinian policymakers. Leaders on each side have not shown the leadership necessary to come to terms. Prime Minister Netanyahu conceded the need to find a "creative solution" to the future of the city in his speech to the U.S. Congress. Defense Minister Ehud Barak told reporters last year that "West Jerusalem and 12 Jewish neighborhoods [east of the city] that are home to 200,000 [Israeli] residents will be ours. The Arab neighborhoods in which close to a quarter million Palestinians live will be theirs. There will be a special regime in place along with agreed upon arrangements in the old city, the Mount of Olives and the City of David."[26]

However, Israel continues to expand neighborhoods in East Jerusalem, including recently announced plans to build in the neighborhood of Gilo, while establishing an entirely new neighborhood, Givat Hamatos, on the outskirts of the city. Meanwhile, the Palestinians' refusal to return to peace talks and test Israel at the negotiating table is only ensuring the continued erosion of the Palestinians presence in East Jerusalem. Without direct negotiations, a third party—namely the United States—must work together with the international community and both sides to "bank" the concept of sharing the city and its holy places so that each side recognizes the endgame and can begin in earnest to resolve their conflict when they ultimately return to talks. Preserving progress in this way will be critical if each side is to make steps necessary to conclude a deal.

In the meantime, in the absence of political leadership, it is critical that respected scholars, religious leaders and NGOs on each side begin to convene a concerted dialogue about the future of coexistence in the city, with or without the endorsement of their

---

26   "Barak: Israel Ready to Cede Parts of Jerusalem in Peace Deal," *Haaretz*, September 1, 2010, http://www.haaretz.com/news/diplomacy-defense/barak-israel-ready-to-cede-parts-of-jerusalem-in-peace-deal-1.311450.

constrained political leaders. To be sure, a network of walls and tunnels can never divide the city. However, ideas must be shared and shaped by civil society leaders as to what future coexistence in the city could look like.

The only prerequisite to such dialogue should be a commitment to finding solutions to coexistence in a shared city. Coupled with this commitment should be an understanding of the most critical component of any discussion with regard to the city: its religious importance to each side. If God had desired for only one faith to control the city, he would have made it so. Religious leaders must stop using religion to justify their exclusive sovereignty over the city. Instead, religious figures must play a critical role in beginning to communicate how Judaism, Islam, and Christianity are destined by God to coexist in the city. As such, each faith can contribute to making the city a unique symbol of peace.

Furthermore, respecting the religious significance of the city can lead to greater dialogue and new ideas from leading scholars about how the city could be administered. For example, a system of citizenship and permanent residency could be created whereas Palestinians on the Israeli side have permanent residency in Israel but vote for elections in Palestine. Similarly, Israelis within the Palestinian jurisdiction of the city would be permanent residents of Palestine, but would vote in Israeli elections. Within this context, scholars must begin to analyze how best to protect socioeconomic and political rights for all. In addition, such a politically divided city would demand strong and sound internal security cooperation between Israelis and Palestinians.

As long as both sides agree on security arrangements—for example, what happens if a crime is committed in one sovereign area and the criminal flees to the other?—then other issues can be resolved as well. Joint efforts to administer necessary municipal services would be simple to arrange should Israel's chief concern—security—be effectively addressed. Forming such details can and should be worked on now to provide resources for political leaders to move forward when they return to negotiations.

Most important is for civil society leaders to begin to change the narrative from one that regards the city as indivisible and completely sovereign to that of a symbol of coexistence and peace. Too many rejectionists continue to deny the reality that the status quo is untenable. Others argue for an unrealistic division of the city along the 1967 lines. Still more critics argue that coexistence between the two sides is impossible. However, without a reasonable solution to Jerusalem, the deep disagreements over the future of the city will continue to serve as a tinderbox of potential violence. My answer to such critics is therefore rather simple: under conditions of real peace and amity, anything is possible; under conditions of hostility, little, if anything, is possible. Political will and courageous leadership can generate vast public support and meaningful coexistence in Jerusalem and beyond. Today, the absence of political will and leadership requires civil society to take the lead.

Rather than serve as a core issue of division, Jerusalem can indeed serve as a symbol of coexistence and peace. To achieve this goal, scholars, religious leaders, and NGOs must get serious about recognizing the religious significance of the city and the existing realities on the ground. They must create a blueprint for coexistence in the city to serve as a launching point for a lasting two-state solution. If they do, the city aptly called "Ir Shalom" or "City of Peace" can deservedly live up to its name.

FACING THE TRUTH ABOUT JERUSALEM

SEPTEMBER 26, 2013

Those who are privy to the ongoing Israeli-Palestinian peace negotiations appear to be more optimistic than ever before about the prospect of reaching an agreement. Yet there are those who believe that, regardless of American prodding, no agreement is likely to emerge because neither Prime Minster Netanyahu nor President Mahmoud Abbas is in a position to make the necessary concessions to make peace and survive politically.

That said, the future of Jerusalem remains at the epicenter of a negotiated settlement, now or at any time in the future, and could make or break any deal their respective publics, especially the radicals among them, can accept which run contrary to their deep beliefs.

For these reasons there is an urgent need to seriously engage in public discussions about the future of Jerusalem because sooner or later the Israelis and Palestinians must be prepared to accept the inevitable—a united Jerusalem, yet a capital of two states.

In a recent interview with the Associated Press, Jerusalem's Mayor Nir Barkat (who is running for re-election) insisted that "There is only one way this city can function-it is a united city that all residents and visitors are treated honestly and equally. It is the only model."[27]

Whereas there is little argument among most Israelis and a substantial number of Palestinians that the city should remain "united," what Barkat is saying is that Jerusalem cannot be divided by walls and fences and remain united as the eternal capital of Israel.

---

27   Aron Heller, "AP Interview: Mayor Says Jerusalem Can't Be Split," *Associated Press*, September 3, 2013, http://bigstory.ap.org/article/ap-interview-mayor-says-jerusalem-cant-be-split.

He is imploring Israeli officials, presently engaged in the peace negotiations with the Palestinians, "to take any talks about dividing Jerusalem off the table."

One critical thing that Barkat seems to ignore is that there will be no Israeli-Palestinian peace unless much of the old city in East Jerusalem, which is largely inhabited by Palestinians, becomes the capital of a future Palestinian state.

Not only will the Palestinians reject anything less, but all Arab and most Muslim states will not accept any peace agreement with Israel that excludes Jerusalem.

The Israeli position:

From the perspective of many Israelis, it is inconceivable to surrender any part of Jerusalem to the jurisdiction of any other peoples or an international governing body.

This unique attachment and affinity to the holy city, which has for millennia symbolized the Jewish sense of redemption, created a powerful motivation to capture the city when it came within their grasp during the Six Day War in 1967. The fall of Jerusalem in the wake of the war remains an unmatched event and came to symbolize Jewish absolution.

This historic development created a renewed awakening that vindicated the religious premise which was embedded in the Jewish psyche for centuries. The realization of what was believed to be a far-fetched dream under the most difficult of circumstances was now seen as the work of the Almighty, which no force can alter.

The Palestinian position:

Due to religious convictions tied to Islam's third holiest shrines in Jerusalem—the Al-Aqsa Mosque and the Dome of the Rock—Muslim leaders will not compromise on East Jerusalem as the capital of their future state.

Muslims around the world believe that Muhammad made his Night Journey from Mecca to Masjid Al-Aqsa (literally, "furthest mosque")

ALON BEN-MEIR

in Jerusalem before he ascended to heaven. Although the Al-Aqsa Mosque was built long after the death of the prophet, Surah 17:1 states that Mohammad visited the site where it was subsequently erected.

One other difficulty that adds to the psychological impediment in relation to Jerusalem is the Palestinians' sense of ownership, which has been uninterrupted for centuries. The 1967 Six Day War and the capture of Jerusalem created a tripled sense of urgency to restore the old city to its Palestinian-majority occupants.

The reality on the ground:

The religious, demographic, physical, psychological, and political realities facing the Israelis and Palestinians in Jerusalem today require that it be an undivided—yet shared—city exemplifying Israeli-Palestinian coexistence.

Neither Israel nor the Palestinians can uproot the other from the city. Jerusalem not only represents the largest urban concentration of Israelis and Palestinians coexisting alongside one another, but also the epicenter of the conflict that divides them.

The demographic reality in East and West Jerusalem makes a division of the city impossible. While Palestinian residents are largely concentrated in East Jerusalem, over 40 percent of East Jerusalem's residents today are Jews who live east of the so-called "seam line" that once divided Jerusalem prior to the 1967 war.

In addition to this demographic mix, having annexed the city immediately following the 1967 war, Israel has developed the east and west of the city as a single city with a network of roads and various municipal services such as gas and power lines.

Israel has understood that such structural ties make a future division of the city impossible, and although the Palestinians also understand that the city will not be physically divided, they seek to establish their capital in the eastern portion of the city.

To dismiss the conflict over Jerusalem as simply one among the religious is to ignore the Israelis' and Palestinians' shared psychological and emotional ties to the city as the core of their national aspirations.

The Israelis will support the removal of some settlers from communities outside of the major settlement blocs in the West Bank but will never support the removal of Israelis from the Jerusalem environs. Similarly, Palestinian leaders will never relinquish their demand for the capital of the Palestinian state to be in East Jerusalem.

This consensus view requires one to consider an approach to ending the conflict by sharing the sovereignty of the city and mutually recognizing the endgame, especially now that the negotiations have resumed.

I am not presumptuous to think that the following measures represent a blueprint that would facilitate an agreement over the future of Jerusalem. Several of the following ideas about the future of the city have been discussed at length. What has been and still is missing is a concerted public discussion about the various aspects of any agreement.

This is particularly important because both the Israeli and Palestinian publics must be prepared psychologically to accept the inevitable—a united city but a capital of two states—and conversely provide public support to the leaders to reach such an agreement. At the same time, radical elements from either side that might resort to any means (including violence) to scuttle such an agreement, believing that they are following God's will, must be disarmed.

Any agreement must begin by institutionalizing what is on the ground. Given the demographic inter-dispersement and the infrastructure of the city, very little can change to accommodate the creation of two capitals. Jewish neighborhoods should be under Jewish sovereignty and Palestinian neighborhoods under Palestinian sovereignty.

The holy shrines should be administered in an independent manner by representatives of their respective faiths. A special regime should be established by mutual agreement for the Mount of Olives and the City of David.

A joint security force should be established to ensure public safety and the integrity of the holy shrines. Each side will administer their respective holy sites and allow for mutual visitations by mutual agreement.

There should be no physical borders or fences to separate East from West Jerusalem, and movement of people and goods will remain free as is currently the case. The border between the two capitals will be a political border only for the purpose of delineating municipal responsibilities.

Since uprooting either Israelis or Palestinians from their current place of residence in Jerusalem is almost unthinkable, an agreement should be reached that would not disrupt their way of life.

Palestinians who end up on the Israeli side (unless they are Israeli citizens) would enjoy permanent residency in Israel but vote or be elected in Palestine; similarly, Israelis within the Palestinian jurisdiction of the city would be permanent residents of Palestine and exercise the right to vote and be elected in Israeli elections.

A new Palestinian municipality will be established to administer the eastern part of the city that falls under its jurisdiction, and a joint commission representing their respective municipalities would work to facilitate issues that may arise as a result of cohabitation that may affect either or both sides.

Whereas each has their own internal security forces, joint units will coordinate and cooperate on all security issues that may occur to prevent violence from either side against the other and reach an agreement on how to treat criminals should they commit a crime and flee to the other side.

To prepare for a solution along these lines would require concerted efforts by various civil society leaders and other public institutions. It is not a minute too soon to start such efforts.

First, officials must articulate creative approaches. Political will and courageous leadership can generate vast public support through leaders changing their public narrative from one that regards the city as indivisible under exclusive Israeli sovereignty to a shared city that symbolizes peaceful coexistence.

Ideally, current and former public officials should publicly support the "one city, two capitals" solution. Prime Minister Netanyahu, if he really believes in a two-state solution, should reiterate and further expand on what he stated in the U.S. Congress: "…with creativity and with good will, a solution can be found."[28]

---

28   Benjamin Netanyahu, "Address to U.S. Congress" (May 24, 2011), http://www.cfr.org/israel/netanyahus-address-us-congress-may-2011/p25073.

Former Defense Minister Ehud Barak told reporters in late 2010 that "West Jerusalem and 12 Jewish neighborhoods [east of the city] that are home to 200,000 [Israeli Jewish] residents will be ours. The Arab neighborhoods in which close to a quarter million Palestinian live will be theirs."[29]

Second, the role of the media is of paramount importance to promote the idea of "one city, two capitals." Liberal Israeli media outlets in particular should attract public attention to the need for a solution to the future of Jerusalem, without which there will be no peace. More and more editorials and in-depth analyses can and should be written about the reality that both Israelis and Palestinians must inevitably face.

Third, the absence of political will and leadership requires civil society to take the lead. NGOs, including think tanks, student organizations, women's groups, and labor unions, should begin a concerted dialogue about the future of the city.

Finally, public forums should be created to discuss the pros and cons of Jerusalem's future as a capital of two states. Although this solution may well be inevitable, still debating other possibilities is critical if for no other reason but to demonstrate why other options are not likely to work. Such dialogues could have, over time, a significant impact on Israeli and Palestinian public opinion.

This concept is possible today more than any other time before because of the revolution in communications that allows for the dissemination of information to millions within minutes.

The participants (in small groups of 15–20) should especially include religious scholars, imams, rabbis, and priests representing the three major monotheistic religions, and historians with a focus on the Middle East. They must be independent thinkers, hold no formal position in their respective governments, and be committed to finding a peaceful solution in the context of coexistence.

---

29   Ari Shavit, "Barak to Haaretz: Israel Ready to Cede Parts of Jerusalem in Peace Deal," *Haaretz*, September 1, 2010, http://www.haaretz.com/print-edition/news/barak-to-haaretz-israel-ready-to-cede-parts-of-jerusalem-in-peace-deal-1.311356.

The only prerequisite is that the participants will have to agree in principle that Jerusalem must serve as the capital of two states, without which peace may never be achieved.

To be sure, to resolve the future of Jerusalem and the other conflicting issues between Israel and the Palestinians requires far greater public engagement. Jerusalem in particular can serve either as a tinderbox of potential violence or a microcosm of coexistence and peace.

It is important to note that regardless of how urgent a solution to Jerusalem may be, any agreement between the two sides should be implemented over a period of no less than three years to allow for the development of new structural, political, and especially security regimes.

Moreover, testing each other's resolve and commitment is central in an environment that is subject to challenges and instability. Israeli and Palestinian leaders must fully cooperate and never allow radicals on either side to undermine such a historic agreement.

To all the skeptics I must say without undue optimism: under conditions of real peace and good intentions, anything is possible. Under conditions of hostility and distrust, little, if anything, is possible.

BORDERS AND
NATIONAL SECURITY

ISRAEL'S NATIONAL SECURITY
AND OCCUPATION

MARCH 4, 2010

The relevant validity of linking national security and occupation in the past has totally lost its currency, especially in the wake of the Arab states' expressed desire to forge a comprehensive peace and Israel's unquestioned ability to defend itself in any future confrontation. Now with renewed efforts by the United States to resume the peace negotiations, it is time for the Israeli government to disabuse itself from its national security paranoia by realistically reassessing the regional balance of power and the changing geopolitical realities on the ground. Israel must sooner than later choose between either continued occupation, which is bound to explode time and again and increasingly undermine Israel's national security interests, or peace with security with the Arab states, which will usher in wider regional stability.

Whereas the incessant Arab hostilities toward Israel in the past could explain the occupation on the grounds of national security, the Arab states' offer of a comprehensive peace along the lines of the Arab Peace Initiative (API) in exchange for the territories and a just solution to the Palestinian problem can no longer justify the occupation on security grounds. Moreover, Israel has failed to demonstrate, especially since 2000, how the occupation has enhanced its national security, when in fact it has promoted further enmity, instability, and violence, not to mention the astronomical cost in treasure and blood. Despite the relative socioeconomic and security improvements in the West Bank, recent low-level violent clashes between Israel and the Palestinians in East Jerusalem and Hebron are feared to constitute a forerunner of another major violent outbreak that could torpedo any prospect for a peaceful solution in the foreseeable future. For this reason, 43 years later, the international community sees no correlation between occupation and national security, and views Israel's continued occupation not only as a security liability for Israel but the single most serious impediment to peace and regional strife.

Immediately after the 1967 Six Day War, Israel offered to return the vast majority of the territories captured in exchange for peace but the answer from the Arab states was a resounding no: no peace, no recognition, and no negotiation. No realistic observer thinks now that the Arab states will accept anything less than what Israel has offered more than four decades ago. In lieu of Arab rejection, the Labor government at the time decided to build a few settlements on the outskirts of Jerusalem to protect the city. In subsequent years, successive Israeli governments—especially right-of-center governments—began a systematic entrenchment in the territories under the guise of national security, which gave rise to a powerful settlers' movement anchored in two extraordinary sentiments: reconstituting Jewish life in the land of their ancestors (Judea and Samaria) and living a better and more affordable life. Although this explains why past and present governments have been hard-pressed not to impede the growth of the settlements, it does not mean, however, that an Israeli government committed to peace cannot relinquish the territories, provided it offers the public only one of two realistic choices—continued occupation and unending strife, or peace with security.

While many Israelis understand the repercussions of occupation, they are generally persuaded by the official rhetoric which uses the near-daily Palestinian violent provocations as proof of the need to sustain the occupation, rather than portraying the violence as a reaction to the occupation. After more than four decades and years of peace negotiations, one thing has become abundantly clear: the only remaining value to the occupation is that it can be used as a bargaining chip to forge peace with security with the Arab states, and subsequently with the rest of the Muslim world. This is the only sane end-game; the sooner the Israeli academic community and the media, in particular, understands it and promotes it publicly, the sooner they will prevent another catastrophic development that will spare no one.

Israel has legitimate security concerns that cannot be denied. These national security concerns have been reinforced by decades of Arab enmity and violence, which has exacted a heavy toll on the Israelis. To protect its interests and sovereign rights, Israel has built over the past six decades one of the most powerful and sophisticated conventional military machines in modern history that has and will continue to deter any Arab country, or a combination of countries, from attacking Israel. This military deterrence is further augmented by Israel's "presumed" nuclear deterrence, which will make it suicidal for any country, including Iran, to credibly threaten Israel as it maintains a second strike nuclear capability that could inflict unimaginable damage on any attacker. Surely this does not mean that small extremist Arab groups such as Hamas, Hezbollah, or Islamic Jihad will stop harassing the Israelis, but none can pose an existential threat to Israel.

The question is, what is the purpose of Israel's military prowess? The growing global perception is that instead of using its military might to make the necessary territorial compromises to make peace, Israel maintains such capabilities in order to preserve the occupation, as neither the Palestinians nor the Syrians will dare to challenge Israel militarily to regain their territory by force. How else can Israel explain its insistence on continuing the building and expansion of settlements?

Israel is justified to argue that it has in fact taken several such risks in the past. It evacuated territories in the West Bank in the late 1990s, it withdrew its forces from Lebanon in 2000, and it relinquished the Gaza strip in 2005. Hamas, Fatah, and Hezbollah, on the other hand, instead of building bridges for peace, ended up using the evacuated territories as a staging ground to attack Israel. As a result of the Second Intifada which erupted in 2000, Israel retook most of the areas from which it had withdrawn in the West Bank, waged war against Hezbollah in Lebanon in 2006 and against Hamas in 2008–2009, inflicting massive damage and causing tremendous economic dislocation and hardship, not to speak of the loss of lives. What happened subsequent to the Israeli retaliations on all three fronts, however, offers instructive lessons that many Israelis chose to ignore. In the West Bank, the Palestinian Authority (PA) has officially committed itself to a nonviolent strategy (the Fayyad Plan) to realize the Palestinian national objective of building the infrastructure of a state living side-by-side with Israel in peace. Since the end of the hostilities in Lebanon and Gaza in 2006 and 2009, respectively, there was hardly any violent provocation against Israel coming from either Hezbollah or Hamas.

The Israeli message to the Palestinians and to Hezbollah was loud and clear: Israel has and will continue to have the capacity to enter any of the evacuated territories at will and only a total and permanent cessation of hostilities will end future Israeli incursions. Moreover, notwithstanding international condemnation, Israel's future retaliations will inflict ever-increasing devastation and loss of life as long as violent resistance continues. But if Israel wants to avoid future international condemnation, should it be compelled once again to inflict such damage in Gaza, it must first end the occupation. The argument that Israel does not occupy Gaza is only technical as Israel has full and total control over Gaza from the sea, land, and air and continues to occupy much of the West Bank. If Israel does not ease the burden of occupation and daily humiliation and commit itself to ending the occupation under a calm atmosphere, which is prevalent now, why would the Palestinians continue to adhere to nonviolent resistance? The Palestinians are duty-bound to continue to resist the occupation and Israel will never be able to claim the moral high ground as long as the occupation persists.

Finally, it must be clear that under any circumstances and however legitimate Israel's security concerns are, there will always be certain risks that Israel must take to secure peace. Any nation that seeks to attain absolute security, as Henry Kissinger once observed, renders its enemies absolutely insecure.[30] Under such a scenario very little progress can be made, as the Palestinians and the Syrians for that matter will never relinquish land they feel is inherently theirs and

30   Henry Kissinger, *A World Restored: Metternich, Castlereagh and the Problems of Peace* (London: Ebenezer Baylis and Son Ltd., 1957), 2.

40

will attempt to regain it by whatever means necessary, however long it may take. Moreover, the Arab states are ready to coalesce around Israel to deal with the Iranian nuclear threat; Israel must capitalize on this changing intra-Arab dynamic and look to the north to forge peace with Syria.

I trust that Prime Minister Netanyahu believes in and wants to seek peace, but he cannot lead a coalition government along with Yisrael Beiteinu and Shas, two extremist parties that tie his hands behind his back, and then blame them for the current paralysis. He has an obligation and historic opportunity to answer the national call and forge a new coalition government with Kadima and Labor along with Likud, representing the left, center, and right—a government with a solid majority that can rise above party politics, which the Israeli public is yearning for. It is time to put an end to the self-delusional policies in support of the occupation that will not only undermine the peace process but severely backfire against Israel's core national security interests.

Now that Israel has fought and finally won the Arab states' acceptance, it too must come around and face, in the words of Yehoshafat Harkabi (head of Israel's military intelligence from 1955 to 1959), its fateful hour: Israel must choose between becoming a garrison state with fences and walls and gradually isolating itself from the international community, or make the bold decision to end the occupation and secure its destiny as a free, strong, and prosperous nation.

ISRAEL NEEDS A PALESTINIAN STATE

JULY 23, 2010

Israel's national security and self-preservation depend on its ability and willingness to come to terms with the reality of coexistence with the Palestinians on the basis of a two-state solution. Unfortunately, instead of seeking to promote the creation of a Palestinian state, the current Israeli government has sought to impede it. Although Prime Minister Netanyahu's endorsement of the two-state solution at Bar Ilan University last summer offered a good start, it fell far short of the kind of vision needed to achieve a sustainable, lasting agreement. What he and his government have proposed amounts to an autonomous Palestinian entity, lacking territorial contiguity, with ultimate security responsibility remaining in Israel's hands.

Today, few Israelis view the establishment of a Palestinian state as a national security imperative, and a growing number have resigned themselves to supporting the idea of conflict management rather than conflict resolution. They simply do not believe that the Palestinians will ever accept Israel as an independent state. This particular view gained tremendous currency following the eruption of the Second Intifada in September 2000 in which more than 1000 Israelis were killed, many by indiscriminate suicide bombers. The Intifada prompted then-Prime Minister Ariel Sharon to re-occupy much of the territories from which Israel had withdrawn as part of the Oslo Accords, and fueled Israelis' disillusionment with the peace process. This skepticism was reinforced after Israel's unilateral withdrawal from the Gaza Strip in 2005. Instead of using the Gaza withdrawal as an opportunity to build the foundation for a future state, the territory was used as a staging ground for rocket attacks into Southern Israel, ultimately leading to Israel's Operation Cast Lead. These events, coupled with growing fears of Palestinian militancy following Hamas' takeover of Gaza, have moved the political pendulum in Israel to the right-of-center, even as the concept of a two-state solution has moved more and more into the mainstream.

As Israelis have become disillusioned with the peace process, Israel has strengthened its formidable military power and economic development, creating the false impression that it can sustain the status quo indefinitely. Meanwhile, the settlement movement has gained significant political power, enabling it to exert immense influence on successive Israeli governments. The settlers' commitment to territorial expansion, which is driven by a belief in their divine right to settle the West Bank, coupled with deep skepticism about the Palestinians' intentions, which is fueled by legitimate security concerns, have led the Israeli public to seemingly become immune to the plight of the Palestinian people.

Against this backdrop, the right-of-center government led by Netanyahu appears to be committed to disfranchising Palestinians, suppressing opposition, undermining democratic values, and forsaking the moral tenants on which the state of Israel was created. In this regard, the passing of two abominable measures in the Israeli Knesset speak volumes about how far this government will go to advance the right-wing "Greater Israel" agenda, however perilous this prospect may be. The first bill requires every individual seeking Israeli citizenship to declare his or her loyalty to a "Jewish democratic state," specifically designed to discriminate against Palestinian citizens of Israel. The second bill would punish any Israeli calling for a boycott of any Israeli individual or institution, whether in Israel or in the territories, with a fine of NIS 30,000 (nearly 8,000 USD) plus any proven damages. In addition to such legislative efforts, the government has continued to demolish Palestinian houses, engage in forced evictions, seize land, and deliberately disrupt communal life. Indeed, there is no internationally orchestrated campaign to delegitimize Israel as many Israelis claim. By its own actions and policies Israel itself is doing a very good job at that. Rather than address Palestinian national aspirations for statehood in the context of a secure and independent Israel, the current government erroneously views maintenance of the occupation and expansion of settlements as synonymous with Israel's long-term national security.

The Palestinians have joined Israel in choosing a convoluted course of action that has undermined their aspirations for statehood. The Palestinians' intense and often violent factionalism has prevented them from adopting a unified purpose and an effective strategy vis-à-vis the Israeli occupation. In addition to the political rivalry for power, the dispute between the two main factions—Fatah and Hamas—which intensified following Hamas' takeover of the Gaza Strip, is a battle of ideas over whether a militant or nonmilitant strategy would have a greater effect on Israeli policy. The Fatah-led PA based in the West Bank, although skeptical about the prospect of an agreement, still opts for a nonviolent strategy, having concluded that violence provides justification for Israel to maintain the occupation. However, its inability to make significant progress at the negotiating table has served to further Hamas' contention that Israel is not interested in peace and that only a militant strategy will force Israel to change course. Although Hamas has suspended violence following the conclusion of the Gaza war in January 2009, the Netanyahu government has made no effort to explore a possible rapprochement with a group that it dismisses as an irredeemable terrorist organization that must be eliminated. The building and expansion of settlements in the West Bank—even as Israel has declared a moratorium on such construction—has further strengthened the hand of those who argue that Israel has no intention of allowing Palestinians to establish a state of their own in the West Bank and Gaza.

While the two sides remain deadlocked, Palestinians recognize that the status quo with Israel cannot be sustained, and that the international community is on their side. It is with this recognition that Palestinian Prime Minister Salam Fayyad has begun to build the infrastructure for a future Palestinian state with the goal of ultimately declaring statehood with or without Israeli cooperation. In so doing, he and President Mahmoud Abbas have disavowed the use of violence, thereby evoking tremendous international support and pressure on Israel to ease the condition of occupation. In many ways this has created a historic point of departure in Israeli-Palestinian relations by offering the Israelis what they have always wanted—a nonviolent approach to reach a lasting solution. The Palestinians are thus demonstrating that, contrary to Israeli claims, there is indeed a Palestinian partner ready and able to negotiate an end to the conflict.

That being said, their ability to negotiate is constrained by time, and it is unclear whether the current Israeli government will be willing to offer the minimum that the Palestinians can accept. The Palestinian public, like that in Israel, is disillusioned with failed peace-making efforts. The Palestinian leadership in Ramallah cannot afford to enter into negotiations unless they can demonstrate to the Palestinian people that such talks have a real chance to succeed. Meanwhile, the more time that passes, the more the cases for a nonviolent approach and for continued peacemaking efforts are undermined. As such, it is no wonder that the Palestinian leadership is increasingly looking to the option of a unilateral declaration of statehood, supported by the international community.

The current deadlock does not change the reality that Israelis and Palestinians must coexist in the land between the Jordan River and the Mediterranean Sea. Coexistence is not optional—in one form or another, and regardless of any political and territorial configurations, Israelis and Palestinians are stuck with one another. The welfare and well-being of both nations are interdependent. Now they must make that fateful choice: do they want to live in hatred and debilitating hostility, leaving a shameful legacy to the next generation, or do they want to live in amity and peace, and become a model of prosperous, neighboring democracies?

Should Israel forfeit this historic opportunity to negotiate a conflict ending with an agreement with the Palestinian leadership in Ramallah, the Palestinians will have the right and the obligation to move with full speed to coalesce international support for a declaration of statehood, with or without Israel's consent.

To avoid this scenario, the Israeli government must recognize that the national security of the State of Israel is dependent on the establishment of an independent and viable Palestinian state, and work accordingly to achieve this objective and market it as such to the Israeli public.

RECONCILING ISRAEL'S SECURITY WITH PALESTINIAN STATEHOOD

SEPTEMBER 26, 2010

The two interdependent issues which hover over every aspect of the Israeli-Palestinian peace negotiations are satisfying Israel's national security requirements and meeting the Palestinian demand to end the Israeli occupation. Whereas the Palestinians must understand that unless Israel feels secure, there will be no independent Palestinian state, similarly, Israel must recognize that a two-state solution must mean an end to Israeli occupation in any form. To achieve the two objectives, both sides must carefully consider not only each other's requirements, but also demonstrate sensitivity to each other's mindset, which has been ingrained for decades and continues to fuel their conflicting positions.

Even a cursory review of the Israeli-Palestinian conflict suggests that Israel has legitimate national security concerns that must be alleviated in order to achieve a negotiated agreement on the establishment of a Palestinian state. Despite the fact that there are still several Palestinian groups who openly and consistently seek Israel's destruction, and however arguable Israel's linkage between its national security and its continued occupation, one thing remains indisputable: Israel's withdrawal from a part of the territories in the past did not create the building blocks for peace. Instead, the evacuated territories were used as a staging ground for further violent attacks against Israel. The withdrawal from parts of the West Bank in the late 1990s did not prevent the Second Intifada; the pull-out from Southern Lebanon in 2000 did not stop the violent exchanges with Hezbollah, which led to the 2006 war; and the evacuation of Gaza in 2005, which made Gaza a launching pad for indiscriminate rocket attacks by Hamas, led to Israel's Operation Cast Lead in 2008–2009. Instead of utilizing the partial withdrawals as the basis for improved relations to encourage further withdrawals and an end to the occupation, the Palestinians mistakenly viewed the Israeli pullouts as a

reaction to continued Palestinian violence. The Israelis' painful retaliations against the Palestinians' incessant violent provocations finally convinced the PA in the West Bank that continued violence against Israel is
self-destructive. As a result, the PA determined to build the infrastructure
of a Palestinian state (i.e., establishing the "Fayyad Plan") and advance
negotiations, rather than continue militant resistance.

Because of past experiences and the mindset that evolved from
these experiences, Israelis are extremely skeptical about the Palestinians' true intentions to seek a durable peace. For these reasons,
Israel will insist that four major security concerns are addressed prior
to any significant withdrawal from the West Bank: a) that the PA
is able to independently prevent the takeover of the territories by
terrorist groups and act decisively against violent provocations, b)
that there will be no smuggling of weapons, especially rockets to the
West Bank which could pose an unacceptable security risk to Israel's
urban centers, c) that the PA never enter into a military alliance with
a foreign nation, and finally, d) that the newly-born Palestinian state
be demilitarized, with the exception of robust internal security forces.
Israel's intelligence and defense establishments strongly believe that
these issues can only be addressed by maintaining a significant residual Israeli force along the Jordanian border, because the PA is not
ready, as yet, to meet its border security requirements. Such forces,
Israel argues, will not only deal effectively with the country's security
concerns, but will also ensure the sustainability of the PA as it will
deter both internal and external elements from undermining peace.

The Palestinians reject the Israeli requirements for forces on the
ground in the Jordan Valley, maintaining that such a residual presence on
Palestinian territory would amount to a continuation of the occupation.
The PA further argues that keeping Israeli troops behind, even without
the daily encroachment on Palestinian lives, would provoke tremendous
resistance and provide Palestinian groups opposed to any agreement with
Israel the munitions they need to undermine peace, including violent attacks. Moreover, 44 years of Palestinian yearning to end the occupation
has created a mindset that diametrically rejects not only the continued
presence of any Israeli soldiers, but also the symbols of occupation and
its humiliating effect on their national dignity and pride. The Palestinians
want to feel that they have finally won their independence, albeit not

through militant resistance, but certainly without even a shade of servitude. In this regard, they would rather maintain their current precarious situation than accede to Israel's demands, which, from their perspective, would be tantamount to surrendering their national aspirations for an independent Palestinian state.

To resolve their conflicting positions, both sides must carefully consider each other's core requirements for peace as well the other's national psychological disposition. There are four security measures that can be put in place with the help of the international community that would alleviate Israel's security concerns without leaving a residual force in the Jordan Valley.

First, although Israel is skeptical of multinational forces intended to safeguard its security interests (the ineffectiveness of international peacekeeping forces in Lebanon offer a glaring example), depending on the composition and the mandate of such a force, a multinational effort could potentially be effective. A force stationed along the Israel-Jordan border that includes military personnel from several *leading Arab States, especially Saudi Arabia, Egypt, and Jordan*—as each has a vested interest in keeping the peace—in addition to a contingency of peacekeepers from select NATO member states under U.S. command, could be extraordinarily effective and essential. A robust force with a mandate to take action to stop the infiltration of terrorists and the smuggling of weapons could satisfy in part Israel's security concerns, provided it is further augmented by other security provisions.

Second, although the PA has demonstrated a remarkable capacity to keep the peace during the past two years and prevent violent attacks against Israel, the Palestinians should agree to a phased withdrawal of Israeli forces over a period of three to four years. During this period of time, the Palestinians' internal security forces should be more than tripled to ensure an orderly takeover of all security responsibilities from Israel as they withdraw from Areas B and eventually C as well, and allow Israel to prepare for relocating many settlers. Jordan, with American financial support, has done an impressive job in training the Palestinian security forces and could use this time to expand the effort to a much larger scale. Through this transitional period and beyond, the PA should recognize that the burden of proof—maintaining a nonviolent atmosphere—falls squarely on its shoulders. They must know that Palestinians' independence depends on Israel's national security, and a repeat of the Second Intifada or the firing of rockets at Israel's densely populated areas following a new Israeli withdrawal from the West Bank would be a kiss of death for the hope of a Palestinian state in the West Bank and Gaza.

Third, the Palestinian state must remain demilitarized, not only to satisfy Israel's requirements but also to conserve financial resources to enable investments in the infrastructure of the state, thereby increasing the vested interests in maintaining peace. There are 17 countries in the world who have virtually no armies and need not have one because they are simply not threatened by their neighbors and do not want to invest in military hardware to no avail. Similarly, the new Palestinian state will not be threatened by any of its neighbors—Jordan, Israel, or Egypt—and even if the Palestinians invest billions of dollars to build a military machine, it would never be in a position to challenge Israel militarily or even deter it should Israel feel threatened by the Palestinian state.

Finally, since Gaza must be a part of the equation, the Arab states, especially Saudi Arabia, Egypt, and Syria in particular, should lean heavily on Hamas to join the peace process and accept the stationing of similar forces in Gaza in exchange for lifting the Israeli blockade completely. Whereas Israel could reach a peace agreement with the PA without Hamas, it would be extremely difficult to sustain it without, at a minimum, Hamas' acquiescence. Thus, from a security perspective, notwithstanding Israel's rejection of Hamas as a terrorist organization, ignoring it will continue to pose security problems for Israel. For this reason Syria will be needed to support the peace process, and in order to induce Damascus to use its leverage on Hamas, it must be given a reason to believe that Israel is seeking a comprehensive Arab-Israeli peace that will include Syria.

The Palestinians, including Hamas, must accept the fact that the prospect of establishing a state of their own is intertwined with Israel's national security. Meanwhile, Israel must drop the illusion that it can ensure its national security while maintaining even a semblance of the occupation. Neither side can realize what they want unless they accept this basic bittersweet reality.

ISRAEL'S FALSE SENSE OF INVINCIBILITY

OCTOBER 8, 2010

The military and economic prowess currently enjoyed by Israel has led to a false sense of invincibility and a belief that the status quo between Israelis and Palestinians is sustainable. While Israel's economy is robust and public confidence in its military remains high, Israel's national aspiration for a safe, secure, and prosperous homeland for the Jews has yet to be achieved. Obtaining this goal is inextricably linked to the establishment of a lasting two-state solution; relinquishing occupied Arab land while abandoning the perilous notion held by many Israelis that their country can maintain this false sense of invincibility is necessary to achieve this. Perhaps this attitude explains the Netanyahu government's unwillingness to extend the settlement freeze for a mere two months, because the Israeli public has become complacent and does not care if the negotiations break down completely.

Israelis are currently enjoying life in a mirage. To drive through Israel's state-of-the-art highways and to walk along the Tel Aviv beachfront with carefree Israelis enjoying the sand and sun along the Mediterranean is to witness this illusion in action. With a strong economy and violence significantly reduced, Israelis today have a chilling sense of security. On the one hand they continue to feel victimized and isolated by the international community, yet on the other hand they feel assured in their ability to defend the state against enemy attacks. Meanwhile, Israelis have begun to lose compassion and empathy for those who are suffering so that they may enjoy this false sense of security.

I remember recently having a breakfast in one of Tel Aviv's beachfront hotels with a colleague who said to me in the midst of our heated discussion about the peace process: "Alon, you keep talking about the need for peace and ending the occupation, why should we do that? Look at what we have created, look at the array of food and splendor; we live in a de facto peace and enormous prosperity—why should we give anything back?" Against this backdrop, in a poll last March only 8 percent of Israelis cited a resolution of the conflict with the Palestinians as Israel's most urgent problem.[31] With alarming short-sightedness, Israelis have come to believe that the status quo can be preserved indefinitely. But can this really last? This mirage could be undermined in a single day by a few deadly attacks. Protecting Israel against such a potential catastrophe requires diligent and concerted efforts to end the conflict with the Palestinians, while the whole world is urging for an equitable solution.

Israel's perceived invincibility stems from its military power, economic prosperity, and technological might. Israel's military is among the strongest, most expertly trained, and experienced in the world, with defense spending per capita consistently among the highest in the world. Even as Israel was criticized by the international community for using disproportionate force in wars in Lebanon and Gaza (and in the flotilla affair), the Israeli public has remained fully supportive and confident in the use of the IDF's military power. Meanwhile, despite a sluggish global economy, Israel is experiencing rapid economic growth. In the second quarter of 2010, Israel's economy grew 4.7 percent, the fastest pace in two years.[32] Consumer confidence is high, with spending increasing nearly 9 percent in that same period. Meanwhile, Israel has rebounded from the global financial crises due to the strength of its global exports, which constitute nearly half of Israel's gross domestic product. Finally, Israel's technological might and entrepreneurial spirit are unmatched. Today, Israel enjoys more start-ups per capita than any country in the world, and has more companies listed on the NASDAQ exchange than all European nations combined. Its reputation as a leader in the high-tech sector has led many to call Israel the "Silicon Valley of the Middle East."

---

31   Karl Vick, "Why Israel Doesn't Care About Peace," *Time*, September 2, 2010, http://content.time.com/time/magazine/article/0,9171,2015789,00.html.

32   Gwen Ackerman, "Israel Economic Growth Unexpectedly Accelerates to Fastest Pace Since 2008," *Bloomberg News*, August 16, 2010, http://www.bloomberg.com/news/2010-08-16/israel-economic-growth-unexpectedly-accelerates-to-fastest-pace-since-2008.html.

Are all of these achievements sustainable without peace with the Palestinians? The short answer is no. Without a viable peace process, the Palestinians will have nothing to lose, while Israel has everything to lose. This is a formula for disaster which must be upended before Israel's dream of invincibility devolves into a nightmare. Ten years ago, the situation was quite similar to what we are seeing today. The West Bank was calm and economic growth in the area considerable. Israel was enjoying advances in its economy and a general sense of confidence that despite the failed Oslo process, the status quo could be sustained. The complete breakdown of peace talks and the Palestinians' violent Second Intifada revealed that this was indeed an illusion. It would be tragic if history were to repeat itself.

Winning wars has become expensive for Israel, both in dollars and diplomacy. Israel's defense spending has exponentially grown to over 50 billion NIS in 2010 (over 13 billion USD).33 But Israel cannot spend enough to overcome the international scrutiny and isolation it will receive as a result of "winning" another war. If there is no progress in peace talks, it could become only a question of time as to when a new violent eruption will occur that could make the Second Intifada pale in comparison. Even if the PA seeks to prevent such an escalation, its security forces may not be able to control a widespread popular uprising, which could be fueled by extremists. The strengthened weapons capabilities of Hamas and Hezbollah are well documented; each has thousands of rockets capable of reaching Ashkelon and Tel Aviv. Israel could win another war—even one that would occur on all fronts—but at what cost in lives and property and to the prospects for achieving long-term peace and security?

If the current peacemaking efforts cannot be salvaged, and the situation dangerously devolves, the costs to Israel would be shattering. As Israel refrains from a settlement freeze that would keep peace talks afloat, the international community is of the consensus that Israel's inaction demonstrates that it does not want peace. In addition to the increased isolation of Israel in the international community, the Arab states could abandon their Peace Initiative, giving Islamic extremists the

---

33 Moti Bassok, "Defense Budget to Grow, Education Spending to Shrink," *Haaretz*, September 30, 2009, http://www.haaretz.com/print-edition/business/defense-budget-to-grow-education-spending-to-shrink-1.6974.

opportunity and justification to undermine Israel in any way they can. Meanwhile, the campaign to delegitimize the State of Israel is likely to intensify and gain greater support. While for the time being the United States is likely to remain at Israel's side, it is unlikely that it can fend off Israel's growing isolation in the face of little evidence that Israel is willing to continue peace efforts, and in doing so help the United States to advance its own goals in the region. Israel's economic growth may indeed suffer as one country after another seeks to distance itself from a country that is viewed not only as an obstacle to peace, but one that undermines their strategic interests in the Middle East. Israel could become a liability even to the United States, which would have the direst consequences imaginable.

Opponents argue that the status quo is indeed sustainable and that peace efforts are useless. They argue that no matter what Israel does, the Palestinians will never deliver peace with security, and that the international community—especially the Arab states—will criticize and isolate it. They argue that the withdrawal from Lebanon and Gaza, and the subsequent rocket attacks and wars that followed, prove that the concept of land-for-peace is no longer valid. In short, they now argue, "we made a land of milk and honey"—as my friend said—"why should we give it away when we have means to sustain it?" This is a fallacy. Genuine peace, security, and prosperity can only come with a negotiated agreement established between the parties in good faith, with the assistance and support of the United States, the Arab states, and the international community. Prime Minister Netanyahu is in a unique position to lead efforts to achieve this goal, but today he must show the determination and political will for it to succeed.

Israel is therefore facing a pivotal crossroads—continue dreaming that Israel can maintain the mirage of invincibility and potentially lead itself to a national nightmare, or make Israel's dream a reality by pursuing a two-state solution and do so from a position of strength. As the father of modern Zionism, Theodore Herzl, famously once said, "If you will it, it is no dream." Prime Minister Netanyahu is capable of steering Israel in either direction. To move toward peace, he must now follow Herzl's dream of a Jewish state living in peace and harmony with its neighbors.

THE END OF LAND FOR PEACE!

JANUARY 7, 2011

Prime Minister Netanyahu has demonstrated through his actions—or more specifically, his inactions—that he rejects the
notion of land for peace. This has been clearly illustrated through his
reluctant rhetorical acceptance of a two-state solution rife with ca-
veats, and his refusal to halt settlement construction in the West Bank
for even an additional two months in exchange for a doubling of the
United States' aid package. Thus, it has become increasingly clear that
the framework of Israel's successful peace agreements with Egypt
and Jordan based on "land for peace" no longer holds true. This
represents nothing less than a fundamental change in Israel's peace
posturing in relation to the Syrians and especially the Palestinians. As
such, today the prospect for successful bilateral negotiations is not
only incredibly remote, but creates an extremely dangerous situation.

In forming a government with Avigdor Lieberman, Netanyahu
has prioritized Israel's security and demographic threat not dissimi-
larly to previous Israeli governments, but with the exception of one
critical provision. Today, there are approximately 5.8 million Jews
living in "historic Palestine," the area between the Jordan River and
the Mediterranean Sea. There are a total of 5.3 million Palestinians
living in the West Bank, Gaza, and Israel proper. The growth rate of
Israeli Jews is 1.7%, while among the Palestinians in the West Bank it
is 2.1, and in Gaza, 3.3.[34] The Palestinian Central Bureau of Statistics
recently estimated that the Palestinian Arabs will constitute a majority

---

34   See "The population of Israel 1990-2009: Demographic Characteristics,"
     The Central Bureau of Statistics, December 2010, http://unstats.un.org/
     unsd/wsd/docs/Israel_wsd_brochure.pdf; and "Population Growth Rate,"
     CIA World Factbook, https://www.cia.gov/library/publications/the-
     world-factbook/fields/2002.html (accessed January 6, 2011).

in historic Palestine by as early as 2014.[35] A recent study by the Taub Center for Israel Studies at NYU showed that nearly 50 percent of students in Israel's schools today are either Arab or religious Jews.[36]

Faced with this demographic dilemma, Ariel Sharon responded by unilaterally withdrawing from the Gaza Strip, thereby shedding responsibility for the over 1.5 million Palestinians living in Gaza while strengthening Israel's Jewish majority (if only extending it for a number of years). Netanyahu's apparent plan—together with his partner, Lieberman—is also to unilaterally redraw Israel's borders. However, the key difference in strategy is that whereas Sharon withdrew to the 1967 border between Israel and the Gaza Strip, Netanyahu intends to pay no heed to the 1967 "Green Line" in redrawing the border to distinguish Israel from the Palestinians in the West Bank.

Netanyahu's refusal to halt settlement construction beyond the three major settlement blocs, widely considered to be included in Israel as part of any agreement with the Palestinians, indicates that unlike his predecessors, who sought less than 10 percent of the West Bank as part of a land swap agreement with the Palestinians, he has his eyes set on much more. This conduct is consistent with Lieberman's controversial proposal to "transfer" Israeli Palestinian citizens such as those living in the triangle of Arab villages in the Galilee to the PA's control—against their wishes—in exchange for the areas of expanded Jewish settlement in the West Bank. The Netanyahu government's strategy is therefore two-fold: first, to enlarge the area of Israeli control in the West Bank while relinquishing Palestinian majority areas; and second, to demand recognition of Israel as a Jewish state as a precondition for any agreement. The two tactics combined offer a distorted view of Netanyahu's plan for "peace" in which he remains unconcerned about the fate of an independent Palestinian state, so long as Israel maintains its false sense of security and a solid Jewish majority. Netanyahu's refusal to stop settlement growth and

---

35   "Arab Majority in 'Historic Palestine' After 2014: Survey," *Al Arabiya*, January 1, 2011, http://www.alarabiya.net/articles/2011/01/01/131780.html.

36   Dan Ben-David, "The Rosshandler Bulletin Series," *Taub Center Bulletin* 2(1) (June 2010), http://taubcenter.org.il/tauborgilwp/wp-content/uploads/Taub_Bulletin_final.pdf.

Lieberman's success in advancing the loyalty oath requirement of Israeli citizens indicates that this strategy is already well into motion.

Confronted with this bleak prospect, the Palestinians now feel compelled to turn to the international community. In doing so, they are seeking two critical points: first, a clear statement that continued Israeli settlement activity in the West Bank serves as a roadblock to achieving a lasting peace agreement between Israel and the Palestinians. Second, that a two-state solution based on the 1967 borders and United Nations Security Council (UNSC) Resolutions 242 and 338 is the only viable resolution to the Israeli-Palestinian conflict, both of which enjoy global consensus support. The two points will be framed by the Palestinians in the exact language that the United States has used for many years, making it exceedingly difficult for the White House to oppose them. After all, how could the White House reject a boilerplate statement of support for a two-state solution? Or that settlement construction is unproductive? Support from the United States would send a significant message, but even without the United States, the support of the vast majority of the countries constituting the United Nations General Assembly (UNGA) would provide the Palestinians with significant leverage to further pressure Israel in its continued opposition to peacemaking. It is important to recall that UNGA Resolution 194, regularly cited as the international community's perspective on the issue of Palestinian refugees, is a non-binding measure—but the influence of that resolution, nevertheless, remains central in any future negotiations to settle the Palestinian refugee problem.

Even so, the PA's campaign to win support in the international arena will be undercut so long as groups like Hamas continue to oppose it. As long as Hamas and other rejectionist groups stand against the PA's international effort to mobilize opposition to settlements, and support for two-states, Israel will have justification to maintain an argument that it has no true partner for peace. It will continue to utilize this excuse in waging a public campaign, pointing blame at Palestinian rejection of Israel's right to exist as a Jewish state—not Israeli intransigence—for keeping the peace process suspended.

Therein lies the fundamental mistake that the Palestinians and Arab states have and continue to make: not sufficiently accepting that Israel indeed faces legitimate security threats from extremist groups like Hamas and Hezbollah, which absolutely must be mitigated if Israel is to ever accept an agreed-upon end to the conflict. The 1967 borders are now a source of pride for Palestinians and the Arab world, made more so by the peace treaties with Egypt and Jordan, and the historic API, which offers full normalization of relations between Israel and the Arab states in exchange for the territories captured by Israel in 1967, including an Israeli-Palestinian agreement on a two-state solution based on these lines. But without receiving an endorsement of the Initiative from Hamas and Hezbollah, and even though Israel itself did not embrace the API, Israel's excuse that it remains threatened, that it has no partner, and that the offer is not comprehensive cannot be dismissed. An endorsement of the API by Hamas and Hezbollah would exponentially catapult the impact of the PA's efforts to pressure Israel to remove its excuses for inaction.

Meanwhile, Netanyahu is making mistakes of his own. First, his continued insistence that he is willing to negotiate face-to-face with PA President Mahmoud Abbas until "white smoke" appears, as he recently told reporters, is simply not credible. With his support of settlements and emphasis on new demands, no one believes that he will negotiate in good faith without evidence indicating that his words are genuine and not merely designed to skirt increasing international pressure. Words alone will not bring Israel out of isolation; only actions can accomplish this now. Second, Netanyahu must also understand that no current or future Palestinian leadership—or that of the Arab world—would ever accept anything less than a negotiated agreement based on the 1967 borders. This is why Israel has been misguided in its continued ambivalence to the API. With every passing day, the State of Israel loses an opportunity to lock in the Arab world to a promise of recognition, normalization, and above all, guaranteeing its national security upon the successful conclusion of peace talks.

A recent poll by the International Peace Institute shows that Israelis remain aloof to the API plan, with just 36 percent preferring the API to the status quo.[37] As long as Israel's leadership promotes

37 "Iran, Lebanon, Israelis and Palestinians: New IPI Opinion Polls," *International Peace Institute*, January 5, 2011, http://www.ipinst.org/news/general-announcement/209-iran-lebanon-israelis-and-palestinians-new-ipi-opinion-polls.html.

the fallacy that Israel can maintain its security and Jewish majority without an agreement based on the 1967 lines—and continues to reject the promise of the API—it is effectively forfeiting the opportunity to make peace and subjecting the next generation of Israelis and Palestinians to continued destruction and death.

THE FURY OVER THE 1967
BORDERS IS DISINGENUOUS

*Israel has legitimate national security concerns but they will never be
satisfied by annexing larger chunks of territory in the West Bank*

MAY 23, 2011

Although President Obama stated nothing new during his speech
last Thursday about the 1967 borders with "mutually agreed
land swaps" as a basis for a negotiated Israeli-Palestinian agreement,
he put it in a manner that should give the Palestinians pause before
they go to the UNGA to seek statehood recognition. Moreover, in
doing so he has marginalized the settlement problem, which has
been a major stumbling block in resuming the negotiations, while
encouraging some key member states of the European Union (EU)
to rethink their endorsement of a Palestinian state come September.
The fury of Israeli and Jewish leaders over what the president said is
entirely misguided, misplaced, and disingenuous.

Every American administration since President Carter has
supported the idea that the 1967 borders provide the baseline
for negotiations. Furthermore, in every negotiation between Israel
and the Palestinians since the Oslo Accords in 1993, both sides
have agreed on the same principle: a land swap to accommodate
the Palestinians for the land on which Israel's three major settlement blocs are situated. Indeed, every Israeli government, regardless of its political leanings has—and will continue—to insist
on incorporating these blocs of settlements into Israel proper
under any peace agreement. For most Palestinians and Israelis,
this formulation has become a given. There will be other territorial disputes in connection with Ariel, for example, which is
located deep in the West Bank, and Silwan near Jerusalem. But

59

both sides know that any agreement would entail a land swap, albeit they will argue about the quality, contiguity, and equivalence of the land to be swapped. That said, there is no question that these and many other even more intractable issues can be resolved if both parties are genuinely committed to peace.

However modified the borders will be to accommodate both sides, the contour of the final borders will not substantially enhance or severely undermine Israel's national security. Prime Minister Netanyahu is being fundamentally disingenuous when he proclaims that the 1967 borders leave Israel "indefensible." The annexation of more land two or three kilometers deep into the West Bank will make little difference from a security perspective. A mutually acceptable land swap, required because of demographic necessity, where more than 70 percent of the settlers reside along the 1967 borders is one thing; to go beyond that is a simple land grab in the guise of national security. What Netanyahu and his hardline coalition partners have in mind is to surround the Palestinians from the east, west, north, and south, which theoretically enhances Israel's security while isolating the Palestinians completely and denying them contiguity. This will not only be rejected off-hand by the Palestinians, but will also deny Israel even a semblance of real peace with security.

Israel's ultimate national security requirements rest on five pillars agreed upon by every politically non-biased Israeli defense and security expert. The Obama administration should begin to articulate these requirements to demonstrate that Israel's genuine national security cannot be met by mere annexation of more swaths of land in the West Bank but must rest, first and foremost, with peace augmented by other measures to alleviate Israel's long-term security concerns.

First, a comprehensive peace: all efforts must focus on achieving a peace agreement negotiated to accommodate Israel's legitimate national security and demographic requirements while providing the Palestinians the right and the space in a contiguous land mass to live freely in their own independent state, alongside Israel, with dignity. In the final analysis, only a genuine peace that meets the aspirations of both peoples and the acceptance of one another as partners and neighbors will endure and offer Israel the real security it seeks.

Second, credible deterrence: since there is—and will continue to be—a lingering distrust between the two sides, Israel must maintain a credible military deterrence that will make it abundantly clear to all those who now or in the future harbor ill intent against Israel that they will suffer utter devastation should they threaten Israel's security. In this regard, Israel and the United States can make sure, as they have in the past, that no single country or a combination of states can overwhelm Israel militarily, along with America's continued guarantee for Israel's national security.

Third, international peacekeeping force: the alleviation of Israel's concerns over the smuggling of weapons and the infiltration of terrorists from the Jordan Valley cannot be achieved by maintaining residual Israeli forces along the Jordan River, which for many Palestinians will be tantamount to continued occupation. Instead, an international peacekeeping force (perhaps with some Israeli and Palestinian participation) will have to be stationed along the Jordan River. The force should be assembled from specific countries that have a vested interest in maintaining peace, including Arab states such as Jordan, Egypt, and Saudi Arabia, and EU nations like Britain, France, and Germany, all under the command of the United States. Such a robust force should be empowered by the UNSC to act as it sees fit to maintain calm, to foster close relations with all neighboring states, and to not be removed without an explicit UNSC resolution, where the United States enjoys veto power.

Fourth, a demilitarized Palestinian state: the newly-established Palestinian state must be demilitarized, with its security assured by the same peacekeeping forces. The Palestinians should accept the fact that they will never be in a position to challenge Israel militarily. Moreover, no country, including Israel, will ever threaten a Palestinian state that lives in peace and harmony with its neighbors. Instead of wasting money on military hardware, presumably to boost its national pride, future Palestinian governments should respond to the yearning of the people by investing in economic development, education, healthcare, infrastructure, and democratic institutions that will enable them to take pride in their achievements. This is what the Arab youth demand from their governments throughout the Arab world and the Palestinian people are no exception.

Fifth, a regional security umbrella: once a peace agreement is achieved, the United States could offer a security umbrella, along the lines of what Secretary of State Hillary Clinton proposed more than a year ago, to which all nations in the region at peace with Israel and with each other can belong. Such a regional security umbrella could also serve as a major deterrent against Iran to prevent it from intimidating or threatening any state in the area.

Finally, national security for Israel is a state of mind; no one should fault Israelis for their preoccupation with national security. Indeed, the Jewish historical experience speaks for itself. But national security in the current technological environment—with the sustained exponential growth in social and economic interconnectedness on the world stage—makes it imperative for Israel to recalibrate its national security strategy. Instead of reaching out and demonstrating its willingness to achieve an equitable peace, Israel is becoming a garrison state, building fences and walls, isolating itself not only from its neighbors but also from the international community. Surely there will always be risks involved in making concessions but as long as such risks are calculated and can be mitigated should they come to pass, seeking absolute security becomes a liability as it offers no room for concessions necessary to make peace.

The president's speech was one of the most pro-Israel speeches ever delivered by any sitting American president. Netanyahu's reaction to it was both divisive and counterproductive. It is time for the Israeli public to rise against such hypocrisy and disdain to demand accountability from a government that has led the country astray from Day One. Thanks to Netanyahu's government, no one can say that Israel is better off today than it was two years ago. It is time to put an end to the illusion that Israel will be more secure by further territorial entrenchment in the West Bank.

NETANYAHU'S STANCE JEOPARDIZES ISRAEL'S SECURITY

MAY 26, 2011

The supposed controversy over President Obama's speech on the Middle East, manufactured by Prime Minster Netanyahu and enabled by the media, is disgraceful and insincere. President Obama said nothing new about borders, just the facts: no border will ever be acceptable to the Palestinians that does not carve out a Palestinian state in the West Bank and Gaza, the two territories must be based on the "1967 lines," and no border will ever be acceptable to Israel that does not include the three major settlement blocs. Negotiating the 1967 lines with mutually agreed land swaps meets both demands, which is why it has been the foundation of border negotiations in every peacemaking effort, including UN Resolutions 242 and 338, both of which Israel accepted. However, by misrepresenting the president's remarks, Netanyahu irresponsibly chose to pick a fight with the one man who can safeguard Israel from near-total international isolation, while ignoring the very significant steps the president took in Israel's favor.

Days before President Obama's speech, Netanyahu spoke to the Knesset and identified Israel's core demands: maintaining the settlement blocs, a united Jerusalem, opposing Palestinian refugees' return to Israel, and receiving recognition as a Jewish state. President Obama has now backed them all, but Netanyahu is choosing not to listen. Netanyahu's reaction to Obama's speech, stating that the 1967 lines are "indefensible," simply ignored Obama's call for mutually agreed land swaps, which inherently means an adjusted 1967 border, as President Obama's explained in his remarks to AIPAC. The notion of "indefensible" borders also ignores pure common sense. The width between the Mediterranean Sea and the Jordan River is a mere 44 miles—if an adjusted 1967 border is "indefensible," what

63

is defensible? How many handfuls of acres or kilometers more are needed to maintain the balance of Israel's national security? The inconvenient truth is that expanding territory by a few more acres is not what will maintain Israel's national security. Israel's security can only be guaranteed by four elements:

1) a lasting peace agreement;

2) credible deterrence;

3) enforceable international guarantees; and finally

4) a strong United States-Israel relationship that provides Israel with a security umbrella.

This will safeguard Israel from international opprobrium by supporting its right to self-defense and working alongside it to address regional threats such as that from Iran.

Meanwhile, Netanyahu, much of the media, and the president's critics and challengers also chose to ignore the significant steps Obama took to place the onus on the Palestinians. In fact, Obama's iteration of the 1967 border discussion was geared directly for this purpose. First, it provides the Palestinians—and the Europeans—with a new consideration ahead of the planned UNGA vote in September. That President Obama gave an exclusive interview after the speech to the BBC—addressing a European audience—and soon after embarked on a five-day trip to Europe only underscores his commitment to ensuring that "efforts to delegitimize Israel will end in failure," and that "actions to isolate Israel at the United Nations in September won't create an independent state."[38] Second, the focus on borders was intended to remove the issue of a settlement freeze from continuing to serve as the primary obstacle to negotiations. It appears he has succeeded, with Palestinians now requesting Netanyahu's response to Obama's formulation on borders as a prerequisite to renewed negotiations, rather than a full freeze. Third, the president addressed Palestinian national aspirations in the context of the Arab Spring to maintain credibility for the United States in the region. But

---

38   Barack Obama, "Remarks by the President on the Middle East and North Africa" (State Department, Washington, DC, May 19, 2011), http://www.whitehouse.gov/the-press-office/2011/05/19/remarks-president-middle-east-and-north-africa.

more importantly, he did so without wavering from the United States' commitment to Israel's security "as a Jewish state." In fact, his reiteration of "Israel as a Jewish state and the homeland for the Jewish people, and the state of Palestine as the homeland for the Palestinian people,"[39] were both endorsements of a two-state solution and a rejection of the Palestinian right of return to Israel. Fourth, not only did President Obama state that the Palestinians "walked away from talks," but with regard to the recent Fatah-Hamas unity government, he challenged the Palestinians to produce a "credible answer" to the question, "How can one negotiate with a party that has shown itself unwilling to recognize your right to exist?"[40]

It is one thing to establish maximalist positions, knowing that negotiations will ultimately moderate these stances to achieve one's actual goals. It is entirely another matter to articulate a position that is totally and completely unacceptable to the other side, as Netanyahu has done when he addressed a joint session of Congress, and does not allow any opportunity for negotiation. After all, both parties know very well what the contours of any peace agreement will look like.

On borders, as Obama stated, a negotiated border will be based on the 1967 border with land swaps to include the major settlement blocs. On Jerusalem, the city must remain "united," but the Palestinians must also have some presence in the Arab neighborhoods to form a capital in East Jerusalem for a Palestinian state. On security, Israel must have ironclad security guarantees with an international peacekeeping force (perhaps with some Israeli and Palestinian participation) to be stationed along the Jordan River. The force should be assembled from specific countries that have a vested interest in maintaining peace, including Arab states such as Jordan, Egypt, and Saudi Arabia and EU nations like Britain, France, and Germany, all under the command of the United States. Finally, both sides must face these hard truths: that Israel's recognition as a Jewish state requires a Jewish majority that can only be sustained through a two-state solution, and, in turn, a solution to the plight of Palestinian refugees must be a return to Palestine, not to Israel. No moderate

39   Ibid.

40   Ibid.

Israeli or Palestinian could accept anything less. None of this is new, none of it should be controversial, and none of it can be achieved without the active participation, encouragement, and facilitation of the United States—whether the international community, the Palestinians, or Israel likes it or not.

Still, if this solution is ever to be achieved, Israel and the Palestinians must address those who would rather perpetuate the conflict than end it. For Israel, this means not enabling settlers and other right-wing radicals to hijack the Zionist cause in ways that are weakening the United States-Israel alliance and placing Israel's future in jeopardy. It also means that instead of shielding his eyes from the truth and pointing to obstacles to justify his inaction, Netanyahu must be pro-active in presenting real leadership and a realistic, practical path that can bring Israel toward greater peace and security and away from its growing isolation. For the Palestinians, it is a clear recognition that violence will only lead to destruction. Hamas must be disabused of the notion that Israel can be destroyed. The use of such rhetoric and violence will not just place Hamas at risk, it will completely annihilate it. Israel will not hesitate to respond to such threats by decapitating its leadership and inflicting a severe blow on its infrastructure, even at the expense of international condemnation. But Israel should also welcome any sign of moderation on the part of Hamas, especially if the reconciliation agreement between Hamas and Fatah holds.

Top Egyptian officials have privately conveyed this message to Hamas leaders—if they ignore the advice, they will do so at their own peril, and at the demise of the Palestinian national cause as well as the significant progress that has been made to achieve the goal of Palestinian independence. As one Palestinian recently told me, he is concerned about the unknown changes that will emanate from the recent reconciliation between Fatah and Hamas: "Right now the Palestinians in the West Bank feel as though we are living in Switzerland—except we don't sleep," he said. "Now, we have so much to lose." The same is true of Israelis—the situation can change overnight, and time is running out. In his remarks on Sunday to AIPAC, President Obama was blunt: "If there is a controversy, then, it's not based in substance. What I did on Thursday [in his speech on the Middle East] was to say publicly what has long been acknowledged privately. I've done so because we can't afford to wait another decade, or another two decades, or another three decades to achieve peace. The world is moving too fast...the extraordinary challenges facing Israel will only grow. Delay will undermine Israel's security and the peace that the Israeli people deserve."[41]

Reflecting on these remarks, Israelis must ask themselves: are we better off today than we were more than two years ago when the Netanyahu government came to power? The question, of course, is rhetorical—but the answer is a clear, unequivocal "no." As such, Israeli leaders should be asking themselves a subsequent question: what are we prepared to do about it? If Netanyahu's speech to a joint session of Congress is his answer, the Israelis should expect further isolation while jeopardizing rather than enhancing their national security.

---

41   Barack Obama, "Remarks by the President at the AIPAC Policy Conference 2011" (Washington, DC, May 22, 2011), http://www. whitehouse.gov/the-press-office/2011/05/22/remarks-president-aipac-policy-conference-2011.

ALON BEN-MEIR

ISRAEL'S BORDERS AND NATIONAL SECURITY

FEBRUARY 16, 2012

Israel's National Security: the Psychological Dimension

No one should fault the Israelis for their preoccupation with national security. Indeed, the Jewish historical experience speaks for itself: centuries of persecution, expulsion, anti-Semitism, and segregation culminating with the Holocaust, followed by incessant, violent confrontations with Arab states and the Palestinians. Such things have created a major psychological barrier that places national security concerns at the front and center of Israel's domestic and foreign policy. For this reason, any agreement on the Israeli-Palestinian conflict must take into full account Israel's legitimate national security concerns, which are deeply embedded in the mind and soul of every Israeli. Regardless of how exaggerated Israel's sense of vulnerability may seem to its detractors, the Palestinians cannot afford to dismiss Israel's concerns and hope to strike a peace agreement. Although the Israelis and Palestinians differ about the kind of measures needed to alleviate Israel's security concerns, only if the Palestinians appreciate the psychological underpinnings behind Israel's national security and agree on the security measures needed will both sides reach an enduring peace.

But Israel's national security strategy in the current technological environment (one with sustained, exponential growth in the social and economic connectedness on the world stage) must be recalibrated. Instead of reaching out and demonstrating its willingness to achieve an equitable peace, Israel is becoming a garrison state, building fences and walls, isolating itself not only from its neighbors but also from the international community. Surely there will always be risks involved in making territorial and political concessions but as long as such risks are calculated and can be mitigated should they come to pass, seeking absolute security becomes a liability as it offers no room for the concessions necessary to make peace. That said, there are many voices in Israel that rightfully argue that given the continuing antagonism and hatred toward Israel by extremists groups like Hamas and states like Iran, Israel cannot settle on a peace agreement at face value. For this reason, whereas real peace provides Israel the ultimate security it seeks, other security measures must be in place as a part of any peace agreement, not only to guarantee such peace but to also further enhance it over time and make it irreversible.

Borders and National Security

Israel has legitimate national security concerns that can be satisfied only through multiple security measures. Unfortunately, those Israelis supporting the notion of a "Greater Israel" often promote territorial ambition in the guise of enhancing Israel's security. Yet the Israelis' national and personal security can never, and will never, be ensured by obtaining more land to establish so-called "defensible borders." After all, the land between the Jordan River and the Mediterranean Sea hardly exceeds 42 miles, a short distance by any standards. Territorial depth will not guarantee Israel's security, especially in the age of rockets and missiles, but strategic depth can. Other than the annexation of larger chunks of territory in the West Bank, the only way to effectively protect Israel's security is through a lasting peace agreement made possible by a genuine, effective security regime and cooperation alongside an equitable "land for peace" formula. Such a formula must be based on Israel retaining the major settlement blocs along the "Green Line" while the Palestinians establish their own state on historic Palestine, consisting of the West Bank and the Gaza Strip.

Every American administration since President Carter has supported the idea that the 1967 borders provide the baseline for negotiations. In every negotiation between Israel and the Palestinians since the Oslo Accords in 1993, each side has agreed to the same principle: a land swap to accommodate the Palestinians for the land on which

Israel's three major settlement blocs are situated. Indeed, every Israeli government, regardless of its political leanings, has and will continue to insist on incorporating these blocs of settlements into Israel proper under any peace agreement. For most Palestinians and Israelis, this formulation has become a given. There will be other territorial disputes in connection with the Ariel settlement, for example, which is located deep in the West Bank, and Silwan near Jerusalem. But both sides know that any agreement would entail a land swap, albeit they will argue about the quality, contiguity, and equivalence of the land to be swapped. That said, there is no question that these and many other even more intractable issues, including the continuance of Israelis living in Palestinian territories, can be resolved if Israel's national security concerns are satisfied and both parties are genuinely committed to peace.

However modified the borders will be to accommodate both sides, the contours of the final borders will not substantially enhance or severely undermine Israel's national security. The annexation of more land two or three kilometers deep into the West Bank will make little difference from a security perspective. A mutually acceptable land swap, required because of demographic necessity, where more than 70 percent of the settlers reside along the 1967 borders, is one thing. To go beyond that is a simple land grab in the guise of national security. What those who promote the notion of a "Greater Israel" have in mind is to surround the Palestinians from all directions, which theoretically enhances Israel's security while isolating the Palestinians completely and denying them contiguity. This would not only be rejected off-hand by the Palestinians, but would also deny Israel even a semblance of real peace with security. This is the imperative that both sides must recognize, and thereby they must carefully consider the real security measures needed that can satisfy Israel's requirements without humiliating the Palestinians.

Israel's ultimate national security requirements rest on seven pillars over which every politically non-biased Israeli defense and security expert have agreed upon. Israel's national defense institutions and think tanks, along with current and future American administrations, should begin to articulate these requirements to demonstrate that Israel's genuine national security cannot be met by a mere annexation of more swaths of land in the West Bank. Indeed, Israel's national security must rest, first and foremost, with peace augmented by other measures to alleviate Israel's long-term security concerns.

First Pillar: Maintaining Credible Deterrence

Since there is—and will continue to be for the foreseeable future—a lingering distrust between the two sides, Israel must maintain a credible military deterrence that will make it abundantly clear to all those who, now or in the future, harbor ill intent against Israel and pose a real threat to Israel's existence that they will suffer utter devastation should they attempt to actualize their threats. Israel's enemies should know that aiming for Israel's destruction will bring about their own destruction first. Simply put, Israel will not die alone; the "Never Again" mindset (in reference to the Holocaust) should be taken very seriously by Israel's adversaries, lest they are determined to commit national suicide.

In this regard, Israel and the United States can make sure, as they have in the past, that no single country or combination of states can overwhelm Israel militarily, backed with America's continued guarantee for Israel's national security. As such, no Arab or Persian nation or other terror group would dare challenge Israel militarily. That is why any agreement must ensure that Israel's qualitative military edge is maintained, as well as its right to defend its citizens from unprovoked attacks of terrorism and war. From a psychological perspective, preserving a military edge will give Israel the sense of comfort it needs, which has proven to be decisive in the past and has certainly inhibited Israel's enemies, be they groups or states, from challenging Israel militarily.

Second Pillar: An International Peacekeeping Force

The alleviation of Israel's concerns over the smuggling of weapons and the infiltration of terrorists from the Jordan Valley cannot be achieved by maintaining residual Israeli forces along the Jordan River as Israel has been demanding. Israel's insistence on maintaining such forces does not foster trust and increases resentment, as for many Palestinians it will be tantamount to continued occupation. Instead, an international peacekeeping force (perhaps with symbolic Israeli and Palestinian participation) will have to be stationed along the Jordan River. The force should be assembled from specific countries that have a vested interest in maintaining peace, including Arab states such as Jordan, Egypt, and Saudi Arabia and EU nations like Britain, France, and Germany, all the while including Israelis and Palestinians and operating under the command of the United States. The Palestinians have agreed to the stationing of such an international peacekeeping force and they, as I understand, may well agree to include a small Israeli contingency as a part of the international force.

Such a robust force should be empowered by the UNSC to act as it sees fit to maintain calm, foster close relations with all neighboring states, and of course prevent the smuggling of weapons and the infiltration of terrorists. To ensure durability and cultivate confidence, such a force cannot be removed without an explicit UNSC resolution, where the United States enjoys veto power. Here too, although Israel as a matter of principle does not place any of its national security concerns in the hands of other parties, the participation of small units of the Israeli army with the international force will alleviate some of these concerns, which would also help engender long-term confidence between Israelis and Palestinians.

Third Pillar: A Demilitarized Palestinian State

The newly-established Palestinian state must be demilitarized, with its security assured by the same peacekeeping forces. The Palestinians should accept the fact that they will never be in a position to challenge Israel militarily. Moreover, no country, including Israel, will ever threaten a Palestinian state that lives in peace and harmony with its neighbors. Peace between the Israelis and the Palestinians will not be based on a military equation. Any Palestinian military buildup will run contrary to the spirit of peace while providing the Palestinians no decisive advantage under any scenario of armed conflict with Israel. There are several countries that do not have (for different reasons) any military forces, including Costa Rica, Samoa, Grenada, and the Solomon Islands.

The idea here is to lessen Israel's national security concerns in order to allow it to make important political and territorial concessions to the Palestinians. That is, the Palestinians can increasingly benefit as long as Israel feels increasingly more secure. The past three years have demonstrated this fact as the security collaboration between Israel and the PA in the West Bank clearly benefited both sides. For this reason, instead of wasting hundreds of millions (if not billions) of dollars on military hardware, presumably to boost its national pride, future Palestinian governments should respond to the yearning of the people by investing in economic development, education, healthcare, infrastructure, and democratic institutions that will enable them to take pride in their achievements. This is what the Arab Spring is all about and this is what the Arab youth demands from their governments throughout the Arab world. The Palestinian people are no exception.

Fourth Pillar: Development of Bilateral Relations—People to People

The uprisings of the Arab Spring of 2011 ushered in a new chapter of empowerment for the citizenry of the Arab world. With the masses increasingly sharing their voice and having it heard, people-to-people dialogue, which seeks to overcome the mistrust and animosity on both sides, must be employed. As the Arab masses seek their independence from the oppressive rule of despots, Palestinians too must eventually obtain their voice and their independence. As the Arab states begin to succeed in meeting the needs of their people, they will again return to their concern for the Palestinian plight, only this time armed with the legitimate support of the millions of Arabs who have taken to the streets demanding justice.

Israel's security as a Jewish and democratic state is inextricably linked to its ability to forge the kind of people-to-people relations that can develop a foundation for peace in the region rather than even greater conflict. To be sure, one of the principle requirements to mitigate the psychological security hang-ups inherent within the Israeli experience is the expansion of the day-to-day cooperation and collaboration between the two sides. Indeed, trust cannot be established by agreements. It must be nurtured over a long period of time when each side lives up to the promises and commitments they make. This is particularly important when trust hardly existed before and when it has been betrayed time and time again. For this reason, increasing trade and tourism between the two sides is fundamental to the development of trust and the fostering of mutually beneficial relations. It is these kinds of day-to-day exchanges of people and commodities that would reveal and enhance the humanity of both sides, especially since coexistence is inadvertent under any circumstances.

Fifth Pillar: A Comprehensive Peace

All security measures, however elaborate and sophisticated, cannot guarantee Israel's national security unless they are accompanied by a peace agreement. For this reason, every effort must first focus on negotiating a peace agreement to accommodate Israel's legitimate national security and demographic requirements while providing the Palestinians the right to live freely on a contiguous land mass in their own independent state alongside Israel. In the final analysis, only a genuine peace that meets the aspirations of both peoples and fosters the acceptance of one another as partners and neighbors will endure and offer Israel the real security it seeks.

In this regard, the API, which calls for normalized relations between Israel and all members of the Arab League and the Organization of the Islamic Conference upon the establishment of an end-of-conflict agreement with a Palestinian state, provides a historic opportunity to ensure Israel's future through a resolution of the core issues at the heart of the Arab-Israeli conflict.

Sixth Pillar: Maintaining Full Security Co-operation and Collaboration

By virtue of the Israelis' and Palestinians' past experiences, full security cooperation between the two sides in advance of, and subsequent to, any peace agreement remains a central prerequisite. To prevent the West Bank from becoming a launching ground for rockets, as was the case following Israel's unilateral withdrawal from southern Lebanon in 2000 and from Gaza in 2005, future Israeli withdrawal from the West Bank must be implemented in full coordination with Palestinian security forces. Progress made between Israel and the PA under the sponsorship of the United States Security Coordinator, with assistance from Jordan, Egypt, and the EU, indicates that effective security cooperation is possible, even in an atmosphere of tension.

The success of this cooperation was built on the PA's ability to show tremendous professionalism and commitment, as well as Israel removing roadblocks and expanding their zones of operation as they proved their ability to succeed. Even if the current cooperation breaks down, future cooperation will need to be a prerequisite to the implementation of any peace agreement. Such ironclad security mechanisms have been, and will always be, Israel's chief concern. To encourage further Israeli withdrawal from Area B, which is partly controlled by Israel, and Area C, which is under Israel's complete control, the Palestinians must fully adhere to any and all security arrangements while Israel engages in a phased withdrawal within a mutually agreed upon timeframe.

Seventh Pillar: A Regional Security Umbrella

Once a peace agreement is achieved and all security measures are in place, the United States could offer a security umbrella, along the lines of what Secretary of State Hillary Clinton proposed in June of 2009, under which all nations in the region at peace with Israel (and with each other) could belong.[42] Such a regional security umbrella could also serve as a major deterrent against Iran to prevent it from intimidating or threatening any state in the area. However, such an arrangement could only be implemented following the establishment of an end-of-conflict agreement based on the two-state solution as outlined by the API. In fact, the API could serve as an important precedent of normalization that could lead to the kind of regional security umbrella that would strengthen United States and Israeli

---

42   Mark Landler and David E. Sanger, "Clinton Speaks of Shielding Mideast From Iran," *The New York Times*, July 22, 2009, http://www.nytimes.com/2009/07/23/world/asia/23diplo.html?_r=0.

relations with the Arab world while advancing their shared interests of deterring Iran from obtaining and/or deploying nuclear weaponry through terrorist proxies.

The issues of borders and security are deeply interconnected. An agreement on borders is not possible without the kind of ironclad security guarantees Israel will need to redeploy its forces with confidence. Similarly, an agreement on security arrangements is impossible as long as the territorial dispute regarding the adjustment to the 1967 Green Line are formulated, agreed upon, and implemented. However, despite the considerable challenges to such an agreement, the ideas (as outlined above) provide an achievable solution to these contentious issues that respect Palestinian aspirations for a state with territorial integrity while meeting Israel's short and long-term legitimate national security imperatives.

ISRAEL'S NATIONAL SECURITY: MYTHS AND REALITY

OCTOBER 8, 2012

Israel's national security has, and for good reason, continues to be of prime concern not only to its citizens but to world Jewry and many of its friends and allies around the globe. Israel has every reason to be weary of its enemies, who have time and again demonstrated that they are not trustworthy and remain committed to Israel's destruction both in word and in deeds. For this reason, many Israelis have become increasingly more pessimistic and skeptical about the prospect of peace and, for that matter, its durability even when achieved. This argument, however cogent it may be, has lost much of its significance as time and circumstances have changed. To be sure, although Israel's military power remains central to its national security, no territorial depth or continued military buildup provides Israel the ultimate security it needs. In the final analysis, Israel's security rests on peace with the Arab states, and its formidable military prowess must now be used to secure that peace, however elusive it may seem.

There are those who suggest that Israel's withdrawal from the West Bank will make Israel vulnerable to rocket attacks from the mountains overlooking Israel's population and industrial centers in the coastal strip below, rendering the country indefensible. As one critic wrote in response to my previous article on the Huffington Post, "Only the US Can End the Israeli-Palestinian Conflict," citing an American military expert, "modern weapon systems, most of them with components which require line-of-sight emplacement, if deployed in the [Judean and Samarian] mountains...[Israel's] present width in the central sector of the country would be reduced from 40-55 miles to 9-16 miles...[which] would render the country

77

indefensible."[43] To support this argument, there are those who simply take at face value the statements made by right-wing Israeli officials who link territorial depth to national security without examining the real relevance between the two, especially in the context of the West Bank and the territorial depth involved.

Against the one "American military expert," there are hundreds of Israeli military experts who disagree with this argument. No one is suggesting that a peace agreement in and of itself provides Israel instant security. Indeed, any peace accord will have to be implemented in stages that would entail quid pro quo, requiring both sides to fully adhere to all provisions of the agreement, especially on the matter of Israel's national security concerns. Thus, security measures will have to be in place including, for example, the stationing of an international peace force led by the United States and stationed along the borders with Jordan, replete with enforcement capabilities. More important, however, is Israel's deterrence and its own military that has and can prevent any violation of an agreement with the Palestinians.

With today's military technology and the proliferation of short and medium-range rockets (ranging from 3 to 300 miles) in the hands of Hamas and Hezbollah, modern weapons systems, regardless of where they are placed, can hit every population center in Israel. Therefore, whether the distance from the mountains of the West Bank is 40–55 miles or reduced to 9–16 miles will hardly make any difference. What will make a real difference in the final analysis are Israel's retaliatory capabilities and the potential unacceptable damage that Israel can inflict that would persuade the enemy from provoking Israel.

Ask yourself: why have the Palestinians in the West Bank, Hamas in Gaza, and Hezbollah in Lebanon refrained from provoking Israel in any serious manner since the Palestinians in the West Bank suffered from the Israeli onslaught in the wake of the Second Intifada

---

43 The commenter was citing Edward Saar, "Israel: The West Bank and Modern Arms," *Nativ: A Journal of Politics and the Arts* 1(1) (1990): 64-65. The original quote is as follows: "…the country's width in the central sector would be reduced from the present 40–55 miles to 9–16 miles…the easily concealed control elements of certain weapons systems, many of them requiring line-of-sight emplacement, if deployed in the central mountains…would render the country indefensible."

in 2000, Hezbollah in 2006, and Hamas in 2009? Hamas and Hezbollah in particular have not as of yet recovered from the destruction they sustained, and for them to re-engage Israel militarily would be nothing short of suicide. This is the reason why the PA opted to forsake violence to achieve its political objectives by peaceful means and the reason behind the relative calm that has prevailed. If one adds to that the element of the peace agreement, the likelihood of a new conflagration will become increasingly less desirable.

The issue is not where the border will finally be drawn. Successive Israeli governments have sold the myth to the Israeli public linking the borders to national security, when in fact building settlements such as Ariel deep into the West Bank is ideologically motivated and has little if anything to do with national security. Indeed, what makes the border between Israel and a future Palestinian state defensible is not as much where the final border is finally established, but continued Israeli deterrence and, in particular, on the establishment of a comprehensive peace and normal relations in which both sides develop, over time, a vested interest. Any claim to the contrary is baseless regardless of what the ultimate intentions of the Palestinians are, as many Israelis contend.

It is a common belief in Israel that the Arabs, especially the Palestinians, cannot be trusted. They further argue that even if an Israeli-Palestinian peace agreement is achieved today the Palestinians will annul it as soon as they feel that its dissolution will work to their advantage. Many Israelis insist that the Palestinians are inherently committed to Israel's destruction and that for the Palestinians, forging a peace agreement will amount to nothing more than a tactical move while waiting for a better day to realize their ultimate goal of bringing about the destruction of Israel. The question is, however, who would make peace on the basis of trust alone? Trust can be cultivated only through a constructive and ongoing relationship that only peace can foster.

Let us assume for a moment that the lack of trust is the main obstacle to making peace. When will the day come when both sides begin to trust each other? Will it come after developing commercial, cultural, scientific, and diplomatic ties, or will it come when the occupation continues, the settlements expand, multiple checkpoints remain in place and thousands of Palestinian prisoners languish in Israeli jails? Defying Israel today does not come from religious beliefs, albeit Hamas and others find it convenient to create such a link to convey their convictions. Indeed, notwithstanding the religious component of the conflict, people, including Palestinians, want to live. They know that there is no virtue in dying in vain, especially when the prospect of destroying Israel is virtually non-existent, and more than anything else, when they have something to hold onto, like the prospect of an independent state of their own.

Israel is and remains, for as far as the eye can see, a military power that no individual Arab state or combination of states can overwhelm militarily, and if they try they will do so at their peril. At no time in its history has Israel been stronger militarily. Their mighty military prowess can and will be used to deter, defend, or go on the offensive should Israel's security be threatened. For this reason Israel cannot mortgage its security to a third party; it must remain vigilant, powerful, and ready at all times to take any legitimate military action deemed necessary to ensure its survival.

Such a military power can and indeed must also be used to reach out to the Palestinians and the rest of the Arab states from a position of strength. Otherwise, what is the point of such military prowess if it does not advance peace? Israel will become increasingly more isolated, gradually evolving into a garrison state with ever-diminishing friends and allies. As it is, there is not a single country in the whole world, including the United States, that supports the occupation and calls on Israel to end it for its own sake.

Meanwhile Israel is gradually losing its soul and its resonance as it was envisioned by its founders. It is time for the Netanyahu government to be honest with the public and stop covering for the expansion and the building of new settlements in the name of national security.

SETTLEMENTS AND OCCUPATION

THE SETTLEMENTS AND VIOLENCE ANATHEMA

FEBRUARY 3, 2009

From his first Middle East tour as President Obama's special envoy, George Mitchell must have found that not much has changed since his 2001 report. During his previous mission on the causes of the Second Intifada, Mitchell concluded that ending Israeli settlement activity and violence are intertwined and remain the core impediment to meaningful negotiations. Mitchell has also said that conflicts that are caused by man can be resolved by man, and that negotiation is the singular most effective tool to solve disputes. His core beliefs and emphasis on diplomacy will certainly help him tremendously on his mission, but he may need more than that to pierce through this emotionally- and psychologically-laden conflict that has eluded all of his predecessors.

The proposition that if the Palestinians want a state they must foreswear violence, and if Israel wants peace it must end the occupation, seems logical and practical, though neither logical discourse nor practicality dictate this long and debilitating conflict. From the Palestinian perspective, ending violent resistance cannot be mitigated by anything other than ending settlement activity and the occupation, which are the sources of humiliation and deprivation. As they see it,

81

no Israeli government can do anything to obscure this basic reality. Many Palestinian moderates agree that acts of violence, including firing rockets into Israel, are inexcusable and that Israel has the right to defend itself. But they also insist that the Israeli war on Hamas and future retaliatory attacks will have no moral sustenance and will not change the core of the problem as long as Israel fails to address the root causes of violence in the first place.

Given that Israel is seen as an occupying power, it has been unable to capture the moral high ground even in self-defense. Instead of generating sympathy for being rained on by rockets, it was condemned by the international community for its incursion into Gaza. Israel might wish to separate Hamas from the Palestinian civilians, but Hamas' popularity grows in conjunction with settlement expansion, especially in light of the Palestinian Authority (PA)'s inability to do anything about it. The Israeli contention that settlement activity will not prejudice the final status agreement falls largely on deaf ears as the Palestinians witness the Israelis' daily encroachment on their land and the consequent hardships they endure. Calm will last only if there is a visible end to settlement expansion, even in settlement blocks that Israel is planning to incorporate into Israel proper through a land swap agreement with the Palestinians. Otherwise, ceasefires are no more than tactical moves serving immediate and limited objectives, and renewed violence remains just a matter of time.

From the Israeli standpoint, wanton violence against its civilians is unacceptable under any circumstances. Israelis recall with horror the violence at the break of the Second Intifada in late 2000 and the more than 110 suicide bombings that indiscriminately killed and maimed hundreds of innocent civilians. For most Israelis, the extent of Palestinian violence—especially following the peace proposals made at Camp David—was indicative of the Palestinians' rejection not only of any peace formula but of Israel's very existence. All the confidence-building measures taken up through the summer of 2000 were shattered overnight, leaving most Israelis baffled about any real prospect for peace. By making the cessation of hostilities a precondition to political and territorial concessions, continued occupation has become synonymous with national security. Palestinian extremists vowing to destroy Israel have provided it with further justification for taking extraordinary measures to protect the security of Israelis. Yet targeted killings, arrests of would-be terrorists, and the demolition of homes by Israeli security forces have provoked violent reactions casting a darker cloud on any credible political discourse or territorial concessions.

Given this uncertain climate, the settlement movement has made significant inroads into Israel's political establishment, usurping the political agenda while successive governments have openly supported expansion or the building of new outposts. Israel's unilateral withdrawal from Gaza and the subsequent use of the strip as a staging ground for attacks against Israel has disheartened most Israelis and alienated even the moderate camp. It has further played into the hands of right-wing Israeli extremists who oppose any withdrawal, and deepened their conviction that peace with the Palestinians remains as elusive as ever. The Israeli public has reacted to the firing of rockets from Gaza during the past three years by further shifting to the right, a development that will make it most likely for Likud leader Benjamin Netanyahu to become the next prime minister following the February 10th national election.

The Arab moderate states, especially Saudi Arabia, Jordan, Morocco, and Egypt, who have condemned Hamas and tacitly supported Israel's stand against it, are running out of patience. The Arab masses cannot reconcile the death of Palestinian civilians, especially women and children, with Israel's grievances about violence when the Palestinians are an occupied people and have an inherent right to resist. For the vast majority of Arabs, it is anathema that Israel—a country presumably seeking peace—has refused to embrace the Arab Peace Initiative (API), which offers exactly that: a comprehensive peace in exchange for the territories. Increased Arab militancy and violence are the inadvertent results steadily eroding the position of the Palestinian moderate camp in favor of militant confrontation.

This is the climate in which Mitchell will find himself when he returns to the region for his Herculean mission. Moreover, he will face a new Israeli prime minister, who will likely be Likud Leader Benjamin Netanyahu—a right-of-center leader who staunchly supports the settlements movement. On the Palestinian side, he may well have to deal with a Fatah-Hamas unity government that will also take a hard line in the peace negotiations. In addition, Mitchell will have to bolster and engage with moderate Arab leaders to ensure their direct engagement and perseverance, while coaxing Syria to enter into direct negotiations with Israel. This, however, will not deter a skilled negotiator like Mitchell as there is also a silver lining here: both Israelis and Palestinians bestow greater trust on stronger and more unified governments who don't compromise their national interests. As for the leading Arab states, Saudi Arabia and Egypt, they are eager to see tangible progress on the Palestinian front and are thirsty for genuine American active involvement. Damascus also is anxious for direct dialogue with Washington.

Mitchell, with the full support of President Obama and Secretary of State Clinton, can succeed where other administrations have failed. He must come equipped, however, with carrots and sticks for both sides, remain committed, actively involved and relentless, and be prepared for the United States to be a part of a long-term solution.

To make serious progress toward a final status agreement between Israel and the Palestinians, George Mitchell must first work on restoring confidence in a peace process that years of havoc and destruction have all but destroyed. To that end, he needs to address the two core sensitive issues that both Israelis and Palestinians place tremendous importance on: ending the violence and fundamentally shifting the settlements policy.

The settlements issue has been the most contentious, not only between Israel and the Palestinians but within Israel itself. No issue has eroded the Palestinians' confidence in the peace process more than the settlements. For the Israelis, the settlements and their expansion are a highly emotional and politically charged national subject. Any future Israeli government will face vehement opposition from the settlers' movement, which exercises disproportionate power on the government's policy toward its activities.

Ideally, building a structure of peace and instilling trust in the negotiating process would require a complete freeze of all settlement activities, including the settlement blocks that Israel wishes to incorporate into Israel proper in exchange for a land swap to compensate the Palestinians for the territory. However, that may be easier said than done. To provide some practical suggestions, it is necessary to break down the settlers' movement into its three basic constituencies. In so doing, some possible interim solutions can realistically be made to demonstrate to the Palestinians that Israel intends on changing its settlement policy and evacuating the vast majority of the West Bank.

The quality-of-life settlers are those who moved to the West Bank primarily for economic reasons, the majority of whom live in the settlement blocks located closer to the green line. According to Peace Now statistics, there are about 190,000 residents in these settlements, several of which are no longer considered settlements and officially have been named as cities, home to more than 30,000 people each including Ma'ale Adumim, Modi'in and Beitar.[44] The routing of the security fence leaves most of these settlements on the Israeli side. The pressure on the government to allow for natural growth in these settlements is enormous and no government is likely to completely freeze their natural expansion, even under intense American pressure.

The ideological settlers use mainly religious arguments to justify the settlements and their presence in the West Bank. They view the return of the Jews to the land of Israel as a fulfillment of God's will. They occupy settlements located for the most part deep inside the West Bank, very close to and often in the heart of Palestinian-populated areas. It is quite evident, however, that public support for these settlements is declining. A growing majority of Israelis tend to accept the fact that Israel will need to evacuate most of these nearly 100 settlements that dot the West Bank.

The ultra-orthodox settlers in the West Bank are a function almost exclusively of cheap and segregated housing close to the Green Line. They are descendants of devoutly religious Jews who oppose change and modernization. They have historically rejected active Zionism and continue to believe that the path to Jewish redemption is through religious rather than secular activity. There are eight ultra-orthodox settlements that were built in the 80s and 90s with roughly 80,000 residents, all of which are located within the

---

44 Hagit Ofran and Lara Friedman, "West Bank 'Settlement Blocs,'"
    Peace Now, May 2008, http://peacenow.org.il/eng/content/west-bank-%E2%80%9Csettlement-blocs%E2%80%9D.

settlement blocks that Israel wants to incorporate into Israel proper.[45] These settlements are currently expanding more rapidly than other settlements due primarily to a higher birth rate.

Based on the settlers' ideological leanings and the location of the settlements, Mitchell should focus on four possible areas where he can persuade the next Israeli government to take action, considering the political constraints under which any future Israeli coalition government will operate.

First, Mitchell should push for the dismantling of all new illegal outposts; the government can take this action without losing much political capital and it can certainly justify it by citing American pressure. The mushrooming of new outposts has been a terrible source of Palestinian frustration, as they signify further entrenchment rather than disengagement.

Second on the agenda should be removing small clusters of settlements occupied by ideological activist settlers in places such as Nablus and Hebron that are troublesome and heavily tax Israel's security forces. All of these settlements are deep in the West Bank and most Israelis agree that they must eventually be evacuated for any peace deal.

Third, Israel must create a program of diminishing incentives that will provide settlers who are willing to relocate voluntarily with equal housing an extra incentive, perhaps of $100,000, if they leave within the first year from the program's initiation. (This amount is compelling based on the Israeli standard of living.) The incentive will then be reduced by $25,000 every six months thereafter. The idea is to create reverse migrations to Israel proper while psychologically preparing the Israeli public and the Palestinians for the inevitability of ending the occupation. While many settlers will not accept the compensation and try to hold out for a better deal, the government must be resolute and not give into blackmail. These settlers must eventually be forcefully evacuated with no incentive.

Lastly, whereas a complete moratorium on settlement expansion may be untenable, the United States can exert sufficient pressure on

---

45   Nadav Shragai, "Ultra-Orthodox Jews Deliver a Population Boom to the West Bank," *Haaretz*, August 14, 2007, http://www.haaretz.com/news/ultra-orthodox-jews-deliver-a-population-boom-to-the-west-bank-1.227419.

Israel to be sensitive to Palestinian sensibilities and not commence major development projects at sensitive moments in the negotiations. Meanwhile, the negotiations on the final borders should be accelerated to reach an agreement on the settlements that Israel could incorporate into its own territory. Such an agreement with the Palestinians would greatly facilitate the movement of ideological settlers from their current locations to these settlements while still fulfilling their ideological mission.

The new Israeli prime minister (presumably Likud leader Benjamin Netanyahu) is likely to be under intense American pressure to make meaningful concessions for advancing the peace. Although Netanyahu as Prime Minister will be a tough negotiator and will demand full compliance in return from the Palestinians for any concession he makes, he may also prove to be the more worthy interlocutor and more trusted by the public. It should be noted that the largest territorial concessions—the Sinai, Hebron, and Gaza—were all made by Likud leaders Begin, Netanyahu, and Sharon, respectively.

Mitchell concluded his report of the Sharm el-Sheikh Fact-Finding Committee with the following words: "Israelis and Palestinians have to live, work, and prosper together. History and geography have destined them to be neighbors. That cannot be changed. Only when their actions are guided by this awareness will they be able to develop the vision and reality of peace and shared prosperity."[46]

No American president has taken such a keen and immediate concern with the Israeli-Palestinian conflict this early in his term as President Obama, and no agreement between Israel and the Arab states has been achieved without direct American involvement. If time, circumstances and leadership matter, there may not be a better time to push for a solution than now.

---

46   Reza Aslan, "Can George Mitchell Fix the Middle East?," *The Daily Beast*, January 21, 2009, http://www.thedailybeast.com/articles/2009/01/21/can-george-mitchell-fix-the-middle-east.html.

ALON BEN-MEIR

THE SETTLEMENT ENTERPRISE
HAS RUN ITS COURSE

SEPTEMBER 27, 2010

Settlement construction in the West Bank has historically served four main objectives for Israel: greater security, a stronger connection to ancient biblical lands, a better way of life for residents, and pressure on the Palestinians to accept the reality of Israel's existence. Today, each of these goals has been largely met. The settlement enterprise has therefore run its course. It now represents an albatross that threatens to thwart Israel's chance to achieve lasting peace and security.

Israelis have long argued that settlement construction has enhanced Israel's security. Indeed, in areas surrounding Jerusalem, construction has expanded Jewish settlements, providing a buffer of security against attacks. Similarly, settlement construction in the West Bank was intended to broaden Israel's border eastward to provide Israel with greater land and security, particularly along the central coast, where the distance between the Mediterranean Sea and the West Bank measures approximately eight miles. However, the security rationale for settlements is no longer valid. The combination of the construction of the security fence and the strengthening of Palestinian security forces in the West Bank has significantly enhanced Israel's security. Furthermore, the long-range rocket fire of Hezbollah has shown that incremental appropriation of land will not significantly enhance Israel's security against short or long-range threats.

The settlements have also been created and expanded with the support and fervor of religious nationalists seeking to settle the biblical lands of Judea and Samaria. Driven by messianic fervor, these settlers believe that the messiah will come when Jews have returned to the biblical lands of Israel. This movement is particularly devoted to Jewish settlement in the ancient biblical lands. In this regard, they have been successful in advancing understandings that major settlement blocs, including areas surrounding Jerusalem, will ultimately be incorporated into Israel. Having done so, however, religious nationalists must now begin to question whether God intended for the land to be characterized by dominance and submission, or of prosperity and peace. In this regard, instead of calling for exclusive Israeli control over holy areas in ancient Judea and Samaria, religious nationalists should come to realize the need to create a Palestinian state in order to preserve secure access for both Jews and Muslims to such sites.

The settlements have also been expanded in order to provide greater livelihoods for Israeli citizens. An estimated one-third of the West Bank settlers have moved to these areas because of economic incentives provided at times by the Israeli government and advocacy organizations, as well as reasonable costs of living. However, today, widespread settlement activity simply does not make economic sense—for individual citizens or the Israeli government. Israeli settlements beyond the major blocs are likely to be evacuated. Any investment in continuing to build beyond the blocs amounts to wasted resources that should be allocated to strengthening the core of Israeli society, and preparing for the re-integration of settlers who must inevitably return to Israel proper as part of a peace agreement. Finally, the settlements have served to pressure Palestinians to accept Israeli control of the land, and ultimately accept the permanence of the Jewish state. Toward this end, Israel has also succeeded. Today, the PA in the West Bank has accepted Israel's right to exist, the principle of land for peace, and a two-state solution in which Israel and a Palestinian state would live side-by-side in peace and security. To be sure, even extremist elements who profess their desire to destroy Israel—notably Hamas in Gaza—have come around to accept the principle of establishing a Palestinian state based on the 1967 lines. Moreover, a majority of Palestinians polled consistently support the notion of a two-state solution,[47] and the Palestinian leadership in the West Bank has

---

47   See "Poll: Most Palestinians, Israelis Want Two-State Solution," *Haaretz*, April 22, 2009, http://www.haaretz.com/news/poll-most-palestinians-israelis-want-two-state-solution-1.274607; and "Despite the Gaza Flotilla Incident, Rise in Willingness to Compromise Among Palestinians and Israelis, but Two-Thirds on Both Sides Remain Pessimistic About the Future of the Peace Process," Palestinian Center for Policy and Survey

devoted itself to eradicating the influence of extremism from the West Bank and enhancing security in the region.

With these core objectives achieved, efforts to continue to rapidly extend the settlement enterprise across the West Bank, upon the conclusion of the settlement moratorium which has just expired on September 26th, would serve to undermine the security of the state of Israel. Continuing construction beyond the core settlement blocs would send the international community a clear and distinct message: Israel is not serious about a two-state solution. It has long been estimated in various negotiation rounds that over 80 percent—representing roughly 400,000 West Bank settlers—are likely to stay in their homes following a two-state agreement.[48] These settlers represent those in the settlement blocs and Jerusalem environs that Israel will not abandon due to strong biblical and political beliefs. Israel cannot claim to desire peace on the one hand, and build in areas known to be a part of a future Palestinian state on the other.

Continued settlement building will inadvertently provide fuel to radical extremists who are seeking to recruit terrorists to commit violent acts against Israeli citizens. Renewed tensions with the United States could also emerge, and positive gestures by the Arab states—including the Arab League's endorsement of direct negotiations—could be reversed. Furthermore, the international campaign to delegitimize Israel's right to exist would be intensified as a result of continued settlement expansion.

To avoid such a scenario, Prime Minister Netanyahu must place Israel's national interests above his coalition concerns. In this respect, Netanyahu is being tested: does he have the conviction and leadership qualities necessary to achieve a two-state solution, or will he be held hostage by domestic politics? He should show leadership now by communicating Israel's position clearly, which should include a land swap that would incorporate the vast majority of settlers in the major

---

Research, June 29, 2010, http://www.pcpsr.org/survey/polls/2010/p36ejoint.html.

48 Peter Hart, "The 'Oh Really?' Factor," *Fairness & Accuracy In Reporting*, May 1, 2002, http://fair.org/extra-online-articles/the-oh-really-factor/.

blocs into Israel proper, an option for some of the religious settlers to stay within a Palestinian state through an agreement with the Palestinians, and for the negotiations to begin to immediately address the issue of borders. Negotiating the borders now is particularly important as it would eliminate the questions as to which lands will belong to Israel and which to the Palestinian state. Moreover, it will allow the Israelis to continue to expand the settlements that will be incorporated into Israel proper early in the process before settling every other conflicting issue. Prime Minister Netanyahu has the political strength to present such a platform; with Kadima waiting in the wings as a potential coalition partner, he should demonstrate such leadership to achieve a two-state solution. The only question now is which path Netanyahu will choose.

Critics argue that the Palestinians rejected Israel's 10-month moratorium and only now are raising its importance. This argument suggests that as Israel makes concessions—like freezing construction—it has received little to nothing in return, with the Palestinians staying out of negotiations for months before being coaxed by the United States to participate in direct talks. Others argue that Israel did not have to freeze construction in the past in order for peace talks to be advanced, so why continue it now? The answer is simple: to show that this time Israel is committed to doing all it can to create an environment conducive to achieving a lasting agreement. Furthermore, after years of negotiating with Israel while it simultaneously settled land in the West Bank, the Palestinians must show their people—who are as skeptical as Israelis about the current peace talks—that this time is indeed different.

The objectives of the settlement enterprise have generally been achieved. Today, its continuation in areas which will inevitably be part of a Palestinian state would place Israel's security, and the nascent peace process, in jeopardy. The United States and the international community are watching closely to see how Prime Minister Netanyahu reacts to this test of his leadership. He has the tools to succeed—now he must show that he has the conviction.

ALON BEN-MEIR

THE SETTLEMENTS: THE CANCER
THAT WILL KILL ANY PROSPECT
FOR A TWO-STATE SOLUTION

OCTOBER 3, 2011

Both Prime Minister Benjamin Netanyahu and PA President
Mahmoud Abbas profess to seek a two-state solution, but still
have not discussed the core issues that divide them. These issues are
borders, security, refugees, Jerusalem, settlements, and identity. The
issue of settlements continues to serve as the immediate stumbling
block to renewing negotiations. Far more than a manifestation of the
territorial dispute between the two sides, the settlement issue is intertwined with the principle ideology of Israeli and Palestinian identities.
Every housing unit built beyond the 1967 Green Line has physical,
psychological, and political ramifications, making the issue a formidable
obstacle to overcome if a two-state solution is to be achieved.

From the Palestinian perspective, the settlement issue is the albatross that undermines any prospect for a viable Palestinian state.
Since the Oslo signing of the Declaration of Principles in September
1993, the number of Israeli settlers in the West Bank has nearly
tripled, from approximately 111,000 in 1993 to over 300,000 today.[49]
This number does not include approximately 200,000 settlers in East
Jerusalem, where Palestinians seek to establish a capital for their state,
and where the Netanyahu government last week announced it would

---

49 Eyal Hareuveni, "By Hook and by Crook: Israeli Settlement Policy in
the West Bank" (B'Tselem report, Jerusalem, July 2010) 10.https://www.
btselem.org/download/201007 by hook and by crook eng.pdf.

build another 1,100 housing units.[50]

Physically, settlement construction confiscates land that Palestinians seek for their future state, bit by painstaking bit. Psychologically, construction sends the Palestinians a clear message that Israel does not accept their claim to the land nor their national aspirations, and has no interest in a two-state solution. Herein lies the rationale for the continued Palestinian insistence on a complete Israeli settlement freeze in both the West Bank and East Jerusalem prior to their entering into negotiations.

From the Palestinian view, if Israel were truly willing to accept a Palestinian state, it would cease construction that encroaches further into future Palestinian territory. Prime Minister Netanyahu and his cabinet ministers reinforce the Palestinian assertions that Israel is not interested in accepting a Palestinian state by continually invoking Israel's historic connection to the West Bank by referring to its biblical Hebrew name, Judea and Samaria.

Politically, continued settlement construction has moved Palestinian leaders further away from compromise with Israel. For any Palestinian leader to enter negotiations without a construction freeze would amount to political suicide. As more Palestinians question whether negotiations can truly lead to a Palestinian state, compromising on an issue that contradicts the very notion of the creation of their state has become a political impossibility.

From Netanyahu's perspective, settlement construction is linked with national identity. He has repeatedly placed the idea of Palestinians accepting Israel "as a Jewish state" at the center of the deliberations over renewing peace talks. From his perspective, until the Palestinians and the Arab world accept the legitimacy of this claim, peace will be impossible. Furthermore, Netanyahu can easily point to his 10-month construction freeze, during which time Abbas failed

50   See Alicia C. Shepard, "CIA Gets Numbers Wrong on Jewish Settlers," *NPR*, June 2, 2010, http://www.npr.org/blogs/ombudsman/2010/06/01/127349281/cia-gets-the-numbers-wrong; and Allyn Fisher-Ilan, "Israel approves 1,100 more settlement homes," Reuters, September 27, 2011, http://www.reuters.com/article/2011/09/27/us-palestinians-israel-settlements-idUSTRE78Q3PQ20110927.

to enter into negotiations, as a justification for his refusal to accept another freeze, especially if it includes East Jerusalem.

Netanyahu fundamentally differs from his predecessors, Ehud Olmert, Ariel Sharon, and Ehud Barak, who used the word "occupation" to describe Israel's continued hold on the West Bank. Netanyahu does not view the ancient Jewish lands of "Judea and Samaria" as occupied, and certainly not East Jerusalem, and thus does not believe them to be off-limits to Israeli construction. This explains why he has expended so much political capital in opposing a settlement freeze, despite continued pressure from Washington and the international community. Netanyahu tries to justify his refusal to freeze construction by linking the settlements to Israel's national security, which an increasing number of Israelis accept at face value.

Netanyahu has repeatedly claimed that Israel cannot accept "indefensible borders" based on the 1967 lines. He highlights that Israel would be only nine miles wide if it were to relinquish its territory in the West Bank. However, this security argument is undermined by the reality that for any agreement to be reached, Israel will have to relinquish land. Unless Netanyahu claims that a 12 or 15 mile width is more "defensible" in today's missile technology than a nine-mile width, it is difficult to comprehend what Netanyahu's "defensible borders" look like without a continued substantial Israeli military presence in the West Bank.

If the dispute over settlements was solely based on security or political issues, it could be reconciled through good faith negotiations. However, the settlements represent more than a security and political disagreement. The issue is viewed as a matter of the inherent historical rights and existence of each side. This is what makes this conflict so intractable. All of this begs the question, if the settlement issue is so deeply ingrained, how can it be resolved? Is there any way the Palestinians can compromise on the issue of settlements in order to return to the negotiating table? Will the Netanyahu government cease construction and accept a Palestinian state, or will it remain committed to a losing strategy that is like a self-consuming cancer?

There is absolutely no way the Palestinians will ever compromise on this issue unless they are offered a more plausible alternative. Compromising now would be viewed as a capitulation for Abbas at a moment when Palestinians believe that they have gained momentum in isolating Israel in the international community, especially on the question of the settlements. At the same time, while Israel has a historical claim to the West Bank, Netanyahu has shown no indication that he is willing to reconcile this claim with the reality that a Palestinian state must be created if a democratic, Jewish state is to remain and thrive in the region.

There will be no solution to the settlement problem until both sides are persuaded to heed the pressure of the Quartet (the UN, United States, EU, and Russia), most directly by the United States, to agree on new rules of engagement by negotiating borders first. Borders will not only define the parameters of the Palestinian state but will also address the settlements issue. A land swap in which Israel would keep the major settlement blocs in the context of a border agreement has long been viewed as the answer to this conundrum. This will also give Mahmoud Abbas the political cover he needs to drop his precondition of a construction freeze by negotiating borders first, as long as future construction will be limited to the settlements that will become a part of Israel in a negotiated agreement. With the construction freeze out of the way, Netanyahu and Abbas will then face the moment of truth.

Mahmoud Abbas must know by now that he has been playing into Netanyahu's hand. He must change his strategy to bring him even better results. Negotiating borders will lead directly to the heart of the settlement issue and will require their immediate resolution.

Netanyahu must know by now that his strategy to create more facts on the ground by continuing settlement construction before negotiating borders with the Palestinians in earnest has run its course. The whole world is focused on Israel's settlement activity because they speak volumes about Netanyahu and his government's ultimate intentions.

THE SETTLERS' MOVEMENT IS A THREAT
TO PEACE AND ISRAEL'S EXISTENCE

JANUARY 9, 2012

The attack of hardline Jewish settlers on an Israeli military base in the West Bank[51] must not be seen as a passing incident that can simply be eradicated by punishing the perpetrators, as Prime Minister Netanyahu said in the Israeli Parliament. This dangerous and most deplorable incident is a byproduct of the settlement policies that Netanyahu and his extreme-right coalition partner have zealously been pursuing for the past three years. Netanyahu condemns the attacks on individual settlers while such policies continue to focus on the rapid expansion of the settlements, further strengthening the settlers' movement, which, for all intents and purposes, has acquired de facto veto power over policies affecting the future disposition of the West Bank.

Any attempt to resume serious peace negotiations between Israel and the Palestinians, including recent efforts by Jordan's King Abdullah II, who hosted the representatives of Israel, the PA, and the Quartet, (the United States, EU, Russia, and the UN) in Amman, will go nowhere as long as there is no change in settlement policy. Beyond that, however, continued settlement construction will increase the divide between those Israelis who seek an end to the conflict with the Palestinians and those hardcore ideologues who place the building and expansion of settlements as the singular historic opportunity that will restore Jewish birthright to their homeland.

The attack on the military base will not be the last incident and it is bound to escalate to the detriment of Israel's very existence as long as the settlements issue remains the most contentious issue between Israel and the Palestinians and any future peace agreement requires the

---

51 See Phoebe Greenwood, "Israeli Military Base Attacked by Jewish Extremists in West Bank," *The Guardian*, December 13, 2011, http://www.theguardian.com/world/2011/dec/13/israeli-military-attack-jewish-extremists.

evacuation of scores of settlements scattered throughout the West Bank. Indeed, far more than a manifestation of the territorial dispute between Israel and the Palestinians, the settlement problem is intertwined with the principle ideology encased within Israeli and Palestinian identities. Every housing unit built beyond the 1967 Green Line has physical, psychological, and political ramifications, making the issue a formidable obstacle to overcome if a two-state solution is to be achieved.

From the Palestinian perspective, the settlement issue is the albatross that undermines any prospect for a viable Palestinian state. Since the Oslo signing of the Declaration of Principles in September of 1993, the number of Israeli settlers in the West Bank has nearly tripled, from approximately 116,000 in 1993 to over 300,000 today.[52] This number does not include more than 200,000 settlers in East Jerusalem, where Palestinians seek to establish a capital for their state, and where the Netanyahu government continues to build thousands of new housing units.[53]

Physically, settlement construction confiscates land that Palestinians seek for their future state, bit by painstaking bit. Psychologically, construction sends the Palestinians a clear message: Israel does not accept their claim to the land or their national aspirations, and has no interest in a two-state solution. Herein lies the rationale for the continued Palestinian insistence on a complete Israeli settlement freeze in both the West Bank and East Jerusalem prior to their entering into negotiations, which they have emphasized in their recent encounter with the Israelis in Amman.

The Palestinians insist that if Israel were truly willing to accept a Palestinian state, it would cease construction that encroaches further

---

52   Eyal Hareuveni, "By Hook and by Crook: Israeli Settlement Policy in the West Bank" (B'Tselem report, Jerusalem, July 2010) 10, https://www.btselem.org/download/201007_by_hook_and_by_crook_eng.pdf.

53   See Alicia C. Shepard, "CIA Gets Numbers Wrong on Jewish Settlers," *NPR*, June 2, 2010, http://www.npr.org/blogs/ombudsman/2010/06/01/127349281/cia-gets-the-numbers-wrong; and Allyn Fisher-Ilan, "Israel Approves 1,100 More Settlement Homes," *Reuters*, September 27, 2011, http://www.reuters.com/article/2011/09/27/us-palestinians-israel-settlements-idUSTRE78Q3PQ20110927.

into would-be Palestinian territory. Prime Minister Netanyahu and his cabinet ministers reinforce Palestinian assertions that Israel is not interested in accepting a Palestinian state by continually invoking Israel's historic connection to the West Bank by referring to its biblical Hebrew name "Judea and Samaria," a position that strengthens the fervent nationalist settlers who believe they have a biblical birthright to live wherever they choose in the West Bank.

Politically, continued settlement construction has moved Palestinian leaders further away from compromise with Israel. For any Palestinian leader to enter into negotiations without a construction freeze would amount to political suicide. As more Palestinians question whether negotiations can truly lead to a Palestinian state, compromising on an issue that contradicts the very notion of the creation of their state has become a political impossibility.

From Netanyahu's perspective, settlement construction is linked with national identity. He has repeatedly placed the idea of Palestinians accepting Israel "as a Jewish state" at the center of the deliberations over renewing peace talks. From his perspective, until the Palestinians and the Arab world accept the legitimacy of this claim, peace will be impossible. Furthermore, Netanyahu can easily point to his 10-month construction freeze, during which time Abbas failed to enter into negotiations because it excluded East Jerusalem, as a justification for his refusal to accept another freeze, especially if it includes East Jerusalem.

Netanyahu fundamentally differs from his predecessors, Ehud Olmert, Ariel Sharon, and Ehud Barak, who used the word "occupation" to describe Israel's continued hold on the West Bank. Netanyahu does not view the ancient Jewish lands of "Judea and Samaria" (and certainly not East Jerusalem) as occupied and thus does not believe them to be off-limits to Jewish construction. This explains why he has expended so much political capital in opposing a settlement freeze, despite continued pressure from Washington and the international community. Netanyahu hypocritically condemns the attacks against settlers while simultaneously justifying his refusal to freeze construction by linking the settlements to Israel's national security, which an increasing number of Israelis accept at face value.

Netanyahu has repeatedly claimed that Israel cannot accept "indefensible borders," based on the 1967 lines. He highlights that Israel would be only nine miles wide if it were to relinquish its territory in the West Bank. However, this security argument is undermined by the reality that for any agreement to be reached, Israel will have to relinquish land. Unless Netanyahu claims that a 12 or 15-mile width is more "defensible" in today's missile technology than a nine-mile width, it is difficult to comprehend what Netanyahu's "defensible borders" look like without a continued, substantial Israeli military presence in the West Bank.

If the dispute over settlements was solely based on security or political issues, it could be reconciled through good-faith negotiations and iron-clad security guarantees. However, the settlements represent more than a security and political disagreement. The issue is viewed as a matter of the inherent historical rights and existence of each side. This is what makes this conflict so intractable, and this is precisely why hardline settlers feel that no one can impede their activities, including the military, which is stationed there for their protection. All of this begs the question: will the Netanyahu government recognize that its blind policy on the settlements has set the stage for further escalation of violent confrontations, not only between the settlers and the Palestinians but also between the settlers and the Israeli military? There is no doubt that Jews will kill other Jews in the name of a messianic mission. Those who think that this simply is unthinkable better think again. Nothing will stop the zealot settlers as long as they believe that they are pursuing God's mission and that the Almighty is testing their resolve, tenacity, and willingness to sacrifice themselves before He grants them once again the Promised Land.

This is no longer just a small group of criminals and vandals who are out to burn or daub inflammatory graffiti on the walls of Palestinian mosques or vandalize an Israeli military base. This is a whole movement deeply entrenched and continues to exert disproportionate influence on all Israeli governments, especially the current right-leaning coalition government. It is a clear manifestation of a movement determined to control any future political agenda in the West Bank and will not be, as Netanyahu seems to believe, easily eradicated. Yes, he can incarcerate one, two, or a dozen settlers, but how does he intend to incarcerate a whole movement which represents the core of his own constituency? Notwithstanding the Netanyahu's government "revulsion" to the settlers' criminal acts, these settlers know where Netanyahu and his cohorts really stand as long as the government continues to authorize construction of new housing units in the heart of Palestinian neighborhoods. What is needed here are fundamental policy changes that must first cease construction and second, commit in deeds (not in empty rhetoric) to a two-state solution, or the Netanyahu government will run the risk of the settlements becoming a self-consuming cancer.

The behavior of these radical settlers must be condemned in the strongest possible terms. However, the real culprits are not the settlers but the Netanyahu government, which was committed from day one to defying the Palestinian reality and the international community and has, above all, engaged in excessive self-denial to the very detriment of Israel's future. No one but Netanyahu is to blame for this horrifying development. If he has one ounce of integrity left in him he should resign.

THE SETTLEMENTS: ISRAEL'S ALBATROSS[54]

NOVEMBER 14, 2013

The stalled Israeli-Palestinian peace negotiations that Secretary of State John Kerry worked relentlessly to reinvigorate four months ago have once again been stonewalled. The issue of the continuing building and expanding of Israeli settlements in the West Bank resurfaced as the central contentious issue between the two sides, threatening to torpedo the peace process altogether.

The Israelis and Palestinians view the settlement enterprise from a completely different perspective that defines their strategic objectives, and is becoming increasingly irreconcilable every time Israel announces the building of new housing units.

As the Palestinians see it, if the current negotiations are in fact aimed at reaching a peace accord based on a two-state solution, continued settlement activity and their very existence throughout the West Bank stand in total contradiction to that objective. Consequently, this will inevitably deprive them from establishing a state of their own on the same territory.

Since the signing of the Declaration of Principles at Oslo in September 1993, the number of Israeli settlers in the West Bank has tripled, from 110,066 to over 340,000 today, plus approximately 200,000 settlers in East Jerusalem, where thousands of new housing units are continuously being built.[55]

---

54 All figures, unless otherwise cited, are courtesy of Hagit Ofran, Settlement Watch director for Peace Now, who I thank for sharing her statistics on the settlements.

55 See "The Two State Solution is Still Alive 20 Years After Oslo," *Peace Now*, October 17, 2013, http://peacenow.org.il/eng/OsloSummary; and "Settlements in East Jerusalem," *Foundation For Middle East Peace*, http://www.fmep.org/settlement_info/settlement-info-and-tables/stats-data/settlements-in-east-jerusalem (accessed November 12, 2013).

Physically, settlement construction confiscates land bit by painstaking bit and sends a clear message: Israel does not accept the Palestinians' claim to the land or their internationally recognized right to establish an independent state of their own.

The Palestinians insist that, contrary to his public pronouncements, Prime Minister Netanyahu has no intention of pursuing a peace agreement based on a two-state solution. They point to his relentless efforts to expand the settlements by following the mantra of the late extreme-right Prime Minister Yitzhak Shamir in the mid- to late-1980s, who fiercely promoted the idea that Israel should settle one million Jews in the West Bank, creating an irreversible fact that no one can change.

Although freezing construction was not a precondition to resuming negotiations, the problem for the PA is that the expansion of settlements during the negotiating process is seen by the public as caving in on the core issue, which discredits the whole purpose of the negotiations.

Indeed, continued settlement activity makes it extremely difficult politically for President Abbas to compromise on other critical issues for Israel, such as the right of return of the Palestinian refugees.

This is particularly daunting for the Palestinians when seen in the context of Israel's refusal to compromise on the one issue that determines the future of Palestinian nationhood.

Netanyahu's position is that the settlements will not impede the creation of a viable Palestinian state. How he plans to mitigate that with the reality on the ground, however, remains a mystery, specifically when his repeated public pronouncements about Israel's inherent right to the land point to the contrary.

Prime Minister Netanyahu remains adamant about Israel's right to maintain a considerable presence in the West Bank, justified from his perspective by a number of unadulterated facts:

First, Netanyahu insists that the Jews have a historical affinity to the entire "land of Israel" as envisioned by the Zionist movement, and unlike his predecessors, Ehud Olmert, Ariel Sharon, and Ehud Barak, ideologically he does not view the West Bank as occupied territory (which he refers to by its Hebrew name, Judea and Samaria). Thus, he maintains that the West Bank should not be off-limits to Jewish inhabitants.

Second, Netanyahu and many Israelis with strong religious convictions uphold the view that the land has been bequeathed to the Jews, who have a biblical birthright to live in it. Zealous settlers deeply believe they are pursuing God's mission and that the Almighty is testing their resolve, tenacity, and willingness to make any sacrifice before He grants them the Promised Land in perpetuity.

Third, Netanyahu has consistently linked the settlements to Israel's national security, which an increasing number of Israelis accept at face value. He has repeatedly claimed that Israel cannot accept "indefensible borders" based on the 1967 lines, and highlights that Israel would be only nine miles wide if it were to relinquish much of its presence in the West Bank.

Fourth, the more practical motivation behind the settlements is the desire of many Israelis, with the encouragement of the government, to live in affordable and spacious housing in a clean environment with easy access to urban centers. To attract more settlers, successive governments have and continue to subsidize housing, schools, security, and many other services.

As a consequence, these four factors led to the expansion of the settlements and the rise of the settlement movement as a formidable political force fully entrenched in the body politic of the country. Over time it has acquired a near de facto veto power over policies affecting the future disposition of the West Bank.

The settler movement is not a small group of criminals and vandals who are out to burn or daub inflammatory graffiti on the walls of Palestinian Mosques or vandalize Israeli military bases, albeit many such incidents have occurred. This is a movement on which successive coalition governments came to rely on to engender wide political support.

If the dispute over settlements was solely based on security or political issues, it could be reconciled through good faith negotiations and iron-clad security guarantees. However, the settlements represent more than a security and political disagreement.

All of this begs the question: will the Netanyahu government recognize that its policy on the settlements has set the stage for further escalation of violent confrontations, as Secretary John Kerry recently characterized the settlements as "illegitimate" and warned of the potential eruption of a third Intifada?[56]

Kerry may well have ill spoken by making such an assessment publicly instead of honing it forcefully in Netanyahu's ears, but the message remains a sound one.

Although the PA learned the lesson following the second Intifada in 2000 and will try to avoid violent confrontation with Israel, there are many Palestinian extremists over whom the PA has limited or no control and who would seize any opportunity to capitalize on the Palestinians' state of limbo and the dim prospect for a change in their unending plight.

Kerry's frustration with Netanyahu over the settlements was evident for anyone to see, but what is most worrisome is that United States-Israel bilateral relations have sunk to a level unseen for decades.

What is needed here are fundamental policy changes that must first, cease construction and second, commit in deeds, rather than empty rhetoric, to a two-state solution. Otherwise, the Netanyahu government runs the risk of the settlements becoming a self-consuming cancer.

The attack by militant settlers on a military base and assaults on IDF soldiers in the West Bank in 2011 and in October 2013 would have been unthinkable only few years ago.[57] However, they are bound to escalate, pitting zealous settlers against the IDF. This is a real possibility and only reckless leaders can shrug it off as unrealistic.

---

56   "Kerry: Israeli Settlements are Illegitimate," *Al Jazeera*, November 6, 2013, http://www.aljazeera.com/news/middleeast/2013/11/kerry-israeli-settlements-are-illegitimate-201311613594909400.html.

57   See "PM Calls Urgent Meeting on Settler Attack on IDF Base," *Jerusalem Post*, December 13, 2011, http://www.jpost.com/National-News/PM-calls-urgent-meeting-on-settler-attack-on-IDF-base; and Itamar Fleishman, "Settlers Pepper-Spray Soldiers, IDF Leaves Bat Ayin," *Y Net*, October 31, 2013, http://www.ynetnews.com/articles/0,7340,L-4448121,00.html.

Moreover, continued settlement construction will increase the divide between Israelis who seek an end to the conflict with the Palestinians and hard-core ideologues like Netanyahu, who deny the evidence that the settlements burden ordinary Israelis who are paying for it through the cost of living and lack of affordable housing.

Religiously committed Israelis, on the other hand, need no evidence to justify their convictions as they place the building and expansion of settlements as the singular historic opportunity that will restore Jewish birthright to their homeland.

It is true that the uprooting of a significant number of settlers will be the most divisive issue that will face Israel. But then, no solution to the Israeli-Palestinian conflict is possible without evacuating the 80 settlements scattered across the West Bank inhabited by more than 127,000 settlers.

These settlers can be resettled in the three blocks of settlements along the 1967 border (consisting of 43 settlements in which more than 214,000 settlers reside) which will, by agreement with the Palestinians, likely become part of Israel proper in an equitable land swap.

In an extensive discussion I had a few days ago with former Israeli Prime Minister Ehud Olmert, he was more emphatic than ever that the time to strike a peace agreement is now.[58] He echoed John Kerry's assessment of Mahmoud Abbas' commitment to peace, because he has never been stronger politically and is willing to make the hard decisions to strike an agreement, which he was unable to do in the past.

The time is ripe for peace also because Hamas' strength and popularity is at its lowest; the Gulf states, led by Saudi Arabia, along with Jordan and Egypt are gravitating toward Israel because their concern over Iran's nuclear program, the waning strength of the Muslim Brotherhood, and the ongoing turmoil in Syria and Iraq make the settlement of the Israeli-Palestinian conflict more desirable than ever before to usher in regional stability.

Netanyahu's demand from the PA to recognize Israel as a Jewish state when the expansion of settlements in the West Bank continues unabated is the height of chutzpah.

---

58 Ehud Olmert in conversation with the author, November 11, 2013.

It could only come from a man who puts his ideological principles before the wellbeing of the state and hold to the view of Herzl that "if you will it, it is no dream." The existence of the Palestinians, though, is not a dream; they are there and the settlements can never wish them away.

THE CURSE OF THE OCCUPATION

JULY 16, 2014

At a time when hundreds of rockets are fired by Hamas and Islamic Jihad from Gaza against Israel—threatening population centers, including Jerusalem and Tel Aviv—criticizing Israel's occupation of the West Bank would seem inappropriate at best.

Many Israelis justify the continuing occupation in light of the intensifying violence. They argue that Israel cannot allow the West Bank to become under any circumstances like Gaza—a staging ground for rocket attacks that could cause unimaginable death and destruction.

The repeated acts of violence emanating from Gaza and the relative calm in the occupied West Bank are used to "validate" this claim. In reality, the occupation itself is the root cause behind the unending Israeli-Palestinian conflict and the current deadly flare-up between Israel and Hamas.

Although Israel has legitimate national security concerns and has every right to defend itself, the continuing occupation is largely used as a cover for those expansionists who believe in the right to Greater Israel.

Prime Minister Netanyahu and many members of his cabinet make no secret of their belief that "the Jewish people are not foreign occupiers." In his speech to Congress on May 24, 2011, Netanyahu emphatically stated:

> This is the land of our forefathers, the land of Israel, to which Abraham brought the idea of one god…no distortion of history could deny the 4,000-year-old bond between the Jewish people and the Jewish land.[59]

---

59   Benjamin Netanyahu, "Address to U.S. Congress"(Washington, DC, May 24, 2011), http://www.cfr.org/israel/netanyahus-address-us-congress-may-2011/p25073.

Naftali Bennett, the Economy Minister, reflected the senti-ments of many Israelis when he stated in 2012: "Obviously all of Eretz Yisrael [the entire land of Israel] belongs to us."[60] Now he openly calls for the outright annexation of Area C, which repre-sents 60% of the West Bank.

Given these deep ideological and religious convictions and the failure of the last set of U.S.-sponsored peace negotiations, the little hope left for the Palestinians to establish a state of their own has been further diminished.

To deny that Israel is an occupying power, as many Israelis do, is the height of hypocrisy. The assumption that a historical and biblical right to the "land of Israel" which goes back four millennia super-sedes the right of the indigenous Palestinians defies both logic and the reality on the ground.

Regardless of who is right or wrong, occupation by its very nature erodes the moral values of the occupier, which leads to violations of the occupied's human rights with near-impunity. In this regard, the blockade of Gaza is as bad as, and perhaps even worse than, the occupation of the West Bank.

This in turn engenders hatred and resentment, as the occupied harbor enmity and often resort to violent resistance, revenge and retribution. The abduction and the murder of three Israeli teen-agers, and the kidnapping of a Palestinian boy who was beaten and burned to death as an act of revenge, instigated, at least in part, the current cycle of violence.

As the Greek dramatist Euripides observed, "The strong should not abuse their strength, nor the fortunate think Chance will bless them forever."[61] What he and other Greek playwrights understood was the theme of blood crimes, where one outrage begets another outrage, so that what ensues is a never-ending

---

60   Raphael Ahren, "The New Great White Hope of the Religious Right?," *The Times of Israel*, July 26, 2012, http://www.timesofisrael.com/the-new-great-white-hope-of-pro-settlement-zionists/.

61   Euripides, "Hecuba," in *The Compete Euripides: Volume 1: Trojan Women and Other Plays*, eds. Peter Burian and Alan Shapiro (New York: Oxford University Press, 2010), 99.

cycle of destruction. Or as Aeschylus puts it, "Old arrogance gives birth to new..."[62]

The sad irony is that as long as Hamas openly seeks and promotes the destruction of Israel and violently resists the blockade, it provides Israel with the excuse and rationale it needs to maintain the blockade and, by extension, the occupation of the West Bank.

This explains why the Netanyahu government does not seek the destruction of Hamas and instead chooses to "manage" its militancy by degrading every few years its military capability and destroying much of its infrastructure to keep it at bay.

The question that Greek tragedy keeps coming back to is, can we learn from all this suffering? How much wanton destruction of life has to occur before we "suffer into truth"—that is, before we learn the truth of moderation, self-control, and respect for boundaries and ultimately reconciliation?

Conversely, even though Hamas knows that it will never be in a position to destroy Israel, and regardless of the acute suffering of the trapped and despondent Palestinians in Gaza, continued militancy provides it with its raison d'être, the staying power and the "legitimacy" as it seeks to portray itself as the champion of the Palestinian cause.

This incessant and obsessive repetition of acts of vengeance and retaliation ultimately spells the end of civic morality. But as Aeschylus also observed, there is a final day of reckoning: "sooner or later... the appointed day comes."[63] How long must we repeat this senseless cycle of bloodshed?

Israel and Hamas will sooner or later agree on another precarious ceasefire, which will last only so long as it continues to serve their interests. In the interim, both will be preparing for the next round of fighting at the expense of the majority of Israelis and Palestinians, who are fed up with their so-called leaders whose ideological compulsion and self-denial overshadows national interests.

---

62 Aeschylus, "Agamemnon," in *The Oresteia*, eds. Alan Shapiro and Peter Burian (New York: Oxford University Press, 2003), 70.

63 Cited in Michael Ewans, *Wagner and Aeschylus: The Ring and the Oresteia* (New York: Cambridge University Press, 1983), 136.

Israel must remember that in the wake of World I, and especially following the defeat of Germany in World War II, a new global political order was established and subsequently enshrined in the United Nations Charter; no country has been able or permitted to sustain a belligerent occupation. In this sense, today only Israel is considered to be an occupying power.

Hamas' leadership knows that they cannot destroy Israel and will be unable to indefinitely rule Gaza, not because Israel can destroy them but because the vast majority of Palestinians in Gaza will rise and demand an end to their misery and servitude, for which Hamas is blamed.

They are prisoners in their own land, encircled by Israel from the land, air, and sea and policed by Hamas. The ghastly conditions under which they live are becoming ever more unbearable and hapless every time Hamas challenges Israel.

President Abbas will do well to stay the course and continue to pursue the path of peaceful negotiations, but he must insist that if Hamas wants to remain a part of the unity government, then Gaza must also fall under the overall authority of the PA.

Egypt is rightfully insisting that any ceasefire must involve the PA's security forces guarding the border crossing with Egypt, and Israel should also be firm that the PA be a signatory to any new ceasefire agreement.[64]

Insisting on these conditions now in exchange for some concessions to Hamas could change the dynamics between Hamas and Israel and may well provide a new opening for the resumption of peace negotiations.

To be sure, occupation is a curse that dehumanizes both the occupier and the occupied. It runs contrary to every tenet of humanity.

Israel must take the initiative because its extraordinary achievements and permanence cannot be sustained by its military prowess alone, but rather by its dedication to the moral values for the lack of which millions of Jews have suffered and perished.

---

64   Avi Issacharoff, "For Ceasefire, Abbas Proposes PA Forces Along Gaza-Egypt Border," *The Times of Israel*, July 16, 2014, http://www.timesofisrael.com/for-ceasefire-abbas-proposes-pa-forces-along-gaza-egypt-border/.

REFUGEES

THE PALESTINIAN REFUGEES—
A REASSESSMENT AND A SOLUTION

FEBRUARY 24, 2009

The Israeli-Palestinian conflict has been riddled with many intractable problems for which solutions have eluded both sides for more than 60 years. None, though, have been as politically and emotionally charged and rancorous as the Palestinians' right of return. As the Israelis and Palestinians prepare for renewed American engagement, they will soon find themselves once again confronting the same old dilemma, lest they are better prepared to accept some inescapable realities on the ground that offer the only realistic solutions.

What caused and who is responsible for
the Palestinian refugee problem?

What the root causes of the Palestinian refugee problem are is not in dispute. Certainly Israel's war of independence in 1948, the invasion by the Arab armies of the nascent state and the efforts by both sides in times of war to make strategic gains precipitated the Palestinian exodus. A new wave of Palestinian refugees occurred in the wake of the 1967 Six Day War, which further aggravated an already existing refugee crisis. As to how the initial flight of Palestinians came about remains in dispute to this very day. That is, the effort to pin down the blame on each other from the time these tragic events unfolded was meant to discharge responsibility, but it mainly served to perpetuate the refugee plight. Any objective review of the events of that particular period shows beyond a doubt that both sides are equally to blame.

Although mass expulsion or transfer was not a part of official Zionist policy, even before the creation of the state of Israel Zionist leaders in Palestine and Europe discussed the need to transfer Palestinians from some of their villages to neighboring Arab states. Most Zionists who advocated the transfer of Palestinians believed in voluntary transfer with compensation to make room for the influx of Jews. Eli'ezer Kaplan, who was the head of the Jewish Agency Finance and Administrative Department, said as early as 1937: "The question here is one of organized transfer of a number of Arabs from a territory, which will be the Hebrew state, to another place in the Arab state, that is, to the environment of their own people."[65] In June 1941, Joseph Weitz, Director of the Settlement Department of the Jewish National Fund, wrote in his diary: "Amongst ourselves it must be clear that there is no room for both peoples in this country."[66] And in 1948 he said: "I made a summary of a list of the Arab villages which in my opinion must be cleared out in order to complete Jewish regions. I also made a summary of the places that have land disputes and must be settled by military means."[67] David Ben Gurion, who was the leader of the Jewish community and later became Prime Minister of Israel, offered his advice in December 1947: "We [the Haganah, Israel's defense forces] adopt the system of aggressive defense; with every Arab attack we must respond with a decisive blow: the destruction of the [Arab] place or the

65 Gabriel G. Tabarani, *Israeli-Palestinian Conflict: from Balfour Promise to Bush Declaration: The Complications and the Road for a Lasting Peace* (Bloomington, Indiana: AuthorHouse, 2008), 73.

66 Hasan Afif El-Hasan, *Israel Or Palestine? Is the Two-state Solution Already Dead?: A Political and Military History of the Israeli-Palestinian Conflict*(New York: Algora Publishing, 2010), 90.

67 Nur Masalha, *The Bible and Zionism: Invented Traditions, Archaeology and Post-Colonialism in Palestine-Israel*(London: Zed Books, 2007), 52.

expulsion of the residents along with the seizure of the place."[68] As war broke out, however, Israeli forces did not shy away from terrifying Palestinians into fleeing, although no forcible expulsion was systematically organized.

As to the role of the Arab states, there is considerable evidence to support that at different times Arab leaders encouraged the Palestinians to flee. Believing in their quick victory and desiring to prevent the Palestinians from being caught in the crossfire, they encouraged Palestinians to temporarily leave and then return for the spoils of the war. During a fact finding mission to Gaza in June 1949 Sir John Troutbeck, head of the British Middle East office in Cairo, found that while refugees "express no bitterness against the Jews...they speak with the utmost bitterness of the Egyptians and other Arab states. 'We know who our enemies are', they will say, and they are referring to their Arab brothers who, they declare, persuaded them unnecessarily to leave their homes."[69] According to Near East Arabic Radio, April 1948: "It must not be forgotten that the Arab Higher Committee encouraged the refugees to flee from their homes in Jaffa, Haifa, and Jerusalem and that certain leaders have tried to make political capital out of their miserable situation."[70] Time magazine reported in May 1948: "The mass evacuation, prompted partly by fear, partly by order of Arab leaders, left the Arab quarter of Haifa a ghost city. By withdrawing Arab workers their leaders hoped to paralyze Haifa."[71] And there were many Palestinians who left 'on their own,' fearing the advancing Israeli forces which were falsely rumored to inflict inhuman suffering, largely perpetrated by both Israelis and Arab officials to serve their own purposes.

---

68 Simha Flapan, *The Birth of Israel* (New York: Pantheon Books, 1987), 90.

69 Efraim Karsh, *Rethinking the Middle East* (New York: Routledge, 2003), 165-6.

70 Judith R. Baskin, ed., *The Cambridge Dictionary of Judaism and Jewish Culture* (New York: Cambridge University Press, 2011), 306.

71 Shlomo Sharan and David Bukay, *Crossovers: Anti-Zionism and Anti-Semitism* (Piscataway, New Jersey: Transaction Publishers, 2010), 32.

How many refugees are there and where?

There is no precise number of the original Palestinian refugees who fled in 1948; estimates vary from 550,000 to 750,000.[72] Although the Palestinian refugees have been cared for during the past six decades by the United Nations Relief and Works Agency for Palestine Refugees in the Near East (UNRWA), there is no definitive number of Palestinian refugees currently dispersed in several Arab states and in Palestine. That being said, there is no doubt that the number of Palestinian refugees has swelled at a minimum four-fold since 1948, making it the most enduring refugee crisis of modern history. Moreover, the disbursement of the refugees and their different situations in their current places of residence makes it even harder to gauge how to go about ascertaining who is a refugee and who is not. Adding to this mix is the fact that more than half of the refugees still live in their homeland, namely Gaza and the West Bank, and nearly one-third live in Jordan as full-fledged citizens. But to have a better view of the complexity of the problem and where the solution might be found, it is necessary to sketch out a general map of the refugees and the precariousness of their legal status.

It is estimated by UNRWA that currently there are more than four million refugees scattered in several locations, mostly in Gaza, the West Bank, Jordan, Lebanon, Syria, and the Gulf states.[73] According to UNRWA, nearly one million Palestinian refugees live in Gaza, representing nearly 25 percent of the total refugee population. The majority are descendants of families that fled in 1948 from places like Jaffa and other southern towns in present-day Israel. More than half of Gaza's refugees still live in eight crowded refugee camps.[74] Gaza has one of the highest birth rates, estimated at five percent

---

72   Paul McCann, "The Role of UNRWA and the Palestine Refugees," *Palestine-Israel Journal* 15/16(4/1) (2008/2009): 84.

73   McCann, "The Role of UNRWA and the Palestine Refugees," 85.

74   "Where We Work | Gaza Strip," UNRWA, http://www.unrwa.org/where-we-work/gaza-strip (accessed February 20, 2009).

annually.75 In the West Bank the refugee population is estimated at 600,000 out of a total of nearly two million residents. About one quarter of them live in 19 refugee camps.[76] The majority of Palestinians in Jordan hold Jordanian citizenship and have, by and large, integrated into the country's economic, social, and political life.[77] Those refugees in Jordan who want to get ahead enjoy full freedom of movement and job opportunities and face virtually no obstacles.

In Lebanon the situation is quite different as the Palestinian refugees constitute approximately 10 percent of the population, estimated at 416,000.[78] The Lebanese government has, over the years, made every effort to resist the refugees' integration into Lebanon's social and political life, fearing a serious deterioration in the delicate demographic balance between the Muslim and Christian communities. As one highly placed Lebanese official said, "The permanent settlement of the refugees in Lebanon will dramatically shift the demographic makeup of the Lebanese population, with ominous implications to the stability of the state."[79] In Syria, according to UNRWA, there are roughly 450,000 refugees, the majority of which came from families that fled Northern Israel in 1948 from cities like Haifa and Safed.[80] Although the refugees in Syria enjoy employment and regular education, they are denied citizenship and also experience limitations in securing government jobs.[81] In addition there are over 400,000 refugees in the Gulf States scattered

---

75   "West Bank and Gaza Strip: Cooperation Strategy at a Glance," World Health Organization, April 2006, http://www.who.int/countryfocus/ cooperation_strategy/ccsbrief_pse_en.pdf.

76   "The Palestinian Diaspora: A History of Dispossession," Global Exchange, March 1, 2003, http://www.globalexchange.org/country/ palestine/diaspora.

77   McCann, "The Role of UNRWA and the Palestine Refugees," 87.

78   Ibid.

79   Farid Abboud (former Ambassador of Lebanon to the United States) in discussion with the author, May 2007.

80   McCann, "The Role of UNRWA and the Palestine Refugees," 87.

81   Ibid.

between Saudi Arabia, Kuwait, Oman and others.[82] The Palestinians in the Gulf do not enjoy civil rights but there are well-off economically. There are about 450,000 Palestinian refugees that live outside the region, mostly in the United States, and constitute a large block of the Arab community in the country.[83] The majority is doing well socially and economically, and they enjoy full citizenship.

Who perpetuated the refugees' plight?

For most Palestinians the right of return transcends the value of the actual return—it is about their collective memory, history, and national identity. The "right of return" has remained a constant in Arab narratives for the past 60 years. As such, it has been promoted and became a highly political issue, preventing many Arab leaders from showing any flexibility on the matter, fearing public condemnation. As a result, the right of return among the Palestinians and in many Arab countries assumed over time a life of its own, and for a long time it has been an albatross strangling public debate. The refugee problem was always on the top of the Arab states' agenda, insisting all along that the refugee camps must remain intact to ensure their temporary nature and to find a solution only through the right of return. This is precisely why Arab media and intellectuals treat the "right of return" like a fossil, frozen in time. In 1956, the League of Arab States advised its members that while it is necessary to provide full economic and social rights to the Palestinian refugees, they must not be allowed to naturalize so as to maintain their refugee status. Notwithstanding the Oslo Accords in 1993–94 and subsequent Israeli-Palestinian agreements, the PLO continued to insist on the implementation of the right of return in all international forums to keep the plight of the refugees alive, thereby providing the PLO with a continuing political strength. Over the years Israeli efforts to change the status of the refugee camps in the occupied territories were vehemently resisted by the Palestinians, fearing that any change in the refugees' status would undermine their basic right of return.

---

82 "The Palestinian Diaspora," *Le Monde diplomatique*, June 30, 1999, http://mondediplo.com/focus/mideast/question-3-3-1-en.

83 "The Palestinian Diaspora: A History of Dispossession."

The Israeli position

Israel rejects in principle the Palestinian right of return on a number of grounds and it does not accept responsibility for the plight of the refugees. The Israeli position is generally predicated on the fact that in time of wars many people end up being displaced and that history is replete of examples whereby refugees end up settling elsewhere, especially when the conditions in their country of origin have changed so dramatically. Moreover, Israel insists that the return of any significant number of Palestinian refugees to Israel proper would obliterate the Jewish identity of the state, which was created as the last refuge for the Jews. Israel further insists that the claim of the right of return is based on UN Resolution 194 passed by the General Assembly (UNGA) in 1948. Although the resolution stipulates "achieving just settlement of the refugee problem," it was superseded by the UN Security Council (UNSC) Resolution 242 which was accepted by the Arab states and Israel and which "affirms...the necessity for achieving a just settlement of the refugee problem" without any reference to the right of return. It is noteworthy that Resolution 242 does not mention the Palestinians by name, as there were also Jewish refugees from Arab lands. In any event, the Israelis argue that Resolution 194 is not legally binding, as are all General Assembly resolutions. Furthermore, the Oslo Accords, which were signed in September 1993 at the White House, stipulated that the refugee problem would be discussed as part of talks on a permanent settlement, again without making any reference to the right of return. At Camp David in 2000, the Israeli strategy was to induce the Palestinians to concede the right of return in exchange for Israeli withdrawal from the vast majority of the occupied territories. It should be noted, based on the proceedings at Camp David, that at no point did Israel agree to accept more than 10,000 refugees under the family reunification framework. In subsequent negotiations at Taba, Egypt, in January 2001, no position papers were exchanged concerning the refugee problem, which was seen as a good sign for open-ended talks. Both sides stated that a comprehensive and just solution to the issue of the Palestinian refugees is central to "a lasting and morally scrupulous peace."[84] Both sides also agreed to adopt the principles and references that could facilitate the adoption of an agreement. In addition, the two parties suggested that, as a basis, they should agree that a just settlement to the refugee problem be in accordance with UNSC Resolution 242.

The Palestinian position

The Palestinian position has generally been consistent with the premise of return; from their perspective nothing has transpired since the early exodus in 1948 that could change their inherent right to return. The issue has become deeply ingrained in the psyche of every Palestinian and each remains adamant that Israel must accept the principle of return as a prerequisite to any lasting solution to the conflict. Hassan Abu Asfur, one of the members of the Palestinian delegation at Camp David, summarized the Palestinian position saying "In the Swedish channel [just prior to Camp David negotiation]...our position was decisive: To grant each and every Palestinian the right of return. The Israeli side kept trying to negotiate over compensation that would be given to the refugees instead of the right of return, and we refused."[85]

Although other Palestinians at Camp David might have agreed to forego a sweeping right of return, it appears that the two sides did not reach a full agreement on the right of return issue through the Swedish diplomatic channel. The Palestinians did not want to accept the ambiguous wording designed to solve the problem. They demanded that Israel assume legal and moral responsibility for the plight of more than four million refugees and also apologize to them—a demand Israel categorically rejected. Neither the Palestinians' position nor the Israelis' has changed much since Camp David. In March 2002, however, the Saudis offered a new Plan (the Arab Peace Initiative, or API) and reintroduced it in Riyadh, Saudi Arabia in March 2007, offering Israel a comprehensive peace with all

84   Beverley Milton-Edwards, *The Israeli-Palestinian Conflict: A People's War* (New York: Routledge, 2009), 114.

85   Uriya Shavit and Jalal Bana, "Everything You Wanted to Know about the Right of Return but Were Too Afraid to Ask," *Haaretz*, July 16, 2001.

Arab states in exchange for the territories captured in the 1967 war. In line with the general Arab position, the API also stipulated that "Achievement of a just solution to the Palestinian refugee problem [is] to be agreed upon in accordance with U.N. General Assembly Resolution 194." This provision in the API that addresses the Palestinian refugee problem is viewed by Israel, both literally and figuratively, as a threat to its very existence as a Jewish state. The authors of the API understood, however, that even though it might come to haunt them, changing the narrative now would undermine the entire process. Israel has thus far refused to embrace the Initiative, especially because of the reference to the right of return. Since the Annapolis peace conference in November 2007, the Palestinians have held fast to their public position throughout the negotiations. Privately, though, they have been signaling some creative ways to circumvent the principle of the right of return.

Considering the reality on the ground

Based on a thorough review of Arab sentiments regarding the right of return, it appears that a growing number of Arab officials appreciate that Israel could not accept the right of return and that the solution lies in their resettlement and/or compensation. They also understand that insisting on repatriation in any future negotiations under the Obama administration's auspices would bring any peace negotiation to a quick halt. What most Arabs, including Palestinian moderates, really want is for Israel to first acknowledge that there is a refugee problem and then to show a willingness to be part of the solution. Second, although ideally the "right of return" should be discussed publicly to prepare the Arab public, especially the Palestinians, for the necessary compromises, one top Jordanian official advises that because of the extreme sensitivity of the issue for both sides, the best course is to leave it to private negotiations to work out the details. Basically, open-ended public discourse will create public pressure that could torpedo the negotiations on this issue before they even begin in earnest. To avoid a repetition of the breakdown that occurred during the Israeli-Palestinian negotiations at Camp David during the summer of 2000, both sides need to understand each other's position through quiet diplomacy prior to formal negotiations. Finally, many Palestinian intellectuals and public officials have suggested that the right of return must mean a return to the homeland, the same soil in the West Bank and Gaza, not a return to the 1948 homes. Sari Nusseibeh, the president of Al-Quds University, has called for renunciation of the right of return in order to make it possible to achieve a settlement to the conflict. He argued that the Palestinians cannot simply ask Israel to return all the territories captured in 1967 and then demand that the Palestinian refugees return to their original homes, in what is today Israel, and thereby obliterate Israel as we know it. Rashid Khalidi distinguishes between what he terms 'attainable' rather than absolute justice. He suggested that while "it must be accepted that all Palestinian refugees and their descendants have a right to return to their homes in principle…[it must be] equally accepted that in practice force majeure will prevent most of them from being able to exercise this right."[86] For Israel, the right of return is a nonstarter and the passage of time will not change its position. For the Arab states, and even more for the Palestinians, giving up the right of return is tantamount to tossing away their trump card. They will not, and it is obvious that they cannot, show their hand before Israel indicates its willingness to withdraw from the vast majority of the territories and move clearly in the direction of a two-state solution. To achieve a comprehensive peace agreement, both sides will have to make many painful concessions. Accommodating Israel on the right of return is one of them.

A framework for a solution

Regardless of how sensitive this issue may be for the Palestinians, the existence of Israel as the home for the Jews, in the view of an over-whelming majority of Israelis, rests entirely on securing a sustainable Jewish majority within the state. It is critically important to understand that this is not a question of right or wrong. This is precisely what has been established on the ground and is not subject to change short of catastrophic events. The Palestinians do have a right in their homeland,

---

86   Mohammad Shiyyab, "Two Threats to Regional Stability: Water and Refugees," *Palestine-Israel Journal* 11(1) (2004): 35.

but this right must be addressed justly, primarily through resettlement in the future Palestinian state and through financial assistance from the international community and concerted humanitarian efforts.

First, Israel has a moral responsibility to be a part of the solution by making it possible for all Palestinians wishing to resettle in the West Bank to eventually do so with absolutely no restrictions. That is, while the Palestinians must accept the reality that they cannot return to their original homes in Israel proper, Israel must not impose limitations on those who chose to return to their ancestral home. Israel should also be prepared to accept between 20,000 and 25,000 Palestinians under the framework of family reunification. Moreover, as Israel must eventually evacuate nearly 100 settlements scattered all over the West Bank (other than the settlement blocks west of the fence), it must leave these settlements intact to allow Palestinian refugees to occupy them as the Palestinian Authority (PA) sees fit. More than 200,000 refugees can resettle in these homes and farms. This would represent the greatest humanitarian gesture that may go a long way toward reconciliation. In addition, Israel should offer technical support and expertise in resettlement to pave the way for neighborly relations.

Second, in looking at the Palestinian refugees' current places of residence, it is obvious that nearly 60 percent live in the West Bank and Gaza. They are, in fact, displaced people rather than refugees, albeit the majority live in refugee camps. The solution for these Palestinians must be found through resettlement in their homeland as articulated by Rashid Khalidi—in the West Bank and Gaza. Certainly this would require substantial capital to provide individual compensation, but mostly for development housing projects and job creation.

Third, the majority of Palestinian refugees living in Jordan are likely to stay in their host country as the Jordanian government, unlike any other Arab state, offered to the majority of the Palestinian refugees full citizenship with equal social and economic opportunities. The few who might opt to resettle in Palestine should be able to do so as a part of the general resettlement program. Here too, it will be necessary to fund the resettlement projects.

Fourth, in Lebanon the Palestinian refugees would most likely require a special dispensation as the Lebanese government strongly opposes resettlement of the nearly 400,000 Palestinian refugees, fearing a major tilt in the demographic balance between Christians and Muslims and concerns over breakouts of violence. As a high Lebanese official explained to me, a violent confrontation similar to one that took place in the summer of 2007 between Palestinian militants and the Lebanese army could escalate the conflict and push Lebanon into another devastating civil war. In this case, two options might be available: 1) to grant the Palestinians citizenship with proper compensation while they continue to live in Lebanon as permanent residents with social and economic rights, or 2) to facilitate the resettlement of those who wish to leave and live in the West Bank or Gaza.

Fifth, a similar option may be provided for the refugees living in Syria. Most Palestinians in the Gulf states and the United States who are better off will most likely stay where they are. All in all, only a few hundred thousand refugees may opt to relocate from Arab states, a number that does not represent the nightmare scenarios which many observers have contemplated.

Other than agreeing on the political solution, which is excruciatingly difficult, the question of the cost involved remains central to finding a lasting solution to the Palestinian refugees. Estimates of the cost involved for resettlement and rehabilitation runs between $50 and $100 billion.[87] Unfortunately, there are no shortcuts and the money must be found if a solution to this tragic problem is to be reached. The Obama administration knows only too well that without a solution to the Israeli-Palestinian conflict, there will be no prospect of stemming the rise of Islamic extremism and no end to regional turmoil. The question is, will the United States, the European Union (EU), and the Arab oil-producing countries raise the necessary money that it will take? I suppose that any sum that may be required must be weighed against the consequences of doing nothing.

---

87   Scott B. Lasensky, "How to Help Palestinian Refugees Today," *Jerusalem Center for Public Affairs*, February 2, 2003, http://www.jcpa.org/jl/vp491.htm.

AN EU SOLUTION TO THE
PALESTINIAN REFUGEES

OCTOBER 15, 2009

Since President Obama's long-awaited meeting with Israeli and Palestinian leaders Benjamin Netanyahu and Mahmoud Abbas this past September, there has been increased speculation about progress in the Middle East peace talks. Thus far, it seems as if attempts at reconciliation have not been translated into action on the ground. The continuation of Israeli settlement activity in the West Bank and Jerusalem has kept George Mitchell and the American negotiating team shuttling back and forth to the region, but little has been mentioned about the most historically contentious issue between these parties—the Palestinian refugee crisis. This conflict has disrupted numerous efforts toward a final agreement in the past, and is likely to present the biggest hurdle that negotiators will face in the future.

It is clear at this point that instead of waiting for final status talks to resume, the international community, led by the EU, must now take steps to change the political atmosphere surrounding the Palestinian refugees. There is only one realistic solution that can be realized as part of a two-state solution: compensation, resettlement, and rehabilitation in the West Bank and Gaza will be necessary for solving this dilemma. The EU must take the lead by using its formidable economic resources and political clout to help bring an end to the tragedy of the Palestinian refugees. In doing so, the EU can establish itself as an indispensable interlocutor in the Arab-Israeli peace process, while enhancing its strategic and economic interests in the Middle East.

Of all the conflicting issues between the Israelis and Palestinians, including territorial claims, secure borders, and the future of East Jerusalem, the Palestinian refugee problem continues to stymie any pragmatic solution between the parties. The majority of Palestinians believe that Israel's creation in 1948 precipitated the problem, and the solution, therefore, lies in the right of return to the state of Israel as a matter of principle. Israel has refuted this argument flat out, and in every encounter with the Palestinians since 1988 the Israelis have made it abundantly clear that to sustain its Jewish majority, which the Israelis consider *sine qua non* to any agreement, the solution must be found through resettlement and rehabilitation in the West Bank and Gaza. This will fulfill the call for Palestinians to return to their homeland, albeit not to their original homes. Other refugees may opt to resettle in their current country of residence as long as these countries are open to accept the refugees as their own citizens.

Many Palestinian and Arab leaders have conceded in private and in negotiations with Israel, especially since 2000, that apart from a symbolic number of refugees (20,000–30,000) returning to Israel proper as part of family reunification, the solution lies largely in resettlement and compensation in the new state of Palestine. Such a solution is based on the 1967 UNSC Resolution 242, which calls for "achieving a just settlement of the refugee problem." This is opposed to the 1948 UNGA Resolution 194, where Article 11 states that "the refugees wishing to return to their homes and live at peace with their neighbors should be permitted to do so at the earliest practicable date." It should be noted that in every final status negotiation between the two parties, a solution to the Palestinian refugees was discussed only in the context of resettlement and compensation. The understanding between the two parties was based on the premise of UNSC Resolution 242, which supersedes the nonbinding UNGA Resolution 194.

Considering the historical magnitude and the politicization of the issue of Palestinian refugees, it is necessary at this point to change the political formula. Waiting for an Israeli-Palestinian peace deal to be signed could take years, and as is, the refugee issue could force any final status agreement into collapse, as happened in Camp David. To change the political dynamics for all sides involved, the EU should start taking direct action to ameliorate the crisis as a precursor to a peace deal. That is, instead of first seeking to change the political narrative about the need to resettle the Palestinians in their homeland, the EU must first create the means that will make that possible.

Historically, the EU has championed the cause of Palestinian refugees since Israel's inception, and has been the largest donor to UNRWA. Considering this, as well as the natural alliance the Palestinians have with the EU (as a possible balance to the close United States-Israeli relationship), the EU is in an ideal position to dramatically change the status of the 4.5 million refugees registered by the United Nations. This is also an opportunity for Europe to solidify its role as an international mediator, with a vested interest in the success of the Middle East.

In order to have a substantial impact on the way this conflict has been framed, the EU will need to take a number of steps to change the entire structure in which the refugees exist. This will require ample capital, perhaps up to $10 billion—far more than the €264 million allotted for UNRWA—as well as a close relationship with the PA and neighboring Arab states of Syria, Lebanon, and Jordan, where many of the refugee camps are located. Raising the funds to support the resettlement of refugees into the West Bank and Gaza will help lay the foundation for the state of Palestine, but it must be accompanied by a support system to ensure the project is a success.

This will be in line with the plans of the PA's Prime Minister Salam Fayyad to establish a de facto state in the West Bank and Gaza. Fayyad's state-building vision has engendered Western enthusiasm along with financial and political support from the Obama administration and the EU. Although Mr. Fayyad invokes UNGA Resolution 194 on the question of the Palestinian refugees, he also emphasizes that "the Government...will do all within its power and authority to bolster on the legal rights and living conditions of refugees in the occupied territory, particularly in refugee camps, including the provision of all the resources it can afford to support and alleviate the suffering of refugees in all aspects of their lives."[88]

Every country that speaks of the need to find a solution to the Palestinian refugees must contribute to this effort, including the United

---

88 Salam Fayyad, "Ending the Occupation, Establishing the State," United Nations, August 2009, http://www.un.int/wcm/webdav/site/palestine/shared/documents/Ending%20Occupation%20Establishing%20the%20State%20%28August%202009%29.pdf.

States, Russia, China, the oil-rich Arab states, and Israel as well. The resettlement of the refugees will require large-scale economic investment for the creation of jobs, contracts for housing and schools, and other measures to ensure that existing Palestinian communities can safely absorb an influx of people. To this effect, the EU needs to partner with the PA to create a ministry with the sole purpose of resettling refugees and aiding in the transition to new homes, jobs, and schools. Improving the economic situation in the West Bank and Gaza will be paramount to ensuring that Palestinians have a motive for leaving the refugee camps and are able to invest in the success of their future state.

This approach is fundamentally different than any previous attempts, as it is based on finding a solution to the refugee crisis before final status negotiations. The EU should not only adopt this idea, but promote it publicly as their official political position. Guaranteeing money for resettlement will lure many Palestinians into thinking practically about this issue, rather than using it as a political tool. Billions of dollars for resettlement will have the effect of changing the debate, and forcing people to think about how to use the money constructively rather than fighting over this issue. The EU must reiterate that this is not a controversial idea, as all of the negotiations between the Israelis, Palestinians, and international mediators in the past have been based on the premise of UNSC Resolution 242 and the concept of resettlement into the West Bank and Gaza.

There are those who argue that while the solution to the refugee problem will indeed be financial at the end, with the right of return exercised inside the new Palestinian state, such a solution is difficult to attain now if it is not linked to the political issue of establishing a viable Palestinian state. If such a viable entity is not achieved as part of a package, Palestinians and Arabs will feel they were "bought" and would not accept such a solution. Sixty-two years have passed and no political solution has yet been found. Since we know how the solution will look, providing the means to settle the refugee problem should be done in precisely the context of establishing a Palestinian state in accordance with the Fayyad plan.

Providing the means to move Palestinians out of refugee camps and into viable communities in their future state will also have a huge impact on the Arab community, which has made this issue its principal focus. Not only should the Arab world help the EU fund this project, but they should also help provide logistical and organizational support for a significant transfer of people. Those Arab states that have used the plight of the refugees to cover up for their own shortcomings and misguided policies can use this opportunity to finally do something beneficial for the people who have been living in squalid conditions for decades. Israel should also welcome this development, as it will help to mitigate the call for a return to Israel proper and ease some of the human rights claims against them. By taking the lead and raising money, the EU can assure the Israelis that all the money raised and the needed permits for construction will be for the sole purpose of moving Palestinians into their homeland in the West Bank and Gaza.

Ultimately, the goal of this endeavor must be to change the current situation of the refugees, not by giving them aid—which is a major role for the UN—but by establishing the funding and grounds where refugees, by the thousands, can start returning to their homeland and investing in their new communities. For the 60% of refugees currently living in camps already in the West Bank and Gaza, this will mean working with the PA in an organizational capacity to pull their families out of refugee status and into proper housing.

Resolving the Palestinian refugee problem will require a substantial amount of money on the part of the EU. But above all, it will require the political and organizational savvy to navigate through the thickets of a highly emotional issue to find a practical solution. This will take the resolve to overcome the many detractors who continue to build their political fortunes on the plight of the Palestinian refugees. What is needed to fundamentally change the political narrative of the refugee crisis is a bold and visionary solution which is wholly consistent with the right of return to the future Palestinian state.

A SOLUTION TO THE PALESTINIAN
REFUGEES ISSUE

SEPTEMBER 5, 2010

Of all the conflicting issues Israelis and Palestinians must resolve in the negotiations—including territorial claims, secure borders, and the future of East Jerusalem—the Palestinian refugee problem in particular has the potential to stymie any pragmatic solution to the conflict. As Israelis and Palestinians renew direct talks, the EU can and must begin to play a key role in helping the parties resolve this difficult and thorny issue.

The EU is uniquely suited to utilize its formidable economic resources and political clout to take the lead in initiating and facilitating such a resolution. In doing so, the EU would establish itself as an indispensable interlocutor in the effort to achieve a sustainable Arab-Israeli peace agreement, while at the same time enhancing its strategic and economic interests in the Middle East. Although EU foreign policy chief Catherine Ashton should have been present at the launch of direct talks between Israelis and Palestinians in Washington last week, her absence should not be interpreted as an indication that the EU will not be critical to ensuring that the renewed peacemaking efforts succeed.

There is only one realistic solution to the refugee issue: compensation, resettlement, and rehabilitation in a Palestinian state in the West Bank and Gaza. While a majority of Palestinians support a "right of return" to the State of Israel as a matter of principle, polls have shown that only a small number of refugees actually seek to return to Israel proper. Meanwhile, Israel has refuted the principle of "right of return" in every encounter with the Palestinians since 1988, consistently stating that sustaining its Jewish majority is sine qua non to any agreement. Any solution must, therefore, be based on resettlement and rehabilitation in a future Palestinian state or in

128

the refugees' current countries of residence. Many Palestinian and Arab leaders have also previously conceded that apart from a symbolic number of refugees (20,000–30,000) returning to Israel proper as part of family reunification, the solution lies largely in the new state of Palestine. This formula would fulfill Palestinian aspirations to return to their homeland, albeit not their original homes. Such a solution would be consistent with the 1967 UNSC Resolution 242, which calls for "achieving a just settlement of the refugee problem" as well as with the API, which calls for "a just solution to the Palestinian refugee problem to be agreed upon in accordance with UN General Assembly Resolution 194" [emphasis added]. It should be noted, however, that UNSC Resolution 242 supersedes the nonbinding 1948 UNGA Resolution 194.

To change the political dynamics surrounding the renewed talks, the EU should take the lead in beginning to create the means that would make such a resolution possible. European nations have championed the cause of Palestinian refugees for decades and traditionally have been a leading contributor to Palestinian projects, including collectively serving as the largest donor to UNRWA. Considering its substantial support for the Palestinians—as well as the Palestinian inclination to turn to the EU as a balance to the close United States-Israeli relationship—the EU is uniquely positioned to influence the Palestinian position regarding the status of the 4.5 million Palestinian refugees registered by the United Nations. Facilitating a resolution would require ample capital, perhaps in excess of 10 billion dollars—far more than the $350 million allotted for UNRWA. Guaranteed money for refugee resettlement would provide an incentive for Palestinians to think practically about how to utilize such compensation constructively, rather than continue to use the issue as a political tool.

Of course, the Europeans cannot solve the refugee issue alone. The United States, Russia, China, the Arab states, and Israel must also significantly contribute to this effort. It would also require close cooperation with the PA, Syria, Lebanon, and Jordan, where many of the refugee camps are located. The Arab states in particular should provide logistical and organizational support. In addition, the Arab states can play a particularly important role in promoting a new narrative regarding the "right of return" to a newly established Palestinian state. President Obama's comment at the launch of direct talks that "A lot of times I hear from those who insist that this is a top priority and yet do very little to actually support efforts that could bring about a Palestinian state,"[89] was a call on the Arab states to match their rhetoric in support of peace with greater action—political and material—to achieve it. The Arab states that have historically used the plight of the refugees to cover for their own shortcomings and misguided policies now have an opportunity to answer the president's call while benefiting the people who have been living in squalid conditions for decades and helping to facilitate a resolution of the Israeli-Palestinian conflict. Such a measure would be welcomed by Israel in that it would mitigate calls for a return to Israel proper.

The resettlement of the refugees would require large-scale economic investment for the creation of jobs, contracts for housing and schools, and other measures to ensure that existing Palestinian communities can absorb an influx of new Palestinian citizens. To this effect, the EU should support the PA's creation of a new ministry tasked with resettling refugees and aiding in their transition. Such an initiative is fundamentally different than any previous attempts to address the Palestinian refugee issue, as it is premised on beginning to facilitate a resolution to the issue even before negotiations are concluded. The re-launch of direct negotiations offers the EU an opportunity to begin promoting this concept as their official position, emphasizing that this is not a controversial idea. All of the negotiations between Israelis and Palestinians in the past have been based on the premise of UNSC Resolution 242 and refugee resettlement in a future Palestinian state.

Some Arab leaders who have been involved in previous negotiations argue that while the solution rests with resettlement and compensation, it would be difficult to advocate publicly such a solution in advance of reaching a comprehensive agreement, fearing that it would instigate public backlash. But providing the means to settle the refugee problem now will begin to change the current situation

---

89   Barack Obama, "Remarks by the President in the Rose Garden After Bilateral Meetings" (Washington, D.C., September 1, 2010), http://www.whitehouse.gov/the-press-office/2010/09/01/remarks-president-rose-garden-after-bilateral-meetings.

of the refugees and at the same time serve to modify the public perception about the practical meaning of the "right of return." Moreover, such an approach would bolster PA Prime Minister Salaam Fayyad's plan to establish a de facto state in the West Bank and Gaza by next year, and many refugees can start returning to their homeland and investing in their new communities. For the 60% of refugees currently living in camps in the West Bank and Gaza, this will mean working with the PA in an organizational capacity to pull their families out of refugee status and into proper housing.

Clearly, resolving the Palestinian refugee problem will require a substantial amount of money. But above all, it will require political commitment to navigate through the thickets of a highly emotional issue in order to find a practical solution. There is no party better suited to lead this effort than the EU, and no better time to start than now.

Alon Ben-Meir

THE PALESTINIAN REFUGEES: THE REAL VICTIMS OF ARAB POLITICS

OCTOBER 22, 2011

With each passing day, the Palestinians and most Arab states make the problem of Palestinian refugees more difficult to resolve. Any solution to the Palestinian refugee problem lies in re-settlement and/or compensation and must preclude their return to Israel *en masse*. Regrettably, the right of return remains the narrative on the Palestinian and Arab streets and continues to be exploited for political ends. In the process, it entrenches the Palestinians and the Arab states in an untenable position that pushes the es-tablishment of a viable Palestinian state under the formula of a two-state solution further from reach.

Creating the false hope that the Palestinian refugees will one day return to their homes in Israel made the acceptance of com-pensation or resettlement politically risky to advocate and near-impossible to implement in the current atmosphere for both the PA and Hamas' leaders. Palestinians designated as refugees throughout the Arab world (with the exception of Jordan, where the majority of Palestinian refugees have been absorbed) have been prevented from fully integrating into the societies in which they live for decades. Even those living in the West Bank and Gaza remain designated as refugees in their own homeland for the sole purpose of maintaining their status and making it the main focus of the Israeli-Palestinian conflict while exploiting their plight as a political tool.

Even before the establishment of the PA, Arab states pointed to the dilemma of the Palestinian refugees as a symbol of the Arab-Israeli conflict, using it as a device to divert attention from their domestic shortcomings. The notion of a full return to their homes has been ingrained in the Palestinian psyche. Today, with the third generation of Palestinian refugees demanding their full return, the issue has been compounded. Whereas in 1950 there were just over 700,000 registered Palestinian refugees, today the number is nearly five million.[90]

The refugee issue remains the rallying cause around which different Palestinian factions agree. Both Fatah and Hamas espouse the unfeasible "right of return," providing them with a rare common cause. To promote anything less than a full return would amount to political suicide for either side. Furthermore, because of the consensus on the issue, no one openly discusses the only realistic solution, which must be anchored in compensation and resettlement. The resulting public discourse has created the perception that a full "right of return" is sine qua non to a solution to the refugee problem.

The Palestinian resolve on the refugee issue has a particularly dramatic effect on the way Israelis view the conflict. For the Israelis, the return of Palestinian refugees to Israel represents an existential threat to the country as a democratic homeland for the Jewish people. Thus, when Palestinians today talk of a two-state solution, Israelis are skeptical. They largely believe that the Palestinians' ultimate intention is to eliminate Israel in stages: first by establishing a Palestinian state in the West Bank and Gaza, and then by eradicating Israel as a Jewish state by demographic means through the right of return. From the Israeli perspective, this explains, at least in part, why the PA refuses to recognize Israel as a Jewish state.

If a full return were to happen, the Palestinian refugees plus Israeli-Palestinian citizens will exceed the number of Israeli Jews, thereby destroying the Jewish character of Israel altogether. Although in previous negotiations the Palestinians accepted the return of a token number of refugees under family reunification, they nevertheless demanded to maintain the principle of the "right of return" in any peace agreement. Fearing that the Palestinians may someday

---

90   See Lex Takkenberg, "UNRWA and the Palestinian Refugees After Sixty Years: Some Reflections," *UNISPAL*, June 10, 2010, http://unispal.un.org/UNISPAL.NSF/0/2A53BF73B3DD857B85257 73E00587A16; and "UNRWA in Figures," Public Information Office, UNRWA Headquarters, July 2011, http://www.unrwa.org/userfiles/2011080123958.pdf.

revive the issue of the right of return, Israel continues to reject any reference to it to ensure a sustainable Jewish majority and thereby the Jewish identity of the state.

Palestinian and Arab policymakers admit that perpetuating the refugees' predicament makes it politically risky to offer alternate solutions unless they are part of an overall Israeli-Palestinian peace agreement. This approach has not worked either. In 2000 at Camp David, Yasser Arafat, the then-Chairman of the PA, raised the question of the right of return at the 11th hour as a matter of principle, even after he and then-Israeli Prime Minister Ehud Barak nearly reached an agreement on all issues including the return of a limited number of refugees. The "Palestine Papers," leaked in early 2011 by Al Jazeera, demonstrated that President Mahmoud Abbas and then-Prime Minister Ehud Olmert were preparing to make a deal enabling 5,000 refugees over the course of five years to return to Israel proper, with the ultimate number for "symbolic" purposes to be in the several thousands. Of course, the revelation of the "Palestine Papers," in showing that Abbas was willing to relinquish the full right of return, hardened the Palestinian position today evermore.

For the Palestinians to conclude a two-state agreement with Israel and convince the Israelis of their intentions, a permanent peace based on a two-state solution will today require a dramatically different approach on the right of return. To avoid a serious Palestinian backlash, however, the new approach must be consistent with political developments since 2000, including the introduction of the API in 2002, the negotiations between Olmert and Abbas in 2008, and Hamas' moderated views since the Israeli incursion into Gaza in 2008–2009.

First, the Palestinian leadership must begin to use a new public narrative in connection with the right of return by adopting the language used in reference to the Palestinian refugees in the API: "Achievement of a just solution to the Palestinian refugee problem to be agreed upon in accordance with UN General Assembly Resolution 194." Although Israel rejects the reference to UN Resolution 194, which is non-binding but nevertheless affirms the Palestinian refugees' right of return to Israel proper, the emphasis should be placed on the concept of a "Just solution…to be agreed upon [by the parties]" which is also consistent with the 1967 UN Resolution 242. The Palestinian public must begin to hear the narrative of a "just solution" that can be accomplished only through resettlement and compensation.

Second, think tanks, writers, and academics should take the lead and begin to change the discourse on the Palestinian refugee issue by changing the narrative from one of helplessness and despair to one of self-determination and renewed initiative. Doing so will have a profound effect on the Palestinian psyche and on the Israeli public as well. Scholars should discuss the plight of the Palestinian refugees in search of realistic, viable solutions to the dilemma in the context of a two-state solution. There is no doubt that this will irk and anger many Palestinians, and some may resort to threats or even violence to silence such voices, but it takes courage and conviction to change the discourse on this vital issue for the sake of those who have been suffering the most.

Third, the new public narrative should center on the necessity of building the Palestinian "homeland" in the West Bank and Gaza Strip. Since the West Bank and Gaza are parts of the original homeland (Palestine), the refugees will have the right to exercise their right of return to these areas, but not necessarily to their original homes in Israel proper. This is especially timely with the recent initiative to gain statehood recognition from the UN. Much like the pursuit of self-determination at the UN, the solution to the plight of the Palestinian refugees would not be dependent on Israel, but rather would be a Palestinian and Arab initiative as part of a broader effort to build their newly established state.

Fourth, there is absolutely no reason or justification to maintain the status of refugees for Palestinians already living in the West Bank and Gaza. Instead of depending on UNRWA for handouts, Palestinian refugees should seek international aid for resettlement in their homeland. The oil-rich Arab states, EU member states, and the United States should contribute financially to rehabilitate and settle these refugees who are still languishing in refugee camps in their homeland, the West Bank and Gaza. Israel too will have to contribute to the resettlement process by providing thousands of prefabricated homes as well as by turning over scores of settlements that will eventually be evacuated under the terms of a peace agreement with the Palestinians. The majority of these refugees do not seek to uproot themselves and go elsewhere, but merely a better quality of life and opportunity to raise their families with dignity, leaving behind the stigma of refugee status.

The politics surrounding the issue of Palestinian refugees, especially Israel's concerns over the Palestinians' ultimate intentions, has made the refugee problem a most serious impediment to negotiating a lasting peace agreement between Israel and Palestine. As a result, the issue can no longer be resolved at the negotiating table alone. Attitudes must be changed, and to do so in the absence of genuine discussion on the political level requires solutions to be found at the popular level.

Palestinian self-determination will remain untenable without a resolution to the refugee dilemma. It is time for the Palestinian and Arab civil society to begin a new public discourse that their political leaders have long avoided.

NEGOTIATING UNDER THE SHADOW
OF THE PALESTINIAN REFUGEES

OCTOBER 3, 2013

One of the main issues that Israelis and Palestinians are struggling with in the ongoing negotiations is the Palestinian refugee problem. Although in previous negotiations in 2000 and 2008–2009 both sides agreed on certain modalities that would permit only a small number (25,000–30,000) of refugees to return to Israel, the agreement failed as it was encumbered by other conflicting issues, especially Israel's national security concerns. Since then, Israel's insistence on maintaining the Jewish identity of the state and shifting demographics make the return of any significant number of refugees to Israel or even the principle of the right of return simply impossible.

The problem of the Palestinian refugees has generally been discussed in context of the moral imperative of the "right of return" and is based on subjective judgment of right and wrong.

The circumstances that precipitated the refugee problem, as seen from the Israelis' and Palestinians' vantage points, weighed heavily in shaping two diametrically opposing perceptions between the two sides.

From the Palestinians' perspective, immediately following the establishment of Israel in May 1948, it embarked on a forceful and systematic expulsion of nearly 800,000 Palestinians from their homeland (Palestine). The Palestinians recall these events as "the catastrophe" (Al Nakba).

This scenario has been embedded in the Palestinian psyche and reinforced by consistent and methodical public narratives by Palestinian leaders to perpetuate their plight, and by the Arab states that used the refugees for domestic consumption to cover up their own internal shortcomings.

What has further aggravated the Palestinian refugees is the subsequent and frequent violence between the two sides, especially after the 1967 war, which created another wave of refugees.

Moreover, the Israeli settlements are seen as a deliberate plan to deny the refugees the prospect of returning to any part of Palestinian land.

Sixty-five years later, the Palestinians still see the right of return as a moral imperative that must trump all other considerations, regardless of any changes on the ground.

Israel disputes the circumstances that precipitated the refuge problem. From its vantage point, the UN partition called for the establishment of a Jewish state alongside a Palestinian state. The Israelis accepted the plan, the Palestinians rejected it, and seven Arab states invaded the nascent country and were subsequently defeated.

The Israelis further argue that the Arab states called on the Palestinians to move out of harm's way during the 1948 war, leave their homes and return for the spoils after the defeat of the Israelis.

The Israeli position is generally predicated on the fact that in times of war many people end up being displaced and end up settling elsewhere, especially when the conditions in their country of origin have changed so dramatically.

Moreover, Israel insists that the return of any significant number of Palestinian refugees to Israel proper would obliterate the Jewish identity of the state. At any rate, the claim of the right of return is based on the nonbinding UNGA Resolution 194, passed in 1948.

In the search for a solution there are several other critical factors that must be carefully considered.

First, both Israelis and Palestinians have created a biased historical account that corresponds to their claims as to what actually precipitated the Palestinian exodus. While Israel claims that the Palestinians were encouraged to leave by the Arab states, the Palestinians insist that they were forced to leave by Israel.

Second, whereas over 700,000 Palestinians fled Palestine in 1948,[91] their number, according to UNRWA, has swelled to nearly five million since 1948.[92] A refugee's legal status was therefore treated as an inheritance to be bequeathed from father to son,[93] in which both UNRWA and the Arab states have continuing interests in maintaining.

Third, while the Palestinian authorities understand that Israel will never accept the return of any significant number of Palestinian refugees, they continue to foster the perception that the Palestinian refugees have a birthright impervious to time.

Fourth, in the peace talks in 2000 and in 2008, the Palestinians agreed to repatriate 20,000–25,000 refugees under family reunification over a few years while insisting that the "principle" of the right of return be enshrined in any peace agreement. Israel rejected that on the grounds that such a clause would leave it vulnerable to future claims. **Thus, self-preservation must trump the moral imperative of the right of return, however just it may be.**

The political philosopher Leo Strauss observed that an extreme situation is "**a situation in which the very existence or independence of a society is at stake**…there may be conflicts between what the self-preservation of society requires and the requirements of commutative and distributive justice. **In such situations, and only in such situations, it can justly be said that the public safety is the highest law** [emphasis added]."[94]

---

91   United Nations Conciliation Commission for Palestine, "Final Report of the United Nations Economic Survey Mission for the Middle East" (Lake Success, New York, December 28, 1949), http://domino.un.org/pdfs/AAC256Part1.pdf.

92   United Nations Relief and Works Agency for Palestine Refugees in the Near East, "In Figures" (Jerusalem, January 2013), http://www.unrwa.org/sites/default/files/2013042435340.pdf.

93   United Nations High Commissioner for Refugees, "Convention and Protocol Relating to the Status of Refugees" (Geneva, December 2010), http://www.unhcr.org/3b66c2aa10.html.

94   Leo Strauss, *Natural Right and History* (Chicago: University of Chicago Press, 1965), 160.

The right of return will continue to be a major obstacle in peace negotiations unless Israel and the Palestinian leadership accept the changing realities which in fact lend themselves to find a solution.

Framework for a solution

The humanitarian crisis of the Palestinian refugees should come to an end; their rights ought to be addressed justly through resettlement and compensation. All parties involved—the Palestinians themselves, Israel, the Arab states, the United States, and the EU— need to facilitate a solution not only for the refugees' sake but because a resolution to the Israeli-Palestinian conflict serves their best national interests.

First, for Israel, reaching an agreement with the Palestinians is becoming increasingly more urgent. Israel's growing isolation, its concern about Iran's nuclear weapons program, fear over the explosive situation in Syria, and rapidly changing demographics in favor of the Palestinians have convinced many Israelis that the time to end the conflict has come.

As in previous tentative agreements, Israel should allow 20,000–25,000 Palestinians to settle in Israel over a period of 4–5 years under the framework of family reunification.

In addition, regardless of how uncanny this may seem today, as a gesture of good will, Israel should leave intact many of the settlements that they will eventually evacuate (through a mutual agreement with the PA) for some of the refugees to inhabit. In addition, Israel could offer technical and logistical support to assist the Palestinians.

Nothing will demonstrate a greater humanitarian overture by Israel than making such a direct contribution to help the Palestinians in this herculean task.

Second, an overwhelming majority of Palestinians want an end to the occupation. The PA as well as Hamas' leadership know only too well the public sentiment in this regard, but for too long held onto extreme positions which run contrary to the wishes of ordinary Palestinians.

The PA and Hamas know that time is running out in this current untenable situation, and they know they must provide the refugees the prospect of a better future, give them hope and opportunities, and above all restore their human dignity.

The PA must now gradually but consistently begin to change its public rhetoric and emphasize that Palestinian refugees **can exercise their right of return to their homeland**—in the **West Bank and Gaza, the newly-established independent Palestinian state.**

Many Palestinians are aware that the right of return has been reduced to a principle rather than a real possibility, provided the promise of resettlement and compensation is credible.

Third, more than any time before, nearly all Arab states have come to the conclusion that the continuation of the Israeli-Palestinian conflict undermines their national interests, and they no longer see Israel as the enemy.

Moreover, weary of the rise of Islamic extremism, which is sweeping the Middle East, and Iran's ambitions to acquire nuclear weapons, they now consider settling the Israeli-Palestinian conflict and achieving rapprochement with Israel as central to regional stability. This further explains their support of the Obama's administration efforts to resume Israeli-Palestinian negotiations.

Such a solution must be consistent with the 1967 UNSC Resolution 242, which calls for "achieving a just settlement of the refugee problem," as well as with the API, which calls for "a just solution to the Palestinian refugee problem."

The Arab states should also provide logistical and organizational support while promoting a new narrative regarding the "right of return" to a newly-established Palestinian state.

Fourth, the EU has a special interest in seeing the Israeli-Palestinian conflict come to an end. The EU imports much of its oil from the Middle East and, because of its proximity, has a vested interest in the region's stability.

The EU has all along played a significant role in aiding the Palestinian refugees and has contributed the largest sum of money for their rehabilitation, healthcare, and education. The EU is uniquely suited to utilize its economic resources to take the lead in raising the funds needed, perhaps in excess of $10 billion, for resettlement and compensation.

Fifth, America's strategic interest in the Middle East is extremely important and successive American administrations have been relentless in persuading both the Israelis and Palestinians to reach a peace agreement.

Due to its prominence and influence, along with its ability to participate in funding any solution to the refugees, both sides look at the United States as the ultimate arbiter who can contribute appreciably to a solution for the refugees, and will continue to play a pivotal role in their resettlement and compensation in the context of a comprehensive peace.

At this juncture in the annals of Israeli-Palestinian conflict, little is left to the imagination. The bitter or sweet reality of coexistence is here to stay. A resolution to the refugee problem is now possible. It is time to put an end to the Palestinian refugees' plight and restore their human dignity.

ISRAELI POLITICS

COALITION OF THE UNWILLING

FEBRUARY 13, 2009

The result of the Israeli elections on February 10th expressed clear sentiments of the public's weariness of the political process and deep cynicism about the political rivals. The question that faces the two leading contenders for prime minister, Kadima's Tzipi Livni and Benjamin Netanyahu of Likud, is two-fold: will they rise to the occasion, join forces and put the country on a path of recovery, or will they go their own separate ways to try to form a narrow coalition government and set the country on a course for new failures and political turmoil?

Amid corruption charges against the departing Prime Minister Ehud Olmert and the failure of Tzipi Livni, who assumed the leadership of the party, to form a new government in October, the nation was forced into an early election. The tumultuous events of the past three years weighed heavily on the public, causing a political shift to the right-of-center. This includes the indecisive war in the summer of 2006 against Hezbollah, Hamas' violent provocations across Gaza's borders, the murky consequences of the Gaza war, and a serious lack of progress in the peace negotiations with the Palestinians. As a result, Israelis went in droves to polling stations voting for center-right parties that advocated a tough stance toward Palestinian militancy, albeit the public remained supportive of the peace negotiations.

Netanyahu's claim that the public has generally endorsed the right-leaning block is technically correct. Based on the number of parliamentarians garnered by these parties which includes Shas and Yisrael Betainu with 11 and 15, respectively,[95] Netanyahu can form a coalition government with a majority of about 65 out of 120 members. But such a coalition government is destined to fail long-term, not only because it would be nearly impossible to develop a cohesive policy toward the Palestinians, but because it would most likely set itself on a collision course with the Obama administration. If, on the other hand, Tzipi Livni manages to get the first crack at forming a government, she will have no choice but to offer Avigdor Lieberman—the leader of Yisrael Betainu, who openly advocates segregationist policies against the Israeli Arabs—a significant role and consequently a say on all future government policy. This of course assumes that Ehud Barak, the leader of the Labor party which came in fourth with only 13 Knesset members, agrees to join the government with Lieberman as a big thorn in his side. The disappointing result for Labor, especially in the wake of the Gaza war which was thought to have given Barak a lift, has forced the party's leaders to reassess their political fortunes. They may decide to stay in the opposition with little prospect of rebuilding the base, or opt to join Kadima to create a single center and left-of-center party which will be a formidable block either in the opposition or in the government.

What is best for the country in these trying times is forming a coalition government that is secular in nature and with solid support in the Knesset. Such a government composed of Kadima, Likud, Labor, and Meretz would have a commanding majority of 71 members in the Knesset and stand an excellent chance of serving the full four-year term. This is of course an ideal situation; the question here is whether Netanyahu and Livni can put their personal ambitions aside and place the nation's interest in front of their parties' differences. All four parties agree that the ultimate solution to the Israeli-Palestinian conflict is a two-state solution; they only differ in the approach.

---

95 "Elections in Israel-February 2009," Israel Ministry of Foreign Affairs, February 10, 2009, http://mfa.gov.il/MFA/AboutIsrael/History/Pages/Elections_in_Israel_February_2009.aspx .

Whereas Netanyahu believes that Israel must first pursue economic development in the occupied territories and stable security which can then lead to peace, Livni believes that only peace could lead to security and economic prosperity. Labor has been supportive of the Kadima approach while Meretz is less concerned with how to reach an agreement, as long as one is reached. The big question as to who will be the prime minister can be resolved if Livni and Netanyahu agree on a rotation arrangement whereby each serves two years as prime minister (while the other alternates as either finance or foreign minister), as was once done between Labor and Likud in 1984. President Shimon Peres should be expected to do everything in his power to persuade the three leaders to heed the public's call and form a forward-looking and stable government that can deal with the nation's urgent concerns.

This kind of a coalition government could potentially develop good working relations with the United States. Although President Obama will be as committed to Israel's national security as any of his predecessors, he will not give Israel carte blanche to determine its policy toward the Palestinians as it sees fit under the pretext of national security. Netanyahu knows only too well that he cannot be on the wrong side of President Obama and that the United States-Israel relationship is of supreme importance, especially because of the continuing regional instability and Iran's nuclear ambitions. Any future Israeli government will have to be prepared to demonstrate flexibility on the settlements and ultimately make the necessary territorial concessions. For this reason, an Israeli government with coalition partners who are against territorial concessions in the West Bank will either be a short-lived government or one with extremely tense relations with the United States.

Now that the Israeli public has spoken, it is the task of those who want to lead to listen carefully to what the public really wants. The Israelis want peace with security, so Livni and Netanyahu must either answer the call or fail their country in a muddled political process. This is their inescapable responsibility, and with the daunting tasks ahead, they should not shy away in the name of narrow-minded political gains.

TREADING AN OMINOUS PATH

MARCH 9, 2009

The collapse of the coalition negotiations between Likud leader Benjamin Netanyahu and Kadima's Tzipi Livni over Netanyahu's refusal to commit to the two-state solution may force him to form an ideologically narrow right-of-center government. Such a government is likely to impede any progress or end up disintegrating under domestic and American pressure to make important concessions for the peace process. The Obama administration must remain unequivocal in its pursuit of the two-state solution to prevent a further escalation of the conflict, which would have unpredictable regional implications.

Ms. Livni was absolutely correct in turning down Netanyahu's "generous" offer to join his government, where her party would be granted important portfolios in the coalition but denied any sound assurance that the peace negotiations would continue. Indeed, an Israeli government which is not committed to the two-state solution is sowing the seeds for incessant terror and violence that will do nothing but set the Israelis and Palestinians further apart. A narrow center-right government is a recipe for paralysis as most of Netanyahu's coalition partners' condition for joining the government is based on continuing the expansion of settlements. Netanyahu's slogan that Israel must first obtain security before peace is simply unrealistic, as only peace will in turn provide Israel with the ultimate security. By pursuing this policy, Israel is delegitimizing its right of self-defense with its continued settlement expansion, while Hamas is strengthening its political position as the true defender of Palestinian rights. As a result, Israel is dangerously eroding its moral standing and losing international sympathy, as it is the Palestinians and not the Israelis who are seen as the beleaguered people.

After Operation Cast Lead, the international community responded by sending throngs of official delegations and visitors to

Gaza. The foreign ministers of France, Canada, Turkey, Sweden, and Norway all made visits to the war-torn strip, as well as Britain's Tony Blair, Javier Solana on behalf of the European Union (EU), and John Kerry representing the U.S. Senate. Even more telling is the 75 countries and organizations who participated in February's donor conference in Sharm el-Sheikh, pledging nearly $5 billion in aid to rebuild Gaza.[96] Between the state visits, donor commitments, and media reaction after the Gaza war, the general sympathy for Palestinian citizens has been overwhelming, and far outnumbers any sentiment toward the Israeli side. Hamas, while damaged, has come out of this war claiming victory by virtue of merely surviving the Israeli onslaught and becoming somewhat recognized as a force that must be reckoned with, either directly or indirectly, in peace negotiations.

The Obama administration ought to make it abundantly clear to Israel that settlement expansion runs contradictory to peace, and linking the settlements to national security is nothing but a smokescreen. Taking into full consideration Israel's legitimate national security concerns, the Obama administration must state firmly that America's strategic interest in the Middle East is directly linked to ending the Israeli-Palestinian conflict. Delaying peace negotiations that could lead to a two-state solution is not acceptable. Moreover, it would be impossible to effectively address Iran's nuclear program in isolation. Only by preventing Iran from exploiting the Arab-Israeli conflict and isolating Hamas and Hezbollah from Tehran will progress be made on the Israeli-Palestinian front. The recent overture to Syria by the Obama administration is a prudent move and it must be seen as a part and parcel of the new American strategy to deal not just with the Arab-Israeli conflict but to contain Iran's regional maneuverability.

Concerned Israelis must ask themselves the question as to what will happen 10–15 years from now if there is no solution to the conflict with the Palestinians. The status quo is pushing both Israelis and Palestinians further into extremism and creating conditions in both camps that raise an ominous prospect for the future. The Palestinians are growing increasingly more hopeless and many are left with no choice but to resort to violent resistance. More than 7 out

96   "Billions Pledged to Rebuild Gaza," *BBC News*, March 2, 2009, http://news.bbc.co.uk/2/hi/middle_east/7918105.stm.

of every 10 Palestinians have been born under occupation. They do not dwell on who is right and who is wrong, as they know only one thing: occupation in any form is intolerable and they are bent on ending it. They watch the usurpation of their land day in and day out while laboring under the humiliation of occupation in every turn they make. For Israel to use Hamas and violence as an excuse without trying to deal with the root cause will no longer resonate, as the reaction of the international community to the Israeli onslaught in Gaza has demonstrated. The only way the Sunni Arab states (led by Saudi Arabia) can put real pressure on Hamas and other extremist groups is if the Israeli government suspends the expansion of settlements, dismantles all illegal outposts and enters in earnest the peace negotiations with the objective of reaching a two-state solution.

One would hope that Netanyahu would moderate his views once he assumes the responsibility of prime minister. Should he, however, form a right-of-center government, he may not be able to modify his position without risking its collapse. It was during his last tenure as prime minister in the late 90s that Netanyahu emphasized the three no's: no withdrawal from the Golan Heights, no discussion of the Palestinians' claim to Jerusalem, and no negotiations while under preconditions. The Obama administration must not let this ideology take hold yet again, and he must have clear vision and a realistic strategy about the peace process to push it through. This will not only bring an end to the Israeli-Palestinian conflict, but safeguard Israel's ultimate national security.

NETANYAHU'S SECOND CHANCE

APRIL7, 2009

The new Israeli government led by Likud leader Benjamin Netanyahu has raised many conflicting feelings among those concerned about the fate of the Arab-Israeli peace process. Will Netanyahu scuttle the little progress that was made under his predecessor Ehud Olmert, or will he engage the Palestinians anew? Questions about whether he will resume negotiations with Syria, how he will tackle Iran's nuclear threat, and if he will get along with President Obama remain unanswered. Yet, given the right political environment created by the Obama administration and supported by the leading Arab states and the Palestinians, Netanyahu has the potential to advance the peace negotiations significantly, and may end up surprising everyone in the process.

On the positive side, those who know him well suggest that Netanyahu has matured considerably since he was first prime minister (1996–1999). He is well aware that he may never be given another opportunity as prime minister and that he now stands before a historic crossroad. Netanyahu understands the requirements for peace from being at the negotiating table many times before. He appreciates the Israeli public's sentiments and is certainly not oblivious to what the Obama administration expects from any Israeli prime minister at this juncture in a region laden with multiple crises. Moreover, the eyes of the international community are fixed on him and he is only too aware of the burden he has just assumed and the limited time he has to demonstrate sound policies. Netanyahu has said he wants peace with security for his country. He argues for strengthening the Palestinian economy and engaging in the peace process, while not excluding making progress on the Syrian front. From his perspective, Iran still poses the largest security threat to Israel, and Netanyahu insists that it must be neutralized, preferably by diplomatic means.

There is nothing from his tough campaign rhetoric that precludes the establishment of a comprehensive Arab-Israeli peace. While the appointment of the right-wing Avigdor Lieberman as foreign minister may have signaled to many a shift away from any peacemaking efforts, it is likely that Netanyahu will use Lieberman strategically for his tough rhetoric to satisfy the more hawkish Israeli constituency while lowering Palestinian expectations. When it comes down to the bargaining table, though, once Netanyahu feels he has an honest shot at peace with security he will not let Lieberman get in his way. Persuading Labor to join his coalition government and appointing Ehud Barak as his Defense Minister also shifts the balance of power toward moderation. His coalition may well signal that the future peace process will be anchored in tight security arrangements, and that he and Barak can offer the toughness and leverage needed to secure such a peace. Netanyahu and Barak are capable of negotiating simultaneously with both Syria and the Palestinians. Though the peace negotiations with the Palestinians will be painstaking and take much longer to conclude, a steady progress can still be made aggressively while pursuing the Syrian track.

Alternatively, left to his own ideological convictions and without American pressure, Netanyahu can easily retreat back to his old ways. Palestinian disunity and internal struggle within the Arab states will make finding a partner for peace extremely difficult. He will likely expand the settlements, respond harshly to Hamas' violent provocations, and focus exclusively on Iranian threats while relegating the Israeli-Palestinian peace process to the back burner. He might even ignore Syria's overtures for peace, especially because Damascus is not in a position to regain the Golan by force. It is possible Netanyahu will only attempt to pay lip service to Obama's political agenda in the Middle East, and will cooperate only on matters of national security. This, however, is not the legacy that Netanyahu wants to leave behind.

These are the two sides to Netanyahu, though they are not necessarily contradictory. He can lean either direction depending on the level, intensity, and consistency of American involvement not only in trying to mediate an Israeli-Palestinian peace but also in engaging all other regional players in conflict resolution. To enlist Netanyahu as a partner for peace, President Obama must be specific and clear about what must and can be done to advance the peace process while addressing Israel's main national security concerns, starting with Iran.

The Obama administration needs to heavily cooperate with Israel over Iran's nuclear program, and must demonstrate greater sensitivity to Israel's concerns over this existential threat. Whereas a diplomatic course with Tehran must be fully explored by the United States, it must commence immediately so that any possible resolution to the nuclear impasse can be found before 2010, a timeframe that is considered safe before Israel contemplates taking matters into its own hands. Israel is not likely to rule anything out from here on out.

While President Obama must support Netanyahu's plan to build a strong economic base for the Palestinians, he must at the same time insist that political progress is also being made, especially in the West Bank. In connection, George Mitchell and the Obama administration must be clear with Netanyahu that all illegal outposts must be dismantled and a temporary freeze on all settlement activity been forced. These actions have almost no security implications for Israel, but they create conditions that must exist for the Palestinians and Arab states to take the negotiations seriously. As Obama recently embraced the Arab Peace Initiative (API) when he met with Saudi King Abdullah in London, he must now lean heavily on the leading Arab states, especially Saudi Arabia, Egypt, and Syria (now that Washington and Damascus are talking) to exert whatever pressure necessary on Hamas to moderate and join the political process. They must resolve now to rein in Hamas and establish a unity government with the Palestinian Authority (PA) that can speak in one voice. Moreover, the Obama administration must take every measure necessary to prevent future smuggling of weapons to Gaza. Otherwise, as long as Hamas has weapons and continues to violently resist Israel's existence, it will provide Netanyahu with a valid excuse to freeze the Israeli-Palestinian negotiations.

President Obama must also openly call on Netanyahu to put the Israeli-Syrian negotiations on the fast track and be prepared to become directly involved in the process. By engaging Syria, the Obama administration can re-contextualize the peace process and give it the comprehensiveness that has been lacking, as was articulated in the 2007 API. Peace between Israel and Syria is within reach and could have broad regional security implications serving both the United States' as well as Israel's national security interests. Moreover, without Israeli-Syrian rapprochement, the task of dealing with Iran will be simply insurmountable.

To be sure, Netanyahu knows that this is his second and likely final chance to advance the Arab-Israeli peace process, but he is not prepared to undermine Israel's legitimate national security concerns for the sake of claiming the peace. As long as President Obama discerns those genuine national security issues and addresses them effectively with Netanyahu, he may find the new Israeli prime minister a willing partner for sustainable peace.

WAKE UP, ISRAEL

MAY 28, 2009

I am departing from my usual analysis of the Arab-Israeli conflict as I profoundly feel that these are neither ordinary times nor ordinary circumstances. The challenges and opportunities that Israel faces today will undoubtedly lay the ground for its future coexistence both in the Middle East and as an ally to the West. With new United States and Israeli leadership in office comes a renewed prospect to solve the old struggles and an opportunity to address once and for all the Palestinian question of statehood. Israel must wake up and heed the call of the international community, rise to the occasion, and use the support it has now and its overwhelming power to make the necessary sacrifices for peace. Above all, Israelis must look introspectively and ask themselves where they want to be in 10, 15, or 20 years from now. Do they want to live in peace with security and prosperity, or do they wish to continue the struggle, which is becoming increasingly more threatening if not existential? I believe that Israel is approaching that fateful hour.

Prime Minister Netanyahu's visit to Washington raised many hopes, but then quelled just as many expectations. It appears he was neither ready to deal with the hard choices presented to him by President Obama, nor was he prepared to offer credible alternatives to deal with the simmering Israeli-Palestinian conflict. At this point in the process, coming to Washington to discuss Arab-Israeli peace without acknowledging the two-state solution only hurt Netanyahu's standing with the new American administration. President Obama and Secretary Clinton have made it clear that there will be no peace without a Palestinian state, and there will be no Palestinian state with the continued expansion of the settlements. President Obama's demand that there should be a moratorium on settlement building and expansion is rooted in the simple logic that the settlements not only impede the

153

viability of a Palestinian state, but they also rob the Palestinians of any hope that they have a partner in peace who respects their claims to the land. The settlements, furthermore, tell 22 Arab states that Israel is not interested in their peace initiative. Continued expansion signals to the United States that Israel does not take American strategic interests and friendship seriously, and it tells the EU to mind their own affairs. Most importantly, Israel's inability to control its settlers conveys to the majority of Israelis who are yearning for peace that they should expect nothing but more violence and bloodshed for decades to come.

The Obama administration has stressed that a resolution to the Israeli-Palestinian conflict is at the top of America's national strategic interests, and that the United States will provide the utmost security for Israel. Successive American administrations have committed themselves to Israel's national security and President Obama's commitment is as unshakable as any of his predecessors'. The difference today is that the President has inherited a region in turmoil with an alarming rise in Islamic extremism, terrorism, and sectarian strife as well as a daunting Iranian nuclear threat capable of fundamentally destabilizing the region. The Israeli-Palestinian conflict only feeds into this frenzy, edging ever closer to the precipice. Caring about Israel's national security requires more than supporting Israel's policies and providing it with the military means to defend itself. Support for Israel will not come with a blank check and a blind eye. President Bush offered unmatched cooperation, but he failed miserably to deal effectively with Iran as it threatened Israel existentially time and again. Bush also neglected to pursue a solution to the Israeli-Palestinian conflict for the majority of his two terms, and thereby undermined Israel's only prospect for peace and real security.

Israel has every right to thwart any potential Iranian nuclear threat, but it must first exhaust every peaceful option with its closest and most trusted ally, the United States. President Obama has come to the conclusion that isolating Iran is not making Israel or the United States any better off. He offered a direct dialogue with Tehran and established the end of 2009 as the time to determine whether or not Iran is willing to commit to negotiations on its nuclear program, leaving all military options on the table. But he is also committed to finding a solution to the Palestinian problem that has eluded all of his predecessors.

The president knows as well as anyone that there is no issue that has helped Iran undermine Israel's national security concerns more than the Palestinian conflict. He appreciates Netanyahu's legitimate concerns about Iran, and thus reasons that dealing more effectively with Iran and weakening its resolve in the Mediterranean would in effect distance Iran's mischief from Palestinian interests. Netanyahu must do better than dismantling a few illegal outposts and offering lip service to a president who believes in Israel's destiny and is ready to commit time and treasure to ensure it as a safe and thriving state.

Netanyahu is correct when he suggests that Israel and the Arab states share a common threat in a nuclear Iran, and it would seem logical to invite the Arab states to join hands in dealing with Tehran's bellicose policies. What Netanyahu fails to understand is that while the Arab states—led by Saudi Arabia and Egypt—are gravely concerned about Iran's nuclear program, they will not cooperate with Israel as long as the occupation persists and the Palestinian plight continues to haunt them. Leaving the Palestinians at this stage to their own devices after 62 years of debilitating struggle would challenge the legitimacy of the Arab states' governments. The Arab countries do not wish to see Iran in possession of nuclear weapons, but the prospect of provoking *en masse* anti-government sentiments throughout the Arab world is deemed considerably worse. From their perspective, continued Israeli occupation has not only displaced the Palestinians but provides a constant reminder of Arab humiliation, and nothing reinforces that more than the building and expansion of settlements. Moreover, if they were to see a moratorium on settlements while negotiations began, they would be very likely to offer major concessions, such as state visits to Israel or the opening of economic trade talks.

The Arab states came full circle when their League passed the API (first in March 2002 and again in March 2007), which offered Israel a comprehensive peace with all 22 Arab countries in return for territories captured in 1967 and a fair settlement of the Palestinian problem. Regardless of the imperfections of this resolution (such as how to deal with the refugees, which both sides know cannot be solved in their right to return to Israel proper), it represents nothing less than a historical transformation, especially when compared to the 1967 Arab League resolution which proclaimed no peace, no recognition, and no negotiations. The API should be a major triumph for Israel; after more than six decades of violent rejection, the Arab nations are ready to embrace Israel as a fellow Middle Eastern state to live with its neighbors in peace and security. Israel must know by now the implications of making real peace with each and every Arab state, something that has eluded it for over 60 years. True, the Israelis have many reasons to be skeptical; decades of enmity and bloodshed have left an indelible mark etched in the memory of countless Israelis who suffered tragic losses. But now the Arab states, perhaps out of the desire for self-preservation, have come to accept the inevitable: Israel is here to stay and they must live with it in peace or continue a fruitless struggle that will only endanger the security of their own regimes.

In one form or another, Israel must face the reality of the Palestinian people and commit to finding an equitable solution that can endure long-term. Like several of his predecessors came to understand, Netanyahu must realize that this is not a matter of blame or right-versus-wrong. No solution will be based on such a judgment. The Palestinians have been dispossessed, just as the Israelis have been denied the right to exist and have had to assert their right. No party involved in the Palestinian plight is blameless: the Arab states, Israel, and the Palestinians have all contributed to the tragic unfolding of events. Now it is time to put an end to this saga that has dehumanized both the occupied and the occupier. Each Palestinian has an inherent right to his homeland, and no one can understand this better that the Israelis, who equally feel that deep attachment to the land of their forefathers. Now that the parameters of two states have been repeatedly established and accepted by a majority of Israelis and Palestinians—as well as endorsed by the international community and the Arab states—the Israeli government is duty-bound to move expeditiously to implement a negotiated agreement. If Netanyahu's current right-wing coalition is not fit for the task at hand, he still has the option of forming a government with Tzipi Livni's Kadima party on the premise of a two-state solution.

Netanyahu can no longer use Palestinian disunity or Hamas as an excuse for not negotiating a final status agreement. The Arab states, through their Peace Initiative, are committed to providing Israel with the security it seeks and can tame Hamas once the territories are evacuated. However legitimate Israel's national security concerns may be, the Israelis cannot live in fear with a paralyzed leadership unable to act in the best interest of the country. The process of developing adequate security and confidence-building measures will take a few years to develop, and Israel will not be required to withdraw its forces from the West Bank before such measures are in place. Then again, Israel under no circumstances will relinquish its national security to any other agent and will remain militarily vigilant to deter any future enemy. That being said, the Israelis must face the inevitable and begin to build trust with their neighbors. But how they can engender trust by building more and more settlements, by impeding Palestinian movements with hundreds of road blocks, by incarcerating thousands of Palestinians, demolishing homes and above all by denying psychologically any future prospect of letting the Palestinians live as they see fit?

Every day, month, or year that passes will only add to the alienation and disdain toward Israel, which has become ingrained in the Palestinian psyche. The zealous settlers have wrested the political agenda, and now Israel's leadership has allowed itself to become woefully misguided by a group endangering the very premise of why Israel was created in the first place. Israel was meant to provide a home and a refuge for the Jewish people—not to rule other people against their will. Why have there been no demonstrations in the street by Israelis demanding an end to the occupation? How can Israelis revel in the plenty of today and forget the scarcity endured by a multitude of Palestinians? Imagine peace with 57 Arab and Muslim states and the renaissance that could be ushered into the region. Imagine Israel and its neighbors engaged in business, cultural, and academic exchanges; imagine the power of Israeli and Arab resources put together and the incredible prospect of reaching a new high never known before between both peoples.

It is time for Israel to wake up. Do not allow this historic chance for peace to slip away because of complacency or lack of courage. The United States and the international community are offering an unprecedented opportunity that cannot afford to be squandered this time around. America has offered its utmost support and the Arab states are ready to assume their responsibility. If Israel is destined to bring light onto other nations, this is the moment.

ISRAEL'S DISMAL PUBLIC RELATIONS

NOVEMBER 8, 2010

Israel's public image today is dismal. As Elie Wiesel once joked, "Jews excel in just about every profession except public relations, but this should not surprise us: when God wanted to free the Jews from Egypt he sent Moses, who stuttered."[97] However, today Israel's problem is not that its leaders are stuttering, rather that they are stalling to show leadership toward ending the Arab-Israeli conflict. In doing so, they are sending a message to the international community that Israel does not care what the world thinks, and that it does not want peace after all.

Israel's public relations problem is not due to a lack of attention. The entire world is watching Israel closely, but they do not like what they see. In recent weeks the world community has witnessed near daily vandalism by settlers against Palestinian property in the West Bank, the passage of a "loyalty oath" aimed at marginalizing Israel's minorities, Foreign Minister Avigdor Lieberman's obnoxious speech at the United Nations, and the government's continued refusal to halt settlement construction in order to improve the environment for peace negotiations, despite unprecedented offers from the United States to encourage it to do so. This is not to mention a range of public blunders by the Israeli government in the past year, from Deputy Foreign Minister Danny Ayalon's insult to the Turkish Ambassador, to Israel's harsh blockade of the Gaza Strip—since eased—which is viewed by the international community as collective punishment of the people of Gaza. All of this has served to undercut public relations campaigns regarding the very real threats to Israel's security, its genuine contributions in computer sciences and healthcare technologies, and its leadership in humanitarian relief efforts in times of crisis, such as in Haiti. As a result, Israel is becoming more and more isolated each day, and

---

97 Elie Wiesel, "The Holocaust, Hatred, and Hope for Humanity" (lecture, Adelphi University, Garden City, NY, April 14, 2010).

is increasingly appearing to be the obstinate party keeping the Middle East peace process from moving forward.

Faced with increasing criticism and delegitimization campaigns, Israelis are becoming resigned to the belief that nothing they do will improve their public image. A recent poll conducted and published in August by Tel Aviv University and the Israel Democracy Institute indicated that 56 percent of Israelis believe that "the whole world is against us." Even more Israelis—77 percent—believe that no matter what Israel may do to try to resolve the conflict with the Palestinians; the world will continue to be critical.[98] These are disconcerting statistics with significant implications for Israel's public relations, and more importantly, for its policies.

The perception that Israel's policies and public relations simply do not matter to the world leads Israel to ignore policies which should be advanced, and to neglect communicating its message when and where it matters most. But Israel cannot simply complain about the discriminatory treatment it receives and make hardly any effort to explain itself. The decline of Israeli-Turkish relations offers a prime example. In the period between 2005 and 2009, Israel's efforts to explain to the Turkish public the onslaught of Hamas rocket attacks appeared to be few and far between. As the Turkish public became increasingly critical, Israel dismissed the trend as a sign of the influence of the new Islamic-rooted AK Party in its rise to power, not the result of poor public relations (or policies).

As a result, rather than seeking to mend relations, adapting policies and improving communications, Israel ignored its longstanding ally, and even worse, insulted it. Instead of using quiet diplomacy to address Turkish Prime Minister Erdogan's verbal attacks while focusing on a well-orchestrated public relations campaign to change Turkish public perception, Israel's Deputy Foreign Minister summoned the Turkish Ambassador to have him seated on a lower chair in front of the press. Following the flotilla affair, Israel's failure to explain itself and its continuation in dragging its feet in providing

---

98   Ephraim Yaar and Tamar Hermann, "Peace Index – August, 2010," *The Israel Democracy Institute*, August 2010, http://en.idi.org.il/media/599180/Peace%20Index-August-trans.pdf.

information to the commission appointed by UN Secretary General Ban Ki Moon, yet again further damaged its image.

Much of the blunders of Israel's public relations today are derived from the disunity of Israel's governing coalition. Let's face it: Israel's Foreign Minister Avigdor Lieberman, charged with serving as Israel's messenger to the world, is a man who 60 percent of Israelis (according to a recent Yedioth Aharonot poll) believe is the politician "most responsible for the increase in extreme nationalist and near fascist tendencies" in Israel today.[99] His speech at the United Nations, which was subsequently rebuked by Prime Minister Netanyahu, exemplified the mixed messages Israel has been sending to the international community, and the division within Israel's current coalition.

In fact, disunity in the coalition is significantly damaging Israel's public relations in two important arenas: New York, where outreach and communications with the American Jewish community is critical, and at the United Nations, where Israel faces an onslaught of criticism and delegitimization on a daily basis. Prime Minister Netanyahu and Foreign Minister Lieberman were unable even to agree upon who should serve as Consul General in New York or Ambassador to the United Nations. Only recently the Israeli Ambassador to Colombia, Meron Reuben, who was filling the position of interim Ambassador of Israel to the UN, was finally instated as the Permanent UN Representative. If Netanyahu and Lieberman could not even agree in a timely manner on the messenger, how can they ever agree on a cohesive, positive message, not to speak of a constructive policy? And without that clear message, Israel's image is suffering precipitously.

The combination of the Israeli public's disillusionment that peace efforts will ever improve its global image and the disunity within the government further exacerbate Israel's historic public relations woes across the globe. But Israel is also inept at public relations at home. A recent poll showed that Israelis continue to oppose the API. While 56 percent of Israelis polled reject the plan, 57 percent of Palestinians

---

99 Donald MacIntyre, "Lieberman: The Man Dragging Israel to the Right," *The Independent*, November 3, 2010, http://www.independent.co.uk/news/world/middle-east/lieberman-the-man-dragging-israel-to-the-right-2123561.html.

polled support it.[100] That the majority of Israelis do not recognize the opportunity posed by the API as a historic repudiation of the Arab League's "three no's" at the 1967 Khartoum Conference, in which they declared "no to negotiations, no to recognition, no to peace," is an indictment of the Israeli government. Instead of marketing the plan as a genuine vehicle for negotiating an end to the conflict, the Israeli government has largely ignored the Arab League's peace effort, and the public has followed suit. As a result, the global community gets a clear message: the Palestinians—and Arab states—are pursuing peace, while Israel is not. This failure is more than just one of public relations, but of the Israeli government's responsibility to pursue and advance all possible efforts to end the conflict and provide Israel with the security it requires.

Some may argue that Israel's public relations have in fact never been better. Prime Minister Netanyahu is viewed by many Israelis as a master of PR. Israel's Ambassador to the United States, one of the most important positions for presenting Israel's perspective to its most critical ally, is led by a respected academic and historian, Michael Oren. But Netanyahu and Oren's mastery of the English language cannot overcome the black eye to Israel's image that Foreign Minister Lieberman provides. And without a government that has a positive message, one that embraces efforts to secure peace and aggressively communicate with its allies in times of agreement and differences, Israel's image will continue to suffer. Contrary to the Israeli public's indifference to global opinion, at a time when Israel is facing a strengthening delegitimization campaign across the globe, Israel's dismal public relations are dangerous for the prospect of peace and for Israel's security. In fact, to effectively counter the impact of these campaigns, Israel should send the global community the kind of concerted, positive message which it is sorely lacking today.

Many across the globe believe that Prime Minster Netanyahu can change the dynamics of the peace process—and Israel's image—at any moment if he wished. The world knows that should Netanyahu genuinely wish to achieve a peace agreement, he has Kadima (the

---

100 " Joint Israeli Palestinian Poll 37, October 2010," *Palestinian Center for Policy and Survey Research*, October 2010, http://www.pcpsr.org/en/node/400.

opposition party) waiting in the wings, ready to enter into a coalition to support him. The fact that he has not done so in itself sends the world a negative message: he does not really want peace. The world sees this and rightly concludes that Netanyahu would rather stick with Lieberman and stall the peace process than bring Tzipi Livni into the coalition and seek to conclude it with a lasting peace agreement.

Should Netanyahu finally decide to bring Livni in, and make a genuine effort to end the conflict, he could dramatically improve Israel's image and live up to his reputation as a master of public relations rather than a demagogue.

'AND IF NOT NOW, WHEN?'

What happened to the spirit of Yitzhak Rabin who gave his life for peace? The Israelis must now muster all their human resources and resolve to capture that spirit again.

MARCH 7, 2011

Is now the right time to pursue a peace agreement? This question is being debated vociferously in Israel today, not only by academics and pundits but by Israel's own president and prime minister. In a recent visit to Madrid, President Shimon Peres stated that "Now is precisely the time to resume the talks between us and the Palestinians...this storm [of protests in the region] is also an opportunity for peace."[101] However, days later in remarks to the Knesset, Prime Minister Benjamin Netanyahu squirmed at the thought of negotiating during a time of such upheaval. "There may be debate regarding a peace partner today, but there is uncertainty regarding the existence of a partner tomorrow," he said. "We do not know what will happen to our west, and we do not know what will happen to our east. And who can determine whether the Palestinian state in the middle will endure?"[102] So which perspective is correct? Do the current regional crises provide a moment of opportunity for Middle East peace? Or does the regional uncertainty require peace efforts to be placed on hold?

---

101 "Israel: Arab Protests 'Opportunity For Peace'," *Ahram Online*, February 22, 2011, http://english.ahram.org.eg/NewsContent/2/8/6211/World/Region/Israel-Arab-protests-opportunity-for-peace.aspx.

102 Jonathan Lis, "Netanyahu Warns: Mideast Instability Could Last for Years," *Haaretz*, February 24, 2011, http://www.haaretz.com/print-edition/news/netanyahu-warns-mideast-instability-could-last-for-years-1.345305.

If there has ever been a time to push for a comprehensive Middle East peace agreement, the beginning of 2009 appeared to be it. A new U.S. president had just come into the Oval Office, committed from day one to help the parties reach a two-state solution. Israel had re-established its deterrence against rocket fire from the Gaza Strip following Operation Cast Lead. Hezbollah was also deterred, a fact illustrated by its silence during Israel's campaign in Gaza. By many accounts PA President Mahmoud Abbas had come very close to concluding a peace agreement with Prime Minister Ehud Olmert just a few months earlier, yet was hesitant to do so knowing that Olmert would soon be indicted and out of office. Meanwhile, security co-operation between Israel and the PA was soaring to new heights, mirroring the rapid growth of the West Bank economy. The Arab League continued to stand by its pledge to normalize relations with Israel upon a successfully negotiated agreement to the Arab-Israeli conflict. A new Israeli government was soon formed with a solid coalition. That summer, President Barack Obama made a historic overture to the Arab world in his speech in Cairo, and the right-wing Likud Prime Minister in Israel, Benjamin Netanyahu, accepted the principles of a two-state solution to the Israeli-Palestinian conflict in a speech at Bar-Ilan University. With so many ingredients in place, 2009 appeared to present a genuine opportunity to achieve a long sought-after regional peace that would finally safeguard the independence, security, and prosperity for Israelis and Palestinians alike.

In the end, however, all of the parties failed to seize the moment. The reasons are many, and have been analyzed and re-analyzed by pundits ad nauseam for the past two years. Ever since, the prospects for peace have appeared to significantly regress. Gone are the high hopes that accompanied President Obama into the White House. Hezbollah has re-emerged as a major political force behind the government in Lebanon, reconstituting a significant threat to Israel from the north. At the same time, Hamas remains entrenched in its control of the Gaza Strip and empowered by the Egyptian revolt to the south. Israelis and Palestinians are refusing to budge from their current positions, and are accusing each other of not being a partner for peace. Iran continues its march toward obtaining nuclear weapons, and Israel is under attack by a considerable international delegitimization campaign that is leaving the Jewish state more isolated—and therefore, more defensive—than ever before. Meanwhile, the future of the Arab League's Peace Initiative, like the status of the regimes throughout the region, may be in doubt as the Middle East undergoes a historic and unprecedented wave of unrest, revolution, and reform.

If on the surface the ingredients were in place for a breakthrough in 2009, the recipe today appears to have the region headed for disaster—or is it? There are two main schools of thought with regard to the "window of opportunity" for Middle East peace:

The first argues that there is never a perfect time to pursue peace, to which I wholeheartedly subscribe, and therefore opportunities for peace must be continuously pursued and even created. Furthermore, moments of crises could in fact lead to moments of opportunity for peace. This view is most often predicated on the belief that if Israel does not achieve a two-state solution soon, it may face dire consequences. Former Prime Minister Ehud Olmert is among the adherents of this view, once telling reporters that "If the day comes when the two-state solution collapses, and we face a South African-style struggle for equal voting rights (also for the Palestinians in the territories), then, as soon as that happens, the State of Israel is finished."[103] This "now or else" approach considers that the long-term challenges that will face Israel if it does not achieve peace are likely far worse than the short-term risks posed to the Jewish state by pursuing an agreement.

On the contrary, the second argument posits that without necessary assurances—whether security, political, economic, or social—pursuing peace is an unnecessary risk and a distraction to securing short-term national objectives. This perspective generates the commonly heard arguments that peace cannot be pursued until Israel's neighbors take specific actions to ameliorate the regional atmosphere to be conducive to successful peace talks. Unlike the first perspective, this view fears the risks of the present far more than those of the future, and therefore adherents are reluctant to change a status quo that appears manageable, if not ideal, especially since any peace agreement requires significant Israeli concessions.

---

103 Ravid et al., "Olmert to Haaretz: Two-State Solution, or Israel is Done For."

The debate between these two arguments can be easily resolved today with an additional question: Is Israel better off than it was two years ago? The answer is unequivocal—no. Israel is more isolated in the international community and more threatened from all sides than perhaps ever before.

But what can and should Israel do amid unprecedented regional turmoil and uncertainty? Any major Israeli concession now would be viewed as a sign of weakness. Throughout the Middle East, autocratic regimes are bribing their people with money and instituting some reforms in a blatantly transparent attempt to sidestep the revolts. Any major move by Israel would similarly be viewed as a desperate measure to ride out the current storm. However, Israel cannot afford to do nothing and allow its position to deteriorate even further. The new governments formed in Egypt and elsewhere will eventually address domestic discontent and refocus their attention on foreign policy matters. They will be especially susceptible to populist demands to aggressively counter Israel's continued occupation of the Palestinians. Meanwhile, leaders of nations with which Israel must make peace—Lebanon, Syria, and the Palestinians—have thus far been immune to the revolutions sweeping the region.

Rather than making a major concession under pressure, Israel should send signals that—consistent with the prime minister's speech at Bar-Ilan University—Israel is 1) committed to maintaining peace with Egypt and welcome its continuing mediating role with Hamas; 2) ready to negotiate with the Palestinians regarding future borders; and 3) prepared to engage the Arab League on its API. All three steps would represent a change of tone and substance, but from a position of strength.

The Israel-Egypt peace treaty is critical to Israel's security calculations. Nearly 70 percent of Egyptians were born after the Egyptian-Israeli peace treaty was signed and have lived under conditions of peace with Israel.[104] But inevitably the new Egyptian government will be pressured to downgrade its relations with Israel

---

104 "Interactive Map: The Waiting Generation," *Frontline*, June 23, 2009, http://www.pbs.org/frontlineworld/stories/egypt804/map/map.html (accessed March 4, 2011).

should there be no movement toward an Israeli-Palestinian peace. It is critical that Israel give the Egyptians no pretext that justifies the diminution of Israel-Egypt ties.

The Palestinians have refused to negotiate despite Israel's claim that it is ready to negotiate unconditionally. That is because few among the Palestinians and in the international community believe Israel's calls for negotiations are sincere. Furthermore, Israel has privately insisted that any negotiations start with security matters. By indicating its willingness to begin talks on borders, a key issue of concern for the Palestinians, it would signal that Israel is indeed serious about returning to peace negotiations, and place pressure on the Palestinians to respond. While the unrest in the region is creating an uncertain future, it is clear that without a change to the status quo, Israel will become more isolated than ever. By September, the Palestinians plan to seek a United Nations General Assembly (UNGA) Resolution declaring Palestinian statehood in conjunction with the completion of Prime Minister Salaam Fayyad's state-building plan. Avoiding such a prospect will require Israel to demonstrate seriousness about peace talks, and in so doing disabuse Palestinians and the international community of the belief that Israel is completely opposed to peace.

If the Arab League meets as scheduled on March 29 in Baghdad, it will be addressing unprecedented challenges. However, in the dust of the regional turmoil, Arab confidence is also shining. The future may be murky, but at the moment the peoples of the Arab world appear more hopeful and optimistic. Israel should capitalize on this moment by providing the Arab League another issue to think about in Baghdad: an Israeli overture praising the API and a declaration that Israel is prepared to discuss its contents with Arab representatives as a basis for a comprehensive regional peace. If it does not seize on the API now, and the prospects for peace further deteriorate, the opportunity may be lost. Israel should therefore send an unequivocal message: it welcomes the more transparent, accountable, and democratic trends in the region and is prepared to engage the Arab states to reach a historic peace agreement. However, if, as reported, Netanyahu comes up with his own peace plan, it must be compelling so that the Palestinians take it seriously. Any unilateral steps taken by Netanyahu—presumably to advance the peace process—will fail and will be counterproductive, just like the Israeli withdrawal from southern Lebanon in 2000 and Gaza in 2005 by former Prime Ministers Barak and Sharon, respectively. Only through a negotiated agreement will an Arab-Israeli peace endure.

In navigating the current regional environment, Israeli leaders today should reflect on the famous saying by Rabbi Hillel: "If I am not for myself, who will be for me? And when I am for myself, what am 'I'? And if not now, when?" There will never be a perfect time to make peace with enemies. However, there is never a bad time to take steps toward peace that could ensure Israel's security as a Jewish, democratic state living alongside its neighbors in peace. **Now** is the time.

KILLING THE PEACE IN THE NAME OF PEACE

JUNE 6, 2011

Prime Minister Benjamin Netanyahu's speech to a joint session of Congress brought political theater to a new height—and the State of Israel to a new low. With his unabashed arrogance and demagoguery on display as never before, Netanyahu's address effectively slammed shut any window of opportunity for a peace settlement. Perhaps he could not hear the windows closing through the deafening applause of more than two dozen standing ovations from the members of Congress. If anything, his speech demonstrated that he has not been listening to the warning bells that have been sounding for months.

Netanyahu had an opportunity to articulate a credible diplomatic initiative that would garner the support of the United States and provide President Obama with the tools necessary to derail the Palestinians' attempt to gain recognition from the UNGA. Instead, Netanyahu chose to leave Washington with his country more isolated and scorned than when he arrived. He may have claimed he was presenting an outline of a "genuine peace," yet a parsing of Netanyahu's rhetorical gamesmanship illustrates that—notwithstanding the sycophantic members of Congress—he is not fooling anyone.

"Two years ago," he said "I publicly committed to a solution of two states for two peoples—a Palestinian state alongside a Jewish state."[105] Yet his actions prove otherwise. Even his rhetorical support for a two-state solution is littered with preconditions intended to create obstacles that will render his "commitment" completely meaningless. Even more, he is careful to state, "**I** publicly committed,"—not "the government of Israel." That is because today the

---

105 Benjamin Netanyahu, "Transcript of Prime Minister Netanyahu's address to U.S. Congress," *The Globe and Mail*, May 24, 2011, http://www.theglobeandmail.com/news/world/transcript-of-prime-minister-netanyahus-address-to-us-congress/article635191/?page=all.

government of Israel is clearly not committed to a two-state solution. A majority of his coalition partners—many from within his own party—have denounced even the slightest consideration of a land for peace formula when it comes to negotiations with the Palestinians. Other coalition partners, such as Shas, will not stay in the government if the final status of Jerusalem is placed on the negotiating table. He went on to say, "So why has peace not been achieved? Because so far, the Palestinians have been unwilling to accept a Palestinian state if it meant accepting a Jewish state alongside it."[106] However, most of Netanyahu's colleagues in his own Likud Party are unwilling to accept a Palestinian state. In fact, while the current government of Israel works feverishly to deflect efforts to delegitimize the State of Israel, its policies serve to delegitimize the Palestinian national identity and their aspirations for statehood in the West Bank and Gaza (the territories captured by Israel in 1967).

To add insult to injury, Netanyahu went on to invoke something new that has not been stated in this context by any of his predecessors: "I recognize that in a genuine peace, we'll be required to give up parts of the ancestral Jewish homeland…In Judea and Samaria, the Jewish people are not foreign occupiers."[107] This statement disregards the presence of the Palestinian people and their national identity in the region for generations. Indeed, for how many generations must a people live on a land to call it a homeland? But from Netanyahu's perspective the land of Israel belongs to Israel and Israel alone, and whatever land Israel decides to relinquish would be a national sacrifice for "the sake of peace." Even worse, if Israel is not a foreign occupier, why has Netanyahu not annexed the West Bank and provided the Palestinian population with Israeli citizenship? Because doing so would guarantee the demise of the Jewish state by sheer demographics. The sad irony is that Netanyahu is ignoring the bitter reality that continuing the occupation will do the same thing.

But of course Netanyahu's theatrics do not stop there. He proceeded by stating that: "President Abbas must do what I have done. I stood before my people—and I told you it wasn't easy for me…and I

---

106 Ibid.

107 Ibid.

said, 'I will accept a Palestinian state.' It's time for President Abbas to stand before his people and say, 'I will accept a Jewish state.'"[108] These six words will not bring an end to the conflict, as he alluded, but will make it the largest and most unnecessary obstacle that Netanyahu has created since returning to the Prime Minister's office. The identity of a nation-state on the basis of ethnicity or religion is not granted by another country, let alone one's enemies. Doing so is the task of the nation's leaders and citizenry. Israel has never requested any other country to recognize it as a Jewish state. Israel was accorded recognition on the basis of its own ethnic self-definition. Israel could choose to mirror itself after the Islamic Republic of Iran, and name itself the "Jewish State of Israel" if it chose to do so. True to this name, the state could also impose religious law, much to delight of many of Netanyahu's coalition partners. But as long as Mahmoud Abbas is not an Israeli citizen, it is not his choice to make. Netanyahu should also be mindful that Egypt would not be called an "Arab Republic" if the majority of its citizens were not Arab. Unless Israel ends the occupation, demographics—not the Palestinian president— will dictate Israel's future ethnic character and identity.

Having established, at least in his own mind, the philosophical underpinning of national identity, Netanyahu finally revealed his grand strategy of a future Palestinian state when he declared, "in any peace agreement that ends the conflict, some settlements will end up beyond Israel's borders. Now the precise delineation of those borders must be negotiated. We'll be generous about the size of the future Palestinian state. But as President Obama said, the border will be different than the one that existed on June 4, 1967. Israel will not return to the indefensible boundaries of 1967."[109] Here he offers a minor concession—that "some settlements will end up beyond Israel's borders"—and surrounds it with insults, rendering his minimal declarations pointless. Achieving a peace settlement will not require Israel to be "generous." It will require good-faith negotiations to achieve an agreement that both sides can accept. Furthermore, if the 1967 lines are "indefensible," what is defensible? Netanyahu

---

108 Ibid.

109 Ibid.

does not say. However, this statement follows the manufactured controversy that Netanyahu himself stoked over President Obama's statement that an agreement will require a "mutually agreed [land] swap"[110] along the 1967 lines. Of course, this is the same formula that was used in the Clinton Parameters, Geneva Accord, Ayalon/ Nusseibeh plan, and the Olmert-Abbas talks. Instead of returning to that basis—the only basis upon which a sustainable peace could ever be achieved—Netanyahu has done all he can to delay having to make any real decisions. Furthermore, the truth is that Israel's incorporation of settlements far into the West Bank—such as Ariel—will leave these Israeli communities truly "indefensible," as they will be surrounded on three sides. In this respect, anything that Israel will maintain beyond the major settlement blocs will serve as security liabilities, not assets.

As Netanyahu moved to the next critical contentious issue of Jerusalem, he slammed the door shut in the face of the Palestinians when he said, "Jerusalem must never again be divided. Jerusalem must remain the united capital of Israel. I know this is a difficult issue for Palestinians. But I believe that, with creativity and with good will, a solution can be found."[111] The Palestinians themselves do not want to "divide" Jerusalem per se. They want to keep it united, albeit with a capital in East Jerusalem. When Netanyahu says, "Creativity and goodwill can create a solution," then what is his idea? Where is his creativity and his goodwill? Netanyahu stops short of saying anything meaningful that would give the Palestinians something to hold onto, and create an avenue toward the resumption of peace talks. Anyone who is serious about peace should recognize that the City of Jerusalem should remain united, but it cannot remain Israel's capital *alone*. Peace can only reinforce the current co-habitation of Israelis and Palestinians in a united city, which will make Jerusalem a microcosm for future peaceful coexistence between the two sides.

---

110 Tom Cohen, "Obama Calls for Israel's Return to Pre-1967 Borders," *CNN*, May 19, 2011, http://www.cnn.com/2011/POLITICS/05/19/ obama.israel.palestinians/.

111 Netanyahu, "Transcript of Prime Minister Netanyahu's address to U.S. Congress."

Although Israel has legitimate national security concerns, Netanyahu wants to ensure absolute national security, a result of which will leave the Palestinians without any semblance of independence. He continues, "So it's therefore...absolutely vital—[for Israel's security] that a Palestinian state be fully demilitarized, and it's vital... that Israel maintain a long-term military presence along the Jordan River."[112] Whereas a Palestinian state should indeed be demilitarized, there is no way Israel can maintain an absolute presence on the Jordan River, as doing so would be tantamount to a continuation of occupation. But an international presence along the border with Jordan could effectively safeguard Israel's and Palestine's security. Israel and the Palestinians have already proven that they can achieve successful security cooperation with American support, encouragement, and facilitation. They can do so along the Jordan River as well, in conjunction with nations like Jordan and Saudi Arabia, all under the auspices of the United States. But Netanyahu has expressed no openness to such a possibility. As I have written previously,[113] Israel's security can only be maintained through a peace agreement and the ironclad security guarantees that would come with it. A continuation of the occupation in another—even lesser—form would not provide the security Israel needs. In fact, placing Israeli soldiers along the Jordan River surrounded on all sides would be far more dangerous for Israel than a coordinated, international approach with some Israeli and Palestinian participation.

Unlike the rest of his speech, here Netanyahu makes important, valid points about the Palestinian refugees when he said, "They were simply unwilling to end the conflict. And I regret to say this: They continue to educate their children to hate. They continue to name public squares after terrorists. And worst of all, they continue to perpetuate the fantasy that Israel will one day be flooded by the descendants of Palestinian refugees...the Palestinian refugee problem will be resolved outside the borders of Israel."[114] Indeed, the Palestinians

---

112 Ibid.

113 See "Netanyahu's Stance Jeopardizes Israel's Security," [page 63].

114 Netanyahu, "Transcript of Prime Minister Netanyahu's address to U.S. Congress."

must begin to prepare their public for a peace agreement. This means beginning to prepare their people for the reality that Palestinian refugees cannot return to the State of Israel—only to the State of Palestine. They must also end incitement, and halt the teaching of hate that I have witnessed in Palestinian cities and refugee camps in the region. However, Netanyahu must also understand the difficulty this poses politically for the Palestinian leadership. Instead of conceding this point outright, it should be sufficient that the Palestinians state their intention to resolve the refugee question in a manner consistent with Israel's security, in the context of a two-state solution.

Regarding the negotiations with the Palestinians, Netanyahu cannot have it both ways, a point highlighted by his statement, "… Israel will not negotiate with a Palestinian government backed by the Palestinian version of al-Qaeda."[115] He cannot say that the Palestinian leadership is weak and the public divided, and therefore peace is beyond reach, while at the same time state that a Palestinian unity government is akin to al-Qaeda. The truth is that Hamas—classified by the West and Israel as a terrorist organization—is now also a political party. Many political parties in Israel also reject the mere notion of Palestinian nationalism, yet they are committed to nonviolence. That should also be the requirement of Hamas. Furthermore, democracy cannot be achieved if one's enemy dictates the platform of a major political party. Yet it is valid, and important, that Hamas completely renounce violence. Hamas too cannot have it both ways. It cannot seek to become a part of the political process while openly seeking Israel's destruction, maintaining its armed struggle and conducting terror against Israel. Hamas must sooner than later make a choice because if it continues with its current posture, Israel will have the right and will not hesitate to decapitate its leadership entirely.

Finally, Netanyahu pays homage to President Obama on the question of how peace may be achieved, agreeing with the president that peace cannot simply be imposed. "I appreciate the President's clear position…on this issue. Peace cannot be imposed. It must be negotiated. But peace can only be negotiated with partners

---

115 Ibid.

committed to peace."[116] As President Obama stated in his remarks at AIPAC, "The world is moving too fast."[117] If Netanyahu is not willing to create any opportunity for negotiations, the international community will pass Netanyahu and Israel by. It is true that an imposition of a peace agreement is not acceptable (and may not work), but Netanyahu's delay tactics are only opening up the possibility of outside interference that will pressure Israel in a variety of forms. If Netanyahu is serious about peace and about his opposition to an imposed agreement, he should offer a plausible peace initiative of his own. Instead, he has given the international community an even greater incentive to isolate Israel as never before.

As Meir Dagan, the former head of the Israeli Mossad who left his post in January, recently stated at Tel Aviv University, Israel's top leaders (Barak and Netanyahu) lack judgment. The anticipated international pressure on Israel resulting from the Palestinians' effort to gain recognition of their own state by the UNGA could lead to a rash decision like an airstrike on Iran, which Dagan characterized as "a stupid idea." As a result, he continued, "The regional challenge that Israel would face would be impossible."[118]

Netanyahu can only mislead his nation, his ally the United States, and the international community up to a point. Sooner or later, he must accept that he is facing a moment of choice: he can lead Israel to greater security, prosperity, and international cooperation and integration, or he can be the prime minister who watched a tsunami of unprecedented change in the Middle East engulf the State of Israel while he stood by and did nothing to stop it.

---

116 Ibid.

117 Obama, "Remarks by the President at the AIPAC Policy Conference 2011."

118 Ethan Bronner, "A Former Spy Chief Questions the Judgment of Israeli Leaders," *The New York Times*, June 3, 2011, http://www.nytimes.com/2011/06/04/world/middleeast/04mossad.html.

SUPPORTING NETANYAHU IMPERILS ISRAEL

SEPTEMBER 26, 2011

Regardless of all the protestations by Israel's Prime Minister Netanyahu to return to peace negotiations if only the Palestinians would agree, one simple fact cannot be masked: Mr. Netanyahu does not want a two-state solution. He wants only to delay decision-making at all costs. Thus far he has succeeded, and he is likely to continue to succeed with the unwavering support of the U.S. Congress and pro-Israel advocates in the United States. But in doing so, Netanyahu and his American backers are jeopardizing Israel's national security.

In a recent tongue-in-cheek YouTube video that now has hundreds of thousands of views, Israel's Deputy Foreign Minister Danny Ayalon reasserted what Prime Minister Netanyahu stated at the joint session of Congress: the West Bank should not be considered occupied territory. Ayalon claims that Israel has already compromised by not establishing its state on the east bank of the Jordan River, in what is today Jordan, in addition to the West Bank.

With this kind of position deeply entrenched in the Netanyahu government's policy, getting to a viable, negotiated two-state agreement is a fantasy at best. Meanwhile, members of Congress, like Chairwoman of the House Foreign Affairs Committee Ileana Ros-Lehtinen (R-FL), have introduced legislation to cut off funding for the United Nations and any state that votes in favor of a Palestinian state at the UN, as well as cuts to United States bilateral aid to the PA.

Statements by Republican presidential candidates like Texas Governor Rick Perry, saying President Obama is "throwing Israel under a bus" may be mere campaign rhetoric, but they do nothing but further encourage Israeli intransigence. Pro-Israel advocates in the United States have fueled policymakers to take imprudent but politically advantageous positions by supporting Netanyahu seemingly at all costs. Perhaps with the best of intentions to protect Israel's interest in this

176

highly contested U.S. political campaign season, Israel is being used largely by Republicans to seek a political advantage. Ironically, it is being done to Israel's detriment. The fact that the Republicans have successfully made support for Israel a major domestic political issue has forced President Obama, who is seeking re-election, to wholly support Netanyahu's unyielding stance as well.

Such unmitigated political support for Netanyahu's government certainly helps to undermine U.S. influence and credibility in the region and beyond. Even more worrisome, however, is that with "friends" like these in Congress and the White House, Israeli rejectionists of Palestinian statehood in Netanyahu's governing coalition are encouraged to continue to advance disparaging policies which threaten Israel's long-term national security. Netanyahu and his cohorts may see this as a major victory, but in truth it only serves Netanyahu's self-delusion that Israel will be better off by stalling rather than directly confronting the Palestinian conflict in search of an equitable solution.

To be sure, Israel has legitimate security concerns, perhaps now more than ever. The Israeli experience of withdrawing from Gaza and Lebanon—however unilateral and without a clear understanding with the Palestinians and the Lebanese respectively—only to receive rockets in return alarmed the Israeli public with regard to the "land for peace" principle. The PA controls only the West Bank, leaving many Israelis doubtful that any agreement could be implemented on the ground. Hamas and other extremist groups like Hezbollah in Lebanon, who have the open support of Iran, still seek Israel's destruction and systematically engage in acts of violence and terrorism.

Certainly the prevailing security conditions in the West Bank are dramatically different from those that existed prior to the Israeli withdrawal from Gaza or southern Lebanon. Even so, no one should expect Israel to simply withdraw from the West Bank without iron-clad security arrangements that build upon and exceed the already-existing Israeli-Palestinian security cooperation.

This raises the question whether Israel is better off today than it was when Netanyahu assumed the premiership nearly three years ago. The answer is clear: Israeli-Egyptian peace is the most precarious it has ever been, Israel's relations with Turkey have appreciably deteriorated, and its ties with the Obama administration have been strained. The international community, including many EU members, largely identifies Israel as the culprit behind the prolonged stalemate in Israeli-Palestinian relations.

Meanwhile, the uncertainty engulfing the broader Middle East as a result of the Arab Spring redoubles Israeli anxiety. To suggest that this state of affairs and Israel's growing isolation would have happened regardless of Netanyahu's policy and the continuing occupation is groundless. The occupation continues to nurture anti-Israeli sentiments throughout the international community and especially in the Arab and Muslim worlds. Israel can walk the moral high ground and claim its rightful place among the free nations only by ending the occupation.

The burden of proof now rests on Netanyahu's shoulders. His policy to date has been simply "delay." In his speech to the UNGA, he missed yet another golden opportunity not only to make the case that Israel is seeking a genuine peace with security, but also identify what Israel will be willing to do to move toward a genuine two-state solution. Instead, he placed Israel on the defensive by justifying the occupation and the settlements, offering no new initiatives or ideas, and most noticeably, no new gestures of good will, like a temporary freeze on settlement construction, to lure the Palestinians to the negotiating table. Whereas today the Palestinians and the Arab world have a clear strategy, to use the United Nations to enhance their international position by advancing the API, Netanyahu has no plan. Indeed, Netanyahu's policy is to reject any opportunity to pursue peace if it is predicated on and must lead to a two-state solution.

Until his backers in the United States stop politicking and recognize their culpability in contributing to Israeli isolation, they will continue to delegitimize and further endanger Israel's national security, which U.S. officials are presumably trying to safeguard. Meanwhile, Netanyahu is placing Israel on a dangerous course that will further increase its isolation and renew violence that will place the security of Israeli citizens and the future of Israel in jeopardy.

THE IRONY OF NETANYAHU'S "SUCCESS STORY"

NOVEMBER 14, 2011

It is ironic how those loyal to Prime Minister Benjamin Netanyahu have created a narrative of a success story of Netanyahu's achievements where failure is clearly rampant. They point to the solidity of the governing coalition, the halting of the Gaza flotillas, the failure of the Palestinian UN gambit, the release of Gilad Shalit, the expansion of settlements, and the standing ovation from Congress, all while defiantly opposing any of the peacemaking moves proposed by President Obama.

For Netanyahu's supporters this is success, when in fact the precise opposite is true. Israel is more isolated in the international community than ever before, relations with its allies have been frayed, it faces unprecedented threats from Iran and its proxies, and an uncertain regional security environment has emerged in full force. Meanwhile, inequality and soaring costs of living throughout the country have brought masses to the streets. To be sure, for the safety and security of Israel and its future as a democratic state, Netanyahu's record is disastrous. His achievements are nothing short of utter defeat for Israel as a country and the Israelis as a people, making the nation appear increasingly like a pariah state.

I did not support the Palestinians' UN bid for recognition of statehood precisely because of the expected reactionary policies of Netanyahu and his supporters. We have begun to see Netanyahu's efforts to punish the Palestinians for their UN gambit emerge. These policies will only further undermine Israeli-Palestinian relations and make it even harder to get to the negotiating table and safeguard regional security. Netanyahu has withheld tax transfers to the Palestinians and sat idly by as his coalition partner, Foreign Minister Avigdor Lieberman, seeks to "Arafatize" Mahmoud Abbas as the

179

chief obstacle to peace. Most disturbingly, Netanyahu has shame-lessly introduced expedited settlement construction in response to Palestinian actions as a form of punishment. In reality, these policies only serve to punish Israel, making it more and more unlikely that a two-state solution can be achieved and shaping Israel into the kind of pariah, apartheid state that peacemaking efforts have sought to avoid for so long.

These policies send a clear message to the Palestinians and to the Arab world at large that diplomacy does not work. Rather than supporting moderation by working with the Palestinians to expand their national project without placing the security of Israel or its citizens in jeopardy, the Netanyahu government has done all it can to show that only violence pays. It ignores Mahmoud Abbas' plea for a settlement freeze to return to peace talks, while negotiating with Hamas on the release of Gilad Shalit in exchange for more than one thousand Palestinian prisoners. One would think that if Netanyahu wanted to moderate Palestinian behavior he would support Palestine's efforts to join international organizations such as UNESCO, where they could have the opportunity to behave more responsibly and legally, so long as they did not seek singularly to isolate the Jewish state. Instead, Netanyahu has placed the future of Israeli-Palestinian diplomacy on hold, while disingenuously calling for negotiations with constructive talks that could lead to a permanent solution that he has no intention of supporting.

Meanwhile, instead of encouraging Hamas to enforce a ceasefire by reigning in other Islamic militant groups while gradually easing the blockade through Egyptian mediation and coordination, Netanyahu chooses the status quo. He refuses to see that Egypt is working closely with Hamas to ensure that the border is secure and the situ-ation is not inflamed. He apparently does not recognize that it is in Egypt's interests—and Hamas' interests—to maintain relative calm. Instead of threatening Hamas, Netanyahu and company should rec-ognize that Hamas has tried to stop other extremist groups from firing rockets. They should begin to encourage Hamas to prove with its actions that it can be a responsible player in the region and bolster its relationship with the fledging Egyptian government by improving the situation in Gaza.

The blockade is a stigma on Israel. It further isolates the state by enabling its detractors to point to what appears to be a clear injustice perpetrated by the Jewish state. To be sure, the blockade has not starved the Palestinians in Gaza or led to any humanitarian crisis of the sort. But Israel can and should work with Egypt to calm the situation in Gaza and better reward Hamas' behavior in an attempt to improve the current status quo which is volatile, unpredictable, and risky for Israel. Unfortunately, this status quo suits Netanyahu while endangering Israel's citizens.

Furthermore, instead of looking for ways to maintain and enhance the security arrangements with the PA and build on it, Netanyahu and his cohorts are jeopardizing Israeli-Palestinian security cooperation through their own misdeeds. It takes the uniquely Israeli chutzpah (naked audacity) to demand further moderation in Palestinian behavior when settlement construction continues and further expands. Does this government ever connect the continued occupation with the Palestinians' growing frustrations, desperation, and despondency? Hundreds of millions of dollars are being spent in the territories in projects to serve ultra-Orthodox and right-wing ideologues. Not only are these resources being squandered at the expense of ordinary Israelis living and serving their nation, but these government policies which cater to religious zealots are making Israel increasingly resemble its arch-enemy Iran.

Hundreds of thousands of Israelis protest against the unaffordable cost of living, economic inequality, and other social inequalities. But where are the Israelis demanding an end to the debilitating occupation that has and continues to sap Israel's financial recourse and bankrupt its moral standing? Where are the opposition parties such as Kadima? Netanyahu is unlikely to lose his hold on power in this political environment when there is no opposition that offers a sound alternative to Netanyahu's perilous policies.

Meanwhile, the considerable threat from Iran will increasingly capture headlines and distract the Israeli public from the Palestinian question. The new revelations made by the International Atomic Energy Agency (IAEA) that Iran is clearly advancing toward the acquisition of nuclear weapons, which from the Israeli perspective represents an existential threat, should also provide the Netanyahu government with the incentive to reach an understanding with the Palestinians. However small or large the potential of conflagration between Israel and Iran may be, it would be in Israel's best interests to focus on Iran and prevent the emergence of a new front in Gaza that could sap much of its military resources when it needs them the most.

This is a shameful state of affairs. The inevitable spark of violence—which could occur at any moment—will only serve to embolden Netanyahu's hardened positions, and he will be quick to say "I told you so." He will sidestep any blame for the deteriorating conditions and he will claim another "success" in not making any diplomatic efforts toward ending the conflict with the Palestinians.

The current status quo, which Netanyahu holds dear, is extremely dangerous for Israel. Violent conflict, whether with the Palestinians or Iran, could substantially change the equation to Israel's detriment. What is needed now is an actual vision for removing Israel from its current path to despair, with Netanyahu's arrogance and intransigence being the first things to go.

WELCOME TO ISRAEL'S SEASONAL POLITICAL CHARADE

APRIL 18, 2012

With the victory of Shaul Mofaz in the leadership contest of the Kadima party, the fractious nature of Israeli politics once again haunts what remains of Israel's peace camp. Mofaz is by no means a perfect candidate, but he at least came up with a peace plan with the Palestinians that, regardless of its merits, presents a basic political platform to achieve peace. At a time, however, when the Palestinian conflict places Israel in real danger of losing its national Jewish identity and its democratic nature, its centrist and left-of-center political parties should unite and form a partnership that could provide a serious alternative to the Likud-led ultra-nationalist coalition of Prime Minister Netanyahu.

Unfortunately, all Israeli politicians are driven by blind personal ambitions. I do not believe that there is a single issue in connection with the Palestinian conflict that Labor, Kadima, and even Barak's Independence party could not agree on to move along a unified political agenda to solve the Israeli-Palestinian conflict. What prevents them from doing so are personal struggles over who should occupy this or that post and what prerogatives they may or may not be able to exercise. Jealousy over the titles of "party leader" and "Prime Minister" has manifested itself in the decisions by the outgoing Kadima chairwoman, Tzipi Livni, who is considering the establishment of a new party,[119] and the television TV anchorman-turned-politician, Yair Lapid, who is also forming a new party, Yesh Atid (There is a Future), in which, Lapid insists, no serving

---

119 Adrian Blomfield, "Tzipi Livni Overthrown as Leader of Kadima," *The Telegraph*, March 28, 2012, http://www.telegraph.co.uk/news/worldnews/middleeast/israel/9172338/Tzipi-Livni-overthrown-as-leader-of-Kadima.html.

politician will be allowed—only "new people with new ideas."[120] Shelly Yachimovich, the Labor party leader, commented that Mofaz's victory makes her a "significant alternative" to Netanyahu.[121]

Moreover, not only do these so-called "leaders" have huge egos, they are also suspicious and distrustful of each other. Lapid does not talk to Livni or to Yachimovich, who has accused him of having Ehud Olmert, the corruption-charged former Prime Minister, as his political consultant.[122] Moreover, they have also been outright dishonest with people as each one of them is trying to hijack last summer's social protest by the Israeli youth over the high cost of living. In newspaper headlines, one can read that Mofaz would lead Israel's protest this summer, Lapid is leading an anti-government campaign entitled "Where is the money?", and Yachimovich initiated serious socioeconomic legislation only after the Israelis took to the streets.[123] The real test for these leaders, who are capitalizing on the demands of the Israeli middle class, is to publicly condemn the expansion of the Israeli settlements and the added expenditure of hundreds of millions of dollars for the military to protect the settlers.[124]

---

120 Ophir Bar-Zohar, "Yair Lapid Dismisses Joining Forces with Tzipi Livni," *Haaretz*, March 30, 2012, http://www.haaretz.com/news/national/yair-lapid-dismisses-joining-forces-with-tzipi-livni-1.421595.

121 Ophir Bar-Zohar, "Yachimovich: Mofaz Victory Only Strengthens Labor Party," *Haaretz*, April 1, 2012, http://www.haaretz.com/news/national/yacimovich-mofaz-victory-only-strengthens-labor-party-1.421863.

122 Ophir Bar-Zohar, "Yair Lapid: Jerusalem Belongs Only to the People of Israel," *Haaretz*, February 2, 2012, http://www.haaretz.com/news/national/yair-lapid-jerusalem-belongs-only-to-the-people-of-israel-1.410642.

123 See Yossi Verter, "Shaul Mofaz to Haaretz: I Will Lead Israel's Social Protest This Summer," *Haaretz*, March 29, 2012, http://www.haaretz.com/news/national/shaul-mofaz-to-haaretz-i-will-lead-israel-s-social-protest-this-summer-1.421349; "Where Is The Money?," *Y Net News*, January 13, 2012, http://www.ynetnews.com/articles/0,7340,L-4175195,00.html; and Mati Tuchfeld, "Yachimovich Says Her Goal is to Become Prime Minister," *Israel Hayom*, April 1, 2012, http://www.israelhayom.com/site/newsletter_article.php?id=3765.

124 See Shmuel Even, "Israel's Defense Expenditure," The Institute for National Security Studies, updated May 25, 2010, http://www.inss.org.

To overcome Israel's debilitating political party structure, there is an urgent need to support the creation of a single party consisting of the left and left-of-center parties. The leaders of Kadima, Labor, Yesh Atid, and others should group their blocks of supporters to create a single party—something that is not unprecedented in Israel's political history. The creation of the Labor party itself in 1968 was only made possible by the merger of the similarly-minded Mapai, Ahdut HaAvoda, and Rafi parties, based on the commitment to a two-state solution. Mofaz, Yachimovich, and Lapid are intelligent enough to recognize the reality that it is security and the continued occupation of Palestinian territories, rather than socioeconomic issues, that distinguishes the political Left from the Right.

For these leaders to campaign on something other than the Israeli-Palestinian conflict is to risk compromising the center's internal logic by gathering points of disaffection from the left and right instead of presenting a cohesive, distinctive political alternative. This is the lesson that they learned from the late Yitzhak Rabin, who wished to fundamentally change Israel and campaigned in 1992 on peace and managed, thanks to his willingness to rely on largely non-Jewish parties, to form a clear majority of at least 61 seats in the Knesset.[125] National interest must prevail and override any personal ambitions or party gains, and a singular party is the only chance to garner significant electoral support that can seriously challenge the Likud-led coalition, which currently has a majority of 63 seats and could further increase its presence if the left and left-of-center parties remain in disarray.

Surprisingly enough, the sole politician who recognized this reality cannot run for elections. Former Mossad head Meir Dagan had the courage and vision to acknowledge that Israel should accept the 2002 API, which demanded Israeli withdrawal from the occupied territories in return for full peace and normalized relations between Israel and the Arab world, and for good reason. In Dagan's words,

---

il.cdn.reblaze.com/upload/%28FILE%291267608515.pdf.

125 Sefi Rachlevsky, "For Fear of a Political Turnaround, Israel's Government is Destroying Democracy," *Haaretz*, April 10, 2012, http://www.haaretz.com/opinion/for-fear-of-a-political-turnaround-israel-s-government-is-destroying-democracy-1.423494.

"We have no other way, and not because [the Palestinians] are my top priority, but because I am concerned about Israel's wellbeing and I want to do what I can to ensure Israel's existence."[126] Right now, the Sunni Arab world is far more eager to make peace, not through their love of Israel, but rather through their hatred of Iran. True, the Iranian nuclear program is a serious threat to Israel, but the greater threat to Israel is the colonization of the West Bank. If Israel persists in its current path, it will neither remain democratic, nor maintain its Jewish identity, nor ensure its national security, as the Palestinians might very well abandon the two-state solution and opt for one state while focusing instead on acquiring equal political rights.

That said, regardless of what peace plans any of these parties come up with, they will not work unless the political leaders demonstrate a real understanding of the critical need of changing Israeli and Palestinian public perceptions of each other. This has been, and continues to be, the prerequisite for any peace agreement. Part and parcel of any political agenda by any party is to have a plan on how to involve the Israelis and the Palestinians publicly in the peace process and realize the concessions needed to reach an agreement. Indeed, every conflicting issue between the Israelis and the Palestinians has a psychological and emotional dimension that must be mitigated by changing the public narratives on both sides. Even when Israel and the Palestinians have almost reached an agreement, as in the 2000 Barak-Arafat negotiations and the 2008 Olmert-Abbas negotiations, they still failed to deliver because neither the Israelis nor the Palestinians were publicly prepared to make the required concessions. What is absolutely critical at this stage is for these parties to prepare the public by encouraging think tanks, NGOs, universities, and synagogues to engage in public debates to seek a solution to the conflict only through peaceful means, while encouraging the Palestinians to do the same.

The Netanyahu government is charting a clear path toward disaster and it must be stopped before it is too late. This can be done only through forming one party comprised of centrist and left-of-center parties. Mofaz, Yachimovich, and Lapid do not have much

---

126 Jason Koutsoukis, "Former Mossad Head Advocates Saudi Peace Plan," *The Sydney Morning Herald*, June 3, 2011, http://www.smh.com.au/world/former-mossad-head-advocates-saudi-peace-plan-20110602-1fivf.html.

time to lose. Secure in the knowledge that he would win another term because of the current charade of the left and left-of-center parties, Netanyahu might well call for early elections. This is particularly attractive as he currently enjoys perplexing popularity and is preparing to pass a law in the Knesset to allow Israeli citizens living overseas to vote in the next election.[127]

Unless the leaders of these parties act immediately by coalescing around one party and abandon, in the name of national interests, their personality-driven ambitions, they risk becoming politically marginalized while jeopardizing Israel's very existence.

---

127 Rachlevsky, "For Fear of a Political Turnaround, Israel's Government is Destroying Democracy."

Alon Ben-Meir

THE PRIME MINISTER'S SPEECH

JUNE 11, 2012

Having been engaged in the Arab-Israeli conflict as an advocate for peace, an interlocutor, a keen observer, and a commentator for much of my adult life, I fantasize once in a while about the regional, if not the global, implications of an Arab-Israeli peace. I allow myself to dream what seems to be an impossible dream because I believe in the dynamism and wealth of the human resources and creativity that both Israelis and Palestinians have in abundance. Peace between Israel and the whole Arab world would usher in a renaissance period to the Middle East that history pages have yet to record.

When Prime Minister Netanyahu announced the expansion of his coalition government to include Kadima, which granted him a historic majority in the Israeli Parliament, I found myself fantasizing again about the prospect of such a comprehensive peace. Truthfully, if a coalition government representing three quarters of the Israeli electorate cannot muster the will and the courage to forge peace, who can, and under what conditions? Israeli and Palestinian leaders, regardless of their political coloration, must sooner than later face, under any circumstances, the inevitability of coexistence. Israel in particular, who is on the defensive for continuing the occupation and the expansion of settlements, must strive to end its increasing isolation.

There are those who understandably argue that this is not the right time for Israel to reach out to the Arab world when Islamists are waging vicious verbal assaults against Israel and even preparing for violent confrontations. Even though this may be the case, is there a better time to diffuse the tension and resolve the conflict with Palestinians, which remains at the very core of the Arabs' resentment of Israel? If from past experiences Israel does not trust the Palestinians, why not shift the onus and let them prove to the entire international community where they really stand? The prime minister should reach

188

out to the whole world, especially to the Arabs and Muslims, and begin a constructive dialogue with the Palestinians. He should project a vision for the future with strength and conviction that will resonate in every corner of the globe.

I have no illusions that Netanyahu or any current political leader in Israel can or will deliver such a speech. It sounds like a fantasy and it may well tragically remain within the realm of fantasy. But stop and think for a moment. The general framework for peace is not likely to change dramatically over time, so the question is: will Israel improve its position as the months and years pass by, or will time become its own worst enemy? The imperatives and choices for Israel are clear: Israel must now take the initiative and choose wisely. And yes, Israel can still become a "light onto other nations" as long as it walks the high moral ground with confidence and determination.

And so I envisage a dream speech that Netanyahu or his successor could deliver to the world about Israel's new transformational political horizon to achieve peace, the consequences of which, I believe, would be incomparable to any development in Israel's history, other than the very birth of the state itself.

And so, here is the Prime Minister of Israel.

I stand before you with pride and humility,
the citizens of Israel,
the citizens of the world, friends and foes alike.
In this momentous hour in our region,
when upheaval is sweeping one country after another,
when young men and women are dying for freedom,
when children perish on the altar of despotism,
when tyrants have their way,
when religion is used to prey,
when extremism is still on the rise,
and when reformers are struggling to stay alive.

But when new opportunities appear on the horizon
We must be worthy of rising to the occasion
Now is the time to correct our ways.

It is the hour to redress our mistakes.
It is the moment when we must say
enough is enough.

Enough of agony and pain,
enough to displacement and terror,
enough to bloodshed and suffering,
enough to blaming and recrimination,
and enough to violence and the never-ending horror.

We must change course
And we must begin now.

First, I want to extend our hand to the Palestinian people.
We share the same land.
We must now share the same destiny.
Sixty-four years of enmity and disdain
must come now to an end.
An end to wanton violence,
an end to hatred and distrust,
an end to displacement and discrimination,
and an end to detention and occupation.
We coexist and will continue to coexist;
we must now decide on the quality of our coexistence.
Do we want to continue to hate, conspire, mistrust, and slay
or do we want to prosper together?
A two-state solution is not one of many choices,
it is the only viable choice
that will preserve our national identities.
We must avoid unilateral disengagement
and be ready to negotiate a fair solution,
a resolution that answers the yearning
of Israelis and Palestinians alike:
a Jewish state and a Palestinian state,
living side-by-side in peace and harmony.
We have no preconditions and no other stipulations
but permanently forsaking violence
and an irreversible recognition of our right

to a state of our own
by every Palestinian political faction
that seeks to lead a Palestinian state.
We will begin by suspending all settlement construction.
Release most Palestinian prisoners
as a gesture of good faith.
Guided by previous negotiations
and the mutuality of agreements
we have reached on several key conflicting issues,
we will be ready to enter immediately into new talks:
starting with the border dispute through a land swap.
Seek a fair solution to the Palestinian refugees
with the support of the international community,
through resettlements in their homeland—
the West Bank and Gaza—
or through rehabilitation and compensation
for those who seek to stay
in their current place of residence.
Establish a solid framework for national security arrangements
for all our people
to ensure peace for generations to come.
And most importantly,
we will make Jerusalem the symbol of coexistence,
a capital for a two-state solution,
the microcosm of peace between our people.

True, these conflicting issues have been intractable
and we made them ever more inflexible
with biases and selective perceptions,
perceptions nurtured by historical bitter experiences,
and sealed with deep conviction
about the wrongs that have been done by the other,
locking both sides into immobile positions.
The outcome was mutual denial
and delegitimization of the other's rights.
But now, as we commit ourselves to ending the conflict
we must begin by mitigating
the psychological dimension of every conflicting issue.

Instead of publicly promoting our differences,
and emphasizing the injustices and wrongdoings
perpetrated by the other
we must now alter our public narratives.
We must speak openly about the inevitability of coexistence,
and express our commitment to reconcile.
Thus, the need to make painful compromises
and allow our respective publics
to live and thrive together in peace.

We do not stretch our hands for peace
out of weakness or fear,
but with confidence in our ability
to defend ourselves and prevail.
Those extremists who will continue to harbor
ill intent against us,
and are bent on our destruction
will do so at their peril first.

Grasp our hands in peace now.
Let us forge a peace with dignity,
equitable peace that will endure.
Peace on the promised land
To which our peoples
have boundless reverence and affinity.

To the whole Arab world we say:

Jews and Arabs have lived for millennia together.
We are ready to rebuild with you the bridges of peace,
ready to embrace the principles of the Arab Peace Initiative,
work with the newly elected democratic governments
regardless of their political or religious leanings.
We will live up to our treaties' obligations,
and honor all previous commitments
as long as all parties concerned adhere to the same.
We are ready to make peace with our remaining neighbors

once a government of the people is established
and demonstrates its commitment to a lasting peace.
We are ready to cooperate
on regional security arrangements,
ready for expansive trade relations,
ready for scientific and technological exchanges,
and ready for tourism and full diplomatic relations.
We know that much of this
must await peace with the Palestinians,
and time to build renewed trust.
The whole Arab world
can assist to bring this about.
We ask current and newly emerging Arab governments
to influence extremist Palestinian factions,
to change their attitude toward Israel
and accept our irrevocable reality
as was affirmed by the Arab Peace Initiative.

We know that peace must come.
Extend your hand to us
and peace will be in our grasp.
Now, in our time.

The time has also come to renew our relations with Turkey.

Jews the world over are indebted to the Turkish people
for providing refuge and protection over the centuries,
for being the first Muslim country to recognize our state,
and for the friendship and alliance between us
that has evolved over times of tranquility and turmoil.
We deeply regret the precipitous decline in our relations.
Many mistakes have been made on both sides,
and we have had our share of errors.

With the Middle East in turmoil,
the perilously unfolding crisis in Syria,
and the concerns over Iran's nuclear program,

Turkey and Israel must bond together again.
Our strategic national interests remain intertwined.
We must now put the Marmara episode behind us.
We apologize for the lives that were lost.
Indeed, the death of any one innocent person
at any time, in any place and
under any circumstances is unfortunate.
So we must learn from this sad episode
and look with great anticipation
to renewed vigorous bilateral relations.
Our apology is not a sign of weakness
but one of strength of conviction.
It would not be a victory for Turkey
but a victory for the human spirit
that transcends the hour and brings nations together.

Jews and Persians have had a millennia-long history

of amity and peace.
We wish to enjoy the same relations
for hundreds of years to come.
Yet, we will not engage in wishful thinking
when we are existentially threatened
by a repugnant regime that has gone mad.
While we extend our hand in peace to the Iranian nation,
we will stop short of nothing to defend our people.
Iran will be prevented from acquiring nuclear weapons.
Because Iran with nuclear arsenals
runs the risk of a nuclear conflagration,
the consequences of which
are far more terrifyingly destructive
than obliterating Iran's nuclear facilities.
The Iranian regime should never doubt
our unshakable resolve
to live and persevere by our convictions,
fortified by our will and military might.
But peace is what we seek.

We will be ready to discuss
a Middle East as a zone free
of Weapons of Mass Destruction
once a comprehensive and enduring peace
between Israel and the Arab world
and with Iran, in particular, has been achieved.

To our friends and allies in Europe:

We understand your concerns over the region's stability,
your trepidation about new conflicts,
and your vast national interests in our region.
We are most sincere in our efforts
to mitigate any conflict in which we have a say.
We deeply appreciate your support
and are grateful for taking to heart our national concerns.
As much as Israel is and will further be
integrated into the Middle East,
it remains beholden to European values.
Now that you know where we stand,
we welcome your continued involvement in the peace process
and deeply appreciate your assistance.
We look forward to our continued security collaboration,
to promote further economic and technological cooperation,
and make Israel and Europe
united in their dream of regional peace
and human dignity for all inhabitants.

And finally, I turn to the beloved:

the United States of America.
A trusted friend and a staunch ally.
Throughout our short history,
America stood by us
Never wavered

Never equivocated
Never hesitated
To provide us with the political support
and means to protect ourselves and prosper.
We look up to you America
with praise and respect.
We look up to you America for guidance
to help us navigate through
the hazardous road ahead.

May God bless America,
bless the people of Israel,
bless all peace seekers
and the dreamers of the brotherhood of man.

NETANYAHU'S SELF-INFLICTED
MULTIPLE DEFEATS

JANUARY 2, 2013

In the past several weeks, Prime Minister Netanyahu suffered four defeats that will undoubtedly have serious repercussions on Israel's global standing, especially if he succeeds in forming the next Israeli government. President Obama's re-election humiliated Netanyahu, who openly supported Mitt Romney; he suffered a second defeat when the PA secured non-member observer state status at the UNGA. It was also a slap in the face for Netanyahu when much of the European community overwhelmingly voted in support of the Palestinians' UN bid while the rest abstained, sending an ominous signal to Israel where the EU stands in dealing with the Israeli-Palestinian conflict. His string of defeats continued with the flare-up in Gaza, from which Hamas emerged with a stunning political victory.

With uncommon audacity, PM Netanyahu openly supported Mitt Romney.[128] Blatant vocalizations concerning U.S. political affairs in general and on elections in particular are uncharacteristic of foreign leaders, let alone Israeli PMs who must demonstrate careful sensitivity. By openly challenging a popular sitting President of the United States, a nation on whom Israel depends for military, political, and economic support and powerful affinity, Netanyahu demonstrated a lack of political savvy. He also acted contrary to Israeli public opinion, which considers United States-Israeli bilateral relations of critical importance to Israel's national security.[129] Obama's victory was

128 Robert Mackey, "Israeli Left Mocks 'Bibi's Bet on Romney,'" *The New York Times*, November 7, 2012, http://thelede.blogs.nytimes.com/2012/11/07/israeli-left-mocks-bibis-bet-on-romney/?_r=0.

129 Shibley Telhami, "Israeli Public Opinion After the November 2012 Gaza War," *Brookings*, November 30, 2012, http://www.brookings.edu/research/presentations/2012/11/30-israel-public-opinion-telhami.

explicitly and directly translated into Netanyahu's defeat, forcing him to rush to rectify his self-defeating miscalculation by being the first to congratulate Obama upon the President's victory. As a result of this brash behavior, Netanyahu lost clout with Obama. One obvious repercussion may be that President Obama takes a much harder stance on Netanyahu's policies; it remains to be seen how much Israel will suffer from Netanyahu's mistake.

The Israeli government's failed attempt to prevent the PA from elevating their status at the UN to a non-member observer state represents another colossal defeat for Netanyahu. Although the Palestinian victory will not have an immediate effect on the reality of the Palestinian people, it has already introduced a new psychological dimension to the Israeli-Palestinian conflict with serious practical repercussions for the future. The position of the PA will never return to the status quo ante; nearly the whole world views Palestine as an "occupied state" rather than as occupied through a land dispute. This real and symbolic victory immediately earned the Palestinians international legitimacy as a state, which they never before enjoyed. Israel cannot afford to ignore this enormous change in circumstances. New limits to the defiance of the will of the international community, with heavier political and economic consequences for noncompliance, will be set for the Jewish State. Regardless of whether or not we see a resumption of peace negotiations or substantial progress therein, the PA has other options to resort to in furthering Israel's isolation. With the momentum of its UN victory at its back, the PA can punish Israel by turning to the International Criminal Court (ICC), charging Israel with human rights violations and illegal expropriations of occupied land.

In losing on the diplomatic front, Israel must also learn the difficult lesson that the Israeli-Palestinian conflict can never be resolved by its renowned military prowess. Israel has supreme military power in the Middle East with more than a thousand assorted jet fighters, three times as many tanks, and precision short, medium, and long-range missiles. It is considered the fourth largest nuclear power with a standing army of over 180,000 troops.[130] While formidable military

---

130 Ben Piven, "Iran and Israel: Comparing Military Machines," *Al Jazeera*, April 24, 2012, http://www.aljazeera.com/indepth/features/2012/03/2012326131343853636.html.

prowess can defend against invasion and even wipe out most any country or combinations of countries, it cannot practically defeat even a small group of terrorists, perhaps numbering 15,000 or less, possessing primitive rockets with a maximum range of 50 miles.[131] If the Cast Lead incursion into Gaza in 2008–2009, devastating the Strip, was not instructive enough, Hamas emerged more determined and far better equipped four years later. During the latest flare-up of violence between Israel and Hamas, the sirens sounded, alerting the public of incoming rocket fire; yet the country with the awesome military power witnessed thousands of its civilians cowering in fear and dashing toward the nearest shelters for cover. The Israelis were no less terrified or vulnerable than the Palestinians in Gaza, who were also running for cover in the face of bombings that rained havoc on much of their government's infrastructure.

Following the exchange of rocket fire, Israel was internationally rebuked while Hamas was rewarded with visits from nine Arab foreign ministers and their Turkish counterpart.[132] Israel was then pressured to accept a ceasefire jointly brokered by the United States and Egypt, which included considerable concessions in easing the blockade on Gaza such as allowing building materials to enter the territory, expanding the range of nautical miles for fishing, permitting farmers to work closer to the border with Israel, and gradually easing restrictions on imports and exports. For Hamas, it was a watershed moment; the group scored an enormous political victory, allowing Khaled Meshal to return to Gaza after decades in exile.[133] Upon his arrival, he was received by hundreds of thousands of Palestinians, putting Hamas back in the center of the Israeli-Palestinian conflict.

---

131 D.B. Grady, "How Hamas' Rockets and Israel's Missile-Defense System Work," *The Week*, November 21, 2012, http://theweek.com/article/index/236734/how-hamas-rockets-and-israels-missile-defense-system-work.

132 "Davutoglu Pays Hospital Visit to Gazans Injured in Israeli Offensive," *Today's Zaman*, December 7, 2012, http://www.todayszaman.com/newsDetail_getNewsById.action?newsId=300464.

133 Adel Zaanoun and Selim Saheb Ettaba, "Hamas Chief Kisses Gaza Soil on First Ever Visit," *AFP*, December 7, 2012, http://www.google.com/hostednews/afp/article/ALeqM5imTamunRDlzLee81e-8bqRwJwAQA?docId=CNG.19a5f06becd20ab6e0f183d0b94b8247.4b1&hl=en.

The loss of support from the EU was particularly stinging, especially after Israel launched a diplomatic offensive in the hope of securing several crucial "No" votes against the PA's UN bid. These efforts failed miserably, with only the Czech Republic having voted against, major countries such as France, Spain, and Italy voted in favor, and much of the EU chose to abstain.[134] Although the resolution would have passed with or without the EU, the fact that Europe took such a position, including by staunch supporters of Israel like Germany, suggests that Israel may be losing the last vestiges of EU support, increasing its international isolation, and becoming more vulnerable to political pressure from the West than at any other time in the past.[135]

Prime Minister Netanyahu may well form the next Israeli government,[136] yet the Netanyahu of 2013 will not enjoy the same political sway he commanded in 2009. In his second consecutive term (third overall), he will face an alienated international community baffled by his general behavior, his defunct policies in relation to the conflict with the Palestinians, and Israel's utter defiance of the international community and its strong opposition to the settlement program. The symbolic decision to build in the "E1" area between Jerusalem and Ma'ale Adumim, regardless of if and when it comes to fruition, and to withhold taxes from the PA, have only increased the international community's bewilderment over Netanyahu's actual vision of Israel's future.

---

134 "General Assembly Votes Overwhelmingly to Accord Palestine 'Non-Member Observer State' Status in United Nations," United Nations General Assembly, November 29, 2012, http://www.un.org/News/Press/docs/2012/ga11317.doc.htm.

135 Barak Ravid, "European Security Council Members to Condemn Israel's Settlement Construction," *Haaretz*, December 18, 2012, http://www.haaretz.com/news/diplomacy-defense/european-security-council-members-to-condemn-israel-s-settlement-construction.premium-1.485666.

136 Yossi Verter, "Haaretz Poll: Majority of Israelis Say Netanyahu Will Retain Premiership," *Haaretz*, December 10, 2012, http://www.haaretz.com/news/national/haaretz-poll-majority-of-israelis-say-netanyahu-will-retain-premiership.premium-1.483720.

Over the past four years, Netanyahu has sought to convey to the world that he is the ultimate defender of the Jewish people, standing alone in a hostile region bent on Israel's destruction. The facts on the ground suggest a different reality. Through Netanyahu's tenures as PM, Israel rambled down the path of international isolation, reaching a low point where even its most strident allies are now questioning Israel's sincerity in the search for peace with the Palestinians and its Arab neighbors. While the Palestinians (especially Hamas) have done their share in contributing to the impasse, Netanyahu's settlement policy and the continuing occupation have drastically shifted the sympathy of the international community toward the Palestinians. Israel stands accused of being the culprit behind the dangerously escalating conflict.

Every thoughtful, sincere, and concerned Israeli, and those who genuinely care about Israel's future, might carefully contemplate Netanyahu's track record. What has he accomplished in the past four years? Is Israel better off today than it was four years ago? Where will Israel be in the peace process and in the eyes of the world if Netanyahu leads the country for four more years?

ISRAELIS MUST RISE UP TO AVERT NATIONAL DISASTER

JANUARY 10, 2013

I believe it is about time for the Arab Spring to reach Israeli shores. It is time for the Israelis to rid themselves of the bondage of occupation and be free again. It is time to stop zealots and messianic leaders from gradually bringing Israel to the brink of national disaster. Israelis can no longer remain complacent in the face of their country's growing isolation and the mounting danger of forsaking the prospect of a two-state solution, which remains the only viable option to save Israel as a democratic Jewish state. It is time for the Israelis to rise up before it is too late and demand an end to the conflict with the Palestinians.

Notwithstanding the failure of successive Israeli governments in the past to reach a peace agreement and regardless of the fact that the Netanyahu government, contrary to its public utterances, implemented policies that torpedoed any prospect for an agreement, it is time for the Israelis to ask themselves the question: where do we go from here? The nature of the Israeli political system, along with the current political landscape that lacks visionary and courageous leaders, will more than likely dim any hope for a peaceful breakthrough any time soon. Only the Israelis who are not deceived by the relative calm and economic prosperity, and who are not swayed by demagoguery and siege mentality, will realize that the country is on a path of self-destruction. They must now rise and demand the restoration of Israel to the principles set by its founders: a free, democratic, and strong home for the Jews, living in dignity, walking the high moral ground with their heads held high.

Nearly a year and a half ago, hundreds of Israelis went to the streets demanding affordable housing, better wages, and less taxation while bitterly complaining about the rising cost of food and gasoline,[137] but no one demanded an end to the occupation on which the government on average spends over $6 billion annually for overall security and military expenditures.[138] Besides the misappropriation of funds, how many Israelis really believe that Israel can 'keep on growing and prosper' while it continues to occupy Palestinian land against the will of its people at a staggering cost? Then again, is Israel really becoming more prosperous when 20 percent of Israeli families (representing 1.7 million people, including 840,000 children) live under the poverty line?[139] If Israelis are not conscious of their internal socioeconomic malaise, how can they possibly be conscious of the Palestinian plight?

Equating the settlement enterprise with national security is not only illusionary, but it also robs impoverished Israelis of a dignified living while allowing the conflict with the Palestinians to simmer. How much longer can the relative calm be sustained before it explodes in the face of Netanyahu and his cronies? The billions spent on settlements and the most sophisticated security apparatus did not stop Hamas from terrorizing tens of thousands of Israelis.[140] The last flare-up with Hamas does not explain or justify continued occupation or the blockade; on the contrary, it points out the futility of military prowess in the absence of peace.

The dismal failure of successive Israeli leaders to end the humiliating conditions for Israelis and Palestinians alike demands that the Israeli public rise by the hundreds of thousands, day in

---

137 Isabel Kershner, "Protests Grow in Israel, With 250,000 Marching," *The New York Times*, August 6, 2011, http://www.nytimes.com/2011/08/07/world/middleeast/07jerusalem.html?_r=0.

138 Shir Hever, "The Economics of Occupation," *Newsweek*, September 18, 2011, http://www.thedailybeast.com/newsweek/2011/09/18/the-economic-costs-of-israel-s-occupation.html.

139 "Facts and Figures 2012: Poverty in Israel," Myers-JDC-Brookdale Institute, April 2012, http://brookdale.jdc.org.il/_Uploads/dbsAttachedFiles/Facts-and-Figures-2012--Poverty-in-Israel.pdf.

140 Seth Freedman, "The Real Price of Israel's Settlements," *The Guardian*, March 25, 2010, http://www.theguardian.com/commentisfree/2010/mar/25/israel-settlements-palestinian-territories-price.

and day out, to put an end to the occupation. They must end the travesty committed by corrupt political leaders, stuck in dead-end ideology and engaged in intrigue and political manipulation to preserve their personal interests at the dire expense of the state. It is time for the public to rise as it takes a short time for preparation, especially when the timing is right and a window of opportunity presents itself.

Effective leaders emerging from academia and student organizations are needed to serve as the catalyst for uniting the general public in an uprising around the common cause of ending the occupation—leaders who can provide a sense of purpose, a true vision for a democratic and free Israel unshackled from the harsh and discriminatory policies that have converted the historically oppressed Jews to oppressors. The behavior of the Netanyahu government runs against every tenant of Jewish values and the principles by which Jews live and die—the principles of equality, justice, and human dignity. Young and old Israelis alike must reclaim these noble values that have sustained the Jews throughout history and will now provide the ultimate security guarantees for Israel.

One cannot over-emphasize the importance of keeping the uprising nonviolent at all costs. Only peaceful protesters can genuinely convey the importance of peaceful resolution to the conflict. Moreover, since the success of such a movement will largely depend on attracting an increasing number of supporters from within and outside the country, maintaining the peaceful nature of the uprising becomes even more critical. The protesters must never allow themselves to be intimidated by the presence of security forces; should limited and inadvertent violence occur, it must never be dealt with counter-violence, which is the only way to reinforce the peaceful intent of the uprising. Indeed, the more peaceful the protesters are, the higher the moral ground they stand on.

The uprising must be en masse with hundreds of thousands pouring into the streets, especially in Tel Aviv and Jerusalem, to demand a change in the status quo. A sizeable public display of democratic expression will not only fuel the spirit of the demonstrations, but will send a clear message to the government, regardless of its political coloration, that the public will no longer rest unless a demonstrable change of policy is at hand. The public must remain unwavering in its commitment to bring about peace and use the plentiful means of modern communications to raise public consciousness.

A consistent and systematic approach to a peaceful uprising is the only way to guarantee the overall success of public demonstrations. Public relentlessness must be the hallmark of the uprising. The protesters should use symbols and banners to convey their indignations such as: Down With Occupation, We are Against Moral Decadence, Only Peace Provides Safety, Must End Illegal Detention, Democracy Cannot be Part of Militarism and Racism, End Creeping Apartheid, End the Expansion of Settlements, and so on. Some of these slogans should be accompanied by drawings, creating unforgettable images that can make injustices visible and stir strong public emotions.

The failure of the government to respond favorably to the public outcry must be followed by selective labor strikes and civil disobedience: for example, walking out en masse from classrooms at universities across the country while making full use of popular media to disseminate blow-by-blow information about what is happening in various parts of the country. Students, faculty, and think tank strikes can provide powerful symbolism of not only intellectual resistance, but a generational manifestation that opposes subjugation of another people, which is contrary to what they believe and stand for.

From all across the land, Israelis and Palestinians should draw on the timeless example of Mahatma Gandhi, whose practice of satyagraha succeeded in ending British rule in India. Satyagraha translates loosely as "insistence on truth" or "truth force"—and nothing is more necessary right now than for Israelis and Palestinians to join hands in insisting on the truth of human dignity and self-determination.

Repeated polls reveal that a majority of Israelis, ranging between 65 and 70 percent, want a two-state solution to end the conflict which will disabuse many Palestinians of the notion that Israel does not want peace.[141] This, of course, does not suggest by any means that the

---

141 Gabriella Tzvia Weiniger, "Poll: Majority of Israelis Prefer Two-State Solution," *Jerusalem Post*, December 18, 2012, http://www.jpost.com/Diplomacy-and-Politics/Poll-Majority-of-Israelis-prefer-two-state-solution.

Palestinians have no part to play or responsibility to shoulder.[142] The point here is that we must start with Israel only because the whole world, including the United States, places the onus on Israel, accusing it of intransigence, defiance, and committed more to the settlement enterprise than to peace. Moreover, as Israel is the more powerful party, it can take the initiative even with limited risks without appearing weak, and with the ability and capability to change course at will.

The call for an uprising against the system may not be popular and certainly may be objectionable to the vast majority of right-of-center Israelis who believe in their cause and their right to the land of their ancestors. These Israelis, however, must ask themselves the simple question: where will Israel be in 10 or even 20 years from today? The fact that Naftali Bennett, leader of the new Jewish Home party and rising star in the Israeli political scene, stated "I don't know" in response to a question on Israel's future direction[143] is a crass and dangerous indication that Israel's potential leaders may be the engineers of their country's demise.

No leader, however dedicated he or she may be to Israel, has the right to chart a course that could threaten the existence of the state without knowing where Israel will be a generation down the line. The future of Israel cannot be placed in the hands of such reckless and misguided leaders who are blind to what the future might hold in store for the only Jewish refuge.

---

142 "The Palestinians Must Wake Up To Their Bitter Reality," [page 278].

143 Jodi Rudoren, "Dynamic Former Netanyahu Aide Shifts Israeli Campaign Rightward," *The New York Times*, December 26, 2012, http://www.nytimes.com/2012/12/27/world/middleeast/naftali-bennett-pushes-netanyahu-rightward.html?pagewanted=all&_r=0.

HERE WE GO AGAIN

MARCH 25, 2013

At the 11th hour, Prime Minister Netanyahu hustled to put his coalition government together only two days before President Obama's visit to Israel. Undoubtedly, Netanyahu's last-ditch effort was prompted by his incontrovertible desire to be the sitting, rather than the caretaker, prime minister in his meeting with President Obama.

Being the political animal that he is, Netanyahu calculated that first he needed to remind Obama that he must deal with him for the next four years, stating: "I look forward to working with you over the next four years to make the alliance between our two countries even stronger"[144]—that is, if his coalition holds together, but then again Netanyahu is no stranger to wishful thinking.

He further calculated that since Obama wants to prevent another failure in his peace efforts, he will avoid locking horns with him again and instead settle for diplomatic niceties. Here is where Netanyahu is wrong.

President Obama bypassed him and appealed directly to the Israeli people as he addressed young students who received his words with repeated applause, even when he emphatically called for the right of the Palestinians to establish their own state and for Israel to treat the Palestinians justly.[145]

The fact that the president linked Israel's ultimate national security to the establishment of a Palestinian state, however, is not

---

144 Benjamin Netanyahu, "Welcome Speech to Obama" (Tel Aviv, Israel, March 20, 2013), http://www.timesofisrael.com/full-text-of-benjamin-netanyahus-welcome-speech-to-obama/.

145 Rick Gladstone, "Obama Lays Out Case for Israel to Revive Peace Talks," *The New York Times*, March 21, 2013, http://www.nytimes.com/2013/03/22/world/middleeast/obama-lays-out-case-for-israel-to-revive-peace-talks.html?_r=1&.

going to move Netanyahu to change course. He is fixated on grabbing more Palestinian land, which only serves to undermine rather than enhance Israel's national security.

The Likud political platform is explicit in this regard: "Settlement of the land is a clear expression of the unassailable right of the Jewish people to the Land of Israel and constitutes as an important asset in the defense of the vital interests of the State of Israel."[146]

Meanwhile, Netanyahu lured three other unseemly ideological parties, Yair Lapid's Yesh Atid, Naftali Bennett's Jewish Home, and Tzipi Livni's Hatnua, to join him in a coalition government. He promised them lots of benefits but with the intention of delivering only what suits his political agenda.

Sadly, considering Israel's political factionalism, it is necessary that top officials are appointed, perhaps with the exception of the Defense Ministry, not because of their special skills, but because of which party they belong to, how many Knesset members the party commands, and accordingly what portfolio they receive.

And so, here we go again. Other than Netanyahu, the three other leaders have joined this unseemly coalition partly because it serves their party's political agenda but mainly because of their personal interests, at least for now.

To start with, Netanyahu, who proclaims that he stands for a two-state solution, is in fact doing everything in his power to prevent that very outcome from happening.

How serious can Netanyahu really be when his Likud party's platform unambiguously states, "The Jewish communities in Judea, Samaria and Gaza are the realization of Zionist values"?[147]

---

146 "Likud Party Platform from the 15th Knesset," Jewish Virtual Library, 1999, http://www.jewishvirtuallibrary.org/jsource/Politics/likudplatform15.html (accessed March 24, 2013).

147 Porter Speakman, Jr., "Netanyahu's Party Platform 'Flatly Rejects' Establishment of Palestinian State," *Mondoweiss*, November 3, 2011, http://mondoweiss.net/2011/11/netanyahu%E2%80%99s-party-platform-flatly-rejects-establishment-of-palestinian-state.html.

To promote his so-called "two-state solution" he gave Tzipi Livni, who was the first to jump on his wagon, the Justice portfolio and put her also in charge of peace negotiations with the Palestinians—a characteristically conniving move.

Netanyahu knows her limitations—she failed in her negotiations with the Palestinians under Prime Minister Olmert, who was actually serious about a peace agreement. How successful can she be under Netanyahu, who loathes the idea of negotiating with the Palestinians?

Livni probably knows only too well that there is no hope for a negotiated peace agreement with the Palestinians as long as Netanyahu is in power, and that he is simply playing for time to build new and expand existing settlements.

The fact is that she has willingly become a conduit for Netanyahu's scheme to claim that he is ready to negotiate, immersing her in a dead-end negotiating process—if and when it is resumed—without giving an inch, and will ultimately blame the Palestinians for not negotiating in good faith.

If this is not cynical enough, Netanyahu gave the Ministry of Economy and Trade to a no lesser person than Naftali Bennett, and the Construction and Housing Ministry to Bennett's partner, Uri Ariel. What a joke! Netanyahu, in his wizardry, has placed a hungry lion in charge of a herd of lambs.

Here is a guy (Bennett) who openly advocates the outright annexation of nearly 60 percent of the West Bank (Area C) and doesn't believe that peace is possible. When asked what he expects to happen in 10–15 years, he plainly said "I don't know."[148]

Bennett's political platform speaks for itself: "[The] Palestinian leadership does not want the West Bank, but rather the entire State of Israel—so that there is no perfect solution for our generation."[149] Oh yes, the annexation of Area C will provide a "perfect solution" that will await him, because by then the Palestinians will simply vanish.

---

148 Rudoren, "Dynamic Former Netanyahu Aide Shifts Israeli Campaign Rightward."

149 The Bayit Yehudi, http://baityehudi.org.il/englp/our.htm (accessed March 23, 2013).

How pathetic to place the future of Israel in the hands of so-called "leaders" with no vision and no strategy as to where Israel should be in 10 or 15 years. Their hunger for ever more Palestinian land is plainly insatiable, never mind that they are putting Israel's future at grave risk.

The biggest joke though is on Lapid, the leader of Yesh Atid ("There is a Future"). I wonder what future Lapid is talking about. He ran on bread-and-butter issues, offering only a scant reference in his political platform about the need for peace with the Palestinians.

He now heads the Finance Ministry, though admitting that he knows little about financing. "Perhaps the finance minister's seat," he said, "does not need an external expert to sit on it, but a politician backed by significant political power."[150] Well, that says it all.

On peace with the Palestinians, here is what his platform informs us: "[We will] strive for peace according to an outline of "two states for two peoples," while maintaining the large settlement blocs and ensuring the safety of Israel."[151]

How much sway will he really have to push for immediate peace negotiations when the two other main partners, Netanyahu and Bennett, are dead set against the establishment of a Palestinian state?

What is most absurd, however, is Lapid's support of the proposed Basic Law, which was initially submitted to the previous Knesset—a law that would annul Arabic as an official language and **make Jewish law the basis for legislation** while barring any other interpretation.[152]

---

150 Moran Azulay, "Lapid: If I Fail as Finance Minister, PM Will Suffer Too," *Y Net News*, March 15, 2013, http://www.ynetnews.com/articles/0,7340,L-4356937,00.html.

151 Neve Gordon, "Yair Lapid: The Southern Man and His Cosmopolitan Ghetto," *Al Jazeera*, February 12, 2013, http://www.aljazeera.com/indepth/opinion/2013/02/2013211112856254494.html.

152 Robert Tait, "Israel to Define Itself as 'National State of Jewish People' – Despite Arab Population," *The Telegraph*, March 17, 2013, http://www.telegraph.co.uk/news/worldnews/middleeast/israel/9935954/Israel-to-define-itself-as-national-state-of-Jewish-people-despite-Arab-population.html.

Congratulations, Netanyahu and his cohorts are finally showing some respect by joining the club of Iran's Ayatollah Khamenei and Egypt's President Morsi, who made Islam the basis for legislation.

Should it be passed by the present Knesset, the law will obliterate Israel as a democracy and subordinate it to religion while dividing the population between Israelis and Palestinians—a wonderful prospect.

If all this seem a little wacky, here is another mocking revelation: Netanyahu will keep the Foreign Ministry portfolio until his buddy, former Foreign Minister Avigdor Lieberman, is cleared of corruption charges so that he can resume his job.

Putting Israel to shame again in the eyes of the international community with Lieberman heading the Foreign Ministry does not matter, as long as Lieberman and his boss agree on the unilateral redrawing of Israel's borders.

And so Israel's political charade continues;[153] Netanyahu and his enablers are charging ahead, making the country ever more isolated and gravely risking its Jewish national identity while destroying its democratic institutions.

As we celebrate Passover, Israelis, particularly the young, should remember that after millennia of servitude, oppression, persecution, and death, their elders have come back to the promised land to be free and live with dignity. They must also remember that their freedom will not endure unless every Palestinian is also free from the bondage of occupation.

---

153 "Welcome to Israel's Seasonal Political Charade," [page 183].

SHARON'S LEGACY

JANUARY 13, 2014

People around the world have passed judgment on the life of Israel's most controversial leader; while some expressed deep admiration for his uncompromising devotion to Israel's security and wellbeing, others, especially the Palestinians, reviled him for being cruel, morally corrupt, and a war criminal.

I doubt that history will render a judgment that supports with no reservation one or the other characterization of this unique individual. As for me, he was a leader's leader who demonstrated the vision, courage, and commitment to what he believed in—qualities that are sorely lacking on the global stage today and especially in the Middle East.

Yes, he had on a number of occasions demonstrated poor judgment that caused great grief and loss to many Palestinians. I can say, however, with no reservation that he had no malice in his heart but that his overzealousness obscured, at times, his better judgment about what was right or what was wrong.

Perhaps the best way to survey Sharon's life is to look as his unique characteristics and the imprint he left behind which will have a lasting impact for generations to come.

Visionary:

He was a hardcore ideologue who believed in Israel's right to occupy all of the land between the Mediterranean and the Jordan River. But when he concluded in 2004 that the only way to preserve Israel as a democracy with its Jewish national identity, he acted and withdrew all Israeli settlers and military personnel from Gaza with the intention of withdrawing from much of the West Bank.

Leadership:

Sharon exuded unmatched leadership qualities both as a soldier and as a political leader. When he was required to fight as a soldier he stood in the forefront and was never fazed by any danger. As a politician, he never hesitated to make the most sensitive political decisions to change course and seek a two-state solution, overriding the objections of many in his cabinet, including Netanyahu, who served as his finance minister at the time.

Courageous:

Sharon's courage was exemplary in leading his troops or his government—he always stuck to the motto that a commitment to achieve anything requires corresponding courage, especially when it appears that all odds are against you. Once he decided to bulldoze ahead with his plan to evacuate Gaza, he never feared the threats to his life from extremist settlers, especially when the assassination of Yitzhak Rabin was still fresh in the mind of the Israelis.

Statesman:

Sharon, who suffered several failures, understood that true statesmanship is not only a product of successive successes but also the lessons learned from failures. Realizing that occupation is not sustainable, Sharon had little compunction to propose a final peace agreement with the Palestinians.

Brilliant military strategist:

Although Sharon was the soldier's soldier and demonstrated from his early career that he was a superb military strategist, he will be remembered in the military annals as one of the greatest. In the 1973 war against Egypt, after Israel's initial retreat he commanded 27,000 Israelis in a drive across Egypt's Suez Canal that helped turn the tide of the war, and was poised to crush the Egyptian Third Army, albeit he was prevented from doing so by the United States.

Relentless:

Sharon's deep convictions about what was best for Israel made him one of the most relentless leaders who never succumbed to failure or circumstances. He was a warrior both in his military and political life. He pursued his goals with zeal by chasing terrorists across enemy lines or changing political course when his party did not go along with him to seek rapprochement with the Palestinians.

Deep ideologue:

Sharon was an uncompromising ideologue; not only did he believe that the Jews have every right to reside in their ancient homeland, he also openly advocated grabbing every inch of Palestinian land to realize the Jews' historic right. He came to be known as the father of the settlements and the architect of building a barrier of fences and walls to separate Israel from the West Bank.

Pragmatist:

Former Israeli Prime Minister Olmert, who served as Sharon's deputy, put it best when he said "He [Sharon] was a smart and realistic person and understood well that there is a limit in our ability to conduct wars."[154] Sharon believed that a practical, realizable solution must be found, regardless of Israel's military prowess.

Focused:

Sharon's many setbacks did not sway him from his ultimate goal to serve his beloved country in any way possible. After his setback in the 1982 Lebanon War he began a process of self-rehabilitation, serving in parliament and in a number of Cabinet posts while endearing himself in the eyes of the settlers. He ended this period by achieving a landslide victory in 2001, which bestowed on him the premiership.

Dismissive:

In many ways, Sharon was dismissive of his opponents, especially when he was convinced of the correctness of his moves. In

---

154 "Leaders, Others React to the Death of Ariel Sharon," *Associated Press*, January 11, 2014, http://bigstory.ap.org/article/world-leaders-react-death-ariel-sharon.

late 2003, he unveiled his "unilateral disengagement" regardless of what his political opponents had to say and without prior consultation or agreement with the Palestinians.

Bold:

Probably the best way to describe Sharon's excessive confidence and boldness is his engineering of the 1982 invasion of Lebanon, portraying it as a limited campaign to rout Palestinian terrorists infiltrating from Southern Lebanon.

Sharon reached the outskirts of Beirut, which was seen by many Israelis as a bold and daring military move that could lead, as Sharon envisioned, to the establishment of a pro-Israel regime in Lebanon. This military adventure, however, ended up in a major debacle which kept Israeli forces in Lebanon for 18 years and most likely precipitated the rise of Hezbollah.

Defiant:

Sharon's defiance may be best described by his provocative visit to the Temple Mount, or Haram al-Sharif, the third holiest site in Islam. This incident was followed by Palestinian riots which escalated into a full-fledged uprising. Whether or not the Palestinians had planned this in advance, the visit provided the impetus. This second Intifada claimed the lives of more than 3,000 Palestinians and 1,000 Israelis, and laid much of the West Bank in ruin.

Sharon's death, in my view, leaves a legacy that the Israelis and the Palestinians would do well to remember: Israeli-Palestinian coexistence is a fact of life, and time and circumstances will change little other than to inflict more pain and suffering and further deepen the hatred and animosity that will continue to poison one generation after another.

Sharon came to this realization and made a historic turn. He had the vision, courage, leadership, and wisdom to act.

It is a historic irony that the two leaders who reached out to the Palestinians, Rabin and Sharon, who both took concrete steps for peace, were struck down before they could accomplish their goal. A true leader must not fear death, because the future of their people and their destiny demands and deserves the highest sacrifice.

A DAY OF RECKONING FOR
ISRAEL'S LEADERS

ALON BEN-MEIR—MAY 15, 2014

The sentencing of former Prime Minister Ehud Olmert to six years in prison by Tel Aviv District Court Judge David Rosen may well be a day of reckoning for Israel's political and business leaders, but is the age of impunity over for crimes committed by such high ranking individuals? The answer to this question is **no**—not only because power often corrupts, but also due to the endemic generational corruption that has infected successive political and business leaders, the majority of whom have escaped justice. Thus, the sentencing of Olmert will not deter corrupt individuals. It will make them only more careful in their dealings as they cannot resist the temptation of accepting the largesse that businesses and politics present.

Israel certainly is not alone: there is hardly any country that does not have its share of corruption at the highest echelons of business and government. But for Israel, corruption charges against top officials appear to be more prevalent.

The question is, are there specific reasons behind that, and what are the implications when leaders begin their careers as suspects who cannot be trusted? The result is that many Israelis dismiss their elected officials as self-serving politicians whose interests trump their political parties' interests and even those of the state.

There are four psychological dimensions to this phenomenon. First is the sense of impunity, as any charges leveled by prosecutors against high profile individuals must provide undisputed evidence beyond any shadow of a doubt; it often takes years to establish guilt or innocence.

As a result, the list of those accused of wrongdoing but ultimately never charged with a crime is long and particularly revealing. It includes Prime Minister Netanyahu, accused of influence-peddling, former

President Ezer Weizman, accused of accepting illegal gifts of money, and former Housing Minister Avraham Ofer, accused of embezzlement. Moreover, in 2011, current Foreign Minister Avigdor Lieberman was charged, though not convicted, with fraud and breach of trust.

This allows for greater infractions by would-be offenders, especially because they are guided by skilled defense attorneys who are waiting in the wings to take on corruption cases and mostly succeed in exonerating their clients.

Indeed, a condition of rampant, endemic political corruption is known as a "kleptocracy"—literally, "rule by thieves." Aristophanes, the Greek dramatist, put it succinctly when he said, "look at the orators in our republics; as long as they are poor, both state and people can only praise their uprightness; but once they are fattened on the public funds, they conceive a hatred for justice, plan intrigues against the people and attack the democracy."[155]

The second dimension is more cultural in nature as many Israelis accuse their elected officials of being ganavim (thieves), thereby justifying their own wrongdoings. The pressure of the high cost of living, unaffordable housing, and high taxes invite corruption. As Henry Kissinger is attributed as saying, "Corrupt politicians make the other ten percent look bad."

The third is that nearly all Israeli officials feel that they are serving their country well and many do; accepting "gifts," from their perspective, is not bribery, albeit most is given in cash to facilitate a transaction, such as the Holyland building project. Olmert may well fit into this category, as well as the real estate developer of the Holyland project, Hillel Cherny.

The fourth is the persistence of the occupation and the settlement enterprise continue to produce an abundance of shady deals and hold many politicians of all political stripes in bondage.

The powerful settler movement and real estate developers, who both have special interests in building and expanding new settlements, spare no money to entice public officials to support their underhanded schemes.

---

155 Aristophanes, "Plutus," in *Wealth, The Complete Greek Drama, vol. 2*, ed. Eugene O'Neill, Jr. (New York: Random House, 1938), via http://www.perseus.tufts.edu/hopper/text?doc=Aristoph.+Pl.+535.

Even more corrosive for the state is that when corruption of senior officials is, or at a minimum is perceived to be, rampant, it has major implications both domestically and internationally.

Lack of public trust of political officials is the first casualty, which makes nearly all governments suspect as a result of widespread corruption. Moreover, since all Israeli governments have always been a coalition of several political parties, the wheeling and dealing to reach a consensus often precipitates compromises akin to corruption at the expense of the general public.

The second casualty of the indictment and trial of Olmert is the Kadima party. It was the one centrist political party Israel needed, and had indeed filled that vacuum. What happened to Olmert has basically destroyed the political center.

Formed by the late Prime Minister Ariel Sharon, Kadima was the one party that actually attempted to change the dynamics of the Israeli-Palestinian conflict, which began with the withdrawal from Gaza with the intention of continuing withdrawal from most of the West Bank.

The corruption charges against Olmert, who succeeded Sharon, may have scuttled the prospect of a peace agreement with the Palestinians. Olmert left office when he was, according to his own public statement, on the brink of forging a peace accord. It is entirely possible that a historic opportunity for peace was squandered as result.

On the international scene, Israel is seen as the intransigent party in the peace process, and many global leaders view political corruption as an extension of the occupation, which spans over two generations of Israelis and corrodes the moral values on which the state was created.

Israel draws a special international focus, not only because of the egregious corruption cases of top officials, but particularly because of the perpetual Israeli-Palestinian conflict. For this reason, Israel is judged by a different standard and is expected to conduct itself wisely to continue to earn international support.

In the final analysis, Israel as a democracy is in danger not because of external enemies but because of self-consuming moral compromises. As Edmund Burke wisely said, "Among a people generally corrupt liberty cannot long exist."[156]

In his verdict, Judge Rosen correctly stated that crimes of bribery pollute civil service, destroy governments, and represent one of the worst crimes in the penal code. "A public official," he added "who accepts bribes is tantamount to a traitor," because they betray the trust of the public.[157]

Yes, the message of Judge Rosen is clear, but as long as the public remains complacent at best, the extent to which government officials will heed it remains in serious doubt.

---

156 Edmund Burke, *The Works of the Right Honourable Edmund Burke* (London: John C. Nimmo, 1887) 242, via Project Gutenberg, http://www.gutenberg.org/files/15198/15198-h/15198-h.htm.

157 "'Traitor' Olmert Jailed Six Years Over Bribes," *The Australian*, May 14, 2014, http://www.theaustralian.com.au/news/world/traitor-olmert-jailed-six-years-over-bribes/story-e6frg6so-1226916373705.

ISRAEL: THE DANGER FROM WITHIN

JUNE 11, 2014

The nearly seven decades-old Israeli-Palestinian conflict continues to overshadow the brewing conflict between the Jewish majority and the Arab minority in Israel. There is overwhelming evidence that successive Israeli governments failed to reconcile between maintaining both the Jewish national identity of the state and a democracy that also connotes equality, the two principles on which the state was founded.

Israeli governments, with strong support from the private sector, can and indeed must fully integrate the Arab citizens into the socioeconomic and political streams of the country. Failing to do so will inescapably move Israel toward becoming an apartheid state (however distasteful such a term may be) and turn the Israeli Arabs into sworn enemies rather than loyal and contributive citizens.

The ongoing discriminatory practices have deepened the Israeli Arabs' sense of alienation, and they continue to foster collective resentment against the establishment as well as against a large segment of the Israeli Jews for their acquiescence, if not their outright participation in these practices.

Repeated pledges by the government to improve the lives of Israeli Arabs amounted to nothing more than a propaganda tool to create the perception that it is taking measures to alleviate the problem when in fact the opposite is true.

To be sure, successive Israeli governments and many Israeli Jews view the indigenous Arabs as a security threat. The current government under Netanyahu has introduced scores of discriminatory and racist laws in the Knesset, designed to segregate Israeli Arabs from their Jewish counterparts.

These laws include the Nakba Bill, which forbids state-funded organizations, and in effect individual Israeli Arabs, from commemorating what they term the "Catastrophe" of 1948, the Loyalty Oath, and the Basic Law stipulating that "Israel [is] the Nation State of the Jewish People,"[158] which by its own definition suggests that the Israeli Arabs are not part of the state.

Another reprehensible law, the "Citizenship and Entry Law into Israel," which restricts immigration into Israel under family reunification, was recently extended by the Knesset and worded as a temporary order. In addition, the government continues to practice job discrimination by inhibiting appointments to government posts, and provides unequal financing for public projects in Jewish versus Arab areas.

To prevent the Arabs from 'becoming a majority' and maintain the Jewish national identity of the state, Foreign Minister Avigdor Lieberman proposed in 2004 a brazen plan that called for Israel to retain areas in the West Bank in exchange for giving the PA populous Israeli Arab areas within Israel.[159]

Whereas a recent report by the Central Bureau of Statistics suggests that by 2035 the Israeli population will grow to 11.4 million with the Arab population reaching 2.6 million, Israeli officials are creating the perception that there is a "dangerous demographic shift" in favor of Israeli Arabs, even though the proportion between Israeli Jews and Arabs will remain roughly the same in 2035.[160]

This is another absurd manifestation of how right-wing Israeli leaders are incapable of contemplating even the possibility that Jews and Arabs can live and prosper together, and readily resort to ethnic cleansing, from which historically the Jews have tragically suffered.

158 Elie Rekhess, "The Arab Minority in Israel: Reconsidering the '1948 Paradigm'," *Israel Studies* 19(2) (Summer 2014): 193.

159 Peter Beaumont, "Plan to Transfer Arab-Israelis to New Palestinian State Seeks Legal Approval," *The Guardian*, March 25, 2014, http://www.theguardian.com/world/2014/mar/25/transfer-arab-israeli-citizens-palestinian-state.

160 Tali Heruti-Sover, "Peering Into the Crystal Ball: How Israel Will Look, Statistically, in 2035," *Haaretz*, June 26, 2013, http://www.haaretz.com/news/national/.premium-1.532152#.

Nurturing the loyalty of Israeli Arabs to the state takes more than false assertions by the Israeli government or some "righteous" individuals who insist that there is no discrimination against Israeli Arabs.

Although the government claim that many Israeli Arabs attend top universities in the country and thousands work hand in hand with their Jewish counterparts is true, it is still nothing but a façade to obscure the reality of systematic discrimination.

The government and especially the private sector must work together to ameliorate this endemic problem with all the danger that would entail if not acted upon, as time is of the essence.

The role of the government

The government must recognize the Israeli Arabs as a national minority with full and equal rights under the law, which must extend to all areas where the government has control, including political appointments. It must also reverse all discriminatory laws and introduce no new laws that distinguish between the Jewish majority and other ethnic national minorities.

Although ideally Israeli Arabs should also serve their country in the military, this may be a stretch at this juncture as neither Israeli Jews nor the government will sanction the induction of a large influx of Israeli Arabs into the military.

This does not mean that the government should not require young Israeli Arabs to serve by performing community service, which will greatly enhance the process of integration and the development of trust between the two communities.

The government must also make every effort to settle the many claims by Israeli Arabs regarding confiscation of properties by compensating the legitimate claimants, many of whom feel displaced, as if they are refugees in their homeland.

The mutual affinity between Israeli Arabs and the Palestinians in the occupied territories has a direct effect on the plight of each other. As long as the Israeli Arabs continue to suffer from socioeconomic and political discrimination, a solution to the Israeli-Palestinian conflict becomes ever more elusive.

Conversely, even if the Israeli Arabs are fully integrated and enjoy full civil rights, as long as the occupation persists they will remain torn between their expected loyalty to the state and kinship to their brethren.

In this regard, Israeli security forces in the West Bank must demonstrate zero tolerance to settlers' attacks on the Palestinians, as this directly affects how the Israeli Arabs perceive the future prospect of Israel-Palestinian coexistence and its long-term effect on the nature and quality of their own existence and loyalty to the state.

The role of the private sector

Civil society, educational institutions, and NGOs should play a greater role to further promote an open dialogue to allow Israeli Arabs to voice their frustration and for these institutions to join in collective efforts to help them integrate into society.

They should also support cohabitation between Jews and Arabs, *à la* Neve Shalom ("Oasis of Peace"), fight for government subsidies, and seek investors and developers to build new housing units in mixed areas. Such efforts will improve the socioeconomic conditions of these areas, mitigate conflicts, and promote amity instead of hostility.

Conversely, Orthodox Israelis are "invading" mixed communities by buying and converting rundown Arab areas in cities such as Jaffa, Acre, and Lod.[161] They openly confess that their intention is **displacing Israeli Arabs** instead of encouraging peaceful and cooperative cohabitation.

The appalling call, by rabbis no less, to refuse renting or selling properties to Israeli Arabs is yet another despicable effort to change the demographics in these communities, which will eventually lead to social unrest if not outright violent confrontation.

Finally, the private sector ought to play an active role by providing the Israeli Arabs with business opportunities to facilitate their integration into becoming active contributors to Israel's growth and successes while fostering a sense of ownership.

---

161 Amy Tiebel, "Orthodox Israelis Moving into Arab Areas of Mixed Cities," *The Times of Israel*, October 4, 2012, http://www.timesofisrael.com/settler-movement-moves-to-jewish-arab-cities-in-israel/.

All Israelis and the government must come to terms with the reality of the Israeli Arabs. They exist and will stay where they are short of a forced expulsion, which is unthinkable even by the most ardent lunatic right-wing Israeli.

The Israeli public, more so than their misguided political leaders, must wake up to this fateful reality and decide what kind of future to chart for themselves and for future generations.

They can choose a course marred with discriminatory practices that sacrifice democracy and gradually push the country into becoming an apartheid state with all that implies, or strive for peaceful and cooperative coexistence.

By choosing the latter, both sides can grow, prosper, and make Israel a true democracy without risking its national identity. This will eliminate the danger from within and also facilitate the solution to the Israeli-Palestinian conflict.

THE MAKING OF A PALESTINIAN UPRISING

JUNE 26, 2014

The abduction of three Israeli teenage boys is a criminal act, and hopefully the perpetrators will be caught soon, face the full weight of the law, and end the heart wrenching ordeal of the boys' parents and relatives. Yet regardless of who is responsible, Prime Minister Netanyahu made matters much worse for both Israelis and Palestinians. His sweepingly harsh response has already led to more deaths and may potentially lead to more abductions, if not an outright Palestinian uprising.

It is legitimate for Israeli security forces to go into the West Bank and investigate in an effort to find the missing boys and capture the perpetrators, especially when President Abbas demonstrated in words and deeds his unreserved cooperation. Abbas condemned the kidnapping, not just for Israeli and American ears but also the Arab world, as he "delivered [his comments] at a high-profile gathering of Muslim and Arab officials in Saudi Arabia."[162]

Instead of working diligently with Palestinian internal security to demonstrate how the two sides can fully cooperate on matters of security now and in the future, Netanyahu sent his security forces on a rampage throughout the West Bank. More than 1,150 locations were searched including charities, media outlets, and university campuses.[163]

---

162 "President Abbas Defends Helping Israel Find Kidnapped Teens," *Epoch Times*, June 18, 2014, http://www.theepochtimes.com/n3/744598-president-abbas-defends-helping-israel-find-kidnapped-teens/.

163 Jodi Rudoren, "Israeli Troops Kill Palestinian Teenager Protesting Arrests in the West Bank," *The New York Times*, June 20, 2014, http://www.nytimes.com/2014/06/21/world/middleeast/israeli-troops-kill-palestinian-teenager-protesting-west-bank-arrests.html?partner=rss&emc=rss&_r=2.

Around 400 Palestinians were arrested, more than half of whom are Hamas operatives and politicians.[164] Netanyahu, who vehemently rejected the Palestinian unity government, seized upon the agonizing kidnapping to play politics with the lives of three innocent youths.

Instead of challenging Hamas to help in the search for the missing teenagers to demonstrate their commitment to the unity government, he immediately accused Hamas of being the "usual suspects" behind such a hideous crime, without producing any evidence.

The subsequent death of four Palestinians, the youngest only 15 years old who was killed while throwing stones at Israeli soldiers,[165] provoked massive demonstrations during his funeral. This sad episode has outraged the Palestinians and only deepened their resentment and hatred of the Israelis, further damaging the already deeply frayed bilateral relations between the two sides.

Regardless of how wrong the Palestinians are and how the extremists among them contribute to this sad state of affairs, the vast majority who seek peace still live a life of servitude, intolerable by any civilized standard. Every Israeli of conscience should put himself in the shoes of an ordinary Palestinian, who wakes up in the morning feeling besieged and goes to sleep trampled upon in his own home.

How absurd and cynical it is to maintain an occupation for 47 years and expect the Palestinians to simply obey and feel sanguine about it.

How outrageous it is to build new and expand existing settlements on Palestinian land, robbing them of their dream to build a state of their own, and then blame them for harboring malice toward Israelis.

Why should any Palestinian feel compassion toward the abducted teenagers when Israeli security forces conduct night raids in private

164 Nick Cumming-Bruce, "Mother Seeks U.N.'s Help to Return Israeli Youths," *The New York Times*, June 24, 2014, www.nytimes.com/2014/06/25/world/middleeast/mother-of-missing-israeli-teenager-appeals-to-un-for-help.html?ref=world.

165 Dennis Lynch, "Israeli Boys Kidnapped: 15-Year-Old Palestinian Boy Killed During Israeli Search Raid," *International Business Times*, June 20, 2014, http://www.ibtimes.com/israeli-boys-kidnapped-15-year-old-palestinian-boy-killed-during-israeli-search-raid-1607706.

homes (often unnecessary and unjustified), terrifying the young who cower in fear? They witness with horror their relatives being humiliated and violently dragged away.

How could Netanyahu bolster restrictive and discriminatory laws against the Palestinians, build physical barriers and endless checkpoints, and make their lives ever more miserable but then expect them to take these abuses with equanimity?

Netanyahu, who claims to be the champion behind Israel's security, is driven by blind ideology and consistently acts in a manner that in fact is dangerously eroding instead of enhancing Israel's legitimate security concerns.

While Netanyahu professes to seek a two-state solution, he spares no effort to undermine the peace process in every way possible. With typical chutzpah, he insists that there is no partner with whom to negotiate.

He accuses the Palestinians of being divided and unable to uphold any agreement, but he then suspended peace negotiations because the Palestinians created a unity government with Hamas that represents all Palestinians in an effort to end their division.

In spite of the fact that the unity government committed itself to the three Quartet principles (recognizing Israel, honoring prior agreements, and forsaking violence), Netanyahu argues that he will not negotiate with any Palestinian government that includes Hamas instead of giving it a chance to demonstrate its commitment to peaceful negotiations.

Three years ago, Netanyahu released 1,027 Palestinian prisoners in exchange for one Israeli soldier.[166] What kind of message has he sent to the Palestinians, and to the whole world for that matter? One that says the release of one Israeli captive is worth more than the lives of over 1,000 Palestinians.

How should the fathers and mothers of more than 5,000 incarcerated Palestinians, among them scores of teenagers the same age

---

166 Lee Glendinning, Warren Murray, Matthew Weaver, Haroon Siddique, and Ben Quinn, "Gilad Shalit Exchange for Palestinian Prisoners – As it Happened," *The Guardian*, October 18, 2011, http://www.theguardian.com/world/blog/2011/oct/18/gilad-shalit-release-palestinians-live.

as the kidnapped Israelis,[167] feel about their kids who are languishing in jail, many without being put on trial and with no end in sight?

Why should there be any surprise if within a few weeks or months the abductors of the Israeli youths demand the exchange of their three captives in return for the release of 3,000 Palestinian prisoners? Netanyahu himself, and no other, is responsible for the development of this unfortunate state of affairs.

Many Israelis, including members of Netanyahu's coalition, are outraged by this brazen response to the abduction of the Israeli teenagers.[168] Friends of Israel the world over are puzzled by his extraordinarily brutal exploit with utter disregard for human rights.

Those who cheer Netanyahu's crackdown are severely undermining Israel's future security and its place among the nations. They must stop and think about how the collective pain and punishment being inflicted on the Palestinians will play out, and why these conditions could lead to a nightmarish explosion.

Netanyahu is simply incapable of grasping the implications of his own actions because neither he nor any of his cohorts know where Israel should be 10 or 15 years down the line.

The question is, how can any leader govern his country without a strategy that will take his people to the intended destination? Netanyahu's strategy, if he has one, is to torpedo the peace process and hope by some miracle that somehow the Palestinians will just disappear.

If Netanyahu genuinely cares about the wellbeing of the three teenagers, he must also demonstrate sensitivity and empathy toward Palestinian youth to cultivate trust and constructive neighborly

167 See "Statistics on Palestinians in the Custody of the Israeli Security Forces," *B'Tselem*, http://www.btselem.org/statistics/detainees_and_prisoners (accessed June 24, 2014); and "Why They Count," *The Economist*, August 17, 2013, http://www.economist.com/news/middle-east-and-africa/21583674-release-prisoners-touches-palestinians-their-core-why-they-count.

168 Spencer Ho, "Abbas: IDF Operation Excessive but PA Committed to Help Find Teens," *The Times of Israel*, June 21, 2014, http://www.timesofisrael.com/abbas-idf-operation-excessive-but-pa-committed-to-help-find-teens/.

relations. Instead, he is nurturing hatred and hostility between the next generation of Israelis and Palestinians, and is condemning them to a cruel and violent future.

It is time for all Israelis to wake up and ask the simple question—where are we heading?—and demand a clear and unequivocal answer from Netanyahu himself. It is only a question of when, not if, the Palestinians will rise again, and though they would be crushed, they have little left to lose and Israel's "victory" will be its greatest defeat.

WILL NETANYAHU SEIZE THE MOMENT?

AUGUST 7, 2014

There is a growing consensus among Israelis and Arabs that the Israel-Hamas war will end just like the 2009 and 2012 encounters. Hamas will declare victory by pointing out the casualties and pain inflicted on the Israelis and the likely limited relief it will obtain from the crippling blockade. Israel will be satisfied that Hamas' military capability and infrastructure is destroyed or seriously degraded while leaving Hamas' governing structure basically intact, as Netanyahu prefers the lesser of two evils—a weakened Hamas rather than the rise of a Jihadist authority in Gaza.

The status quo that existed before the war will gradually be restored, Hamas will rebuild its shattered forces, tunnels, and a new cache of rockets with greater sophistication, and Israel will prepare for the next round of fighting to keep Hamas at bay.

This scenario is sadder than sad; it projects hopelessness about the prospect of a solution to the Israeli-Palestinian conflict and disregards the repeated heavy toll these mini-wars exact in destruction, death of innocent civilians, and human suffering, further deepening emotional scars and making peace ever more elusive.

Can this appalling scenario be avoided? What would it take, and by whom?

The answer lies at the heart of two principle requirements:

Israel rightfully insists that Hamas must permanently renounce violence and disavow its stated objective to destroy Israel as a precondition to lifting the blockade; Hamas demands the lifting of the blockade to allow for the free flow of goods and travel as a precondition to any enduring ceasefire. Both demands are extraordinarily difficult to accept as neither is prepared to concede without meeting the other's demand.

Both sides have agreed in the past on ceasefires, which met their objectives only in part. Unfortunately, the lull in hostilities during those periods was not utilized by either side to foster more sustainable peaceful relations.

Although Israel and Hamas view each other as mortal enemies, this war has forced them once again to recognize that neither can destroy the other, and they must now begin to moderate their religious or ideological narratives, necessitated by the changing circumstances. In reality, Israel can reoccupy Gaza and topple Hamas, but Netanyahu does not want, and wisely so, to assume the burden of administering the Strip and caring for nearly two million Palestinians without a viable exit strategy and without leaving behind sustainable calm. Equally, Hamas realized that firing over 3,000 rockets at Israel and its efforts to kill or kidnap Israelis has had little effect.

The fundamental difference in this war, however, may well change Israel's and Hamas' calculus:

Never before has Hamas been so strapped for funds and isolated. Egypt destroyed the tunnels leading to Gaza, virtually ending the flow of goods and depriving Hamas of collecting taxes, and closed the Rafah border crossing. Iran's financial aid was reduced to a trickle, and the continuing Israeli blockade and the lack of financial and political support from the Arab states and the PA (with the exception of Qatar and Turkey) added immeasurably to Hamas' woes.

All combined have left Hamas with no prospect of improving the conditions of its despairing populace to stem the growing public restiveness and discontent. With little left to lose, Hamas ignited a new crisis to shake up the status quo, hoping to change the dynamic of the conflict from which it could benefit, regardless of the risks involved.

Conversely, Netanyahu's popularity has soared; public trust in his leadership has never been deeper. He has understood the limits of what Israel can do and shown restraint by rejecting calls from his right-wing political partners to expand the war beyond his stated objective—the destruction of the tunnels and Hamas' infrastructure.

The question for Netanyahu is whether he would be willing to return to Gaza in the future and "mow the lawn" again, and if that would secure Israel's future despite the lack of a solution to the Israeli-Palestinian conflict before he departs the political scene.

Netanyahu is a zealous ideologue who believes that Israel is not an occupying power and that the entire Holy Land, including the West Bank, is an inseparable part of the Jews' existence and whose redemption is intertwined with the redemption of their land.

With this deep conviction, can Netanyahu change his position and take a historic leap of faith to work toward ending the Israeli-Palestinian conflict?

I disagree with those who suggest that Netanyahu will never change his stripes. Many deeply ideological leaders before him have unexpectedly risen to the occasion to answer the call from their people and the international community for a drastic change.

Former Israeli Prime Ministers Begin and Sharon, de Klerk of South Africa, and Gorbachev of the former Soviet Union are some prominent leaders who unpredictably changed their political convictions and direction; Netanyahu himself had unpredictably accepted the Wye River Memorandum.

Netanyahu is a skilled and astute politician; he knows how to rally the people around him, is not deterred by obstacles, believes in himself, and is totally dedicated to Israel's national security.

The time and circumstances in which he finds himself now place his deep ideological convictions against the unmitigated reality of the Palestinians. As a leader, he now realizes that the conditions in which he finds himself provides him a pivotal moment in time to seek an end to the Israeli-Palestinian conflict that may not be repeated. As John F. Kennedy once said, "leadership and learning are indispensable to each other."[169]

The current 72-hour ceasefire provides an opportunity for Netanyahu to demonstrate leadership, courage, and vision, and shift the onus entirely on Hamas and those countries critical of the blockade.

He should offer a complete lifting of the blockade in phases over a period of time (two to three years), provided that Hamas agrees to

169 John F. Kennedy, "Trade Mart Speech" (Undelivered speech, Dallas Citizens Council, Dallas, TX, November 22, 1963).

renounce violence and demilitarize Gaza. Hamas must also agree to the stationing of a robust international force to monitor the borders and PA security forces to supervise the crossings from Gaza into Israel and Egypt.

In addition, Hamas must adopt the API, which would mean implicitly recognizing Israel and at the same time offering Hamas a face-saving way out.

Whether or not Hamas agrees to this Initiative, Netanyahu will emerge as a statesman who is ready to strike a deal that the whole world would embrace while achieving a remarkable feat without risking much, radically changing the outlook for the resumption of serious peace negotiations.

Ultimately, Israel's long-term national security rests on ending the blockade and neutralizing the threat from the West Bank in particular by negotiating with any representative Palestinian government and ending the occupation under mutually accepted terms.

Netanyahu has served as Prime Minister longer than any of his predecessors, with the exception of Israel's founder, David Ben-Gurion. Like any other leader, Netanyahu is surely thinking about his legacy and likely wants to be remembered as the prime minster who led his people to a lasting peace, rather than leaving Israel even more insecure and vulnerable.

Will Netanyahu seize the moment and give the next generation of Israelis and Palestinians the greatest gift—to live, grow, and prosper together in peace?

Perhaps I am a dreamer, but as Victor Hugo once observed:

"There is nothing like a dream to create the future."[170]

---

170 Victor Hugo, *Les Misérables* (New York: Simon & Schuster, 2009), 243.

PALESTINIAN POLITICS

THE PALESTINIANS AT A
PIVOTAL CROSSROADS

JUNE 2, 2009

President Obama's push for a solution to the Arab-Israeli conflict has given the Palestinians a historic opportunity to end their disastrous state of affairs. Although many parties involved in the conflict—especially the Arab states and Israel—have contributed directly or indirectly to Palestinian suffering, the Palestinians have undoubtedly inflicted the greatest injury upon themselves by forgoing numerous opportunities to make peace with dignity. With the best of intentions from the international community, and even with unwavering American and Arab support, only the Palestinians united in their purpose and committed to a peaceful solution can end their hardship and realize a state of their own. Sixty-two years of dislocation and despair can come to an end; the question is, will the Palestinian leadership be able to present a united front and rise to the historic occasion?

There are five prerequisites that the Palestinians must collectively meet to achieve a state of their own. Certainly no one should expect either the Palestinian Authority (PA) or especially Hamas to adopt all of these simultaneously or immediately. One thing, however, must be clear: no Israeli government—regardless of its ideological leaning—will compromise on these five issues, nor will the Obama administration break its resolve in backing them. These demands on the

Palestinian leadership are consistent with the requirements imposed by the United States, the EU, and Israel, calling on the Palestinians to renounce terrorism, accept prior agreements and recognize Israel's right to exist. Hamas has shown in the past an unwillingness to cooperate with demands from the international community, but it seems that with new U.S. efforts to push for reconciliation, Hamas has a unique opportunity to join the political process as a recognized party. The PLO under the leadership of Yasser Arafat went through the same pain, and in 1988 recognized Israel and renounced terrorism. In a recent interview with Hamas leader Khaled Meshal, he agreed not only to a Palestinian state based on 1967 borders, but conceded that "'when the time comes,' Hamas will make some of the moves demanded of it by the West."[171]

Form a united front

As the Egyptian-brokered talks between Fatah and Hamas continue, it is becoming more imperative that the Palestinian leadership show a united front as they face upcoming negotiations with the U.S. and Israeli governments. A Palestinian unity government will allow Hamas to save face as it can commit to the two-state solution that the Hamas charter forbids. This will give the radical yet undeniably popular group a voice and stake in the negotiating process, and can bring Hamas to the table as a significant political force rather than an armed faction with a devious political agenda. Both Hamas and the PA (which represents the Palestinian Liberation Organization) know that the prospect of reaching a viable peace deal with Israel requires that the Palestinians speak in one voice. Hamas as a popular movement has secured a place in the Palestinian body politic and no one can effectively deny Hamas a say in negotiations. This is why it is critical that Hamas is included in the Palestinian government, because left to its own devices and with no prospect of exercising some power over Palestinian affairs, it will undoubtedly resort to violence to disrupt the process. It appears, though, that the Egyptian-mediated

---

171 Paul McGeough, "Hamas Comes Out of Hiding," *The New York Times*, April 12, 2009, http://www.nytimes.com/2009/04/13/opinion/13mcgeough.html.

negotiations between the PA and Hamas to form a unity government have advanced considerably, and the two sides may well reach an agreement this summer.

That being said, Hamas must nevertheless drop the illusion that it can control the Palestinian political agenda entirely. It must realize that the PA, with the support of the United States and other powers, will soon have a military powerful enough to confront Hamas' future challenges and prevail. The recent clash in the West Bank proved that Fatah soldiers are willing to take on Hamas if necessary. Hamas must further be disabused of any illusion that it can overthrow the PA by political or violent means and take over the West Bank. The continued training of PA security forces in Jordan with American funding, monitoring, and equipment remains essential. It sends a clear message to Hamas' leadership that there will be no chance of unseating the PA and that time is not in its favor. Finally, if Israel is to make any major concessions to the Palestinians, it will only do so knowing that they are in agreement with a united leadership supported by the Arab street. Israel will not risk giving up an inch of land to the PA if it feels threatened that Hamas can hijack it and use it to launch violent attacks. If Hamas wants to gain legitimate political credibility in all of Palestine, it must demonstrate to the international community and to Israel in particular that it can act as a credible and responsible political partner along with the PA.

End all acts of violence

Cessation of violence is fundamental, not only to the resumption of peace negotiations but for fostering confidence between all parties. Decades of violence and counter-attacks have not improved the Palestinian prospect for statehood in any capacity. Although the PA has acknowledged this reality and worked to quell violence in the West Bank, Hamas has made violent resistance against Israel the pillar of its strategy. Hamas too has realized—especially following the Gaza war—that continued rocket fire can only get them so far. During the war, Hamas' fighters could not confront the Israeli army and assumed defensive postures as they were no match to Israel's overwhelming military prowess. Furthermore, the militants used civilian homes and other populated areas to stage attacks, effectively using the civilian population as a collective human shield to raise the collateral damage and to bring international pressure on Israel to end the fighting. Now that Hamas has suspended violent resistance, it must continue to reinforce it at all costs in order to become a party to the peace negotiations. Should Hamas choose instead to violently disrupt the political process that the United States is leading with the active involvement of the Arab states, it will risk losing all the political capital it gained throughout the past decade.

Ending the calls for Israel's destruction

Challenging Israel's right to exist will get the Palestinians nowhere, as has been demonstrated in the past. If Israel feels threatened that it must fight for existence, it will justify all means, however severe, to ensure its long-term safety and survival. Moreover, Israel does not need Hamas' recognition, though in ongoing negotiations Hamas has indirectly had to acknowledge Israel's existence as a reality. Hamas' leadership has agreed to the 1967 borders, a long-term ceasefire and the possibility of living in peace with Israel, as was conveyed by former President Jimmy Carter. Khaled Meshal may come much closer to accepting Israel in his upcoming policy address. Moreover, Hamas is also fully aware of the changing political dynamics in the region as the Arab states are moving toward reconciliation with Israel. The Obama administration has repeatedly reaffirmed America's unshakable commitment to Israel's security and a viable Palestinian state. Hamas should not forsake this opportunity for an unrealistic goal of calling for Israel's destruction. This is a chance that Hamas may not want to miss, especially after watching Hezbollah's recent defeat in the Lebanese Parliamentary elections.

Give up on the Palestinian right of return

This may be the most difficult demand for the Palestinians to come to terms with. It represents one of their toughest bargaining chips and in large part caused the collapse of the negotiations at Camp David in 2000. While in theory the Palestinian right of return appears logical, no solution to the Israeli-Palestinian conflict could possibly envision the return of any significant number of Palestinian refugees to Israel proper. From the Israeli perspective, any sizeable influx of Palestinian refugees will change overnight the demographic makeup of the state. This is not a question of right and wrong; it is simply a matter of Israel's survival as a Jewish state for which it was created, and Israel will never abandon or compromise on this principle. That being said, any Palestinian refugee who opts to resettle in their homeland should be able to do so in the West Bank or Gaza once a Palestinian state is created.

In past negotiations between Israel and the Palestinians, the Palestinian representatives understood that a solution to the refugee problem lies in resettlement and/or compensation. United Nations General Assembly (UNGA) Resolution 194 (1948), which called on Israel to allow the refugees to return to their original homes and serves as the basis for the right of return, is not binding, as is the case with all General Assembly resolutions. Moreover, Resolution 194 was superseded by the binding United Nations Security Council (UNSC) Resolution 242 (1967), which instead called for "achieving a just settlement to the refugee problem." Having preached the gospel of the right of return so consistently over so many years, the Palestinian leadership may not be in a position to simply drop the issue altogether unless it is a part of the whole package of a peace agreement. Yet, the sooner they begin to modify their narrative, prepare the public, and indicate to the United States their readiness to address the refugee problem in the context of resettlement and compensation, the easier it will be for the Israelis to make concessions in other areas such as the settlements, where they feel less threatened.

Embrace the Arab Peace Initiative

The leading Arab states—especially Saudi Arabia and Egypt—must persuade Hamas to embrace the Arab Peace Initiative (API) and rejoin the Arab fold. The API generally calls on Israel to give up the territories captured in the 1967 war and find a just solution to the Palestinian refugee problem in exchange for peace with all Arab countries. This offers Hamas a clear way out of its self-imposed isolation. This is an opportunity Hamas should not forsake, as the

Initiative represents the collective Arab will and provides the basis for a comprehensive Arab-Israeli peace. Its merits have been acknowledged outside the Arab world by President Obama and Israeli President Shimon Peres among others, and it will likely be included in the Road Map as the official framework for negotiations. Moreover, the leaders of the Arab states are determined to end the Israeli-Palestinian conflict, which has been feeding extremism to the detriment of their own regimes. Once Syria joins the peace process on that basis, which may be sooner than later, Hamas will stand alone in the Arab world in its struggle against Israel. Moreover, if Hamas is seen as an obstructionist undermining the prospect of a comprehensive peace, it will force many Arab states that support President Obama's peace offensive to take severe punitive measures against Hamas. Hamas' leadership can see the writing on the wall, and to maintain its political viability it must find a way to join the Arab states. While it will take time and a concerted effort to include Hamas in the Annapolis process, in the interim it should accept the Initiative created by the Saudis, who are instrumental to its survival.

Although these requirements for peace are not new, they have eluded the Palestinians for decades. These years of struggle have also been instructive, however, as the Arab states led by Egypt have gradually concluded that Israel cannot and will not be marginalized or destroyed. A majority of Palestinian civilians have also finally come to accept the premise of a two-state solution. Time and circumstances matter greatly and now both Israel and the Palestinians face an unprecedented opportunity to forge a lasting peace.

SUPPORTING FAYYAD'S VISION

AUGUST 28, 2009

Palestinian Prime Minister Salam Fayyad's unveiling of his government program to build the apparatus of a Palestinian state within two years is an admirable, bold, and welcome initiative. For 60 years the Palestinians have been accused by Israel and the international community of being weak, fragmented, and harboring extremist ideologies. The plan of the 13th Palestinian National Authority government not only represents a blueprint for the government to address these inherent problems, but it is the first outline for a viable Palestinian state based on freedom, democracy, nonviolence, and international law. It should be supported by all those who seek a peaceful solution to the Israeli-Palestinian conflict, as this commitment suggests that the culture of blame and violence must come to an end. The program further affirms that the Palestinians' nation-building must be founded by the Palestinian people, for the Palestinian people, and according to all international standards of human rights and law. Israel in particular should embrace this initiative as it would strengthen the efforts of Palestinian moderates, and set in motion a peaceful process leading to final negotiations and the two-state solution to which Netanyahu has agreed.

Israeli detractors of this plan have condemned the PA for acting unilaterally and imposing a timeline, while Palestinian extremist groups Hamas and Islamic Jihad have claimed the plan is far too accommodating to Israel. The irony here is that a feeble and dependent Palestinian government has gotten the Palestinian people nowhere in the past, just as ideologies of violent resistance have only resulted in more deaths, as the war in Gaza demonstrated. How can the Israelis justly accuse the Palestinians of being incapable and then rebuke the PA's plan to build a strong government? And how can Hamas reject a plan for a nonviolent de facto Palestinian state when violence has

241

only exacerbated the Palestinians' plight? For Israelis to align themselves with Hamas in opposition to a moderate Palestinian plan for
good governance is absurd.

The PA's outline for statehood offers hope to the third generation
of despondent Palestinians that there is a better and brighter future
where they can develop a vested interest in creating of a state of their
own. A commitment to build a future based on equality and restoration of self-dignity in a nonviolent atmosphere will fundamentally
change the mindset of nearly every individual in this conflict. The
forward of the plan by Salam Fayyad states specifically that:

> Palestine will be a peace-loving state that rejects violence,
> commits to co-existence with its neighbors, and builds
> bridges of cooperation with the international community.
> It will be a symbol of peace, tolerance and prosperity
> in this troubled area of the world. By embodying all of
> these values, Palestine will be a source of pride to all of
> its citizens, and an anchor of stability in this region.[172]

The majority of Palestinians who will benefit from the Fayyad
plan will oppose the resumption of any violence against Israelis. An
overwhelming majority of the Palestinian public already approves
of a two-state solution and peace with Israel. The mere fact that
the Palestinians can now take matters into their hands to build their
nation will place the burden of proof on their heads. Indeed, the
development of democratic, political, economic, and social programs
that the Fayyad plan calls for will empower the people and offer a
stark choice between the prospect of a better life or more bloodshed.
Israel will commit a serious strategic error if it chooses to stifle this
effort, as it will give ammunition to Palestinian extremists that Israel
has no intention of allowing the peaceful rise of a Palestinian state,
giving credence to continued violent resistance.

The PA's program is a fulfillment not only of the Palestinians'
national aspirations, but Israel's as well. A commitment to building the
infrastructure of a viable Palestinian state in the West Bank and Gaza
will foster acceptance of Israel as a recognized independent state. The

---

172 Fayyad, "Ending the Occupation, Establishing the State," 4.

plan emphasizes peaceful co-existence with all neighboring states and a policy against any form of religious or cultural discrimination. Is this not what Israelis have been wanting since the inception of their state? Those Israelis skeptical about the Palestinians' ultimate intentions should find some solace in a written government document confirming the Palestinian government's vision of peace and democracy. The Palestinians know only too well from past experiences that any challenge to Israel's national security will render their nation-building efforts obsolete. The consequences of the second Intifada remain etched in the memory of the Palestinian people, and may well have contributed to the emergence of the current program of moderation.

The concept of a democratic Arab state with an open market economy governed by the rule of law is no small feat. The United States has every reason to promote this goal in any way possible, and Israel should welcome the plan's premise of expanding and promoting regional trade. In addition, the Fayyad plan will also have serious implications for the Palestinian internal political struggle. Hamas operatives will have a hard time finding support for their opposition, as it will be interpreted as rejecting the principle of realizing the long-held goal—a Palestinian state. The PA is planning general elections in January of 2010, and Hamas will be hard-pressed to resist joining a political process with an agenda to provide goods and services to the Palestinian people.

Finally, it is important to note that the Fayyad initiative does not call for the unilateral establishment of a Palestinian state, but focuses on building the foundation for such a state, leaving all conflicting issues with Israel—including final borders, East Jerusalem, and Palestinian refugees—to a negotiated agreement. What this plan states is that the Palestinian people do not need permission from anyone to prepare for such an eventuality, the principle parameters of which are recognized by the international community—including Israel. The plan's Foundation of Principles states that "We are building a democratic system of government founded on political pluralism, guarantee of equality, and protection of all its citizens' rights and freedoms as safeguarded by the law and within its limits."[173] This

---

173 Ibid.

should be encouraged by Israel if it wants to have a strong partner with whom to negotiate. But if a state is declared before reaching a final agreement, it will have only provisional borders that will still have to be negotiated with Israel. What is important here is that the path chosen for Palestinian statehood is the path that of necessity precludes violence. Had the Palestinians started this process after Israel's evacuation of Gaza, there is no question that the last four years would have been dramatically different, preventing the rise of Hamas and the Israeli incursion into Gaza.

As the American-sponsored Israeli-Palestinian negotiations will likely resume soon, there is no better atmosphere under which to conduct these negotiations than the nonviolent climate that the Fayyad plan will hopefully foster. It is this commitment to true nation-building that will at last put an end to the tragic Israeli-Palestinian conflict and discredit those who still advocate violent resistance.

HAMAS' CENTRALITY TO A TWO-STATE SOLUTION

SEPTEMBER 21, 2009

As the Obama administration continues to push for the resumption of the Israeli-Palestinian peace negotiations, one of the main questions still looming pertains to who will ultimately represent the Palestinian people. As Mahmoud Abbas comes to the UN this month to speak on behalf of Fatah, it is unlikely that Israeli-Palestinian peace talks will make measurable progress unless Hamas is brought into the political process in some capacity. The social and geopolitical reality of the Israeli-Palestinian conflict is steeped in mutual distrust, so that any concessions made or breakthroughs achieved must come from parties representing the mandate of the people. There can be no lasting peaceful solution without recreating a single Palestinian entity in the West Bank and Gaza, governed by a single administration representative of the majority of the Palestinian electorates. Future Palestinian governments must be elected democratically and Fatah, Hamas, and other parties must able to compete freely. This must be the premise on which to base any future negotiations about the two-state solution, and efforts to exclude any party from the political process—including Hamas—could severely undercut the prospect for peace.

Hamas' participation is essential not only because it is in control of Gaza, but because it is a disciplined grassroots movement with social, political, and security apparatuses, and coupled with an economic structure that provides for hundreds of thousands of Palestinians. While many would like to dismiss Hamas as a radical or militant group, which it rightly is, Hamas wields too much influence over its followers to be discounted, and ignoring it has not helped to marginalize it in the past.

So how do President Obama and the leaders of moderate Arab states go about bringing Hamas into the peace process? Thus far,

245

Hamas' political participation has been conditional upon the organization's acceptance of the Quartet's (UN, United States, EU, and Russia) three requirements: recognizing Israel, renouncing terrorism, and accepting prior Israeli-Palestinian agreements. Hamas' leadership has refused to heed the Quartet's call and is unlikely to do so any time soon as it would be seen as a major concession to Israel. From Hamas' perspective Israel is the aggressor, and so long as it continues its egregious occupation of Palestinian land, it must be resisted by all means available. At the same time there exists serious policy disagreements and personal animosity between Hamas and the PA that continue to stifle any meaningful discourse between the two sides. This has prevented the Palestinian camp from entering into negotiations with a united front, something it will need should Israel contemplate further withdrawal from land in the West Bank.

That being said, it is important to note that the conditions created since the Gaza incursion that ended in a ceasefire earlier this year offer a greater opportunity to move the peace process forward with the participation of Hamas. This includes the early push for the resumption of the negotiations by the Obama administration. Since January there has been a general lull in violence, and Hamas has adhered to the ceasefire. The economic and security progress in the West Bank has been notable, with an expected economic growth rate of 7%, partially due to an easing of roadblocks by Israel in the West Bank.[174] Notably, there has been growing receptivity of the API in Israel, especially by Israeli President Shimon Peres and also by numerous officials in the Obama administration. Looming over all of this is the Iranian threat, as its potential acquisition of nuclear weapons affects both Israel and the Arab states. All of these events combined make the time ripe for the Palestinian parties to unite for the sake of a two-state solution. But to utilize this environment and translate it into a real progress, the negotiating strategy must first be modified.

The three preconditions placed on Hamas by the Quartet should be realistically assessed in light of the changing dynamics to prevent what may be obsolete requirements from seriously hindering the

---

174 Ethan Bronner, "Signs of Hope Emerge in the West Bank," *The New York Times*, July 16, 2009, http://www.nytimes.com/2009/07/17/world/middleeast/17westbank.html?_r=0.

peace process. To that end, it is critical to capitalize on the API, which can provide a common denominator for both Israel and Hamas as a framework for peace. This would offer Hamas a face-saving way out to deal with Israel indirectly, and become a part of the negotiating process acceptable to both the Israelis and the Quartet.

Hamas's refusal to recognize Israel in advance of any agreement is in fact in line with the other 19 out of 21 Arab states that still do not officially recognize Israel before all conflicting issues are settled. Israel does not and should not need Hamas' recognition, nor is it required to recognize Hamas or its ideologies separately from the PA. It is absurd that Israel should feel it needs the recognition of a group it deems a terrorist organization; it should only need recognition from the Palestinian government once a Palestinian state has been negotiated and agreed upon. Moreover, Israel is not expected to negotiate directly with Hamas or any other Palestinian group unless such a group wins general elections and forms a representative government that seeks to reconcile its differences with Israel peacefully. For these reasons, establishing recognition of Israel as a precondition is premature and unnecessary, as it complicates matters and stalls the process from moving forward. Because of the bitter split between Hamas and the PA led by Mr. Abbas, the Palestinians must first settle their differences by allowing the people to pick who they think can best serve their needs. Once they have agreed on general elections for President and parliament, only then will the elected Palestinian government and Israel exchange mutual recognition and establish rules of engagement.

Unlike the question of recognition, renouncing violence by Hamas is an absolute requirement under any circumstances. Within or outside the Palestinian government, Hamas must accept the simple fact that violent resistance is unacceptable and its leadership must make that choice if it wishes to become a political partner in future negotiations. Any acts of violence against Israelis obligate the Israeli authorities to respond violently, not only to ensure the safety of their citizens but also because it evokes a moral imperative of safeguarding its sovereign right which cannot be violated with impunity. Hamas must resolve to permanently forsake violence and build on the current ceasefire in preparation for the general Palestinian elections scheduled for early next year. This will pave the way for Hamas' future participation in negotiations with Israel as a representative of the Palestinian government, should it win an outright majority or become a partner in a coalition government.

As for the condition that Hamas must accept all prior agreements, this issue can be resolved almost entirely on its own once Palestinian elections are held and a new government is installed. Any future Palestinian government must accept prior agreements or modify them with Israel by mutual agreement. Neither the Quartet nor Israel should treat Hamas as an independent state. Hamas is and must be seen as a Palestinian political party, and if its leadership wants to be a part of the political process they can run on any political platform they desire except militant resistance to Israel. If Hamas sits in the opposition, their acceptance or refusal of prior agreements becomes irrelevant, but as part of a government they must adhere to the norms of conduct between nations including prior agreements or obligations they have entered into.

The API is a means to unravel this political conundrum between Hamas, the PA, Israel, and the Quartet, and provides a dignified way out for all the players involved. The API, which was adopted first in Beirut, Lebanon in March of 2002 and reintroduced in March of 2007 in Riyadh, Saudi Arabia, provides a comprehensive formula for an Arab-Israeli peace. Moreover, it provides a perfect cover for Hamas to enter into peace negotiations with Israel indirectly. The Initiative establishes the following principles: 1) full Israeli withdrawal from all the territories occupied since 1967; 2) achievement of a just solution to the Palestinian refugee problem; 3) the acceptance and the establishment of a sovereign, independent Palestinian state on the Palestinian territories occupied since the 4th of June 1967 in the West Bank and Gaza strip, with East Jerusalem as its capital; 4) the Arab-Israeli conflict ended, a peace agreement with Israel, and security for all the states of the region, and finally; 5) the establishment of normal relations with Israel in the context of this comprehensive peace.

Although the Netanyahu government has not yet formally endorsed the Initiative, it would be wise as it provides a solid foundation for a comprehensive Arab-Israeli peace. The United States and the EU should formally endorse it and make every effort to persuade Israel to do likewise. There is nothing in the API that negates Israel's ultimate objective of establishing peace and normal relations with all of its neighbors. The Initiative was never meant to be presented on an all or nothing basis, and within the general framework of the document everything is negotiable to achieve a secure and durable peace.

Egypt, Saudi Arabia, Syria, and the leading Arab states who wish Israel to accept the Initiative must now use all the leverage they have to persuade Hamas to adopt it as well. The Initiative offers Hamas a way to achieve land and peace for the Palestinians without having to concede to directly to Israel, as signing on to the API would be seen as joining the collective will of the Arab states. By accepting the Initiative, Hamas need not necessarily accept the Quartet requirements, as Hamas will fall in line with the 19 Arab states that are willing to recognize Israel only upon reaching an agreement based on the provisions of the Initiative. On more than one occasion, Hamas leaders have suggested that they can see themselves accepting a solution to their conflict with Israel based on Israeli withdrawal to the 1967 borders. In fact Hamas' political leader Khaled Meshal told the New York Times that "We are with a state on the 1967 borders, based on a long-term truce. This includes East Jerusalem, the dismantling of settlements and the right of return of the Palestinian refugees."[175] Although this is not the exact formula that will eventually be adopted, especially in regards to the right of return—which many Arab leaders have accepted will be mutually agreed upon—there is no doubt about the fact that Hamas is beginning to move into a more constructive direction.

The social, security, and economic progress achieved in the West Bank offers a glaring contrast to the continuing despondency in Gaza, which presents a serious challenge to Hamas' strategy. If Hamas intends to represent the Palestinian people, they are in dire need of a new strategy to deliver goods and services to their constituents. Israel's incursion into Gaza in December of 2008 left an ineradicable mark on Hamas militants that violent resistance will further diminish, rather than strengthen, their position vis-à-vis Israel. Polls have clearly indicated that continued military resistance has actually undermined their popular support.

---

175 Taghreed El-Khodary and Ethan Bronner, "Addressing U.S., Hamas Says It Grounded Rockets," *The New York Times*, May 4, 2009, http://www.nytimes.com/2009/05/05/world/middleeast/05meshal.html.

Hamas remains central to the two-state solution, but its leadership must know that while Hamas retains the capacity to disrupt the peace process, there is no other viable option to ensure its survival as an influential political organization other than the two-state solution.

THE FAYYAD DIFFERENCE

JULY 13, 2010

When the PA's Prime Minster Salam Fayyad first introduced his plans to build the infrastructure for a future Palestinian state, many Israelis and Palestinians thought of it as nothing more than another Middle Eastern mirage that will leave no lasting impression. A little more than a year later, the plan is showing not only tremendous promise, but has become indispensable to the emergence of a democratic Palestinian state—one living side-by-side with Israel in peace and security. Israel, the United States, and the European community in particular must do everything in their power to support Fayyad's plan and ensure that the difference he has already made becomes irreversible and leads to the only viable option to resolve the Israeli-Palestinian Conflict—the two-state solution.

Having just returned from a visit to the West Bank where I met with Prime Minister Fayyad, I was struck by the remarkable socio-economic progress in many parts of the West Bank, especially in Ramallah. Even more impressive was Dr. Fayyad's determination to continue in his path with total conviction that the prospect of establishing a Palestinian state rests in the Palestinians' hands, provided they focus on building the tenets of statehood which, from his perspective, rest on four pillars.

First, he stressed that militant resistance and violence have run their course. Committing acts of violence against the Israelis simply plays into their hands, offering justification for continued occupation and enabling Israel to link national security with occupation. The Palestinians must disabuse the Israeli public of this notion. The only way this can be done is by insisting on a nonviolent approach to resolving differences with Israel, especially now that the international community supports the establishment of a Palestinian state. For this reason, the preparation for statehood will be peaceful, and as Dr. Fayyad proposes, "Palestine will be a peace-loving state that rejects violence, commits to co-existence with its neighbors, and builds bridges of cooperation with the international community."[176] Although the Palestinians, especially Hamas, he cautioned, are still not united in this regard, it is up to the PA to demonstrate that a nonviolent policy provides significant gains for a public that develops vested interests and demands to maintain it. He strongly suggested that if Israel is seeking peaceful coexistence, it must support his efforts not only by further easing the burden of occupation but also by investing in the Palestinian enterprise, from which both sides can greatly benefit economically and develop mutual trust—critical for good neighborly relations.

The second point that Dr. Fayyad emphasized was the importance of building the infrastructure of the state, including industrial zones, electricity networks, roads, crossing points, and other critical services such as schools and hospitals. He noted that no state can be established if it lacks the basic infrastructure or the bureaucracy that can respond to public needs. Interestingly, he chose Israel as an exemplary model, not only of developing the infrastructure prior to statehood, but also for its political system and the need for unity to maintain national identity. Israel, he said, was not created in 1948; this was only the official declaration. The foundation of the state, for all intents and purposes, was established several decades before. For example, the Histadrut, Israel's trade union, was created in the beginning of the British Mandate in 1920, and was responsible for all social services for workers, including healthcare, education, banking, and housing, forming the building-blocks of the state and remaining influential to this day. Another critical institution during this time was the Jewish Agency, which was recognized by the British Mandate as the governing organization that oversaw political, economic, and cultural relations. After Israel's declaration of statehood, the Jewish Agency remained the primary organization for facilitating immigration to Israel. For Dr. Fayyad, providing such infrastructure offers not only a sense of belonging but also a strong sense of accomplishment that makes the goal of political independence look increasingly realistic. In the end, he observed,

---

176 Fayyad, "Ending the Occupation, Establishing the State," 4.

only visible and sustainable progress changes the negative political narrative of the past, which made virtues of hatred and misery in the name of defiance of occupation.

The third pillar in Fayyad's plan is a vibrant and dynamic political system. "Palestine," he said, "will be a stable democratic state with a multi-party political system…founded on political pluralism, guarantee of equality, and protection of all its citizens' rights and freedoms as safeguarded by the law and within its limits."[177] The Palestinians, he continued, will not settle for anything less. They have lived alongside the Israelis for more than six decades, and regardless of the long and often bloody conflict, the Palestinian people witnessed firsthand the working of democracy in Israel, appreciating its values and the advantages it offers. "The formation of a democratically-elected leadership that enjoys popular and factional support, as well as regional and international recognition, is an essential step towards realizing the supreme national goal of establishing the State of Palestine."[178] In this regard, Dr. Fayyad is ruling no one and no faction out because, from his perspective, only a true democracy in which every Palestinian has the right to participate will provide Palestinians with a political system that can sustain their independence as well as their socioeconomic progress.

Finally, Fayyad's fourth pillar is the creation of a single, independent state for all Palestinians. Whereas the people may differ in their political or ideological views, they must remain united in their aspiration to maintain national unity. "The Government also bears considerable responsibility for facilitating the national dialogue aimed at ending the state of political fragmentation and restoring national unity,"[179] Fayyad says, referring to Hamas and other Palestinians factions that still reject Israel's existence. But he feels sanguine about the prospect of Palestinian unity as long as the principle of a Palestinian state along the 1967 borders, with some limited land swaps, is maintained and the Palestinians enjoy the freedoms accorded to citizens of

---

177 Ibid., 6.

178 Ibid., 8.

179 Ibid.

other developed nations. Fayyad believes that under these conditions, all Palestinians will eventually support the emerging Palestinian state, living side-by-side Israel in peace.

The picture, of course, is not completely rosy. Fayyad faces a number of serious obstacles that he must overcome, and to do so he needs both internal and external help. Other than being rejected by Hamas and other extremist groups, he still experiences major difficulties from within the Fatah organization. He is generally viewed as an outsider and even detached from the day-to-day reality of the Palestinian people. His plans need far more public exposure, especially outside the Palestinian territories, and his state-building effort must be bolstered by tangible progress in the political process. The United States, in particular, should do everything possible to enable him to show increasingly more progress on these fronts in order to strengthen his public support. Israel must also make far greater and more visible concessions to ease the bondage of occupation, particularly because of the demonstrable and consistent ability of the Palestinians' internal security to keep the peace by preventing acts of violence against Israeli targets.

One can only imagine what a difference the Fayyad plan would have made had it been introduced immediately after the Oslo Accords, which were signed in 1993. A Palestinian state may have been already created, thousands of lives on both sides may have been spared, and the entire Middle East may have flourished beyond present recognition. The question is: will the rejectionists among both Israelis and Palestinians grasp the historic significance of what Fayyad has advanced, which represents the only sane exit from an otherwise terrifying race toward the abyss? The Fayyad plan offers a noble and exquisite option.

HAMAS MUST PLAY A ROLE IN
THE TWO-STATE SOLUTION

SEPTEMBER 13, 2010

The negotiations between Israel and the PA can potentially succeed, but such a success cannot be sustained unless Hamas is brought into the political process in some capacity. The concessions made or breakthroughs achieved must represent the majority of the electorates, as there can be no lasting peaceful solution without recreating a unified Palestinian polity in the West Bank and Gaza. The Arab states should therefore heed President Obama's call to meaningfully contribute to the peace process by pressing Hamas to renounce violence and accept the principles of the API as a common frame of reference for advancing Palestinian unity and a comprehensive resolution of the Arab-Israeli conflict.

Israel must accept that Hamas is a reality, which it cannot simply wish away. Hamas' participation is essential, not only because it is in control of Gaza, but also because it represents a disciplined grassroots movement with a substantial social, political, and security apparatus. To be sure, Hamas is a radical militant organization, yet it wields too much influence over its followers—and over the Gaza Strip—to be discounted. While Israel will continue to defend its citizens, Hamas—as an ideology—cannot be removed completely by military force, and ignoring Hamas has not been a successful strategy to marginalize it. Thus far, Hamas' political participation has been conditional upon its acceptance of the Quartet's three conditions: recognize Israel, renounce terrorism, and accept prior Israeli-Palestinian agreements. Hamas' leadership has refused to do so and is unlikely to comply any time soon, perhaps with the exception of adhering to a nonviolent atmosphere.

The renewed peace talks offer a new chance to press Hamas to forsake violence and become part of the political process. Notwithstanding Hamas' recent attacks on Israelis in the West Bank coinciding with the launch of direct talks, the group has largely refrained from such violence since the conclusion of Israel's Operation Cast Lead in January 2009. That is because Hamas recognizes that escalating violent terror acts against Israelis would be self-destructive. Israel would not hesitate to respond militarily to an escalation of violence by decapitating Hamas' leadership. In this sense, Hamas is already tacitly acknowledging that violence is ineffective, and will only lead to more destruction. Meanwhile, the social, security, and economic progress achieved in the West Bank offers a glaring contrast to the continuing despondency in Gaza, presenting a serious challenge to Hamas. Hamas is therefore in dire need of a new strategy to deliver goods and services to their constituents. Just as Israel can no longer ignore the reality of Hamas, Hamas must accept the reality and the security of Israel as a prerequisite to its own political survival.

At this stage, the Quartet's conditions on Hamas to enter the political process should be replaced by an insistence that Hamas explicitly renounce violence and accept the API. Two of the three Quartet conditions are unrealistic. Hamas' refusal to recognize Israel in advance of any agreement is consistent with the position of the Arab states (besides Egypt and Jordan). Israel does not and should not need Hamas' recognition, nor should it be required to recognize Hamas or its ideologies. Furthermore, Hamas will not explicitly accept past agreements, as doing so would also amount to recognition of Israel. However, by participating in past elections, Hamas has already recognized the governance structure of the PA—a body created following an agreement with Israel—as legitimate. Hamas should be viewed as a political party, and if its leadership wants to be a part of the political process they can do so as long as they do not advocate violence. In this regard, neither the Quartet nor Israel should elevate Hamas' status by treating it as an independent state. However, the third Quartet condition, Hamas' forsaking of violence, should be an absolute requirement for it to enter any political process. Doing so could pave the way for both Palestinian unity and Hamas' participation, albeit indirectly, in negotiations with Israel.

Meanwhile, the Arab states—particularly Egypt, Saudi Arabia, and Syria—should now pressure Hamas to accept the Initiative as a face-saving way of entering the political process that could be acceptable to Israel, the Arab states, and the Quartet. These three Arab states have a particular interest in the Israeli-Palestinian talks and must now support efforts that could bring about a Palestinian state. Egypt shares a border with the Gaza Strip and has experience addressing Hamas and the Muslim Brotherhood, mediating the dispute between Fatah and Hamas, and working with Israel. It has a vested interest in Hamas' moderation and calm along its border. Saudi Arabia—as the initiator of the API—now must show that it is capable of the leadership necessary to advance it.

As the custodian of the Islamic holy sites, Saudi Arabia can be uniquely influential in addressing Hamas' Islamic ideology. Moreover, Saudi Arabia has the power of the purse and it can offer substantial financial aid as a further inducement for Hamas to sign on to the API. Finally, by advocating Hamas' acceptance of the Initiative, Syria—as host to Hamas leader Khaled Meshal in Damascus as well as a signatory to the API—could demonstrate that it is determined to improve its relations with the United States. In this regard, the statement following the recent meeting between King Abdullah of Jordan and Syrian President Basher Assad in support of the API is a welcome sign.

The API is not an all-or-nothing deal. The general framework of the document offers a common frame of reference to which all parties to the conflict could relate as a basis for negotiations toward a secure and durable peace. Critics may argue that just as Hamas has not accepted the Quartet's conditions, it would similarly reject the API. It should be noted that on more than one occasion, Hamas leaders have suggested that they could accept a formula of a cessation of hostilities for a Palestinian state along the 1967 borders. For example, Hamas' Khaled Meshal told the New York Times in May 2009 that, "We are with a state on the 1967 borders, based on a long-term truce. This includes East Jerusalem, the dismantling of settlements and the right of return of the Palestinian refugees."[180]

---

180 Taghreed El-Khodary and Ethan Bronner, "Addressing U.S., Hamas Says It Grounded Rockets," *The New York Times*, May 4, 2009, http://www. nytimes.com/2009/05/05/world/middleeast/05meshal.html?_r=0.

Although such statements contain problematic elements for Israel—especially the right of return of refugees—the comments do suggest that Hamas recognizes the benefits of principles of the Initiative. Others may question whether the Arab states would have any meaningful influence on Hamas, since its principal supporter—Iran—is dedicated to obstructing the political process. However, the relationship between Sunni Hamas and Shiite Iran is one of convenience and necessity, not ideology. Hamas' joining the Arab states' endorsement of the API would serve to bring Hamas into a more suitable alliance with its Sunni Arab brethren.

The API is the only peace plan that offers a common denominator, with elements acceptable to all parties to the conflict including Hamas and Israel. Saudi Arabia, Egypt, and Syria should take the lead in advocating it as a way forward for Hamas to become part of the political process, and in doing so advance the prospects of the recently launched peace talks.

PALESTINIAN INCITEMENT AGAINST ISRAEL

*Nothing harms the Palestinian cause more than
their continuing incitement and the spread of hatred
against Israel, especially among the youth*

APRIL 11, 2011

The adoption of nonviolent methods by the PA to advance the Palestinian cause is admirable and represents the most promising strategy to affect change. But for a nonviolent movement to serve the intended purpose of advancing the peace process, it must be accompanied by a public narrative supportive of both the strategy and the reality of Israel. The continued incitement against Israel emanating from Palestinian private institutions, media, schools, and refugee camps defeats the nonviolent strategy and instead serves to strengthen the voices of radicals on both sides of the Green Line. Rather than advance Palestinian independence, this vitriol contributes to the solidification of the Israeli occupation in the name of security. It is time for the Palestinians to realize this, because continuing verbal and written onslaughts that support the use of violence and perpetuate radical political narratives are detrimental to their cause and must be stopped.

A renewed focus has been placed on the issue of Palestinian incitement, as the indiscriminate violence that it helps to create has returned. After the horrific murder of five members of the Fogel family,[181] Prime Minister Netanyahu pointed to Palestinian incitement as a root cause. Subsequently, 27 U.S. Senators sent a letter to Secretary of State Hillary Clinton stating that "...the Palestinian

---

181 For more information, see Harriet Sherwood, "Israelis and Palestinians in Shock After Fogel Family Massacre," *The Guardian*, March 14, 2011, http://www.theguardian.com/world/2011/mar/14/fogel-family-massacre-israelis-palestinians.

Authority must take unequivocal steps to condemn the incident and stop allowing the incitement that leads to such crimes. Educating people toward peace is critical to establishing the conditions to a secure and lasting peace."[182] A House version of the letter will soon be sent to President Obama. The legislators are right.

Palestinian Prime Minister Salaam Fayyad and President Mahmoud Abbas condemned the murder of the Fogel family and the subsequent terror attack at a bus station in Jerusalem. They have also worked to dismantle much of the Hamas infrastructure in the West Bank, which served to widely disseminate violent anti-Israel rhetoric and imagery. Even more, in recent years, the PA has built a security apparatus that has dramatically reduced the number of terror attacks, led to greater freedom of movement for Palestinians, and consequently, economic growth. Meanwhile, the Fayyad plan to build the foundation for a Palestinian state has garnered historic levels of international sympathy and support for Palestinian independence.

Naming public infrastructure and roads after suicide bombers and their organizers, providing financial assistance to families of "martyrs" who have been killed while plotting or carrying out terror activities, honoring them in public ceremonies, and depicting Israelis as ruthless murderers in Turkish television programs, all threaten to derail Palestinian independence.[183] Yet, President Abbas and Prime Minister Fayyad have presided over all of the above in just the past several weeks. It is one thing to witness this type of incitement in

---

182 Jordana Horn, "US Senators Ask Clinton to Help End Anti-Israeli Incitement," *Jerusalem Post*, March 30, 2011, http://www.jpost.com/International/US-Senators-ask-Clinton-to-help-end-anti-Israel-incitement.

183 See "PA Names Ramallah Street After Hamas Terror Mastermind," *Haaretz*, April 7, 2010, http://www.haaretz.com/news/pa-names-ramallah-street-after-hamas-terror-mastermind-1.891; Julia Preston, "Emirates Aided Kin of Palestinian Militants," *The New York Times*, March 20, 2006, http://www.nytimes.com/2006/03/20/international/middleeast/20emirates.html?pagewanted=print; Isabel Kershner, "Palestinians Honor a Figure Reviled in Israel as a Terrorist," *The New York Times*, March 11, 2010, http://www.nytimes.com/2010/03/12/world/middleeast/12westbank.html; and "Israel Protests Turkish TV Series About Palestine," *The New York Times*, October 15, 2009, http://www.nytimes.com/2009/10/16/world/middleeast/16israel.html?_r=0.

Gaza, where Hamas openly professes its desire to destroy Israel. However, it is an entirely different matter to witness it in the West Bank, where the PA espouses a two-state solution alongside Israel. Furthermore, Israel is not completely convinced that the PA has fully disavowed violence, as evidenced by recent WikiLeaks documents indicating that the U.S.-backed PA security forces have been reluctant to collect arms from, and apprehend, those linked with the Fatah af-filiated Al-Aqsa Martyrs Brigades, which has carried out numerous terror attacks against Israelis.

Many top PA officials privately recognize the severity of the problem. However, rather than address it, they are too often pointing at Israeli actions that undermine the voice of moderates in favor of radicals, arguing that they make it too difficult politically to oppose venomous statements against the occupier and be accused of collabo-ration. Particularly with the PA now in unity discussions with Hamas, officials are hesitant to clamp down on incitement and appear to be "soft" on Israel. To be sure, Israel's settlement construction in disputed areas and the ongoing nighttime raids in the West Bank by the Israel Defense Forces (IDF) add fuel to the fire of incitement. Still, an envi-ronment conducive to peace must be established if a lasting two-state solution is to be achieved. Even more, what appears politically disad-vantageous will ultimately prove to be quite the opposite. Creating an atmosphere that encourages peacemaking rather than incitement will lead to greater support from the international community and equally greater pressure on Israel to make concessions. After all, peace must start at home. Today, on both sides, the message entering the homes of too many Palestinians—and Israelis—is that of perpetual conflict, marketed by the ideology of extremists in the refugee camps on the one hand, and radical settlers on the other. Addressing these problems requires leadership that today is sorely lacking.

Meanwhile, the psychological damage caused by the radicalization of the two national narratives is enormous. Palestinians are soon to produce a fourth generation of children who will know nothing except the hated occupation and the continuing violent conflict. The previous generation is already poisoned by the pervasive glorification of terror and violent "resistance." It now falls to the responsibility of the PA, and Palestinian teachers, parents, and community leaders to ensure that the next generation focuses on the potential of its future as a nation, rather than on demonizing an enemy that it cannot, and will not, defeat.

Moreover, although trust between two entities alone cannot offer the basis for any lasting peace agreement, incitement undermines the building of trust. Without a measure of trust, there is no room for even calculated risks, especially on matters of national security and peacemaking. A review of the reasons behind the collapses of the bilateral negotiations in 2000 and in 2008 show that a lack of trust was a major factor that led the Israeli side to rethink its position, as the gap between the Palestinian public narrative and the required Israeli concessions was simply unbridgeable. Whereas the PA has legitimate grievances against Israel, including territorial claims, it must nevertheless acknowledge at least in words to the Palestinian public the existence of the State of Israel. That is, the reality and acceptance of co-existence alongside Israel will not be established, among the youth in particular, as long as the central reality on the ground is ignored. This is precisely why the PA has had major difficulties in making required concessions—in the minds of too many Palestinians, concessions are unnecessary to an entity that they have been taught does not have the legitimacy to exist or, even worse, can be defeated through violence.

Finally, with the PA now in discussions with Hamas regarding Palestinian unity, this becomes even more acute. For a unity government to succeed in its stated purpose—to advance the cause of Palestinian independence—Hamas too must end its self-destructive violent provocations against Israel, permanently renounce violence, and end incitement. Such a first political step would offer a significant leap toward a sovereign Palestinian state, as well as the establishment of the beginning of trust and confidence between Israelis and Palestinians. Otherwise, even international recognition of an independent Palestinian state based on the 1967 lines—as might be passed by UNGA this September—will change very little on the ground because Israel has every right to protect its legitimate national security concerns.

Much is made of the weakness of the Palestinian leadership and the divisions within Palestinian society. But as the Fayyad Plan has shown, the PA is capable of capturing the attention and imagination of the international community in support of the Palestinian cause through proactive institution building and nonviolence. Palestinians cannot allow incitement to jeopardize their national aspirations by providing such a clear and legitimate excuse for Israel to be reticent about negotiations toward an eventual two-state framework.

The PA can and must demonstrate that it is prepared to build a responsible government by ending incitement in all its forms. Doing so would make a lasting and meaningful impact on Palestinian and Israeli societies alike, by serving to simultaneously advance Palestinian independence and Israeli recognition.

ALON BEN-MEIR

FATAH-HAMAS RECONCILIATION

Will demonstrate how committed the Palestinians—Hamas and Fatah—and Israel are to a lasting two-state solution

MAY 9, 2011

The Fatah–Hamas reconciliation agreement is a byproduct of the Arab Spring, and is designed to position the public of both the West Bank and Gaza Strip for Palestinian statehood. The questions that the deal raises are numerous—yet so are the possibilities. Should this new Palestinian understanding hold, and should it serve to advance national aspirations for a Palestinian state living at peace alongside the State of Israel, the Fatah-Hamas agreement could prove to be a critical step toward securing Palestinian independence based on a two-state solution.

The Fatah–Hamas deal comes after more than a year of reconciliation talks and two previously failed attempts (in 2007 and 2009)—so why now? After all, the agreement calls into question Israeli-Palestinian security cooperation and continued aid from donor countries (particularly the United States), just as the Palestinians are gaining momentum for international recognition of a Palestinian state. For Fatah, the agreement serves three purposes. First, it ensures that its agenda, a state in the West Bank and Gaza Strip come September, is feasible. Just days ago, Prime Minister Salam Fayyad, the architect of Palestinian institution-building in preparation for statehood who will be forced to step down as part of the unity deal, stated that establishing a Palestinian state required an urgent end to Palestinian disunity. Second, it addresses the demands of the Palestinian people in the midst of the radical change sweeping the Arab world. Those who have protested in Ramallah and Gaza have not used "down with the regime" or "down with Israel" as their rallying call, but rather "the people want to end the split."

264

Third, it serves to reconnect Fatah with Gaza, where Fatah's operations have been all but erased by Hamas' grip on the territory. For Hamas, the reasons are also clear. First, the unrest in Syria threatens Hamas' operations and support base in Damascus, weakening its overall position. Second, Hamas was more comfortable with the mediation of the caretaker government in Egypt after its clear friction with the ousted President Hosni Mubarak, whose alliance with Abbas and opposition to the Muslim Brotherhood were well-documented. Reports that the new Egyptian government will permanently open the Gaza-Egypt border indicate the new tenor of the Hamas-Egypt relationship. Finally, just as Fatah seeks to gain a foothold in Gaza, Hamas seeks gain a foothold in the West Bank. The next several months will be critical as both factions compete for influence and political power in advance of the general elections for a president and parliament.

To be sure, while announcing that they have reached an agreement on five points—forming an interim government, convening elections, combining security forces, activating the Palestinian legislative council, and exchanging prisoners—there was no mention of any consensus as to how to pursue peace with Israel. However, there was a clear statement that the agreement would pave the way for the Palestinians to seek recognition of an independent Palestinian state along the 1967 Green Line at September's UNGA. In announcing the agreement, Hamas official Mahmoud Zahar stated "Our plan does not involve negotiations with Israel or recognizing it. It will be impossible for an interim government to take part in the peace process with Israel."184 The emphasis on an interim government is critical. Officials on both sides have emphasized that the unity agreement is intended to address internal Palestinian governance and set the stage for elections in less than one year, while the Palestinian Liberation Organization (PLO) headed by Mahmoud Abbas would continue to represent the Palestinian people in negotiations with Israel. Yet should the United Nations recognize a Palestinian state in September, the next Palestinian elections will be those of a state, which will have full authority (and responsibility) for both domestic

---

184 Khaled Abu Toameh, "'Unity Gov't Won't Take Part in Peace Talks,'" *The Jerusalem Post*, April 28, 2011, http://www.jpost.com/Middle-East/Unity-govt-wont-take-part-in-peace-talks.

and foreign affairs. As such, the new Palestinian government will be faced with a choice: negotiate with Israel, or fight it. Many members of the United Nations, especially some of the European countries, are not likely to move forward in recognizing a Palestinian state if they believe that the newly admitted member that includes Hamas is committed to the destruction of another member state, Israel.

Unfortunately, the possibility that a unity government might serve Israel's strategic interests has eluded Prime Minister Benjamin Netanyahu. His knee-jerk reaction to the Fatah-Hamas deal, stating that Fatah must choose between Israel and Hamas because there is "no possibility of peace with both," fundamentally misreads the implications of the agreement. In the past, Netanyahu has pointed to Palestinian disunity as a significant obstacle to a two-state solution. He cannot have it both ways. Just two weeks ago in Tunisia, PA President Mahmoud Abbas proved yet again that he is a partner for peace when he renounced violence and stated his clear opposition to a third intifada. With over 130 nations prepared to recognize a state under his leadership, and the United Nations, IMF, and World Bank all endorsing the PA's preparedness for statehood, Abbas would not risk entering into an agreement with Hamas unless he felt it would advance, rather than hinder, this statehood effort, the viability of which depends on continuing Israeli cooperation. Furthermore, Abbas' remarks against violence were not made to the western media in English, but to the Arab world in Arabic—he understands that a renewal of violence will inflict a major setback to Palestinian national aspirations and severely undercut the considerable progress they have made toward achieving them in the past two years. Meanwhile, by entering a unity government, Hamas has indirectly taken on a significant level of responsibility. A renewal of violence from Gaza would seriously impede Palestinian statehood efforts, in addition to halting international financing of Palestinian projects, to the detriment of Hamas' political standing in Palestine. In this context, the unity agreement is a renewed challenge for Hamas to behave in a responsible way.

But Netanyahu's quick dismissal of the agreement signals that he did not read the agreement for what it is: a potentially significant shift in the Palestinian political dynamic in preparation for independence. Instead, Netanyahu seized the announcement as a political tool to shift away the pressure that had been building on him to announce a peace initiative of his own. Indeed, the pressure for now has shifted to the Palestinians, who are being watched closely by the international community to see if this deal holds and if it will lead to responsible governance. However, while the sudden shift of attention away from Netanyahu may be welcome to the Prime Minister now, it may not be long before attention returns to his government. In fact, should the Palestinian unity agreement hold without a renewal of violence, as Khaled Meshal, Hamas' political guru, suggested during the signing ceremony of the reconciliation agreement, the Palestinians will be in an even stronger position to gain international recognition for a state of their own.

Although from the Israeli perspective Hamas must first meet the Quartet's three conditions that it renounces violence, recognizes Israel, and accepts past agreements before Israel can engage Hamas, it is not likely that Hamas will accept all of these requirements in advance of the Palestinian elections other than informally halting all violent activities against Israel. In fact, Russia's hailing of the agreement, and EU Foreign Policy Chief Catherine Ashton's statement that she would "study" the deal, suggests that members of the Quartet may be weakening their demands. Indeed, only one condition should matter going forward: a complete cessation and permanent renunciation of violence by Hamas as a means by which to achieve Palestinian statehood. This would signal the unified Palestinian polity's willingness to negotiate with Israel, and could ultimately produce the recognition and lasting peace agreement that both sides profess to seek. Instead of dismissing the report of unity, Israel should join other nations in studying it, and should signal its readiness to welcome a change of attitude on the part of Hamas to permanently renounce violence and annul the clause that calls for the destruction of Israel from its Charter. However, just as the Israelis have every right to demand that the Palestinian unity government permanently rule out all forms of violence, they must recognize that such a government should be able to recognize Israel, defined by mutually acceptable borders as the result of a negotiated accord, not as a precondition to talking.

The United States should respond similarly. The Israeli-Palestinian peace process in the past two years based on a two-state solution was not possible without the inclusion of Hamas—who could undermine peace talks at any time with renewed violence—and the blockade policy of Gaza has worked to entrench Israel's isolation, not Hamas'. The United States should recognize that Hamas is unlikely to accept the Quartet's conditions, although challenging these conditions amounts to a misguided policy. After all, many figures in Fatah today view their own recognition of Israel in 1993, prior to a final peace agreement, as a strategic mistake for which they have paid dearly. The United States should lead by example, and encourage Israel to follow, by challenging Hamas to utilize unity to demonstrate that a Palestinian state with a unified government will be a responsible member of the international community seeking to coexist in peace alongside Israel.

The reconciliation agreement between Fatah and Hamas—should it withstand the test of time—offers Israel and Hamas the opportunity to face what they have denied each other for nearly three decades. Hamas must accept Israel's reality not only because it will never be able to destroy Israel, but because if it ever poses a real danger to Israel, it will be destroyed first. Conversely, Israel must accept a nonviolent Hamas as an integral part of the Palestinian community because without Hamas' active participation, no Israeli-Palestinian peace agreement based on a two-state solution is sustainable.

THE PALESTINIAN AUTHORITY: STRATEGIC MOVES ON THE INTERNATIONAL FRONT

OCTOBER 31, 2012

The stalled Israeli-Palestinian peace negotiations and the lack of prospects for their resumption anytime soon have persuaded the PA to chart its own course by applying to the UNGA as a nonvoting member state. However uncertain the prospect of such a move may be from the PA's perspective, there is very little to lose at this juncture and perhaps much to gain in taking such a unilateral step.

The Palestinians are counting on Israel's increasing isolation in the international community and the overwhelming political support for their cause, which is also the official policy of the United States.[185] The forthcoming elections in the United States as well as in Israel, regardless of their outcomes, will provide the Palestinians with an opportunity to thrust the nearly forgotten Palestinian problem into the Israeli and American political agendas while ensuring that the conflict returns to the forefront of the international community's attention.

From the Palestinian standpoint, the Netanyahu government does not want to negotiate in earnest and does not believe in seeking a resolution to the conflict based on a two-state solution. They point to the continuing expansion of existing settlements and the building of new ones as evidence of this. Moreover, the fact that Israel refuses to accept, after four years of calm, a renewed freeze on settlements, a release of additional prisoners, broader freedoms of movement and its acquiescence to the settlers' harassment of Palestinians, suggests that the Israeli government only talks about a two-state solution but has no intention of preparing the groundwork to achieve such an outcome. The recent union of Netanyahu's Likud Party with Yisrael

---

185 Ethan Bronner, "Netanyahu Responds Icily to Obama Remarks," *The New York Times*, May 19, 2011, http://www.nytimes.com/2011/05/20/world/middleeast/20mideast.html?partner=rss&emc=rss.

Beiteinu, led by Foreign Minister Avigdor Lieberman,[186] seriously suggests that the new Israeli coalition government will be led by Netanyahu, and will hold onto even more extremist views than the current one, which will further diminish any hope for achieving a peaceful solution if the political dynamics are frozen in place.

In addition, a growing majority of Palestinians believe that many Israelis have given up on the prospect of a two-state solution, as they have taken several one-sided actions in the past, including the unilateral withdrawal from Gaza and the expropriation of Palestinian land. Even now Israel is considering further unilateral actions, as was recently suggested by Defense Minister Ehud Barak who proposed withdrawing from 60 percent of the West Bank.[187] From the Palestinian standpoint, Israel's contemplation of taking these steps further justifies unilateral action on their part while being assured that their quest to become a nonvoting member in the UNGA is guaranteed to pass by an overwhelming majority.

From the Israeli perspective, the regional turmoil in the wake of the Arab Spring, the Iranian threat, the PA's refusal to negotiate unconditionally and the notion that the Palestinians do not really seek peace has made it impossible to restart negotiations as the outcome may prove to be as futile as previous peace talks. Moreover, Israel does not trust the Palestinians to negotiate in good faith and certainly does not believe they will adhere to any agreement that may be reached. The Netanyahu government further insists that as long as Palestinian extremists (i.e., Hamas, Islamic Jihad, and others) continue to advocate the ultimate destruction of Israel, there is hardly any point in discussing peace negotiations, particularly when the Palestinian public is continuously being fed this narrative. In addition, Israel maintains that as long as the Palestinians remain politically divided between Hamas and Fatah, any agreement that may be reached will be torpedoed by extremist Palestinian factions with the support of outside players such as Iran.

---

186 Yoel Goldman, "Liberman Says Plans for Joint Knesset Run with Likud Began a Year Ago," *The Times of Israel*, October 26, 2012, http://www.timesofisrael.com/liberman-says-plans-for-merger-with-likud-began-a-year-ago/.

187 "Barak Floats Unilateral Israeli Withdrawal in West Bank," *BBC News*, September 24, 2012, http://www.bbc.co.uk/news/world-middle-east-19700213.

The passage of the Palestinian application to the UNGA will undoubtedly carry a big price tag. It could, for instance, instigate Israel to impose greater restrictions of movement in the West Bank, withhold collected taxes from the PA,[188] restrict trade between Israel and the West Bank, accelerate the expansion of settlements, and even annex additional Palestinian territory and institute harsher policies in order to put greater pressure on the Palestinians. In addition, since the United States does not support unilateralism from either the Israelis or the Palestinians, it may take punitive action against the Palestinians including the cutting, at least temporarily, of financial aid and political support by other countries that the United States can exert influence on.

The advantages, however, outweigh the disadvantages. The Palestinians' unilateral action is consistent with the upheavals sweeping the Middle East. The message of the Arab Spring has not been lost on the Palestinians. If Arab youth are dying by the tens of thousands in Syria and elsewhere to gain freedom, why should they continue to live under occupation? The pressure of the restive Palestinian youth on the PA to act is mounting, leaving President Abbas little choice but to do so before he loses what is left of his legitimacy. Thus, UNGA membership will internationalize the Palestinian cause and provide transparent support by the international community that will have a propelling political effect. Moreover, regardless of who wins in the U.S. and Israeli elections, the victors will have to confront this new reality and can no longer ignore it without repercussions. Finally, the main advantage is that it thrusts the Israeli-Palestinian conflict back into the spotlight, forcing the international community, especially the United States, to take a new look and push to restart the negotiations with an end game clearly in sight.

For Israel, the Palestinian move will force Israel to face a new reality, which will inherently engender overwhelming pressure from the international community to support and act on a two-state solution. Even if the United States objects to the proposed Palestinian UNGA membership quest (which is all but assured), the prospective support

---

188 George Hale, "Why The Palestinian Authority Is Broke," *The Daily Beast*, October 25, 2012, http://www.thedailybeast.com/articles/2012/10/25/why-the-palestinian-authority-is-broke.html.

of the majority of the European Community in particular will lend the Palestinians a major moral and practical victory that no Israeli government can afford to dismiss. No matter what measures Israel takes to retaliate against the move, it will not provide Israel with any meaningful advantage, as the entire peace process will assume a new momentum and Israel's international isolation will be exacerbated. Regardless of the political makeup set to emerge following the U.S. and Israeli elections, the Israeli-Palestinian conflict will become front and center for both countries, forcing them to deal with this new reality which Israel is assiduously trying to prevent.

How Israel and the United States handle the aftermath of the Palestinians' UN membership could dramatically advance the peace process, provided that the new U.S. administration commits to becoming directly involved in mediation and remains persistent and consistent. If the Israelis simply retaliate against the Palestinians and the U.S. acquiesces, the situation will become extremely more volatile and dangerous. The United States needs to reign in both sides in order to stop the potential deterioration and come up with a practical framework, using the Palestinians' new standing as an opportunity to constructively push the process forward. To that end, the United States should advance its own framework for peace based on prior negotiated agreements reached between Israel and the Palestinians in previous negotiations in 2000 and 2007/2008. The United States must employ both coercive and interest-based strategies to pressure both the Israelis and the Palestinians to make the necessary concessions to reach an agreement.

Notwithstanding Israeli and American objections to the Palestinians' move, it may well unfreeze the peace process or at a minimum demonstrate whether the Israeli and Palestinian claims to seeking a viable two-state solution are mere political posturing or based on an honest desire to end the conflict. Indeed, the changing political dynamics resulting from the Palestinian bid can be turned into an advantage for Israel as well. It will keep the two-state solution alive which ultimately is in Israel's best interest, provided that vision and realism prevail and the new emerging opportunity is not squandered.

PALESTINIANS' UN BID FOR OBSERVER STATE STATUS: WILL IT ADVANCE OR STIFLE THE PEACE PROCESS?

NOVEMBER 13, 2012

There are furious discussions and commentaries being made by top officials from the United States, Europe, Israel, and the PA on the wisdom of the Palestinians' attempt to upgrade their status in the UN from a non-Member Observer Entity to a non-Member Observer State. What the consequences would be for the Palestinians and the peace process resulting from such a move remains to be seen. Regardless of the pros and cons, the frozen Israeli-Palestinian peace process must be defrosted. Whether or not this is the opportune time for the Palestinians' bid remains subject to varied speculations. However, one thing must be clear: the status quo is not sustainable and a new dynamic must be introduced to prevent dire consequences for both the Israelis and the Palestinians.

The efforts to postpone or prevent the Palestinians' UN bid on the premise that such a move will undermine future peace negotiations does not hold much water, as the peace negotiations have been frozen since 2010 and the prospect of their resumption is not in sight. Speaking to reporters in Tel Aviv, U.S. Ambassador to Israel, Dan Shapiro, implored the Palestinians to go to the negotiating table: "This is the only way it [the conflict] can be addressed, so I am certain we will continue to look for opportunities to bring the parties together and try to resolve the conflict together, through direct negotiations."[189] The irony is that there was hardly any progress made to mitigate the Israeli-Palestinian conflict in the past three years, and to "look for opportunities to

---

189 Tovah Lazaroff, "Barak: Palestinian UN Bid Must be Delayed," *Jerusalem Post*, November 8, 2012, http://www.jpost.com/Diplomacy-and-Politics/Barak-Palestinian-UN-bid-must-be-delayed.

bring the parties together"[190] seems hollow, as one has to wonder what opportunities he is talking about when the peace process continues to languish.

The two-state solution has become increasingly more rhetorical and loses significant impetus every day that passes with Israelis and Palestinians speculating, as the creeping one-state "solution" gains more credence. The Israelis have become increasingly more complacent, satisfied to live with the status quo of no peace and no violence while the ground underneath them is gradually shifting toward a one-state solution with ominous consequences for both the Israelis and the Palestinians. The Palestinians are counting on the growing international support for their cause while demographics are shifting in their favor. Current and future Israeli governments will have to choose, sooner rather than later, between a true democracy with a sustainable Jewish majority or an apartheid state. Many Israelis already consider the policies of the Netanyahu government toward the Palestinians apartheid-like, which are utterly inconsistent with the Jewish moral values that are central to Israel's very survival.[191]

In a previous article,[192] I supported the Palestinian UN bid not only because of the slim prospect of resuming the negotiations "unconditionally" (as Prime Minister Netanyahu demands), which is a condition in and of itself, but precisely because without changing the dynamic of the conflict there will be no progress to the detriment of both sides. To persuade the Palestinians to hold off on their UN bid, they should be provided with an idea as to what they can realistically expect if they were to agree to either postponement or withdrawal of their planned application. The international Quartet's special envoy to the Middle East, Tony Blair, is correct in arguing that "We have to understand the position the Palestinians find themselves in. It is all about the credibility of the

190 Ibid.

191 Gabe Fisher, "Controversial Survey Ostensibly Highlights Widespread Anti-Arab Attitudes in Israel," *The Times of Israel*, October 23, 2012, http://www.timesofisrael.com/survey-highlights-anti-arab-attitudes-in-israel/.

192 "The Palestinian Authority: Strategic Moves on the International Front," [page 269].

steps toward statehood. It is very much in our interest to offer them [the Palestinians] a way forward that allow us, one way or the other, to get back to the negotiating table."[193]

Those countries or individuals who are asking the Palestinians to wait until the new Obama administration gets its bearings, or after the Israeli election as Israel's Defense Minister Ehud Barak recently suggested, are not saying what will in fact happen should the Palestinians decide to wait. The failure of the Obama administration to come up with any credible plans for the past two years offers no hope to the Palestinians that there will be significant progress in sight. Other than issuing statements in support of a two-state solution and urging both sides to resume negotiations, the Obama administration left the Israelis and the Palestinians to their own devices. While the Netanyahu government continued to expand the settlements, the Palestinians conditioned the resumption of the negotiations on freezing the very same settlements, making the situation increasingly more intractable. As German Foreign Minister Guido Westerwelle (whose country stands behind Israel) aptly put it a few days ago, "As the whole of the E.U., we share the view that the settlement policy is a hindrance to the peace process."[194]

That said, the Palestinians must keep in mind that their quest to become an observer state must be promoted as a vehicle to advance the peace process rather than as a tool to threaten or undermine Israel's international standing. Abbas Zaki, member of the Central Committee of Fatah, was quoted by the Jerusalem Post a few days ago as saying that "Once the status of a Palestinian state is upgraded, the Palestinians would be able to pursue Israel for 'war crimes' in the international criminal court." He went on to say, "We will go to all U.N. agencies to force the international community to take legal

---

193 Crispian Balmer, "Obama Win Opens Way for New Mideast Push: Blair," *Reuters*, November 7, 2012, http://www. reuters.com/article/2012/11/07/us-palestinians-israel-blair-idUSBRE8A61M320121107.

194 "Europe Condemns Israel's OK for New Settler Homes," *Associated Press*, November 7, 2012, http://www.ynetnews.com/articles/0,7340,L-4302623,00.html.

actions against Israel."[195] This is not the kind of message that the PA wants to convey to the outside world, especially if they want to court the support of the EU.

One other significant point that could undermine the Palestinians' draft resolution to the UN is the phrase that relates to the delineated borders on which to base the negotiations. In three different passages the document "reaffirms the right of the Palestinian people to self-determination and to independence in their State of Palestine on the basis of the pre-1967 borders"[196] [emphasis added]. This particular phrasing is especially troubling to many EU members as it could also mean going back to the UN partition plans of 1947, which is a non-starter. A top Palestinian official told me that this could readily be amended to read instead "the June 4th cease fire line of 1967," which is universally accepted as the basis for any future peace negotiations.

The EU is currently divided between those who object to the PA bid (led by Germany), those who tend to support it (led by France), those who seek to delay it (led by Britain), and those who will abstain because they do not wish to irk either the United States or Israel. Although the Palestinians can garner the endorsement of at least 115 countries, significant support from the EU matters greatly and such reckless statements by Zaki may well alienate several key European states that would otherwise support the Palestinian bid.

The two-state solution based on the 1967 borders of necessity requires an end to Israel's constant encroachment on Palestinian territory. The concept of a two-state solution otherwise loses what is left of its meaning or credibility. PA President Abbas is correct in insisting that a freeze on all settlement expansion should precede the resumption of peace negotiations. If this requirement is to be dropped as demanded by the Netanyahu government, however,

195 Khaled Abu Toameh, "Fatah: Oslo Accords Will Cease to Exist After UN Bid," *Jerusalem Post*, November 8, 2012, http://www.jpost.com/Middle-East/Fatah-Oslo-Accords-will-cease-to-exist-after-UN-bid.

196 "Palestinians Seek New U.N. Status as Observer State," *USA Today*, November 8, 2012, http://www.usatoday.com/story/news/world/2012/11/08/palestinians-un-status/1692837/.

Netanyahu must also relinquish his condition of "unconditionality" and agree to establish credible rules of engagement, as no serious negotiations can take place on an open-ended basis.

Thus, to persuade the Palestinians to postpone or drop their bid, a credible third party such as the United States must come forward with a framework for negotiations. Such a framework must include a mutually-agreed upon agenda with specific conflicting issues to be discussed and a sequence of implementation, coupled with a time-frame to instill confidence in the deliberations and allow for concessions to be made by both sides in order to reach an agreement. The duration of the negotiations should be established in advance to persuade the Palestinians that although Israel may continue to expand certain settlements during the negotiating period, it will make little difference in changing the reality on the ground. Ideally, the negotiations should first start by negotiating the borders, which will define the future parameters of the Palestinian state.

Whether or not the Palestinians accept such a compromise or decide to proceed with their UN bid, they have already managed to change the dynamic of the conflict. The Obama administration should seize the opportunity to break the impasse by using its leverage on both sides and insist on meaningful peace negotiations that can bring an end to a nearly century-long conflict.

THE PALESTINIANS MUST WAKE UP TO THEIR BITTER REALITY

JANUARY 15, 2013

Although repeated polls taken in the West Bank and Gaza consistently show that a majority of Palestinians support a two-state solution, their leadership has failed miserably to capitalize on this unmistakable consensus.[197] Instead, Fatah, Hamas, and a score of other small factions have over several decades been engaged in unending infighting, political intrigue, corruption, and blind ideological rivalries while feeding the public false information about Israel, promising what they know they were and still are unable to deliver. The question is: for how much longer must the Palestinians live with subterfuge, humiliation, and the indignities of occupation before their leaders wake up to the reality that an Israeli-Palestinian peace requires significant concessions, uncompromised credibility, and an unshakable commitment to enduring peace?

Although PA President Mahmoud Abbas has demonstrated consistency and keenness in the search for peace, he too remains a prisoner of a decades-long Palestinian narrative insisting on, among other demands, the "right of return" of the refugees, which is a complete nonstarter for any Israeli government. Concurrently, Hamas continues to resist the existence of Israel, knowing full well that seriously threatening Israel will be at its own peril. By way of example, Hamas' political guru Khaled Meshal said the following in Gaza early December 2012 on the occasion of Hamas' founding celebration: "Palestine is ours from the river to the sea and from the south to the north. There will be no concession on any inch of the land."[198]

---

197 "PPC: Palestinian Public Opinion Polling June 2012," Palestinian Peace Coalition, June 2012, http://www.geneva-accord.org/mainmenu/ppc-polling-june-2012.

198 Steven Erlanger, "Leader Celebrates Founding of Hamas With Defiant Speech," *The New York Times*, December 8, 2012, http://www.nytimes.

Many Palestinians and Israelis dismiss such a statement as nothing more than political posturing designed for domestic consumption. Even if this was the case, however, there is a much larger Palestinian constituency whose anti-Israeli sentiment and hatred tends to become more potent as a result of such statements. Moreover, this gives right-of-center Israelis further ammunition to justify their increasing entrenchments in the territories, making matters worse for both sides. The fact that Meshal, in an earlier interview with Christiane Amanpour, said "I accept a Palestinian state according to 1967 borders with Jerusalem as the capital, with the right to return"[199] is of little comfort to the Israelis who view Hamas as an irredeemable terrorist organization bent on Israel's destruction.

Caught in the cycle of this viciously irresponsible and destructive public narrative, President Abbas, who undoubtedly seeks a peace agreement based on the 1967 borders, is unfortunately a victim of the acrimonious rhetoric and violent actions promoted by reckless militant Palestinian leaders. Following a visit to the city of Safed in Israel in November 2012, Abbas was vehemently condemned by Palestinians from all quarters when he said: "I visited Safed before once but I want to see Safed. It's my right to see it, but not to live there." Referring to the internationally-recognized pre-1967 border, he went on to say: "Palestine now for me is '67 borders, with East Jerusalem as its capital. This is now and forever...This is Palestine for me. I am a refugee, but I am living in Ramallah. I believe that the West Bank and Gaza is Palestine and the other parts are Israel."[200] Abbas' courage is admirable, but sadly he does not have the public support and the mandate he needs to change public perception on issues such as "the right of return," which has over the decades become embedded in the public psyche, even though it will never come to pass.

---

com/2012/12/09/world/middleeast/khaled-meshal-hamas-leader-delivers-defiant-speech-on-anniversary-celebration.html?_r=0.

199 Khaled Meshaal, interview by Christiane Amanpour, *CNN*, November 21, 2012, http://edition.cnn.com/TRANSCRIPTS/1211/21/ampr.01.html.

200 Harriet Sherwood, "Mahmoud Abbas Outrages Palestinian Refugees by Waiving his Right to Return," *The Guardian*, November 4, 2012, http://www.theguardian.com/world/2012/nov/04/mahmoud-abbas-palestinian-territories.

To make matters worse, the Palestinians in the West Bank, especially on the local level and in Gaza, continue to characterize Israel as the ultimate enemy and malign it in schools and in many public places. Moreover, they offer nothing but empty slogans and false hope to the young and old about Israel's ultimate demise while prolonging the miserable existence of millions of Palestinians with no end in sight.

The PA's successful efforts to obtain nonmember observer state status at the UNGA and the emergence of Hamas' politically advantageous stance in the wake of the latest flare-up with Israel, coupled with the current negotiations between the two sides to form a unity government, all offer Hamas a momentous opportunity to abandon violent resistance from a relative position of strength. In any event, should the unity discussions prove successful under the leadership of Abbas, he should not expect to enter into peace negotiations with Israel until the "united Palestinian government" commits itself to nonviolence in order to achieve a peace agreement.

The collective body of the Palestinians needs to demonstrate its commitment to a peaceful resolution. They must enhance their credibility in the eyes of the Israeli public. Indeed, even Israeli liberal/centrist governments, led by Barak and Olmert, respectively, could not conclude peace because of the Palestinians' lack of credibility and unwillingness to sign a final agreement to permanently end the conflict.[201] The Israelis point to Yasser Arafat, who refused to do so when the opportunity presented itself at Camp David in 2000.

Just as the Israelis must stop the settlement enterprise to establish their credibility and commitment to a two-state solution, the Palestinians must also disabuse the Israelis of their belief that the Palestinians ultimately seek the destruction of their state. Here is where the big dilemma lies, although it is not insurmountable. On the one hand, the Palestinian public has been indoctrinated to view Israel as

201 Robert Malley and Hussein Agha, "Camp David: The Tragedy of Errors," *The New York Review of Books*, August 9, 2001, http://www.nybooks.com/articles/archives/2001/aug/09/camp-david-the-tragedy-of-errors/?pagination=false; and Diego Baliani, "After Annapolis' Failure: The Chances of the Israeli-Palestinian Peace Process in the Light of Hamas' Control of Gaza," International Institute for Counter-Terrorism, March 23, 2009, http://www.ict.org.il/Articles/tabid/66/Articlsid/673/currentpage/8/Default.aspx.

a temporary phenomenon, that its demise is inevitable, and that the continuing suffering and sacrifices will eventually be handsomely rewarded. It does not appear, however, that this day of redemption will come any time soon, if ever. In the interim, Israel continues to expand current as well as build new settlements, and the Palestinian refugees continue to languish in camps while their leaders keep asking them to make more and more sacrifices, as if three generations of suffering is not enough.

Meshal, Hamas' Prime Minister Ismail Haniyeh, and other lost souls continue to preach the gospel of death. They should know that there is no glory in martyrdom, no salvation in death, no hope in illusions, and no future in a bankrupt ideology. It is time for the Palestinians to rise up against this madness and the mendacity of their so-called leaders who have led them astray, using and abusing them solely for self-gratification under the guise of a higher purpose. Truth and human decency have been lost to the zealots, the bloodthirsty militant Palestinians who robbed their own brothers and sisters of a life with dignity.

The Palestinian people must decide if they want to live in peace and freedom, or if they want to continue to despair for another 65 years. Israel is a reality; it exists and will continue to exist for as far as the eye can see. Only peace, genuine and lasting, will end the indignities and deprivation and usher in a prosperous future that the Palestinians deserve. I have advocated to the Israeli academic community and student bodies to rise up against their misguided leaders and reach an agreement with the Palestinians; I believe it is time for young Palestinian men and women to also engage in collective peaceful civil disobedience and demand from their leaders an end to the Israeli-Palestinian conflict and to stop misleading the public by making promises that they can never deliver.[202] Palestinian women can be of special importance if they resolve en masse to defy through peaceful demonstration the debilitating and unforgiving status quo, akin to the protests led by Catholic and Protestant women in Northern Ireland that changed the face of the conflict and ultimately helped lead to its resolution.

---

202 "Israelis Must Rise Up To Avert National Disaster," [page 202].

It is time for Palestinian youth, especially those affiliated with Hamas, to heed the example of such figures as Gandhi, Mandela (after abandoning armed struggle), and Martin Luther King Jr. to forsake violence as a political tool and protest by the hundreds of thousands to proclaim their right to human decency, a better future, and a life with dignity. It is time for young and innocent Palestinians to have a real sense of belonging and purpose, to feel safe and secure, and to grow up as free men and women with all the potential that a free society can offer. It is time to end the invocation of religion as a tool to subjugate and to enslave; rather, it should be used to liberate and offer guidance for a better and more wholesome life. President Abbas, the most moderate and courageous Palestinian leader, needs the public to rally behind him to provide him with the political cover and mandate to make the necessary concessions to achieve peace, and in so doing, force Israel's hand to seek a genuine and viable two state-solution.

In the final analysis, all sides from militant to moderate must take a hard look at what they are doing and preaching to avoid a major confrontation with Israel, from which neither side can expect to emerge with any significant gains. The situation has fallen to an alarmingly low point that has allowed minority extremists to assume and steer the political agenda while marginalizing moderate voices.

It is imperative, therefore, for the Palestinians to begin to develop a culture of civil disobedience and collective nonviolent resistance. They must demand the truth from their leaders and no longer fall prey to the cynicism and doubletalk of militant leaders who have been riding on their backs in the name of national salvation while ravaging their lives for so long.

FATAH AND HAMAS RECONCILIATION: RUSHING TO JUDGMENT

MAY 1, 2014

Characterizing the Fatah-Hamas unity, or rather reconciliation, agreement as helpful or harmful to the Israeli-Palestinian peace process is premature at best. Determining the viability or the lack thereof in such an agreement must first be examined in the context of Hamas' changing state of affairs and the status of the Israeli-Palestinian peace negotiations.

The fact that two similar agreements failed to materialize in the past does not suggest that this one will necessarily meet the same fate. My understanding is that both Fatah and Hamas have concluded that unlike past agreements, the new accord is essential to adjust to the changing dynamics in the region and their bilateral relations.

Hamas was motivated by a number of factors, including the extremely difficult task of meeting Palestinian needs in Gaza, who are despairing with unemployment reaching nearly 40 percent,[203] substandard medical services and education, and a new generation living the daily indignities with little prospects for a better future.

Hamas has been cut off from Egypt as the new military-controlled government destroyed most tunnels, preventing the smuggling of goods to Gaza, which have in the past provided a financial lifeline to the Hamas government.

The turmoil in Syria and Hamas' decision to support the rebels deprived it of the political and logistic support that had been provided by the Assad regime. Moreover, because of the sanctions

---

203 Nidal al-Mughrabi, "Gaza's Economic Woes Pile Up, Unemployment Soars," *Reuters*, February 21, 2014, http://www.reuters.com/article/2014/02/21/us-palestinians-gaza-blockade-idUSBREA1K09R20140221.

imposed on Iran, Tehran has substantially reduced its financial aid and military supplies on which Hamas relied heavily in the past.[204]

The Israeli blockade of Gaza, though somewhat eased during the past two years, still prevents the free flow of goods, especially building materials, not to mention the extraordinary travel restrictions and the near-isolation of the Palestinians from the rest of the world.

Finally, Hamas' inability to challenge Israel militarily now and in the future has finally sunk in, leaving it to conclude that the only viable option left is joining Fatah in a bid to ease the financial pressure, enjoy, over time, greater political acceptance by the international community, and become an integral part of the peace process.

For the PA, the agreement with Hamas is accepting the inevitable: no peace agreement with Israel can be reached, fully implemented, and endure without the support of Hamas. For Abbas, since the peace negotiations have thus far made hardly any progress, he concluded that he stands to risk little by reaching out to Hamas, consolidating his role as the leader of all Palestinians while gaining wide Palestinian political support.

With Hamas, the PA will be in a position to present a united front, prevent Israel from continuing its policy of "divide and conquer," deny Israel's claim that there is no partner with whom to negotiate, strengthen its mandate to govern, and gain, over time, enhanced international support.

Finally, given Hamas' diminishing popularity, Fatah is more than likely to emerge as the winner in the elections, scheduled to take place within a few months. For Hamas, other than easing the financial pressure, joining the Arab fold appears to trump its policy of violent resistance toward Israel.

Abbas' assessment of the Israeli reaction was on target. Notwithstanding Netanyahu's decision to suspend the negotiations, which are already moribund, and his threats to squeeze the PA financially, Netanyahu wants to prevent the collapse of the PA. He is terrified

204 Adnan Abu Amer, "Iran Resumes Monetary Aid to Hamas," *Al Monitor*, March 24, 2014, http://www.al-monitor.com/pulse/originals/2014/03/iran-hamas-finance-economy-resistance-axis-gaza.html#.

of being forced to assume the financial and security burden of over 2.5 million Palestinians in the West Bank.

Although the United States expressed disappointment with Abbas' surprise decision to reconcile with Hamas, the Obama administration will, too, find it extremely difficult to punish the PA as such punishment, including withholding financial assistance, will not only scuttle what is left of the peace process but damage its ability to influence the PA in the future.

Netanyahu's insistence that Abbas must chose to make peace with either Israel or with Hamas is disingenuous at best. For Netanyahu, the reconciliation agreement is heaven-sent; it gave him a timely opportunity to end the negotiations over a two-state solution to which he has never subscribed, while conveniently blaming the PA.

Netanyahu and most of his coalition partners do not want to even entertain the idea that Hamas can moderate its position, and refuse to consider that time and circumstances have brought this about. Israel itself precipitated much of this change, but is now refusing to accept the results of its own policies.

Indeed, regardless of Hamas' current political posture toward Israel, its leaders know full well that they cannot now or at any time in the future pose an existential threat to Israel. They cannot stay outside the main political currents, which potentially bear significant developments in months and years to come, and they know that there is no other viable alternative if they choose to remain relevant.

Yes, Hamas was rightfully designated as a terrorist organization by Israel, the United States, and the EU, but so was the PLO less than two decades ago. The changing political conditions and the reality on the ground forced the PLO to change its stance toward Israel, which eventually led to canceling the articles in the PLO charter that denied Israel's right to exist on April 24, 1996.[205]

In fact, Hamas' position and its precondition to establish peace with Israel is not much different than the current PA stand. Hamas'

---

205 "The Palestinian National Charter," *Israel Ministry of Foreign Affairs*, July 17, 1968, (accessed April 28, 2014), http://www.israel.org/mfa/foreignpolicy/peace/guide/pages/the%20palestinian%20national%20charter.aspx.

political guru Khaled Meshal told CNN in November 2012 what he has stated twice before: "I accept a Palestinian state according [to] the 1967 borders, with Jerusalem as the capital, with the right to return."[206]

Moreover, even though Israel considers Hamas to be a terrorist organization and has blockaded Gaza for the past nine years, it has been dealing and negotiating directly and indirectly with Hamas on many fronts including prisoner exchanges, trade in both directions, and the exchange of some information to prevent accidental flare-ups.

Instead of rejecting outright the reconciliation agreement, both Israel and the United States should encourage Hamas to take additional steps to demonstrate its intentions and ask friends of Hamas, such as Turkey, to persuade Hamas to change its public posture toward Israel.

In this regard, Hamas may well be persuaded to embrace the Arab Peace Initiative (API), which offers Israel a comprehensive Arab-Israeli peace based almost exactly on the same provisions that both the PA and Hamas are demanding.

This would allow Hamas to return to the Arab states' fold without losing face, and allow the United States and the EU to remove Hamas from their terrorism lists.

It should be noted that the reconciliation agreement between Hamas and the PA requires Hamas to refrain from calling for Israel's destruction, not provoke Israel, and prevent other Palestinian extremists from provoking Israel, which Hamas has, in any case, been doing for the past three years.

To be sure, the idea behind the unity agreement is for Hamas to become an integral part of the Palestinian body politic and permanently abandon violent resistance to the Israeli occupation in favor of peaceful political resistance.

The latest unity agreement at this particular juncture will more than likely survive and offers new opportunities for the United States and Israel to build on it rather than dismiss it. Hamas and the

---

206 "Mashaal: I Accept a Palestinian State on '67 Borders," *Jerusalem Post*, November 22, 2012, http://www.jpost.com/Middle-East/Mashaal-I-accept-a-Palestinian-state-on-67-borders.

Palestinians in Gaza are a fact of life and for the United States and Israel to choose to be oblivious to their existence is not only short-sighted but dangerously misguided.

Indeed, neither the United States nor Israel could wish Hamas away. Both will have to deal with Hamas as long as it moderates its ways and challenges Israel to make peace rather than challenging its right to exist.

CHARTING A NEW COURSE

JUNE 4, 2014

The success or failure of the newly-established Palestinian unity government rests on its ability and willingness to chart a new course in its relations with Israel and its commitment to peace. Having Hamas as a partner in this government is critical for two reasons: the Palestinians can now present a united front, and Hamas may have finally come to terms with the reality of Israel.

While the road ahead remains cluttered with many logistical, political, and ideological differences, it offers a historic opportunity to reach a breakthrough in future peace negotiations with Israel. The fact that the new government was recognized by a majority of the international community gives it the opportunity not only to unite the Palestinians, but to make genuine efforts to realize their long-held dream of establishing an independent state.

To that end, the unity government must begin by addressing the most critical issues that have blunted the Palestinians' efforts in the past to realize the two-state solution.

There is probably nothing more relevant to the success of the unity government than earning the trust of the Israeli public. The government must recognize that the average Israeli believes that the Palestinians do not seek real peace and are still committed to Israel's destruction. As a result, Israelis have resigned themselves to live with the status quo. The lack of imminent threats, the absence of terrorist attacks, and the economic boom have further removed any sense of urgency to change anything.

Nevertheless, Israelis remain security-conscious and will support any government on the question of national security. Indeed, regardless of how powerful the Israeli military is, the public still feels insecure; this goes back to its collective historical experience. This state of mind makes the Israelis extremely sensitive and inflexible on matters of national security, and the unity government would be wise to take this aspect of the Israelis' psychological vulnerability seriously.

Under any circumstances, the unity government must maintain its security cooperation with Israel, build on it, and maintain its credibility and commitment on matters of security. This is one area where the Israelis have praised the PA in the past for their full cooperation. Moreover, Palestinian internal security should do everything possible to prevent violent attacks against Israel from Gaza and the West Bank. The purpose here is to disabuse the Israeli public of the commonly-accepted dictum that the Palestinians cannot be trusted.

In this respect, regardless of how abhorrent some of the settlers' provocations may be, it would be extremely unwise on the part of the Palestinian government to engage in a tit-for-tat. The government, however, must condemn any premeditated acts of violence, as it has done in the past, to demonstrate to the Israeli public in particular that it takes Israel's security very seriously.

What I am suggesting is to engage in a diplomatic offensive with a focus on security, because threatening the use of or resorting to force against Israel has not worked and it will not work in the future. Israel is a formidable military power and is capable of dealing with any threat, regardless of its source and intensity.

Moreover, the Palestinians' worst enemy has been their own repeated public condemnations of Israel and their failure to distinguish between the public and the government's action and policy toward the Palestinians. It is critical that Palestinian officials tone down their public denunciation of Israel because as long as expressions of animosity and hatred are constantly leveled against Israel, it will only reinforce the Israelis' perception that the Palestinians were and remain the ultimate enemy.

Saeb Erekat, who is a member of the PLO Executive Committee and head of the Palestinian negotiating team no less, causes more damage to the Palestinian cause than any sworn enemy of the Palestinians because of his constant condemnation of Israel and irresponsible public statements. In the past two days alone, Erekat issued several statements including one under the title: "The Israeli government is celebrating 47 years of occupation and war crimes with the approval of thousands of new settlement units in the Occupied State of Palestine." Another is titled "Israel is marking 47 years of Israeli occupation: 'We are marking another year of occupation, oppression and colonization.'"

This particularly has had an adverse effect on the Palestinian cause as it plays into the hand of the Israeli government, especially the current one led by Netanyahu's right-of-center party, who would readily capitalize on the continuing (perceived or real) Palestinian enmity, regardless of its merit.

For this reason, the Palestinians need to drastically change their public narrative to demonstrate to the Israeli public, whose support of the peace process is central, that there is a genuine change of attitude in the pursuit of peace and that the Palestinians can be trusted, which is in their best interest.

Only the Palestinians can modify and subsequently change the Israelis' mindset. Only the Palestinians can make the Israelis understand that the status quo is not sustainable, because as bad as the occupation is for the Palestinians, its continuation will be worse for the Israelis.

The Palestinian government must capitalize on the different political ideologies in the Israeli coalition government. They must keep in mind that Netanyahu is not politically immune; he relies on a coalition government of four parties that give him a majority of 68 out of 120 Knesset members.

Two of these parties, Yesh Atid (led by Yair Lapid with 19 members) and Hatenua (led by Tzipi Livni with six members), are committed to reaching an agreement with the Palestinians. Even without the two Arab lists, there are four other parties in the opposition from the center and left. Those parties combined with Yesh Atid and Hatenua would total 52 members. After including the religious parties Shas and United Torah Judaism,[207] they would muster a solid majority of 70 members.[208]

---

207 Contrary to popular belief, the main political concern of the religious parties is the domestic and economic needs of its religious constituents, not settlement for ideological reasons in the West Bank.

208 "Current Members of the Nineteenth Knesset," *The Knesset*, http://www.knesset. gov.il/mk/eng/mkindex_current_eng.asp?view=1 (accessed May 28, 2014).

Netanyahu's rejection of the Palestinian unity government and his refusal to negotiate with it will only further isolate Netanyahu both domestically and internationally, as it stands in total contrast to the position of all major powers that are willing to give this government a chance to demonstrate its readiness to seriously negotiate with Israel.

Thus, it is immensely important for the Palestinian government to be cognizant of the fact that if it demonstrates determination to negotiate in earnest and is ready to make important concessions, and Netanyahu still refuses to negotiate faithfully, both Lapid and Livni are on record saying they would leave the government. This would open the door for new elections or the formation of a new coalition government that can actively pursue a peace agreement.

In an op-ed published in Time, Lapid stated that "Our goal was and remains to continue talks until an agreement is reached. But before that, we must know something very basic: with whom exactly are we talking?"[209]

Lapid was clearly alluding to the unity government and to what extent Hamas' commitment is to peace. The unity government must capitalize on the "fragility" of the Netanyahu government by demonstrating their readiness to end the conflict politically based on mutually accepted terms.

Finally, the unity government must now strive to earn and solidify the continuing American and EU support, which will depend on the Palestinians' keenness to adhere to the above points.

Furthermore, the Palestinian government can make it easier for Obama, who wants the unity government to succeed, by ensuring that Hamas embraces the API, which could offer both a face-saving way out for Hamas and a way for the United States to potentially remove Hamas from the terrorist list.

To be sure, the Palestinian unity government provides a historic opportunity to either advance peace and realize the long-hoped-for Palestinian state, or destroy any hope for the resumption of talks toward that end. What matters is the action the

---

209 Yair Lapid, "A Final Agreement Is Still Possible," *Time*, May 8, 2014, http://time.com/91886/a-final-agreement-is-still-possible/.

unity government takes, the public narrative it engages in, and how constructive a role Hamas will play.

All must be designed to persuade the Israeli public that time and circumstances have changed. Neither Israel nor the Palestinians can allow themselves to be prisoners of the past.

ISRAELI-PALESTINIAN NEGOTIATIONS

ISRAEL AND HAMAS:
AN UNTENABLE STATUS QUO

JULY 18, 2011

Israel and Hamas are currently locked in a perpetual standoff. Hamas is emboldened by the flurry of international attention on the situation in Gaza, despite the improved conditions following the ease of the blockade by Israel after the first flotilla episode and Egypt's opening of the border crossing. The Hamas-Fatah unity talks, currently on hold and in danger of collapse, have aided the transformation of the international perception of Hamas as a terror organization to that of a legitimate political party, alongside Hamas' refrain from violence against Israel. However, without an outright rejection of terror and recognition that Israel cannot be destroyed, Hamas' growth as a political force for the Palestinian people will remain limited and potentially mired in failure. Similarly, without Israel recognizing that lasting security is unlikely unless Hamas is included in the political process, efforts to advance a two-state solution will be fruitless. Overcoming these obstacles will require new thinking to find a formula that enables each side to save face in altering their positions to move forward in a political process.

Hamas has been strengthened by the international community increasingly discarding the notion that it is a terror organization

293

and realizing that it must, nevertheless, be brought into a political process if efforts to achieve regional peace and security are to succeed. The recent attempt to deliver aid via a second flotilla, (and when that failed, via a "fly-tilla") was not about delivering aid, but rather about demonstrating solidarity with the people in Gaza. Despite its failure to reach Gaza, the international attention paid to the activists in and of itself is a victory for Hamas' portrayal of the people of Gaza as innocent victims of cruel Israeli oppression. Gaza's economy jumped by 16 percent at the end of 2010 after Israel eased the blockade last summer, but nearly 70 percent of the population still relies on handouts and nearly half of the work force remains unemployed.[210] Today, the focus on Gaza is on the economic situation, not on Hamas' rejection of Israel's right to exist or its refusal to release captured Israeli Corporal Gilad Shalit.

Hamas has been further strengthened by the ongoing Palestinian unity talks, which it has entered into without relinquishing any of its avowed positions to oppose peace with the State of Israel. Hamas' chief, Khaled Meshal, has in the past told reporters that he would be willing to accept a two-state formula along the 1967 lines, but without taking any action to bring about conflict resolution. Meanwhile, Hamas members have denigrated international efforts to gain Palestinian statehood at the United Nations and remain fiercely opposed to Israel's existence. These inconsistent postures have enabled Hamas to navigate international circles with the aura of possibility that it could be a partner for peace, even without espousing a unified, clear position or easing its hardline stance as a "resistance movement" against Israel. This ambiguous posturing causes Hamas, like its partner in arms Hezbollah, to force Israel to spend disproportionately on defense and maintain a state of readiness with ever-escalating debilitating financial and human costs.

---

210 See Alisa Odenheimer, "West Bank Economy Grows 9% in First Half While Gaza Expands 16%, IMF Says," *Bloomberg*, September 14, 2010, http://www.bloomberg.com/news/2010-09-14/west-bank-economy-grows-9-in-first-half-while-gaza-expands-16-imf-says.html; and "Easing of Blockade Helps Gaza Economy," *Y Net News*, July 7, 2011, http://www.ynetnews.com/articles/0,7340,L-4091854,00.html.

However, Hamas' recent gains may be reaching an apex. First, the Hamas-Fatah unity agreement is in jeopardy today over Hamas' refusal to keep Salam Fayyad as prime minster and adopt a technocratic government that might be acceptable to the Palestinian Authority (PA)'s Western donors. A recent poll by the Palestinian Center for Policy and Survey Research indicated that 61 percent of Palestinians want "the new government of reconciliation to follow the peace policies and agendas of President Abbas and the PLO rather than Hamas'."[211] Another poll by the Center indicated that 45 percent prefer Salaam Fayyad to remain prime minister as opposed to only 22 percent support for Hamas' candidate, Jamal Khoudari.[212] Since nearly 60 percent of the Palestinian public expects the unity agreement to succeed, Hamas risks being blamed for its failure.

Furthermore, Hamas' recent downplaying of efforts to gain a unilateral declaration of statehood at the United Nations is inconsistent with Palestinian public opinion. A week ago, Hamas' Khalil al-Hayya called the plan for statehood a mere "mirage,"[213] but 65 percent of the Palestinians support the move.[214] Whereas unity talks were initially seen as a mechanism to improve the prospects of the UN move, Palestinians are increasingly realizing that Hamas could be placing the UN effort—and future international aid—in serious jeopardy. Finally, Hamas has been weakened by the uprising in Syria which has thrust its patron, Bashar Assad, in a fight for the survival of his regime, which has consistently provided political and logistical support for the organization and asylum to its leaders.

211 "Palestinian Public Opinion Poll No (40)," *Palestinian Center for Policy and Survey Research*, June 16-18, 2011, http://www.pcpsr.org/en/node/213.

212 "Survey: Majority of Palestinians Want Fayyad as Prime Minister," *Haaretz*, June 20, 2011, http://www.haaretz.com/news/diplomacy-defense/survey-majority-of-palestinians-want-fayyad-as-prime-minister-1.368749.

213 "Hamas Leader: Armed Resistance Best," *USA Today*, June 20, 2011, http://usatoday30.usatoday.com/news/world/2011-06-19-palestinian-leader-violence_n.htm.

214 "65% of Palestinians Support UN Statehood Bid, Poll Finds," *The Jerusalem Post*, June 28, 2011, http://www.jpost.com/Breaking-News/65-percent-of-Palestinians-support-UN-statehood-bid-poll-finds.

Most importantly, Hamas' growth is stuck between two realizations. The first realization is that under no circumstances can Israel be destroyed. Even more, Hamas knows that should it reengage in a campaign of terror against Israel, Jerusalem will not hesitate to respond by decapitating its leadership in an effort to wipe out the movement's core structure, regardless of the international condemnation that would likely follow. Furthermore, as long as Hamas wears the "terror group" label assigned to it by the Western world, its ability to shape the future of Palestine remains handicapped. The second realization is that Hamas knows that it too cannot be destroyed. Indeed, although Hamas' public support has been steadily declining during the past several years and it is unlikely to garner more than 25 percent of the votes if elections were held today, it remains a strong grassroots movement. Whether through a unity government or free and fair elections, Hamas and its ideology of "resistance" will persist as a potent force in the Palestinian body politic. The question facing Hamas today is how to reconcile these two contradictory realities: that the organization will endure, but its ultimate objective—the destruction of Israel—will never be fulfilled.

A similar question regarding Hamas faces Israel. While previous and current Israeli governments know that it can wipe out Hamas' leadership, it cannot destroy its ideology, and as long as it remains on the outside of the political process, it can spoil any Israeli efforts to advance negotiations with its rival Fatah. Israel has succeeded in containing Hamas' violent activity, including rocket attacks, due to its considerable deterrence, but it is at least in part constrained by the international opprobrium that has followed its blockade of Gaza, which has further served to strengthen Hamas' position in the international arena.

The result of this policy limbo gripping both sides is a hardened status quo. Each side remains vigilant and troubled by the actions of the other, but is unable to simply wish their adversary away. At the same time, neither Israel nor Hamas is prepared to publicly recognize this fact and adjust their policies accordingly. Therefore, instead of re-framing their policies and public narratives, each side is merely treading water by maintaining these contradictory postures. What is needed is a face-saving way out of this deadlock. The status quo will not produce peace or security. If Israel wants peace with Palestinians based on a two-state solution, now or in the future, it simply cannot make peace with half of the Palestinians and leave Gaza out of the equation. Even if the PA manages to gain recognition without a unity agreement in place, a divided Palestinian state is not a viable option. Meanwhile, if a unity government is reached, the United States and a number of European nations will have the pretext to oppose the UN initiative on the grounds that Hamas has not met the three Quartet conditions: renouncing violence, recognizing Israel, and accepting past agreements.

As a result, on the surface the status quo between Israel and Hamas appears sustainable for the foreseeable future. However, the elevated expectations caused by the lead up to the United Nations General Assembly (UNGA), the revolutions of the Arab Spring, and the decrease of Hamas' marginalization internationally could all lead to this status quo being shattered come October. If Hamas loses any potential of becoming a player in shaping the Palestinian national cause, they are likely to upset the process in order to maintain their relevance. That is why new thinking must be applied, in order to create a face-saving formula that will enable each side to adjust its positions.

The long-dormant Arab Peace Initiative (API) could serve as the basis for such a formula. The Initiative could enable Hamas to soften its stance on the political process with Israel by aligning itself with the stated position of the entire Arab League, but without having to relent on its long-held opposition to the three Quartet conditions. In turn, the Israeli public, notwithstanding the objections of the Netanyahu government, should be persuaded to accept the centrality, and in fact the indispensability, of the API in principle as the basis for renewed negotiations with all who support it as a framework for talks. Israel could do so with its own reservations that aspects of the Initiative, like the ultimate status of Palestinian refugees and secure borders, as in the past, must be negotiated. In fact, doing so could provide Israel with a more generic formula for talks than the security and borders-first approach advanced by President Obama. The acceptance of the API by either side would be a game-changer that could inject life into the Palestinian movement on the one hand, as well as represent the

Israeli initiative that many are calling for on the other. Creating such a game-changer will not only require political leadership on the part of Israel and Hamas, but also outside pressure and encouragement.

The United States, with the support of the European Union (EU), should be pressing Israel to adopt this formula. Bearing in mind that the Netanyahu government is not likely to make any progress toward a two-state solution, these efforts must begin now in preparation for the next Israeli elections in late 2012. To be sure, educating the Israeli public about the critical importance of the API and the perilous impasse the Netanyahu government has created would engender vitally important discussions in Israel about the desperate need for a change of direction.

In the same token, the Arab states, especially Egypt and Saudi Arabia (Egypt because of its proximity, centrality in Arab affairs, and security interests, and Saudi Arabia because it is the custodian of Sunni Islam), must press Hamas to do the same. Given Hamas' increasingly precarious situation in wake of what is happening from within and outside the organization on a regional scale, its leadership is also looking for a face-saving way out. The API could offer Hamas exactly just that, not only because it allows the organization to join the Arab fold but also because of their changing posture toward a solution to their conflict with Israel, which has become increasingly closer to the API. As I indicated in previous writings,[215] Turkey too could play a significant role in persuading Hamas to make the leap at this particular juncture.

Since the Gaza war, Israel and Hamas have been engaged in a chess game, with each side making marginal gains and losing critical pieces vis-à-vis the other side. Today, they are in a deadlock, with neither side able to put the other in checkmate. The Gaza war showed clearly that Israel cannot destroy Hamas, just as it showed

215 See "Is Turkish-Israeli Reconciliation Imminent?," *Jerusalem Post*, July 1, 2011, http://www.jpost.com/Magazine/Opinion/Is-Turkish-Israeli-reconciliation-imminent; "Iran Is At The Core of the Turkish-Israeli Rift," *Huffington Post*, January 10, 2011, http://www.huffingtonpost.com/alon-benmeir/iran-is-at-the-core-of-th_b_806980.html; and "Israel and Turkey: What Went Wrong?," *World Policy Institute*, June 18, 2010, http://www.worldpolicy.org/alon-ben-meir-israel-and-turkey-what-went-wrong.

that Hamas' acts of terror have enormous consequences for the Palestinian people. While the current standoff appears sustainable, it is not. Beginning a détente between the two sides will require finding a common denominator that could be utilized as a face-saving measure for adapting positions without appearing to have relented to the demands of the other side.

The API offers many common denominators that both Israel and Hamas can relate to and accept. Although Israel and Hamas today are not politically prepared to accept it, their friends and allies in the United States, the Arab world, and Turkey, respectively, should begin pressing them to prepare to do so. Otherwise a dangerous, violent explosion could occur as the current status quo is not sustainable and undoubtedly will unravel. The only question is when.

ALON BEN-MEIR

ISRAEL AND HAMAS: IN THE WAKE OF THE PRISONERS EXCHANGE

OCTOBER 25, 2011

The prisoner swap in which Hamas released Israeli captive Gilad Shalit in exchange for 1,027 Palestinian prisoners in Israeli prisons suggests that Israel and Hamas recognize each other's unmitigated reality and prerogatives. The deal was unquestionably motivated by mutually beneficial political calculations made on both sides, including a desire to overshadow President Abbas' efforts to seek UN recognition of a Palestinian state, to which Hamas and Israel object. Nevertheless, without an outright rejection of terror and recognition that Israel cannot be destroyed, Hamas' growth as a political force will remain limited and potentially mired in failure. Similarly, without Israel recognizing that lasting security is unlikely unless Hamas is included in the political process, efforts to advance a two-state solution will be fruitless.

The growing influences of Egypt and Turkey on Hamas, the Arab Spring, and the promise of the API all provide avenues to bridge the gaps between Israel and Hamas. To do so, the Quartet must rethink its three demands on Hamas (renounce violence, accept Israel's existence, and agree to past agreements), which will keep the two sides mired in a dangerous status quo. Overcoming these obstacles will require new thinking to find a formula that enables each side to save face by altering their positions to move forward in a political process.

Israel's negotiations—even though they were through Egypt—are the first public indication that Israel recognizes it cannot militarily eliminate Hamas. Israel could not rescue Shalit through military assaults, despite its pummeling of Gaza in the winter of 2008/2009. Hamas was emboldened as a result of the prisoner exchange. In a poll taken by Al-Najaf University in Nablus just after the prisoner swap

300

was announced, 67 percent of Palestinians said that they believe that the deal "will increase the popularity of Hamas among Palestinians."[216]

Hamas has been further strengthened by the on-again, off-again Palestinian unity talks, which it has entered into without relinquishing any of its avowed positions to oppose peace with Israel. Hamas' chief, Khaled Meshal, has told reporters in the past that he would be willing to accept a two-state formula along the 1967 lines,[217] but without acting on it to bring about conflict resolution. Meanwhile, Hamas members have denigrated international efforts to gain Palestinian statehood at the United Nations and remain fiercely opposed to Israel's existence.

These inconsistent postures, including the generally self-imposed ceasefire for the past three years, have enabled Hamas to navigate international circles with the aura of possibility that it could be a partner for peace, even without espousing a unified, clear position or easing its hardline stance as a "resistance movement" against Israel. This posturing forces Israel to spend disproportionately on defense and maintain a state of readiness with ever-escalating debilitating financial and human costs.

However, Hamas' rise may be reaching an apex. According to the Al-Najaf poll, 77 percent of Palestinians believe "that the surrounding Arab and international circumstances necessitate concluding a national reconciliation agreement between Fateh [sic] and Hamas."[218] An equal number supported the Palestinian bid to gain statehood recognition at the United Nations. But with Hamas' Prime Minister Ismail Haniyeh calling the UN gambit a mere "mirage," Hamas could in fact be blamed for the bid's failure, as well as for the failure of reconciliation talks. Even more, whereas 57 percent of Palestinians expect a third intifada, the same number opposes the use of violence. Hamas' political viability could be undermined if it is

216 "Results of Palestinian Public Opinion Poll No. 43," *Independent Media Review Analysis*, October 17, 2011, http://www.imra.org.il/story. php3?id=54127.

217 Ethan Bronner, "Hamas Leader Calls for Two-State Solution, but Refuses to Renounce Violence," *The New York Times*, May 5, 2011, http://www. nytimes.com/2011/05/06/world/middleeast/06palestinians.html.

218 "Results of Palestinian Public Opinion Poll No. 43."

blamed for another round of violence that dramatically sets back the Palestinian cause. Hamas' challenge is made more difficult as a result of the uprising in Syria which has thrust its patron, Bashar Assad, in a fight for the survival of his regime.

Most importantly, Hamas' growth is contingent upon two realizations. The first is that under no circumstances can Hamas destroy Israel. Hamas knows that should it reengage in a campaign of terror against and seriously threaten Israel, Jerusalem will not hesitate to respond by decapitating its leadership, regardless of the international condemnation that would likely follow. Furthermore, until Hamas disavows violence as a tool, achieving Palestinian statehood and its ability to shape the future of Palestine remains handicapped.

The second realization is that Hamas knows that it too cannot be destroyed. Although Hamas' public support has steadily declined in the past several years, it maintains a strong grassroots following. Whether through a unity government or free and fair elections, Hamas and its ideology of "resistance" will persist as a potent force in the Palestinian body politic. The question facing Hamas today is how to reconcile these two contradictory realities: that the organization will endure, but its ultimate objective—the destruction of Israel—will never be fulfilled.

A similar question regarding Hamas faces Israel. While previous and current Israeli governments know that it can wipe out Hamas' leadership, it cannot destroy its ideology, and as long as it remains on the outside of the political process, it can spoil any Israeli efforts to advance negotiations with its Fatah rival. Israel has succeeded in containing Hamas' violent activity, including rocket attacks, due to its considerable deterrence, but it is at least in part constrained by the international opprobrium that has followed its blockade of Gaza, which has further served to strengthen Hamas' position in the international arena.

This policy limbo gripping both sides hardens the status quo. At the same time, neither Israel nor Hamas is prepared to publicly recognize this fact and adjust their policies accordingly. Each side is merely treading water by maintaining these contradictory postures. What is needed is a face-saving way out of this deadlock. The status quo will not produce peace or security. If Israel wants peace with the

Palestinians based on a two-state solution, it simply cannot leave Gaza out of the equation. Meanwhile, if a unity government is reached, and talks are currently being held between Fatah and Hamas, some in the international community are likely to withdraw Palestinian aid on the grounds that Hamas has not met the three Quartet conditions.

Hamas and Israel must adopt a new strategy in order to create a face-saving formula that will enable each side to adjust its positions. So what can be done?

First, as the prisoner exchange deal attests, the growing influence of Egypt in Hamas' internal calculations could serve toward an easing of direct hostilities between Hamas and Israel. Israel has a strategic interest to maintain ties with the Egyptian authorities, particularly in the military establishment. With Bashar Assad's future in doubt, Hamas too has significant interests in maintaining solid ties with its Egyptian neighbors. Egypt's role can be expanded to issues related to security and economic concerns along the Gaza-Israel and Egypt-Gaza borders, as well as along the Gaza coastline.

Second, just as Egypt has deepened ties with Hamas as its ties with Israel were placed into doubt following the ouster of Hosni Mubarak, Turkey-Israel ties have deteriorated as Turkey-Hamas relations have strengthened. Israel could signal to Turkey to play a mediating role between Jerusalem and Gaza, as Israeli President Peres acknowledged it did in the prisoner swap, bolstering Israeli-Turkish relations in the process. Turkey was a quiet but key player in Gilad Shalit's release, agreeing to accept some of the released Palestinian prisoners in Turkey for exile. Turkey's assistance in helping Israel and Hamas reach sustainable security, economic, and political arrangements will be essential in restarting a process of mending ties between Jerusalem and Ankara.

Third, the Arab Spring forced Israel to listen to the demands of the Palestinian street. Palestinians in Gaza and the West Bank are not likely to remain silent in a region that is undergoing a transformation of epic proportions. The Palestinian street cannot be left out of the revolutionary freedom wave crossing the Middle East for long. It is in Israel's strategic and security interests—and Hamas' political interest—to keep Palestinian protests peaceful so as to not derail any hopes of riding the Arab Spring's momentum toward a realization of Palestinian national aspirations.

Fourth, the long-dormant API could enable Hamas to soften its stance on the political process with Israel by aligning itself with the stated position of the entire Arab League. In turn, the Israeli public, notwithstanding the objections of the Netanyahu government, should be persuaded to accept the centrality, and in fact the indispensability, of the API in principle as the basis for renewed negotiations with the Arab states and a framework for talks. Egypt, because of its proximity to Israel, centrality in Arab affairs, and security interests, and Saudi Arabia because of its status as the custodian of Sunni Islam, must press Hamas to give up violence and accept the principles of the API.

Finally, the Quartet should reexamine its formula for engaging Hamas, particularly in connection with recognizing Israel and accepting prior agreements. There are members of the Israeli cabinet who do not renounce violence, recognize the right of Palestine to exist, or accept previously negotiated agreements. To ask it of Hamas is simply a ploy to avoid the inevitable—negotiating with them. Instead of these unrealistic conditions, the Quartet should publicly state one clear condition to be accepted by the international community: Hamas must renounce violence in any form, a condition which Hamas has de facto accepted. Challenging Hamas to rise to the occasion could spur the kind of change necessary to break the deadlock that is currently gripping the Middle East peace process.

Since the Gaza war, Israel and Hamas have been engaged in a chess game, with each side making marginal gains and losing critical pieces in relation to the other side. Today, they are in a deadlock, with neither side able to put the other in checkmate. Egypt and Turkey, with the support of the Quartet, can help the parties find a common denominator, utilizing the momentum of the Arab Spring and the promise of the API. Now is the time to make concerted efforts to force a game-changer, without which the region could be headed toward a dangerous and violent explosion.

ISRAEL AND HAMAS: IS IT TIME FOR A NEW DEAL?

NOVEMBER 14, 2011

The one important lesson that should be drawn from the last few weeks' interaction and conflict between Israeli and Palestinian forces is that a new deal between Hamas and Israel is timely, possible, and necessary to gradually move toward ending the conflict between them. In lieu of this, southern Israel could once again become a target of rockets fired by non-Hamas Palestinian militants in Gaza, and Israeli retaliatory attacks could further escalate violence along the lines of the 2008–2009 Gaza war. To be sure, since any incident could trigger an outbreak of renewed violence, it is in the interest of both Israel and Hamas to build on the recent prisoner exchange and seek a new agreement that would ease the Israeli blockade and gradually end it. Similarly, Hamas would officially suspend violence and eventually renounce it as a means by which to achieve the Palestinians' aspiration for statehood.

The two agreements that Hamas has reached recently through Egyptian mediation—the Palestinian reconciliation agreement in May with the Fatah movement and the prisoner swap agreement in October with Israel—offer an opportunity to provide the building blocks for improved relations between Israel and Hamas. After the signing of the reconciliation agreement in Cairo, Hamas chief Khaled Meshal not only confirmed that they will abide by the cease-fire with Israel for at least one more year but, more importantly, reiterated that Hamas is willing to accept a Palestinian state within 1967 borders, something which he had said two years ago.[219] The prisoner swap in which Hamas released Israeli captive Gilad Shalit in exchange

---

219 "Meshal: Hamas Seeks Palestinian State Based on 1967 Borders," *Haaretz*, May 5, 2009, http://www.haaretz.com/news/meshal-hamas-seeks-palestinian-state-based-on-1967-borders-1.275412.

for 1,027 Palestinian prisoners being held in Israeli prisons suggests that Hamas and Israel recognize each other's unmitigated reality and prerogatives. Neither side could retrieve their captives through the use of force nor, as some Hamas members have suggested, that the prisoners exchange would allow for the exchange of more Palestinian prisoners in the future should Hamas succeed in capturing new Israeli soldiers. This is certainly not a given because the conditions and the circumstances could be dramatically different at any point in time.

These two agreements therefore imply that the positions of the two parties are actually much closer than they appear on the surface. For that reason, a new win-win deal between Israel and Hamas would greatly benefit both sides, allowing each to save face while bringing them closer to recognizing each other's unmitigated existence. Under the proposed deal, Hamas would commit itself to the suspension of all violent activities against Israel emanating from Gaza. In return, Israel would, in phases, lift the blockade it has imposed on the Gaza Strip since 2006 and open all the Israel-Gaza crossings to allow the free flow of people and commodities in both directions.

At first sight, this proposed deal might look far-fetched. There are those who can persuasively argue that it is unthinkable for Hamas to renounce the "armed struggle" on which it has built its legitimacy in the Palestinian territories. This argument, however, can be mitigated on several grounds. First, Hamas de facto adheres, even voluntarily, to the cease-fire and works aggressively against other radical groups in Gaza from firing rockets at Israel. Second, the prisoner exchange has shown that Hamas can extract concessions from Israel only through negotiations and not violence while recognizing the futility of continued armed struggle against Israel, which now also runs against Egypt's national interests given its increased involvement with Hamas and its desire to maintain peace with Israel. Third, Hamas' challenge is made more difficult as a result of the uprising in Syria which threatens the collapse of its base in that country, compelling Hamas to work much closer with the Egyptian authorities than ever before. More importantly, the proposed deal requires neither direct negotiations between Israel and Hamas, nor formal recognition of Israel, nor a surrendering of arms, but simply an official suspension of violence to give the nonviolent approach a chance.

For Israel, some would certainly argue that the Netanyahu government would be disinterested in such a deal because it has, by and large, already secured a cease-fire. And in case Hamas reengages violently or allows others to engage in a campaign of terror against it, the Israeli Defense Forces has the capability to retaliate and inflict painful destruction, including decapitating its leadership. But this argument is myopic for a number of reasons. First, the blockade is degrading Israel's moral international standing, increasing its isolation, and reinforcing the image of Israel as an indifferent and reclusive state. Recent private comments caught on open mics by France's President Sarkozy that Netanyahu is a liar and President Obama's repartee that he must deal with him (Netanyahu) every day is a telling example.[220] Additionally, European diplomats are baffled by Netanyahu's confrontational policies, especially in reaction to the Palestinians' bid for UN recognition and precisely when the Palestinians are pursuing moderation.

Second, removing the blockade would be gradual. Hamas' commitment would be tested and monitored by the Egyptians, who have a vested interest in keeping the peace. It should be noted that removing the blockade has not been ruled out even by the staunchest right-wing elements in Israel. Foreign Minister Avigdor Lieberman in 2010 suggested disengaging entirely from Gaza including lifting the blockade and leaving Hamas to its own devices as long as it does not commit acts of violence against Israel.[221]

Third, new revelations made by the International Atomic Energy Agency (IAEA) that Iran is clearly advancing toward the acquisition of nuclear weapons[222] represents an existential threat from the Israeli

---

220 Yann Le Guernigou, "Sarkozy Tells Obama Netanyahu is a 'Liar,'" *Reuters*, November 8, 2011, http://www.reuters.com/article/2011/11/08/us-mideast-netanyahu-sarkozy-idUSTRE7A720120111108.

221 Shimon Shiffer, "FM Presents: 2nd Disengagement from Gaza," *Y Net News*, July 16, 2010, http://www.ynetnews.com/articles/0,7340,L-3920724,00.html.

222 Julian Borger, "Iran Nuclear Report: IAEA Claims Tehran Working on Advanced Warhead," *The Guardian*, November 7, 2011, http://www.theguardian.com/world/2011/nov/07/iran-working-on-advanced-nuclear-warhead.

perspective and should also provide the Netanyahu government with the incentive to reach an understanding with the Palestinians. However small or large the potential of conflagration between Israel and Iran may be, it would be in Israel's best interest to focus on Iran and prevent the emergence of a new front in Gaza that could sap much of its military resources when it needs them the most.

Finally, the gradual removal of the blockade would also provide a good start toward mending relations with Turkey, especially at a time when Turkey is playing an increasingly important role in dealing with the uprising in Syria, which has serious direct and indirect national security effects on Israel.

The third party that would enormously benefit from the agreement and whose contribution to it is indispensable is, of course, Egypt. The ruling military in Egypt would be interested in reaching an agreement between Israel and Hamas out of the concern that a renewed violent conflict would only complicate the domestic situation in Egypt and severely undermine its relations with both Israel and the United States. Egypt could not simply come to Hamas' aid in case of a new Israeli incursion without risking these relations, nor could it ignore the death of hundreds of Palestinians without public outcry. While Egypt is perfectly suitable to take the initiative and hold indirect negotiations (à la the Gilad Shalit deal), its terms of engagement should be clear: Hamas should not provoke Israel into a new incursion and Israel should refrain from tit-for-tat retaliations to allow for further negotiations and progress.

Inherent in the proposed deal is the inclusion of phases that would engender trust in the mechanism and help Israel and Hamas maintain an ongoing dialogue, albeit indirectly, to develop the confidence needed to move to the next phase of any agreement they reach. As Hamas suspends violence and the mutual cease-fire is reinforced, Israel would reciprocate by gradually easing the blockade, provided that the Egyptians would take verifiable and transparent measures to prevent weapons from being smuggled into Gaza. There should be no doubt that the United States and the Quartet have a role to play in this agreement by signaling to Hamas that taking such a step would pave the way for providing finance for the reconstruction of Gaza to help the Palestinian population. In turn, this would discourage

Hamas from accepting funds from Iran that have traditionally been used by Tehran as a tool to foil any rapprochement between Israel and the Palestinians, particularly Hamas.

If conducted in good faith through the genuine interests of both parties, this deal would create a new dynamic that induces both Israel and Hamas to accept the inescapable reality of each other's existence as people and neighbors. This would be particularly timely, especially since the PA and Hamas have nearly come to a full agreement leading toward national elections sometime in the first half of 2012, in which Hamas will still represent a strong Palestinian constituency, regardless of Israel's wishes.

TURKEY: RECONCILING BETWEEN ISRAEL AND HAMAS

JANUARY 16, 2012

While the representatives of Israel, the PA, and the Quartet (the United States, EU, Russia, and the UN) were recently hosted in Amman, Jordan, in an effort to revive the Israeli-Palestinian peace process, Turkey's Prime Minister Erdogan met in Ankara with Hamas' Prime Minister, Ismail Haniyeh, who openly remains committed to Israel's destruction and opposes any peace negotiations with Israel. This does not suggest that Erdogan's support of Hamas' position is against Israeli-Palestinian peace, but this raises the question as to whether or not Erdogan is willing to play a constructive role in mitigating the Israel-Hamas discord or continue to shore up Hamas' obstructionist position to the detriment of Israeli-Palestinian peace.

For Turkey to play a leading and constructive regional role, especially in the Israeli-Palestinian peace process, it first needs to regain its credibility with Israel. The prudent thing for the Turkish Prime Minister to do is to openly balance his tenacious demands of Israel to modify its position toward Hamas, for example, by putting an end to the blockade in Gaza. Similarly, he should equally demand that Hamas' leadership change its posture by accepting Israel's right to exist and renouncing violent resistance as the means by which to achieve a solution to the Israeli-Palestinian conflict.

Erdogan's open-ended support of Hamas, which is mainly rooted in his Islamic affinity to the organization (as many observers suspect of being the case), places the Turkish Prime Minister in a position to persuade Hamas' leadership to permanently abandon violence and accept a two-state solution through peaceful negotiations for its own sake. Indeed, however indispensable Hamas may be to a permanent and secure Israeli-Palestinian peace, as Erdogan clearly and correctly stated, unless Hamas accepts Israel's reality, it will eventually be marginalized even by its own followers, the majority of whom want to put an end to the debilitating conflict with Israel that has led to only more pain and suffering. Repeated polls conducted over the past year have clearly revealed a growing support for the PA while Hamas' popularity shrinks.[223] Hamas recognizes that it needs to change its strategy toward Israel and that Turkey can play an increasingly important role by helping Hamas' leadership take the final leap toward peace negotiations with Israel. Such an effort on Turkey's part is most timely because intense internal deliberations among Hamas' leaders about the pros and cons of ending militant resistance against Israel are taking place, which also remains a point of contention within the unity negotiations between Hamas and the PA.

More than any other party, Turkey has earned the trust and confidence of Hamas by being the first to invite to Ankara Hamas' political guru, Khaled Meshal, more than four years ago. Even though Hamas has been designated as a terrorist organization by the United States and the EU, Turkey has remained a vocal and ardent supporter of the organization ever since. In fact, Ankara has done so even at the expense of undermining its relations with Israel, especially after the Mavi Marmara incident on May 31, 2010, where nine activists (eight Turks and one Turkish-American citizen) were killed by Israeli soldiers.

It is at this particular juncture that Turkey is perfectly positioned to bring Hamas in line with the PA due to the fact that a) Hamas' political base in Damascus is in tatters due to the upheaval in Syria and is seeking a new political base outside Gaza; b) Iran, Hamas' main benefactor, is under tremendous international economic and political pressure because of its suspected pursuit of a nuclear weapons program; and c) Egypt's Muslim Brotherhood, Hamas' political supporter, is marred in a continuing struggle with the military over power sharing, but gave up violence long ago to get to this point—an abject lesson for Hamas.

Notwithstanding the victories of Islamic political parties in the elections held in Tunisia, Morocco, and Egypt (however encouraging that might be to Hamas), none of these parties have gained national

---

223 Dahlia Scheindlin, "End of Year Poll Updates: Israel and Palestine," *+972*, December 29, 2010, http://972mag.com/end-of-year-poll-updates-israel-and-palestine/7371/.

popularity because of their pronounced hatred and animosity toward Israel. They won because they focused on domestic issues: their ailing economy, healthcare, education, and human rights. In fact, it is precisely because they did not resort to scapegoating Israel or the United States for their respective countries' ailments, a habitual practice of which the Arab youth is weary. Hamas knows its limitations and will not be carried away by the illusion of the "Islamic Spring." Israel will not be wished away and no party to the Israeli-Arab conflict appreciates that better than Hamas, especially following Israel's 2008/2009 incursion into Gaza. This further explains why Hamas is seriously deliberating abandoning violence against Israel as a means by which to realize Palestinian statehood.

Erdogan himself might well think that this is the age of Islamism and further enforce the general perception, in and outside of Turkey, that he favors any organization or country with strong Islamic credentials over others, regardless of the conflicting issues involved. However, Erdogan is realistic enough to understand that Turkey's continued economic developments and future leadership role in the Middle East depends on its ability to reconcile between the conflicting parties in the region. In particular, improved relations with Israel is one of the prerequisites to achieve that objective. Should Ankara continue to support Hamas without attempting to moderate its attitude toward Israel, Ankara will not only forsake the opportunity to lead but will be labeled as an obstructionist, especially in the eyes of the Arab-Sunni states that Turkey is trying to court, at a time when the entire region is in the process of geopolitical realignment.

Ankara can be sure that Iran will strongly and continuously encourage Hamas to hold onto its anti-Israel line under the pretext of serving the Palestinian cause. In fact, Iran is only looking to serve its regional ambitions and will go to great lengths to protect its national interests, especially by supporting its surrogates Hamas and Hezbollah in carrying out its bidding. It is time for Turkey to realize that Tehran's and Ankara's national interests do not coincide and that in fact the two countries may soon be on a collision course, not only over post-Bashar Assad Syria but also over their overall regional ambitions. If Ankara considers regional stability central to its own national interests, then Turkey must spare no efforts to wean Hamas off of Tehran. Should Turkey decide to act in this direction, it can certainly count on both the United States' and the EU's support.

Turkey is well positioned to persuade Hamas to renounce violence, which is a pre-requisite to becoming an active partner in the peace negotiations, and at the same time provide Hamas' leadership with the political cover they need to transition from a militant to a nonviolent resistance movement. Once the label of terrorist organization is removed, Turkey may then invite Khaled Meshal to move his political headquarters from Damascus to Ankara. In so doing, Ankara will not only further distance Hamas from Iran but will help legitimize Hamas in the eyes of the United States and the EU. Moreover, Ankara will be in a strong position to assert itself as a significant player in the Israeli-Palestinian peace process while beginning to mend its relations with Israel.

Regional leadership is not a given and it cannot be built on divisions and discord. Turkey must earn the regional leadership role it seeks to play. There is no better time than now for Ankara to use its influence on Hamas to make a crucial contribution to the Israeli-Palestinian peace process while enhancing its leadership role in a region in transformation.

ISRAEL'S CONTINUED INDEPENDENCE
RESTS ON PALESTINIAN INDEPENDENCE

MAY 1, 2012

As Israel recently observed 64 years of independence, it is critical that Israelis reflect on the path they have taken and ask if the current one is sustainable in the long term. Much has been achieved since the nation's founding, and Israelis should take immense pride in what they have accomplished in a relatively short period of time. In the midst of celebration, however, there is a dangerous obliviousness to the "dark side" of Israel, one that could jeopardize Israel's very existence far more than threats from Iran or any other country. Indeed, none of Israel's achievements will be sustainable if Israel ignores the gathering storm and continues on its current perilous course.

Whereas Israel has achieved a near economic miracle, touting itself as the "start-up nation," hundreds of thousands of Israeli citizens, including a quarter of Holocaust survivors, live below the poverty line.[224] The social gap between rich and poor continues to grow, and according to the Organization for Economic Cooperation and Development (OECD), Israel ranks alongside Chile, Mexico, and the United States in its levels of inequality. The increasing frustration of the poor and middle class was on full display last summer, when nearly 400,000 citizens took to the streets to demand equal opportunities, a reigning in of the cost of living, affordable housing, and most importantly, credible government efforts to respond to their demands.[225] Strong support for the protests (as high as 90% in some

224 Harriet Sherwood, "Holocaust Survivors Struggling to Make Ends Meet in Israel," *The Guardian*, April 19, 2012, http://www.theguardian.com/world/2012/apr/19/holocaust-survivor-struggle-money-israel.

225 Isabel Kershner, "Summer of Protest in Israel Peaks With 400,000 in City Streets," *The New York Times*, September 3, 2011, http://www.nytimes.com/2011/09/04/world/middleeast/04israel.html.

polls)[226] underscores the level of dissatisfaction that exists today in Israeli society. This is certainly not what the elder Zionists of the state, notably Herzl, had envisioned.

Whereas the Netanyahu government strives to maintain the Jewish national identity of the state and demand from the PA recognition of such, close to one million Israelis have left the country for more than one year and have not returned.[227] Moreover, public opinion has been favorable toward those that have left and has been laden with expressions of sympathy that do not bode well for the future Jewish identity of the state. There is a clear and present generational shift in attitude. As the noted journalist Gideon Levy rightly points out, "If our forefathers dreamt of an Israeli passport, there are those among us who are now dreaming of a foreign passport."[228] Whether motivated by opportunities abroad or fears of future uncertainty, there is a growing uneasiness about the direction that Israel is taking. This certainly defies the dream of the ingathering of the Jews to live in their homeland, as they now run the risk of becoming a minority in their last and only refuge.

Whereas there is a constant stream of rhetoric about the desire to make peace with the Palestinians, the Israeli government's actions on the ground belie its words. Instead of moving toward a solution to the Palestinian problem, Israel is taking steps that will jeopardize any hope of a peaceful settlement. The Netanyahu government's recent decision to retroactively legalize three West Bank settlements is nothing short of a shameless move that highlights the government's willingness to surrender to the whims of the settlement movement.[229] Jerusalem's mayor, Nir Barkat, is promoting the establishment of a new settlement in East

---

226 Harriet Sherwood, "Israeli Protests: 430,000 Take to Streets to Demand Social Justice," *The Guardian*, September 4, 2011, http://www. theguardian.com/world/2011/sep/04/israel-protests-social-justice.

227 Chamie and Mirkin, "The Million Missing Israelis.

228 Levy, "Fear is Driving Israelis to Obtain Foreign Passports."

229 Jodi Rudoren, "Israel Retroactively Legalizes 3 West Bank Settlements," *The New York Times*, April 24, 2012, http://www.nytimes.com/2012/04/25/ world/middleeast/israel-legalizes-3-west-bank-settlements.html.

Jerusalem,[230] a move that is bitterly antagonistic toward the Palestinians and threatens to diminish what little hope is left to forge a peace agreement, which is sine qua non to Israel's own existence as an independent Jewish state. Out of desperation, the Palestinians may opt for a one-state solution, which will force Israel to choose between being a bi-national state with a Palestinian majority in control or becoming an apartheid state, earning international condemnation, increasing isolation, and eventually, crippling sanctions. Is this how the Netanyahu government tries to realize the Jews' millennium-old dream to live in security and peace?

Instead of reaching out to the Arab and the Muslim world by embracing the API, Israel managed to alienate the only three Muslim countries that it had enjoyed good relations with. Since the 2010 Gaza Flotilla Raid, a precipitous free-fall in Israeli-Turkish relations has taken place. Recently, Turkey vetoed Israel's bid for attendance at an upcoming NATO conference in May[231] and has spoken out forcefully against Israel's latest moves regarding its settlement program. Jordan also has denounced Israel's decision to legalize three West Bank settlements,[232] and Israel stands to lose the Hashemite Kingdom's important role in solving the Palestinian question as was demonstrated in recent talks that were, albeit unsuccessfully, held in Jordan between Israeli and Palestinian delegations. The political rise of the Muslim Brotherhood (MB) in Egypt has also led to heightened tensions. A recent contract cancellation of natural gas delivery to Israel from Egypt was fraught with political concerns and implications.[233] The shifting

---

230 Akiva Eldar and Nir Hasson, "Jerusalem Mayor Aims to Establish New Settlement in East Jerusalem," *Haaretz*, April 3, 2012, http://www.haaretz.com/news/national/jerusalem-mayor-aims-to-establish-new-settlement-in-east-jerusalem-1.422228.

231 "Turkey Vetoes Israel's Latest NATO Partnership Bid, Despite Criticisms," *Tehran Times*, April 25, 2012, http://www.tehrantimes.com/middle-east/97271-turkey-vetoes-israels-latest-nato-partnership-bid-despite-criticisms.

232 "Palestinians Condemn Legalization of 3 Outposts," *Jerusalem Post*, April 24, 2012, http://www.jpost.com/Diplomacy-and-Politics/Palestinians-condemn-legalization-of-3-outposts.

233 "EMG: Egypt Didn't Halt Gas Merely Over Money," *Haaretz*, April 27, 2012, http://www.haaretz.com/business/emg-egypt-didn-t-halt-gas-merely-over-money-1.426814.

nature of Egypt's political landscape reveals a newly-found willingness on the part of Egypt to question one of the most important regional relationships since signing the bilateral peace treaty of 1979. Past, current, and future Egyptian governments have been and will always be particularly sensitive to the Israeli-Palestinian conflict. The lack of a resolution to this debilitating struggle will remain the single most daunting obstacle to the normalization of relations between Israel and the Muslim world. Can Israel otherwise survive in a sea of Arab hostility quickly approaching half a billion people?

The most talked-about issue in Israel today, the nature of the Iranian nuclear program, reveals an often-erratic display of behavior on the part of the Netanyahu government. Yuval Diskin, who retired last year as Director of Shin Bet (the Israeli equivalent to the FBI), recently said in a public forum that he had no faith in the leadership of Netanyahu and Barak in matters pertaining to relations with Iran, relations that present "a false view to the public on the Iranian bomb."[234] He further stated, "I don't believe in a leadership that makes decisions based on messianic feelings."[235] Although Iran may represent a certain threat, the government is overly focused on Iran when it should be focused on immediate concerns such as achieving peace with the Palestinians while maintaining its security, national identity and territorial integrity.

Israel's former head of the Mossad, Meir Dagan, was even blunter in his criticism of the Netanyahu government when only a few weeks ago he stated, "We are in a situation in which the national agenda, long-term planning, the handling of the urgent or the politically sensitive national problems, simply don't exist. The only thing

---

234 Kevin Flower, "Former Israeli Security Chief Slams Handling of Iran," *CNN*, April 29, 2012, http://www.cnn.com/2012/04/28/world/meast/israel-iran-criticism/.

235 Jodi Rudoren, "Remarks by Former Official Fuel Israeli Discord on Iran," *The New York Times*, April 28, 2012, http://www.nytimes.com/2012/04/29/world/middleeast/yuval-diskin-criticizes-israel-government-on-iran-nuclear-threat.html?pagewanted=all&_r=0.

of interest to the leaders is to maintain the coalition and survive."[236] A chorus of past top Israeli officials including former Prime Minister Olmert, former IDF Chief of Staff Gabi Ashkenazi, and former Air Force Commander Eliezer Shkedy, along with the current Chief of Staff Benny Gantz, expressed the same concerns. They all suggested, in one form or another, that although Israel should remain vigilant about the Iranian nuclear program and be prepared for any eventuality, Netanyahu's bellicose statements about Iran are dangerous.

Diplomacy must be given time to work; attacking Iranian nuclear facilities must absolutely be a last resort and must be made in full coordination with the United States. That said, Israel should reserve the option to strike Iran's nuclear facilities, even unilaterally, should diplomacy along with sanctions fail, or if Iran is about to reach the point of no return to acquire nuclear weapons and the United States is not prepared to take military action under such circumstances. Otherwise, acting prematurely against Iran would have disastrous global consequences for which only Israel would be blamed and suffer unimaginable consequences.

One would think that given the looming threat to Israel's national security, if not its very existence, the Israelis would demand from their leaders a unity of purpose by coalescing around a single movement that places national interests, not personal ambitions, first. But sadly, instead of forming such a movement consisting of the center, left-of-center and left, and agree on a general framework for peace with the Palestinians, political factionalism and opportunism is what characterizes Israel's political landscape today. It should be recalled that it was internal division and infighting that destroyed ancient Israel, and those who aspire to lead should learn a page or two from the Jews' instructive history. As Israel moves toward new elections (perhaps this fall), more political parties are mushrooming and sowing the seeds for more division and inner discord, which would allow Netanyahu and his cohorts to win another election, something that will bring Israel to the brink of a national disaster.

---

236 Ben Kaspit, "Former Mosad Chief Interviewed on Israeli Gov't System, Elections, Regional Issues," *Biyokulule Online*, April 27, 2012, http://www.biyokulule.com/view_content.php?articleid=4630.

The father of modern Israel, David Ben-Gurion, offered a wise counsel to the Israeli people to deal with the Palestinians with restraint and wisdom. If Israel wants to celebrate the next 64 years, or even the next 10 years, of independence with ample praise and adulation for its progress, it must correct its errors, change its current course, and above all else, work tirelessly to achieve a peace agreement with the Palestinians.

ALON BEN-MEIR

THE ARAB UPRISING: AN IMPEDIMENT OR AN OPPORTUNITY FOR PEACE?

AUGUST 13, 2012

There is an ongoing debate in and outside of Israel as to whether or not this is the right time to forge peace with the Palestinians in light of the regional upheavals and instability. At this juncture, the peace process is hopelessly frozen while the expansion of the Israeli settlements[237] and the continued internal Palestinian strife and factionalism increasingly dims the prospect of reaching an agreement. That said, the Arab Spring, which has triggered the rise of the Arab youth against their governments and has been accompanied by uncertainty, is not an impediment but an opportunity to solve the Israeli-Palestinian conflict based on a two-state solution. The reality on the ground strongly suggests that maintaining the status quo will be particularly detrimental to Israel.

Those inside the Netanyahu government who suggest that now is not the right time to seek a peace agreement with the Palestinians because of regional turmoil and existential threats that Israel now face are both misguided and disingenuous. On the contrary, given the threats from Iran and its surrogate Hezbollah, and the potential consequences of a failed state in Syria, it is a particularly critical moment for Israel to forge peace with the Palestinians. By doing so, Israel would be in a position to focus on the vastly more serious threats emanating from its real adversaries and would prevent the rise of a Palestinian fifth column, should Israel become mired in these

---

237 Harriet Sherwood, "Israeli Spending on West Bank Settlements up 38%," *The Guardian*, July 31, 2012, http://www.theguardian.com/world/2012/jul/31/israeli-spending-west-bank-settlements?newsfeed=true.

regional conflicts.[238] To enhance their positions, those who oppose peace now offer three faulty arguments to justify their stance.

First, the Palestinians cannot be trusted and Israel "correctly" points to the precedents of the partial disengagement from the West Bank between 1993 and 2000, the complete withdrawal from southern Lebanon in 2000 and the withdrawal from Gaza in 2005. From the Israeli perspective, all of these moments attest to the Palestinians' inability or unwillingness to forge a permanent peace, despite having ample opportunities.

Second, due to Palestinian factionalism and infighting, there is no credible partner with whom Israel can negotiate as the Palestinians have been unable to sustain a unity government. The Netanyahu government is convinced that even if an agreement is reached, it will still prove transient.

Third, there are extremist Palestinian groups, such as Hamas, Islamic Jihad and others, along with non-Palestinian factions, including Hezbollah and Al Qaeda, that are vehemently antagonistic toward Israel and remain committed to its destruction.

However, none of the three arguments above can pass careful scrutiny. These types of arguments are used as excuses and a cover for the Netanyahu government's deep conviction that the Jews have an inherent right to the whole "land of Israel." This remains a nonstarter to reaching a peace agreement that requires significant territorial concessions, including the conversion of Jerusalem to the capital of both Israeli and Palestinian states. From the Netanyahu government's perspective, the conditions of no peace and no war that currently prevail are preferable to a compromise of the Jews' historical rights, and through a strong and determined will, Israel will eventually triumph.

In light of the reality on the ground, which both the Israelis and the Palestinians alike must face by virtue of their inevitable coexistence, Israel must act now because the passage of time may well be to its detriment, if not its very existence. There are three critical issues that increasingly work against Israel.

---

238 David Ignatius, "Israel's Arab Spring Problem," *The Washington Post*, July 6, 2012, http://www.washingtonpost.com/opinions/david-ignatius-israels-arab-spring-problem/2012/07/05/gJQAV5JrRW_story.html.

Considering Israel's demographic situation,[239] its evolutionary path has shifted radically as emigration from Israel over the past two decades (about one million) is roughly equal to the immigration into Israel for the same period. This, along with low birth rates relative to the Palestinian population, continues to erode the sustainability of Israel's national character as a Jewish state. Should this growing demographic imbalance between the Jewish and Palestinian populations continue,[240] Israel will be forced to either establish a single state (an unacceptable proposition for them as it will instantly make the Jewish population a minority) or resort to apartheid policies that will be vehemently rejected by the international community.

In recent years, Israel has been fortunate that Gaza and the West Bank were generally quiet with limited resistance to the occupation and only launched marginal rocket attacks from Gaza that the Israeli military was able to handle with ease. Maintaining the occupation, however, and continuing the creeping expansion of the settlements, coupled with the uprisings of Arab youth against their own governments, now make it only a matter of time before the Palestinians will be inspired, if not forced, to rise against the occupation. They will not remain indefinitely passive, as they clearly see that the longer they wait, the more their land will be consumed, resulting in an irreversible reality on the ground that will deny the rise of an independent and viable state.

Moreover, Israel will continue to face intensifying pressure from the international community due to the perpetuation of the status quo, which will dramatically increase Israel's isolation.[241] For the United States and the EU, who continue to be steadfast supporters of Israel, the lack of progress has a destabilizing effect

---

239 Chamie and Mirkin, "The Million Missing Israelis."

240 Murray Fromson, "'The Arabs are Multiplying Twice as Fast as the Israelis,'" *The Jewish Journal*, April 8, 2010, http://www.afhu.org/files/HUArticles/The%20Arabs%20are%20multiplying%20twice%20as%20fast%20as%20the%20Israelis.pdf.

241 Edmund Sanders, "Israel Under Pressure to Offer Peace Plan," *Los Angeles Times*, April 19, 2011, http://articles.latimes.com/2011/apr/19/world/la-fg-israel-peace-plan-20110419.

on the region, which directly and indirectly impacts their national strategic interests and undermines Israel's national security. Israel should not be surprised if its closest allies, especially the United States, decide to advance their own frameworks for peace largely based on prior Israeli-Palestinian negotiations in an attempt to save Israel from charting its own disastrous path.

In a broader context, Israel's current enemies, specifically Iran and Hezbollah, will continue to exploit the Israeli-Palestinian conflict to their advantage. To counteract this encroaching threat, Israel can at least begin to neutralize its antagonists' positions by taking steps that open the door for a negotiated solution and normalization of relations with the Arab states by accepting the API as a basis for negotiations. While this strategy may not initially and necessarily change the principle objection to Israel's very existence by actors such as Iran and Hezbollah, Israel could shift the geopolitical conditions in the region in its favor. As I was convincingly told time and time again by top Arab officials, the Arab states are prepared to move toward establishing full diplomatic relations with Israel once an Israeli-Palestinian peace is achieved. They cite the changing dynamics in the region in the wake of the Arab Spring and the ensuing battle between Sunnis, led by Saudi Arabia and Turkey, and Shiites, led by Iran who seeks regional hegemony.

Despite the complex situation that Israel finds itself in, the basic question remains: how much longer can it sustain its present course without experiencing horrific and self-inflicted wounds? Israel must face the inevitable now while it is still in a strong position to negotiate an agreement with the Palestinians, a population that has and can continue to withstand the test of time. Unlike the precipitous withdrawal from Southern Lebanon and Gaza, any agreement with the Palestinians should be made with the PA in the West Bank and should be based on a quid pro quo that would involve phased withdrawals from the West Bank over a few years in order to foster mutual trust and normalization of relations while ensuring Israel's national security.

Set against the context of the Arab Spring, Israel remains an oasis of stability with its economic, military, and technological advantages continuing to strengthen over time.[242] The inability of the Palestinians to change the dynamics in their favor has deepened the Israelis' complacency while removing any sense of urgency to solve the conflict, as they remain intoxicated by their military prowess and the deceptive calm before the storm. Simply put, passively waiting for the region to achieve a modicum of stability while Israel further entrenches itself in the territories is a nonstarter as the Arab upheavals are not a fading phenomenon and will remain an engine of change for years, if not decades, to come. The Palestinians' turn will come sooner than expected.

I must emphasize that the Palestinians, by their own violent actions and hostile public utterances, have directly contributed to the Israelis' skepticism and deepening of their conviction that the Palestinians are not partners to be trusted, nor are they a population with whom they can negotiate a lasting peace. That said, it is up to Israel not to allow past experiences to blur its vision for the future, and it must now chart its own future course by ending the occupation under specific "rules of disengagement" with the PA. Israel must never abandon the principles of equality and human rights regardless of race, color, or religion, as they are the very basis on which the state arose from the ashes of the Holocaust.

Netanyahu will eventually have to answer to the Israeli public as to what he has achieved over the past four years. The Israelis must now determine whether or not Netanyahu has made the conflict with the Palestinians considerably worse since he took office in 2009 and what price Israel will have to pay for his misguided and ominous policies.

---

242 Fareed Zakaria, "Under Netanyahu, Israel is Stronger Than Ever," *The Washington Post*, May 9, 2012, http://www.washingtonpost.com/opinions/under-netanyahu-israel-is-stronger-than-ever/2012/05/09/gIQAcTH2DU_story.html.

ISRAEL AND HAMAS:
HOW BIASES ARE DRIVING THE
CONFLICT TO THE PRECIPICE

NOVEMBER 21, 2012

When listening to Israeli and Hamas officials about the nature of their conflict and what precipitated the current conflagration, one comes to a definite conclusion: they are both right. At close scrutiny, however, one finds that while both may indeed be "right," they are also dead wrong. Both sides have successfully managed over the years to foster public perceptions that support both their respective narratives and the notion that the other has wronged them. It is this conviction and the lack of unbiased and credible voices to the contrary from inside and outside the region that allows this violent and self-consuming conflict to fester, pushing both sides ever closer to the precipice.

It is pointless to try to establish which side is to blame for the current flare-up. Indeed, whether it was ignited by the deliberate firing on an Israeli jeep by an Islamic Jihadist from Gaza that wounded four Israeli soldiers,[243] or by the pinpointed air assault that killed Hamas' al-Qassam Brigade commander, Ahmad Jabari,[244] is hardly relevant. The tit-for-tat that followed was not simply the result of these initial attacks and counter-attacks. These incidents simply ignited a long-simmering tension that would have exploded anyway, as both Israel

---

243 Gili Cohen, Yaniv Kubovich, Jack Khoury and Avi Issacharoff, "Four IDF Soldiers Wounded when Gaza Anti-Tank Missile Hits Jeep on Border," *Haaretz*, November 10, 2012, http://www.haaretz.com/news/diplomacy-defense/four-idf-soldiers-wounded-when-gaza-anti-tank-missile-hits-jeep-on-border.premium-1.476521.

244 Ibrahim Barzak and Aron Heller, "Israeli Airstrike Kills Hamas Military Chief," *Associated Press*, November 14, 2012, http://bigstory.ap.org/article/israel-officials-warns-against-palestinian-un-bid.

and Hamas were determined to change the equation on the ground to their advantage at this particular juncture.

Israel was determined to end Hamas' and other Islamists' largely unprovoked rocket attacks (nearly 750 were fired at Israel in the past 12 months)[245] and weaken, if not destroy, Hamas' infrastructure. Known for his national security credentials, Prime Minister Netanyahu opted to act forcefully now not only to send a message to Hezbollah, Iran, and militants in Syria that Israel is prepared to deal with all contingencies, but also because of the Israeli general election in January 2013 and his determination to consolidate his political base.

Hamas, on the other hand, has several objectives in mind. First, it aims to demonstrate its resolve and strength against the weaker PA, which has achieved little for its peaceful posture toward Israel, and undermine the PA's efforts to seek UN non-Member Observer State status as the representative of all Palestinians. Hamas also wants to test the affinity and commitment of the new Islamic Egyptian government and the extent to which it will rally behind their cause. In addition, Hamas wishes to garner the support of other Arab and Muslim states in the wake of the Arab Spring. Finally, Hamas aspires to alleviate the plight of the Palestinians in Gaza by refocusing the world's attention on the Israeli blockade.

From the Israeli perspective, Hamas is a terrorist organization and is recognized as such by the United States and the EU.[246] It is an irredentist foe, irredeemably committed to Israel's destruction, and openly calls for and relentlessly supports other Islamic jihadists that attack Israeli targets. Hamas is further seen as the conduit for Iran's regional misadventure; it has no interest in peace and, to the contrary, devotes much of its resources to buying weapons instead of feeding their people and hatching plots to undermine Israel's security while fostering and exploiting regional instability.

---

245 Dan Murphy, "How Many Rockets were Fired from Gaza at Israel this Year?," *Christian Science Monitor*, November 15, 2012, http://www.csmonitor.com/World/Backchannels/2012/1115/How-many-rockets-were-fired-from-Gaza-at-Israel-this-year.

246 Bryony Jones, "Q&A: What is Hamas?," *CNN*, November 24, 2012, http://www.cnn.com/2012/11/16/world/meast/hamas-explainer/.

Hamas sees Israel as a ruthless occupying power behind the plight of the Palestinian refugees, who have been languishing in camps for more than six decades. They view Israel's settlement enterprise as a clear manifestation of its intentions to continuously usurp Palestinian land and prevent them from establishing their own state. They accuse Israel of deliberately limiting the Palestinians' mobility while enacting discriminatory policies that stifle the Palestinians' growth and prosperity. Moreover, Hamas views the Israeli blockade around the impoverished Gaza as inhumane, as it forces people to live in poverty and denies them the basic right to live with dignity.

A cursory review of Israel's and Hamas' perceptions of each other suggests that their respective citizenry commonly accepts their assessments. Their daily denunciations and portrayals of each other in evil terms have done nothing but deepen their distrust, intensify their hatred and hostility, and shatter any hope for reconciliation. It is no wonder then that this mindset evolved into a siege mentality, leaving no room for any mitigation, moderation, and certainly no accommodation. Yet both sides know deep inside that the other exists and will continue to exist. The death and destruction of recent days will leave nothing more than deeper scars and haunting nightmares. A new ceasefire will eventually be established in the wake of the current violence, even if it were to follow a major Israeli incursion into Gaza. Unless the new ceasefire is established on a different basis, it will more than likely follow the pattern of previous ceasefires that served as nothing more than respites to prepare for the next round of ever-intensifying violence.

Hamas may think that they are riding high and will seek to gain politically from the ashes of the destruction and deaths of men, women, and children whom they use as human shields. Hamas impresses itself by the outcry of relatively few Palestinians who want revenge and the show of support from the Arab states, but Hamas is deaf to the voices of the majority of Palestinians in Gaza who want to live in peace. They are sick and tired of being subjected to the whims of extremist leaders who wage wars in their names while destroying the very fabric of the society they presumably seek to protect. Hamas has done nothing but use the people as sacrificial lambs to promote its blind ambitions that will do nothing but bring greater havoc, helplessness, and hopelessness to the people.

The Israeli government, on the other hand, pretends to walk the high moral ground when in fact it too subjects its own people to a long and protracted conflict that has robbed the country of much of the values upon which it was founded. The occupation is a curse that justifiably portrays the historically oppressed Jews as oppressors. Israel has created intolerable conditions in the territories by expropriating land, erecting barriers, building new (and expanding existing) settlements, uprooting olive trees, and depriving ordinary people of the opportunity to live normal lives. By its own actions, Israel is planting the seeds of discontent and extremism among the Palestinians and then blames them for their militant and violent behavior.

Neither side can or will change their attitudes toward the other overnight, not only because of the lack of trust and open hostility that have been ingrained in their psyche, but because they have their own agendas that preclude the right of each other to exist in their present form. For these reasons, it is not enough to establish a new ceasefire to end the cycle of violence, as this limited objective will only, as in the past, be violated time and time again. Both Israel and Hamas have legitimate claims and each must meet the other's basic requirements in order to chart a new course that can be sustained in the long run.

Israel is correct in demanding that a more permanent security arrangement be established that will prohibit the firing of rockets in the future by Hamas or any of its surrogates. Israel is also seeking some assurance that Hamas will be prevented from acquiring more sophisticated rockets. In return, Israel must agree to lift the blockade, albeit in stages, conditional upon the complete cessation of hostilities and allowing international monitors to join Israeli inspectors to inspect all cargo going in or out of Gaza. The international monitors will also be charged with ensuring that steel and cement are used strictly for building homes, hospitals, government institutions, and infrastructure, not bunkers or tunnels. Only full adherence to a ceasefire and the expansion of trade (which is ongoing even as the fighting continues) between the two sides will allow, however gratingly, for the gradual building of trust which is sorely absent. This will also permit the creation of a new environment conducive to peaceful coexistence, as the United States is currently pushing for, while building the foundation for bilateral relations and leaving the prospect of a peace agreement a possibility sometime in the future.

None of this can happen without the direct and indirect support of Egypt, who can exercise tremendous influence on Hamas, and the United States who likewise can persuade Israel to accept a deal based on mutuality of interest. Both Egypt and the United States have major stakes in ending the conflict. Notwithstanding his public condemnation of Israel, the last thing that President Morsi seeks, regardless of his ideological and religious leanings, is to entangle his country in the Israeli-Hamas conflict, which could spin out of control and place Egypt in a terrible bind. Egypt has a profound national interest in maintaining the peace treaty with Israel and is in dire need of the United States' financial and political support. If President Morsi wants to survive as president, he must first and foremost focus on the Egyptian economy. Paying lip service to Hamas is the minimum he must do to calm his own public, but he remains the central figure that can effect a real change in Hamas' behavior toward Israel. In the main, President Morsi must, at one point or another, pressure Hamas to permanently forsake violence as the tool of choice to achieve its "political objective," which must be based on a two-state solution.

The United States, on the other hand, is the only country that can exert the kind of influence necessary to encourage any Israeli government to look at the Israeli-Palestinian conflict from a different perspective and work in earnest toward a permanent solution. The United States can exercise tremendous leverage on Israel as it is the only country that supports Israel financially, politically, and militarily, as well as economically. Israel trusts the United States to watch its back and ensure its ultimate national security. The new Obama administration must now, however, assume a direct and active role and remain relentless in supporting peace between Israel and the Palestinians. Secretary of State Hillary Clinton's mission at this moment of crisis must not end with the establishment of a ceasefire but with the beginning of a renewed and sustained American effort to bring an end to the Israeli-Palestinian conflict, however long and difficult it may be.

Hamas might feel emboldened by the wide range of political support it has received from the Arab states, Turkey, Iran, and other countries, but it also knows that rhetoric is not equal to realpolitik. No Arab or Muslim state will venture to confront Israel militarily only to save Hamas' skin. In the final analysis, Hamas will be left to wallow in its own mess while the Palestinians in Gaza will continue to suffer from their leaders' misadventures. Israel, on the other hand, must too come to terms with the reality on the ground. Hamas cannot be wished away and even if Israel succeeds in destroying Hamas' infrastructure and decapitating its leadership, Hamas will rise again.

The current bloody and destructive conflict can serve both Israel and the Palestinians (including Hamas) well, if they only let reason and reality dictate their future course of action.

NETANYAHU'S BRAZEN AND PERILOUS DEFIANCE

DECEMBER 3, 2012

O ne would think that Prime Minister Netanyahu and his cohorts would one day come to their senses and realize that there are limits to which they can defy the international community, including the United States, without serious, if not perilous, repercussions for the State of Israel. As long as he is in power, Netanyahu has no intention, now or ever, to allow for the establishment of a functioning and independent Palestinian state. His talk of a two-state solution is nothing but an empty slogan designed to mislead the international community, and tragically he is leading the Jews' third commonwealth to a historic disaster akin to the destruction of the Second Temple. Those Israelis from the left and center of the political spectrum must wake up and stop him in his tracks before it is too late. Otherwise, they will be judged as harshly and mercilessly as history will judge Netanyahu by not preventing the looming disaster from destroying the Jews' last refuge.

I may sound overly dramatic, but anyone who witnessed last week's events at the United Nations and condemned the General Assembly's overwhelming support in granting the Palestinians a non-Member Observer State is contributing to the demise of a two-state prospect, which offers the only solution that preserves and safeguards Israel's very existence. Leading Israeli figures, including former Prime Minister Olmert, applauded the UN resolution not because they care about the Palestinians, but because they are concerned about the future of Israel itself.[247] Israel's isolation has already reached its zenith, as was displayed at the UN vote, and further defiance of the international community

---

247 Dan Murphy, "Who Backs Palestine UN Bid? Ehud Olmert, Among Others," *Christian Science Monitor*, November 28, 2012, http://www. csmonitor.com/World/Backchannels/2012/1128/Who-backs-Palestine-UN-bid-Ehud-Olmert-among-others-video.

will make Israel a pariah state living in darkness and uncertainty, with no friends left to watch its back.

Due to the converging political events and circumstances in Israel and in the region, I for one feel, like millions around the world and in Israel, that the PA's successful UN bid offers a momentous opportunity to resume in earnest the Israeli-Palestinian peace process. Israel and the United States for that matter, who claim that the PA's unilateral action only undermines the peace negotiations, have yet to produce a shred of evidence that supports their contention. In fact, Israel has been taking unilateral measures in the occupied territories, including expropriating Palestinian land with impunity, to which the whole world is opposed.

There are several central reasons why I feel that further delay in resuming the negotiations for tactical or strategic reasons by either side will erode the last vestiges of a mutually accepted agreement with dire consequences for both.

First, as the peace negotiations have been frozen for the past three years, I believe that the PA's elevated status could change the dynamic of the conflict in an unprecedented manner, compelling the Israelis to face a new reality. For many years now, as long as there was no spike in violence or threat of imminent danger emanating from the West Bank, the Israelis became increasingly complacent, preferring the status of "no peace, no war." This condition allowed Netanyahu to have it both ways, which is precisely what he wished to accomplish as he continued unabatedly with the expansion of settlements. President Abbas' effort at the UN has now shaken that status quo. Olmert expressed his support stating that the move "is in basic line with the strategy of a two-state solution,"[248] and any attempts to stifle this momentum will herald a return to the status quo ante, which will severely cripple the viability of the two-state solution and acutely harm Israel's national interests.[249]

248 David Ariosto and Michael Pearson, "U.N. Approves Palestinian 'Observer State' Bid," *CNN*, November 30, 2012, http://www.cnn.com/2012/11/29/world/meast/palestinian-united-nations/.

249 Samuel Burke, "Israel's Former Prime Minister: 'Time is Running Out for Israel,'" *CNN*, November 29, 2012, http://amanpour.blogs.cnn.com/2012/11/29/israels-former-prime-minister-time-is-running-out-for-israel/.

Second, although the Obama administration voted against the UN resolution, the timing of the PA move is particularly important as President Obama prepares for his second term where he must now deal with the ever-changing conditions in the Middle East. Recent events in Gaza have added further urgency for direct U.S. involvement in solving the Israel-Palestine conflict. The Obama administration has largely neglected the conflict after attempts were made in 2010,[250] but the latest flare-up of violence between Israel and Hamas provided a rude awakening: the United States cannot ignore the Israeli-Palestinian conflict without consequences to America's strategic interests. The fact that the United States has backed Israel at the UN does not suggest that President Obama supports Netanyahu's obstructionist policy toward the Palestinians.

The Netanyahu government's announcement, the day after the PA's successful bid, that it was moving ahead with plans to build a new city in the contentious area known as E1 between Ma'ale Adumim and Jerusalem (making a contiguous Palestinian state virtually impossible), was nothing short of a slap in the face to President Obama. Defying Israel's sole ally is not only short-sighted but also extremely damaging to Israel as the United States is becoming increasingly frustrated with a prime minister who has lost his bearings and his mind. Regardless of Netanyahu's loathsome behavior, however, the PA move should prompt the United States to interject itself directly, actively, and consistently to push for an accord while making it abundantly clear to the Netanyahu government that it can no longer take U.S. blanket support for granted.

Third, regardless of who wins the January 2013 elections in Israel, the next prime minister will have to face the Palestinian problem in one way or another. Playing for time, as Netanyahu has done over the past four years, will no longer work. The election in January can be fateful only if the center and left parties come to grips with the danger that Israel will face should Netanyahu be given another chance to form a new government. These are no ordinary times; the splintered political groups in Israel must either rise to the occasion

---

250 "Israeli-Palestinian Talks 'Progress' on Settlements," *BBC News*, September 15, 2010, http://www.bbc.co.uk/news/world-middle-east-11308678.

and literally save the country from sliding toward the abyss, or allow their personal interests and inflated egos to stand in the way of fighting for their country. I know this is a tall order, but if they do not match their criticism of Netanyahu with action, they will have sacrificed the future of the nation on the altar of their blind self-indulgence. Then again, should Netanyahu form a new government, he will have to face, or must be made to face by the United States, the changing dynamics. The Palestinians now have other tools by which to constantly refocus the attention of the international community on their plight by going, for example, to the International Criminal Court (ICC) and exercising their newly gained leverage. Israel should look at the changing conditions constructively. Instead of opting to punish the Palestinians, the next government must respond to the majority's demands that Israel exorcize the evil of occupation and restore dignity to both Israelis and Palestinians alike.

Fourth, the overwhelming support from the international community has sent a loud and clear message to current and future Israeli governments that Israel has no friends left.[251] The biggest blow to Netanyahu's policy came from the European countries that either chose to support the resolution (like France) or abstain (like the United Kingdom and Germany). Denying Netanyahu even a minimal face-saving outlet exposed his unseemly bankrupt policy. The disproportionate vote at the UN (138-9, with 41 abstentions)[252] provided a glaring testimony to Israel's near-complete isolation, which necessitates that something must now be done to face the conflict squarely. No new Israeli government, even if led by Netanyahu, can afford to ignore the consensus of the international community, provided that the leading European nations (especially Britain, Germany, and France under the leadership of the United States) are determined to use whatever diplomatic tools and leverage they can muster to resolve the conflict. In that sense, what happened in the UN provided a new momentum because the stakes for all countries concerned are extremely high.

---

251 Ethan Bronner and Christine Hauser, "U.N. Assembly, in Blow to U.S., Elevates Status of Palestine," *The New York Times*, November 29, 2012, http://www.nytimes.com/2012/11/30/world/middleeast/Palestinian-Authority-United-Nations-Israel.html?ref=world&_r=0.

252 Ibid.

Finally, the Palestinians are not likely to remain idle in the wake of the Arab Spring when young men and women have and continue to die for their freedom and dignity in places such as Libya, Egypt, and Syria. It would be only a question of when, not if, they will rise against the humiliating occupation. The PA's success is likely to forestall the potential uprising in the territories and give more time for negotiations. Moreover, the successful UN bid strengthens the PA's position as well as that of other moderate voices over Hamas, whose political standing along with other extremist groups was boosted in the wake of the latest Israel-Hamas flare-up. This development offers the United States in particular a new opportunity to re-engage Israel and the Palestinians in a productive dialogue.

To fully benefit from these developments, the Palestinians would be wise to use their elevated position in a constructive way. Instead of threatening to go to the ICC, they should focus intensely on the resumption of negotiations unconditionally and leave it to the United States to establish the rules of engagement. In so doing, they will deprive Netanyahu of playing for time, particularly because it was he who insisted on resuming the negotiations unconditionally. Israel, for its part, would be wise to refrain from taking even symbolic punitive actions against the PA. Doing so will not only worsen the situation but weaken Israel's hand, as it would be acting against its own interest while further alienating the entire international community. The recent decision by Netanyahu's government to build 3,000 units in East Jerusalem and West Bank settlements[253] is exactly the wrong prescription for the immediate resumption of negotiations, but since this project is still at the planning stages, the United States can play a direct role in diffusing this conflicting issue.

The Obama administration has an equally important task in resolving the conflict by demonstrating that it can be an honest and impartial mediator. The United States should retract its own threat

---

253 Jodi Rudoren and Mark Landler, "Housing Move in Israel Seen as Setback for a Two-State Plan," *The New York Times*, November 30, 2012, http://www.nytimes.com/2012/12/01/world/middleeast/israel-moves-to-expand-settlements-in-east-jerusalem.html?hp.

of taking action against the PA.[254] President Obama can make a convincing argument to Congress that taking punitive action would further undermine U.S. influence in the region and that withholding aid from the PA will only strengthen the extremists among the Palestinians.

It should be made clear, though, that none of the above exempts the Palestinians from responsibility. They have all along obstructed the peace process and resorted to violence, especially the second Intifada, which was a turning point for Israel providing justification for its concerns, suspicions, and complete lack of trust. In that regard, while "the Palestinians never miss an opportunity to miss an opportunity,"[255] Israel cannot afford to miss this opportunity and bring an end to the seven-decades-old debilitating conflict with dignity.

Fundamentally, the dwindling prospect of achieving a two-state solution demands a creative and principled approach by the United States and Israel. The latest move by the PA may well provide the impetus to seek a solution, however elusive it may seem.

254 Elise Labott, "Palestinian Bid Could Put U.S. Funding at Risk," *CNN*, November 29, 2012, http://security.blogs.cnn.com/2012/11/29/palestinian-bid-could-put-u-s-funding-at-risk/.

255 David Harris, "The Palestinians: Once Again Missing an Opportunity?," *The Jerusalem Post*, July 19, 2011, http://blogs.jpost.com/content/palestinians-once-again-missing-opportunity.

SHOW THE LEADERS THE ROAD TO PEACE

AUGUST 5, 2013

If there was even a small chance of success in the Israeli-Palestinian negotiations, they would have to be based on three fundamental tenets. First, they must come to an agreement on the critical issue of borders, delink it from other difficult conflicting issues (e.g., Jerusalem and the refugees), and remain committed to it, rather than aiming for achieving a comprehensive peace which is not attainable at this juncture. Second, the United States should remain resilient, advance ideas of its own, and use its leverage on both sides to keep them on track. Finally, trust must be cultivated between Israelis and Palestinians through people-to-people interactions, which is the subject of this article.

Repeated polls suggest that a clear majority of Israelis and Palestinians want peace.[256] Now that formal negotiations have started, they must no longer remain complacent. It is up to them to initiate people-to-people interactions that must occur concurrently with the peace talks.

This is the only way to build trust between the two sides and allow them, over time, to see each other in a starkly different and positive light, instead of the prevailing sense of empowerment, which the Israelis enjoy, and defeatism, from which the Palestinians suffer.

The following points are not revolutionary ideas. Some of these measures have been taken in the past and are still being pursued today, albeit on a smaller scale. However, they have not been employed in a cohesive, purposeful, and consistent manner to instill a different set of values that would nurture trust.

---

256 Lydia Saad and Elizabeth Mendes, "Israelis, Palestinians Pro Peace Process, but Not Hopeful," *Gallup*, March 21, 2013, http://www.gallup.com/poll/161456/israelis-palestinians-pro-peace-process-not-hopeful.aspx.

First, mutual visitation: The public must demand that their respective authorities allow them to visit each other with ease. Concerns over security can certainly be mitigated; Israel is in a perfect position to institute background security checks in advance and prevent the infiltration of Islamic radicals and weapons.

Security at the border crossing can be made along the lines of security procedures in airports that are both quick and thorough. It is hard to exaggerate the value of such mutual visits when ordinary people meet, share experiences, and get a real sense of each other's humanity.

Second, female activism: Israeli and Palestinian women, who are doubly affected by the unending conflict, should use their formidable power to demand an end to the conflict.

They can insist that their respective governments facilitate the gathering of Israeli and Palestinian women, allowing them to share both the pain and agony of the past and the prospects for a better future.[257]

Women have far greater sway than men if they join hands, go out in force, and remain consistent with the message to cease all forms of violence and gradually bring the occupation to an end. The role of women in ending the conflict in Northern Ireland and throughout the wars in the Balkans offer a vivid picture of how women can impact the course of events.[258]

---

257 A number of organizations have engaged in this type of activity, such as Bat Shalom and Jerusalem Center for Women, as highlighted in a report by Norwegian Church Aid in 2008 (http://www.norad.no/en/tools-and-publications/publications/publication?key=132926).

258 Siobhan Byrne highlights the important role women played in the peace process in Northern Ireland, particularly as those experiences relate to the Israeli-Palestinian conflict (http://irserver.ucd.ie/bitstream/handle/10197/2416/89_byrne.pdf?sequence=1). In the Balkans, the most recognizable womens' group involved in the peace movement there is Women in Black (http://zeneucrnom.org/index.php?lang=en), the Serbian branch of which was founded in 1991. Beyond these two conflicts, UN Women has highlighted a number of conflict situations globally where women have played a key role in mediation and conflict resolution (http://www.unwomen.org/en/what-we-do/peace-and-security/conflict-prevention-and-resolution).

Third, joint sporting events: Israeli and Palestinian football, basketball, and other sports teams can meet alternately in Israel and Palestine to train, compete, and develop camaraderie.[259]

The Palestinians will realize that not every Israeli carries a gun and is ready to shoot at Palestinians, and the Israelis will also see the human face of the Palestinians and stop equating Palestinian youth to terrorists.

Fourth, student interaction: It is time for Palestinian students (in primary and secondary schools and universities) to mingle with their counterparts and for Israeli students to look into the eyes of their peers and talk about their aspirations and hopes for the future, free of daily trepidations.

No Israeli or Palestinian child should continue to be fed with poisonous ideas and denial of the other. On the contrary, students should be encouraged to use the latest social technology to communicate with each other, share stories and experiences, and play games.

The future of the Israelis and Palestinians rests in the hands of these youth. What they learn today will either come back to haunt their societies or usher in a future of peace and promise.

Fifth, art exhibitions: There are scores of Israeli and Palestinian artists who have never met or delved into each other's mindset to see how their works reflect their lives.

Joint exhibitions should take place both in Israel and Palestine, touring several cities, to allow people young and old to see and feel what the other is trying to express. These cultural exchanges can expand to include music festivals, theater performances, and other forms of art.[260]

Sixth, public discourse: Universities, think tanks, and other learning institutions should encourage Israelis and Palestinians to

259 Similar to the activities spearheaded by women's groups, a number of sporting organizations in this vein have already been established, most notably the Israeli-Palestinian Peace Team, a collaboration between the Peres Center for Peace and the Al-Quds Association for Democracy and Dialogue (http://www.peaceteam.com.au/about-the-peace-team/).

260 Some of these cultural exchanges are already taking place, in particular, theater performances. Groups such as YTheater Project, Freedom Theater, and Combatants for Peace have been using theater to open dialogues between Israelis and Palestinians.

participate in roundtable discussions on the inevitability of coexistence and how both sides can remove the barriers to make it desirable.

The academic community can play a pivotal role in changing public perceptions. Such small enclaves can be videotaped and disseminated through online media to hundreds of thousands of people instantly. The words "inevitability of coexistence" must become a household phrase for all to embrace.

Seventh, forums to discuss conflicting issues: Joint forums should be established, consisting of qualified individuals with varied academic and personal experiences who enjoy respect in their field, are independent thinkers, hold no formal position in their respective governments, and have thorough knowledge of the conflicting issues.

For example, in addressing the future of Jerusalem, the participants should especially include religious scholars (imams, rabbis, and priests representing the three major monotheistic religions) and historians.

Even though Jerusalem may well become the capital of two states, debating other possibilities is critical if for no other reason but to demonstrate why other options may or may not work.

Eighth, changing public discourse: Israeli and Palestinian officials also have a very important role to play by changing their narrative about the conflicting issues. Now that the negotiations have resumed, it is incumbent on both sides to maintain a positive and optimistic public posture.

Regardless of whether these negotiations succeed or fail, Israelis and Palestinians will sooner or later face each other at the negotiating table. The less acrimonious atmosphere they create now, the easier it will be to meet again and continue with the building blocks for a durable peace.

Ninth, the role of the media: Israeli and Palestinian media should begin to report on positive developments between the two sides to inform the people that the bilateral relations are not all sad and gloomy. For example, they can discuss ongoing trade, security, and healthcare cooperation, Palestinians studying in Israeli universities, and so on.

In this sense, the role of the media becomes critical to disseminate information about the need for people-to-people interaction. The media should publicize these events as they occur and columnists and commentators should encourage more such activities.

The media can play a pivotal role in shaping bilateral Israeli-Palestinians relations, emphasizing the fact that there are two peoples living side-by-side for eternity and that cooperation between the two is imperative to their welfare and future wellbeing.

The aspiration of Israelis and Palestinians for peace is real and realizable. Their leaders have been deaf and failed time and again to answer the public's call. It is now the responsibility of the public to take charge and show the leaders the road to peace.

STUCK IN AN IDEOLOGICAL DIVIDE

APRIL 2, 2014

The common characteristics and stark differences between Israel's Prime Minister Netanyahu and the PA's President Abbas might just explain why the current peace negotiations are stuck and not likely to lead to any breakthrough as long as they remain in power. The irony is that while a majority of Israelis and Palestinians aspire for peace, Netanyahu and to a lesser extent Abbas have become the main obstacles as they remain wedded to certain beliefs and ideologies that have long since lost their merit.

How absurd is it to think that Secretary of State John Kerry's effort could in fact lead to a peace agreement on major concessions, including the Palestinian refugees, Jerusalem, national security, and settlements, when Netanyahu and Abbas cannot even agree on the release of a handful of Palestinian prisoners in exchange for extending the peace negotiations to the end of the year?

Netanyahu claims that if he agreed to the release before securing the extension, his government would collapse, and Abbas feels that if he were to agree to Netanyahu's demand, he would be accused of having caved to incongruous demands coming from a person that the Palestinians dislike and distrust.

A conflict that has exacted so much pain, human lives and material losses for over six and a half decades should not and cannot continue only because Netanyahu and Abbas **presumably disagree** to extend the current negotiations. It is absurd, if not outright insane.

It is even more absurd that Netanyahu is now asking Kerry to secure the release of convicted spy Jonathan Pollard in return for releasing more Palestinian prisoners, extending the negotiations, and also freezing the building of new housing units in the West Bank. The irony is, how many more Pollards will it take to reach an agreement?

The truth is rarely pure and never simple. Netanyahu will not deliver any of the necessary concessions because **he is not committed to reaching a peace agreement** based on two states for two peoples.

Conversely, Abbas, who appears to be more committed to peace, is beholden to old and tired narratives of yesteryear, knowing full well that he simply is not in a position to concede on any issue such as the **principle** of the right of return or the future of Jerusalem as a capital of two states, which he has held sacred for decades.

While Abbas has correctly taken the unilateral step of applying to 15 UN international conventions to pressure Israel,[261] he has stated that he still remains committed to the negotiations but left the door open to join other UN agencies, including the ICC, should the talks fail, a move Israel fears the most.

Kerry must know what the strategy of this odd couple is by now. Netanyahu, who is a hardcore ideologue, is not prepared to deviate from his belief in a greater Israel that must include much of the West Bank. For that he must play for time, and he does so skillfully by making demands he knows full well that Abbas cannot accept.

He is convinced that he can go against the tide, believing that the Obama administration will simply not put the kind of pressure needed on Israel, fearing domestic repercussions.

Poor Abbas; his hands are tied behind his back, or rather, he asked that his hands be tied behind his back. There is not one single concession he can make, be that on the future of Jerusalem, the Palestinian refugees, the settlements, etc., without alienating one segment or another among the Palestinians, unless he first exacts significant concessions from Netanyahu.

He does not have the full support of the Arab states, Hamas is breathing down his neck, the public is divided, and many Palestinians feel that he lacks legitimacy. Therefore, his options are limited, he has no one among the Palestinian leadership whom he can trust, and certainly he has no apparent successor.

---

261 Yifa Yaakov, "Abbas Signs Palestine Request to Join 15 Int'l Bodies," *The Times of Israel*, April 1, 2014, http://www.timesofisrael.com/abbas-signs-palestines-application-to-join-15-un-bodies/.

What could have been the difference if you had two leaders who are really and absolutely committed to reaching an agreement based on the only viable option of two states for two peoples? Netanyahu and Abbas would have sat together with their top advisors for weeks or months and done whatever else it takes to hammer out an agreement that meets the necessary requirements to make peace.

Simultaneously, they would have come out and faced their own respective publics and stated loud and clear: we both must make major concessions, however painful these may be. But these two leaders are simply incapable and unwilling to do just that.

As a result of their intractability, the price that both sides will pay is beyond what either could contemplate in their worst nightmare. Many Israelis will die to protect themselves, and many more Palestinians will prefer death over continued subjugation, humiliation, and despair.

It is about time for Kerry to read Netanyahu and Abbas their rights. The United States cannot reform these leaders—one with a messianic mission and the other presiding over a shallow political base frozen in time and place.

Kerry has two options: first, leave the Israelis and the Palestinians to their own devices and let them slug it out at each other for another decade or two until they reach a point of exhaustion, while risking major regional repercussions.

The second option is for Kerry to present his framework to Netanyahu and Abbas and give them one year to reach an agreement on a take it or leave it basis. Should they fail, the United States must be prepared to withdraw its political and financial aid from both Israelis and Palestinians alike.

The sooner the Obama administration comes to this conclusion, the better off the Israelis and the Palestinians will be; but then again, it will take bold American leadership.

The catch is that Obama is not likely to take such a position, and we may have to wait for the rise of new Israeli and Palestinian leaders committed to pursuing peace because the alternative is too dire to contemplate.

WHAT WENT WRONG?

MAY 8, 2014

The failure of the negotiations between Israel and the Palestinians and the causes behind it were absolutely predictable. I, like many others, argued that regardless of the United States' determination to lead both sides to agree on a two-state solution, the energy, resources, and political capital invested by Secretary of State John Kerry toward that end were all to no avail. Indeed, the commitments to reach an agreement, specifically by Prime Minister Netanyahu, and United States' unwillingness to put the necessary pressure were absent.

Kerry made a fundamental mistake by establishing rules of engagement that were not conducive to progress, raising serious doubts about the prospect of a solution.

He caved in to Netanyahu's demands to address Israel's national security concerns first instead of dealing with borders, as it would have defined the contours of the Palestinian state, which Abbas sorely needed to allow him to be more flexible.

Kerry's yielding to Netanyahu's refusal to freeze settlement expansion was nothing short of the kiss of death. Every time a new tender for building housing units was announced, it raised anew psychological and practical doubts about Netanyahu's real intentions.

Continued settlement expansion during the negotiations was seen as creeping annexation of Palestinian land, which was rightfully viewed by the Palestinians as a detriment to the establishment of a Palestinian state.

Kerry did not insist that both Israeli and Palestinian leaders refrain from criticizing each other publicly during the negotiations, which further eroded, instead of mobilized, public support of Israelis and Palestinians alike.

The appointment of Martin Indyk as a mediator was unwise, as he was perceived by the Palestinians to be biased in favor of Israel.

Kerry conceded to Netanyahu's excuse that his government would collapse should he freeze settlement construction when in fact Netanyahu could have mobilized public support if he was really seeking a two-state solution.

Knowing how sensitive settlement expansion is to the Palestinians, Netanyahu's Housing Minister sabotaged the negotiations as he issued tenders for new housing units timed to enrage Kerry and Abbas.

Burned by failure during his first term, President Obama remained indirectly involved in the negotiations, sparing Netanyahu and Abbas the necessary pressure only he could exert.

It should have been more than obvious to Kerry that Netanyahu was never committed to reaching a solution, certainly not one that would lead to the creation of a Palestinian state. Netanyahu counted on the Israelis' complacency about the prospect for peace, as most Israelis accepted Netanyahu's misleading narrative that there is no negotiating partner and that the Palestinians cannot be trusted.

Israel, led by Netanyahu, should bear much of the blame. Netanyahu took advantage of Kerry's indecisiveness, and for good reason—he could count on Congress and the Jewish lobby to prevent Kerry from pressuring Israel to make any meaningful concessions to keep the process going.

Netanyahu cleverly insisted on negotiating national security matters first to prevent negotiations on borders, which would have facilitated the talks over national security and the future of much of the settlements.

As a means by which to prevent reaching an agreement, Netanyahu borrowed a page or two from the Iranian negotiating manual by playing for time and by merely preaching, for example, the two-state solution for international and public consumption but refusing to act on it.

Although Netanyahu appointed Tzipi Livni as chief negotiator, his appointment of Yitzhak Molcho, his personal confidant and relative, to the negotiating team was purposely made to monitor Livni and prevent her from making any concessions to which he might object.

In all fairness, the Palestinians were the least responsible for the collapse of the negotiations. Abbas needed to show that he would not succumb to Netanyahu's whims or Kerry's urging because he felt all along that he has already made several important concessions.

These concessions included allowing Israel to keep residual forces along the Jordan River for five years, finding a solution to the Palestinian refugee problem acceptable to Israel, accepting a demilitarized Palestinian state, and leaving most of the settlers (80 percent) in place along the 1967 border as a part of Israel.

That said, Abbas suffered from a lack of consensus among the Palestinians; he did not feel that he had a full political mandate while Hamas, until recently, was breathing down his neck.

Abbas' legitimacy was questioned as his term expired in 2009, which for several years discouraged him from making any other concessions, like recognizing Israel as a Jewish state, on which Netanyahu insisted.

He negotiated from a position of weakness, especially because Netanyahu refused to make any significant concessions, such as freezing even for a short period of time the construction of new housing units in the West Bank.

For all these reasons and some, it was ironic to hear top American and Jordanian officials with direct knowledge of the negotiations insist that Kerry's initiative, unlike any other previous mediating efforts, will succeed in forging an Israeli-Palestinian peace.

Kerry was quite blunt, and for good reason, in placing the blame on Israel for the collapse of the negotiations. However, he never acknowledged that he too contributed to the impasse because the negotiations were based, from the very beginning, on a flawed process.

Perhaps one critical thing has been learned from this painful exercise, stated by Obama best: "...if you see no peace deal and continued aggressive settlement construction—and we have seen more aggressive settlement construction over the last couple years than we've seen in a very long time—if Palestinians come to believe that the possibility of a contiguous sovereign Palestinian state is no longer within reach, then our ability to manage the international fallout is going to be limited."[262]

Israel will do well to heed Obama's warning.

---

262 Jeffrey Goldberg, "Obama to Israel – Time Is Running Out," *Bloomberg View*, March 2, 2014, http://www.bloombergview.com/ articles/2014-03-02/obama-to-israel-time-is-running-out.

A TRAGEDY SHOULD NOT BEGET ANOTHER

JULY 2, 2014

There are no words that can adequately condemn the tragic death of the three Israeli teenagers, Naftali, Gilad, and Eyal, who have become the latest victims of the long and bloody Israeli-Palestinian struggle. The abduction of any person, be that for exacting ransom or for the purpose of a prisoner exchange, must be vehemently condemned in the strongest words. To summarily execute the three kidnapped innocent boys, however, is beastly and transcends the most awful crime that one can commit against another.

The unfathomable murders should now hopefully serve only the opposite of what the criminal perpetrators intended. If they meant to inflict tremendous pain and agony on all Israelis, especially the families of the victims, they have succeeded, but they also have miserably failed as they set back the prospect of a solution to the agonizing conflict from which many Palestinians, young and old, will dreadfully suffer.

The deaths of these brave teenagers, whose lives were mercilessly cut short, must not be in vain. They must be the catalyst for peace and not the cause that perpetuates the self-consuming conflict that will only poison another generation of Israelis and Palestinians.

Prime Minister Netanyahu has blamed Hamas for the atrocious murders without producing as of yet any compelling evidence. The mere fact, however, that Hamas' leadership extolled the abductions and subsequently condoned the cold-blooded killing strongly suggests that Hamas' leadership is incapable of changing its stripes.

Following the establishment of the unity government, I advocated that the Israeli government should give Hamas a chance to prove that it has finally subscribed, albeit indirectly, to a negotiated settlement of the Israeli-Palestinian conflict.[263]

---

263 See "Charting a New Course," page [288].

348

It is now obvious, to my chagrin, that Hamas joining the unity government was designed only to strengthen its foothold in the West Bank and benefit economically from the merger.

That said, I am convinced that Hamas' leadership does not represent the vast majority of the Palestinians in Gaza, who are captives of these ruthless leaders and are fed up with their unending precarious status quo.

Although Hamas' leaders deny culpability in the horrific murders, and even if their claim proves to be true, Hamas has forfeited any chance to redeem itself while subjecting the Palestinians in Gaza to greater suffering and despondency.

Meanwhile, Hamas' leadership has severely undermined PA President Mahmoud Abbas, who genuinely seeks a negotiated peace agreement to bring an end to the seven decades-old debilitating conflict.

Those in and outside the Israeli government who are calling for massive retaliation to indiscriminately punish the Palestinians, including the Economy and Defense Ministers (Naftali Bennett and Moshe Ya'alon, respectively), have lost their bearing as they seek revenge and retribution. They are clearly short-sighted because they seem to have no idea where the escalation of violence could lead to.

Capturing and punishing the culprits behind the murders is one thing, but destroying the prospect of a peace agreement is as harmful to the Israelis as it is to the Palestinians. Uncompromising Israeli and Palestinian zealots are only paving the way for more tragedies on both sides, which sadly has already led to the death of at least six Palestinian youths.

The Netanyahu government is clearly split over the scope of the Israeli retaliatory measures and what the ultimate objective is. Obviously, deliberating in such a painful and emotionally charged atmosphere often leaves little room for rational discourse.

That said, there are still wise men and women in the Israeli government, including Finance Minister Yair Lapid and Justice Minister Tzipi Livni, who for good reason counsel restraint.

They, like many other Israelis, know that there is no escaping the reality of Israeli-Palestinian coexistence in one form or another.

Every action or reaction taken today will have a lasting impact, either deeply damaging or benefiting their bilateral relations.

The ultimate gain belongs to those Israelis and Palestinians who share the vision of peaceful coexistence and remain focused on the larger picture regardless of how awful the current circumstances are.

Every crisis, regardless of its magnitude, presents an opportunity for a new breakthrough. The United States' call for restraint while consoling the Israelis and sharing their grief is certainly the right first step. But more is needed to be done by the United States to prevent the outbreak of a major violent conflagration.

Given the sweeping turmoil throughout the region and the danger that every state in the area faces, another major Israeli-Palestinian flare-up will only play into the hands of the jihadists, especially the Islamic State of Iraq and Syria (ISIS), who would exploit every opening to promote their menacing agenda, which will pose a direct danger to Israel, Jordan, and the Palestinians.

President Obama must spare no effort to calm the situation first by immediately dispatching Secretary of State John Kerry to the region, and make a personal appeal to the Israeli government and the PA to do everything in their power to preserve their security cooperation.

He should also urge them to further strengthen their collaboration and defy those who are bent on destroying the last vestiges of peaceful negotiations now or in the not-too-distant future.

President Abbas in particular needs all the support and help he can get to hold onto his position and remain the voice of reason. No other leader but the American President can give Abbas the helping hands he now desperately needs.

The President should also invite both Netanyahu and Abbas to the White House and remind them of the perils of not achieving peace, and ask them to publicly reaffirm their commitment to resume negotiations in earnest.

The Israeli and Palestinian public needs to see the two leaders working hand in hand toward that end, and that the tragic events have only strengthened their resolve.

No Israeli or Palestinian child should die in a conflict that could have been resolved decades ago. They deserve and have the right to live in peace and a promising future. The precious loss of life of Naftali, Gilad, and Eyal should not be in vain—may their victimhood be the catalyst for peace.

THE DOUBLE FOLLY

The war between Hamas and Israel has exposed the folly of both sides. Hamas' long-standing objective to destroy Israel has come back to haunt it, which may eventually spell its own demise. Conversely, Prime Minister Netanyahu's unwillingness to end the occupation and the blockade has also shown the folly of his policy.

The sad irony is that Hamas' leaders know that they will never be able to seriously threaten Israel existentially, and every time they challenge Israel, they subject the Palestinians in Gaza to the horrors of war, destruction, and death.

Similarly, Netanyahu does not recognize that continuing the occupation and the blockade is unsustainable and there is no such thing as secure borders in the age of rockets, regardless of how fortified they may be.

Let me first state that I distinguish between the fanatic, violent, and misguided organization Hamas, and the vast majority of Palestinians in Gaza and the West Bank, who want to live in peace and dignity.

The current flare-up vividly demonstrates the cruelty and degenerate morality of Hamas by using men, women, and children as human shields to safeguard its cache of rockets, subjecting innocent Palestinians to abject poverty and despair. This only attests to Hamas' brutal reign, which places its twisted religious bent above the lives of those it presumably wishes to protect.

Driven by blind fanaticism, Hamas' leaders readily sacrifice the precious lives of children and heartlessly prevent ordinary, terrified Palestinians from leaving their homes to avoid death and injuries for the sole purpose of inviting increasing international condemnation of Israel.

Hamas made a habit of provoking Israel, ostensibly to end the Israeli blockade. Instead, it finds itself marred in another bloody confrontation while the vast majority of Palestinians in Gaza end up paying a dear price.

Following the formation of the Palestinian unity government, I advocated that Israel should give Hamas a chance to demonstrate its willingness to adhere, albeit indirectly, to the three Quartet principles of recognizing Israel, accepting prior agreements, and forsaking violence,[264] which the unity government reaffirmed.

Instead, Hamas chose to forfeit a historic opportunity that could have allowed the unity government to chart a new path to bring about the eventual lifting of the blockade and establish the conditions on which to gradually build a durable peace.

Rather than building on Israel's concessions in the 2012 ceasefire agreement, Hamas opted to challenge Israel again in an effort to boost its waning political legitimacy among the Palestinians, who have been reaping nothing from Hamas' militancy but more pain and despondency.

While Hamas was able to generate in times of stress sympathy from the Arab states, today Hamas finds itself more isolated and financially strapped than ever before.

Weary of Islamic extremism, the Arab states are in fact quietly cheering Hamas' beatings by Israeli forces. Not surprisingly, Egypt took pleasure witnessing Hamas' self-inflicted wounds as the Egyptian government loathes Hamas, which has strong affiliations with the now-outlawed Muslim Brotherhood.

Netanyahu, on the other hand, has not fared much better. He insists that Israel is not an occupying power and that in any case it needs defensible borders. The new conflagration with Hamas has once again revealed the folly of his argument as thousands of rockets are raining on Israel, creating mayhem and forcing thousands to scramble in fear for cover.

The argument advanced by right-wing politicians is that the withdrawal from Gaza in 2005 demonstrates that the Palestinians cannot be trusted, as Hamas uses the land as a staging ground for attacks on Israel instead of building the infrastructure of a state.

---

264 See "Fatah and Hamas Reconciliation: Rushing to Judgment," p. [283].

Had it not been for the fact that the withdrawal from Gaza was precipitous, unilateral, and done without security arrangements, economic development plans, or in phases, the picture would be different today. Hamas would not have been able to overthrow the PA, which was in control of Gaza at the time, and seize control of the Strip.

Nevertheless, the decision to withdraw was made on the assumption that a divided Palestine is more advantageous to Israel, and ridding itself of Gaza would free Israel from the responsibility of administering a densely populated area which Israel has no affinity to, and has no ideological resonance or geostrategic value.

The shortsightedness of successive Israeli governments in settling for the status quo is not sustainable given the continuing blockade of Gaza and Israel's unwillingness to ease it in times of calm, the occupation of the West Bank, and the continuing expansion of settlements. A violent eruption such as the current war was predictable.

Here again, Israeli folly is put on full display. A relatively small, fanatic Islamist group is able to inflict incredible havoc all over Israel while boldly facing down the most formidable military power in the Middle East.

Now Netanyahu find himself in a box. He is torn between his desire to crush Hamas and destroy its infrastructure, and international pressure to end the hostilities. Once again, the whole world is watching the unfolding of a Greek tragedy, except this one is very real and unforgiving.

It is a tragedy because both Hamas and Israel are guilty of hubris that transcends bounds and defies reality. The ever-present evidence of Israeli hubris is the unending occupation while denying Palestinians the establishment of their own state; with Hamas, it is its suicidal persistence to seek Israel's total destruction.

It is clear that a ceasefire must be urgently established to immediately provide humanitarian aid organized by the UN, which must be followed by negotiating a more durable accord. But no such agreement will have any meaning unless it addresses the causes and consequences of this never-ending conflict.

The current crisis offers an opportunity for a major breakthrough:

To begin with, no concession should be made to Hamas unless

it first surrenders its cache of weapons to a UN-sponsored group in return for easing the blockade and gradually lifting it altogether.

Security coordination between Israel and the PA should be put in place in Gaza under the auspices of the unity government, allowing the PA security forces to take charge of all crossings from the Gaza side.

Israel must pledge to resume the peace negotiations in earnest and recommit itself to the two-state solution to give all Palestinians hope that the occupation will eventually come to an end.

I am not naïve to assume that Hamas and Israel will readily accept such an agreement. But this is the time to squeeze both as they cannot have it both ways. For Hamas, it is to be free to move people and goods in and out of Gaza while preparing for the next battle, and for Israel, to continue the expansion of settlements, maintain the occupation, and keep the blockade in place.

If the international community, led by the United States, wants to avoid a repeat of these disastrous scenarios, it must insist on these conditions, however untenable they may seem.

Indeed, as long as these dynamics are not fundamentally changed, Israelis and Palestinians will continue to pay the price. It is time to expose the Israeli and Palestinian folly.

Both sides will discover that this mutual folly assures a fate as described by Aeschylus: "So great shall be new sacrifices of clotting blood...so great the piles of bones, even to the third generation they shall be seen by human eyes as speechless warnings that those who must die not overreach themselves: when stubborn pride has flowered, it ripens to self-deception and the only harvest is a glut of tears."[265]

---

265 Aeschylus, "Persians," in *The Complete Aeschylus: Volume II: Persians and Other Plays*, eds. Peter Burian and Alan Shapiro (New York: Oxford University Press, 2009), 73.

A LESSON ISRAEL AND HAMAS
SHOULD REMEMBER

AUGUST 22, 2014

The ongoing war between Israel and Hamas is only reinforcing the notion that unlike previous ceasefire agreements, preventing repeated violent confrontations requires a fundamental change in the status quo. Hamas' demand for the complete lifting of the blockade and Israel's insistence on the demilitarization of Gaza suggests that small incremental steps, including easing the blockade by Israel and in return adhering to a ceasefire by Hamas, will no longer suffice.

While Hamas is still committed to a self-styled religiously-anchored doctrine that calls for Israel's destruction, Israel is convinced that Hamas is irredeemable. Ironically, neither side wants to restore the status quo ante, yet they are holding on to what appears to be irreconcilable positions which are at the core of the conflict.

Both sides are stuck and are looking for a way out; nevertheless, neither is willing to make the far-reaching concessions necessary to avoid future violent confrontations and their destructive consequences.

Israel can reoccupy Gaza and eliminate many, if not all, of Hamas' leadership, but it would come at a prohibitive cost in blood and treasure. Israel will have to administer and care for more than 1.8 million Palestinians, risking the lives of tens of thousands of soldiers and instigating an insurgency that would terrorize Israeli forces at every turn.

In the interim, new Hamas cells will mushroom and once Israel withdraws its forces (as it cannot and does not want to maintain the occupation indefinitely) and passes the reins to the UN or any other international agency, Hamas will re-emerge with greater vehemence and commitment to destroy Israel, however elusive that goal might be.

Under such a scenario, there is also the possibility that a plethora of jihadists will converge on Gaza, i.e., ISIS and Al-Qaeda, who will join other local jihadists and create a reign of terror that will pale in comparison to Hamas.

As a result of these probable developments, Netanyahu is correct in rejecting the call to reoccupy Gaza and resisting the introduction of substantial ground troops to destroy Hamas' rocket stockpile, as this will not be possible short of reoccupying the Strip.

The other option is to agree on another tactical ceasefire fashioned along previous ones to provide both sides with some breathing room. By definition, such a ceasefire is not likely to hold as it would once again subject Israel to the terror of rockets raining indiscriminately, wreaking havoc and forcing thousands to flee in panic to shelters, which the public is unwilling to tolerate any longer.

For Hamas, merely easing the blockade while Israel continues to maintain tight restrictions on the free flow of goods and people to and from Gaza will no longer meet the public outcry for a fundamental change in their miserable daily lives.

Although Hamas still enjoys grassroots support, the overwhelming majority of Palestinians in Gaza want an end to the conflict with Israel. For too long they have been subjected to abject poverty and indignity, and suffered greatly from repeated conflagrations with Israel.

Moreover, Hamas no longer has any appetite to provoke Israel only to suffer tremendous destruction and death of innocent civilians, which explains why Hamas is looking for a fundamental change in the status quo and to be in a position to deliver significant relief to the public and restore confidence in its leadership.

One might think that Israel and Hamas would be well disposed to accepting each other's demands and establishing a permanent ceasefire on which to build, over time, peaceful coexistence.

This regrettably is not the case. But under no circumstances will the negotiations resume and produce what both sides ultimately want (lifting the blockade against demilitarization), which is completely inconsistent with their public positions.

They need a face-saving way out, but they remain haunted by a deep distrust of each other, which makes it much harder and ever more complicated to reach any agreement.

Ideally, the solution will have to be based on the establishment of a long-term ceasefire that will provide the basis for demilitarizing Gaza and ending the blockade over time and in phases, with an eye on reaching a more comprehensive Israeli-Palestinian deal.

Sadly, we are not living in an ideal world, but then what lesson have both sides learned from this continuing miserable state of affairs? This war and its repercussions have demonstrated once again the limits of the use of force alone, as neither side can emerge unscathed from continuing to slug it out.

Israel, with its mighty military prowess, could not force Hamas to submission; it still remains capable of wreaking havoc on the Israeli population. Conversely, Hamas cannot exact one meaningful concession from Israel by force or by evoking international outcry for the terrible human tragedies and material losses it has sustained. It is a bitter lesson both sides will do well to remember.

Should they now begin to contemplate taking bold steps and change direction, which appears to be inconceivable at this juncture? I believe that in the long run they will have no other choice. Yet, however incongruous this may seem, it is better to be a fool who tries than a wise man who never dares.

UNITED STATES AS PEACE BROKER

OBAMA'S ISRAELI CHALLENGE

MAY 13, 2009

President Obama's May 18th meeting with Israel's Prime Minister Benjamin Netanyahu will introduce a new dimension to the long-standing American-Israeli alliance. The changing circumstances in the Middle East and the potentially diverging views each leader holds in connection with the Arab-Israeli conflict could make finding common ground more challenging than in the past. To preserve the integrity of the bilateral relations, both leaders can be expected to engage in some serious give and take. Obama is likely to insist that there must be significant progress made in the Arab-Israeli peace process, especially regarding the Palestinian front. Similarly, Netanyahu, a master tactician, will find a way to accommodate the President while also exacting assurances that the United States will deal pointedly with the Iranian nuclear threat.

The U.S.' commitment to Israel's national security is embedded in the American psyche and transcends shared values or an influential lobby. A long history of moral commitment to a homeland for the Jews, strategic cooperation, evangelical grassroots support, and cultural and political affinities have all cemented the relationship over the years, making Israel the closest U.S. ally, perhaps with the exception of the United Kingdom. That being said, however powerful

359

militarily Israel might be, the country's ultimate security still depends on the United States, and only together can they fashion a solution to the Arab-Israeli conflict while safeguarding Israel's national security. This has guided previous American presidents and will certainly guide President Obama—no Israeli prime minister is oblivious to this reality.

The U.S.' dedication to the two-state solution is not a new policy; it has been central to the Road Map, Oslo Accords, the Madrid Peace Conference, and to every interim agreement between Israel and the Palestinians and previous American administrations. Netanyahu cannot simply deny or defer the discussion in hopes of persuading or coercing the Palestinians and the Arab states to settle for much less. Obama finds himself in a unique position to push for the resumption of Israeli-Palestinian negotiations, not only because he feels committed to the idea, but because of the conversion of events and developments that offer the opportunity for a solution yet also bear ominous implications if nothing is done.

Obama has inherited the wrath of the Arab and Muslim world, precipitated mainly by his predecessor's policies: two wars in Iraq and Afghanistan and a third shaping up in Pakistan, a potentially nuclear Iran, and the continuing rise in extremism, terrorism, and jihadi movements. By every conceivable account the Israeli-Palestinian discord feeds into these violent conflicts, making it impossible for any American president to articulate practical solutions without attending to the Israeli-Palestinian issue first. Neither Netanyahu nor any of his coalition partners can avoid this reality. Obama faces an international community that was less than supportive of Israel's recent military incursion into Gaza, and allies who want to see once and for all a final solution for the Palestinian people. For Obama to unravel some of these menacing developments with the support of any international partners, he must first put out the Arab-Israeli fire.

Driven by their concern over Iran's nuclear program, the growing Sunni-Shiite schism, and threatened by Islamic extremism, the Arab states—for the first time since the creation of Israel in 1948—appear ready to negotiate in earnest a comprehensive peace deal with Israel. Anyone who underestimates the significance of the Arab Peace Initiative (API) in this regard misses the historic dimension of the

Initiative, which offers Israel the ultimate security it seeks. Fortunately, it was not missed by Obama. The President's embrace of the Initiative, which he expressed personally to Saudi Arabia's King Abdullah, is pivotal to changing the dynamics of the conflict and reaching a solution. For Israel, this represents nothing less than a revolutionary transformation in the Arab states' attitude and it must find a way to capitalize on its long-term implications.

Obama is as keen as Netanyahu that Iran's nuclear program is, at a minimum, politically destabilizing and may indeed pose a threat to Israel's national security. To suggest, however, that a resolution to Iran's nuclear ambitions must take precedence over a resolution to the Israeli-Palestinian conflict is based on a false premise. As long as the Palestinian conflict persists, one can count on Tehran to fan the flames and continue to undermine the prospect of a comprehensive solution which will have to include Syria.

In one form or another, President Obama's commitment to pursuing the Israeli-Palestinian track has already paid some dividends. Hamas leader Khaled Meshal—under pressure from the Arab states and certainly in a nod to Obama—has indirectly supported the idea of a two-state solution by supporting a Palestinian state based on the 1967 borders. This development considerably improves the prospect of a Palestinian unity government that can speak in one voice and has the potential to deliver on a long-term ceasefire. Hamas is here to stay and it is now impractical to count them out of the equation on any peace agreement. Netanyahu can take solace in the fact that Hamas moderated its stance under his watch and responded with a favorable gesture, especially now that Hamas has suspended all acts of violence against Israel.

As he understands Syria's central role in any future Arab-Israeli negotiations, Obama's outreach to Damascus is most significant and overdue. Damascus is ready and eager to resume, this time directly, serious peace negotiations with Israel while seeking normal relations with the United States. Surely the price tag is the return of the Golan Heights—a price that Israel will have to pay if it ever chooses to end the Arab-Israeli conflict. But for Obama, this also represents a historic opportunity not only to end the Israeli-Syrian conflict but forge a grand regional security arrangement that would address Iran's ambitions. Indeed, only a comprehensive Arab-Israeli peace that can eventually draw in Iran will usher in a period of real calm and open the door to credible talks about a Middle East free of nuclear arms.

In the end, the incredible bond between Israel and the United States will prevail, as it is stronger than any one administration or leader. Obama has the maneuverability to push on Netanyahu because it is guaranteed that the United States would never compromise Israel's security. It is with the Arab states that the United States has lost major capital, and Obama knows that if he does not deliver soon, he can risk losing any partner in peace. If he cannot regain the confidence of Arab leaders in countries like Jordan, Egypt, and Saudi Arabia, the United States will have another major conflict on its hands.

There is no doubt that the discussions between the two leaders will be tough, but neither can lose sight of what is really at stake here. Netanyahu knows only too well that in the final analysis, only a comprehensive peace will offer Israel the ultimate security it seeks. President Obama sees a historic opportunity to achieve just that, while both understand the ominous implications if they fail.

OBAMA'S PEACE OFFENSIVE

JULY 21, 2009

On a recent trip to the Middle East, I had the opportunity to meet with many Israelis and Palestinians from all walks of life including high officials, settlers, and members of the Peace Now movement. I also met with academics from the left, center and right, poll takers, journalists, and scores of other ordinary people. Paradoxically, while repeated polls confirm that a majority (between 68 and 72 percent) on both sides seek peace based on a two-state solution,[266] what I heard simply reconfirmed an old adage about a profound lack of political cohesiveness within both Israeli and Palestinian communities, which has and continues to plague both sides.

While it seems that a serious disconnect exists within the Israelis themselves about the requirements for peace, a similar disconnect exists within the Palestinian community. Political factionalism in both communities, coupled with intense personal rivalry, prevents the rallying around one leader or party that can garner popular support to advance the peace agenda. More alarming is that while the disconnect within each community persists, there is still a lost perspective between Israelis and Palestinians about each other's national aspirations, concerns, requirements, hopes, and fears. Generally they remain oblivious to each other's psychological disposition while mutual suspicion and lack of trust of each other marks the essence

---

266 See Darya Shaikh, "Most Israelis, Palestinians Still Support 2-State Solution: Poll," *Huffington Post*, May 23, 2009, http://www. huffingtonpost.com/2009/04/22/most-israelis-palestinian_n_189596. html; Khalil Shikaki, interview by Bernard Gwertzman, Council on Foreign Relations, September 25, 2006, http://www.cfr.org/israel/ shikaki-palestinians-support-hamas-but-most-favor-negotiated-peace-israel/p11522;and "Poll: 58% of Israeli Jews Back Two-State Solution," *Y Net News*, May 14, 2009, http://www.ynetnews.com/ articles/0,7340,L-3715759,00.html.

of their relationship. The question is, since a majority on both sides want peace, why then is there no national drive in either camp to push for a solution? The answer may be attributed to the following:

First, generally both sides have little faith in their own leadership's ability to deliver peace with security and dignity any time soon. Israel and the Palestinians lack determined, visionary, and courageous leadership. In Israel, the nature of a coalition government often prevents the prime minister from rising above the fray and taking decisive measures toward peace without risking the collapse of the government. The Palestinians, on the other hand, suffer from chronic factionalism, making it impossible for a leader to make the necessary concessions without risking assassination. Moreover, both sides often use internal division and a lack of consensus as an excuse for inaction.

Second, many Israeli and Palestinian leaders still feel that time may further improve their position and hence they argue against "rushing" into an agreement when more time may allow them to exact greater concessions. This is coupled with strong rejectionist elements in both camps; in Israel there are those who still seek a greater Israel, especially among the settlers, and among the Palestinians there exist several groups, such as Islamic Jihad and Hamas, who want all of mandated Palestine (including Israel).

Third, neither the Israeli nor Palestinian governments have been preparing the public over the years for the inevitability of peaceful coexistence based on a two-state solution. Whereas Israeli officials talk about the lack of a worthy Palestinian interlocutor and complain about continued violence perpetrated against Israel, the Palestinian media and public condemnation of Israel continues to incite hatred against Israel often using venomous language and a tone that makes the idea of coexistence sound far-fetched at best and even undesirable.

Fourth, both societies remain internally conflicted as to how far they can go to accommodate each other while remaining doubtful if they can actually meet the other's requirements to make peace. For example, on the surface it appears that the Israeli government would not compromise on the future unity of Jerusalem as "Israel's eternal capital" while the Palestinians would presumably not compromise on the issue of the right of return of the refugees. In reality, however, both sides have in previous negotiations substantially modified their positions and reached agreements on these two critical issues.

Five, there has not been consistent pressure exerted from the outside to prompt both Israelis and Palestinians to settle their differences. Although the United States has exerted some efforts over many years, it was neither consistent nor absolutely determined to bring parties together to forge peace. Clinton and Bush focused on the Israeli-Palestinian conflict largely at the 11th hour of their presidencies. The Arab states have been using the Palestinian plight to cover for their domestic failures and only in the past few years have they advanced the Arab Initiative. Although historic in its dimensions and implications, the Arab Initiative remains static because neither side is ready or willing to translate it into a real peace process.

The above explains why, in spite of the fact that there is a clear majority on both sides that seek peaceful coexistence, very little was accomplished toward that goal. Considering this paradoxical reality, both Israelis and Palestinians have shown that they are simply incapable of resolving the conflict on their own. This is why the Obama administration must pursue a specific political agenda with determination that could unravel the internal intricacies in both camps to facilitate an agreement. The United States cannot equivocate with the Israelis, the Palestinians or the Arab states as to what is required to forge a lasting peace. But for that to occur, the Obama administration must secure a number of prerequisites to avoid the pitfalls of previous administrations and capitalize on the changing political environment in the Middle East, especially among the Arab states that favor peace with Israel.

Ending Settlement Expansion

Ending settlement expansion is absolutely one of the most critical elements in changing the dynamic of the Israeli-Palestinian negotiations. More than anything else, it sends a clear message that Israel has no sovereign right to these territories and that the idea of a two-state solution is not dead. Moreover, it will strengthen Mahmoud Abbas' hand as he would be able to claim credit for an extraordinary Israeli concession. To resolve the conflict on this issue between the

Obama administration and Israel, both sides must agree on a moratorium for a specific period of time (instead of an open-ended freeze) pending a resolution to the borders dispute. The expansion can then be resumed on the settlements that would be incorporated into Israel proper by agreement with the Palestinians. In return for an Israeli moratorium on the settlements, the Obama administration must demand and receive from the Palestinian Authority (PA) an immediate cessation of all incitements against Israel, which must include electronic and print media in Arabic in particular as well as textbooks, as is being promoted by the Peace Research Institute in the Middle East. In addition, the PA must demonstrably take whatever action needed to end any and all violent attacks against Israelis. In addition, the PA must undertake a major public relations campaign to foster the virtues of peaceful coexistence with Israel. Short of that, Israel should continue to expand the settlements as it sees fit and it should be under no obligation to accommodate the Palestinians. Such a quid pro quo between Israel and the Palestinians will go a long way toward building trust, which is sorely lacking between the two sides.

Promoting a Palestinian Unity Government

Establishing a unity government remains central to promoting a lasting Israeli-Palestinian peace. The Obama administration must exert tremendous pressure on Egypt and Saudi Arabia to do everything in their power to advance a Palestinian unity government between Hamas and the PA. Every effort must be made to pressure Hamas to accept the API as an alternative to their refusal to specifically recognize Israel, renounce terrorism, and accept prior agreements, which may provide its leadership a face-saving way out. Although the Netanyahu government may not negotiate directly with Hamas, its leaders will have an indirect say at the negotiating table. Hamas is not just another wild bunch; they are highly organized and disciplined. Hamas is a grassroots movement and cannot be ignored as they remain capable of disrupting the peace process at will. However, having been substantially weakened by Israel's Gaza offensive late last year, and with the continuing closure of border crossings and the growing disenchantment of the Palestinians in Gaza with its policies, Hamas may now be more inclined to forge a unity government than any time before. Otherwise, continuing the split between

Hamas and the PA will not serve the interest of any of the players in the conflict and will instead serve only to perpetuate a lack of progress, which will inadvertently lead to renewed large scale violence.

Reducing Tension in the Territories

Although there has been significant progress in the West Bank and the Palestinians are enjoying greater freedom and relative economic prosperity, Israel can do considerably more to make life for the Palestinians in the West Bank easier. Moreover, Israel cannot weaken Mahmoud Abbas, and then blame him for being weak and inconsequential. Israel should continue to remove scores of road blocks, release thousands of prisoners, and allow thousands more Palestinians to work in Israel and make it publicly known that it was Mahmoud Abbas who has successfully negotiated these concessions. This first and foremost will strengthen him in the eyes of ordinary Palestinians and allow him to make important concessions to Israel, especially in connection with border adjustment and the Palestinian refugees. In addition, these efforts would further strengthen Abbas in his negotiations with Hamas to form a unity government, as he can demonstrate that he is the more effective interlocutor with the Israelis. Finally, Israeli concessions will help to create the contrast in the quality of life and personal freedoms for Palestinians in the West Bank that Israel and the United States want to foster between Gaza and the West Bank to demonstrate that moderation pays and is rewarded.

Translating the Arab Peace Initiative into confidence-building measure

The Obama administration must persuade the Arab states to translate the Initiative into confidence-building measures. Such a historic document, which calls on Israel to return territories captured in 1967 for peace while finding a just solution to the Palestinian refugees, is not only momentous but can provide the foundation for a comprehensive Arab-Israeli peace. No one put it better than the Crown Prince of Bahrain, Sheikh Salman bin Hamad al-Khalifa, when he said in his Washington Post op-ed that "We must stop the small-minded waiting game in which each side refuses to budge until the other side makes the first move. We've got to be bigger than that. All sides need to take simultaneous, good-faith action if peace is to have a chance."[267] The Arab states, for example, can take specific action, however symbolic, including allowing Israeli passenger and cargo aircrafts to fly over Arab territories, opening trade offices in other Arab states other than Jordan and Egypt, holding cultural exchanges, and lifting the ban on Arab officials from meeting with their Israeli counterparts to demonstrate their sincerity behind the Initiative. It should be specifically noted that the Arab Sunni states, Saudi Arabia, Egypt, and Jordan among others, have grave concerns over Iran's nuclear program and want to put the Arab-Israeli conflict behind in order to focus on Tehran's threat. They should be far more in tune to make important concessions to Israel at this juncture as they view Israel ultimately as the best defense against Iran's nuclear ambitions. In return, to assuage the Israelis, the Obama administration will need to work closely with Israel on the Iranian threat and consequently be in a better position to coax them to embrace the Initiative as a basis for negotiating a comprehensive Arab-Israeli peace.

Advancing the Israeli-Syrian Peace Process

Advancing Israeli-Syrian peace negotiations has to be part and parcel of Obama's peace offensive. Syria still holds the key to regional stability and enjoys a very important geo-strategic position with far-reaching regional implications. Although the Obama administration seems to be leaning toward Israeli-Palestinian accommodation first, it must pursue the Israeli-Syrian track with the same tenacity. Peace between Israel and Syria will have serious ramifications on Damascus's influence over Hamas, Hezbollah, and its relationship with Iran, and consequently could facilitate an Israeli-Palestinian agreement. Israel's deep concerns over Iran's nuclear program should encourage its government to focus on Syria. Indeed, the way to distance Iran from the Mediterranean is to distance Syria from Iran, and that can happen only when Israel comes to the conclusion that peace with Syria is

---

267 Shaikh Salman bin Hamad al-Khalifa, "The Arab Peace Initiative for Israel and the Palestinians," *The Washington Post*, July 16, 2009, http://www.washingtonpost.com/wp-dyn/content/article/2009/07/16/AR2009071602737.html.

more valuable than the Golan Heights. For this reason, the Obama administration must bring whatever pressure necessary to bear on Israel to reach an accord with Syria. In return, Damascus must demonstrate that peace with Israel remains Syria's strategic option and the leadership is prepared to fully embrace complete normalization of relations with Israel.

Staying the Course

The question is, will the Obama administration stay the course? Having started his peace offensive on day one of his administration, President Obama has shown his commitment to peace; he must now demonstrate his resolve to stay the course. Yes, the Obama administration must expend tremendous political capital, at least initially, to achieve some tangible results as a 62-years old intractable conflict surely demands. Indeed, President Obama must remain relentless as both the Israelis and the Palestinians will continue to check his resolve. The president must exert equal pressure on all relevant players, not only to demonstrate evenhandedness, but because this is what it will take to change the dynamic in favor of peace. Moreover, President Obama must also go on a public relations offensive to extol the virtues of a two-state solution and why the administration is investing so much political capital behind its push for peace. Both the Israeli and Palestinian publics must be made fully aware about what the enormous benefits are and what would be the price of failure. The Israeli public does not tolerate a government that alienates the United States, which is viewed as the indispensable guarantor for their national security. Orchestrated pressure on Netanyahu and Mahmoud Abbas will provide both leaders the political cover they need to make the necessary concessions for peace.

The administration cannot retreat in the face of Israeli or Arab resistance, because the price of failure will be impossible to fathom. Deferring the peace process will not offer a respite for reassessment but will be a prelude for an unimaginably violent escalation of the conflict from which only the detractors of peace can reap the greatest benefit.

A STRATEGIC NECESSITY

JULY 30, 2009

The Obama administration's push for a comprehensive Arab-Israeli peace may have a much stronger likelihood of succeeding this time around because of the prevailing political and security dynamics. For an agreement to be realized, however, Israel must concede the inevitable by relinquishing territories captured in the 1967 war, and the United States must provide a new security umbrella to its regional allies. This would lead not only to a comprehensive Arab-Israeli peace, but it could seriously impede Iran's ambitions for regional hegemony replete with nuclear weapons capabilities.

The administration's ambitious agenda came in focus this past week as Special Envoy George Mitchell, Secretary of Defense Bob Gates, National Security Advisor Jim Jones, and Obama's Iran strategist Dennis Ross all converged in the region for a series of high-level security meetings with Israeli officials. Subsequent visits by Mitchell to Ramallah, Cairo, and Damascus are clear evidence of this administration's emphasis on a regional diplomatic push that goes well beyond the Israeli-Palestinian track.

With the international spotlight on Israel, it now must find a way to work harmoniously with the Obama administration if it wants to be viewed as a genuine partner in the peace process. The United States remains indispensable to Israel's national security and is ultimately the last line of defense against any threat—including Iran—so for Israel to appear flippant to U.S. pressure at this juncture is a dangerous gamble. The territorial concessions necessary to forge a comprehensive Arab-Israeli peace could further cement Israel's relations with the United States by upgrading Israel's U.S. strategic cooperation into a new security arrangement akin to a defense treaty. If Israel has full American backing in security and defense, it will have more flexibility to concede the occupied territories because ultimately ensuring Israel's security takes away its main rationale for keeping Palestinian and Syrian territories.

Such a security agreement with Israel does not mean that the Obama administration has resigned itself to the inevitability of a nuclear Iran. Israeli Minster of Intelligence and Atomic Energy Dan Meridor recently alluded to this in an interview with Army Radio, noting that, "Now, we don't need to deal with the assumption that Iran will attain nuclear weapons but to prevent this."[268] A U.S.-Israel security agreement, and possibly a larger security umbrella that covers Arab allies as well, would likely make Iran's nuclear ambitions less compelling. This agreement, combined with potentially crippling sanctions, might provide enough deterrence for Iran to consider co-operating with the international community on its nuclear program. Moreover, since Iran never admitted to pursuing nuclear weapons, the U.S. strategy might offer Iran a face-saving way out. But if diplomacy nevertheless fails and Tehran continues with its refusal to settle the nuclear conflict through negotiations, then Israel will still have gained from the United States' full cooperation and security partnership, as long as the negotiations with Iran are not open-ended.

Israel's other significant advantage would be an opening to the rest of the Arab world. The Arab states, led by Saudi Arabia, Egypt, Jordan, and Morocco, deeply dread the Iranian nuclear threat, and many would be willing to work with Israel to mitigate their deep concerns. However, they are loath to cooperate with Israel, and right-fully so, as long as Israel continues to occupy Arab land and expand the settlements, which symbolize to them an indefinite occupation. The Iranian nuclear menace has created a new power equation in the Middle East, where Israel and the Arab states share a common threat. Israel, which for decades has been seen as the enemy of the Arab world, could now become a potential ally through various cooperative defense deterrents against Iran. For Israel, this represents not only a historic opportunity to forge a comprehensive peace, but to form a de facto united Arab-Israeli front while working closely with the United States for sustained regional security.

---

268 Barak Ravid, "Israel Slams Clinton Statement on Nuclear Iran," *Haaretz*, July 22, 2009, http://www.haaretz.com/news/israel-slams-clinton-statement-on-nuclear-iran-1.280505.

Finally, there is international public opinion, which is unified on the issue of occupation and sees Israel's intransigence as not only cause for regional instability, but as a threat to global energy resources. In case of a major conflagration between Israel and Iran, the effects of oil and gas volatility could be potentially devastating. As for the Israeli-Palestinian issue, much of the international community, with the European Union (EU) at the forefront, has become far more forthcoming in its opposition to Israeli policies. Recently, 27 EU foreign ministers decided to put off the planned upgrading of EU-Israel relations to an "association agreement," which would have large trade benefits, until they can see a stronger commitment from Israel to a Palestinian state. No one should expect Israel to compromise its national security only to please the international community. That being said, Israel has made tremendous strides in becoming a respected member of the international community in terms of diplomatic and trade cooperation. However, the scores of countries affected by the continuing turmoil in the Middle East are fed up with a conflict they believe can be resolved by ending the occupation. From their perspective, linking territory to national security no longer holds the weight it used to, not only because of Israel's technological superiority but because the Arab world has come full circle to accept Israel's reality. If Israel were to forfeit this opportunity, it will be blamed for many of the regional ills as well as the growing rift with the United States, which most Israelis will not tolerate.

The Obama administration is investing tremendous political capital in its effort to forge a comprehensive Arab-Israeli peace. Moreover, for the Obama administration to restore its moral leadership, neutralize Iran's nuclear ambitions, and reach a major breakthrough in U.S.-Middle East relations—following eight years of President Bush's disastrous policies—it has no alternative but to tackle the Arab-Israeli peace process head on. If these efforts require a regional security umbrella by the United States, as was suggested by Secretary of State Hilary Clinton,[269] Israel can come out of this not only with a comprehensive Arab-Israeli peace deal but with stronger security ties with the United States.

---

269 Landler and Sanger, "Clinton Speaks of Shielding Mideast From Iran."

This prospect offers what most Israelis yearn for—peace with security. Any Israeli government that refuses to see that will have forfeited its mandate to govern and should give way to a new Israeli government capable of delivering peace.

WINNING BACK ISRAEL

AUGUST 21, 2009

During his recent meeting with Egypt's President Mubarak, President Obama expressed cautious optimism about the progress being made in the Arab-Israeli peace process. While both presidents noted that there was "movement in the right direction,"[270] eight months of American direct engagement in the Arab-Israeli conflict has produced few tangible results. Middle East envoy George Mitchell, who has been shuttling back and forth to the region to negotiate between parties, has yet to persuade the Israelis, Palestinians, and the surrounding Arab states to undertake the necessary parallel confidence-building measures needed to breathe life back into the process. The Netanyahu government's ongoing refusal to declare a moratorium on settlement expansion has been met with Arab leaders' obdurate resistance to offer Israel concessions of their own, raising questions about Mitchell's strategy and the viability of the process. For this reason, the Obama administration can no longer afford to wait for the Israelis and Palestinians to see eye-to-eye, and instead it must interject itself more forcefully by establishing the general parameters for a peace agreement.

Before the Obama administration launches this new initiative, it must first take a number of corrective measures to create a more positive atmosphere in the region, especially among the Israelis. As a proponent of the two-state solution based on the 1967 borders, President Obama's envisioned peace agreement between the Arabs and Israelis does not differ much from his predecessors', including the efforts at Camp David and Annapolis. Yet President Obama's

---

270 Barack Obama and Hosni Mubarak, "Remarks by President Obama and President Mubarak of Egypt During Press Availability," The White House, August 18, 2009, http://www.whitehouse.gov/the_press_office/Remarks-by-President-Obama-and-President-Mubarak-of-Egypt-during-press-availability.

strategy and advocacy have been much more pronounced since his first days in office, where he has championed the role of a committed and evenhanded interlocutor. In his efforts to repair the relationship between the United States and Arab world that was left in tatters after the Bush administration, President Obama has along the way created an atmosphere of doubt among many in the Israeli camp.

A growing number of Israelis are concerned that in his efforts to win the hearts and minds of the Arab world, President Obama has not been as sensitive as his predecessors to Israel's specific plights on national security issues. Moreover, many Israelis have become less trusting of President Obama and feel that his speech from Cairo to the Arab and Muslim world sought improved relations with Arab states at Israel's expense. As a result, an increased number of Israelis are showing greater forbearance to Netanyahu's rejection of Obama's demand to freeze the settlements—even at the expense of creating tension with Washington.

It is critical at this juncture that President Obama now personally appeal directly to the Israeli public. This must include a massive public relations campaign, where the U.S. President can reach out to Israelis through op-eds in Israeli papers, interviews on Army Radio, and appearances on Israeli television channels. The purpose would be not only to restate America's unshakable commitment to Israel's national security, but also to show that Israel's ultimate security and prosperity lies in peace with the Arab states. The president ought to explain that he seeks to realize what President Clinton attempted to achieve at Camp David in 2000 and what President Bush continued with his efforts to strike an Israeli-Palestinian peace through the Road Map. He must make it abundantly clear that his focus on the settlements is not arbitrary, but represents a critical point of departure if Israel is to ever to seek peace with the Palestinians. Indeed, the settlements not only reinforce the occupation practically and psychologically, but they also diminish the Palestinians' hope for establishing a state of their own. President Obama in his own words must make it clear to Israelis that as much as the Palestinian extremists will never be able to build a Palestinian state on Israel's ruins, Israel will not see peace unless an independent Palestinian state is established in the West Bank and Gaza.

The requisites for a peace agreement have been discussed and negotiated at length by countless administrations; what the president ought to project now to the Israelis is a vision of an overall solution consistent with previous discussions between the parties. While parallel confidence-building measures are still vital to the process, they must be seen as building blocks that clearly point to an endgame visible by all sides. The President must also explain that in order to keep his commitment to seeing out a final agreement, the parameters must cover all conflicting issues, especially the final borders, settlements, the fate of Palestinian refugees, and the future status of East Jerusalem. By providing a vision of the "big picture," President Obama would be able to foster the confidence that incremental building measures will indeed lead to the desired structure of peace. For Israel to make progress on halting settlement growth, Netanyahu must be able to trust that Obama will apply equal pressure on the Arab states to deliver concessions with the goal of normalizing relations with Israel.

Finally, the president must invoke the historic dimension of the API, which offers Israel peace with all 22 Arab states in exchange for the occupied territories and a just resolution for the Palestinian refugees. The president must be vehement about this timely opportunity for the Israelis while the conditions on the ground are ripe and they have moderate partners in the process. The choice for the Israelis, he must emphasize, will be to end more than 60 years of bloodshed and destruction and live in peace. Should they choose not to acknowledge the collective will of the moderate Arab community, they risk dealing with a much more extreme Arab world as a result.

Moreover, for the President to regain the trust of the Israeli public that has substantially diminished in the past few months, he must be more fervent in his resolve to counter Iran's nuclear agenda, which Israelis dread the most. While there is an ongoing dialogue between United States and Israeli intelligence and security communities concerning Iran's nuclear ambitions, President Obama must assure the Israeli public as well that it is in their best interest that all diplomatic options are first exhausted with Iran. He must intimate that all other options, should diplomacy fail, will be thoroughly discussed with the Israeli government. To be sure, the Israelis must feel confident that the

Obama administration will resort to any means necessary to eliminate what they consider an existential threat from Iran.

Whereas it was critically important for the Obama administration to improve its relations with the Arab states to regain its moral footing and influence, it absolutely cannot undermine the nature of U.S.-Israeli special relations. This unique bond has offered successive American administrations greater leverage with Israel, allowing it to exact important concessions in negotiations, as Clinton was able to do with Netanyahu in the Hebron agreement in 1997. Although Arab states have in the past complained about America's lack of evenhandedness, they understand that the U.S.-Israeli relationship gives the American president leverage to deliver for them. Any erosion of that relationship will create serious difficulties in future negotiations, as President Obama is currently finding out for himself. President Obama must now correct that impression before he can move the peace process forward and restore the trust and confidence of the Israeli people.

THE PROSPECT FOR A BREAKTHROUGH

SEPTEMBER 23, 2009

Although the Obama administration's efforts to resume Israeli-Palestinian peace negotiations have not, as yet, produced tangible results, the prospect for a breakthrough in negotiations may be closer today than it has been in many years. Notwithstanding the inherent skepticism about the prospect of real progress, the conversion of certain regional and international developments has altered the political dynamic and created a new set of opportunities for a negotiated settlement. The Obama administration has a greater chance for success than any of its predecessors, as long as it remains consistent and unwavering while keeping the end-game in sight. There are six factors that have made this moment ripe for significant progress, if not actually achieving an Israeli-Palestinian peace.

There is no doubt that the early push for the resumption of negotiations by the Obama administration has created a sense of urgency that the time has come to put an end to this debilitating conflict. President Obama's early involvement signals that the United States views the Israeli-Palestinian conflict in a wider context, and sees that its continuation reverberates and impacts other regional conflicts, as well as prevents many Arab and Islamic states who wish to normalize relations with Israel from doing so. Moreover, the United States is aware of its central role in facilitating peace, and Obama's insistence on a renewal of negotiations illustrates that he understands that the intractability of the conflict and the innate skepticism of all the players involved requires time to build confidence between the conflicting parties.

Whereas previous administrations spoke about the requirements for peace, the Obama administration is taking action to insist that some of these requirements be met—asking the Israelis to declare a moratorium on the expansion of Israeli settlements in the West Bank, and the Arab states to open a trade section in Israel and allow Israel to fly planes over Arab territory are two cases in point. Early engagement offers a clear indication that the Obama administration's heavy investment of political capital will not allow the United States to cut and run. Obama has made clear his intentions of seeing negotiations through at the trilateral meeting he hosted this week between Netanyahu, Abbas, and himself. All sides must now be prepared for the long haul while the United States is able to provide them with the political cover they need to make the required concessions.

The second significant factor that came on the heels of the administration's early involvement is the present general lull in violence. For obvious reasons, nothing disrupts the peace process more than acts of violence, which shatter any desire by either party to cooperate politically. In the West Bank, the PA has recognized that progress can be made only under the condition of a tangible calm, and the genuine efforts of the PA Security Forces to prevent any wanton acts of violence against Israelis has persuaded Israel to begin to ease the brunt of the occupation on Palestinian civilians. Scores of road blocks have been removed by the IDF, and economic development has been on the rise throughout the West Bank. To this regard, Palestinian Prime Minister Salam Fayyad's unveiling of his government program to build the apparatus of a Palestinian state within two years is an admirable, bold, and welcome initiative. Fayyad and the PA's commitment to build a future based on equality and restoration of self-dignity in a nonviolent atmosphere changes in a fundamental way the mindset of nearly every individual in this conflict. The forward of the plan by Salam Fayyad states specifically that:

> Palestine will be a peace-loving state that rejects violence, commits to co-existence with its neighbors, and builds bridges of cooperation with the international community. It will be a symbol of peace, tolerance and prosperity in this troubled area of the world. By embodying all of these values, Palestine will be a source of pride to all of its citizens, and an anchor of stability in this region.[271]

---

271 Fayyad, "Ending the Occupation, Establishing the State," 4.

Israel in particular should embrace this initiative as it would strengthen the efforts of Palestinian moderates, cementing this lull in violence and setting in motion a peaceful negotiating process.

This development has not been lost on Hamas. The clear evidence of economic growth and prosperity in the West Bank has created a stark contrast to the situation in Gaza, which illustrates to all parties involved in the conflict that moderation leads to results. Although Hamas' adherence to the ceasefire may in fact be tactical, its actions are still motivated by the organization's desire to change the dynamic of its relations with Israel—especially after Israel's incursion into Gaza in December 2008 and Hamas' subsequent terrible political and military losses. Moreover, as Hamas seems to be losing popular support compared to the PA, its leaders are eager to show some progress on the political front. To that end, Hamas has been working through Egyptian mediators to negotiate a prisoner exchange with Israel and an agreement to ease the border crossings into Gaza to allow for goods to pass through. Most importantly, on more than one occasion Hamas' leaders have said that they can see themselves accepting a two-state solution based on the 1967 borders, which signals that they have been taking to heart the changing Arab political winds toward Israel.

This development is better understood when examined against the third important development in the current political climate, which is the evolving nature of the Israeli-Palestinian conflict and the fatigue that seems to have engulfed all sides. That is, it is entirely possible that the Israelis and Palestinians have reached a mutually disadvantageous stalemate, where they have both realized that the continuation of violence diminishes, rather than enhances, their bargaining posture. This is not to suggest that Israel and the Palestinians are ready to settle their differences and sign a peace treaty today. It only suggests that both sides seem to have concluded, without publicly admitting, that regardless of how much longer this conflict persists, neither side can improve appreciably their position enough to warrant further hostilities and suffering. This can be seen in the recent International Peace Institute poll which showed that nearly two-thirds of Palestinians now support a two-state solution and the steps it would involve to see it come to fruition.[272] The two-state solution is not one of many possibilities, but the only outcome of any negotiated settlement. Surely, the hard bargaining will continue throughout the negotiation process, and only a naïve person would predict that peace is just around the corner. But given other regional developments, the resumption of large scale violence akin to the second Intifada seems increasingly more remote, as the political climate is shifting more toward reconciliation and the benefits derived from moderation.

The fourth element contrasts the view that the rise of a right-of-center government in Israel is a detriment to peace, when in reality no lasting Israeli-Palestinian peace can be forged without the full support of the center and right-of-center parties. The current Israeli coalition government, led by Benjamin Netanyahu with Labor's leader Ehud Barak as Defense Minister, is in a strong position to conduct the initial hard bargaining necessary to move negotiations forward while still meeting some of Israel's core requirements. Although this government may not be in a position to make significant concessions, such as those on East Jerusalem, and still remain in power, Netanyahu may end up forming a unity government with the centrist Kadima party, and will thereby encompass the left, center, and right, representing the majority of Israeli public opinion. Historically, major concessions in the Israeli-Palestinian conflict were made by prime ministers of the Likud party; Begin withdrew from the Sinai as a part of a peace agreement with Egypt in 1979, Netanyahu pulled out from Hebron under the Wye River agreement in 1998, and Sharon evacuated Gaza in 2005.

Moreover, the Israeli public is ready for peace with security, and the Israelis are fully aware that there is a demographic time bomb in the making. Israel must choose between a democratic state with a sustainable Jewish majority, which necessitates giving up most of the West Bank, or risk losing the Jewish majority in Israel, in which case Israel will be thrust into two untenable situations—either accept the

---

272 Douglas Hamilton, Joseph Nasr, and Samia Nakhoul, "Palestinians Want Peace Deal but don't Reject Hamas," *Reuters*, September 25, 2009, http://www.reuters.com/article/2009/09/25/us-palestinians-israel-poll-idUSTRE58O1OF20090925.

one-state solution, which if democratically elected would be governed by a Palestinian majority, or disfranchise the Palestinians to stay in power, which would inevitably lead to catastrophic consequences. Netanyahu will not miss an opportunity to sign a peace treaty that meets Israel's principle requirements: a sustainable Jewish majority, territorial integrity, and national security, none of which negate the establishment of a Palestinian state living in peace side-by-side with Israel.

The growing receptivity of the API in Israel and by the Obama administration presents the fifth critical element in the evolution of the peace process. The API provides a comprehensive formula for an Arab-Israeli peace and the means to unravel the political conundrum between Hamas, the PA, and Israel. The Arab Initiative was adopted first in Beirut, Lebanon in March of 2002, and reintroduced in March of 2007 in Riyadh, Saudi Arabia. The Initiative establishes the following principles: 1) full Israeli withdrawal from all the territories occupied since 1967; 2) achievement of a just solution to the Palestinian refugee problem; 3) the acceptance and the establishment of a sovereign independent Palestinian state on the Palestinian territories occupied since the 4th of June 1967 in the West Bank and Gaza strip, with East Jerusalem as its capital; 4) the Arab-Israeli conflict ended, a peace agreement with Israel, and security for all the states of the region, and finally; 5) the establishment of normal relations with Israel in the context of this comprehensive peace. The conditions are now ready for all parties involved in the Israeli-Palestinian conflict to endorse this historic initiative, which will facilitate an end to the conflict and still meets the fundamental requirements of the stakeholders involved.

The sixth and final factor that may accelerate the peace process and bring Israel and the Arab states closer to a settlement is the Iranian nuclear program, which threatens both Israel and the Arab states. Although the Arab states—with the exception of Egypt— have thus far refused to cooperate with Israel publicly and have sought first to extract some concessions from Israel on the Palestinian front, there is no doubt that these countries count on Israel to obstruct Iran's regional ambitions. There is certainly no love lost between Shiite Iran and the majority Sunni Arab states, and when viewed with this incentive, Israeli-Arab cooperation is bound to grow.

Motivated by self-interest and national security concerns, the Arab states will become increasingly more accommodating to Israel, as the Egyptian government and some of the smaller Gulf States have already amply demonstrated. Iran, which has effectively undermined the peace process in the past, may now inadvertently aid the process by virtue of its regional ambitions and pursuit of nuclear weapons.

To capitalize on this new environment, the Obama administration must first and foremost stay on course and remain unwavering in its effort to resume Israeli-Palestinian negotiations. President Obama's successful efforts to arrange a trilateral meeting between Netanyahu, Abbas, and himself on the sidelines of the United Nations General Assembly (UNGA) is a positive move, regardless of how little it might have achieved in the short term. The president made his determination clear when he stated "It is past time to stop talking about starting negotiations; it is time to move forward."[273]

To further facilitate the progress of the Israeli-Palestinian negotiations, the Obama administration must allay Israeli concerns over Iran's nuclear weapons program. To that end, there must be a complete understanding between Israel and the United States about the course of action needed to dissuade Iran from pursuing its nuclear ambitions, as well as a close collaboration between the two countries on matters of intelligence. Moreover, President Obama must assure the Israelis that his call for a nuclear-free Middle East will not bring Israel's nuclear program into question—especially as the P5+1 countries (United States, Russia, China, United Kingdom and France + Germany) enter into negotiations with Iran on October 1. Doing so would allow Iran to tie the development of its nuclear program to the existence of an Israeli program, and would cause serious rifts between the United States and Israel.

In addition, the Obama team must now capitalize on the existing calm in the West Bank and along the Gazan borders, and work with the Egyptians to secure the release of the Israeli soldier Gilad Shalit in a package prisoner exchange. Such an agreement would

---

273 Helene Cooper and Mark Landler, "White House Pivots in Mideast Peace Bid," *The New York Times*, September 22, 2009, http://www.nytimes.com/2009/09/23/world/middleeast/23prexy.html.

dramatically reduce the tension between Hamas and Israel, and would also pave the way for opening the border crossing with Israel and allow much-needed goods to enter Gaza. In the same vein, with continued American prompting and support, Israel and the PA must continue their security and economic cooperation in the West Bank, which will deepen their vested interest in the evolving, mutually gainful relationship.

Although the Netanyahu government has not yet formally endorsed the API, the United States and the EU should first officially endorse it and make every effort to persuade Israel to do likewise. There is nothing in the API that negates Israel's ultimate objective of establishing peace and normal relations with all of its neighbors. That being said, Egypt, Saudi Arabia, Syria, and the leading Arab states who wish Israel to accept the Initiative must now use all the leverage they have to persuade Hamas to adopt it as well. The Initiative offers Hamas a way to achieve land and peace for the Palestinians without having to concede directly to Israel, as signing on to the API would be seen as joining the collective will of the Arab states. By accepting the Initiative, Hamas will fall in line with the 19 Arab states that are willing to recognize Israel only upon reaching an agreement based on the provisions of the API.

Finally, there is a need to create an economic incentive for the Israelis and Palestinians to come together and cooperate on such contentious final status issues as the Palestinian right of return. It is necessary for all countries who endorse peace in the Middle East— including the United States, Russia, China, Japan, the EU, and wealthy Arab states—to prove their commitment to a peaceful solution through a financial commitment of $15 to $20 billion dollars for the resettlement and rehabilitation of the Palestinian refugees. This not only implies that a solution to the Palestinian refugee question will be reached through negotiation, but more importantly, it redirects the various parties' focus away from fighting over the political issue, and toward how to appropriately spend the money toward a just solution to the Palestinian refugee problem. This also assures Israel that the international community, along with some of the Arab states, is committed to a solution to the refugee problem that precludes the right of return to Israel proper without saying so publicly. Such a pool of funds should be placed under the umbrella of the International Monetary Fund (IMF), the World Bank, or the UN. President Obama can play an important role in seeing this through, but the United States cannot be seen as the only power endorsing this campaign.

Skeptics and pessimists will view the current geopolitical climate in the Middle East as nothing more than a mirage, and will conclude that President Obama's efforts to push for peace in the Israeli-Palestinian conflict are futile. Yet it is not a question of the level of optimism needed to create peace, but rather a question of whether the Obama administration can afford not to act and thus squander a historic opportunity for a breakthrough—however remote that possibility might be. President Obama has demonstrated leadership and courage, the two qualities surely needed to push the process forward. Now he has to demonstrate that he possesses the iron will necessary to stay the course and translate this positive political climate into a major transformation in the conflict. As Obama himself stated to Netanyahu and Abbas, "So my message to these two leaders is clear: despite all the obstacles, all the history, all the mistrust, we have to find a way forward."[274]

---

274 Ibid.

TIME TO CHANGE THE STATUS QUO

MARCH 23, 2010

The last few weeks have looked like a crash course in Middle East diplomacy, replete with the grandeur of talks and lofty speechmaking, and the lows that shamed even those most committed to the peace process. As the media frenzy played out, the public watched as Israel and its closest ally celebrated proximity talks, clashed over the untimely announcement of new construction in Jerusalem, and worked through their differences during the American Israel Public Affairs Committee (AIPAC) conference in Washington and Prime Minister Netanyahu's subsequent meeting with President Obama. Through all these ups and downs—and the criticisms that have ensued—one thing remains clear: the dynamics of the U.S.-Israeli-Palestinian axis have shifted and a new momentum has been generated as a result. It is now incumbent upon all sides to take this momentum and translate it into concrete action on the ground.

Secretary Clinton should be commended on all accounts for an honest and thorough presentation to AIPAC, outlining a U.S. position which is willing to prod and pressure Israel when needed while still allaying Israel's ultimate concern: national security. Clinton was right to proclaim that "Staying on this course means continuing a conflict that carries tragic human costs...Both sides must confront the reality that the status quo of the last decade has not produced long-term security or served their interests. Nor has it served the interests of the United States."[275] Clinton's point here, which distinguishes this administration from the previous two, is that the United States is finally willing to acknowledge that the Israeli-Palestinian conflict is inextricably linked not only to U.S. strategic interests, but also to the

---

275 Hillary Rodham Clinton, "Remarks at the 2010 AIPAC Policy Conference" (remarks, AIPAC Policy Conference, Washington, DC, March 22, 2010), http://m.state.gov/md138722.htm.

complex power structures throughout the greater Middle East. For the United States to support Israel's security, especially when it comes to garnering support against Iran's nuclear advancements, it must continue multilateral tracks to make progress on a political level, a security level, and a people-to-people level.

The United States must continue to put pressure on ending the continued expansion of Israeli settlements without making the entire peace process beholden to the inevitable ups and downs of these activities. The settlement agenda is a highly contested issue within Israel itself, with myriad opinions coming from diverse political parties and ministers in and outside Netanyahu's fragile coalition. The United States should enforce the continued moratorium in the West Bank, and pressure Israel to refrain from public construction announcements like the recent one in East Jerusalem, yet understand that Netanyahu has to appease his coalition in some respects in order to deliver needed concessions for the time being. For this reason, the United States should ensure that proximity talks, continued institutional and economic development in the West Bank, and an easing of the humanitarian situation in Gaza are all tended to regardless of the latest settlement uproar.

One of the most promising ways that the United States can actively support the peace process without subjecting itself to the vicissitudes of Israeli domestic politics is to reinforce the Fayyad Plan. Palestinian Prime Minister Salam Fayyad, a moderate economist and technocrat whose vision for the Palestinian people is a state with viable institutions and economic opportunity—all achieved through nonviolent means—should have the unequivocal support of the Obama administration at every step. Fayyad has started a movement where in lieu of any political progress, Palestinians can still move forward with the development of infrastructure, institutions, and even a central bank. Beyond helping with security training and economic aid, the United States should up the ante on its support of this plan, and lean on Israel to allow for more land to be devoted to industrial zoning so that moderate Palestinians can feel the rewards of nonviolence. A 7% growth rate in the West Bank is one of the surest ways to draw a stark reality between violent resistance and moderation. By championing the Fayyad Plan and encouraging Israel to be cooperative in these efforts, the United

States can see to it that progress continues for Palestinians even when negotiations are stalled.

The Arab states too should not shirk from their responsibilities or sit back as spectators while the United States attempts indirect mediation between Israel and the Palestinians. The Arab states have taken a huge step toward moderation by being willing to recognize Israel and normalize relations with it in a land-for-peace agreement outlined in the historic API. Yet by and large, they have watched as their plan for peace has languished for years without doing any substantial legwork to promote it. What the Arab League must understand is that whatever political and economic maneuvering is being done by the United States, the EU, the Quartet, or Turkey to solve this crisis will only benefit it if the collective Arab states can muster the will to promote their plan for how the future of their own region should look. Redoubling efforts to promote the API as proximity talks ensue should be top of the agenda for the upcoming summit in Libya. Syria in particular should be vocal in this effort, as the United States has started normalizing relations with it while ensuring its claim on the Golan is addressed.

In the context of these deliberations, a player like Turkey should not be dismissed, even as official ties between the Turkish and Israeli governments have been tense since Israel's offensive into Gaza. While Turkey's official role as a mediator in the Arab-Israeli conflict has waned, people-to-people development continues as the Turkish Chamber of Commerce has pushed for expanding private sector development in industrial zones throughout the West Bank. Turkey has asserted its interest in seeing an end to the Arab-Israeli crisis, and in lieu of a sound political process has continued to push for development in the future Palestinian state without seriously compromising its close military and trade ties with Israel.

Lastly, Israel needs to start delivering concessions on the ground or it will find itself increasingly more isolated as the international community coalesces around the push for a two-state solution. Although Netanyahu has emphasized Israel's willingness to enter direct and unconditional negotiations, this suggests that the accomplishments and agreements of prior negotiations can be ignored. The United States should be abundantly clear that the parameters of a solution have been established time and again; proximity talks should focus on dealing with core issues where progress has been made and back such agreements so that they will not be subject to renegotiations time and again. While the Jews' historical and biblical ties to Jerusalem must be respected, this Israeli government cannot use that as a crutch to sabotage talks or prohibit it from moving forward with concessions. Netanyahu should brace himself for the pressure and persistence that President Obama will put on Israel when it comes to settlements, a subject that even General Petraeus has listed as a threat to U.S. interests and security abroad. If Netanyahu's current center-right coalition is preventing him from making the necessary concessions, he has every obligation then to bring Kadima back in as a strategic partner in peace. With a major domestic victory under his belt, President Obama will have more time and energy to see that Israel is making progress on the Palestinian track.

On the security front, Obama, Vice President Biden, Special Envoy Mitchell, and most recently Clinton have all made it profusely clear that "for this entire administration, our commitment to Israel's security and Israel's future is rock solid, unwavering, enduring and forever."[276] The United States has gone above and beyond to prove to Israel its commitment when it comes to national security, which should dispel any of the concerns about the nature of the current U.S.-Israel relationship. Nonetheless, this does not mean that the United States will or should back down from pressuring Israel to make necessary concessions for peace, as this is directly related to Israel's ultimate security needs and American strategic interests.

Beyond that, as Israel continues its campaign to get widespread support against Iran's nuclear agenda, President Obama must make one thing clear: if the United States is to confront Iran with sanctions or a military threat, both of which will require international cooperation, there must be significant progress, if not a full agreement, on the Arab-Israeli track. With the war in Afghanistan and continued instability in Iraq, the United States simply cannot and will not confront

---

276 Glenn Kessler, "At AIPAC Conference, Clinton Pledges White House Commitment to Israel Security," *The Washington Post*, March 22, 2010, http://www.washingtonpost.com/wp-dyn/content/article/2010/03/22/AR2010032200820.html.

Iran, especially militarily, before it can secure a real calm on the Israeli-Palestinian track. The Iranian regime, Hamas, Hezbollah and al-Qaeda all in some form gain support for their causes through the fact that Israel is still an occupying force and the United States supports it as a staunch ally. Trying to separate the rise in power of these groups from the progress on the Israeli-Palestinian front is a futile exercise, and Israel should know that if it wants full support from the United States, EU, Arab states, and the UN Security Council against Iranian threats, it must prove its commitment to seeing out the peace process. The regional alliances that balanced the ambitions of Iran, Iraq, Syria, and other leading states drastically changed with an aggressive U.S. military and foreign policy in the Middle East during the Bush era. The last thing the United States wants is another regional conflagration where it will need to mobilize support for an unpopular effort. Israel should be well aware of this, as progress on the Arab front will make it much easier for the United States to resort to even greater coercive actions against Iran should it become necessary.

Because of the unraveling balances of power that have shifted immensely this past decade—which have played out on political, military, and religious fronts—security has been globalized in such a way that the conflict between Israel and the Palestinians is no longer just regional. Benjamin Netanyahu has some serious soul-searching to do if he is going to get his coalition to act in Israel's long-term interests instead of presumed short-term gains. This includes reigning in his coalition ministers and presenting a unified Israeli public voice as well as taking the necessary risks needed to reach an agreement.

Netanyahu should know that while he now has a partner in the United States, EU, and the Arab League, this may not last, nor will the current lull in violence. The recent scuffle over settlements started as a disaster for Israel's public image, but can end in such a way that Israel could be seen as a country willing to govern constructively for the future instead of hiding behind the perilous status quo.

PREREQUISITES FOR THE SUCCESS
OF THE PROXIMITY TALKS

MAY 28, 2010

This year, May 15th came and went without too much noise, relatively speaking. While the 62nd anniversary of the State of Israel was celebrated with fireworks and praise by Israelis throughout Jerusalem, noticeably absent was Mahmoud Abbas' speech commemorating what is known by Palestinians as the "Nakba," or catastrophe. Currently, as proximity talks mediated by the United States are underway for the second time following a series of public missteps by all parties, it seems that there is a concerted effort not to make any moves that might sabotage the fragile nature of the trilateral relationship.

In this tense climate, it is doubtful that a deal feasible to all parties will come in the four-month time period allotted. But if President Obama and his team can play their cards right, the looming threats from Iran and the current lull in violence from the Palestinians may give them the advantage needed to make significant progress. There are a few issues that the Obama administration will need to carefully consider to ensure these negotiations bear some fruit.

First, President Obama must keep in mind that any talks conducted strictly in isolation will likely end that way. In a region where, as the dictum goes, no war is possible without Egypt, no peace without Syria and the support of Saudi Arabia, these countries (as well as Jordan) should be present in negotiations. Palestinians will need political cover and support from the leading Arab states to make difficult concessions, and the states that will be instrumental in ensuring the success of a future Palestine should be privy to the decision-making process from the very beginning. Inclusivity will also address Israeli qualms about their future status with the larger Arab world and allay some of the Israeli concerns over their long-term national security. In addition, if negotiations are comprehensive, Israel will not only feel that the deal on the table has the backing of the Arab states, but that normalization of relations with these states is possible. While George Mitchell has secured some progress with the PA, he needs to look wider in scope if he wants a solution credible enough for Israel and palatable to the Arab states.

The next consideration that must be kept a priority throughout the proximity talks is Syria's special interest in the conflict. As a central player in the region with its own land claims with Israel and the reigns to Hamas, Hezbollah, and a powerful Iranian influence, Obama cannot afford to marginalize Syria's role. If excluded from the process, Bashar Assad can and will undermine negotiations through proxy groups if he feels Syrian interests are being neglected. He recently outlined the Syrian position as being ready for peace or war at all times, a statement which should not be pushed aside. Damascus' improved regional political fortunes have emboldened Syria to take a much more assertive posture. The political tactics by the U.S. Senate—stalling Robert Ford's appointment as ambassador to Syria—are not helping U.S. efforts at engagement. Yet any Syrian track that is pursued with the United States or Israel will also be futile without any progress on the Palestinian front. The best way to avoid failure in this case is to make proxy talks a segue into what should be a broad and comprehensive strategy toward Syria and the other Arab League member states.

In this sense, putting proximity talks in the context of a grand picture will be paramount to this process. While the negotiations of the 1990s and 2000s fell short of establishing peace, they made great headway and set a precedent for the current status quo. Oslo, Madrid, Camp David, Annapolis, and the countless other efforts by previous administrations should absolutely serve as a frame of reference for the current negotiations. The atmosphere has not changed in such a dramatic way that the agreements made by all parties in previous negotiations should not hold true for the most part today. Some of the final status issues that remain on the table such as refugees, Jerusalem, and final borders have been negotiated time and again and should therefore take off from where they were left at the last round of talks.

In formulating a comprehensive Arab-Israeli strategy, the Obama administration would be best served by looking at the API as the main framework for moving forward with negotiations. The document, which is backed and signed by the entire Arab League, is the only peace plan thus far with the outreach to bring normalization and peace between Israel and all 21 Arab states in exchange for an end to the occupation. If the United States were to adopt the API's principles into its own peace plan, it would give the document much more legitimacy in the eyes of the Israelis and encourage the Arab states to reign in Palestinian extremist elements. In this regard, the United States must encourage Israel to look more favorably at the API and take advantage of such opportunities like the Qatari offer to engage in reconstruction efforts in Gaza in exchange for normalization of relations. This is how the API can be translated into practical measures for all to see, including Iran, and for Israel to strengthen its position as it normalizes relations with one Arab country following another.

While Obama should get credit for his tenacity in resuming negotiations despite early setbacks, he cannot afford another failure at this point. This could have the deleterious effect of painting the Obama administration as helpless in the eyes of both allies and detractors. In order to remain a credible interlocutor with enough political capital to sway both parties to the center, he will need to start showing some deliverables. Netanyahu has insisted that direct negotiations between Israel and the Palestinians should be the next phase, provided that some discernible progress is first made in the proximity talks with the American mediation. The fact though is that throughout the Oslo, Taba, and Annapolis negotiations, direct talks with no mediation were not successful in achieving a breakthrough. If Obama wants to ensure success, he needs to start showing the Israeli and Arab public that he has a plan and a grand strategy for dealing with not only the Israeli-Palestinian conflict but U.S. engagement as a whole toward the Middle East. U.S. mediation is and will continue to be indispensable to ultimately achieve the desired outcome, both through direct and indirect negotiations between Israel and the Arab states.

Finally, and perhaps most importantly, President Obama should use the occasion of Prime Minister Netanyahu's formal visit to the White House to allay the concerns of the Israeli public. The visit will certainly serve to mend much of the tension between Obama and

Netanyahu, but the President must also use the opportunity of a joint press conference with Netanyahu to address the Israeli public directly. President Obama needs to reaffirm not only American commitment to Israel's national security but also explain why many elements of American national security concerns are linked to the Middle East's stability and how American and Israeli strategic interests are parallel and complementary. He needs to tell the Israelis why America is seeking a comprehensive peace, why an Arab-Israeli peace offers Israel the best security guarantees, and how the United States intends to see this through. The Israelis need to hear from the President why painful concessions must be made and why the prospect of regional peace, security, and prosperity will by far outweigh these concessions.

Such a message will not only serve to alleviate much of the Israelis' anxiety over the necessary concessions, but will also send a powerful message to the enemies of peace that the United States standing shoulder-to-shoulder with Israel is the prerequisite to peace and the anchor to regional stability.

A DEFINING MOMENT IN AMERICAN-ISRAELI RELATIONS

JUNE 10, 2010

Regardless of the intended purposes of Israel's blockade on Gaza, the tragic incident surrounding the Mavi Marmara flotilla raid on May 31, 2010 has brought the blockade into international focus, and Israel will find itself under increasing pressure from friends and foes alike to lift the blockade in the coming weeks. Although Israel has legitimate security reasons to maintain the blockade (to prevent certain materials, including weapons, from entering Gaza), that should not preclude finding an alternative arrangement that can still satisfy Israel's security concerns. The tragic events on the flotilla should serve as a catalyst for Israel, Turkey, and the United States to change the regional political environment for the better before the conflict and the region's rising tensions spin out of control.

Israel must do what best serves its national security interests, but at this point it is necessary to take a much wider view of those interests because the prospect of regional instability is forcing other players, such as the leading Arab Sunni states, to reassess their position, especially in the wake of the growing Iranian nuclear threat. Added to this is the uncertainty about Iraq's future stability and how the brewing Israeli-Lebanese tension might play out.[277] Since the Gaza incursion in 2008, Israel has had ample opportunities to demonstrate a gesture for peace, ease the blockade, and show that it rewards nonviolence. Yet little progress has been made by the Netanyahu government, and unfortunately Israel now has less maneuvering room and faces mounting pressure to act. To prevent a continuation of this downward spiral, there is no better time for Israel than now to take the lead, demonstrate

---

277 Long-standing tensions between Israel and Hezbollah came to a head in mid-2010 with reports of weapons being sold to the group and overt threats from leader Hassan Nasrallah towards Israel.

creativity, and take a number of steps which could change the dynamics without being apologetic.

To start with, Israel must waste no time expanding its own inquiry into the tragic flotilla events by inviting other international investigators to join the Israeli team. As it has been said time and again, the investigation must be credible, thorough, transparent, and comprehensive. To do this, Israel should invite the United States and Turkey along with EU representatives to take part in the investigation. Israel should have nothing to hide, but even if its military is found responsible of terrible negligence leading to the death of nine Turks, there is no better way to settle the matter than through such a multinational investigation, while leaving no doubt about the integrity of the inquiry. An investigation with Turkish participation could, at a minimum, offer the hope that the arduous process of reconciling Israeli-Turkish relations could begin sooner rather than later. The investigation will also make public the nature of the conditions in Gaza, which have been distorted by all sides. In the final analysis, it is up to Israel to demonstrate that political pandering has been at play by those self-described champions of the Palestinian cause, but that can be proven only if Israel shares with outside powers the true picture about and inside Gaza.

Next, Israel must take the lead in demonstrating that the blockade was not arbitrary, and regardless of its effectiveness, Israel is willing to lift it as long as its legitimate security requirements are fully met. Israel must work closely with the United States and select European nations, such as Germany and France, along with Egypt and Turkey, to find a way to end the blockade while making absolutely certain that any and all construction materials are used strictly for civilian purposes. The Obama administration could spearhead the creation of such a monitoring group that Israel can trust. This will also allow the monitors to have a much better sense about Hamas' internal operations and may in fact reduce rather than increase Hamas' militancy. Whether or not Hamas accepts the new arrangement, Israel will succeed in internationalizing the Gaza burden, rather than own it lock, stock, and barrel. Under any circumstances, Israel must develop a new strategy to deal with Hamas. The present situation is not only unsustainable, but extraordinarily volatile and dangerous. The current policy does nothing but play into Iran's hand. To be sure, the blockade has run its course and become a major liability to Israel's international standing, rather than an asset from which the Israelis might still realize some future gains.

Whereas the first two measures are critical and require immediate attention, Israel must also move deliberately to make significant progress with the PA in the proximity talks. The Obama administration has invested heavily in its effort to restart Israeli-Palestinian negotiations. Although Israel must under any circumstances make some important concessions to move the peace process forward, making such concessions now is particularly important because this can achieve a number of Israeli and American objectives. Other than help mending Israel's strained relations with its most critical ally, it would also enhance America's credibility in the region. Discernible progress would also shift from proximity talks to direct negotiations—something that the Netanyahu government seeks—and encourage the Saudis and other Arab states to be more openly supportive of U.S. and Israeli efforts in dealing with Iran.

It has now become increasingly evident that the Israeli-Turkish crisis over the tragic flotilla affair was driven by political ambitions rather than by human compassion to provide the Palestinians with more humanitarian aid. Turkey must demonstrate that it really cares about the Palestinians rather than using their plight for domestic political gains, all which could have averted the flotilla crisis. Turkey—who seeks to assume regional leadership—must too play a more constructive and responsible role. What happened on the decks of the Turkish ship Mavi Marmara was not murder or massacre as some Turkish officials have portrayed it, and it certainly was not "state terrorism" as Mr. Erdogan most regretfully characterizes it.[278] To describe the tragic deaths in these terms simply further aggravates the already tenuous relations between the two countries and pushes them to the brink of crisis at a time of extraordinary regional volatility. This is a development that serves neither Israel's nor Turkey's ultimate strategic interests.

---

278 Harriet Sherwood, "Israel Accused of State Terrorism After Assault on Flotilla Carrying Gaza Aid," *The Guardian*, May 31, 2010, http://www.theguardian. com/world/2010/may/31/israel-accused-state-terrorism-assault-flotilla-gaza.

It is abundantly clear that the situation in the Middle East is becoming increasingly more dangerous. Iran is speeding toward acquiring nuclear weapons, the tension between Israel and Hezbollah is rising, Syria is assuming a steadily more aggressive posture toward Israel, and Hamas is riding high on the waves of the flotilla disaster. The room for miscalculation is forever present, and any small incident could trigger a regional conflagration. Israel must work closely with the United States to change the equation for the better. This is the moment that will define American-Israeli relations for decades to come.

THE PALESTINIANS' ULTIMATE OPTION

JULY 27, 2010

The Arab foreign ministers meeting on July 29th in Cairo to discuss the Israeli-Palestinian negotiations must keep in mind that endorsing direct negotiations between Israel and the Palestinians is not necessarily a favor to the Israelis. In fact, the opposite is true; direct negotiations will compel the Netanyahu government to deal with substantive issues—such as borders—as a precursor to negotiating a two-state solution. The Arab states should link direct talks to negotiating borders, instead of waiting to make more progress in the proximity talks. The United States, along with the leading Arab states, Israel, and the Palestinians, must do all they can to change the current dynamic of the negotiations. To that end there are specific realistic steps that must be taken not only to avoid failure but to set in motion the inevitability of establishing a Palestinian state.

For the United States, it must work to bring the parties to direct negotiations while seeking to bolster the credibility of its leadership in the region. Doing so will require bridging the gaps between the two sides in bringing them to direct talks, engaging their publics, and working with regional actors that have strong stakes in the success of peacemaking efforts, especially the governments of Saudi Arabia, Egypt, and Jordan. In this connection, strengthening Israeli trust and confidence in President Obama and his commitment to Israel's security is critical if Israel is to make the kind of concessions necessary to achieve a negotiated two-state accord. Obama should visit Israel and speak directly to the Israeli people regarding his commitment to enhancing U.S.-Israel security cooperation—particularly regarding the threat from Iran—and to resolving the Arab-Israeli conflict such that Israel's future as a democracy with a sustainable Jewish majority is ensured. He should not wait for progress in the peace process to do so. On the contrary, increasing Israel's confidence in President Obama, and enhancing overall trust in the relationship between the United States and Israel, will be critical to affect progress in the negotiations.

While reaching out to Israel, the United States should work to bring Prime Minister Netanyahu to direct negotiations with the issue of borders as the initial point of departure. The Palestinians refuse to enter into direct talks because they do not believe Netanyahu is sincere in his stated desire to achieve a two-state solution. But addressing the issue of borders (excluding Jerusalem, which should be negotiated at the conclusion of direct negotiations) would signify Netanyahu's seriousness. Even more, addressing the borders issue ultimately offers a chance to kill two birds with one stone: achieving an agreement on the contours of a border between Israel and the future Palestinian state, while taking the issue of Israeli settlement construction—a constant point of tension and distraction—off the table. It would also lead to an understanding that the major settlement blocs will remain part of Israel based on land swaps along the 1967 Green Line—a key and necessary achievement for the success of the peace talks that has been the basis of nearly every previous Israeli-Palestinian peacemaking endeavor.

The United States must also bring the Palestinians to direct talks. To do so, the United States must assure Palestinians that the White House is committed to hosting negotiations that are meaningful and sincere. The United States should welcome the Palestinians' recent proclivity to turn to the Arab League for endorsement of steps in the peace process, and go even further to encourage Arab League representatives to join the Palestinian team in direct talks in order to augment the Palestinians' position and utilize the API as a resource for advancing negotiations. The Arab foreign ministers must endorse the American approach and not press for a tactical advantage, if any, while undermining the strategic objective.

Israel too must make significant steps to improve the atmosphere in the region if negotiations are to succeed and Palestinian unilateral actions are to be avoided. Israel should agree to negotiate borders first in order to demonstrate its seriousness, and to address the issue of settlement construction. It also should encourage the economic and security advancements in the West Bank by permitting and even encouraging Israelis to visit Area A and invest in the West Bank.

At the same time, Israel should continue to remove unnecessary roadblocks and expand the areas in which Palestinian security forces may operate, including into Area B. In the context of renewed direct talks, Israel should work toward freeing a significant number of Palestinian prisoners to the PA leadership in Ramallah to show that negotiations—and not violence—produce meaningful results. In this respect, continuing to ease the blockade on the Gaza Strip and enabling the import and export of goods from the territory will also be important measures to be taken as negotiations proceed, while also crediting the PA for any progress made in this regard.

Finally, the Palestinians must also do all they can to give negotiations a chance to succeed. To start, they should enter into direct talks with support from the Arab League and aforementioned assurance from the United States. The benefits of entering direct talks are two-fold: they demonstrate the Palestinians' commitment to the two-state solution—which enjoys strong international support—while pressuring Netanyahu to reveal his positions. The Palestinians should continue to stress that borders be negotiated first, but reduce their emphasis on an Israeli settlement freeze. As long as any Israeli building is done quietly and does not take place in sensitive areas that are to be negotiated, the Palestinians should provide Netanyahu with space to maneuver politically. At the same time, as the Palestinians move forward on the political track, they should continue to pursue economic growth in both the West Bank and Gaza while promoting a concerted nonviolent campaign to oppose Israel's occupation. In this regard, the movement to refuse work in Israel's West Bank settlements and boycott settlement products is useful and legitimate as a tool of the nonviolent approach to send a clear message.

While pursuing these steps to advance negotiations, the Palestinians should concurrently prepare the groundwork for a Palestinian declaration of statehood in the event that negotiations fail to produce a viable two-state solution. They should continue to build the infrastructure for a future state while canvassing the international community in an effort to obtain their readiness to recognize its establishment. The support of the EU and the Arab League will be particularly critical in the effort to obtain a United Nations Security Council (UNSC) Resolution recognizing the newly declared state.

The Palestinians should continue to make public their intentions in this regard, and consider appointing a special envoy who is tasked with advancing this diplomatic initiative in full coordination with the Palestinian leadership in Ramallah. Key to the success of this effort—as well as to the potential for successful negotiations—is the maintenance of permanent calm in the region and the Palestinians' repeated publicly stated commitment to nonviolence. This is the key to guaranteeing Israel's national security, which is a prerequisite to the realization of the Palestinians' national aspirations for statehood.

By working to advance negotiations on the one hand while preparing the groundwork for a declaration of statehood on the other, the Palestinians can take control of their future—but only through nonviolent means. In fact, the greatest threat to Palestinian statehood today is not a breakdown of negotiations, but a return to violence that would renew an open-ended bloody conflict, relinquish the vast international support the Palestinians enjoy, and squander Prime Minister Salam Fayyad's impressive state-building efforts which are bringing the Palestinian people to the brink of independence.

DIRECT TALKS AND THEIR
POTENTIAL CONSEQUENCES

AUGUST 23, 2010

The Obama administration's success in moving the Israeli-Palestinian talks from proximity to direct negotiations is an important achievement for making real progress. However, direct talks will not produce substantive results unless the United States takes a number of pivotal steps to ensure that the progress made in the negotiations is irreversible, and will eventually lead to a final agreement. This is the only way the United States can avoid the pitfalls of past bilateral negotiations, so that if—for whatever reasons—the negotiations stall or break down, they can be resumed from where they were left off. Moreover, the United States must remain directly and actively involved in the negotiations, serving as the "depository" of any incremental agreement achieved, while delinking progress on any particular issue from the remaining unresolved issues. To that end, the Obama administration ought to focus on four different steps:

First, the Obama administration must persuade Israel to start the direct negotiations with the Palestinians by focusing on the issue of borders. Addressing the final borders would first and foremost signal to the Palestinians that an issue at the core of the conflict—the parameters of a two-state solution—is to be negotiated in earnest, something that will dramatically strengthen Abbas' position. This will also have a tremendous psychological and practical impact on the Palestinians as it will inadvertently address the status of the majority of the Israeli settlements in the West Bank. Delineating the borders will allow both sides to determine through negotiations which of the settlements will be incorporated into Israel proper through a land swap of equal size and quality, which settlements will be turned over to the Palestinians, and which will be dismantled. As a result, settlement construction should no longer be a point of contention, as Israel would build only inside the settlements that are determined to be part of Israel proper. Borders have been comprehensively discussed twice before—in 2000 at Camp David and in 2008 between the Olmert Government and the PA, with a general agreement achieved in both sets of the negotiations. Utilizing this experience, it is conceivable that an agreement on borders could be achieved within six months. The critical point here is that once there is an agreement on borders, it should be "banked" by the United States and delinked from any other issue, including the Palestinian refugees and the future of East Jerusalem. Moreover, the Palestinians in particular will develop a vested interest in continuing the negotiating process and will be far more inclined to negotiate to the finish line as the vision of their own state will be in sight.

Second, the United States must expand the negotiations beyond the scope of the Quartet and the Roadmap by officially embracing the API as the central framework for a comprehensive Arab-Israeli peace accord, with the objective of changing the dynamic of the negotiations. Such a step is critical at this juncture for six reasons. First, it would give the Arab states confidence that the United States is committed to a comprehensive solution, and therefore they would be more inclined to invest greater political capital in the process.

Second, it would allow the Obama administration to insist that some of the leading Arab states such as Saudi Arabia and other Gulf and North African states make certain concessions to Israel in return, including goodwill gestures such as overflights and opening trade. Such measures would go a long way toward ameliorating the attitude of many Israelis who oppose the API, and disabuse many others who do not believe that the Arab states intend on making peace. In addition, it would strengthen Prime Minister Netanyahu's hand with his coalition partners by providing him with the necessary political cover to make concessions as negotiations are advanced.

Third, it would increase the stakes of the Arab states in the peace process and strengthen their resolve to deal with any rejectionist groups such as Hamas, by bringing them back to the Arab fold in one form or another, including coercive diplomacy. Fourth, representatives of leading Arab states should continue to be present as observers at the negotiating table beyond the first session in the White

House on September 2. Their participation will bolster Mahmoud Abbas' position, serving as a political shield that will provide Abbas with the backing he needs from the Arab world to make difficult decisions in the negotiations.

Fifth, embracing the API would also provide a useful and necessary context with which to try to co-opt Hamas into the political process as well as advance Israel-Syria talks. Notwithstanding Hamas' extreme positions, it would be wise for the United States, the PA, and Egypt to encourage Hamas to accept the principle of the API in order to become part of the process, as long as it also maintains its current nonviolent posture. If Hamas is ignored, it will stop short of nothing to undermine the peace negotiations. Similarly, the Obama administration must prepare the groundwork to reopen Israeli-Syrian negotiations. Peace between Israel and Syria remains central to achieving regional stability. Finally, throughout these efforts, the United States must remain directly and actively involved, advancing new ideas, bridging differing positions, and inducing collaborative approaches to get results.

It is extremely important that President Obama address the Israeli public directly, preferably by visiting Israel or, at a minimum, by dedicating an exclusive press conference on the heels of the resumption of direct talks at the beginning of September. Although Obama has repeatedly stated America's unshakable commitment to Israel's national security, there is still considerable consternation among Israelis about the President's personal commitment. The bilateral American-Israeli relations during the first 18 months of his presidency were rocky for a variety of reasons, including the conflict over a settlement freeze. Now it appears that President Obama and Prime Minister Netanyahu have reached a much better understanding about the requisites for conducting meaningful negotiations with the Palestinians, particularly following Netanyahu's visit to the White House on July 6. Going forward, it is critical that the President demonstrate to Israelis not only America's non-negotiable commitment to their national security, but that pursuing peace with the Palestinians based on a two-state solution offers Israel long-term security guarantees and remains the only viable option to resolve the conflict. Indeed, the president must emphasize that America's strategic interests in the Middle East are intertwined with Israel's national security interests. Our shared interests in security and stability throughout the region would significantly be advanced by a comprehensive peace between Israel and the Arab states. Moreover, Israelis must understand that dealing with any threat emanating from Iran or its surrogates, Hamas, Hezbollah, and others, requires an end to the Israeli-Palestinian conflict with the full backing of the United States and the Arab states.

A visit by Obama to Israel at this particular time may evoke criticism from some who may accuse the president of political pandering in an election year. Conversely, a visit at this time could blunt the impact of the Obama administration's critics who have begun to use the past friction between the Obama White House and Israel as a political tool during this election season. Putting such cynicism aside, there is nothing more powerful than the presence of the President of the United States in a country which is eagerly seeking to restore the unflinching bond that has symbolized the relations between the two nations. Furthermore, only when the Israelis are confident in the state of U.S.-Israel relations will they be more likely to make the kind of meaningful concessions needed to conclude a peace agreement. Only under such circumstances will the Israeli public demand its own government to make the necessary concessions to achieve peace with security.

The President should use his visit to Israel to reassure Israelis that the United States is committed to preventing Iran from acquiring nuclear weapons. Israelis are terrified of the prospect that, if not stopped, Iran will eventually acquire nuclear weapons and Israel will face an existential threat. Spelling out the United States' commitment to avert such a scenario in unequivocal terms will send an important message not only to the Israeli people, but to Iran as well. Delivering this point from Israel will clearly signal where the United States stands on Iran's nuclear program while making a compelling case to the Israelis that America stands shoulder-to-shoulder with their country. The President does not need to threaten the Iranian regime with military force to show solidarity with Israel. However, such a message would be particularly important because if force is ultimately used as a last resort against Iran's nuclear facilities by either country, both the United States and Israel would be implicated.

President Obama has already invested substantial political capital in trying to resume meaningful negotiations between Israel and the Palestinians, and must now invest even more to bring an end to the decades-long debilitating conflict. The resumption of direct negotiations gives the President his first chance since he came to office to meaningfully pursue an Israeli-Palestinian peace through a two-state solution. It most likely will be his last chance. A failure to achieve a breakthrough this time around will not simply delay a peace agreement or restore the status quo ante; it will seriously erode the President's credibility and could usher in a period of intense violence and instability (if not all-out war), setting back the prospect for a solution to the Arab-Israeli conflict by a whole generation, with potentially terrifying consequences. Neither Israel, the United States, nor the Arab states can afford such a breakdown at this particular juncture, especially when the war in Afghanistan continues to rage, violence is still inflicting Iraq, tension between Israel and Lebanon is simmering, and Iran is racing toward acquiring nuclear weapons.

The experiences from former negotiations strongly suggest that the measures stipulated here must be carefully considered in order to avoid the pitfalls of the past. In particular, the United States must become the "depository" and final arbiter of all interim agreements achieved, such as borders, and must commit both sides to honor these agreements in the future should the negotiations falter at any stage and for whatever reason, including a change of government. To be sure, the United States must insist that future talks resume from where current negotiations leave off; otherwise, they could be used as a tool to stall from reaching an agreement rather than achieving a permanent solution.

This is the time when the United States must insist that all the parties to the conflict put their cards on the table and demonstrate once and for all that their protestations to seek peace are genuine. By demonstrating leadership, the United States can ensure that the parties no longer claim to seek "peace" without making the difficult decisions necessary to achieve it.

"CHANGE WE CAN BELIEVE IN"

OCTOBER 22, 2010

With the peace process at a standstill, President Obama must shake up the current efforts, and his Mideast peace team, in order to get the Israelis and Palestinians back on track toward a peaceful resolution of their conflict. The Obama White House has invested an enormous amount of political capital to advance Middle East peace since taking office, yet has little to show for it. Even so, the United States cannot abandon its efforts and leave Israel and the Palestinians to their own devices. It is therefore time to recognize that the current U.S. strategy is not working, and that significant changes are needed if there is to maintain any hope for reaching a breakthrough in the coming year.

The new strategy must begin with President Obama's visit to Israel after the midterm election. Rightly or wrongly, Obama's decision not to visit Israel following his June 2009 Cairo speech and other trips to region was interpreted as a slight to Israel. This month, the president will make his third official overseas visit as president to four Asian countries, including a heavily Muslim country—Indonesia—once again skipping Israel and sending the message to the Israeli public that he is uninterested in engaging the Israelis directly. Because of President Obama's long overdue visit to Israel, the Israeli public is becoming increasingly more skeptical of the president and his administration. Although the majority of Israelis support a two-state solution, the public remains passive and acutely cynical with regards to the current peace efforts. This relatively silent majority will only become aroused in support of the peace process if they understand what is at stake, and why it is in Israel and the United States' best interests to achieve peace now. The Israeli public needs to hear it directly from the President of the United States. President Obama must connect with ordinary Israelis and forcefully deliver the message that while America's commitment to Israel's national security is unequivocal and unconditional, only sustainable peace offers Israel ultimate security. A personal appearance by President Obama before the Israeli Knesset would have a decisive impact on Israel's public opinion and on his own personal standing and credibility in the Israelis' eyes. The president needs to explain that America and Israel are in this together, and that the United States will stand with Israel shoulder-to-shoulder at all times to confront any potential threat from any direction. What the president needs is a game changer, and only when the Israeli public subscribes to the peace process with confidence and a belief that peace can be achieved with security, will they raise their voice in support of peace "now."

During Netanyahu's visit to the United States in July he said to President Obama in the Oval Office, "You know, I've been coming here a lot. It's about time you and the First Lady came to Israel, sir." "I'm ready," was Obama's response. "We look forward to it. Thank you."[279] Whether or not Netanyahu wishes for the President to visit Israel at this juncture, President Obama has been invited. He should, as soon as possible, announce his readiness to visit Israel because there may not be a better time to do so if he wants to seriously impact the peace process.

For President Obama to execute a new strategy, he requires a new team. Special Envoy George Mitchell is overrated as a skilled negotiator, and although he has a clear understanding of the Arab-Israeli conflict, he has failed to advance more compelling scenarios that deal with the psychological and emotional perspectives of the conflicting parties—the settlement debacle offers a case in point. In an effort to deflect criticism of the failing peace efforts, Mitchell has noted on several occasions that in his experience in Northern Ireland, he had "700 days of failure and one day of success."[280] He will soon

---

279 Barack Obama, "Remarks by President Obama and Prime Minister Netanyahu of Israel in Joint Press Availability" (Washington, D.C., July 6, 2010), http://www.whitehouse.gov/the-press-office/remarks-president-obama-and-prime-minister-netanyahu-israel-joint-press-availabilit.

280 Chris McGreal, "Israel and Palestinians to Resume Peace Talks in Washington," *The Guardian*, August 20, 2010, http://www.theguardian.com/world/2010/aug/20/israel-palestinians-resume-peace-talks.

reach that 700-day mark, and there is still no sign of progress on the horizon. Meanwhile, although Dennis Ross has reportedly been playing a more assertive role in the White House's peace efforts, he is an old hat, and does not have the trust of the Palestinians. Ross has little to show for his years of intimate involvement in Israeli-Palestinian negotiations.

The recent offer by the United States to provide security guarantees for a 60-day extension of Israel's settlement moratorium exemplifies how the president's Mideast team has failed. The United States' commitment to Israel's security should not be a bargaining chip to advance the negotiation process. Even though Netanyahu is reportedly still entertaining the offer, to make such an offer touches on the most sensitive issue for Israelis and suggests that Israel's security is negotiable or could be enhanced by additional security guarantees from the U.S. and military hardware. This is exactly the wrong message to send to the Israelis, and it is high time to get the message right that Israel's national security will never become a part of the negotiating mix.

Both Mitchell and Ross should resign and be replaced by an envoy that will stay in the region and work daily with both sides so that he/she cannot be ignored. One of the keys to recently retired Lt. Gen. Keith Dayton's success as the United States Security Coordinator charged with training the Palestinian security services in the West Bank was that he lived in the region and spent each day earning the trust of Israelis and Palestinians on the ground. This same principle should now apply to an envoy tasked with advancing peace talks. What is needed is someone who is trusted by both sides, knows the issues intimately, enjoys a solid mandate and provides a blunt no-nonsense approach to moving the talks ahead.

With a new team in place, the Obama administration must not allow Israeli settlements to remain the foremost obstacle impeding progress. The White House made the mistake of making a settlement freeze a precondition for negotiations without taking into consideration that Netanyahu might reject such a freeze, and failed to have a "Plan B" in the event that he would do so. The Palestinians latched onto the position of the United States and now the process—yet again—is stuck over the issue. To move forward, the United States must change the dynamics completely by persuading the Palestinians to let go of the issue of the freeze for now, in order to focus on something larger and more important to the Palestinians—a border agreement. Netanyahu continues to say he would be willing to discuss all issues with the goal of reaching a two-state solution. The Palestinians, with the support of the United States and the Arab League in particular, should take him up on the offer. In doing so, the issue of borders should be the new launching point, with a goal to resolve the issue within six months. In addition, if any incremental agreement is reached, including on borders, the United States should institute new rules of engagement, such as any agreements that are established in the negotiations should be deposited with the United States. Too much time has been wasted determining the point of departure for the negotiations. The United States' depositing agreements would ensure that should talks breakdown, future negotiations could start where this effort left off.

The United States' stakes in the Middle East are extremely high, and Washington cannot play a meaningful leadership role and lose what is left of its credibility in the region without some kind of solution to the Israeli-Palestinian dispute. For this reason, should nothing move forward, the United States must prepare a peace plan of its own. Although the Netanyahu government is on record opposing any plan imposed from the outside—including one from the United States—by indicating that the United States is preparing to go that route should it become necessary, it will send a clear message about the seriousness and the urgency the United States attaches to solving the Israeli-Palestinian conflict. Furthermore, the knowledge that such a plan is in the making will put the Netanyahu government on notice that it must sooner than later change course. That said, in preparing the plan, the Obama administration needs also to communicate to the Israelis that although an Israeli-Palestinian peace serves America's strategic interest in the region, any peace plan will be consistent with Israel's legitimate security concerns and requirements. The contours of an agreement are already largely known. Any plan would naturally take into consideration the numerous negotiation efforts of the past, and include areas of general agreement between Israel and the Palestinians.

Without negotiations toward a two-state solution, the Palestinians are already exploring the possibility of gaining international recognition for the unilateral declaration of a state along the 1967 borders through various international forums, including the UNSC. As recently stated by French Foreign Minister Bernard Kouchner, "one cannot rule out in principle the Security Council option." Based on current international sentiments, the Palestinians are likely to gain broad support for such a move in the UNGA. Even though a resolution in the UNGA in favor of creating a Palestinian state is not binding, it would have a tremendous psychological effect and may well pave the way to a similar resolution in the UNSC. Should the peace process continue to dissolve and this UN campaign materialize, the United States will be forced into a no-win situation—if the Obama administration were to veto such a resolution in the Security Council, it would enrage the Arab world; if it were to pass it, it would infuriate Israel. The United States also cannot abstain and absolve itself from influence over the peace process. Moreover, the United States voted in favor of UNSC Resolution 1850 in December 2008, which called for a two-state solution and support for the "Palestinian institution-building programme in preparation for statehood," which is being feverishly implemented in the West Bank on the basis of PA Prime Minister Fayyad's plans.[281] Can the United States go against statehood now? To avoid such a scenario, the United States needs to get negotiations back on track—and soon.

Skeptics may argue that the Mitchell team needs more time, that a U.S. plan—even as a last resort—will undoubtedly fall flat, or that the United States should give up and stop its efforts altogether, particularly if the president emerges from the midterm elections in a significantly weaker political position, which is more than likely. But the Obama administration cannot give up under any circumstances. America's strategic interests throughout the Middle East are incalculable, and its credibility across the globe—especially in the Arab and Muslim world and in Israel—is now at stake. A new strategy, a new message and

---

281 United Nations Security Council, Resolution 1850, "The Situation in the Middle East, Including the Palestinian Question," December 16, 2008, http://unispal.un.org/UNISPAL.NSF/0/7F7430A137000C4E85257523 004CCADF.

a new team are sorely needed. President Obama must create a new dynamic moving forward that will demonstrate the kind of leadership and resolve that is necessary to end this festering malaise.

President Obama was elected with a promise to deliver "change we can believe in." His election raised expectations (perhaps too high) both in the United States and in the Middle East. Thus far he has achieved very little. However, he still has an opportunity to be a transformative leader who can deliver peace and security in the Middle East. To do so he must now deliver on his promise of change.

CALLING ON ROBERT WEXLER

NOVEMBER 3, 2010

It is time for the White House to bring on a new Mideast peace team. At various points in the past several months, Special Envoy for Middle East Peace George Mitchell has responded to reporters' questions about the stalled peace process by recalling his experience mediating the conflict in Northern Ireland, stating that he had "700 days of failure and one day of success."[282] Unfortunately, this analogy was never an apt one. In the Middle East, 700 days of failure serves to undermine credibility and trust—and that is exactly what has happened to Mitchell and his team.

In less than two months, Mitchell will reach his 700th day working to end the conflict between Israelis and Palestinians, with no semblance of "success" achieved thus far and none on the horizon. As a result, Israelis, Palestinians, and the international community are deeply cynical as to the United States' peacemaking efforts led by the former Senator from Maine, and the two-state solution is being openly questioned like never before. It is time for Mitchell to resign. He should be replaced by someone who already has the trust of both sides, who can effectively communicate to leaders in the Mideast and to domestic audiences in the United States, and who can live in the region to work face-to-face with the parties on a daily basis. There is one individual who fits this description to a T—former Congressman Robert Wexler.

Wexler already has the trust of the President and both Israelis and Palestinians. As a surrogate for President Obama during the presidential election season, Wexler was a lead voice in promoting Obama's credentials to Jewish audiences in particular. William Daroff, the Washington director of the Jewish Federations of North America, told reporters when Wexler left Congress that "It was a

---

282 McGreal, "Israel and Palestinians to Resume Peace Talks in Washington."

crucial tipping point to have someone of Robert's stature in the Jewish community to vouch for (Obama)."[283] Wexler could now have the same impact for Obama in the Middle East. As a Congressman from Florida, Wexler was described by AIPAC as "one of the stalwart leaders of the American-Israel alliance in Congress."[284] But he has also earned the trust of Palestinian leaders. In recent months, PA President Mahmoud Abbas and Prime Minster Salaam Fayyad have held two high-level, off-the-record meetings with prominent leaders of the American Jewish community in Washington, DC and New York, respectively. Both were hosted by Wexler in his current role as head of the Washington-based Center for Mideast Peace. Even more, he enjoys the trust of one of the most aggressive and critical actors in the Middle East today—Turkey. Wexler co-founded the Congressional Caucus on U.S.-Turkey relations and today is a frequent visitor to the country. Few, if any, match Wexler's experience, credentials, and knowledge of the interrelated issues at play in this volatile region.

With trust in place, Wexler would have the ability to speak with the parties and domestic audiences in a way that Mitchell never could. Immediately upon his appointment, Mitchell was viewed with skepticism, perhaps unfairly, by some in the pro-Israel community in particular, but Mitchell still has yet to earn the trust of either side. The emphasis he placed on settlements has proven ineffective for advancing the peace process and actually served to undermine the already tenuous trust between the White House and the Israeli public. In fact, in order to obtain a settlement freeze or any other concession from the Israelis, trust with the Israeli public and pro-Israel advocates must be achieved. Mitchell has been unable to help President Obama do this, but Wexler could. As the former Congressman from the most heavily Jewish-populated district in the United States, Wexler is not a novice when it comes to addressing the concerns of Israel and pro-Israel Americans. He fully understands and appreciates the mindsets of the players involved and would be able to provide both

---

283 George Bennett, "Wexler Leaves Congress, Pursues Challenge of Middle East Peace-Making," *Palm Beach Post*, January 2, 2010, http://www.palmbeachpost.com/news/news/wexler-leaves-congress-pursues-challenge-of-middle/nLtx4/.

284 Ibid.

sides with the confidence needed to support significant concessions for advancing the peace process.

Rumors have been swirling for months that Wexler could be named the new U.S. Ambassador to Israel. He would be a good choice for that position. However, it would be even better to give him the task of advancing the peace process: post him in Jerusalem and put him to work capitalizing on the trust he has earned from both sides. One of the keys to the success of recently retired Lt. Gen. Keith Dayton, the United States Security Coordinator charged with training Palestinian security services in the West Bank, was that he lived in the region and worked daily to earn the trust of Israelis and Palestinians on the ground. The same approach should now be applied to advancing peace talks. Also key to Dayton's success was his no-nonsense approach, which Congressman Wexler fully shares.

What the peace process needs today is a messenger with a presidential mandate to mediate and offer new and creative ideas, and who can also be blunt and honest with the parties to communicate what is at stake and the obligations that both sides must meet. Wexler wears his toughness and frankness as badges of honor, so much so that he titled his memoir "Fire-Breathing Liberal." For the sake of ending the Israeli-Palestinian conflict based on the two-state solution, it is time to appoint former Representative Wexler as the fire-breathing envoy.

THE GREAT CHESS GAME

APRIL 25, 2011

Amid the stalemate in Israeli-Palestinian peacemaking, a storm of diplomatic activity is brewing. The Palestinians, Israel, and the United States are carefully calculating what moves to make next. Only the Palestinians appear to have a clear-cut strategy: to bring the conflict to the international arena through a UNGA Resolution recognizing a Palestinian state in the West Bank and Gaza Strip, within the 1967 borders. Meanwhile, the United States and Israel are feverishly working to develop counter-strategies of their own that will shelve the Palestinians' United Nations plan and maintain some semblance of the prospect that a two-state solution can be reached through good-faith negotiations. For that to succeed, however, Israel must come up with a *credible* peace plan that the Palestinians are willing to accept as a basis for negotiations and that the Obama administration can also embrace. But with the September UN General Assembly just five months away, the time to make such a move on the Mideast chessboard is now.

The PA's recognition strategy has, on the surface, been quite successful. Over 130 nations have already endorsed the proposed resolution for statehood and many other countries are prepared to recognize a Palestinian state. In the interim, many South American nations have already recognized Palestine over the last several months. Western European nations that support the two-state solution and have generously funded Palestinian civil society programs and institutions are eager to see the benefits of their decades-long investments. In advance of another donors' conference in Paris in June to discuss new aid to the Palestinians, PA Prime Minister Salam Fayyad met the donor's coordination group for the Palestinian territories, the Ad Hoc Liaison Committee, on April 13 in Brussels. In the forward of the report, Fayyad wrote: "We stand today on the verge of national readiness for the birth of the State of Palestine." He presented them with his new National development Plans for 2011–2013 titled "Establishing the State, Building our Future."[285]

Strengthening Fayyad's arguments, reports have been issued by the United Nations Special Coordinator for the Middle East Peace Process Robert Serry, the IMF, and the World Bank, all expressing enthusiastic support for the progress toward a self-sustaining Palestinian state. The UN report indicated that "[i]n six areas where the UN is most engaged, governmental functions are now sufficient for a functioning government of a [Palestinian] state."[286] The IMF stated that "...the PA is now able to conduct the sound economic policies expected of a future well-functioning Palestinian state."[287] In addition, the World Bank said that "If the Palestinian Authority (PA) maintains its performance in institution-building and delivery of public services, it is well-positioned for the establishment of a state at any point in the near future."[288] Even more, President Barack Obama himself stated to great applause in his address to last year's UN General Assembly that "when we come back here next year, we can have an agreement that will lead to a new member of the United Nations—an independent, sovereign state of Palestine, living in peace with Israel."[289] With so many elements coalescing to-

---

285 Salam Fayyad, "National Development Plan 2011-13: Establishing the State, Building our Future," Palestinian National Authority, April 2011, 5, http://lllp.iugaza.edu.ps/Files_Uploads/635063697861151130.pdf.

286 *Palestinian State-Building: A Decisive Period* (Brussels: Office for the United Nations Special Coordinator for the Middle East Peace Process, 2011), iii, http://www.un.org/depts/dpa/qpal/docs/2011%20Helsinki/UNs%20Report%20to%20the%20AHLC%2013_April_2011.pdf.

287 "Macroeconomic And Fiscal Framework For The West Bank And Gaza: Seventh Review of Progress," International Monetary Fund, April 13, 2011, http://unispal.un.org/UNISPAL.NSF/0/A35B30B2051C33A38525786A006A23F8.

288 "The Underpinnings of the Future Palestinian State: Sustainable Growth and Institutions," The World Bank, September 21, 2010, http://go.worldbank.org/DWNMPJRX50.

289 Barack Obama, "Remarks by the President to the United Nations General Assembly" (United Nations General Assembly, New York,

gether, the Palestinian plan for recognition come September seems to be in place—or does it?

Privately, some Palestinians recognize the drawbacks of the UN option and even admit that this is not a solution, but only a change in the nature of the conflict. UN recognition cannot remove Israeli soldiers or West Bank settlers. It cannot enable the flow of goods into or between Palestinian territories, nor does it solve the Fatah-Hamas split. Should there be no political progress after September, even with recognition, President Mahmoud Abbas has threatened to resign. But what would be next? While much has been invested in developing the threat of a unilateral declaration, there appears to be little strategy as to what to do with that recognition. Prime Minister Salam Fayyad's institution building plan continues to be an admirable enterprise, but is it unsustainable without continued co-operation, coordination, and negotiations with Israel, especially since an important part of Palestinian successes—as suggested by the IMF report—are attributed to Israel's security cooperation and support of the Palestinians' economic development programs? And how does the Gaza Strip factor into the UN's recognition if it is still under the control of Hamas, who seeks the destruction of Israel, another UN member state? These uncertainties, coupled with regional unrest, have led Fatah and Hamas to renewed reconciliation talks. Although both sides know that reaching a unity agreement before going to the UNGA is critical, whether a Fatah-Hamas agreement is imminent, or even possible, remains to be seen, especially since each has adopted a different strategy toward Israel, if not a different objective altogether. However, it is clear that with uncertainties and questions mounting, the PA would be eager to grasp at a new diplomatic initiative if it offered a way for the Palestinian leadership to save face, and provided the Palestinian people with confidence that their national aspirations are being met, and that the conflict with Israel is finally ended.

Only the United States and Israel can give the Palestinians such assurances—but will they do so? Israeli officials have publicly recognized the potential chaos that would erupt should a Palestinian state be declared. Recently, Defense Minister Ehud Barak told a conference at

NY, September 23, 2010) http://www.whitehouse.gov/the-press-office/2010/09/23/remarks-president-united-nations-general-assembly.

the Institute for National Security Studies in Tel Aviv that in such a scenario, Israel would face a "diplomatic tsunami."[290] In his meeting two weeks ago with President Barack Obama, Israel's President Shimon Peres is widely believed to have laid the groundwork for the possibility of an Israeli initiative that would head off the Palestinian one. When Prime Minister Benjamin Netanyahu arrives in Washington in late May for the annual AIPAC conference, all eyes will be awaiting a much-anticipated "Netanyahu plan." And, perhaps to President Obama's chagrin, Netanyahu was invited by the House Speaker, John Boehner, to address a joint session of Congress where he is expected to be received with a warm welcome, especially by Republicans.

Rumors thus far indicate that Netanyahu's plan could include a withdrawal of IDF soldiers from some areas in the West Bank and transfer security responsibilities to Palestinian control, allowing Palestinian security forces to operate with greater freedom and autonomy. Yet while Netanyahu has put the brakes on recent Jerusalem construction plans, his rumored plan does not include removing any settlers from the West Bank (at least at this juncture) and a freeze on housing construction in the settlements which the PA made sine qua non to the resumption of negotiations. To be sure, Netanyahu stands to lose the support of his two main coalition partners, Shas and Yisrael Beiteinu, who respectively reject compromises on Jerusalem and sweeping territorial concessions that will include uprooting scores of settlements. If he seriously discusses these sensitive issues which the Palestinians insist upon, he will also lose the support of many members of his own Likud party in the Knesset. With such political obstacles in place, Netanyahu's ability to deliver a plan that will be sufficient to keep the Palestinians from using the UN option is doubtful. However, what is abundantly clear based on his own history is that Netanyahu will market any plan he develops during his trip to Washington as if it is a monumental leap toward peace—and many U.S. legislators are likely to buy it. But will the Palestinians?

---

290 Natasha Mozgovaya, "Barak: Israel Facing Regional 'Earthquake' and Diplomatic 'Tsunami,'" *Haaretz*, March 23, 2011, http://www.haaretz.com/news/diplomacy-defense/barak-israel-facing-regional-earthquake-and-diplomatic-tsunami-1.351285.

Today, President Obama is boxed in by all sides. His remarks at the UN General Assembly last year (and in Cairo before that), the consistent development of the PA hailed by international bodies, the democratic revolutions of the current "Arab Spring," and the potential fallout should a solution to the current stalemate not be found all suggest that it is high time for a Palestinian state. But there are also constraints on the other side. Obama surely realizes that Israel feels threatened by the uncertainty that has gripped the region as a result of the Arab revolts, and is particularly reluctant to pursue peace as a result. Without Israel's consent, any arrangement for the Palestinians is unlikely to be sustainable. Even more, the "diplomatic tsunami" that could face Israel should the President be unsuccessful in navigating the peace process out of its current malaise will be on his watch, during an election season in which 63 percent of Americans sympathize with Israel.

President Obama would like nothing more than to expand upon a meaningful initiative by Prime Minister Netanyahu that he could package to the Palestinians and the reshaping Arab world. He would also undoubtedly love to travel to Jerusalem—as he is rumored to be contemplating attending Shimon Peres' "Tomorrow Conference" in June—with a message of friendship and peacemaking in-hand, in order to place the highly publicized tension between him and the Israeli prime minister in the past. But he cannot do so without Netanyahu's help.

The United States is eager to advance an initiative that will provide ample grounds to renew negotiations between Israelis and Palestinians, rather than see them pursue unilateral measures. The parameters of a two-state solution are known and have been rehashed ad nauseam. It is likely that most Israelis and Palestinians want the same. But for now, in the Mideast chess game, all eyes remain on the Israeli prime minister—it is now Netanyahu's move.

AIPAC'S MISGUIDED ADVOCACY

AUGUST 22, 2011

The effusive standing ovations Prime Minister Benjamin Netanyahu received during his speech to a joint session of Congress, despite his recent public clashes with President Obama, raised
anew questions of the power and influence of the so-called "Israel
lobby," led by AIPAC. Suggestions that AIPAC is all-powerful in
Washington, or that its aims and actions are nefarious, are baseless.
AIPAC is an effective interest group that has wielded grassroots
activism and political contributions to foster a closer relationship
between the United States and the State of Israel based largely on
common interests, values, and cultural affinity. Yet criticism of
AIPAC is not unwarranted, especially with regard to its muted efforts to support actions to achieve a lasting peace in the Middle East.

It is one thing to be supportive of Israel, but it is another to
simply be a rubber stamp for its policies, however self-destructive
they are. On its website, AIPAC touts itself with a quote from The
New York Times describing the organization as "the most important
organization affecting America's relationship with Israel." It is time
that AIPAC wield this position of influence in support of peacemaking efforts that will keep the U.S.-Israel relationship strong not
only in this generation, but also in the next.

In many ways, AIPAC has written the playbook on how to be
an effective Washington lobby. By mobilizing grassroots constituencies across the country consisting of many religious and cultural
backgrounds, AIPAC has brought the cause of Israel and the U.S.-
Israeli relationship to the attention of the masses. Today, the "Israel
lobby" is not a "Jewish lobby" exclusively, but one that incorporates
all faiths, most prominently the Christian Evangelical and Meth-
odist movements, through organizations like Christians United for
Israel (CUFI). AIPAC has successfully advocated for an annual aid

422

package that has helped Israel maintain its qualified military edge in the volatile Middle East. It has brought countless congressional delegations to Israel, linking American policymakers with their Israeli counterparts. The American Israel Education Foundation, which is affiliated with AIPAC, sponsored 81 House members this month on a visit to Israel and the West Bank, the largest group of Congress members to ever make the trip during a single recess.[291] In addition, while it is not a formulated political action committee (PAC), it has steered millions of dollars of political contributions to candidates and elected officials across the country for decades. Any lobby should be envious of AIPAC's success.

Yet too often AIPAC's advocacy has become synonymous with silencing debate when it comes to the United States' role in promoting an Israeli-Palestinian peace. This issue exploded with the publication of "The Israel Lobby" by Professors Stephen Walt and John Mearsheimer, which in my view went too far to suggest that Mideast policy issues are explicitly driven by Israel-centric policymaking. Still, the debate further intensified with the establishment of the aggressive, liberal-minded J Street, as well as publications like Peter Beinart's "The Failure of the American Jewish Establishment" in the New York Review of Books. The book pointedly challenged the American Jewish community's traditional thinking about Israeli advocacy and warned that the status quo is alienating younger Jews in particular—a constituency that AIPAC claims to represent when in fact it does not.

These criticisms cannot be dismissed. Indeed, pro-Israel organizations, led by AIPAC, have too often sought to advance short-term goals over long-term interests, to the detriment of genuine advocacy in support of peacemaking. Historically, AIPAC has presented a distinctly conservative approach. At AIPAC's 2007 "policy conference," then-House Speaker Nancy Pelosi was booed, albeit by a few dozen attendees, after suggesting that the Iraq war had been a failure. Many were also concerned that President Obama would be booed this year. Although he ultimately was not, the question is, why should there have been any concern that the U.S.

---

291 Jennifer Steinhauer, "A Recess Destination With Bipartisan Support: Israel and the West Bank," *The New York Times*, August 15, 2011, http://www.nytimes.com/2011/08/16/us/politics/16congress.html.

President could be booed in a conference that promotes close ties between Israel and the United States?

In the 1990s, Prime Minister Yitzhak Rabin was famously concerned that he would not receive sufficient support from AIPAC in promoting the Oslo peace process. Notably, AIPAC has been known to promote counterproductive legislation in Congress. It did so in the 1990s promoting the U.S. embassy's move from Tel Aviv to Jerusalem prior to an Israeli-Palestinian peace agreement, a move that would have surely led to widespread global condemnation and compromise the United States' ability to serve as a Mideast peace broker. There are those who argue that in spite of these legislative agendas, the United States successfully mediated the 1997 Hebron Agreement and the 1998 Wye River Memorandum followed by the Sharm al-Sheikh Accord. However, this does not alter the reality that the United States' regional influence is declining.

AIPAC has also promoted legislation to limit U.S. funding options to nations like Egypt and Lebanon, as well as the Palestinians, in an effort geared to limit funds for Islamists, but which could make funding moderates much more difficult. In reaction to recent legislation along these lines, just last month Secretary of State Hillary Clinton sent a letter to the House Foreign Affairs Committee, stating that the recently proposed legislation "would be debilitating to [her] efforts to carry out a considered foreign policy and diplomacy, and to use foreign assistance strategically to that end."[292]

The recent standing ovations from Congress for Prime Minister Netanyahu were only the most recent indirect display of such influence. Each year, at AIPAC's policy conference, which had over 10,000 attendees this year, AIPAC directors list one-by-one the names of the members of Congress that are in attendance, with over 350 attending this year alone. In this sense, AIPAC has always straddled a difficult line: on the one hand dispelling claims of its influence, while on the other making sure policymakers believe it. This has created the perception that the U.S. Congress is in Israel's pocket, a perception

---

292 Mary Beth Sheridan, "Clinton, in Letter, Blasts Bill Restricting Foreign Aid," *The Washington Post*, July 27, 2011, http://www.washingtonpost. com/blogs/checkpoint-washington/post/clinton-in-letter-blasts-bill-restricting-foreign-aid/2011/07/27/gIQATIeccI_blog.html.

that undercuts U.S. interests and influence in the Middle East. It is no wonder that the PA has concluded that President Obama cannot persuade or pressure Netanyahu to change direction and decided to defy the United States by going to the UN to seek recognition of a Palestinian state against American advice.

Principal to AIPAC's arguments has been that Israel is under siege, surrounded by enemies seeking its complete destruction. It is an argument that has been effective on Capitol Hill, but it has not served to develop effective U.S. peace proposals that keep Israel from self-destructive policies. Today, despite AIPAC's best efforts in Washington, Israel is more isolated than ever in the international arena and is increasingly equated to apartheid South Africa, as settlement construction continues unabated in the West Bank.

Moreover, Israel's leadership lacks the courage or desire to make peace with a Palestinian leadership supported by the international community, including the United States, yet AIPAC has done little to suggest that Israel should change its posture. Although the PA does not fare much better, it is Israel and not the Palestinians that holds the key to breaking the impasse. This is exactly why Israel today is on the defensive and is being widely blamed for the lack of any progress in the peace process.

Furthermore, Israeli legislation, such as the recent boycott ban and effort to downplay its democratic nature in favor of its Jewish one, fundamentally threatens the notion of Israel's democracy, and yet AIPAC is silent. Meanwhile, resentment of Israel and AIPAC by Washington and an increasing number of European capitals is rising.

The future stability of the U.S.-Israel relationship demands that AIPAC change its approach. AIPAC has successfully built bipartisan support for a U.S.-Israel relationship on the foundation of shared democratic values and the search for peace based on a two-state solution. Both are being threatened today. Yet AIPAC can use its influence, however overblown it may actually be, to advance a new narrative: that in order for the U.S.-Israel relationship to remain as strong in our children's generation as it is today, the countries must work together to advance peace with the Palestinians and the entire Arab world. It is not enough to have this kind of narrative plastered on AIPAC's website; it must be actively, publicly, and relentlessly promoted. This can and must be AIPAC's primary objective today. The blind support of the Netanyahu government is achieving the precise opposite results.

The future of Israel as a Jewish and democratic state is at stake. As Israel's democracy and the prospect for peace unravel, so too will the U.S.-Israel relationship. It is only a matter of time. If AIPAC truly cares about the state of Israel and the U.S.-Israel relationship, it should be spending every waking hour making sure this does not happen.

OBAMA'S LAST CHANCE TO END
ISRAELI-PALESTINIAN CONFLICT

NOVEMBER 8, 2012

It is hard to imagine that the Israeli-Palestinian conflict can be resolved without the direct and active involvement of the United States. I believe that if the conflict, which is simmering beneath the surface, is not addressed in the near foreseeable future, it will violently explode with dangerous ripple effects that could spin the whole region out of control and render the prospect of a two-state solution untenable. Such developments will also inflict a lasting damage to the United States' security, economic interests, and credibility in the region while denying President Obama his last chance to end the Israeli-Palestinian conflict. For these reasons, Obama now has a momentous opportunity to revitalize the Israeli-Palestinian peace negotiations and inform the two sides of his resolve to end the conflict for the sake of all concerned.

Notwithstanding the multiple domestic and foreign problems Obama faces, I do not subscribe to the argument that he will not be in a position to devote much time and energy to the Israeli-Palestinian conflict, which appears to be less urgent compared to the crisis in Syria, the ticking time bomb behind Iran's nuclear program, and the economic problems at home. Indeed, the United States as the global leader not only cannot afford to neglect such an explosive conflict, but it also certainly has the capacity and the resources to deal with multiple global issues simultaneously. In terms of priority and urgency, President Obama must place the Israeli-Palestinian conflict at the top of his agenda. The United States has serious stakes in the region and a responsibility toward its allies. The lack of an Israeli-Palestinian peace will continue to undermine the United States' interests, erode its influence, and jeopardize its role in shaping the outcome of the multiple upheavals sweeping the region in the wake of the Arab Spring.

As the Palestinians watch young men and women in several Arab states fighting and dying for their freedoms, their own relative passivity at the present will not last forever. If the Palestinians feel that the United States continues to be detached from the conflict, they may well rise up out of desperation and hopelessness to end the occupation and be prepared to die for their freedom. The United States' inaction on the peace front will also seriously endanger not only the Jewish national identity of Israel but its very existence, which the United States is committed to protect.

Throughout his first term and in his speech at the UN General Assembly this year, the President has insisted that the only solution to the Arab-Israeli conflict rests on creating two independent Jewish and Palestinian states living side-by-side in peace while growing and prospering together as neighbors.[293] Any other message coming from the White House will fundamentally be injurious to both the Israelis and the Palestinians. The notion from some American politicians who have said that the United States should not have a greater desire for peace than the parties to the conflict is shortsighted. To advance the prospect for peace between Israel and Palestine, regardless of who will be the next prime minister in Israel, the President must take a number of critical steps:

First, the President must correct a strategic error in failing to visit Israel when he travelled during his first term three times overseas, visiting four Arab and Muslim states: Turkey, Saudi Arabia, Egypt, and Indonesia. For most Israelis, skipping Israel three times was nothing short of a slap in the face. Thus, within a few months after the inauguration, the President should visit Israel and Palestine and directly address the Israeli people as well as the Palestinians, emphasizing that only peace will serve their greater interests. The President must look into the eyes of both publics and stress that the United States is committed to a two-state solution and will remain consistent and resilient until such a resolution is achieved. Such a visit to Israel would have a transformational effect on many Israelis, akin to the

---

293 Barack Obama, "Speech to the United Nations General Assembly" (New York, NY, September 25, 2012), http://www.nytimes.com/2012/09/26/world/obamas-speech-to-the-united-nations-general-assembly-text.html?pagewanted=all.

visit of the late Egyptian president Anwar Sadat to Israel in 1977 that made the Israeli-Egyptian peace possible.

Second, the President should develop a general framework for an Israeli-Palestinian peace based on prior agreements negotiated between the two sides, especially those achieved in 2000 (at Camp David between Yasser Arafat and Ehud Barak), and in 2007–2008 between Ehud Olmert and Mahmoud Abbas. In both sets of these comprehensive negotiations, the two sides were able to resolve the majority of the conflicting issues. In the 2007–2008 talks, then-Israeli Prime Minister Olmert stated both sides had come "very close, more than ever in the past, to complete a principle agreement that would have led to the end of the conflict."[294]

Third, to increase the framework's effectiveness, a new internationally recognized special envoy of the caliber of President Clinton should be appointed with a clear presidential mandate. The envoy should remain relentless in his efforts to advance the negotiating process while keeping a top-level American official in the region to press on with the negotiations during the occasional absence of the special envoy.

Fourth, to avoid deadlocks, the rules of engagement should be based on an incremental agreement on various conflicting issues, ideally starting with borders. The Palestinians should abandon their precondition to freeze the settlements before they enter the negotiating process. An agreement on borders will in and of itself resolve 70–80 percent of the final status of the settlements and define the parameters of the Palestinian state. Such an agreement will also facilitate the negotiations of other conflicting issues, including the status of Palestinian refugees, Jerusalem, and Israel's national security. Finally, the negotiations should not be open-ended; a timeline must be established, albeit with some flexibility, to prevent either party from playing for time.

Fifth, it is imperative that the United States reaches out to other leading Arab and Muslim states (such as Saudi Arabia, Qatar, and Turkey) to exert pressure on the PA to make necessary concessions. Egypt must also be approached to play a role in influencing Hamas to forsake violence as a tool to achieve Palestinian statehood. These

---

294 "'I Felt Weight of Jewish History on my Shoulders,'" *Y Net News*, January 28, 2011, http://www.ynetnews.com/articles/0,7340,L-4020432,00.html.

Arab states have serious stakes in finding a solution to the Israeli-Palestinian conflict. Indeed, any new Israeli-Palestinian conflagration will impact directly and indirectly not only on their own interests, but could also draw them into the conflict which they want to avoid at all costs given their own internal political combustion and uncertainty.

Sixth, once the Israelis and Palestinians engage in negotiations, the United States should press both to immediately begin the process of changing their public narratives about each other by mutually ending acrimonious statements and expressions of hatred and distrust. To that end, both governments should encourage universities, nonpartisan think tanks, and media outlets to deliberate publicly about the psychological dimensions of the conflicting issues and begin a process of changing mindsets about some of the inevitabilities of reaching an agreement.

Finally, in reaching out to the Arab and Muslim world, the President should help reignite the API, which still represents the most comprehensive solution to the Arab-Israeli conflict. The revival of the API remains critically important as even top Israeli officials, including the former head of Mossad, Meir Dagan, have stated that the plan is central to resolving the conflict.[295] The API will have a special importance in reaching a comprehensive peace and long-term stability. The creation of a "sovereign, independent Palestinian state," which the API calls for, will greatly contribute to stabilizing the region.

The Arab-Israeli conflict has been overshadowed in recent months by international concerns over Iran's nuclear program, the bloody civil war in Syria, and the unending insurgencies and terrorism that plague many nations. Meanwhile, the Israeli-Palestinian conflict is quietly simmering underneath the surface and is becoming ever more perilous. Israel continues to expand existing settlements and legalize others while the Palestinians remain hopelessly factionalized and aimless, unable to present a unified front to be taken seriously, thus leaving the festering conflict in the hands of radicals on both sides.

For President Obama, finding a solution to the Israeli-Palestinian conflict should remain one of his top priorities. The status quo is explosive and it can only lead to a new violent confrontation. The

295 Koutsoukis, "Former Mossad Head Advocates Saudi Peace Plan."

United States has both the interest and the responsibility to put an end to the self-consuming Israeli-Palestinian conflict in a region where the stakes for all concerned cannot be overestimated.

EARNING THE NOBEL PEACE PRIZE

JANUARY 31, 2013

Awarding the Nobel Peace Prize to President Obama early on in his first term was largely based on the premise that he would pursue peace and end existing violent conflicts to make the world a better and safer place for all people. The President's efforts to end the war in Iraq and wind down the war in Afghanistan are admirable, regardless of what may befall these countries in years to come. However, he fell short in his effort during his first term to forge peace between Israel and the Palestinians, which remains extraordinarily pivotal to regional stability. The raging conflicts throughout the Middle East—the horrific civil war in Syria, the unending violence in Iraq, the instability in Egypt, Jordan, Bahrain, and Libya, and the simmering conflict with Iran—may *appear* to have little to do with the Israeli-Palestinian conflict, yet they are interconnected. A resolution to this decades-long explosive conflict will have an immediate and direct impact on the stability of the entire region and *singularly earn* President Obama the Nobel Peace Prize he was awarded.

With the confirmation of John Kerry as Secretary of State, the Obama administration must develop a comprehensive strategy geared toward stabilizing the region and remain engaged to preserve its sphere of influence and ensure continuing stability while maintaining its strategic interests. There is not a single Arab country that does not seek American support to end the civil war in Syria and to protect its own turf; there will be no solution to Iran's nuclear weapons program and no solution to the Israeli-Palestinian conflict without direct and active American involvement. President Obama may well be reluctant, especially following the two bruising wars in Iraq and Afghanistan, to involve America in other conflicts which may require direct or indirect military intervention. The United States, however, will have little choice but to project its multi-faceted powers—economic, political, and military—to influence, if not shape, the outcome of these conflicts before they explode in America's face and spin the entire region out of control.

A solution to the Israeli-Palestinian conflict stands out as the singular most troubling conflict because the Palestinian problem continues to feed into the Arab frenzy, especially in the wake of the Arab Spring. Although the Israelis and Palestinians are not slugging each other day in and day out, that does not suggest that the relative quiet can last as the conflict continues to simmer beneath the surface. Given the regional turbulence and the continuing debilitating status of the Palestinians, I strongly believe that unless the United States initiates a new peace offensive, it will only be a matter of time until the Israeli-Palestinian conflict explodes with more far-reaching regional repercussions than can be envisioned. In Prague, on his first European visit in April 2009, President Obama emphatically stated "When we fail to pursue peace, then it stays forever beyond our grasp."[296] No individual, let alone the President, can ignore a conflict that has spanned over three generations in such a pivotal region when the stakes are so high for the United States and its allies.

It is interesting to note that throughout the Israeli election campaign, all political parties from the extreme left to the far right focused primarily on domestic socioeconomic issues, while the conflict with the Palestinians received scant attention. In his confirmation hearing, John Kerry stated "There were elections yesterday [in Israel] and we still don't know which government it's going to be...I pray that maybe this will be a moment that will allow us to renew the effort to the one they were on in the last few years. I would like to try and do that."[297] Mr. Kerry's efforts to "bring the parties to the negotiating table and go down a different path" should not be mere wishful thinking. The United States must realistically assess where Netanyahu, who will most likely form the next Israeli coalition gov-

---

296 Barack Obama, "Speech on Nuclear Weapons" (Prague, Czech Republic, May 6, 2009), http://www.huffingtonpost.com/2009/04/05/obama-prague-speech-on-nu_n_183219.html.

297 Yoel Goldman, "Kerry Heading Here to Try to Restart Peace Talks," *The Times of Israel*, January 25, 2013, http://www.timesofisrael.com/kerry-will-try-to-restart-peace-talks-says-us-envoy/.

ernment, really stands on the prospect of the two-state solution and what kind of measures the United States is prepared to take if it wishes to lead Israel and the Palestinians toward a peace settlement.

The result of the Israeli elections will more than likely force Netanyahu to invite Yair Lapid, the leader of left-of-center party Yesh Atid (who made bread-and-butter issues and social justice his central political themes), to join his government. This should not mislead anyone to think, however, that Netanyahu will automatically moderate his views about the Palestinians and actually act to advance the two-state solution as the only practical option to end the conflict. He will publicly support such a solution to pacify the United States, but will certainly be guided by his convictions and play for time, as he does not believe that Israel is an occupying power and believes that the West Bank is an integral part of the Jewish people's ancestral land.[298]

The Palestinian victory in becoming a non-member observer state at the UNGA has yet to yield any improvements in their condition on the ground; on the contrary, the PA is now facing dire financial problems.[299] The Obama administration's opposition to the Palestinian bid for UNGA membership has in fact encouraged Netanyahu to accelerate the expansion of settlements while withholding tax revenue from the Palestinians, making their acute financial crisis even worse, albeit he recently transferred $100 million to the PA.[300] Adding to their financial difficulties, Palestinian factionalism and infighting (i.e., the rivalry between Fatah and Hamas) further complicates the prospect of genuine peace negotiations, especially since Hamas continues to openly seek Israel's destruction. Here, the

---

298 Benjamin Netanyahu, "Address to U.S. Congress" (Washington, DC, May 24, 2011), www.theglobeandmail.com/news/world/transcript-of-prime-minister-netanyahus-address-to-us-congress/article635191/?page=all.

299 Yolande Knell, "Stifled West Bank Economy Drains Palestinians' Hopes," *BBC News*, October 16, 2012, http://www.bbc.co.uk/news/world-middle-east-19911902.

300 Joel Greenberg, "Israel to Transfer Withheld Tax Revenue to Palestinians," *The Washington Post*, January 30, 2013, http://www.washingtonpost.com/world/middle_east/israel-to-transfer-held-tax-revenues-to-palestinians/2013/01/30/b0bf2c36-6aca-11e2-ada3-d86a4806d5ee_story.html.

Obama administration must rethink its position in relation to the Palestinians and how it must treat Hamas, which ultimately cannot be excluded from the peace process if the United States wishes to pursue sustainable peace.

While it seems logical that the Israelis and the Palestinians should sort out their own problems, history has shown that they have simply been unwilling or unable to do just that. Indeed, the conflict transcends territory, security, refugees, settlements, and the future of Jerusalem; it is highly emotional and shrouded with intense hatred and distrust, further hampered by psychological hang-ups emanating from deep historical experiences and religious beliefs.

In his speech at the United Nations in September 2011, President Obama said: "Ultimately, it is the Israelis and the Palestinians who must live side by side. Ultimately, it is the Israelis and the Palestinians—not us—who must reach agreement on the issues that divide them: on borders and on security, on refugees and Jerusalem."[301] If the President feels today the way he felt then, he should not expect a breakthrough in the peace process any time soon. The United States' role has been and remains indispensable, as was reflected in John Kerry's speech in March 2009 at the Brookings Institution when he said: "While I believe there must be an enhanced role for the regional players, nothing can substitute for our [the United States'] crucial role as an active and creative agent for peace[emphasis added]."[302]

Given the current regional upheavals and the Iranian threat of regional ambition, if the Israeli-Palestinian conflict remains unresolved over the next couple of years it could ignite a massive violent conflagration that will undermine the prospect of achieving a settlement and severely damage the United States' strategic interests and credibility in the region. Notwithstanding Obama's failure to achieve a

---

301   Barack Obama, "Remarks by President Obama in Address to the United Nations General Assembly" (New York, NY, September 21, 2011), http://www.whitehouse.gov/the-press-office/2011/09/21/remarks-president-obama-address-united-nations-general-assembly.

302   John Kerry, "Middle East Peace" (Brookings Saban Center, Washington, DC, March 4, 2009), http://www.brookings.edu/~/media/Events/2009/3/04%20leadership/0304_leadership.PDF.

breakthrough in the peace process during his first term, he now has one last chance to push for an agreement. John Kerry, who is only too familiar with the travails of the conflict, may succeed with the full support of the President where others have failed.

In the wake of the Arab Spring, however, as Palestinians watch young men and women in several Arab states fighting and dying for their freedoms, their own relative passivity will not last forever. In his speech after he was awarded the Nobel Prize in December 2009, Obama said, "For peace is not merely the absence of visible conflict. Only a just peace based on the inherent rights and dignity of every individual can truly be lasting."[303] The President must now live up to that premise. He cannot kick the ball down the field and leave the region to the whims of other powers—Russia and Iran—that will go to any length to undermine American interests while tearing the Israelis and Palestinians further apart without any prospect of reconciliation.

For these reasons, what President Obama and his Secretary of State do within the next few months will have a clear and immediate effect on how the Israelis and Palestinians conduct themselves in anticipation of a new American initiative to resolve the conflict. The notion that the United States should not have a greater desire for peace than the parties to the conflict is flawed. The lack of peace will continue to erode the United States' interest and influence and undermine its role in shaping the outcome of the multiple upheavals sweeping the region in the wake of the Arab Spring. The United States may well have to save the Israelis and the Palestinians from themselves and use both inducement and coercive measures if necessary to that end.

To advance the real prospect for peace between Israel and Palestine, President Obama must take a number of critical steps:

First, within the next few months, the President should visit the region and directly address the Israeli as well as the Palestinian people. For most Israelis, Obama's failure to visit their country when he traveled three times to the region during his first term

---

303 Barack Obama, "Nobel Lecture" (Oslo, Norway, December 10, 2009), http://www.nobelprize.org/nobel_prizes/peace/laureates/2009/obama-lecture_en.html.

(visiting four Muslim states) was nothing short of a slap in the face. Skipping Israel and the Palestinians seemed odd, especially in light of the fact that President Obama made a solution to the conflict a top priority in his first term by appointing former Senate Majority Leader George Mitchell as a Special Envoy to the region only a few days after his first inauguration.[304]

A visit to Israel in particular could be a game changer, where the President can explain why only peace will ultimately ensure Israel's national security, democracy, and the Jewish national identity of the state. The President should reiterate his commitment to a two-state solution and emphasize that the United States will use all means available at its disposal to advance the peace process while maintaining an unshakable commitment to Israel's national security. President Obama's visit to Israel will further reinforce the belief that nearly all Israelis share—that the United States is the only ally they can trust without any reservation. The President may also expand the existing strategic agreement with Israel by offering to enter into a mutual defense treaty with Israel once a peace agreement with the Palestinians is achieved. Such a bilateral defense treaty could then develop and become a part of a regional security umbrella between Israel and every Arab state that is at peace with Israel.[305]

Second, the President must carry with him a general framework for peace based on a prior understanding negotiated between the two sides, especially those achieved in 2000 (at Camp David between Yasser Arafat and Ehud Barak) and 2007–2008 (between Ehud Olmert and Mahmoud Abbas). In both sets of comprehensive negotiations, the two sides had been able to resolve the vast majority of the conflicting issues; in the latter, then-Israeli Prime Minister Olmert stated both sides had come "very close, more than ever in the past, to complete a principle agreement that would have led to the end of the conflict."[306] These prior

304 Mark Landler, "Seasoned Negotiator to Serve as a Mideast Envoy," *The New York Times*, January 21, 2009, http://www.nytimes.com/2009/01/22/us/politics/22diplo.html?_r=2&hp&.

305 Landler and Sanger, "Clinton Speaks of Shielding Mideast From Iran."

306 "'I Felt Weight of Jewish History on my Shoulders.'"

agreements should be placed on the table anew and modified to factor in the changing conditions on the ground, creating a clear basis for negotiating a comprehensive agreement with the United States' direct and active participation. The United States must use all means available at its disposal, including political, economic, and coercive measures, to exact the necessary concessions from both sides to reach an agreement.

Third, to increase the framework's effectiveness, a new independent envoy should be appointed with a clear presidential mandate to work relentlessly to advance the negotiation process while maintaining a top-level American official in the region to keep up the momentum and the pressure in case of the occasional absence of the envoy. By way of example, former President Clinton would be a remarkable choice, or for that matter former Secretary of State Hillary Clinton, or someone in their caliber—namely, a widely respected figure who would be welcomed by both sides. The envoy should be present in every single session to find out how sincere the Israelis and the Palestinians are in the search for peace and to what extent they are prepared to make the painful concessions needed to reach an agreement. The Israeli and Palestinian contention that there is no partner with whom to negotiate or that the other cannot be trusted to negotiate in good faith would be dispelled or confirmed in these face-to-face negotiations (only, however, with an American presence).

Fourth, it is imperative that the United States reaches out to leading Arab and Muslim states, such as Saudi Arabia and Qatar, that can exert pressure on the PA in the West Bank to make necessary concessions. Similarly, Egypt and Turkey, who both enjoy great leverage on Hamas, should persuade its leadership to change its acrimonious public pronouncements against Israel, as well as its antagonism and hardline policy against Israel. In particular, Hamas must renounce violence as a tool by which to reach its political objective of establishing an independent Palestinian state and remove from its charter the clause that calls for Israel's destruction, in return for the promise of American recognition. Hamas must be treated as a political party who does not need to recognize Israel or accept prior agreements (the principles stipulated by the Quartet), but would be required to do so as a precondition to being a legitimate partner in the negotiations.[307]

The Arab states, especially Egypt (under the Muslim Brotherhood or any other regime), will always have serious stakes in finding a solution to the Israeli-Palestinian conflict and could play a leading role in persuading Hamas to change course. Indeed, the government of Egypt has mediated several times between Hamas and Israel in the past under the Mubarak regime. More recently, the Egyptian government arranged for a ceasefire between Israel and Hamas with American involvement. In fact, Israeli officials had direct contact with Hamas in Cairo in order to negotiate the terms of the latest ceasefire, following the violent flare-up between the two sides in mid-November 2012.[308]

Fifth, in reaching out to the Arab and Muslim world, the President should help reignite the API, which still represents the most comprehensive solution to the Arab-Israeli conflict. The revival of the API remains critically important, as even top Israeli officials including President Shimon Peres and former head of the Mossad Meir Dagan have strongly endorsed the API as central to resolving the Arab-Israeli conflict.[309] In the wake of the Arab Spring, restarting the API will have special thrust; as the whole region undergoes revolutionary change, the API represents a key factor in maintaining and enhancing the momentum toward positive and constructive regional change. In his Brookings speech, Kerry rightly invoked the API when he said, "This bold step never received the focus it deserved when Saudi King Abdullah proposed

---

307 "Statement by Middle East Quartet," *United Nations*, January 30, 2006, http://unispal.un.org/UNISPAL.NSF/0/354568CCE5E38E5585257106007A0834.

308 Nidal Almughrabi, Michael Shields, and Alison Williams, "Israel, Hamas Teams in Cairo for More Truce Talks," *Reuters*, November 26, 2012, http://www.reuters.com/article/2012/11/26/us-palestinians-israel-egypt-talks-idUSBRE8AP0VG20121126.

309 Yitzhak Benhorin, "Peres Lauds Arab Peace Plan," *Y Net News*, November 12, 2008, http://www.ynetnews.com/articles/0,7340,L-3622251,00.html; and Koutsoukis, "Former Mossad Head Advocates Saudi Peace Plan."

it in 2002. We cannot underestimate the importance that, through this initiative, every Arab country and all Muslim states have now agreed to the basic formulation of land for peace, recognition of the state of Israel, and normalization of relations."[310] The creation of a "sovereign independent Palestinian state," which the API calls for, will greatly contribute to stabilizing the region. Indeed, most if not all Arab and Muslim countries will begin normalizing relations with Israel and foster a lasting peace that will ultimately improve the lives of millions of ordinary citizens throughout the region.

Sixth, the perception that Congress is more supportive of Israel than the President must be dispelled, and no one can do that better than the President himself. During his first term, Obama provided Israel with greater political, economic, and military support than any of his predecessors. Before he embarks on a new peace initiative, he should use the opportunity of his upcoming State of the Union Address, or seize any other opportunity, to articulate to the American people and to Congress how critical it is for Israel to forge peace and why it is in the best interests of the United States to take the lead, however uncertain the prospect may be, to help Israel reach peace with security. The President needs to explain that by not taking action now, Israel's future as a democratic and Jewish state could be jeopardized. Being a trusted friend of Israel, Secretary of State John Kerry can further articulate and emphasize to Congressional leaders the need to act soon, because Israel's peace with the Palestinians is an integral part of the United States' commitment to Israel's national security and key to regional stability.

Seventh, one of the most difficult impediments between the Israelis and Palestinians is mutual distrust and the psychological underpinning of the conflict. It is critical for the United States to exert every conceivable pressure on both the Israelis and Palestinians to begin changing their public narratives about each other, ending mutually acrimonious statements, expressions of hatred, and distrust. In addition, the United States should insist that both governments encourage universities, nonpartisan think tanks, and the media to begin a process of changing mindsets about some of the inevitabilities which will be required to reach an agreement

---

310 Kerry, "Middle East Peace."

Even if Israeli and Palestinian leaders reach an agreement behind closed doors, they cannot simply come out with pronouncements of concessions that were made without first preparing the public. For example, an agreement on Palestinian refugees might entail the return of only a small fraction of refugees to Israel proper, so as to preserve the Jewish identity of the state, but the vast majority of Palestinians still believe in the right of return. In addition, there can be no two-state solution without East Jerusalem becoming the capital of both Israel and Palestine, and though the city will remain united, this will be difficult for the Israeli public to accept.[311] For this reason, the groundwork must be laid concurrently with the resumption of the negotiations, if not before, in order to shift the public narrative and psychologically prepare the populations on both sides to accept the necessary concessions. The willingness to encourage public discourse on these sensitive issues and others will further indicate the extent to which either or both sides are committed to reach a mutually gainful agreement. In addition, to avoid deadlocks, the agreement should be implemented in a number of phases, making sure that any concession made by one side is reciprocated by the other based on prior agreements to gradually engender trust.

The Arab-Israeli conflict has been overshadowed in recent months due to international concerns over Iran's nuclear program, the bloody civil war which continues to rage in Syria, and the unending insurgency and terrorism that continue to plague many nations in the region. Meanwhile, the conflict is quietly simmering underneath the surface and is becoming worse as Israel continues to establish new and expand existing settlements while the Palestinians remain hopelessly factionalized, unable to present a unified front and demonstrate the keenness necessary to make peace.

Finding a solution to the Israeli-Palestinian conflict, which has gone on for more than 60 years, should now be a top priority for Obama as it is central to Arab-Israeli peace and will dramatically enhance regional stability. The status quo is not sustainable, and it can only lead to a new violent and perilous conflagration that will leave no victors—only horrifying destruction, irreparably deepening

---

311 Boaz Fyler, "Netanyahu: Jerusalem Will Remain United," *Y Net News*, May 20, 2012, http://www.ynetnews.com/articles/0,7340,L-4231748,00.html.

the already existing gulf between the two sides. The United States has both the interest and the responsibility to put an end to this self-consuming conflict in a region where the stakes for all concerned cannot be overestimated.

President Obama may well deserve the Nobel Peace Prize, but by successfully forging peace between Israel and the Palestinians he will have earned it, and that will be his greatest legacy.

WINNING PEACE THROUGH
HEARTS AND MINDS

APRIL 3, 2013

Much has been said about President Obama's journey to the Middle East but little about the substance and the implications the visit might have. I believe that if the President was set to win the hearts and minds of the Israelis, he certainly made considerable strides toward that end.

Unfortunately, most Palestinian commentators misread the implications of his visit to Israel and to the Palestinians in particular. They failed to understand that even the President of the United States cannot exact the necessary concessions from the Israelis to advance the peace process unless he earns their trust and makes them feel confident that the United States will always remain committed to their national security.

The many Palestinians who criticized President Obama for showering the Israelis with lavish praise and for his unfettered commitment to Israel's security seem to miss the central point that he wanted to convey and expected to achieve.

To suggest the President "spent three days in Israel and almost as many hours in [the West Bank]" to presumably explain where the President stands and what are his priorities, as was observed by the Economist's N.P. under the title "A fleeting visit," is simplistic and completely out of touch. That Obama's visit "was an insult to the Palestinian people on every count," was another cynical assessment by Ghada Karmi of Al Jazeera.

The trip does not have a diminishing return, as Osama Al Sharif observed in Arab News, or that "it did significant damage to America's ability to play the role of honest broker between Israelis and Palestinians if negotiations ever begin," as was proclaimed by MJ Rosenberg (not a Palestinian) in his Huffington Post column.

The truth of the matter is that even without the observation from Ismail Mahmoud Rabah that Obama's visit had "crucial implications for the approaching end of the Israeli Occupation," criticism of the trip was almost entirely misperceived, and here is why.

Regardless of the fact that the Obama administration has provided Israel with more financial and military aid and political support while extending unprecedented cooperation on countless levels than any of its predecessors, Israelis generally distrust President Obama.

They recalled his speech in Cairo in June 2009, which they interpreted as being one-sided in favor of the Palestinians, and they recollected with dismay that he traveled three times overseas during his first term, visiting several Arab and Muslim states while skipping Israel.

In addition, they resented the fact that he placed undue pressure on Israel to freeze settlement construction without demanding specific counter-measures from the Palestinians.

His critics are dead wrong in their assessments of the President's intentions and the approach he took toward the Israelis during his visit to Israel, Palestine, and Jordan.

His expressed purpose was to win the hearts and minds of the Israelis because he knows that any concessions he can secure on behalf of the Palestinians depend on how much the Israelis trust him and how confident they feel that the United States will watch Israel's back in a moment of real need.

The President also knows only too well that he must engage the Israeli public in the search for peace and make them understand the hazards of continuing occupation—that time is dangerously running out and they can no longer remain complacent.

For this reason, he went over the head of Prime Minister Netanyahu and appealed directly to the Israeli public, especially the young, to take the lead, emphasizing that "governments respond to popular will" and they must now make their voice heard.[312]

---

312 Barack Obama, "Remarks of President Barack Obama To the People of Israel," The White House, March 21, 2013, http://www.whitehouse.gov/the-press-office/2013/03/21/remarks-president-barack-obama-people-israel.

He implored the young Israelis to put themselves in the Palestinians' shoes, who have been stripped of their dignity, and "look at the world through their eyes." "It is not right to prevent Palestinian from farming their lands," he emphatically stated, "or to displace Palestinian families from their home. Neither occupation nor expulsion is the answer."

Those who criticized the President for his presumed lack of evenhandedness in addressing the Israelis and Palestinians do not seem to grasp that the President did not need to convince the Palestinians that continued occupation is unacceptable. He did not need to remind the Palestinians of their plight and suffering. These words were directed to the Israelis who can do something about it.

He passionately stated that "Israel must also live up to its obligations to ensure that Palestinians can live, and work, and develop their society. And just as it devastates Palestinian families, the continuing humanitarian crisis in Gaza does not serve Israel's security; neither does the continuing lack of opportunity in the West Bank."

This is what the Israelis need to hear, provided it is said in the context of the United States' uncontestable commitment to guard Israel from outside threats, especially from Iran, and their trust in him. The Palestinians must remember that the President could hardly wring one meaningful concession from the Israelis during his first term as long as he was perceived as an antagonist and unsympathetic to their concerns.

Just as Obama sought to change the Israelis' perception of himself and successfully touched the hearts and minds of the Israeli multitude, his administration must now focus on its renewed peace efforts to which he committed.

Other than insisting on the resumption of negotiations between Israeli and Palestinian officials, he must exert equal pressure, though quietly, on both sides to begin changing their public narrative on the conflicting issues that separate them.

Two critical conflicting issues, the "right of return" of the Palestinian refugees and the continuing expansion and building new settlements, should top the agenda to provide mutually acceptable solutions which require a drastic change in the Israelis' and Palestinians' respective public perceptions.

PA President Mahmoud Abbas cannot possibly speak about a real prospect of a two-state solution while he continues to preach the gospel of the "right of return," which is utterly unacceptable to the Israelis as it will wipe out Israel's national Jewish identity overnight.

This issue cannot be resolved at the negotiating table without first preparing the Palestinian public to accept that the right of return can be exercised only through resettlement of the refugees in their own homeland—the West Bank and Gaza—or compensating those who elect to remain in their current country of residence.

Prime Minister Netanyahu too cannot be serious about a two-state solution as long as he continues to insist on the expansion of old and the building of new settlements in the name of national security, which "violates previous agreements and undermines efforts to achieve peace."[313]

If President Obama believes, as I do, that governments listen to the will of the people, then Israeli and Palestinian public perceptions must first change on these fundamental conflicting issues and about each other.

This is a moment in time that neither the Israelis nor the Palestinians can afford to squander because the passage of time will acutely undermine their ultimate national interests and make the conflict ever more intractable and increasingly perilous.

No one, however, should expect current officials on either side to voluntarily change their narrative in order to induce a change in their respective public perceptions. On the contrary, Israeli and Palestinian governments alike have used the prospect of a two-state solution for public consumption only while continuing to pursue policies that torpedo any possibility of such an outcome.

Here is where the United States' role becomes crucial. As much as Obama needs to press Israeli and Palestinian officials to resume formal peace talks, he must simultaneously exert tremendous pressure to change their public narrative and stop misleading their publics about the requisites for peace based on a two-state solution that he so ardently advocated.

---

313 Dana Milbank, "Barack Obama Makes Small Successes in Israel," *The Oregonian*, March 23, 2013, http://www.oregonlive.com/opinion/index. ssf/2013/03/barack_obama_makes_small_succe.html.

If President Obama did not privately counsel Netanyahu and Abbas during his visit to do just that, he should do so now. Without public support, peace negotiations will go nowhere and an Israeli-Palestinian peace will remain a pathetically self-consuming illusion.

"IF YOU WIIL IT, IT IS NO DREAM"

MAY 14, 2013

In talking to scores of people from the diplomatic corps, the academic community, and many from the media here in the United States, the Arab states, and Israel about the Israeli-Palestinian conflict, the majority seem to agree that unless the United States **puts its foot down**, the renewed efforts to achieve peace launched by Washington will certainly end up in failure.

I subscribe to this notion and vehemently disagree with many American officials who suggest that the United States should not want peace more than the parties themselves. They insist that the onus falls on Israeli and Palestinian shoulders to demonstrate their willingness to engage in serious peace negotiations, which the United States will then be happy to facilitate.

If that were the case, why then does the Israeli-Palestinian conflict continue to persist even though majorities on both sides want peace?[314] I maintain that if President Obama wills it, he can forge an agreement provided he invests the necessary resources and political capital, which were lacking in previous efforts.

There are many impediments to realizing peace between Israel and the Palestinians, including mutual distrust, misperceptions about each other, differing domestic pressure, radical ideologies, and contrasting religious precepts. I believe that notwithstanding these impediments, they can all over time be overcome.

Israeli and Palestinian leaders have fallen victim to their own uncompromising public narratives, making it extraordinarily difficult to change course without losing their political base. To facilitate the terms of an agreement, they need powerful and relentless pressure to provide them with political cover, which only the United States can exert.

---

314 Saad and Mendes, "Israelis, Palestinians Pro Peace Process, but Not Hopeful."

Current efforts by Secretary of State John Kerry to restart Israeli-Palestinian negotiations are imperative to the security of Israel and the United States' Arab allies, and for regional stability.[315] President Obama, however, needs to unambiguously warn both sides that the United States intends on pursuing peace unremittingly and will be prepared to use any tools at his disposal to that end.

Otherwise, neither Prime Minister Netanyahu, for ideological reasons, nor President Abbas, because of his political vulnerability, will heed the warning. These efforts would consequently end in failure, just like the President's previous foray into the Israeli-Palestinian quagmire during his first term.[316] His administration back then lacked a clear action-oriented strategy and the resolve to nudge both sides out of their long-entrenched positions.

In addition to an indispensable forceful approach, Obama must challenge other important players that can, in turn, further influence the Israelis and Palestinians to come to terms with one another.

First, Kerry's appeal to the Arab League must now translate into action.[317] The API, which was first introduced in 2002 by the Arab League, offered new horizons and laid out a plan central to any comprehensive Arab-Israeli peace. It must now be reinvigorated to offer a new hope to end the conflict.

The United States needs to insist that Saudi Arabia, which originally initiated the API, take the lead by reintroducing it and publicly suggest that while the API's wording need not be modified, it should not be treated on a take it or leave it basis and must, in any case, be negotiated.

---

315 "Kerry in New Push for Israel-Palestine Talks," *Al Jazeera*, May 9, 2013, http://www.aljazeera.com/news/middleeast/2013/05/201358233629703392.html.

316 Matti Friedman, "Reversing Policy of First Term, Obama Says no Preconditions to Talks," *The Times of Israel*, March 21, 2013, http://www.timesofisrael.com/reversing-policy-of-first-term-obama-says-no-preconditions-to-talks/.

317 "Possible Breakthrough for Middle East Peace at US-Arab League Talks," *DW*, April 30, 2013, http://www.dw.de/possible-breakthrough-for-middle-east-peace-at-us-arab-league-talks/a-16780307.

Given the regional turmoil and the Iranian threat, the Gulf States (led by Saudi Arabia), Turkey, and Egypt in particular can no longer engage in double talk, presumably supporting peace while allowing Hamas and Hezbollah to torpedo such prospects.

The United States should demand that these countries do their share by exerting whatever pressure necessary to bring the two renegade organizations to heel.

The Palestinians are not innocent victims; they have contributed to their own plight and some of them (i.e., Hamas) continue to this day to seek Israel's destruction. As long as these two extremist factions continue to threaten Israel and the leading Arab states accept that with indifference, current and future Israeli governments have legitimate reasons to suspect Arab intentions.

The United States can insist that these Arab states can no longer preach the gospel of peace while they look the other way by allowing Hezbollah, which serves its masters in Tehran, and Hamas' militancy to continue to split the Palestinians, thereby undercutting the prospect of peace.

Second, Obama needs to appeal to congressional leaders, especially those with strong Evangelical backing and who overwhelmingly support Israel (right or wrong), to understand that Israel's national security interests are best served by peace.

They must realize that the status quo is becoming increasingly perilous and they are contributing to it by their inadvertent support of the occupation. This reflects appallingly on Israel's moral standing in the eyes of the international community and portrays Congress as complicit in the occupation.

Whereas political, financial, and military support for Israel is necessary, every congressional leader must ask: where does Israel's current policy lead? The longer the conflict persists, the greater the risks are for Israel, which these leaders paradoxically seek to safeguard.

Both Democrats and Republicans, who admire Israel's democracy and its incredible achievements under constant conditions of hostility, must now rise to save Israel from itself. They must urge the Netanyahu government to accept the API in principle.

Their unmitigated support over the years provides them with the moral responsibility and the obligation to join Obama in his quest for peace.

Third, the American Jewish community's support of Israel is natural by virtue of the Jewish people's affinity to each other and the belief in a shared destiny. Israel was created to provide all Jews, regardless of place of residence, a sense of security born from catastrophic historical experiences and cultural heritage, perhaps unlike any other nation.

Whereas their support of Israel is a given, it should not translate to a blind endorsement of Israel's policies, which could undermine the very reason why Israel was established in the first place.

Although some American Jewish leaders privately counsel Israeli leadership to moderate its policies toward the Palestinians, historically the majority of American Jewry supported the Israeli government's policies, however extreme they happened to be.

In recent years, however, the emergence of J Street, which promotes peace and calls for the end to the occupation, in contrast to AIPAC, which generally supports the policies of any Israeli government, suggests a discernible shift of sentiment among American Jews.[318]

In addition, there is growing disenchantment by American Jewish youth who object to the occupation which they view as immoral and inconsistent with the values on which they were reared.

These developments provide a new opening for the administration to strongly advocate to American Jewish leaders that notwithstanding the United States' unshakable commitment to Israel's security, Israel cannot live by the sword and it must break out of its growing isolation.

Everyone can point out the difficulties of reaching an agreement because they involve many thorny issues, the risks entailed, and the fear of failure. That said, President Obama must nevertheless resort to any means necessary, including coercion, to resolve the conflict

---

318 Bradley Burston, "Will 2013 be the Year American Jews Secede From Israel?," *Haaretz*, January 1, 2013, http://www.haaretz.com/blogs/a-special-place-in-hell/will-2013-be-the-year-american-jews-secede-from-israel.premium-1.491286.

because the consequences of no action far outweigh any political risk or the potential of failure.

The administration's new push for peace may well be Obama's last chance before the Middle East potentially plunges into a regional war precipitated by the disintegration of Syria and/or Iran's persistent pursuit of nuclear weapons. The United States has placed itself as the ultimate arbiter to end the debilitating Israeli-Palestinian conflict; it must now deliver.

In his 1902 book "The Old New Land," the founder of Zionism, Theodor Herzl, proclaimed in reference to the establishment of a Jewish state the everlasting phrase, "If you will it, it is no dream."

It was inconceivable at the time that a Jewish state would be created, but it happened 45 years later. The Israeli Palestinian conflict has endured for 65 years; it can end, but only if the United States wills it.

KERRY'S LAST DITCH EFFORT

JUNE 11, 2013

In his upcoming visit to Israel and Palestine, Secretary of State John Kerry will attempt a last-ditch effort to persuade Israel's Prime Minster Netanyahu and the PA's President Abbas to resume peace negotiations. If there is, however, the slightest chance of getting the two sides to start talking it would require substantial American pressure and commitment to see the peace process through.

Given the regional turmoil, the question is, will the United States be prepared to invest that much time and political capital on an uncertain venture when it must now focus on the far more urgent conflict in Syria, which has the potential to spark regional conflagration?

Moreover, while a small chance may exist to resume the negotiations, neither Netanyahu nor Abbas have a political strategy in place, nor are they taking action on the ground to suggest that they are ready and willing to reach an agreement.

In fact, they have assumed certain positions and pursued policies that have impeded rather than advanced the peace process. Sadly, both Netanyahu and Abbas lack the vision and the courage to change course, depriving their own people of the opportunity to realize their aspirations for peace.

This theme on leadership was pointedly cited by President Nixon in his 1982 book Leaders: "Prescience—knowing which way to lead—lies at the heart of great leadership. The very word leader implies the ability to act as the guide, to see beyond the present in charting a course into the future."[319]

---

319 Richard Nixon, *Leaders* (New York: Warner Books, 1982), 46.

Netanyahu is an ideologue who has no known political strategy for resolving the Israeli-Palestinian conflict and no clue where his policies of expansionism and militarization will lead to in 10 or 15 years.

He is fixated on maintaining a strategy of deterrence, backed by a superior military prowess that can simultaneously tackle military confrontations on multiple fronts while making Israel a garrison state surrounded by fences and walls.

Publicly, he insists that Israel is not an occupying power and that Israel has an inalienable right to the whole "land of Israel" (Israel plus all Palestinian territories).[320] Furthermore, he does not accept the 1967 borders as the basis for negotiating a two-state solution.[321]

He argues that the Palestinians cannot be trusted and that Israel's national security depends on defensible borders, which of "necessity" requires the annexation of a substantial part of the West Bank.

On the practical level, he has and continues to be an ardent advocate of building new and expanding existing settlements; he provides massive financial assistance to settlers and devotes substantial resources for their security.[322]

Meanwhile, he continues to restrict Palestinian movement, limits Israeli-Palestinian interaction and cooperation, and inhibits joint economic projects and mutual visitations between Israelis and Palestinians which could serve to build the very trust which he claims is lacking.

Conversely, President Abbas has for some time been a strong advocate of a two-state solution and sought to achieve it through peaceful means. Other than maintaining the calm, though, he did little to prepare the public for peaceful coexistence.

---

320 Benjamin Netanyahu, "Address to U.S. Congress" (Washington, DC, May 24, 2011), http://www.cfr.org/israel/netanyahus-address-us-congress-may-2011/p25073.

321 Harriet Sherwood, "Binyamin Netanyahu Rejects Calls for Palestinian State Within 1967 Lines," *The Guardian*, January 20, 2013, http://www.theguardian.com/world/2013/jan/20/binyamin-netanyahu-palestinian-state-1967.

322 Nir Hasson and Jonathan Lis, "Netanyahu: Settlement Construction Will Continue, But Israel Must be Smart About It," *Haaretz*, June 11, 2013, http://www.haaretz.com/news/diplomacy-defense/1.528978?localLinksEnabled=false.

He insisted on a total freeze on building new and expanding existing settlements.[323] When Netanyahu finally agreed, under American pressure, to freeze settlement activity for a year in 2009, he waited 10 months before agreeing to enter negotiations (which lasted only two months, to no avail).

While Abbas painted himself into a corner by insisting on a complete freeze on settlements as a precondition to resuming negotiations, he sought and succeeded to elevate the Palestinian status at the UNGA to a nonmember observer state.[324]

Although this might have been the right move to make, it made little headway as it has further hardened the Israelis' position on the settlements problem and been found unhelpful by the Americans who insisted that only direct negotiations could advance the peace process.

Politically, Abbas is deeply troubled by Hamas' rancorous rivalry with Fatah and its insistence on continuing militant resistance to Israel, which inhibited his ability to maneuver politically and increased his political vulnerability. To make up for his precarious political standing, he negotiated a unity agreement with Hamas, which remains unfulfilled and has further soured relations with Israel.[325]

He remains saddled by pervasive corruption, constrained by continuing financial hardships and infighting within his immediate circle. He failed to support his former Prime Minister Salam Fayyad, an internationally respected economist, to press for more reforms and stem corruption. Instead, Abbas made his displeasure with Fayyad public knowledge, which led the latter to resign in April 2013.

---

323 "Abbas Asks Spain to Push for Settlement Freeze," *The Jerusalem Post*, April 20, 2013, http://www.jpost.com/Diplomacy-and-Politics/Abbas-asks-Spanish-FM-to-push-for-Israeli-settlement-freeze-310470.

324 "General Assembly Grants Palestine Non-Member Observer State Status at UN," *UN News Centre*, November 29, 2012, http://www.un.org/apps/news/story.asp?NewsID=43640#.Uh5Erj9cXe8.

325 "Fatah, Hamas Agree to Form Palestinian Unity Government," *Al Arabiya*, May 15, 2013, http://english.alarabiya.net/en/News/middle-east/2013/05/15/Fatah-Hamas-agree-to-form-Palestinian-unity-government.html.

On the practical level, he continues to promote untenable goals such as the right of return of the Palestinian refugees, giving the Palestinians false hope. Although this was more rhetorical than real, he gave the Israelis another reason to doubt his sincerity.

He turned a blind eye to the systematic maligning of Israel in schools, denying Israel's very existence in textbooks, while indirectly aligning himself with the Palestinian media that portrays Israel as the source of all evil.

Even a cursory review of the strategic, political, and practical approaches that Netanyahu and Abbas pursue explains why they insist on a negotiating strategy that fits their political positions and the respective negative public perception they have shaped.

For all intents and purposes, Netanyahu does not accept the two-state solution and is merely paying lip service to Kerry's efforts in order to not further alienate the Obama administration.

He borrowed a page or two from the Iranians by playing for time, which is evident in his insistence on restarting the negotiations unconditionally (which in and of itself is a precondition).

Should the negotiations resume under his terms, Netanyahu will certainly seek to first negotiate peripheral issues such as water or discuss trust-building measures, and avoid any substantive matters, especially borders, to define the parameters of two states.

Although Abbas' demand to freeze settlements activity in advance of the resumption of negotiations is justifiable, in hindsight, Abbas made a major tactical mistake by not dropping his precondition of the settlements freeze and calling Netanyahu's bluff.

Unfortunately, instead of siding with Netanyahu to commence the negotiations unconditionally, Kerry should have insisted on negotiating mutually accepted rules of engagement that could at least offer a precedent for future negotiations and even a chance for making modest progress.

Ideally, Kerry should be able to persuade both Netanyahu and Abbas to abandon any preconditions, clearly identify the conflicting issues and the order in which they should be negotiated, and a time-frame to prevent protracted negotiations.

Starting with borders would clearly be the most practical way, as negotiating borders first would define the parameters of the Palestinian state, which is the single most important issue to be agreed upon.

Moreover, an agreement on borders would resolve at least 75% of the settlements problem; establishing the extent of the land swap would also demonstrate the seriousness of both sides to reach an agreement.

An American presence at the negotiating table at all times would demonstrably show which side, if any, is indeed committed to reaching an agreement. The failure to agree on such principled rules of engagement should leave no doubt as to where Netanyahu and Abbas stand.

The irony here is that repeated polls taken during the past decade consistently show that a majority of Israelis and Palestinians want peace based on a two-state solution.[326] Yet both Netanyahu and Abbas are delaying the inevitable, at a terrible cost in blood and treasure to their people.

Although a resolution to the Israeli-Palestinian conflict remains central to regional stability, the horrifying turmoil in Syria and its potential to engulf other states in the region will likely trump the relative calm on the Israeli-Palestinian front.

Thus, should Netanyahu and Abbas fail to seize Obama's likely last effort to achieve an Israeli-Palestinian peace, Secretary Kerry may well abandon his mediating efforts.

The Israeli and Palestinian peoples will have to await the rise of wise and visionary leaders, unshackled by the illusions of their predecessors—leaders who can muster the courage to chart a new path to a peaceful coexistence.

---

326 Saad and Mendes, "Israelis, Palestinians Pro Peace Process, but Not Hopeful."

ENOUGH TALKING ABOUT TALKS

JULY 25, 2013

Secretary of State John Kerry is to be highly commended for his tireless efforts to persuade the Israelis and Palestinians to resume peace negotiations soon in Washington. Although the prospect of success of these negotiations is very slim, if there is any opportunity for a breakthrough, it will ultimately depend not only on major concessions both sides must make, but also on other critical elements, without which the prospect of success stands at zero.

I am not entirely sanguine that either the PA's President Mahmoud Abbas or Israel's Prime Minister Netanyahu are ready, willing, or able to make peace.

Netanyahu is an ideologue who does not really believe in a two-state solution, or at any rate, not one that would be established in most of the West Bank. From his perspective, Israel's historic and biblical claim to the entire "land of Israel," which includes the West Bank, is a given, if not divinely ordained, leaving little room for significant territorial compromises.

Conversely, Abbas is politically weak; his public support is limited and he is challenged by Hamas, which inhibits him from taking any step that would add to the prevailing perception of his weakness. At heart he wishes for peace, but his circumstances prevent him from taking the necessary bold steps required to reach an agreement.

Short of a change in Israeli and Palestinian leadership, if there is even small chance of forging peace with the current leaders, the United States must take a number of critical steps concurrently with the peace negotiations once they resume.

Only by adopting these measures will Netanyahu and Abbas clearly demonstrate how serious they are about reaching an agreement while helping the United States to determine early on the real prospect of achieving that goal.

These steps are critically important to engender public support from the start and help maintain the momentum, as the negotiations will inadvertently face a number of obstacles.

First, there exists profound distrust between the two sides which cannot be mitigated at the negotiating table. Israeli and Palestinian leaders must make every effort to change public perceptions about each other by simultaneously taking constructive measures to cultivate trust parallel to the negotiations on substantive issues.

All pronouncements by public officials must support the peace efforts and no longer portray each other as the eternal enemy. If Netanyahu and Abbas believe in a two-state solution, as they profess they do, they must portray it as the only viable outcome from the inevitability of coexistence.

The Palestinian leadership must openly advocate that the purpose of these negotiations is to bring an end only to the occupation of Palestinian land (the West Bank with some land swaps), which does not include any part of Israel.

The Israeli and Palestinian media can certainly play a pivotal role if they are regularly briefed by both sides about the progress in the negotiations, which can help generate increased public support.

Moreover, Israeli and Palestinian schools should change their attitude toward each other. The Palestinians, in particular, must demonstrably start modifying their textbooks to reflect Israel's existence.

Changing public perceptions must not be held prisoner to reaching an agreement first, because whether it happens now or later it remains indispensable to reaching a peace agreement.

Actions on these fronts by Israelis and Palestinians must be visible and convincing in order to nurture trust. The Obama administration needs to insist that both sides engage in such public discourse and that failing to do so will only attest to their lack of commitment to reaching an agreement.

Second, Hamas must sooner than later be engaged in the negotiating process, initially through back channels by Western powers to seek some input from Hamas' leadership.

To be sure, unless Hamas' leadership feels that they have stakes in the negotiations, they will not hesitate to torpedo the whole negotiating process. Firing even a few rockets at Israel will cause some casualties and deliberately invite Israeli retaliation that could kill scores of Palestinians.

Such a scenario could easily bring the negotiations to an immediate halt because neither side can continue with the negotiations as if nothing happened.

This is not to suggest that Hamas enjoys veto power to reject Israeli-Palestinian negotiations, but no keen observer can argue that a peace agreement between them is possible and can endure without Hamas' involvement.

Saudi Arabia and Egypt in particular are in a strong position to persuade Hamas to adopt the API, which requires Hamas to abandon violence to resolve their conflict with Israel, and become legitimate partners in the negotiating process.

The United States should encourage Abbas to reopen negotiations with Hamas' leaders to agree on general elections and subsequently form a government that represents the majority of the Palestinians.

Given their loss of Syrian support, their weakened position with the new Egyptian government, and the substantially reduced financial aid from Iran along with their diminishing popularity and the painful realization that Israel is here to stay, Hamas may well be inclined to cooperate at this juncture.

Third, enlisting key Arab states, in particular Egypt, Saudi Arabia, and Jordan, not only to lend public support to the peace talks but also to participate as observers, would provide political cover for Mahmoud Abbas to make significant concessions.

The right of return of the Palestinian refugees, for example, will be nearly impossible to resolve (as Israel resolutely rejects the return of any significant number of refugees) without explicit support from key Arab states. Their presence will make such a concession appear as coming from the collective Arab body.

Moreover, considering the Iranian threats, most Arab states are eager to put the Israeli-Palestinian conflict behind as long as it meets key provisions of the API.

Fourth, the United States must insist on starting the negotiations with the most conflicting issue by focusing on borders first.

An agreement on borders would resolve 70–80 percent of the settlements problems, address Israel's major security concerns, and give the Palestinians every reason to believe that a Palestinian state is in the offing.

Finally, both Israelis and Palestinians must believe that the United States is serious and committed to resolving the conflict. Neither side will take risks by making any major concessions unless they know the United States is fully behind them.

The United States must also be prepared to advance its own ideas and prepare to use its leverage—economic and political—to narrow the gap between them.

Finally, both Israelis and Palestinians must also believe that President Obama will use the power of his office to exact the needed concessions to reach an agreement by resorting to coercive measures if necessary.

The agreement to release dozens of long-held Palestinian prisoners—a most sensitive issue for the Palestinians—the appointment of Martin Indyk, a skilled and respected diplomat, and insisting on continuing negotiations for at least six months, adds credibility and perceptibly improves the prospect of the United States' efforts to mediate a peace agreement.

The idea of submitting any peace agreement to public referendums in Israel and Palestine is both necessary and desirable, especially if they pass with an impressive majority.

Israeli and Palestinian leaders can garner such a majority only if they demonstrate a resolute commitment to peace and create the environment from day one of the negotiations to that end.

WHERE ARE THE LEADERS
TO ANSWER THE CALL?

JANUARY 20, 2014

No one can accuse Secretary of State John Kerry of not doing his very best to forge an Israeli-Palestinian peace agreement. His tenacity, commitment, and perseverance are exemplary, and if anyone can remotely succeed in ending the conflict, Kerry unquestionably tops the list. Logically, if Kerry did not believe in the prospect of reaching an agreement, he would not have invested this much time, resources and political capital on an enterprise that has eluded so many before him.

The question is why I, like so many other observers, doubt that the current Israeli-Palestinian negotiations will lead to a solution in spite of Kerry's Herculean efforts and Prime Minister Netanyahu's and President Abbas' presumed commitment to peace.

There is no easy answer, but what has characterized the intractability of the conflict in the past remains in play today, which is further aggravated by a faulty framework for the negotiations and a lack of commitment to reach an agreement that would of necessity require mutually painful concessions.

The rules of engagement: Kerry stated that "[the negotiations] would address all of the core issues that we have been addressing since day one, including borders, security, refugees, Jerusalem, mutual recognition and the end of conflict and of all claims."[327] This sounds compelling, but in reality it is a recipe for failure.

To begin with, the inherent flaw in setting these "rules of engagement" is that it did not place negotiating the conflicting issues in a sequence where a resolution of one would facilitate a solution to another.

---

327 Scott Bobb, "Kerry Holds Talks With Palestinian Leader," *Voice of America*, January 3, 2014, http://www.voanews.com/content/kerry-to-meet-israel-pa-leaders-as-peace-talks-continue/1822578.html.

Although the negotiations involved all the issues that Kerry enumerated, Netanyahu insisted that Israel's national security must top the agenda. His demand, however, that Israel retain residual forces in the Jordan Valley only reinforced the Palestinians' suspicion that the Israeli occupation will indefinitely continue only in another form, which naturally evoked stiff resistance.

Had Kerry insisted that reaching an agreement on borders must come first instead of succumbing to Netanyahu's demand, he could have paved the road to coming very close to reaching an agreement, not only on Israel's security concerns but the settlements problem as well.

Ironically, Netanyahu has consistently invoked the need for defensible borders while adamantly refusing to discuss borders first, because he simply does not want to establish at the onset the parameters of a Palestinian state, to which he has not really subscribed.

An agreement on borders would have provided both the practical requirement and the psychological comfort the PA needs to engage in a quid pro quo with the Israelis. This would have allowed Abbas to demonstrate that he has achieved something that has never been achieved before and make him far more flexible to permit certain residual Israeli forces to remain in the Jordan Valley as a part of a UN peacekeeping force for a specified period of time.

Netanyahu's argument that such a major concession will certainly unravel his government does not explain or justify why holding onto the coalition government is more important than peace. Reaching an agreement with the Palestinians requires a dramatic change in the political landscape and discourse inside Israel.

Any Israeli political leader must place peace on top of his political platform and any prime minister must risk his position or even his life and lead the people to peace, not to the abyss where Netanyahu is leading the country. As of now there is still no agreement on this contentious issue of keeping residual Israeli forces along the Jordan Valley; instead, it is compounding the overall difficulties in negotiating other thorny issues which may well be Netanyahu's intention.

Settlement expansion: Although the rules of engagement did not stipulate that Israel must suspend the construction of new housing units during the negotiations, Kerry's failure to persuade Netanyahu

463

to suspend construction, or at a minimum do so discreetly and at a slower pace (without deliberate provocation of the Palestinians), has poisoned the atmosphere and deepened the PA's doubts about Netanyahu's real intentions.

For good reasons, Abbas was furious when he said "We will not remain patient as the settlement cancer spreads, especially in Jerusalem, and we will use our right as a UN observer state by taking political, diplomatic and legal action to stop it."[328]

Here too, an agreement on borders first would have established the status of most settlements and determined which will become a part of Israel proper and which will not. Such an initial agreement would allow Israel to expand any of the settlements that fall under its jurisdiction by agreement on the basis of equitable land swaps, even before a comprehensive accord is achieved.

Recognition of Israel as a Jewish state: What has further complicated the negotiations is Netanyahu's demand that the PA recognize Israel as a Jewish state. The irony here is that Israel does not need any Palestinian government, now or in the future, to recognize Israel as a Jewish state in order for Israel to maintain its Jewish national identity.

There are undoubtedly sinister intentions behind Netanyahu's demand and unfortunately Kerry fell for it, however illogical and counterproductive it may be. Whether Netanyahu is making this demand to please his hardcore conservative constituency or as a ploy to play for time, or even if he believed that such recognition has real merit because of shifting demographics in Israel's disfavor that would affect its future national identity, he is being disingenuous at best.

As I have said in an earlier article, Israel's Jewish national identity can be preserved only through a sustainable Jewish majority.[329] This can be achieved by solving the Palestinian conflict based on a

---

328 Marissa Newman, "Abbas Threatens to Rally UN Against Settlement 'Cancer'," *The Times of Israel*, December 31, 2013, http://www.timesofisrael.com/abbas-threatens-to-rally-un-against-settlement-cancer/.

329 "'The Jewish State of Israel,'" [page 5].

two-state solution, providing greater subsidies to large families, discouraging emigration of Israelis and increasing immigration.

The latter two requirements can be realized only by reaching a comprehensive Arab-Israeli peace based on the API, which will offer new and exciting opportunities for growth, but it can happen only when an Israeli-Palestinian peace is achieved.

This is what Netanyahu should focus on if he really wants to preserve the Jewish national identity of the state. The continuation of his current policy of prolonged occupation and settlement expansion will, in fact, jeopardize rather than safeguard the future of Israel as a Jewish state, and no recognition by any country will change this basic sad reality.

Negative public narratives: Contrary to the spirit of cooperation and commitment needed to advance the negotiating process, both sides continue to engage in public narratives that raise serious doubts about their real intentions and willingness to make peace.

Netanyahu, Abbas, and other officials on both sides accuse each other, and for good reason, of not negotiating in good faith, thereby further polarizing their respective publics and instilling serious misgivings, which inevitably diminish the prospect of reaching an agreement.

In order to reinforce the notion that there is no partner in the negotiations and to delegitimize the Palestinian claim, Netanyahu said:

> "There's growing doubt in Israel that the Palestinians are committed to peace. In the six months since the start of peace negotiations, the Palestinian Authority continues its unabated incitement against the State of Israel."[330]

---

330 Michael R. Gordon and Isabel Kershner, "While Kerry Pushes Peace Talks, Israeli Leader Airs Criticism," *The New York Times*, January 2, 2014, http://www.nytimes.com/2014/01/03/world/middleeast/while-kerry-pushes-peace-talks-israeli-leader-airs-criticism.html? r=2.

And to further undermine the negotiations, Economy Minister Naftali Bennett said that the ongoing negotiations "have only brought us terror."[331] On another occasion, he stated that "The nation elected us…to guard the values of the state of Israel, not to pawn our future to Abu Mazen."[332]

The most outrageous of all public utterances came from Moshe Ya'alon, Israel's Defense Minister no less, who said that Kerry, "who…is acting out of an incomprehensible obsession and a messianic feeling—cannot teach me a single thing about the conflict with the Palestinians. The only thing that can save us is if Kerry wins the Nobel prize and leaves us alone."[333]

It is unfortunate that Kerry did not insist that both sides refrain from such negative public narratives just as he insisted on maintaining secrecy about the substance of the negotiations.

Much damage has already been done, which was worsened by Kerry's own off-hand public utterances, specifically when he said that "The alternative to getting back to the talks is the potential of chaos. I mean, does Israel want a third intifada?"[334] This kind of statement did nothing but further entrench both sides in their positions.

Truth and reconciliation: Aside from the conflicting issues, there are profound feelings of hatred, mistrust, and unsettled

331 Tovah Lazaroff and Gil Hoffman, "Bennett Dismisses Land Swaps with Palestinians For Peace, Security," *The Jerusalem Post*, January 7, 2014, http://www.jpost.com/Diplomacy-and-Politics/Watch-live-Naftali-Bennett-gives-speech-on-peace-process-337351.

332 Ben Sales, "Sparring by Livni and Bennett Shows Cracks in Coalition," *The Times of Israel*, January 9, 2014, http://www.timesofisrael.com/sparring-by-livni-and-bennett-shows-cracks-in-coalition/.

333 James M. Dorsey, "Israeli Pitches: A Tale of Racism, Bigotry and Double Standards," *The Turbulent World of Middle East Soccer*, January 19, 2014, http://mideastsoccer.blogspot.com/2014/01/israeli-pitches-tale-of-racism-bigotry.html.

334 Hannah Strange, "John Kerry Warns of Third Intifada if Israeli-Palestinian Talks Fail," *The Telegraph*, November 8, 2013, http://www.telegraph.co.uk/news/worldnews/middleeast/israel/10436109/John-Kerry-warns-of-third-intifada-if-Israeli-Palestinian-talks-fail.html.

historical accounts that cannot be mitigated on their own. I am prepared to venture that even if an agreement on all other issues is achieved (which is far-fetched), it will be transitory at best.

Concurrent with the negotiations, Kerry should have demanded (and still can) the creation of a Truth and Reconciliation Commission, made up of apolitical and respected Israelis and Palestinians, to address the grievances against each other to create an atmosphere conducive to **enduring** peaceful coexistence.

I am absolutely convinced that unless the Israelis and the Palestinians look at each other in the eyes and listen, understand and demonstrate genuine sympathy to each other's painful history and agonizing concerns for the future, current and future peace negotiations will continue to falter.

The process of truth and reconciliation is difficult and disquieting; it has been avoided because it requires self-searching as much as understanding the other's core emotional outrage. But then, Israelis and Palestinians must co-exist in one form or another and cannot continue to live in denial. They need to be shaken to understand that truth and reconciliation is not just an addendum for good measure; it is central to facilitate current negotiations and affect how future Israeli and Palestinian generations view each other.

If both sides are indisputably seeking peace, they must demonstrate that they are ready and willing to engage each other on that human level instead of engaging in continuing mutual recrimination that does nothing but push them further apart and make peace ever more elusive.

Enforcing U.S. framework: The above point becomes more cogent given the growing skepticism about the possibility of reaching a final agreement by the original deadline in April, which now has given way to a more modest goal of reaching an interim understanding, based on a loose framework soon to be advanced by Kerry.

Perhaps this is the most that Kerry can hope for. That said, given the region's volatility, the spiraling of violent conflicts that surround Israel and the Palestinians, and the growing impatience of the Palestinian public, an interim agreement or even a general framework for peace will not stand the test of time.

Unlike the late Prime Minister Sharon, Netanyahu remains a blind ideologue who has no vision where Israel will be 10 or 15 years down the line and no courage to take corrective steps now to safeguard Israel from compromising its democracy and endangering its Jewish national identity. He continues to wallow in wishful thinking, bringing a greater danger to Israel every day that passes.

Abbas, on the other hand, may be willing to strike a deal but only on his own terms, as he is extremely constrained by limited public support and is running out of time. While Abbas claims to represent all Palestinians, Hamas, which is in total control of Gaza, does not recognize Abbas' authority and is unlikely to accept an accord with Israel that does not fit its self-destructive political agenda.

The lack of courageous and visionary leadership: To be sure, neither Netanyahu nor Abbas have demonstrated bold and visionary leadership, which is surely needed at this fateful juncture. The Israeli-Palestinian annals are saturated with self-denial and resistance to the inevitable and there is little evidence that much has changed.

Thus, it is illusionary to assume that presenting the Israelis and Palestinians with a framework will in fact pave the way for a peace agreement at some point in the near future. To put it bluntly, only direct American pressure can produce real results, provided that both Netanyahu and Abbas fully understand that there will be serious consequences if they defy the United States.

There is no better or closer ally to either Israel or the Palestinians than the United States and it is the only country that can provide both sides the political cover they need; it can also use coercion and/or inducements to compel them to find the middle ground to reach an agreement.

The threat of withholding political support from Israel in international forums will go a long way in convincing Netanyahu and other Israeli leaders that the day of reckoning is here. Similar political and economic pressure on Abbas will seriously resonate with the Palestinians, who cannot afford to dismiss America's crucial support.

In this context, Kerry should reinvigorate the API and ask the leading Arab states, especially Saudi Arabia, Egypt, Morocco, Jordan, and others that actually support the Israeli-Palestinian peace negotiations, to be more publicly vociferous in support of his peace offensive. Abbas needs the Arab states' political and economic support and the Israeli public needs to be persuaded that the Arab world overwhelming supports the peace negotiations.

There are those who claim, and rightfully so, that considering congressional resistance and the stiff opposition of the powerful evangelical constituency and the so-called Jewish lobby, the Obama administration will be reluctant to force Israel to make any concession to the Palestinians which is not to its liking.

This of course may well be true, but then again if the United States is serious about achieving peace and believes that it is best for Israel and that time is of the essence, it can no longer dilly-dally with mediation efforts that go nowhere. Here too, leadership matters; the president cannot settle for preaching the gospel of peace and leave John Kerry to sink or swim.

The United States has massive strategic interests in the Middle East and it needs an Israeli-Palestinian peace just as much as they need it to prevent another major conflagration that is certain to come if the current conditions persist.

The Middle East will experience unprecedented turmoil for years to come. There may not be a better time to achieve an Israeli-Palestinian peace than now, but where are the leaders that can answer the call?

AMERICAN JEWS MUST SUPPORT, NOT HINDER, KERRY'S EFFORTS

FEBRUARY 14, 2014

I am one of those who certainly support J Street's ongoing efforts to promote Israeli-Palestinian peace, and I applaud their repeated outreach calling on congressional leaders and Jewish groups to support Secretary of State John Kerry's peace offensive. I am puzzled though by J Street President Jeremy Ben-Ami's call for financial assistance to "help send more pro-Israel, pro-peace candidates to Congress and stand-up to the personal attacks on Kerry."

Regardless of how well-intended, there are three major concerns over Ben-Ami's appeal:

To begin with, anyone who follows Congress' deliberations and sentiments regarding the Israeli-Palestinian peace process witnesses overwhelming support of Israel, and many congressmen have called on the Obama administration not to pressure Israel to make concessions it does not wish to make voluntarily.

The problem here is not that there is no congressional support for Israel, but there are not many who specifically support Kerry's peace efforts, as stated in Ben-Ami's call. What this sadly means is that American Jews should elect only representatives that support a certain policy related to Israel and that should be the sole criteria that would qualify them to be elected.

The message that this sends, especially to non-Jewish voters, is that Israel, and only what is good for Israel (albeit from different ideological perspectives), is what should be the litmus test for old or new representatives. What this misguided approach does is reinforce the notion that Congress is in Israel's pocket, serving one pro-Israeli interest group or another.

The second problem with Ben-Ami's appeal is that congressional elections will be held toward the end of the year, and all new and veteran members of Congress will effectively start working at the end of January 2015. Considering the urgency to make some serious progress in the Israeli-Palestinian negotiations, how will the election of "pro-peace candidates" now help Kerry's efforts, when time is of the essence?

There is a desperate need to make progress at this very juncture in the negotiations. Not that I expect a comprehensive peace agreement will be achieved within the next 12 months, but if there is no significant progress to keep the Israelis and the Palestinians engaged and hopeful, I seriously doubt that the negotiations will continue for another year.

Ben-Ami himself reaffirmed in his own words that time is critical when he stated: "The next couple of months will be a decisive moment for the peace and security of Israel. As Kerry prepares to roll out his framework agreement, we cannot afford to stand idly by…"

To that end, J Street should rally current members of Congress in support of Kerry's tireless efforts and present each and every one with the terrible prospect of a new conflagration if Kerry's efforts fail.

Every congressman should be hearing not only from representatives of the strongly conservative-leaning AIPAC, which blindly supports the current Israeli policy of intransigence, but also from the heads of the plethora of major Jewish organizations who fully support Kerry's efforts.

The third problem is that although J Street touts itself as an "organization that primarily focuses on nonpartisan education and advocacy on important national issues,"[335] it has done little to educate congress members with the real conflicting issues between Israel and the Palestinians. It is not enough for a congressman to hear from a lobbyist why he or she should support what is best for Israel.

To educate these representatives about the real issues that separate Israelis from Palestinians, they should be invited to see and listen to Israelis and Palestinians discussing the perils of no peace. They should witness the plight of the Palestinians under occupation and understand why continuing occupation dangerously erodes Israel's moral standing, which affects every Jew regardless of his or her place of residence.

---

335 "About," *J Street*, http://jstreet.org/about (accessed February 12, 2014).

J Street must counter AIPAC's argument that Israel is under siege, surrounded by enemies seeking its destruction. This argument has been effective on Capitol Hill, and instead of pushing for peace now by supporting Kerry's efforts, they are unwittingly contributing to Israel's self-destructive policies.

The fact is, despite AIPAC's best efforts in Washington, Israel is becoming increasingly isolated in the international arena. The potential failure of the current negotiations will squarely fall on AIPAC's and its surrogates' shoulders.

J Street must challenge AIPAC on its own turf and demonstrate that the preservation of Israel as a viable and secure state rests on peace even though it requires painful concessions. Regardless of how painful these concessions may be, they will pale in comparison to the self-inflicted wounds that Netanyahu's policies are leading towards.

J Street is an organization worthy of support by every person who cares about Israel's future and ensuring that the American-Israeli bond continues to grow stronger. No one, however, should take that for granted.

The United States and the West in general are running out of patience and soon there will come a time when Israel can no longer count on their automatic political support, not to mention a host of other collaborative relations critical to Israel's national security and well-being.

The monumental time, energy, and political capital that Kerry has and continues to invest must not be squandered by so-called Jewish leaders who are sitting on their cushy chairs 6,000 miles away and counsel no concessions at the expense of Israeli blood.

They should go not only to Israel but also to the occupied territories and experience the life of a Palestinian, deprived of his or her personal freedom, with no opportunity and no hope for a better future. What do they expect them to do?

Israel is creating its own time bomb through self-destructive policies, and every American Jew who does not raise his or her voice in support of the peace process is complicit in the bloodshed that will inescapably unfold.

Every congressional candidate needs money to run for office and that is legitimate. But none should take a dime if it is conditioned upon supporting any political position that affects Israel one way or the other.

They must be educated, not bought, in order to become conscientious of the high stakes involved that will come from failure.

They must understand that Israel's very existence rests on peace with the Palestinians.

They must act accordingly if they truly care not only about Israel but the Palestinians as well, because the Israelis' and Palestinians' futures are intertwined and neither can live in peace and security without the other.

INTERNATIONAL
NEGOTIATIONS

A SELF-DEFEATING FIXATION

MAY 24, 2010

Last week, an effort by the Qatari government to improve diplomatic relations with Israel and aid the reconstruction effort in Gaza ended with a freeze in all official ties between the two countries. Qatar's offer to carry out infrastructure reconstruction projects in Gaza in exchange for re-opening up Israel's diplomatic mission in Doha would have been a positive development for both sides. The rejection of this offer by the Israeli government is both short-sighted and self-defeating. The Netanyahu government's failure to seize an opportunity to normalize relations with an Arab state—against a limited risk that Hamas would act against the Qatari government and seize some of the construction materials for fortification of its defenses—demonstrates not only intransigence but a lack of a coherent policy as to how to bring about an end to the Arab-Israeli conflict. The Israeli government may justifiably suspect Hamas' menacing intentions, but that too must be balanced against the reality of Hamas which cannot simply be wished away by the Israelis. At some point a pragmatic policy must be introduced to demonstrate how Israel is going to calibrate its risks and opportunities and better manage its relations with the Arab states that are making goodwill gestures.

By now it has become abundantly clear that Israel's blockade of Gaza has not weakened Hamas, but rather increased its popularity in the Arab street and heightened international sympathy to the beleaguered Palestinians in Gaza. The fact that Israel allows ample supplies of food and medicine to pass through the crossings to Gaza while denying other critical materials to rebuild has created the widespread perception of indifference and disdain by Israel toward the plight of ordinary Palestinians. Tens of thousands continue to live in squalor, which defies any political logic the Netanyahu government may wish to employ and from which Israel could conceivably benefit. Israel will have to coexist with the Palestinians in Gaza under any political configuration, regardless of who may govern the area. The question is, does the Netanyahu government have a specific plan to change the current dynamics to entice Hamas into the political process? Engaging in wishful thinking that may in fact scuttle other peace overtures, such as ones from the Qataris, is futile and profoundly counterproductive.

Had the Qatari offer been accepted by Israel, it could have had serious positive implications from which Israel could greatly benefit. To begin with, Israel would have sent a clear message to the international community that although it has genuine concerns about Hamas' continuing militancy, in light of Qatari assurances that the material will be used for housing and other civilian institutions, the welfare of the Palestinians will override such concerns. In addition, unlike a similar offer made by Turkey's Red Crescent organization, which came on the heels of growing tension between the two countries and was seen by Israel as pandering for domestic and Arab political support, the Qatari offer provides Israel with a critical opportunity to establish formal relations with an Arab state. This would have allowed other Gulf states such as Bahrain and the Emirates to follow suit. Qatar in particular has taken several initiatives toward Israel in the past, including inviting then-Foreign Minister Tzipi Livni to speak in Doha, and its current offer represents a continuation of a policy which has received, albeit tacitly, the endorsement of other Arab states. Moreover, the timing of the Qatari offer is particularly auspicious as it comes when the proximity talks are underway and a goodwill gesture is both needed and expected of Israel.

More important is the fact that involving other Arab governments in the internal affairs of Gaza and working with Hamas' leaders would have the effect of moderating Hamas' position over time. Indeed, the only way to distance Hamas from Iran is by encouraging it to return to the Arab fold. But that can happen only through constructive, gainful, and lasting engagement of Hamas, especially by official Arab governments which are much harder to rebuke than aid organizations or nonprofit groups. Qatar could have paved the way for other Arab countries to be involved in the reconstruction efforts in Gaza, something that the Israeli government must support if it ever wishes to end the Israeli-Palestinian conflict. Egypt has voiced its dissent of the deal, as it jealously guards its hegemony in Israel's relations with Hamas due to its own problem with the Muslim Brotherhood, and because of its shaky ties to Qatar after much criticism from Doha-based Al Jazeera. Yet ultimately, Egypt has not yet proved to be effective in dealing with this problem of Hamas and ameliorating the situation in Gaza, so Israel needs to start looking at this problem on a wider scale. Allowing other Arab players into Gaza could open up various channels of communication between Israel and Hamas that were heretofore unproductive under Egypt's ownership.

Although the Qatari offer was rejected, it is not too late to revive it and unfreeze ties, particularly since Israel's rejection was carefully deliberated and even the astute right-wing National Security Advisor to the Prime Minister, Uzi Arad, argued in its favor. Israel's security concerns about Hamas' potential threats are genuine and cannot be dismissed on the grounds of simple paranoia. The problem here is to what extent Israel should allow itself to be fixated on Hamas as an irredeemable militant group bent on Israel's destruction without searching for ways to reconcile with its existence. The Gaza war has clearly demonstrated that Israel cannot change Hamas' current militancy either by brutal force or by a continuing blockade, which has not worked and has deleterious effects on Israel's standing in the international community.

Regardless of why Hamas is currently pursuing a nonviolent posture toward Israel, the Israeli government must demonstrate its willingness to reward such behavior. After all, Israel has rightfully demanded in the past cessation of all hostilities as a precondition to improved relations; it must now demonstrate the readiness to respond and deny Hamas the pretext of resuming violence under the continuing unbearable conditions. Unlike other foreign attempts to reconstruct Gaza, Qatar's offer comes from a moderate Arab state and has the potential to influence the nature of relations with Hamas by accepting it as a political movement and by allowing the Palestinians in Gaza to develop a vested interest in the improved conditions.

This experiment may entail some risk for Israel, but such a risk needs to be seen in the bigger picture, because the tremendous benefit Israel could potentially garner should the effort work far outweighs the potential risk. Without a long-term strategy, Israel's fixation on Hamas will prove to be self-defeating, playing willfully into Hamas' hand, especially when the patience of the international community is wearing thin.

A PARADIGM SHIFT

OCTOBER 22, 2010

The Arab League's decision to give more time for efforts to resume the stalled Israeli-Palestinian negotiations provides more than just political cover for Palestinian Authority (PA) President Mahmoud Abbas; it also signals a more prominent role for the Arab states in determining the fate of the peace process. The Obama administration must further encourage this apparent shift by the Arab states to expand the scope and change the direction of the negotiations to provide the peace process with the comprehensiveness that has been sorely lacking.

President Abbas has reached out to the Arab League at three crucial moments in the past year: to enter proximity talks, to move to direct talks, and now to defer the decision as whether or not to leave the talks because of Israel's refusal to extend the settlement freeze. By playing this key role in the Israeli-Palestinian peace process, the Arab states may have finally decided to collectively assume responsibility for its success or failure. If so, this represents nothing less than a paradigm shift on the part of the Arab states in dealing with their conflict with Israel. This new role for the Arab League could breathe new life into the Arab Peace Initiative (API), first proposed by Saudi Arabia and endorsed by the Arab League in 2002. The Initiative offers Israel normal relations with the 22 members of the League once Israel and the Palestinians reach an agreement on a two-state solution and Israeli withdraws from other occupied Arab land. However, since being introduced the API has languished, with the Arab states refusing to advance it beyond sending the Jordanian and Egyptian foreign ministers for a brief visit to discuss it with their Israeli counterparts. That could now be changing, and it is up to the Arab states to seize the opportunity.

President Obama has used recent speeches on the Mideast peace process to stress the importance of Arab support. By actively participating in the negotiations and placing the API on the negotiation table, the Arab states could heed this call. The current talks are already following the parameters of the API; the question now is whether the Arab states are willing to go further to support the peace process that transcends the settlement freeze. They can do so by using the Initiative as a political tool to fashion solutions while ensuring that a conflict-ending agreement would be comprehensive. Doing so would effectively replace the already diminishing importance of the Mideast Quartet (United States, European Union [EU], UN, and Russia—which Israel continues to doubt if not mistrust), with the Arab states, which is the only body that can provide both political support to the Palestinians and the recognition and normalization that Israel desires.

The United States should encourage the Arab League to not only endorse the continuation of direct talks at this critical juncture, but also be more creative, take the initiative, and change the dynamic of the negotiations regardless of how the settlement quandary is resolved. The Arab League should take a macro view of the Israeli-Palestinian peace process and focus on the larger picture of how to advance a two-state solution on the ground and do so now. It is true that the settlements have impeded and continue to impede progress; however, this hindrance is much more psychological than physical. Since Prime Minister Netanyahu declared his willingness to discuss the parameters of a Palestinian state, why not put him to test by insisting on negotiating borders first (which is central to defining statehood) and leave the settlement building alone? As long as the parties, with the United States' direct and active involvement, agree on a timeline to end the negotiations on borders, what does it matter if in the interim Israel builds an additional one or two thousand housing units? The initial focus on the settlement expansion by the Obama administration, without anticipating possible Israeli objection, and without a Plan B in place should the Israeli government do so, was misguided in the first place. Continuing to insist on a freeze simply plays into the hands of Netanyahu's right-wing coalition partners. What would happen if there was no progress during the extension of the freeze by the two or three months that the Obama administration is asking for? It makes far more practical sense to focus on negotiating borders, which should be considerably more meaningful to the Palestinians, instead of remaining stuck with the settlement freeze problem, which is exactly what Israel's Foreign Minister Avigdor Lieberman and his right-wing coalition partners want.

However legitimate the Palestinians' demand to extend the freeze, at least from a symbolic perspective and as a matter of principle, and regardless of how shortsighted Israel's rejection is, elevating the issue of the freeze to the level of "make or break" is foolhardy and imperils the negotiations. After all, the settlements physically occupy one percent of the land mass of the West Bank. It should be particularly noted that there is no mention of the settlements in the API, and that Israel and the Palestinians have always negotiated in the past while settlement activities were ongoing because what mattered then and what matters now is whether or not there is the will to reach an agreement. To reach an agreement, the Palestinians must not—at least at this juncture—seek international recognition for statehood until they exhaust all possibilities to negotiate borders.

The Arab League's involvement should further expand by sending observers to the Israeli-Palestinian negotiating table. Although Israel may initially object, the Netanyahu government cannot have it both ways by seeking Arab recognition but then preventing them from participating in the peace negotiations. The United States ought to insist on this requirement. While Israel has every right to ensure that the Arab states are sincere about real peace with security and normal relations, it can achieve this only through the continuing presence of representatives of other leading Arab states, especially those who have no formal peace with Israel, such as Saudi Arabia, Morocco, and even Syria. Their participation as observers would not only give the Israeli-Palestinian negotiations the comprehensiveness needed, as stipulated by the API, but precipitate the critical change in public perceptions both in Israel and the Arab streets about the prospect of real peace. That is, the more visible other Arab states are engaged in the Israeli-Palestinian peace negotiations, the greater vested interest all parties will have in a successful outcome.

In this connection, the United States should also leverage the newfound activism of the Arab League. Shortly after taking office, President Obama's request for Saudi Arabia to take confidence-building measures toward normalization with Israel was rebuffed. But the new Arab League role offers the Obama administration a new opportunity to engage Arab states, such as Saudi Arabia in particular, by providing the Saudi Kingdom, the initiator of the API, a chance to demonstrate leadership among the Arab and Muslim states. Moreover, the increased role of the Arab states would serve two other important purposes. First, it would alleviate Israel's skepticism about their intentions. The Arab states have now encouraged the Palestinians to keep talking at three critical junctures. By collectively supporting the negotiations, the Arab states have effectively become a responsible party for the outcome of the talks. Second, a more visible Arab role provides the Arab states with an avenue to dealing indirectly—and in some cases, even directly—with Israel, something that Israelis have been seeking for a long time.

Some critics argue that the Arab League's meetings to endorse the negotiations have been counterproductive, that rather than providing support for the Palestinians, the Arab states have undercut Mahmoud Abbas' ability to negotiate independently. Others claim that the Arab states are merely providing lip service to talks that they are certain will fail. Still others argue that the Arab states are too preoccupied with internal issues to play a meaningful role in facilitating peace, and that Israel itself has shown little interest in making meaningful steps to advance the peace process. Indeed, there is deep skepticism on all sides and perhaps for good reason, as the squabble over the settlement freeze has shown. But the Arab states can—and must—play a more meaningful role if they want to realize actual progress. Past experience can be extremely instructive: whether or not Yasser Arafat was ever serious about peace is questionable— what is not in doubt is that without support from the Arab states, he would never have been able to implement a peace agreement that would have met Israel's security needs. In short, Arafat never obtained the necessary broad Arab support that Mahmoud Abbas firmly enjoys today. Furthermore, by endorsing the process, the Arab states are providing more than just lip service—they are providing tangible political support while using their influence to quell efforts by extremist groups to disrupt the process. The Arab-Israeli conflict thrives on distrust, with each side claiming the other does not have true intentions to make peace. Now, with an opportunity for the Arab states to engage in a comprehensive process, we may find out who wants peace, and who does not.

The time of reckoning has arrived—there is a growing realization that time is running out on the only viable two-state solution, and the concern over another regional war and the threat from Iran is high. The opportunity for a committed American president should not be missed. The Arab states must capitalize on this moment by putting the Netanyahu government to the test and insisting on restarting the negotiations on borders, instead of focusing on a settlement freeze. They must not allow the historic API to die when it may well offer the only real chance to reach a peace agreement.

A DISMAL FAILURE OF
LEADERSHIP ALL ROUND

DECEMBER 11, 2010

It is hard to describe the state of affairs of the Arab-Israeli conflict at this particular juncture without using adjectives such as "sad," "unfortunate," or even "tragic," which I think is the most appropriate description. The collapse of the so-called Israeli-Palestinian peace process is indicative not only of the failure of the Israeli and Palestinian leadership, but of the other parties involved, in particular the Arab states and the Obama administration. It is a tragic situation because all the parties seem to focus on political expediency to explain away their failing policies while they lose the capacity to show the vision and courage needed to avert the great regional disaster that is in the making.

I am not sure how Israel's Prime Minister Benjamin Netanyahu wants to be remembered. As things stand today, he will surely be recalled as the Prime Minister who twice lost a historic opportunity to forge peace with Israel's remaining conflicting parties—the Palestinians, the Syrians, and the Lebanese. It is one thing to miss such an opportunity if the status quo remains frozen and can be revisited at leisure without major losses or risks. It is an entirely different matter, however, when the enemies of peace like extremist groups and Iran are steadily gaining power and will certainly pose a far greater danger to Israel in the absence of an Arab-Israeli peace. Netanyahu has shown not only a lack of ability to lead, but has been systematically engaged in deceiving his interlocutors—the Americans as well as the Palestinians—while misleading his own people. Using his right-wing government as an excuse for his inability to engage the Palestinians in earnest is nothing short of demagogy. He knows that he could have made basic—and for that matter inevitable—concessions to lure the Palestinians to the negotiating table. He could have also changed the composition of the government by dumping Shas and Yisrael Beiteinu and inviting Kadima to join him to put the Palestinians to the real test. But he opted not to, simply because he and his coalition partners are unwilling to make any meaningful concessions—regardless of what the Palestinians are doing or saying. Netanyahu may see a hopeful sign in the fact that the Obama administration has given up its effort to persuade Jerusalem to freeze construction in Jewish settlements, but the judgment of time will be much harsher than Netanyahu can imagine. The Israelis will end up paying a dear price for the tragic mistakes that he has willfully and even proudly committed.

Just as tragically, the Palestinian leadership does not fare any better. It is "understandable" that for ideological and political reasons Hamas will continue to hold onto its extreme position, albeit to the detriment of the Palestinians. But then, the same cannot be said about Fatah and its leader Mahmoud Abbas. Surely he has internal and external—from the Arab states—constraints, but that does not explain his failure to demonstrate leadership and go against the political grain to rise above past prejudices and skepticism. No leader can claim to want peace but then allow certain preconditions—i.e., the settlements' freeze—to stop him from entering into serious negotiations. Moreover, President Abbas and Prime Minister Salam Fayyad have failed to utilize the remarkable progress they made in maintaining security throughout the West Bank and their impressive economic developments to change the dynamic of the negotiations with Israel by changing the rules of engagement, including—however legitimate—the settlement freeze. Abbas remained bogged down in negotiations with Hamas, who he fears and detests, which unavoidably limited his maneuvering room in trying to negotiate with Israel. Although Abbas appears to be sincere and certainly committed to a nonviolent solution to the Israeli-Palestinian conflict, he remains politically weak and isolated. Instead of taking new initiative, he relied heavily on the Americans to deliver the Israelis and on the Arab League to provide him with the political cover to engage or disengage the Netanyahu government, missing yet again another opportunity to reach an agreement.

The Arab states too have not fallen much shorter behind the Israelis and the Palestinians. Whatever happened to the API? Why is it that the Arab League, led by Saudi Arabia, has done next to nothing to promote their historic Initiative, especially among the Israelis who know very little about the document and even less about the Arab states' real intentions to make peace? More than any other time, especially because of the growing Iranian threat, the Arab states have every reason to sort out their differences with Israel and begin some serious back-channel diplomacy to assure the Israelis of their true intentions behind the Initiative. It is not enough to present the Israelis with a general framework for a comprehensive peace; they must next translate it into action. The Israelis, who have and continue to be extremely skeptical about the Arab states' ultimate intentions, want to see a concrete move in the direction of normalization as virtually nothing has changed since the Arab League first introduced the API in 2002. The Arab states, to be sure, have become the victims of their own rhetoric, consistently maintaining the same political narrative. For example, the rhetoric about the right of return of Palestinian refugees gives Netanyahu the excuses he needs not to engage in serious negotiations.

The Arab states have a critical role to play; they can no longer blame a lack of peace solely on the Israelis. They have to do more to moderate Hamas' position and take advantage of the changing regional geopolitical dynamic, especially in confronting Iran. The WikiLeaks cables reveal with clarity the Arab states' sentiment and profound fear of Iran's growing influence. It is time to abandon their hypocrisy and take a stand against Hamas and Hezbollah to demonstrate that they are committed to regional stability by using their collective power to moderate the extremists. It is also time for the Arab League to make real use of the remarkably important API in order to foster the prospect of equitable peace.

Finally, the United States should take a much harder look at its initial failure to mediate an Israeli-Palestinian peace. Whereas the Obama administration received high marks for starting the peace process in the first days of assuming power, it must now accept the deserved blame for failing to properly assess the political and physical realities on the ground. It is time for the Obama administration to realize that even with the best of intentions, neither the Israelis nor the Palestinians will forge peace without a forceful American diplomacy and without a clear vision for the future. The Obama administration needs a new strategy and a new team while insisting on a much more active and direct involvement by the leading Arab states. The current team, led by former Senator George Mitchell, is tired and perhaps out of touch with the reality and the political constraints under which the Israelis and the Palestinians live. Moreover, Mitchell has demonstrated a lack of understanding of the underlining mindsets in both camps, specifically in connection with Israel's national security and the future of the Palestinian refugees.

I maintain that it is time for the Obama administration to come up with its own plan for a solution based on prior agreements and on negotiating borders first. President Obama has barely a year to achieve a breakthrough. He must make it abundantly clear to all parties that American national interests are being systematically undermined by the continuing conflict, and that an Israeli-Palestinian peace serves American strategic interests as much as it serves the interests of the Israelis and the Palestinians themselves. Neither Israel nor the Palestinians can seek continued American support and security guarantees but then ignore vital American interests in the area that are being undermined by Iran and Al-Qaeda. The United States has every right to demand that both sides come to grips with what is required to move toward a political solution. The Obama administration should not hesitate to bring all pressure to bear on both the Israeli and Palestinian authorities to make the necessary concessions. If this precipitates the collapse of either government or both, so be it.

No single entity, be that Israel, the Palestinians, the Arab states, or the United States, can achieve a comprehensive peace unless all parties are prepared to really make—and not just talk about making—critically necessary concessions or take a new initiative to achieve peace. While the conflict continues, the one and only country benefiting from—and contributing to—the impasse is Iran. Iran virtually controls all of Iraq, exerts enormous influence in Syria, and holds tremendous sway in Lebanon. Iran is bent on developing nuclear weapons and is poised to become the region's hegemon. Neither Israel, the Arab states, nor the United States can or should allow that to happen. But this will happen as long as the Arab-Israeli conflict continues to simmer and as long as the leadership on all sides fails to rise to the historic call and instead pave the way for another catastrophic conflagration.

Alon Ben-Meir

THE PALESTINIANS' TREACHEROUS PATH TO THE UN

The Palestinians' plans to seek UN recognition of a Palestinian state augur a bad omen for both Israel and the Palestinians. Instead, President Obama should seek a UN resolution that reflects his own conviction of a two-state solution for the two peoples.

JULY 24, 2011

Pundits and policymakers today are frantically grappling with the various pros and cons concerning the PA's plans to seek recognition from the United Nations General Assembly (UNGA) in September. Regardless of the merit or wisdom behind such a move, the Palestinians seem determined to proceed with their plans unless a viable alternative is provided that could lead to the same result—the establishment of a Palestinian state—within a reasonable and credible timeframe. Although detractors and supporters of the plan among Israelis and Palestinians make convincing arguments to back up their positions, neither side has been willing or able to agree on rules of engagement to support their professed desire to enter into serious negotiations to conclude a peace agreement that meets each other's principal requirements.

The failure to reengage in negotiations before September or the failure to modify any resolution passed by the UN to produce positive momentum would usher in a period of instability with unpredictable consequences for all—the United States, Israel, and the Palestinians.

First, one clear consequence of the UN plan is marginalization of the United States. Long believed to be the only credible mediator of the Arab-Israeli dispute, the internationalization of the conflict serves as a de facto vote of no confidence in the Obama administration's ability to bring the parties back to the negotiating table with a chance to succeed in reaching an equitable peace agreement.

Second, Israel would face an unprecedented wave of delegitimization efforts. Increasingly, the international community will join in solidarity with the Palestinians, whether for demonstrations in the newly declared "state" of Palestine, boycotts of Israeli products, or in supporting putting Israel on trial at the International Criminal Court (ICC). Furthermore, the marginalization of the United States, which will further decrease its influence in the Arab-Israeli arena, is likely and as a result will increase the tensions between Washington and Jerusalem.

Finally, the Palestinians will face an unprecedented test. After a systematic two-year period in which the Palestinian leadership has devoted itself to prepare for statehood, where will the Palestinian public now turn to advance their national cause and put an end to Israeli occupation? The test for the PA will be managing the strategy for the post-UNGA environment alongside the elevated expectations that have come with the international push to recognize Palestine. All the while, the PA will be challenged from its rival Hamas and other extremists groups who are ready, willing, and prepared a return to violence as a means to advance the Palestinian agenda, a ploy that could have horrific consequences for the Palestinian people.

So what can be done?

Both Israel and the Palestinians are weary of the unending conflict, and yet they have been pursuing counterproductive policies undermining the very premise on which a lasting peace can be erected. If Netanyahu wants to prevent the Palestinians from going to the UN, he must put on the table luring and realistic proposals to give Mahmoud Abbas a face-saving way out. Meanwhile, the Palestinians must demonstrate that they mean what they say and stop promoting old narratives, particularly about the return of Palestinian refugees, thereby deterring the Israelis from taking the Palestinians seriously.

The Arab states' endorsement of the Palestinian move at the UN would have had far greater resonance in Israel had they demanded that the endorsement be conditional upon Hamas permanently renouncing violence and committing itself to a political solution, as did its counterpart the PA, by accepting the API. By failing to do so, they too have signaled to Israel that they are motivated by political posturing rather than trying to genuinely advance the cause of peace.

The stark reality is that each side is heavily invested in their political posturing and is unable to relent in advance of the September showdown. The only way to avoid what will be an unprecedented period of uncertainty that could lead to a resumption of violence is for the United States and the EU to lead the way. They must find an alternative before September that can help each side save face in order to avoid a potential catastrophe. To that end, the Obama administration could choose between two options:

Reaffirming the 1967 borders with land swaps

In his recent speech about the Arab Spring and the Israeli-Palestinian conflict, President Obama reaffirmed publicly what has been the basis for negotiations between Israel and the Palestinians in all previous negotiations when he stated that:

What America and the international community can do is to state frankly what everyone knows—a lasting peace will involve two states for two peoples: Israel as a Jewish state and the homeland for the Jewish people, and the state of Palestine as the homeland for the Palestinian people, each state enjoying self-determination, mutual recognition, and peace...We believe the borders of Israel and Palestine should be based on the 1967 lines with mutually agreed swaps, so that secure and recognized borders are established for both states.[336]

The United States should ask the United Nations Security Council (UNSC) to adopt this position and empower the United States to see to its implementation. It has been recently reported that Prime Minster Netanyahu has privately intimated to the United States that he is willing to accept the President's proposals provided that the Palestinians recognize Israel as a Jewish state. Mahmoud Abbas has already indicated that he is willing to enter into negotiations with Israel on the basis of Obama's proposals, without asking to amend

---

336 Obama, "Remarks by the President on the Middle East and North Africa."

the reference to the Jewish state in Obama's speech and dropping his plans to go the UN for recognition.

There is no doubt that such a resolution will be adopted by the Security Council. As such, recognition by the United Nations of a Palestinian state based on the 1967 borders with land swaps would reaffirm the existence of two entities between the Mediterranean Sea and the Jordan River. In this sense, it would be a motion—with the support of a vast majority of the international community—declaring that the solution to the Israeli-Palestinian conflict is two states, not one. Only this time the Palestinians and Arab states will be at the forefront of promoting the formula, rather than rejecting it in favor of renewed violent conflict. With this support for two states in place, Israel's position against radical groups like Hamas, Hezbollah, and Islamic Jihad will be considerably strengthened. The UN vote's locking in the two-state formula would undermine extremist arguments to wipe out the Jewish state. As such, the international community is likely to be more receptive to Israel's security concerns vis-à-vis these fringe groups, who will not only be opposing peace with Israel but also the formula for a two-state solution endorsed and re-endorsed by the international community, as well as the entire Arab world.

Offering specific parameters for a solution

The second option, which is less preferable especially to the Israelis, would be for the Obama administration to lead a campaign to introduce a resolution that could garner the support of the UNSC with provisions that will inevitably have to be accepted by both Israel and the Palestinians. The United States should join leading EU members like Britain, France, and Germany, who are considering proposing four parameters that any future negotiations will have to accomplish: 1) the future border to be established based on the 1967 borders with mutually agreed land swaps; 2) security arrangements that both end any sign of occupation and prevent terrorism; 3) a shared capital in Jerusalem; and 4) a just solution to the Palestinian refugee issue. Rather than offer a detailed framework for an agreement that would be rejected by each side, these terms provide a general framework with regards to the need to establish two states and to address the core final status issues, starting with borders and security as proposed by President Obama. In doing so, the resolution should be framed as a continuation of the efforts the UN has made on this issue since the end of the 1967 Six Day War. In this regard, the resolution could serve to reaffirm the spirit of UN Security Council Resolutions 242 and 338 (which endorse the land for peace formula), which will be critical to realize the vision of a two-state solution. Finally, such a resolution must recognize the legitimate security needs of both Israelis and Palestinians, and renounce all forms of incitement and terrorism.

Having failed since taking office to advance the Arab-Israeli peace process, it would be understandable if the Obama administration simply tries to veto the resolution in an effort to curry favor with Israel's advocates in the United States prior to the upcoming presidential election. But it would be a major mistake. Without successful diplomacy to find an alternative path forward, the U.S. position will be considerably undermined in the Middle East, where the United States is in need of influence at a time of change and upheaval. The administration must be realistic in its outlook. A final peace agreement in the short-term simply is not possible given the current political postures of the two sides.

Yet a different, nuanced, and creative resolution that provides international support for the two-state solution and a workable framework to bring the parties back to negotiations could prevent both Israelis and Palestinians from racing toward a new quagmire with unpredictable consequences.

THE PALESTINIANS' UNCHARTED MARCH TO THE UN

SEPTEMBER 5, 2011

No serious observer of the Israeli-Palestinian conflict should have any doubt that both the Netanyahu government and the PA have been pursuing self-destructive policies over the past 30 months. President Obama's failure to persuade the Israelis and Palestinians to reengage in serious negotiations has added another significant layer of uncertainty to an already untenable environment. The decision of the PA to go to the United Nations to seek recognition of a Palestinian state is likely to make matters worse, leading both sides to further entrench themselves into longtime, hardened positions which could potentially lead to a renewed cycle of widespread violence.

Prime Minister Benjamin Netanyahu has been working hard to create a posture that suggests he is ready to enter immediately into peace negotiations, if only PA President Mahmoud Abbas would return to the negotiating table unconditionally. Netanyahu, however, has set his own conditions, creating new obstacles to negotiations: He demands that Israel be recognized "as a Jewish state" at the outset of negotiations, even though this was never a requirement in previous peace negotiations with the Palestinians.

Netanyahu refuses to accept the 1967 borders as the base line for negotiating a two-state solution with some land swaps. He insists that Jerusalem's future status is not negotiable and that Israel must be allowed to maintain residual forces along the Jordan River. Meanwhile, Netanyahu has refused to consider an even nominal renewal of the settlement construction freeze to test Abbas' resolve to enter into serious negotiations.

In reality, Netanyahu has said little and done less to convince the Palestinians that his professed desire for a two-state solution is genuine. He has skillfully led his public into believing that the status quo is sustainable and perhaps even beneficial for the State of Israel. Of course, the heinous and abhorrent terrorist attack in Eilat and the exchange of fire between Israel and Hamas along the Gaza border and the deteriorating relations with Egypt have shown otherwise. To be sure, Netanyahu has given the Palestinians plenty of ammunition to make the argument that there is no genuine Israeli partner. Even though Netanyahu's popularity has somewhat dimmed in the past few weeks over the civil protests, to many Israelis he remains the kind of "tough" leader that is needed to navigate Israel through its equally "tough" neighborhood. Yet in reality, he is not delivering to improve the prospects for real peace that most Israelis yearn for. As a result, Israel is becoming more isolated than ever in the international arena. Its relationship with the United States is fractured, and public opinion of Israel in Europe has dipped to unprecedented depths.

Tragically, the Palestinians have not fared any better. They have continued their campaign to distort the history of the conflict. They have been working day-in and day-out to perpetuate the fantasy of a return of Palestinian refugees to Israel, giving Israel no reason to believe that a two-state solution will indeed be the endgame of the conflict. Furthermore, they have miserably failed to demonstrate a united front truly committed to a lasting peace. Hamas, in spite of the so-called "unity" agreement, which is faltering and has become a major liability for the PA, continues to preach the gospel of Israel's destruction and refuses to renounce violence as a means to achieve their national objective. Moreover, contrary to Abbas' revisionism in his May 16th op-ed in The New York Times, it was the Palestinians who refused to accept the UN partition plan in 1947 and it was the Arab states that declared war on Israel in 1948.

To be sure, neither side has been willing or able to agree to rules of good-faith negotiations to support their professed desire to enter into serious talks to conclude a peace agreement that meet each other's principal requirements of security and political independence.

The phenomenon of the frantic lead up to the UNGA has been striking. The success of Prime Minister Salaam Fayyad's state-building enterprise has led to rising international support for the Palestinian statehood initiative. Since the Palestinians do not believe that Netanyahu is sincere about a two-state solution, they are equally convinced that Obama's failure to persuade or pressure Netanyahu to change his posture has undercut his ability to effectively mediate the conflict.

Hence, the Palestinians were left with "no choice" but to turn to the UN in an effort to achieve statehood. Recognition of statehood by the UN, they insist, will internationalize the Palestinian problem and open the door for other players, such as the EU, to play a more active role. The idea, as Mahmoud Abbas has stated, is to level the playing field, and to re-enter negotiations with Israel as equals. In the process, statehood will presumably enable the Palestinians to pressure Israel through the ICC and other international forums. Abbas has been further emboldened by the fact that of the world's 20 most populated nations, only five (the United States, Japan, Mexico, Germany, and Thailand) have yet to recognize Palestine.[337]

However sincere or contrived the UN initiative may be, what will happen the day after the UNGA could be more ominous than the Palestinians have ever contemplated. Israel may annex parts of the West Bank, as was proposed by MK Danny Danon, in retaliation for a UN vote, which would likely ignite a violent and defensive reaction from Palestinians. Israel may further respond by withholding tax transfers collected from Palestinian workers to the PA.

The U.S. Congress will likely be driven to halt aid for the PA and for the security forces should they not continue cooperation with Israel. This could aggravate an already major financial crisis facing the PA. Even if the aid from the United States and other Western donors is not cut completely, the Palestinians already have been experiencing a financial test; after a UN vote it will likely only get considerably worse.

Furthermore, with expectations elevated that a Palestinian independence day is on the horizon, the disappointment among Palestinians when the Israeli occupation continues unfettered beyond September's UNGA recognition of a Palestinian state will be palpable.

Mahmoud Abbas has painted himself into a corner. Reversing the progress made in the West Bank could be a dangerous course

---

337 John Whitbeck, "On Palestine, the US is a Rogue State," *The Guardian*, December 29, 2010, http://www.theguardian.com/commentisfree/2010/dec/29/us-israel-palestine-independence.

of action. Already, protests are being planned similar to those conducted on Nakba ("catastrophe") Day. What may start as a nonviolent movement could lead to a third violent intifada. Meanwhile, the Israeli government has begun training and arming defense teams in the settlements in anticipation of Palestinian violence that may deliberately or accidently be ignited.

Both Israel and the Palestinians have become victims of their own self-destructive policies, undermining the very premise on which a lasting peace could be erected. Netanyahu and Abbas should prevent the UN from taking any action that would equally damage their national interests. The Obama administration's last-ditch efforts at the present time to prevent both sides from sliding into the abyss could prove to be successful only if both sides recognize the dangerous course they have charted and agree to sit down and face the inevitable.

Both must put their cards on the table and demonstrate that they are ready, willing, and able to make the necessary concessions that could lead to a lasting peace agreement, however impossible this may seem at the present. Reaching such a compromise before the UNGA acts on the Palestinian request next month is essential if both Israelis and Palestinians are to be prevented from racing toward a new quagmire with unpredictable consequences.

ARAB PEACE INITIATIVE

THE ARAB PEACE INITIATIVE:
NOW OR NEVER

MAY 4, 2010

It has been almost a year since President Obama set out for Cairo early in his presidency to deliver what has been seen as one of the largest overtures by the United States to publicly engage the Middle East. Unfortunately, despite the high hopes that this new administration garnered and the continuous efforts of high-level American officials to put an end to the Arab-Israeli conflict, there is little fruit to bear on the ground. More often than not, the diplomatic breaches and hurdles to even get to the negotiating table have consumed the headlines, and two years later the multilateral relations in the region seem tepid at best. The repeated failures of the bilateral negotiations between Israel and the Palestinians and Israel and Syria may be attributed to a number of factors, including a deep-seated mistrust that has not been addressed, concerns over long-term security, and domestic political constraints to make the required concessions to reach an agreement. Yet while all of these elements contribute to the despondent current state of affairs, the one critical missing ingredient has been the absence of a *comprehensive* framework for peace representing the collective will of the Arab states.

Now more than ever, the Arab Peace Initiative (API) offers the best possible chance of achieving an inclusive peace, provided that all parties to the conflict understand its significance and historic implications that have eluded Arabs and Israelis for more than six decades. The likelihood that the current lull in violence will continue if no progress is made on the political front is slim. If the Arab states want to demonstrate a united front, especially as Iran's nuclear advances threaten the regional balance of power, they must finally and publicly resolve to promote the API in earnest. Conversely, Israel too must take a much harder look at the API and not dismiss it off-hand because of certain objectionable clauses. Indeed, the API offers the only viable framework for an Arab-Israeli peace and it will be nothing less than tragic to let it languish and eventually die.

Historical significance against a dim reality

The API represents a monumental historic transformation, especially when compared to the infamous Arab League Khartoum resolution of 1967, known for its three no's: no peace, no negotiations, and no recognition. Given the critical importance of the API, why have the Arab states and Israel failed, thus far, to appreciably advance the Arab-Israeli peace process? The answer lies in four interrelated reasons.

First, it should be noted that the API was launched in the midst of the Second Intifada, while intense violence was raging and scores of Israelis and Palestinians were losing their lives daily. The Israeli government, then led by Prime Minister Ariel Sharon, was determined to apply an iron fist to deal with the indiscriminate violence, while Arab governments were faced with public outrage instigated by graphic images of death and destruction. Under such circumstances, active promotion of a comprehensive peace with Israel under the banner of the API would have prompted even greater public outrage. The reoccupation of all territories previously evacuated by Israel in the West Bank further eroded any modicum of trust left between Israel and the Palestinians. It was not until 2005 that relative calm was restored, only to be shattered by the war between Israel and Hezbollah in 2006. By this point, the API had lost any wind left in its sails. The Israelis hardly took any notice of its existence, while the Arab states made no substantial legwork to promote it between 2000 and 2005.

Second, it was not until the meeting of the Arab League in Riyadh, Saudi Arabia in March 2007 that the Arab states resolved to promote the Initiative in the United States, the European Union (EU), and Israel in order to persuade their respective governments and public of its historic dimension. Unfortunately, other than a brief visit by the foreign ministers of Jordan and Egypt to Israel in 2007, and a translation of the text into Hebrew by the Jordanian foreign ministry, no other effort to advance its merit took place anywhere. Instead, in subsequent Arab League gatherings, threats to rescind it were echoed by several member states, presumably because of Israel's refusal to adopt it. The irony here is that while the API is transformational by its very nature, it was perceived by even the limited number of Israelis who knew about it as a trap due to the language concerning the solution to the problem of Palestinian refugees. Thus, rather than exposing the Israeli public to its far-reaching significance for normalization in the region, Arab officials retreated and blamed Israelis for their disinterest. To this day, neither Saudi Arabia nor any of the other leading Arab states has made concerted efforts to promote it to the Israeli public, making it much easier for Israel's leadership to ignore it in its entirety.

Third, from the moment the API was launched in Beirut, Lebanon in 2002, not a single change was introduced in the political narratives by Arab officials to reconcile Israel's legitimate requirement for peace with the API. The mention of United Nations General Assembly (UNGA) Resolution 194 in the official document, which calls for the right of return of any Palestinian refugees to their original homes in Israel proper, was never explained in the context of previous negotiations. All Arab governments understand that the more realistic solution to the refugee problem rests with resettlement and compensation. Israel rejected the API on the grounds of the nonbinding 194, despite the fact that the Initiative calls for a "just solution" to the refugees, based on the United Nations Security Council (UNSC) Resolution 242, which superseded UNGA 194. This shows a level of political pandering to the Arab street, which often used the plight of the Palestinian refugees as a scapegoat for their domestic shortcomings, while expressing their frustration with Israel. Moreover, in every recent negotiation between Israel and Palestinian officials, the Palestinian representatives have agreed that only a token number of refugees would in fact return to Israel under family unification if Israel accepts the principle of the right of return. For Israel, this clause in the Initiative represented the single most objectionable provision, and unfortunately the language of Resolution 194 trumped the call for a realistic solution and thus Israel cannot accept it.

Finally, the failure of the Arab states to persuade the United States, in particular, to officially embrace the API has severely undermined its currency. The generally unsettled relations between Washington and Arab capitals such as Damascus throughout the Bush presidency also made it somewhat politically awkward for the Bush administration to adopt the Initiative. Instead, Bush sought a different venue in the Quartet to promote the Israeli-Palestinian peace process. Certainly the United States' preoccupation with the wars in Iraq and Afghanistan further shifted the focus from the Israeli-Palestinian conflict, leaving the API with no support while Israelis and Palestinians were left to their own devices. Although President Obama has shown a general support of API, he has yet to adopt it as the principle frame of reference for all future Arab-Israeli peace negotiations.

The Quartet—a poor substitute

The Quartet, consisting of the United States, EU, UN, and Russia, and the Annapolis Conference in November 2007, meant to create a credible mechanism to promote the peace process, proved incapable of enforcing any real implementation by the parties involved. The Bush administration, with only one year left in office, did not commit the time to iron out all the details that the Clinton administration had worked so fastidiously on for two terms. The singular most important achievement of the Quartet, however, was the consensus around the establishment of a Palestinian state to co-exist peacefully side-by-side with Israel. Yet ultimately the roadmap for Middle East peace could not be force-fed to Israel or the Arab states, and it too was unable to sustain momentum.

Unlike the Quartet, which is composed of diverse power centers outside the region, the API represents the collective Arab will. It represents the consensus of the Arab governments, and therefore naturally resonates well among the Arab populace. Moreover, whereas the Quartet focuses on solving the Israeli-Palestinian conflict through the establishment of a two-state solution, the API offers a broad Arab-Israeli peace that also provides solutions to all outstanding conflicts, including those with Lebanon and Syria. In addition, the API promises a formal peace treaty between Israel and all the Arab states with security guarantees and normalization of relations, which are critical requirements for any Israeli government that will agree to relinquish the vast majority of the territories. One other critical element in the API is that its formal adoption by the United States and Israel in particular would put enormous pressure on radical Arab groups, including Hamas and Hezbollah, to join the Arab fold. Instead, the members of the Quartet remain bogged down with the requirement that Hamas recognize Israel and accept all prior agreements between Israel and the Palestinians, which at this point is highly unrealistic. Now that there have been increased efforts by Egypt and other actors to include Hamas in the political process, as well as a toning down of anti-radical rhetoric on the U.S. front, the time is ideal to include these players into the overall peace strategy.

Why now more than ever

To be sure, time is of the essence. The prevailing conditions on the ground strongly support the need for immediate action to move the peace process forward toward a comprehensive peace under the framework of the API. To begin with, since February 2009 there has been a general state of calm devoid of violence on the part of Palestinians and Israelis. No one can or should take this condition for granted. The existing calm must be built upon to demonstrate that the prerequisite of a nonviolent atmosphere to advance the peace process is taken very seriously. It serves Israel's best interests to alleviate the intolerable conditions of the Palestinians—especially in Gaza—to demonstrate to the world that the Israelis will reward nonviolent behavior. Otherwise, the notable progress, prosperity, and security the Israelis experience today will be in jeopardy if they do not show movement when there is moderation. Calls for a one-state solution, either by Israelis who believe in the historical concept of *Eretz Yisrael* and delegating the Palestinians to Jordan, or by Palestinians who feel if they wait long enough they can overwhelm the Jewish majority demographically, are only perpetuating the myth that either side can simply wish away the other over time. The governments of Israel and the Arab states should dispel such notions whenever they gain momentum, as they only serve to distract the public away from the realities on the ground and from the only viable option of a two-state solution.

Israel has long-term national security concerns that top its domestic agenda, many of which can be addressed only in the context of the API because the Palestinians themselves cannot offer a sustainable framework for regional security. Moreover, since other regional actors have a stake in the outcome of any peace agreement, they would want to ensure that such an agreement satisfies their needs and territorial requirements. Whereas Iran, for example, will do anything it can to undermine Israel, it would be hard-pressed to go openly against the collective Arab will should the Palestinians strike a deal with Israel under the API principles. The lack of a comprehensive frame of reference enables other political groups such as Hezbollah to pursue their agenda operating at the behest of non-Arab states such as Iran. Each holds different views of how to achieve their objectives, which often run contrary to the Arab states' collective interest. Moreover, this also applies to other rejectionist groups such as Islamic Jihad, who still wish to see the destruction of Israel but will be pressured not to sabotage the collective Arab security arrangements with Israel. Indeed, the ultimate intentions of the extremist groups remain central in Israel's domestic debate. Only when the Arab states together speak with one voice and have the support of all Muslim states that embrace the API will there be the kind of international legitimacy needed for longevity.

Finally, the greatest advantage of the API is the acceptance of Israel as an integral part of the Middle East. If there is currently one overarching impediment to peace, it is the prevailing misconceptions among the Israeli and the Arab masses about one another. Promoting the API directly and effectively remains indispensable to changing the mindsets of the masses, without which very little if any progress can be made. No piecemeal approach can mitigate the embedded lack of trust and cynicism which consumes Israelis and the Arabs. The API is the singular framework that can change the dynamic of the conflict and create new and more compelling conditions on the ground conducive to peace.

Reconciling the API with Israel's requirements for peace

Promoting the API on a take-it-or-leave-it basis will not achieve the document's intended purpose. Whereas the Arab states cannot convey that every clause in the Initiative is subject to an open-ended nego-tiation, Arab officials can use quiet diplomatic channels to express that while the Initiative will not compromise certain pillars—like the estab-lishment of a Palestinian state with East Jerusalem as its capital—there is room within these principles to reconcile Israel's requirements for peace with the API. In particular, since the Israelis have legitimate long-term security concerns, these concerns must be allayed in unequivocal terms. The Arab League must emphasize that the API should be seen as the singular frame of reference for a comprehensive Arab-Israeli peace and that Israel's national security will be collectively assured. Any mutually accepted agreement will be *final and permanent*. In particular, the Arab states should categorically declare that they will enforce it *by whatever means necessary*, including the use of force on any Arab radical groups, as long as they are part and parcel of the Arab body politic and occupy Arab land. This will partially alleviate the Israeli concerns over national security matters, and it will prompt the Israeli public to exert greater pressure on their government to seriously engage the Arab states on the basis of the API.

Promoting solutions by changing the political narratives

The general framework for a comprehensive peace to the Arab-Israeli conflict has been hashed and rehashed ad nauseam. The two-state solution, a fair resolution for the Palestinian refugees through a combination of resettlement and compensation, and the return of the Golan Heights to Syria provides the only viable solution. The API is very clear on all of these issues. The Arab states must now actively and relentlessly promote these solutions. But to do so successfully, they must begin to change their political narratives and openly state to the Arab masses that peace with Israel is in the Arab states' best collective national interests. The academic community and the Arab media in particular must write about and analyze the importance of the API, and why peace with Israel under its framework should be pursued. Finally, it is critically important to note that the greatest impediment to peace between Arabs and Israelis is not territory. The real impediment is the complacency with the status quo, and the psychological hurdles involved in taking risks to change it. Both the Israeli and Arab public must now recognize the inevitability of peaceful coexistence and advocate that if there was ever any benefit to prolonging the conflict, it has outlived its usefulness. Neither side can improve their position regardless of how much longer the conflict persists. At this point, the longer the conflict continues, the greater the diminishing return will be.

The geopolitical conditions in the Middle East have dramatically changed since the API was initially introduced in 2002. The wars in Iraq and Afghanistan have drastically altered the regional power equation, as have the new administrations in power. Iran, which has benefited the most from the collapse of the Saddam Hussein regime, poses a serious threat to both Israel and the Arab Sunni states. It is plausible that the Obama administration will roll out its own Middle East peace plan in the coming year, which may well include the Syrian and Lebanese tracks as well as the Palestinian. Yet unless this plan is conducted under the framework of the API, with the backing of leading Arab states such as Saudi Arabia, Egypt, Jordan, and Syria, it will not bolster long-term normalization and peace in the region.

If there is any time when such an initiative should be taken to end the Arab-Israeli conflict, it is now. While Israel must be open to earnestly reexamining the API and adopting it as a basis for comprehensive peace, the Arab League must seize the opportunity to promote the API, and remain relentless until it is fully implemented.

'ARAB AND PEACE' IS NOT AN OXYMORON

AUGUST 9, 2010

Earlier this summer I was in Jerusalem meeting with various officials and catching up with old friends. Minutes after meeting a friend, a former top official in Israel's Foreign Ministry, he ran back to see me. "Alon, come quick, you have to speak with this guy," he told me. After our meeting, he had walked into a pharmacy where the pharmacist saw that he was carrying the brochure I published, "Israel and the Arab Peace Initiative." I went to the pharmacy to speak with the pharmacist and after I confirmed that I was the author of the brochure, he said, "You do not really believe that peace with the Arabs is possible, do you? 'Arab and peace' is an oxymoron. There is no such thing."

The pharmacist, like many Israelis, was simply unaware of the API and the groundbreaking opportunity that it represents. A recent joint poll by Hebrew University's Truman Institute and the Palestinian Center for Policy and Survey Research indicated that 59 percent of Israelis are opposed to the API.[338] It is a troubling statistic, but one that reflects the failure by successive Israeli governments to embrace and market this critical initiative to its people. To be sure, Israelis have reason to be skeptical. Repeated violent conflicts with Arabs and the Arab states' rejection to past peace overtures have traumatized Israelis to believe that an "Arab Peace Initiative" is indeed an oxymoron. Following the 1967 war, the Arab world rejected the possibility of negotiating with Israel for a withdrawal from the lands Israel captured in the Six Day War. Instead, they delivered their answer through the infamous declaration at the Khartoum Conference in 1967 stating "no to peace, no to recognition, no to negotiations," which has been ingrained in the mindset of Israelis ever since.

---

338 "Joint Israeli Palestinian Poll, June 2010," Palestinian Center for Policy and Survey Research, June 2010, http://www.pcpsr.org/en/node/404.

To make matters worse, the API was first adopted by the Arab League at the Beirut Summit on March 27, 2002, the same day as a horrific suicide bombing which killed 30 people and injured 140 at a Passover Seder at the Park Hotel in the Israeli coastal city of Netanya, at the height of the violent Second Intifada. Thus, good ideas presented at the wrong time seemingly become bad ideas. This was certainly the case with the API in March 2002. Indeed, had the API been presented in 1967 instead of the declaration at Khartoum, the region might look very different today. But it is no longer the spring of 2002 and it is no longer 1967—Israel should act accordingly. It cannot allow the trauma of the past to distract it from its obligation to its people to seek ways to safeguard the security of the Jewish state which can be attained only through peace. While there are aspects of the Initiative that concern Israel, it should still fully embrace the effort as a historic opportunity and landmark repudiation of the message the Arab states delivered at the Khartoum conference.

In fact, Israel's silence in response to the Arab world's bold gesture in support of a comprehensive regional peace sends the message that it is rejecting peace today—a notion that was reaffirmed to me during my recent trip to Strasbourg, France, where I met scores of EU parliamentarians who, without exception, insisted that Israel—and not the Palestinians—is the obstacle to peace. Israel must recognize that time and circumstances have changed, and that the Arab states also recognize that Israel is here to stay—albeit peace can be forged only through the exchange of territory for peace. There are six key reasons why the Arab states recognize the need to make peace today, and why they have yet to remove their initiative from the table despite Israel's rejection, and in spite of the currently stalled negotiating process.

First, the ability of the Arab states to exploit the Palestinian problem for domestic consumption has run its course. It is no longer advantageous for the Arab states to use the Palestinian problem to distract their publics from domestic problems. The Arab states are deeply troubled by extremism and dissatisfaction within their own societies, which are fueled to a large extent by the Israeli-Palestinian conflict.

Second, resolving the conflict is not only an Arab concern today—it is a global concern. The Palestinian problem is now one that has been adopted by the international community, with the United Nations, Europe, the United States, and the Arab world all heavily engaged. In this regard, the Arab world has succeeded in making Palestinian nationalism a focus of the international community. No longer can the Arab states claim it is an issue that is being ignored. Now it is an issue that must be resolved.

Third, the Arab states realize that Israel is too powerful to be defeated. Israel is a powerful nation with a vibrant economy and strong military. In 1967, it was not clear to the Arab states—despite their defeat in the Six Day War—whether the "Israel phenomenon" was insurmountable. In 2010, it is clear that Israel is a reality that must be reckoned with. Those Arab extremists who still dream of destroying Israel do so now at their peril.

Fourth, the Arab states see Israel as a buffer against the growing influence of Iran in the Middle East. The Arab world is deeply concerned with Iran's determination to acquire nuclear weapons and its hegemonic ambitions in Lebanon, Gaza, Iraq, and throughout the region. In addition, the possible failure of sanctions against the current Iranian regime and the concerns that the Obama administration may not be willing to use force to halt Iran's nuclear ambitions leave Israel (from the Arab world's perspective) as the only credible power with the capability to stop Iran. In this regard, the concept of "the enemy of my enemy is my friend" is applicable.

Fifth, Israel is increasingly viewed as a useful economic partner in the Middle East. As the West seeks to transition from its oil dependence, so too do the Arab states. Many Arab states also realize that Israel has much to offer in terms of advanced technologies and economic developments. In fact, currently there are nearly a dozen Arab states that have established some kind of relations with Israel in these fields. They indeed realize that they have much to learn—and benefit—from Israel's thriving economy and educated citizenry.

Sixth, for the Arab states, peace is no longer a luxury—it is a necessity. The regional powers in the Middle East today are Israel, Iran, and Turkey—all non-Arab actors. To turn the tide, which has placed the Arab world lagging behind, requires the Arab states to begin to look to the future and resolve the conflicts of the past. To overcome the Arab world's frustration with its malaise, the Arab states need to begin to provide the kind of economic development and security that can enable prosperity—and that is only possible through a comprehensive peace with Israel.

There is a very strong likelihood that the Palestinian Authority's (PA) President Mahmoud Abbas will soon agree to enter into direct negotiations with Israel. Israel will now have a golden opportunity to demonstrate its commitment to peace by agreeing to negotiate substantive issues—such as borders—with the intention of finalizing peace with the Palestinians before the end of 2011.

Israel should begin to communicate to its public exactly what I told the Israeli pharmacist: 'Arab and peace' is not an oxymoron today, just as 'Israel and peace' need not be. The Arab world has dramatically changed since 1967, and the time has come for Israelis to recognize it.

RESOLUTION 194—THE ACHILLES' HEEL OF THE ARAB PEACE INITIATIVE

AUGUST 19, 2010

Israel's chief reservation regarding the API is the way in which the text addresses the issue of Palestinian refugees. Specifically, the Initiative calls upon Israel to affirm: "achievement of a just solution to the Palestinian refugee problem to be agreed upon in accordance with UN General Assembly Resolution 194." Israelis have largely rejected this passage, believing that it is in effect calling for the "right of return" of Palestinian refugees to Israel, something that would destroy the Jewish character of the state. But a closer look at the Initiative indicates that its mention of 194 need not be the Achilles' heel that Israel has made it out to be.

The Arab states'—and Palestinians'—inclusion in the API of UNGA Resolution 194, adopted in the wake of the 1948 Arab-Israeli War, is less about the text of the resolution and more about the principle it represents. Resolution 194 addressed the refugee issue as follows:

> "Resolves that the refugees wishing to return to their homes and live at peace with their neighbors should be permitted to do so at the earliest practicable date, and that compensation should be paid for the property of those choosing not to return and for loss of or damage to property which, under principles of international law or inequity, should be made good by the Governments or authorities responsible."

To be sure, the Arab states have used this passage in Resolution 194 in an effort to make the refugee issue fundamental to any Arab-Israeli peace agreement, and to further extract and mobilize sympathy from the Arab public. However, the Arab states are not chiefly concerned with Israel accepting the exact wording of 194; after all, the text also calls for United Nations control over Jerusalem. They do, however, want Israel to accept the principle of addressing the plight of Palestinian refugees in the context of a comprehensive solution to the Arab-Israeli conflict.

In this regard, Israelis should not be fearful of the API's mention of Resolution 194. The resolution was adopted by the UNGA—not the Security Council—and as such is non-binding. Furthermore, it has not been accepted by all of the parties to the conflict. Meanwhile, UNSC Resolution 242, which Israel and the Arab states have each signed onto, effectively supersedes UNGA Resolution 194. UNSC Resolution 242 addresses the refugee question by calling for a "just settlement of the refugee problem," yet it does not mention the Palestinian refugees by name. Arabs have long interpreted the word "just" in Resolution 242 to mean the arrangement that had been described in UNGA Resolution 194, while Israelis have been averse to the word "just," interpreting it to mean that Israel should assume responsibility for the refugees. Neither is an accurate interpretation. A "just" resolution is one that both parties agree to and one that effectively settles the disputed claims at the heart of the conflict—and this is where the API gets it exactly right. The API is worded such that Israel does not need to accept the wording of 194; rather, it needs to accept a negotiated agreement on the Palestinian refugee issue as a key component of the framework of a comprehensive Arab-Israeli agreement. In this regard, the key words of the API are "a just solution to the Palestinian refugee problem to be agreed upon…" It should also be noted that in every previous negotiations between Israel and the Palestinians, especially at Camp David in 2000 and during the Israeli-Palestinian negotiations in 2007–2008, the Palestinians have accepted the principle that only a limited number of Palestinian refugees (between 20,000 and 30,000) would be allowed to go back to Israel over a period of a few years, under family unification.

Opponents in Israel of the API point to the refugee question— and the Initiative's mention of UNGA Resolution 194 specifically—to discredit the effort entirely. With their interpretation of the text, they argue that the plan effectively calls for the eradication of the State of Israel by diluting the Jewish state with Palestinian refugees. A cynical view of the Initiative—and the intentions of the Arab states—might claim that it is no wonder the 22 nations of the Arab League have offered normalized relations with Israel—they know Israel would never accept the plan, and if they did it would mean the end of the Jewish state. To further augment their arguments, those Israelis who oppose the Initiative suggest that had the Arab states really sought a realistic solution to the refugee problem, they would have stated publicly their willingness to settle for partial resettlement and compensation. The Arab states and the Palestinian leadership, however, refuse to single out the Palestinian refugees and want a solution to the problem to be part and parcel of an overall peace agreement.

Such arguments not only misinterpret the text of the Initiative and the intentions of its backers, they also do a disservice to the Israeli public by ignoring the valuable components of the Initiative, which should be embraced. This includes a proper interpretation of a negotiated agreement on the issue of Palestinian refugees and a comprehensive resolution to the conflict on the basis of UNSC Resolution 242, which would lead to normalized relations with the 22 member states of the Arab League in addition to 34 other Islamic countries (altogether the 56 member states of the Organization of the Islamic Conference). By focusing on what it interprets to be negative aspects of the Initiative, Israel effectively sends a message to the Arab world and the international community that it is not interested in negotiating for peace. It is regretfully ironic that while the API represents a historic repudiation of the Arab League's Khartoum conference in 1967 which declared "no to negotiations, no to recognition, no to peace," it is now Israel which appears to be the party rejecting a momentous opportunity for peace.

The API's approach to Palestinian refugees has been the key source of the current deadlock that has caused the Initiative to languish until today. Those Israelis who are skeptical of the text—and its mention of UNGA Resolution 194—should take a closer look. If they remain skeptical of the intentions of the Arab states, there is only one way to find out—test them. They can do so by accepting the framework of the API and calling for negotiations with the Palestinians and Arab states using the Initiative as a basis for a comprehensive settlement.

By taking this approach, Israel would effectively turn the table on those who believe it is disinterested in peace, place the burden of proof onto the Arab states, and challenge their groundbreaking promise for a comprehensive peace.

RESURRECTING THE ARAB
PEACE INITIATIVE

APRIL 25, 2013

The resurrection of the API by the United States,[339] which was initially introduced by the Arab League in Beirut, Lebanon in 2002, is a strategic and timely move. Sadly, however, the API should have all along constituted the basis for a negotiated Israeli-Palestinian peace agreement which was, and still is, the pre-condition for a comprehensive Arab-Israeli peace.

This is not high insight; for years I have been preaching that the Israelis and the Palestinians could have forged a bilateral agreement had Israel accepted the API as the framework of a comprehensive Arab-Israeli peace.

Israel's national security concerns (real and imagined) could have dramatically been allayed had the Arab states, and by extension all Muslim countries, been at peace with Israel. By rejecting the API, successive Israeli governments have made a mistake of historic proportions.

For the Palestinians, given their political factionalism and their approach to the conflict with Israel, only a comprehensive Arab-Israeli peace could have ended the occupation and established a Palestinian state. Here too, the Arab states failed to aggressively promote their own initiative and left the Palestinians to their devices.

Why now? There are a number of compelling reasons behind the United States', the Arab states', and Israel's lukewarm desire to resurrect the only peace initiative that provides the basis for a comprehensive Arab-Israeli peace. This will still take supreme efforts by the United States in particular because of the pervasive

---

339 Josef Federman, "Kerry Visit Revives Possibility of Arab Peace Plan," *The Times of Israel*, April 8, 2013, http://www.timesofisrael.com/kerry-visit-revives-possibility-of-arab-peace-plan/.

apprehensiveness, especially in Israel, regarding the unquantified change that will of necessity occur.

The failure to engage Israel and the Palestinians in productive negotiations during President Obama's first term and the growing concerns and frustrations over the continuing stalemate forced the United States to look into other viable options. The API stands out as the single most viable framework, especially because it was the initiative of the collective Arab political body.

The sweeping upheavals in the Middle East and the concerns over renewed Israeli-Palestinian violent confrontations resulting from the continuing stalemate are making the Arab states increasingly concerned. Thus, settling the Israeli-Palestinian conflict, which they view as the main source of regional instability, has assumed greater urgency. The API provides the vehicle around which all Palestinian factions can coalesce, with the full backing of the Arab states, in the search for an equitable solution.

Finally, in the wake of the Iranian threat and the uncertain outcome in Syria's civil war, the Arab states are looking to engage the United States in a meaningful effort to resolve the Israeli-Palestinian conflict. From their perspective, only the United States can bridge the gap between Israel and the Palestinians at a time of extreme uncertainty.

What would it take to succeed?

First, although the Arab states refuse to make any changes in the language of the API, the Secretary General of the Arab League (AL), Nabil El-Arabi, should publicly announce that Israeli acceptance of the API would of necessity require negotiations to iron out the details for any potential accord. That is, the API was never presented on a take it or leave it basis, albeit the various components of the Initiative must be dealt with and agreed upon in any peace agreement.

If such a statement is made following the meetings between the Arab League representatives (Foreign Ministers from Saudi Arabia, Qatar, Egypt, Morocco, and Jordan, a PA representative, and the Secretary General of the AL) and John Kerry in Washington next week,[340] it will go a long way toward persuading the Netanyahu government to accept the API in principle.

Second, the API offers Hamas, which must be an integral part of future negotiations, the opportunity to accept the API without requiring it to recognize Israel in advance and without accepting prior agreements as stipulated by the Quartet.[341]

That said, the Arab states, especially Egypt, must exert every effort to persuade Hamas to formally forsake violence and focus on a political solution as required by the API. Hamas' leaders, including Khaled Meshal and Ghazi Hamad, have already stated on more than one occasion that they will accept a two-state solution based on the 1967 borders. According to Hamad, "all factions in the movement agree to this and are prepared to accept it."[342]

Third, Israel should offer goodwill gestures by releasing Palestinian prisoners, which is an extremely sensitive issue for President Abbas, and declaring a temporary halt on building new and expanding old settlements in sensitive areas. In addition, as suggested by Secretary Kerry, Israel should release all tax revenues collected on behalf of the PA from Palestinian laborers.[343]

Fourth, although the API calls for the return of all territories captured in the 1967 war, the Arab states should not demand, at this phase, that Israel relinquish the Golan Heights. Given the civil war in Syria and the uncertainty that will surely follow the ouster

---

340 Laura Rozen, "Arab League to Meet With Kerry to Revive Arab-Israel Peace Initiative," *Al-Monitor*, April 18, 2013, http://backchannel. al-monitor.com/index.php/2013/04/5024/arab-league-may-reissue-arab-israel-peace-initiative-at-meeting-with-kerry-april-29/.

341 David Horovitz, "Editor's Notes: Still the Optimist," *The Jerusalem Post*, June 25, 2010, http://www.jpost.com/Opinion/Columnists/Editors-Notes-Still-the-optimist.

342 Shlomi Eldar, "Ghazi Hamad: Hamas Agrees To Accept State Within '67 Borders," *Al-Monitor*, April 4, 2013, http://www.al-monitor.com/pulse/originals/2013/04/razi-hammed-palestinian-state-67-borders.html.

343 "Israel Restarts Flow of Revenue to Palestine," *DW*, March 25, 2013, http://www.dw.de/israel-restarts-flow-of-revenue-to-palestine/a-16698641.

of Assad, it would be impossible for Israel to consider withdrawal from the Golan. The eventual Israeli withdrawal will have to follow an Israeli-Palestinian peace agreement and a stable Syria, which will provide Israel further assurance of what lies ahead.

Fifth, the United States must lean on Ankara to not muddy the waters, as intimated by John Kerry, by making unreasonable demands on Jerusalem in connection with lifting the blockade over Gaza.[344] Instead, Ankara should adopt a balanced approach by first restoring full diplomatic relations with Israel (especially now in the wake of the Israeli apology) and exert its substantial influence on Hamas to refrain from any violent provocation to encourage further easing of the blockade by Israel.

Sixth, Secretary General El-Arabi should reiterate publicly that the API clearly affirms that the Arab states will recognize Israel and establish full diplomatic relations once an accord with the Palestinians is achieved. This public statement will have a profound psychological impact on the Israeli public, which doubts the ultimate intentions of the Arab states.

The Israelis require these public assurances to engender grass-roots support for the API, especially following Obama's visit to Israel and his appeal to Israeli youth to lead the march for peace.[345] Any Israeli prime minister, including Netanyahu, will find himself in a difficult position not to embrace the API under such circumstances.

Seventh, Israeli think tanks, the academic community, youth and labor organizations, synagogues, the media, and all political parties that seek an end to the Israeli-Palestinian conflict should engage in new public narratives about each conflicting issue between Israel and the Palestinians. All options should be aired out so that the general public understands the imperatives they face and the concessions needed to reach a comprehensive solution.

344 Paul Richter, "John Kerry Urges Turkish Leader to Delay Gaza Strip Visit," *Los Angeles Times*, April 21, 2013, http://www.latimes.com/news/world/worldnow/la-fg-wn-john-kerry-turkey-20130421,0,2876820.story.

345 Barack Obama, "Speech in Jerusalem" (Jerusalem, Israel, March 21, 2013), http://www.theguardian.com/world/2013/mar/21/barack-obama-speech-jerusalem-text.

Finally, it is not far-fetched to suggest that Sheikh Hamad bin Khalifa al Thani, the Emir of Qatar, who is politically progressive and open to new ideas, invite Israeli President Shimon Peres to visit Doha. Al Thani, in a meeting with President Obama, has already voiced his support for the peace process, stating that "it's very important for us to see peace between Israel and the Palestinians, and to see also a good relationship between Arab countries and Israel once a Palestinian-Israeli peace agreement is reached."[346] Peres is a staunch supporter of the API and such a visit to an active Arab country in the pursuit of peace will send a clear message to Israelis and Palestinians alike that the Arab world is determined to end the Israeli-Palestinian conflict.

This will not be the first time that an Israeli official is invited to Doha. Former Foreign Minister Tzipi Livni (currently the Justice Minster) was invited to speak at the Doha conference in April 2008.[347] A state visit by President Peres will go a long way to demonstrate to skeptical Israelis that the Arab world is serious about peace.

Resurrecting the API offers the most promising prospect for a breakthrough; however, it will take the collective resolve of the Arab states, the Palestinians, Israel, and the United States to see it through.

346 Barack Obama and Amir Hamad, "Remarks by the President and Amir of Qatar After Bilateral Meeting" (Washington, DC, April 23, 2013), http://www.whitehouse.gov/the-press-office/2013/04/23/remarks-president-and-amir-qatar-after-bilateral-meeting.

347 Herb Keinon, "Senior Diplomatic Source: Qatar is a Bitter Enemy," *The Jerusalem Post*, November 28, 2012, http://www.jpost.com/Diplomacy-and-Politics/Senior-diplomatic-source-Qatar-is-a-bitter-enemy.

NO BETTER TIME TO REINSTATE
THE ARAB PEACE INITIATIVE

MARCH 14, 2014

As U.S. Secretary of State John Kerry is about to unveil his proposed framework for an Israeli-Palestinian peace agreement, there may not be a more opportune time than now to reinvigorate the API in support of Kerry's efforts. Certainly the geopolitical conditions in the Middle East have dramatically changed since the API was first introduced at the 2002 Arab League Summit in Beirut, Lebanon. Paradoxically, at this juncture of turmoil sweeping the region, the API is more relevant than ever before to generate new, badly-needed momentum for the peace process.

The meeting of Arab foreign ministers in Cairo on March 10th urged for the establishment of an independent sovereign Palestinian state in line with the API; they further reinforced the "continuing Arab commitment to the initiative as a strategic option."[348]

Although the Arab ministers' reference to the API as a strategic option and their call for an end to the conflict based on a two-state solution is positive and necessary (regardless of their merit), their outright rejection of Israel as a Jewish state or their demand that Jerusalem must become the capital of two states preempts and may well undermine Kerry's arduous efforts.

Instead of rehashing old slogans and making new demands on Israel, the Arab states should utilize the platform the API provides to push the peace negotiations forward rather than establish new red lines that can only harden the Israeli as well as the Palestinian positions.

---

348 "Peace in Mideast Remains Strategic Option – Arab Ministers," *Kuwait News Agency*, March 10, 2014, http://www.kuna.net.kw/ArticlePrintPage.aspx?id=2365524&language=en.

The efforts Kerry has and continues to exert to advance the Israeli-Palestinian peace process toward a comprehensive peace agreement may well be the last attempt by the Obama administration. Given the regional instability and the growing tension between Iran and the Arab states, Saudi Arabia and Egypt in particular have special interests in pushing for an Israeli-Palestinian peace and no longer need to obscure that with unhelpful public narratives. Here is why.

First, it is an open secret that relations between the Arab Sunni states and Israel have never been closer because of the perceived common threat of a nuclear-armed Iran. Israel and the Arab states are consulting each other, exchanging Iran-related intelligence, and developing a joint strategy to effectively deal with Iran's nuclear program.

Even if the proxy Shiite-Sunni war currently being waged in Iraq and Syria (led by Iran and Saudi Arabia) subsides, the long historic rivalry between the two sides will not be mitigated by Iran's current charm offensive. There is no love lost between them where centuries of enmity and hatred still looms high, which makes Arab-Israeli rapprochement not only desirable but also a strategic necessity.

Second, as John Kerry is preparing to disclose his framework for peace, demonstrable support by the Arab states along the lines of the API (which is consistent with Kerry's framework) will send a powerful message to both Prime Minster Netanyahu and President Abbas that the whole Arab world stands behind Kerry's initiative.

For the Israelis, it will be a reassuring message that the Arab states are now more than any time before committed to backing the peace efforts and providing the incentive to compromise. The Israeli and Palestinian governments know they must make significant concessions to reach an agreement. They also know that regardless of the inevitable changing regional dynamics in the years to come, the fundamental concessions required now to reach an agreement will not drastically change.

Third, given the turmoil in Syria, Israel would not need to grapple, at least not at this juncture, with the API's requirement to withdraw from the Golan Heights. This was one of the main impediments behind Israel's refusal to embrace the API in the first place.

Interestingly, in their formal statement from Cairo, the Arab ministers made no reference to the Golan Heights. In an earlier meeting with Kerry in April 2013, the Arab foreign ministers agreed to a "comparable and mutual agreed minor swap of the land,"[349] which the Israelis found to be very helpful.

In addition, an Israeli-Palestinian peace will be seen as another phase toward the establishment of a comprehensive Arab–Israeli peace, following the examples of the Egyptian and Jordanian peace treaties with Israel.

Notwithstanding semantics and public protestations to the contrary, both Israel and the Arab states face a fateful crossroad, and Kerry's efforts to forge an Israeli-Palestinian peace stand in contrast to any similar attempt in the past.

Time is their worst enemy; if the current negotiations fail, the Palestinians should not assume that turning to the UN by joining various agencies and seeking justice through the International Criminal Court (ICC) will bring an end to the Israeli occupation. At the end of the day, they must still sit face-to-face with the Israelis to find a mutually acceptable solution.

For Israel, the situation is even more acute because of the changing demographics in relation to the Palestinians, Israel's growing isolation from the international community, and the United States' weariness to pursue an elusive peace while losing much of its credibility and undermining its strategic interests.

Indeed, ahead of Netanyahu's visit to DC during the first week of March, President Obama warned that the United States may not be able to protect Israel if a two-state solution with the Palestinians fails.[350]

For these reasons, it is not enough for the Arab states to provide Kerry with lukewarm public support; they need to become active participants both publicly and privately and show solidarity with U.S.-led efforts to send a clear message to the Israeli and Palestinian publics where they really stand. Renewing the API as part and parcel

349 Daoud Kuttab, "Fatah Would Accept Land Swaps With Israel," *Al Monitor*, May 13, 2013, http://www.al-monitor.com/pulse/originals/2013/05/israel-qatar-land-swap-palestine.html#.

350 Goldberg, "Obama to Israel – Time Is Running Out."

of Kerry's initiative would create a new atmosphere conducive to accommodations, knowing that the future holds no better prospect.

Time and circumstances have changed; the balance of power in the region is being transformed, regional stability is elusive at best, Islamic militancy is on the rise, and the United States and Russia seem engaged in another "cold war," all of which add to the region's travails.

Given this state of affairs, the failure to achieve an agreement now could unwittingly plunge the Israelis and Palestinians into a new violent confrontation and drag the Unites States and the Arab states into a new conflict that they desperately want to avoid.

COEXISTENCE

ISRAEL AND THE PALESTINIANS
MUST FACE THE INESCAPABLE

AUGUST 8, 2011

Coexistence between Israel and the Palestinians is inevitable and, short of catastrophic developments, the two peoples are doomed or destined to live between the Mediterranean and the Jordan River. They must now decide on the quality of that coexistence. Do they want live with mutual hatred and fear while demonizing one another, or do they want to live in peace and amity and realize the biblical prophecy of making their shared land the true Land of Milk and Honey? No peace will ever be forged, let alone endure, unless both sides understand and appreciate each other's fears, concerns, hopes, and dreams. Only through direct social contacts and people-to-people dialogue will they overcome their mutually destructive perception of each other.

The Palestinians' perception of the Israelis as oppressive and uncaring people, determined to deny them basic rights, is anchored in their day-to-day experiences. As they see it, the continuing occupation, road blocks, humiliation, and usurpation of land further diminishes any prospect for peaceful cohabitation. The Israelis are viewed as an enemy to be hated, resisted, and undermined. As they see it, successive Israeli governments offered no reason for the Palestinians to change their minds and no cause to hope for a better tomorrow. And with a complacent Israeli public, what prospect is there for ordinary Palestinians to change their perception about Israel as an occupying, oppressive nation that continues its entrenchment in their land? Yet what effort have the Palestinians made to reach out to their Israeli counterparts and try understanding and appreciating their personal concerns and mindset that continues to feed into their inner tribulations and a sense of uncertainty and insecurity?

The Israelis, however, feel no better about the Palestinians. They see them as violent, unrelenting people who will not settle for anything less than the utter destruction of Israel, especially when such a sentiment is on display by radical Palestinian groups such as Hamas, Islamic Jihad, and others. The Israelis' experiences give them no reason to trust the Palestinians. They view them with ridicule and disdain as backward people wedded to habits and traditions that prevent them from rising to civilians deserving of a better fate. The Israelis too, however, never really fully appreciated the Palestinians' plight, suppression, and daily indignities and how these feeling manifest themselves, when in fact every Palestinian in the Occupied Territories wakes up each morning living in subjugation in his own homeland.

If coexistence is inevitable, however, the change of perceptions about each other becomes imperative. The need to hear each other's stories and life experiences, and the creation of a human connection is indispensable to normal relations. Only day-to-day encounters with each other in different settings can reveal the humanity that everyone shares. Listening to opposing views, understanding each other's pain and agony, and appreciating what the other is experiencing allow for a change of perception of each other. Indeed, being passionate about one cause, as both sides rightfully feel, does not preclude respecting the other's cause. Both must work peacefully to mitigate their differences; the inevitability of coexistence demands this. It is mutuality of respect, not necessarily an overall agreement that bridges the gap. Indeed, one need not change identity, cultural heritage, or religion to live in peace as long as there is mutual acceptance and respect. The realization that the other is just a normal human being with feelings, hopes, and aspirations creates that human connection so desperately needed between the two sides.

Successive Israeli governments and Palestinian authorities have failed miserably for the past 63 years to advance the cause of peace.

They have been engaged in mutual recrimination instead of facing the inevitable and charting a way forward to end the festering conflict that poisoned three generations of Israelis and Palestinians. They continue to be suspicious of each other's sinister intentions. The Palestinians accuse Israel of having a grand design to permanently occupy all of the land west of the Jordan River, and the Israelis accuse the Palestinians of plotting to dismantle Israel in stages.

Regardless of the current political maneuverings and their consequences, the next generation of Israelis and Palestinians must free themselves of these embedded prejudices that the continuing conflict feeds into. They must now begin to build ties to prevent a renewed cycle of violence. How else can trust be built, and to what end does one continue to fight those people with whom one must live indefinitely? The visible and the invisible walls between the two people must be torn down, but it takes determined people on both sides to do so. Both sides have the responsibility and the power to leave the past behind. Only the people can mold the present to whatever future they wish to have. Their governments, which failed them time and again by perpetuating mutual fear, will have no choice but to heed to their call. Peace and reconciliation must first be envisioned by the people because it can only come from the people. They must rise and demand change. Only they can bring an end to the dehumanization, mutual recrimination, and the ever-festering wrong perception of each other.

Past injustices and agonizing human tragedies and loses cannot be settled by acts of vengeance and retribution, which is the recipe for a continuing cycle of violence, but through dialogue and identification with each other's inner feelings, concerns, and trepidations. Dr. Izzeldin Abuelaish, the Palestinian physician who lost three daughters to Israeli shells in Gaza, had every reason to feel angry and hate every Israeli while seeking revenge, but he refused. "Many people" he said, "were expecting me to hate. My answer to them is I shall not hate. Let us hope for tomorrow."[351] Yitzhak Frankelthal, an Israeli father whose 19 year old son was kidnapped and then killed by Hamas, did not seek revenge either. Instead, he established Parent Circle, an organization of bereaved Israeli and Palestinian parents who too lost a

---

351 Lucy Ash, "The Palestinian and Israeli who Give Obama Hope," *BBC News*, May 20, 2011, http://www.bbc.co.uk/news/world-13469588.

loved one to this senseless violent struggle. "I gradually realized," he said, "that the only hope for progress [to bring an end to the Israeli-Palestinian struggle] was to recognize the face of the conflict."[352] More and more communities like the Oasis of Peace, Neve Shalom, must be established, where Israelis and Israeli-Palestinians choose voluntarily to live side by side. Neve Shalom remains the only place where their children live and grow together and foster relationships on which to build a new future.

Palestinians and Israelis must learn to overcome decades of mutual fear and lack of trust and together seek a new horizon. They must defy the present conditions that deepen their estrangement and begin to socially and openly connect. It is absurd that Israeli Jews can move everywhere between the Mediterranean and the Jordan River while the Israeli government deprives the Palestinians of the same privileges. Every Israeli who wants to live in peace must demand that this discriminatory law that prevents the Palestinians from entering Israel be annulled. Notwithstanding Israel's national security concerns, which must be considered, hundreds of thousands of Palestinians could readily and easily receive security clearance and be allowed to see and mingle with the "enemy," only to realize that the Israelis are not their nemeses, but simple people who yearn to live in peace. The same must also be applied to the Israelis who should flock into the West Bank the way they used to before the Second Intifada and reengage the Palestinian people with whom they must coexist. As Gene Knudsen Hoffman, a Quaker peace activist, said, "an enemy is one whose story you have not heard." If the Israelis do not take matter into their hands, who will? Who will bring an end to this debilitating anomalous existence that does nothing but breed more hatred and disdain?

The time has come for the people on both sides to tear down the shameful fences and walls and demand an end to this consuming madness. Only the people, Israelis and Palestinians alike, can begin to reconcile their national narratives and embrace the inevitability of coexistence to build a promising future for both people.

---

352 Ibid.

FACING THE INESCAPABLE REALITY

SEPTEMBER 8, 2011

The Palestinians' efforts to seek UN recognition of their own state will not serve the national interests of either the Palestinians or the Israelis. Such recognition, should it come to pass, will not change the reality on the ground in any significant way and may in fact further undermine Israeli-Palestinian relations, potentially leading to a violent confrontation. The solution to the Israeli-Palestinian conflict has and continues to depend on good faith negotiations based on the 1967 borders with some land swaps leading to a two-state solution, which both sides profess to seek.

The Netanyahu government and the Palestinian Authority (PA) must face the inescapable reality and agree to the realistic proposals set forth by President Obama, with the support of the Quartet, to start negotiations with borders and security without any other pre-conditions. Negotiating borders first will resolve the future status of more that 70 percent of the settlements, which is critical to the Palestinians. It will also mitigate Israel's security concerns, which is of extreme importance to the Israelis.

Only such an approach could lead to a two-state solution living side-by-side in peace and security. Indeed, Israeli-Palestinian coexistence is inevitable because both peoples are literally stuck between the Mediterranean and the Jordan River. Neither can dislodge the other short of a catastrophe of unimaginable magnitude.

There are extremist right-wing and ultra-Orthodox Israelis and extremist Palestinian groups like Hamas who seek to realize a greater Israel and greater Palestine respectively. They will continue to resort to any measures, including incessant violence, to realize their hopeless dreams. They have thus far failed and their eventual complete failure will be dictated by the reality on the grounds of coexistence.

The Palestinians will never defeat Israel militarily, and Israel will never succeed in sustaining the occupation and indefinitely subjugating the Palestinian people.

Israel was created as the last refuge for the Jewish people. It must remain free, independent, and democratic. Israel can—indeed it must—maintain the Jewish national identity of the state through a sustainable Jewish majority. The only way this vision can be realized is the creation of two states: a Jewish state and a Palestinian state.

To ensure the sustainability of the Jewish majority, the Israeli government must create the socioeconomic and political conditions that will make Israel the haven for all Jews. The failed Netanyahu/Lieberman policies have created the precise opposite conditions, forcing many Israelis to run away from Israel rather than staying and flourishing in their homeland. By last credible estimates, more than one million Israelis have emigrated to different countries seeking better opportunities. The growing socioeconomic gap between rich and poor and the lack of any prospect for peace with the Palestinians will force a still-growing number of Israelis to emigrate from the land once called the last refuge for the Jewish people.

It is not for the Palestinians to recognize Israel as a Jewish state as Netanyahu demands; it is for the Israelis themselves and their government to ensure the continuing Jewish identity of the state through a sustainable Jewish majority without racism and discrimination.

Israel's territory must be based on the 1967 borders with some land swaps of roughly five percent to allow for the incorporation of all Israeli settlements (three blocks of settlements) along the 1967 borders into Israel proper.

The territory of the Palestinian state must encompass the Gaza Strip and 95 percent or so of the West Bank, plus five percent of current Israeli territory to swap for five percent of the West Bank that will be incorporated into Israel proper.

Israel's national security under any peace agreement with the Palestinians cannot be achieved through the annexation of more territory as Netanyahu insists, but only through six comprehensive security and political measures:

1. Maintaining credible deterrence that will inhibit any Palestinian group or states in the region from posing a serious threat to Israel;

2. Insisting on a demilitarized Palestinian state with the exception of maintaining internal Palestinian security forces that cooperate fully with their Israeli counterparts;

3. Stationing of a robust international peacekeeping force along the Jordan River under American command to prevent the penetration of terrorists and the smuggling of weapons;

4. Establishing a regional security pact among all the states in the area with a vested interest in maintaining peace with Israel;

5. Encouraging people-to-people cultural exchanges, trade, and tourism to foster neighborly relations between the two sides;

6. And finally, changing the political narratives about each other to disabuse a growing number of Israelis and Palestinians of the notion that one harbors the eventual destruction, displacement, or domination of the other.

As the security situation gradually stabilizes and the extremists on both sides accept the inescapable reality of coexistence, Israel can eventually remove all security barriers to allow for the unimpeded movement of goods and people in both directions across the borders.

Under any peace agreement, there will be some Israelis who will continue to live in the Palestinian state and Palestinians (other than the Israeli-Palestinians) who will continue to live in Israel. Those Israelis and Palestinians who will live in each other's state will be given the status of permanent resident who can vote or be elected only in their respective countries. This will not only solve the problem of some settlers who by agreement with the Palestinians choose to stay in the West Bank under the Palestinians Authority, but will also sustain the national identity of both Israel as a Jewish state and Palestine for the Palestinian Arabs.

The Israelis must now rise not only against the vast socioeconomic gap between the rich and poor, but against the defunct Netanyahu/Lieberman policies toward the Palestinians that, if not changed, will bring Israel to the brink of socioeconomic and political disaster.

ALON BEN-MEIR

THE LESSONS OF BUDRUS—
SEVEN YEARS LATER

SEPTEMBER 12, 2011

I recently spoke at the New York United Nations Association following a screening of the documentary *Budrus*, named after a Palestinian village in the West Bank. Although I carefully followed the
events in that small village as they occurred in 2003–2004, when I
previewed the documentary, I realized how little has changed since
that time in Israeli-Palestinian relations. A village of 1,500 residents
was determined to use peaceful protests to prevent the Israeli Defense Department from building a security fence that would separate
the village from the rest of the West Bank.

Events that could have had tragic consequences ended in the
villagers' triumphant peaceful resistance that accommodated Israel's
security requirements while restoring their way of life with dignity.
Now, what lessons have Israelis and Palestinians learned from this
compelling story of nonviolent resistance against occupation?

First, only peaceful resistance can improve the dynamic on the
ground. This was proven over the past nearly three years when the
PA in the West Bank determined that only by renouncing violence
as a means to achieve their national objective of statehood will the
inevitability of peaceful coexistence finally set in.

The contrast between the West Bank and Gaza is extraordinarily
stark. Whereas the West Bank has developed state infrastructure with
social and political institutions, shopping centers, and movie theaters,
while internal security maintains law and order with full cooperation
with Israel, much of Gaza remains a wasteland.

This is not because of the Israeli blockade, but primarily because Hamas refuses to renounce violence and still calls for Israel's
destruction. This position forces Hamas to focus on security by

acquiring offensive weapons against Israel instead of providing the people with economic opportunities and the building of the foundation of state in cooperation with its counterpart in the West Bank.

The second lesson from the Budrus experience is that Israel's legitimate security concerns can be mitigated by minor border adjustments through land swaps without displacing a single Palestinian and without uprooting hundreds of olive trees, which is one of the main sources of the villagers' livelihood.

Contrary to Netanyahu's contention that the 1967 borders are not defensible, in the age of missiles and rockets one might ask, what borders are indeed defensible? Is Gaza's border defensible? Will acquiring swaths of land by Israel in Gaza make any difference from a security perspective?

The truth is that only peace that meets the mutual requirements of both sides makes nearly any border peaceful and even a source of cooperation, trade, and a host of other exchanges. Budrus has demonstrated that Israel remains as secure by building the fence along the 1967 lines without infringement on Palestinian territory. Under conditions of sustainable peace, the fence could eventually be removed altogether and allow for free movement of people and goods in both directions.

The Budrus story further suggests that extremism will serve neither the Israeli nor the Palestinian cause. Extremists on both sides can disrupt and delay the peace process, but will never be able to prevent peace from being realized because a majority on both sides yearns for peace. This was further emphasized by the Hamas supporter featured in the film, a father of seven children and a teacher who initially was skeptical about "peaceful" resistance. But once he realized that many Israelis were also against the occupation and came out in droves in support of the Palestinians in Budrus by joining them hand in hand, he too came to the conclusion that there is reason to believe that the conflict can be resolved without bloodshed.

Budrus highlights an important and often overlooked element in the process of peaceful resistance, namely the role of women. Unlike military and political processes which often exclude women and families, these parties can participate and support nonviolence resistance. Women were at the forefront of the protests in Budrus, which empowered them to take a stake in protecting their village. By protesting alongside men, both Israeli and Palestinian, the women of Budrus showed that this conflict transcends cultural boundaries to unify and bolster their community and home.

The story of Budrus also uncovered mutual misperceptions of Israelis and Palestinians while revealing the basic humanity and the sheer desire to live in peace. The Palestinians realized that not all Israelis are gun-wielding, ready to kill any Palestinian, as they have been portrayed by Palestinian extremists and the media.

In turn, the Israelis who joined the Palestinians' protest against the fence realized that these villagers simply want to live a peaceful life. They harbor no ill feelings toward the Israelis and accept Israel as a neighbor with whom they want to cooperate as long as Israel does not infringe on their autonomy.

The inescapable conclusion of this poignant story is that Israeli-Palestinian coexistence is not one of many choices, but the only choice. Israelis and Palestinians must now choose between continuing strife, bloodshed, and poison one generation after another, or live in peace and prosperity together.

Unilateral action by either side will go nowhere. Neither continued occupation nor the quest to attain UN recognition of a Palestinian state will serve either side's national interest. The solution to the Israeli-Palestinian conflict rests on good-faith negotiations, provided that both sides accept what the villagers of Budrus and the Israelis who came to support them have accepted all along: live and let live.

DISTRUST AND THE REALITY
OF COEXISTENCE

DECEMBER 10, 2012

One of the main impediments to resolving the Israeli-Palestinian conflict is the complete lack of trust between the two sides. What makes the conflict even more intractable is that neither side believes that their distrust can be mitigated given the history of the conflict, their contrasting objectives, and the day-to-day experiences reinforced by the constant maligning of each other through their public narratives. This results in an ever-diminishing prospect for reconciliation which inhibits concessions and drives both sides to resort to a zero-sum negotiating posture. Moreover, due to their respective public sentiments (hate and animosity toward the other), pessimism, and resistance to change, neither side wants to appear weak. As a result, they refuse to show flexibility, and in so doing, distrust becomes further ingrained intellectually and emotionally, creating a vicious cycle which defies reason and reality.

It is clear that if the Israelis and the Palestinians hold fast to their positions, it will be near-impossible to allay distrust, leading to a permanent deadlock, because distrust cannot be negotiated by simply agreeing to establish a new trusting relationship. In fact, even if the two parties negotiate and reach an agreement, such as the 1993–1994 Oslo Accords, there is still no way to ensure that such agreements could endure given the embedded distrust that both had and continue to harbor against one another, as neither side lived up to their obligations as stipulated by the Accords. But since Israeli-Palestinian coexistence, in one form or another, is the only option, any agreement reached must be based on certain provisions, mechanisms, logistics, and a timeline designed to ensure compliance based on reciprocity that would nurture trust, which is a prerequisite to lasting agreements.

The claims and counter-claims by Israeli and Palestinian officials that distrust prevents them from reaching a peace agreement is baseless, not only because they coexist and neither can change this reality, but because distrust cannot be mitigated in a vacuum. Their relationship must be established on the fact that coexistence is irrevocable. Trust can then be nurtured not only as they negotiate and reach an agreement that meets their principle requirements, but through an agreement based on meeting each other's obligations in a specific time frame. For example, in 2000 and 2008–2009, the Israelis and the Palestinians were nearly able to reach an agreement on even the most contentious issues, such the future of Jerusalem and the Palestinian refugees, but nevertheless failed. At close scrutiny, we find that at play were biased and selective perceptions, reinforced by historical experiences and nurtured by distrust and concern over each other's ability or willingness to deliver.

The Israeli withdrawal from Gaza in 2005 reaffirms the concept that mere withdrawal, which was viewed by Israel as a major move to demonstrate its intentions to end the occupation, failed to achieve Israel's "presumed objective." Instead of turning a free Gaza into a prosperous area, building the infrastructure for an independent entity on the way to statehood, Hamas, after wrestling the strip from the PA, used Gaza as a staging ground for launching thousands of rockets against Israel. For most Israelis, this was interpreted as a clear sign that the Palestinians simply do not want peace and cannot be trusted. As a result, Israel was discouraged from further evacuation of Palestinian territories in the West Bank (as was articulated in the Kadima platform),[353] and most Israelis still believe that even if Israel were to withdraw from the West Bank, the Palestinians would still seek the destruction of the state as Hamas repeatedly enunciates.

From the Palestinians' perspective, however, the Israeli withdrawal from Gaza was a tactical move. They insist that Israel simply wanted to rid itself from occupying a densely populated area of Palestinians, which has no strategic value and is prohibitively costly.

353 Mazal Mualem, "Kadima Platform Includes Jewish Majority in Exchange for Territorial Concessions," *Haaretz*, November 29, 2005, http://www.haaretz.com/print-edition/news/kadima-platform-includes-jewish-majority-in-exchange-for-territorial-concessions-1.175413.

Furthermore, the Palestinians are convinced that the Israelis do not consider Gaza an important part of their biblical claim to the entire so-called "land of Israel," and that Israel has no intentions of vacating other occupied Palestinian territories, especially in the West Bank. Moreover, the Palestinians further argue that although peaceful coexistence has generally prevailed between Israel and the PA in the past several years, Israel continues to expand current settlements and build new ones, a fact that cannot be denied. For this reason, the Palestinians have no reason to trust the Israelis, who presumably support the two-state solution while continuing to act contrary to the logical and practical requirements to effectuate such a solution.

The question before us then is, had the Israeli withdrawal from Gaza been done differently, would the outcome have been any different, or at a minimum, vindicated or repudiated the narrative of either side? My answer is absolutely yes. The Israeli withdrawal from Gaza was precipitous and unilateral with no coordination with the PA and without assessing Hamas' power, and entailed no phased withdrawal, with no new security arrangement in place and no agreement on trade and commercial ties to foster human-to-human relations that engender trust. Thus, it can be argued that had then-Prime Minister Sharon reached an agreement with the PA about every aspect of the withdrawal, including the number of phases, the length of time between each phase, specific reciprocal moves on the part of the Palestinians, and tight security arrangements, the move would have nurtured trust between the two sides. Surely, both sides would have known full well that any violation of the specific agreed-upon arrangements would stop the process in place, an action from which neither side could benefit, regardless of their real intentions.

It should be recalled that it took three years for Israel to complete its withdrawal from the Sinai. It is true that the difference between the withdrawal from Gaza and the Sinai is significant in scope and span; there should have been no difference, however, in the principles that guided the withdrawal from the Sinai to those from Gaza. Had Israel followed the same pattern, it would be safe to assume that Hamas might not have been able to overthrow the PA in Gaza or win the elections in 2006. Indeed, the Israeli presence, after announcing its intention to withdraw from Gaza, should have lasted long enough to allow the PA to establish its own security apparatus, engage in economic development over the transitional period, and develop a vested interest in the new peaceful arrangements while fostering trust between the two sides. The same can be said about Israel's abrupt and unilateral withdrawal from southern Lebanon by former Prime Minister Barak under cover of night without any agreement with the Lebanese government, which gave Hezbollah the opportunity to consolidate power. Could a prior agreement with an enforcement mechanism in place have prevented the war between Israel and Hezbollah in 2006? The answer may be speculative but the question remains valid.

Obviously, trust cannot be fostered in an environment of hostility and mutual recrimination. However, distrust is not set in stone; it can and should be alleviated, especially under the circumstances that govern the lives of Israelis and Palestinians. Israel must now learn from its experience with Egypt verses Gaza and Lebanon and apply these lessons to the West Bank. Israeli arguments against withdrawal, citing distrust and national security concerns, are thus unfounded. If these were the real reasons and not the further usurpation of Palestinian land, both concerns could be mitigated by developing a comprehensive planned withdrawal from Area B, followed by C, extending over a period of several years and based on reciprocity on the part of the PA, while continuing and further enhancing security cooperation to ensure an orderly transition. The PA has demonstrated that it has the ability, capacity, and the resolve to deliver and live up to its commitments, to which many Israeli officials attest.[354]

The recent flare-up between Israel and Hamas and the elevation of the Palestinians' status to a nonmember observer state at the UNGA have introduced a new aspect to the Israeli-Palestinian conflict. Notwithstanding Israel's military prowess, Hamas was able to justifiably claim political victory, and the PA's triumph at the UN

---

354 International Crisis Group, "Squaring the Circle: Palestinian Security Reform Under Occupation," Middle East Report no. 98 (September 7, 2010), http://www.crisisgroup.org/~/media/Files/Middle%20East%20North%20Africa/Israel%20Palestine/98%20Squaring%20the%20Circle%20--%20Palestinian%20Security%20Reform%20under%20Occupation.ashx (accessed December 8, 2012). Numerous Israeli officials are cited throughout, attesting to these observations.

demonstrated how isolated Israel has become. Nevertheless, Israel remains the pre-eminent power; the Palestinians and all Arab states must come to term with this reality.

In the final analysis, guided by the imperative of coexistence, genuine efforts can and must be made to mitigate distrust through a peace process based on reciprocal and reinforced provisions, to which both Israelis and Palestinians must commit to reach a lasting peace agreement.

AN OPEN LETTER TO THE
ISRAELIS AND PALESTINIANS

JULY 9, 2014

I have been writing about your conflict for more than three decades. Invariably, I find myself delving into the same themes time and again, as the nature of the conflict remains the same. You coexist, and short of self-inflicted catastrophe, you are destined to coexist until the end of time. You must now choose to live in harmony and peace, or in self-consuming enmity and hate.

No Israeli or Palestinian child should ever die for a cause that defies reality and reason. Taking teens hostage and horrifically killing them in cold blood, or abducting a child and gristly burning him alive defies your religious beliefs and the basic tenets of your humanity.

Like beasts, the militant madmen among you creep in the shadows for their prey, satisfying their lust for revenge and retribution. They disgrace you as a people and a nation, while poisoning the next generations with hostility and disdain, robbing them of their future and destroying the little hope left to live in harmony and peace.

A majority of you Israelis and Palestinians are crying out for peace, yearning still for that elusive day when you can retire to bed without fear and face tomorrow excited about what lies ahead. Every day that exacts blood and torments so many is a day when your graves are dug ever deeper, burying innocent children and any hope for a better future.

The gap between you grows ever wider, feeding the vicious cycle of death and destruction. Instead of reaching out compassionately, you obliterate the last traces of empathy toward one another, knowing that there is no place to go but together.

You, the so-called leaders, are the culprits behind this miserable state of being. Immersed in blind ideology and misguided religious dogmas and possessed by a messianic mission, you incite your people and fan the flames of acrimony and violence.

Shame on you Naftali Bennett, you are a zealous madman. You want to annex much of the West Bank and openly preach the invasion of Gaza. You proclaim that war with Hamas is inevitable and "It's preferable that we're [the Israelis] the ones who initiate it."[355]

You are a menace to the people of Israel whom you presumably wish to protect. It is alright that hundreds of Israelis and Palestinians die as long as you continue to amass fortunes and enjoy the opulence that life can offer.

And what about you, Ismail Haniyeh, Hamas' misguided leader, you are a fanatic fool who refuses to see the light. You extolled the kidnapping of the three Israeli youth, you call for another Intifada, and encourage "the escalation of the resistance,"[356] only to watch thousands of Palestinians die as sacrificial lambs to satisfy your twisted ego and hollow religious convictions.

And Israel's Deputy Defense Minister Danny Danon, you have long since lost your moral bearings; unabashedly you advocate collective punishment of the Palestinians, proudly announcing: "If terrorists find refuge among Palestinians, then Palestinians will pay the price."[357]

Khaled Meshal, Hamas' brazen political leader, you encourage more abduction of Israelis and with venom you "congratulate" the abductors as if this is the recipe to be "[free] from the prisons of the occupation."[358] You invite more misery on so many innocent

---

355 Raphael Ahren and Stuart Winer, "Ministers Split on Military Response to Teens' Killings," *The Times of Israel*, July 1, 2014, http://www.timesofisrael.com/ministers-split-on-military-response-to-teens-killings/.

356 "U.N. Says Palestinian Deaths in Israeli Manhunt 'Alarming'," *Naharnet*, June 23, 2014, http://www.naharnet.com/stories/en/136224.

357 Lahav Harkov, "Danon: Cut Palestinians' Ramadan Perks Until Captives are Released," *The Jerusalem Post*, June 26, 2014, http://www.jpost.com/National-News/Danon-Cut-Palestinians-Ramadan-perks-until-captives-are-released-360682.

358 Jack Khoury, "Hamas Chief Lauds Abductors of Israeli Teens, Says Has No New Information," *Haaretz*, June 23, 2014, http://www.haaretz.com/news/diplomacy-defense/1.600759.

Palestinians, who simply want to live a normal life devoid of constant anguish and pain.

Prime Minister Netanyahu, you cannot hide behind your tempered reaction to the abduction of the three Israeli teenagers and your expressions of sympathy to the family of the young Palestinian boy who was beaten and set on fire. You are now reaping the fruits of your relentless expansionism and blind ideological bent.

You have created this untenable situation between you and the Palestinians and largely contributed to the impasse and the hopelessness of ever reaching a peace agreement.

This is your plight, Israelis and Palestinians alike; you are led by inept, self-centered leaders with no vision and no courage. Have you ever paused and asked the simple question: where do we go from here? None of you—Bennett, Haniyeh, Netanyahu, Meshal, and Abbas—now what will be the fate of Israel and Palestine in 5 or 10 years should you continue to pursue your bankrupt policies.

You, Israeli and Palestinian leaders and people, must come to terms with the harsh reality you refuse to face. You are stuck; there is no escape and no future without the other.

You radical Palestinians who seek the destruction of Israel will do so at your peril. Israel is here to stay and will never die alone. And you Israeli zealots who conspire to thwart the Palestinians' aspiration for a state of their own will irreparably erode Israel as a Jewish state. Israel will become a garrison state, isolated and loathed by the community of nations.

Paradoxically, Netanyahu and Abbas, you can still change the current perilous path. If you truly desire to achieve peace based on a two-state solution, then prove it by rising to the call of the hour and turn the tragedies of recent days into a triumph over the evil of extremism.

This is the time when you must stand tall together and proclaim your unshakable commitment to realize peace now, in our time. You have the moral responsibility to make the sacrifice of innocent Israeli and Palestinian children, whose lives were cut short, the catalyst for peace and not the cause of more violence and death.

Netanyahu, you can no longer use the potential fall of your coalition government as an excuse for making gratuitous concessions to the Palestinians. Do not listen to the hawks and invade Gaza time and again.

Once the calm is restored, you must muster the courage, dissolve your government, and form a new coalition dedicated to the path of peace.

In spite of your past mistakes, you still possess the leadership qualities needed now to prevent the looming disaster. This could be your long career's finest hour, or the hour of infamy and shame for failing to rise above the fray.

Abbas, you too must make the hard choice. Whereas your unity government is preferred for peace negotiations, you must demand that Hamas adhere to the rules of engagement and no longer permit Hamas to have it both ways.

You must insist that Hamas's leaders forsake violence once and for all, or dump them to wallow in their own morass. They will pay dearly for betraying their fellow Palestinians in Gaza, who are despairing for a taste of freedom and a glimmer of hope.

You, Israelis and Palestinians of conscience, must now raise your voices and be heard loud and clear: enough is enough, no more bloodshed, no more waste of precious lives, no more tears, and no more heartbroken mothers and fathers.

The time has come for you to strive for peace, as the continuation of conflict will never yield a winner but only mutual death and destruction. There is no glory, no heroism, no dignity, and no martyrdom in death, when peace is within your grasp.

TRAPPED BETWEEN DELUSION AND DENIAL

JULY 30, 2014

Israelis and Palestinians have been trapped for decades between delusion and denial, and both have resorted to ideological and religious dogmas that dismiss with conviction any factual evidence to the contrary.

A powerful Israeli right-of-center constituency led by Prime Minster Netanyahu insists that Israel is not an occupying power, the settlements are not impediments to peace, Jerusalem will never become the capital of two states, Palestinian hatred of Israelis is at the core of the conflict, the Palestinians do not seek real peace and are committed to Israel's destruction, and the blockade of Gaza is justified for security reasons.

The Palestinians' delusions about their reality are no less absurd as they continue to demand the right of return of the refugees and claim that Israel is a foreign implant in the region and has no right to exist, Israel has no real national security concerns, and all Israelis are sworn to prevent the establishment of a Palestinian state.

Their actions and reactions to each other's transgressions only validated these delusions, which have tragically perpetuated the conflict. Thus, little room is left for any bilateral constructive discourse as suspicion, hatred, and distrust became deeply embedded in their respective public psyches, creating psychological, political, and physical divides.

Not surprisingly, this sad state of affairs is now glaringly manifested, once again, by the war between Israel and Hamas (an organization that represents a relatively small segment of the Palestinian population).

There will be no victors, only losers, emerging from this war, and though both sides are sustaining terrible losses, they still find comfort in their delusions and refuse to face the truth. As Kierkegaard once observed, "We can...be deceived in many ways. We can be deceived by believing what is untrue, but we certainly are also deceived by not believing what is true."[359]

There are many Israelis who strongly believe that Israel now has the opportunity to wipe out Hamas once and for all. In a recent column, Michael Oren, the former Israeli ambassador to the United States, strongly advocated that "Israel must be permitted to crush Hamas in the Gaza Strip."[360]

This is the kind of delusion that blinds him and many of his compatriots who do not comprehend how ominous their position is concerning Hamas. Israel can destroy every tunnel and every rocket and even decapitate Hamas' leadership, but this will prove to be futile and bordering on insanity as Hamas as a movement still enjoys some grassroots support.

Such madness will only give rise to a new generation of radical Islamist Palestinians who will carry the banner of Hamas, but with a far-greater vehemence and determination to violently resist Israel.

No one can accuse Oren of being stupid, but then, as Saul Bellow aptly put it, "a great deal of intelligence can be invested in ignorance when the need for illusion is deep."[361]

Conversely, Hamas can terrorize the Israelis, spread fear and cause havoc among the civilian population, and inflict major human and material loses, but it will never defeat Israel militarily; this only strengthens the Israelis' resolve, however delusionary, to eradicate Hamas as a terrorist organization.

The irony is that all of Israel's military might has failed to deter Hamas. An organization under siege with extremely limited financial resources was able to build a sophisticated network of tunnels, purchase and manufacture more than 10,000 rockets, train thousands

---

359 Søren Kierkegaard, *Works of Love*, trans. Howard V. Hong and Edna H. Hong (Princeton, NJ: Princeton University Press, 1995), 5.

360 Michael Oren, "Israel Must Be Permitted to Crush Hamas," *The Washington Post*, July 24, 2014, http://www.washingtonpost. com/opinions/michael-oren-israel-must-be-permitted-to-crush-hamas/2014/07/24/bd9967fc-1350-11e4-9285-4243a40ddc97_story.html.

361 Saul Bellow, *To Jerusalem and Back* (New York: Viking Press, 1976), 127.

of fighters, and ready itself to face down Israel's formidable military machine from underground and from the air.

Moreover, the disproportionate deaths of Palestinian civilians, especially children, versus the number of casualties among Hamas' combatants evoked international outcry, putting Israel on the defensive. Never mind that Hamas is using innocent civilians as human shields; Israel, not Hamas, is accused of indiscriminate killings, allowing Hamas to win the public relations war.

The war will eventually come to an end. The question is, will the terms for ending the bloody conflict set the stage for the next round of hostilities, or will both sides shed their delusions, recognize each other and stop this vicious cycle of violence?

For Hamas, this is not just a battle for easing the blockade or lifting it altogether; it is a battle for its very existence. However, Hamas painted itself into a corner; after having innocent civilians suffer so much death and destruction, failing to lift the blockade at some point in the future is tantamount to political suicide.

Although Netanyahu cannot crush Hamas as a movement, he hopes to unravel the unity government. Regardless, he no longer accepts, and rightfully so, a long-term ceasefire unless all tunnels are destroyed and Gaza is demilitarized, with the PA's security forces in charge of all border crossings.

For the above reasons, any solution will have to disabuse Israel and Hamas of the illusion that either can rid itself of the other. Now that so much death and destruction has been inflicted on one another, perhaps they can stop and think where all this insanity is leading to.

Thus, any effort to find a solution following the initial humanitarian ceasefire must be based on a formula in which Israel and Hamas share important common denominators that could meet their principal requirements and open the door for serious peace negotiations between Israel and the Palestinian unity government.

Being weary of Islamic extremism, the Arab states have largely abandoned Hamas and are now in a much stronger position to squeeze Hamas to adopt the Arab Peace Initiative (API), which remains the only realistic formula and has been on the table for 12 years.

The API recognizes Israel's right to exist and provides for the establishment of an independent Palestinian state to live side by side with Israel and permanent peace, and the recognition of Israel by the Arab and Muslim states.

There is wide support in Israel for the API, and here is where President Obama must finally put his foot down and insist that the Netanyahu government embrace the API to provide the foundation for credible peace negotiations.

Every Arab and Muslim state has endorsed the API. Qatar and Turkey, in particular, enjoy considerable influence on Hamas and can now exert real pressure on the organization to embrace the API. Several statements made in the past by Hamas' political leaders are very consistent with the main provisions of the API, which recognize Israel's right as a state along with the creation of a Palestinian state.

For nearly seven decades, Israelis and Palestinians have been marred with delusions and denial, planning and plotting to undermine one another instead of building human bridges and coming to accept their shared destiny.

The question is, will Israel's and Hamas' leaders learn anything from this horrifying war, or, to paraphrase Dostoyevsky, will they continue to delude themselves and come to a point where they "become unable to recognize truth, either in himself or in anyone else"?[362]

This war has introduced a new dimension to the Israeli-Palestinian conflict. Whether the Israelis and Palestinians are destined to live and prosper or destroy each other is the question they must ponder, because neither will survive without the other living in peace and security.

---

362 Fyodor Dostoyevsky, *The Brothers Karamazov* (New York: Bantam Dell, 2003), 55.

CONFLICT RESOLUTION

DEFYING THE RULES OF CONFLICT RESOLUTION

JUNE 13, 2011

The study of conflict resolution is prefaced on the notion that two parties in conflict desire a mutually acceptable resolution to end their dispute, however intractable it may be. The behavior by Israel and the Palestinians, however, suggests a different desired outcome. Whereas both talk about their desire to make peace, their actual actions on the ground demonstrate differently. Today, Israelis and Palestinians alike are defying essential principles of conflict resolution, serving to prolong rather than conclude their festering conflict.

Diminishing Returns

To achieve a resolution, parties in conflict must believe that continuing their dispute provides diminishing returns. That is, they must exhaust all possibilities to improve upon their positions and recognize that the situation of both sides can only be improved through compromise and cooperation. Recent developments indicate that neither Israel nor the Palestinians have come to this conclusion.

In fact, their behavior suggests the opposite. Today, each side has contributed to preservation of the status quo: Israel through settlement

547

construction and arrogant intransigence in recognizing any merit to Palestinian positions, and Palestinians through their refusal to return to the negotiating table and insistence on the right of return of the Palestinian refugees, which Israel will not accept. The status quo has become a political asset for each side, even at the risk of serving as a strategic liability for the future of both peoples. Furthermore, with short-term political considerations dominating the political discourse in Ramallah and Jerusalem, neither side has indicated any willingness to take the kind of calculated risk that will be necessary to resolve the conflict. Without calculated risks, or efforts that begin to mitigate the conflict, it is impossible to move forward toward a resolution—and today in Israel and Palestine, there is neither. Furthermore, the cost of maintaining the conflict today is currently acceptable to both sides. The economy in Israel and the West Bank is thriving, and it is even improving in the Gaza Strip, where Hamas' relationship with Egypt is improving with the renewed open border. From each side's perspective, today's conflict is manageable in the immediate term, even if both parties appear headed off a cliff in the not-too-distant future.

A Zero-Sum Game

Successful conflict resolution also requires a non-zero-sum approach based on mutual compromises and mutual gains. Today, there is no such give and take between Israelis and Palestinians. Both sides believe that any compromise constitutes a "loss" and the other side's "gain." This situation is aggravated by the complete lack of trust today between the two sides. Without trust, political or real security risks are perceived to be virtually impossible to take.

Through their hardline postures and rhetoric, each side is discrediting the notion and diminishing the prospect of mutual gains in the future. Their actions are even worse. Here, the "giving," for example, in relation to any territorial concession by either side, is seen as a sacrifice and the "taking" is considered to be deserved and overdue. Positions are not described in terms of what is possible, rather in, "what is ours." This diminishes the value of any give and take, makes it more difficult to conduct negotiations, and it becomes even harder for conflict resolution efforts to succeed.

Lack of Outside Pressure

If the parties in a conflict are under some level of outside pressure to reach a compromise, there is a greater incentive to reach one. Today, the international community is weary of the Israeli-Palestinian conflict, and their resulting approach is one that is serving to perpetuate rather than resolve it. There is no pressure on Israelis or Palestinians to act. In fact, their intransigence has been aided and even encouraged by their international benefactors. For Israel, the image of virtually every member of Congress giving a standing ovation for Prime Minster Netanyahu's diatribe of preconditions and insults confirms the unhelpful and even harmful laissez faire attitude the American Congress has taken with regard to Israel's self-destructive policies.

Meanwhile, the American Jewish community has been similarly idle. Rather than an outcry, the Jewish community is providing support for whatever Israel's policy happens to be, however reckless. For the Palestinians, their refusal to return to the negotiating table has been encouraged by the international community's burgeoning support for a United Nations General Assembly (UNGA) resolution which ignores any possibility of a negotiated agreement. The Palestinians may have greater international support today than at any point in their history. Instead of interpreting this backing as support for calculated risks toward peace, the Palestinians have understood the international support as providing further incentives to refuse a return to talks and hold out for greater gains in the future. In addition, like American Jews standing by Israel in its foolhardy approaches, the Arab world is blindly supporting the Palestinians, rather than encouraging them toward a historic peace agreement. Even worse, Iran is serving to encourage continued conflict through its support of its proxies, Hamas and Hezbollah.

Domestic Complacency

Domestic outcries for conflict resolution create greater political will to generate steps to achieve it. In Israel, economic growth and a stable security environment have blinded Israelis into believing the status quo is sustainable. Support and outcry for making necessary concessions to reach an agreement hardly exists. Prime Minister Netanyahu's approval rating soared by 13 percent after his address to the U.S. Congress in which he provided a blueprint for prolonging the current Israeli-Palestinians stalemate. The public has been similarly complacent on the Palestinian side. The surge of Palestinian activism has been focused on efforts to isolate Israel and to demand an end to the Fatah-Hamas split, not for efforts to reach a historic compromise with Israel.

The reasons for this complacency are three-fold. First, each side fears the unknown. The Arab Spring has the region facing a period of unprecedented change. Rather than proactively seeking to shape this period of change, each side's reluctance is based on a fear that the devil they know—continued conflict—is perhaps safer than the devil they don't—a comprehensive resolution reached through mutual compromises. Second, there is a lack of political consensus on both sides. Without a clear path developed by policymakers on both sides, each is settling for the lowest common denominator. Without consensus, Jerusalem and Ramallah have settled on internal compromises of mediocrity and inaction. Finally, each side is locked into old political narratives against one another while each side is suffering from internal division, which is hardly conducive to united political action. Israel remains focused on an archaic notion of security despite the changed landscape of warfare and defense in the region. Rather than recognize that the only guarantee for security is through a comprehensive peace, Israel is locked into a narrative of an inability to compromise for peace because of the security liabilities they worry it would create. Meanwhile, Palestinians remain committed to the impossible return of refugees to Israel and Hamas' repeated existential threats against Israel. The teaching of this narrative in schools and the espousing of the right of return by politicians to the Palestinian public is politically expedient. These hardened positions are incompatible with genuine efforts to reach a lasting two-state solution.

Prevailing Pessimism

To achieve a resolution to a conflict, both sides must believe that they can succeed. Being positive about the prospect of a deal is an important mindset—if you are entering a room to negotiate without a belief that it will lead anywhere, it will then be a self-fulfilling prophecy. That is what is happening today in the Israeli-Palestinian conflict. Neither side believes in the merits of negotiations at the present time. The two publics are equally skeptical about the prospect for peace. This is a dangerous combination. If peace is not possible, why try? Why create alternatives that could offer mutual accommodations? Why be creative? Without hope that the conflict can be resolved, there is no motivation to work toward a historic compromise—and violence becomes the more likely outcome. In the current pessimistic atmosphere, creative ideas in the search for a solution are being stifled and readily dismissed, if not ostracized and condemned. After years of failure, the parties and the international community are equally wary of concepts which have been tried and failed in the past as they are of new and inventive ones.

The Religious Component

In conflict resolution, different political ideas are considered, argued about, and negotiated ad nauseam if need be until a compromise is reached, provided that the parties are committed to a resolution. Even in intractable conflicts, time highlights the inability to sustain hardened ideologies, leading to an eventual realization in the benefits of a change in tactics toward greater compromise and cooperation. The religious components of the Israeli-Palestinian conflict have obfuscated this process. Religious precepts deem that it does not matter if one side is right or wrong—God ordained it, and so it is so. The Jews' affinity, for example, to Jerusalem and the Palestinians' claim of East Jerusalem to be their future capital are deeply rooted in religious rather than political convictions. Regardless of how much time passes and what developments may occur, religion (particularly in its fundamentalist form) provides a hardened foundation from which parties cannot deviate. It is very difficult, though not impossible, to reconcile these religious convictions.

Peace is still possible, however bleak the picture may appear today. The geopolitical dynamics must be changed in profound ways to overcome the current shortcomings to achieving a successful conflict resolution. Each of the aforementioned obstacles must be addressed because the alternative to the current impasse is mutually perilous. What is needed then are bold actions that can change the dynamic of the conflict in a dramatic way.

A visit by President Obama to Israel and Ramallah to speak directly to the Israeli and Palestinian people would spell out with clarity the advantages of peace and the adverse consequences of a continued stalemate. Such a personal, perhaps overdue, visit by the president could have a significant impact on creating incentives for the parties to act, and to adjust their internal calculations regarding the continuation of the conflict.

Similarly, a push by the leading Arab states to reinvigorate the Arab Peace Initiative (API) could begin to reverse the atmosphere of pessimism and intransigence that pervades the region. Indeed, regardless of the regional Arab turmoil, and perhaps because of it, the API remains central, if not the only viable framework, to any successful negotiations to ending the Arab-Israeli conflict.

Since the conflict has a strong religious component, sustained dialogue among the religious groups will be required. Although today there is virtually none occurring between Jewish and Muslim religious leaders, and no incentives being created to do so, the religious leaders have a special moral responsibility to rise up in the name of their religious teaching to find a solution to the religious element of the conflict, which bears heavily on the overall search for a solution.

Most importantly, any chance to improve the prospects for a resolution will require one critical element that is currently in extremely short-supply: leadership. Without leadership to act in recognition of the danger the current stalemate poses, Israelis and Palestinians will continue blindly prolonging a conflict that appears manageable yet dangerously simmering. Otherwise, one day they will be awakened by the kind of horrific violent eruption that could spin the region out of control.

MITIGATING CONFLICT PERCEPTION

MAY 2, 2013

There are many impediments to finding a solution to the Israeli-Palestinian conflict, including historical and current experiences, claims and counter-claims, the lack of trust, contradictory ideological and religious convictions, and the unwillingness to make painful compromises.

The one critical impediment that has not been addressed and continues to impede resolutions to the conflicting issues is the perception that each side holds for the other, and the continuing public narratives that reinforce that perception.

While changing perceptions may not by itself solve every discordant issue—Jerusalem, refugees, national security, etc.—it will dramatically contribute to finding solutions. Thus, unless we mitigate misperceptions about each other, it will be nearly impossible to find a mutually acceptable and lasting solution.

The negative perception that has been formed over decades of conflict was nurtured by public narratives promulgated by officials, biased media, schools, and other public forums. Both sides have become fixated on what they want to achieve regardless of the other's rights, wishes, and national aspirations.

Although a majority of Israelis and Palestinians have a good idea about the contours of a peace agreement, they resist change because a) they completely distrust each other, and b) they are still struggling to define their nationhood, as that sense remains relatively in its infancy.

This state of mind makes it increasingly difficult for officials on both sides to come to grips with reality and seek resolutions to any of the incompatible issues before changing the perception of their respective publics.

To that end they must first strive to change their public discourse, demonstrate that a negotiated agreement is possible, and convey that the options to resolve the contentious issues are limited while recognizing the inevitability of coexistence.

Obviously, changing public perception takes many forms. Ideally it should start with officials on both sides. Yet, having been locked into public postures that reject the other's, which appears irreconcilable, it becomes impossible for politicians to change their public narrative without serious political repercussions.

Moreover, the lack of courageous and visionary leadership on both sides makes it extremely difficult to change course, especially in the absence of powerful internal peace movements and external political pressure, which can provide the leaders the political cover they need.

Thus, to prompt both internal and external pressure to bridge the psychological gap and alter the perception of each other, a serious change in the public narrative becomes central and urgent.

Such a change can occur, in large measure, through public dialogues between noted Israelis and Palestinians in particular, along with other Jews and Muslims, by establishing forums where they can publicly and freely air out the obstacles that keep Israelis and Palestinians apart.

In the same setting they should discuss the commonalities they enjoy, why their destiny is intertwined, and why they need each other to coexist peacefully.

The participants: Pre-requisites

In each of these forums, the participants' only agenda must be to promote peace, and they should present (not represent) as objectively as possible the views of Israelis, Jews, Palestinians, and other Arabs and Muslims.

What would qualify these individuals is their varied academic and personal experiences, respect in their field, thorough knowledge of the conflicting issue, status as independent thinkers, lack of a formal position in their respective governments, and commitment to finding a peaceful solution in the context of coexistence.

For example, in addressing the future of Jerusalem, the participants should especially include religious scholars, imams, rabbis, and priests representing the three largest monotheistic religions, and historians with a focus on the Middle East.

They all have to agree in principle that Jerusalem must serve as the capital of two states, without which peace may never be achieved. Although that solution may well be inevitable, still debating other possibilities is critical if for no other reason but to demonstrate why other options are not likely to work.

The same thing can be said about the Palestinian refugees; nearly any informed person, Israeli and Palestinian alike, knows that Israel cannot and will not accept the right of return while remaining a Jewish state.

The question is how to explain to the Palestinian public that the right of return can be implemented by facilitating the return of the refugees to their homeland—the West Bank and Gaza—or resettlement and compensation.

On national security concerns, the participants should have a background in security, such as former high ranking military officers with experience in peacekeeping, and scholars specializing in security matters.

Although there are many qualified individuals who would shy away from participating in these public enclaves, fearing criticism or even retribution, there are as many courageous and willing individuals who would be eager to contribute to these efforts.

These open discussions will allow, over time, many noteworthy individuals to come out in the open and provide such forums increasing visibility, credibility, and outreach.

The format

Separate forums will discuss specific contentious issues and need not be held simultaneously and certainly not with the same participants.

Ideally these enclaves would occur frequently, every two to three weeks, and feature a maximum of 20 participants in a roundtable format (lasting 3–4 hours) at a minimal cost.

This would allow all participants ample opportunity to speak and the public to hear and discern different perspectives and engender creative approaches to complex problems, dictated by the inevitability of coexistence.

Even though the solutions may be obvious, they still require a fresh approach as to how they can be achieved, disabusing both Israelis and Palestinians of the notion that they can have it only their way by fostering a new mindset receptive to the changing conditions and reality they face.

Given the plethora of modern mass communication tools, such dialogues could have, over time, a significant impact on the Israelis' and Palestinians' public opinion and how they view each other in the long term.

These forums could initially be held in cities that attract public attention such as Washington, DC, New York, Tel Aviv, and even Ramallah, and later expand to include other cities in Europe and key Arab states.

This entire concept is made possible today more than any other time before because of the revolution in communications that provides multiple ways by which information can be disseminated to millions within minutes.

The means of disseminating should include but not be limited to printed materials, live webcasts, YouTube, Facebook, and Twitter. Certainly there are certain television networks, including PBS, C-SPAN, al-Hurra, and Al Jazeera who might also be interested in airing such enclaves.

These forums should be revisited in a variety of ways including redistribution through interested media outlets, think tanks dedicated to Israeli-Arab peace, and similar organizations, thereby expanding the scope of dissemination as the forums progress.

Indeed, unless there are consistent follow-ups and concerted efforts to promote both the concept and the content of the deliberations in these forums, the net result will not match the efforts made.

In particular, think tanks could share with their members and websites both the concept and content of these deliberations. As the proceedings become available, the general public will be more engaged, further increasing the overall profile of the deliberations.

Such continuing efforts would provide new openings to change public perceptions, prepare the public to compromise, and offer the leaders the political cover they need to make peace that of necessity would entail mutually painful concessions.

PSYCHOLOGICAL
IMPEDIMENTS

ROOT CAUSES BEHIND THE ISRAELI-PALESTINIAN IMPASSE

JULY 11, 2011

On the surface, the current stalemate in the Israeli-Palestinian peace process seems illogical. After all, each side knows, with the exception of the Netanyahu government, that the basic framework of a negotiated settlement is a two-state solution based on the 1967 borders with land swaps that keep the major settlement blocs inside Israel proper. Jerusalem would remain a united capital of two states, and the vast majority of Palestinian refugees would be compensated and remain in their countries of residence or resettle in the newly-created state of Palestine, in the West Bank and Gaza Strip.

These fundamental factors, coupled with appropriate security guarantees for Israel, represent what has been on the table at the conclusion of numerous rounds of negotiations in the past decades, with each round coming closer to finalizing the deal, yet failing to do so. But why? And why the deep reluctance now by either side to return to talks if the foundations are so clear? Because before agreeing on suitable arrangements, both sides must put to rest the deeply embedded and conflicting psychological dimensions, religious convictions, and nationalist narratives of each side. These factors must be recognized, understood, and addressed if a genuine end to the conflict is ever to be reached.

The Psychological Dimension

Underlying the Israeli-Palestinian conflict are the scars each side carries from a traumatic past. The Jewish experience throughout the Diaspora was one filled with discrimination, persecution, and expulsion, culminating in the Holocaust, during which one nation sought to extinguish a defenseless Jewish people. The trauma of the genocide perpetrated by the Nazis is unmatched in size and scope. Without question, the Jews have carried the scars of this past with them to Palestine. Moreover, many Jews were prevented from avoiding death camps by immigrating to Palestine, which added another layer of horrifying experience for the Jewish people. With this past, once the State of Israel was established it was seen not only as the fulfillment of both the secular Zionist mission, but also as a biblical fulfillment of the return of the Jews to their ancient homeland—their last refuge that must be guarded with absolute zeal.

Palestinians have never fully appreciated the psychological implications of this historical experience. Instead of understanding the Israeli mindset that was formed by this horrific experience and the Jews' connection to the land, the Palestinians have either denied the Holocaust altogether, or bemoaned that if it did happen, why should they, the Palestinians, pay the price? For the Palestinians, the experience of the Nakba ("catastrophe"), precipitated by the 1948 war, was indeed "catastrophic." From their view, they were living in their own land—albeit under Ottoman and then British rule—for centuries. During the 1948 war, many were either forced out of their homes by Israelis or encouraged to leave by their Arab brethren in the context of the war and found themselves as refugees—an experience that has lasted decades. Israelis have never fully understood the significance of this traumatic experience, nor how it has served to bind Palestinians together in the same way that the Jews coalesced following the Holocaust.

Israelis often argue that since Jews left their homes across the Arab Middle East to settle in Israel, the Palestinian refugees must be considered as a de facto swap between the Palestinians and Jewish refugees. This view not only dismisses the historic trauma experienced by the Palestinians but also disregards their national aspirations to establish a homeland of their own. It is that psychological fixation, among other factors, that prevented either side from coming to grips with inevitability of coexistence.

Lack of Trust

The trauma experienced by both sides prior to, and as a result of, the founding of Israel has been reinforced by wars and misdeeds by each side that has fostered a deeply embedded culture of mistrust between the two peoples. The Arab states' refusal to accept the 1947 United Nations partition plan was the first such message to Israelis that the Arabs were not interested in peace. The wars, identified by the years they took place (1948, 1956, 1967, and 1973), have only strengthened the Israeli conviction that Arabs seek only the destruction of, rather than peace with, the State of Israel. The Arab League meeting in Khartoum in 1967 codified this view, declaring the infamous three no's: "no to negotiations, no to recognition, no to peace." Finally, with the launch of the Oslo peace process in 1993, Israelis and Palestinians began to speak with one another in an attempt to find a lasting end to their conflict, but with the trauma of conflict underlying their discussions and the utter lack of trust, neither side believed the words of the other. From the Israeli view, they negotiated as Hamas and other extremist Palestinian groups gained strength and committed a savage campaign of suicide bombings across Israel, only to be further intensified by the Second Intifada upon the collapse of the Oslo talks.

The Israeli view that the Palestinians do not really want peace gained further currency following Israel's withdrawals from Lebanon and the Gaza Strip. Instead of using the evacuated territories as an opening for improved relations, they became a staging ground for launching rockets on Israeli cities. Meanwhile, from the Palestinians' perspective, they negotiated as Israeli settlement construction grew exponentially in the West Bank, rapidly grabbing land that the Palestinians imagined for a state of their own. The Palestinians insist that Israel could not possibly negotiate in good faith as long as it continued to deepen the roots of occupation while undermining any real prospect for establishing their own state.

In truth, both sides are right to feel cheated. But it is no longer a question of right or wrong. The perception by each side that the other is not serious must be overcome if peace is to be achieved. However, the leadership on both sides has not made any real effort to correct these perceptions, deciding instead to stroke the nationalist fervor and angst against the other, rather than moving forward with a peace agreement in good faith.

Religious Conviction

The Arab-Israeli conflict is typically viewed as a political and territorial conflict, yet the religious component fuels the conflict and makes it extremely difficult to resolve. The Israeli narrative is one that is based on the biblical connection of the Jewish people to the land of their forefathers. As Prime Minister Netanyahu implored Congress in his May 24 address, "This is the land of our forefathers, the Land of Israel, to which Abraham brought the idea of one God, where David set out to confront Goliath, and where Isaiah saw a vision of eternal peace. No distortion of history can deny the four thousand year old bond, between the Jewish people and the Jewish land."[363] For many Israelis it is extremely painful to relinquish control of the West Bank, known as the ancient biblical lands of Judea and Samaria, and it is inconceivable to surrender the Wailing Wall and have Jerusalem under the jurisdiction of anyone else.

Similarly, no Arab leader would compromise on Jerusalem because of the religious convictions tied to the third holiest shrine of Islam in Jerusalem, the Al Aqsa Mosque and the Dome of the Rock on Haram al-Sharif. Moreover, many Muslims scholars believe that Muhammad made his Journey from Mecca to the Al Aqsa Mosque (Masjid al-Aqsa, literally, 'furthest mosque') in Jerusalem before he ascended to heaven. Although the Al Aqsa Mosque was built long after the death of the prophet, Surah 17:1 says that Mohammad visited the site where Masjid Al Aqsa was to be built. This belief is

---

363 Benjamin Netanyahu, "Text of PM Binyamin Netanyahu's Speech to the US Congress," *The Jerusalem Post*, May 24, 2011, http://www.jpost.com/Diplomacy-and-Politics/Text-of-PM-Binyamin-Netanyahus-speech-to-the-US-Congress.

certainly not limited to the Palestinians but shared by all Muslims, further complicating any solution to the future of Jerusalem.

Defiance of Reality

Although many people on both sides realize that coexistence is inevitable, there are still very strong voices among Israelis and Palestinians who simply don't accept it. There are Israelis who deny that the Palestinians are a people with national aspirations, believing that they can be given independence in municipalities but remain perpetually under the jurisdiction and control of the Israeli authorities. Just as there are Israelis who deny the existence of a Palestinian people, there are Palestinians who deny that Israelis constitute a people worthy of a nation, let alone one that should settle in the land they seek for their own.

Too often, the leadership on both sides has sought to exploit these nationalistic denials for their own political and ideological gains, at the expense of understanding the narrative of the other side. For example, for the Israeli side, this has meant a denial of the dilemma of Palestinian refugees and on the Palestinian side, a denial of Israel's genuine security concerns. As a result, the public discourse has advanced the notion that the other side has no genuine claims and that one day they can be defeated with hardened, resolute positions, and therefore there is no compelling rationale to compromise to find a formula for coexistence. This blind refusal of reality by influential voices on both sides strengthens those on the fringes seeking to delay a solution. The quintessential example of the denial of the need to coexist is the development of unilateralism as a policy of choice. The Israelis' continued settlement expansion and the Palestinians' drive to seek UN recognition of their own state suggest bold attempts to shape their respective national future as if it were possible to do so independent of the other side.

Self-Entrapment

By insisting on far-fetched formulas, each side is creating a state of self-entrapment by imprisoning themselves in positions that are not sustainable, locking themselves into a posture without a face-saving way out. Israelis and Palestinians are addicted to missing opportunities and adopting harmful positions. To illustrate this self-entrapment, consider the following: Israelis insist that the Palestinians should have no jurisdiction over any part of Jerusalem and that they must recognize Israel as a "Jewish state." Palestinians continue to perpetuate the fantasy that refugees will one day return to Israel en masse, thereby destroying Israel's Jewish character. As long as these positions, however untenable they may be, continue to dominate public discourse, they not only impede any serious dialogue or discussion but also paint the Israeli and Palestinian leadership into a corner with increasingly diminishing prospects of finding a dignified way out.

Overcoming these fundamental obstacles to a two-state agreement requires more than negotiations between political leaders. Last month, the French initiative to host peace talks failed when parties could not agree even to attend. Many such conferences in the past have come and gone without introducing any lasting changes for the better in the dynamic of the conflict. So why have another?

That said, the Europeans are uniquely suited to host other types of conferences to address the specific impediments to peace by bringing together noted and respected religious leaders, historians, and NGOs that engage in separate talks about each of these issues without outside political pressure, as long as all participants believe in the inevitability of coexistence. Airing these issues and reaching a better understanding could have a tremendous impact on public opinion on both sides and provide the political leadership with the necessary public support and the political cover they need to accommodate each other. Understanding and appreciating one another's position and mindset while reaching a consensus governed by the reality on the ground will be a game changer.

For this reason, as a case in point, any negotiations about the future of the city of Jerusalem require first an in-depth dialogue between respected and independent Jewish and Muslim religious scholars. It is they who must first reach a mutual understanding about the religious connections to the land, its impact on the conflict, and how the gaps between the two religious narratives can be bridged to preserve the peace and sanctity of Jerusalem in light of the inevitability of coexistence. In a different setting, notable historians from both sides can meet and serve to advance understanding among both peoples of the traumatic history of each side and how the narratives have been shaped in the past and might be shaped in the future to advance coexistence. In a similar vein, other conferences could deal with the problem of a lack of trust, the continuing self-entrapment, and the denial of the realities on the ground. Finally, nongovernmental organizations can help to disseminate these finding across the broader public without the political baggage of the respective political leaderships. The European community would be ideal to host such dialogues because they do not come with the same religious biases of nations like the United States, where there is a strong base of support for Israel among evangelicals, or Turkey, with its natural tendency to support its Muslim brethren.

Doing so would also acknowledge the helpful role that Europe and the broader international community can play in resolving rather than stoking the conflict. Only with such a broader, deeper dialogue, and the shared pursuit of understanding of the issues on the psychological, historical, religious, and emotional levels can the roots of the conflict be addressed and lead to substantive negotiations to end the Israeli-Palestinian conflict.

PERPETUATING HISTORIC VICTIMHOOD BREEDS NEW VICTIMS

JANUARY 23, 2013

Even a cursory review of the Israeli and Palestinian political landscape conspicuously and sadly reveals the overall self-resignation and apathy expressed by many on both sides, strongly suggesting that the Israeli-Palestinian conflict is simply beyond resolution. The sorry truth is that while polls consistently show that a majority of Israelis and Palestinians believe that only the co-existence of two independent states offers a viable solution, they still refuse to divorce themselves from a deep **sense of victimhood**. Both parties continue to define themselves as historic victims, and nourish a kind of vicarious victimhood which ultimately serves to justify the policies and goals they pursue, however counterproductive they may be to a solution.

The genocide perpetrated during the Holocaust was surely something new in history: never before had a powerful state turned its immense resources to the industrialized manufacturing of corpses; never before had the extermination of an entire people been carried out with the swiftness of an assembly line. The question, however, is, does the Jewish people's unprecedented historical suffering somehow transform them from "victims" to "Victims," guaranteeing them, and by extension the State of Israel, an unconditional status of moral untouchability? The French philosopher Alain Badiou is right to suggest that we need to question the presumption "that, like an inverted original sin, the grace of having been an incomparable victim can be passed down not only to descendants and to the descendants of descendants but to all who come under the predicate in question, be they heads of state or armies engaging in the severe oppression of those whose lands they have confiscated."[364] The Israelis' sense of being "Victims"

---

364 Alain Badiou, *Polemics* (New York: Verso, 2006), 160.

has led to a lack of empathy towards the Palestinians' plight. It has further manifested itself through the usurpation of Palestinian land and a shirking of Israel's responsibility toward the refugee problem, all the while promoting self-righteousness. Israelis who would continue occupying land belonging to a future Palestinian state must realize that we do not and cannot honor the dead when we use their memory, and what they suffered, to dishonor and disinherit the living.

For the Palestinians, the experience of the Nakba (the "catastrophe"), precipitated by the 1948 war, was no less calamitous. From their perspective, they were living for centuries in their own land and are absolutely convinced that during the 1948 war, they were forced out of their homes by Israelis—a tragedy that has lasted for decades and which they continue to endure to this day, leaving an indelible impression on their psyche. This traumatic experience has served to bind Palestinians together in the same way that the Jews coalesced following the Holocaust, with each side believing that their tragic historical experiences are unparalleled in scope and magnitude. The Palestinians, as a result, have hardly made any serious effort to appreciate the psychological implications of the Jews' historical experience. They have either denied the Holocaust altogether, or bemoaned that if it did happen they should not be held responsible or pay any price for the Jews' historic tragedy—an attitude reinforced by Israel's building of settlements on their land.

Israelis and Palestinians alike (especially those who, like Hamas, seek the destruction of Israel) must become more self-critical in their use of victimhood; both sides need to realize that neither has a monopoly on the position of "victim" and neither is granted a morally unimpeachable status as a consequence of their historical experiences or the changed reality on the ground.

Israel's national security concerns, however legitimate, have been used as an excuse for expropriating land and expanding settlements under the guise of creating defensible borders. Successive Israeli governments continue to occupy Palestinian territory and by its own actions offer no sign that the occupation will end any time soon, thereby denying the Palestinians not only a contiguous land mass but also the right to live in freedom and dignity. The Palestinians too (Hamas in particular) must understand that their belief in some day recapturing all of Palestine is an illusion, as is the return of nearly five million Palestinian refugees, since that would mean the obliteration of Israel through demographics. Such hopes cannot be fulfilled if the Palestinians want to coexist peacefully and forsake the use of violence to achieve their political objectives.

Neither side's sense of victimhood can be mitigated by reverting to their historical experiences. It is this state of mind that continues to haunt the majority in both camps while allowing the extremist minority to manipulate the conflict in order to stifle any progress. Together, these sentiments and mindsets inherently endure, particularly when reinforced by Israeli and Palestinian officials' public narratives that openly promote the rejection of the other's claim and rights. Perhaps this explains why Israeli and Palestinian leadership has devised policies and made demands that the other could not accept without abandoning decades-old self-serving political agendas (however skewed) to justify their actions. Moreover, being that Israel and the Palestinians are politically factional, coupled with the lack of visionary and courageous leaders around which they can coalesce, there is little hope that their current leadership, which has lost its moral compass, can change course and accept not only each other's reality but each other's rights.

For these reasons, the task must now fall on the shoulders of the silent majority in both camps; it is they who must leave complacency behind, go out to the streets by the hundreds of thousands, and loudly and clearly proclaim that enough is enough and that the conflict must come to an end. The time has come for the Israeli and Palestinian masses to engage in collective civil disobedience, lasting as long as it takes to force the leadership in both camps to change course and seek a peaceful solution to the conflict. This means, of course, that both sides must break with the mechanical way of reacting to injury or harm, namely, by nursing the hurt and resolving to hurt the other in return and in so doing perpetuating the mutual source of victimhood, which provides a psychological comfort.

If revenge involves taking a bit of the past and letting it determine our future, in effect we have no future; the success, then, of nonviolent resistance absolutely rests on its peaceful nature. The smallest violent incident distracts from the purpose of the message and allows extremists on both sides to exploit such incidents to their advantage. Although civil disobedience must not be limited to women, imagine the impact that tens of thousands of Israeli and Palestinian women demonstrating in every major city will have domestically and internationally—the women who no longer want to see their young children die in vain or deprived of a bright future only to serve a blind cause that has long since lost not only its merit but has been rendered morally bankrupt.

Although civil disobedience is essential, it may well be that the Israelis and the Palestinians can no longer resolve this conflict on their own and need an outside power or powers to mediate, pressure, coerce, or even threaten both parties to change course before it is too late. The United States, which has a tremendous stake in the Middle East and enjoys great influence on Israel and the Palestinians, remains pivotal to helping them reach an agreement. Led by Germany, the UK, and France, the European Union (EU) is already preparing a proposal that provides the basis for the immediate resumption of peace negotiations. Outside powers, particularly the United States, will have far more leeway and justification to push for a peace plan when tens of thousands of Israelis and Palestinians are on the streets demanding the same.

Indeed, the people who are paying with their own blood are making the sacrifices and suffer for it; they want their children to grow up in peace, and have a better prospect and an opportunity to prosper and flourish. Those who want to chart their own destiny; Israelis and Palestinians alike, have the inherent right to dream, hope and live in peace. This is what the Israeli and Palestinian silent majority needs and hopes for, but they must first do their share by going to the streets in acts of civil disobedience to make their voices heard.

The continuation of the Israeli-Palestinian conflict is now creating a third generations of victims—not the victims of the Holocaust or the victims of al-Nakba but the victims of misguided leaders. So-called leaders, like Prime Minister Netanyahu (who may well form the next government and continue to lead Israelis astray), are bringing them ever closer to the precipice—he and his ilk on the Palestinian side, such as Hamas' Ismail Haniyeh, must be stopped by the public outcry to head off a potentially catastrophic development.

ALON BEN-MEIR

ISRAELI-PALESTINIAN CONFLICT: THE PSYCHOLOGICAL DIMENSION

Brief Synopsis: The most puzzling aspect of the Israeli-Palestinian conflict is that after 65 years of mutual violence, enmity and suffering, it remains unresolved even when coexistence is inevitable and a two-state solution remains the only viable option. Although there are many contentious issues that must be specifically addressed, it is the psychological dimension of the conflict which directly impacts every conflicting issue and makes it increasingly intractable. To mitigate the conflict, we must first look into the elements that inform the psychological dimension and how to alleviate them as prerequisites to finding a solution.

THE ROLE OF PSYCHOLOGICAL RESISTANCE

FEBRUARY 7, 2013

On the surface, the deadlock in the Israeli-Palestinian peace process seems illogical and unsettling. After all, a majority of Israelis and Palestinians realize the inevitability of coexistence and presumably understand the general parameters of a negotiated peace agreement: a two-state solution based on the 1967 borders with some land swaps, Jerusalem would remain a united city (but a capital of two states), and the vast majority of Palestinian refugees would be compensated or resettled in the newly-created Palestinian state in the West Bank and Gaza Strip. These fundamental *imperatives*, coupled with appropriate security guarantees for Israel, represent what was on the negotiating table in 2000 at Camp David and in 2008/2009 in Jerusalem and Ramallah, with each round coming closer to finalizing an agreement yet ultimately failing to do so. The question is: why?

The answer lies far beyond the political concessions on the ground and is deeply embedded in the psychological dimension of the conflict, which impacts every conflicting issue between the two parties. Biased

568

and selective perceptions, reinforced by historical experiences, religion, and incompatible ideologies, have locked both sides into immobile positions. The factors that maintain and enhance these patterns include emotions such as fear, distrust, and insecurity; the psychological outcome is mutual denial of the narrative of the other and mutual delegitimization. Put together, the operative result is stagnation and polarization. What is therefore needed is a consensus-oriented dialogue at the leadership level, by both officials and non-officials, to resolve the issues of perception—a tall order given the current environment that buttresses rather than ameliorates perceptions.

There are certain psychological concepts which are relevant to understanding the Israeli-Palestinian conflict; the concept of illusion is an essential one. In "The Future of an Illusion," Freud offers the following definition: "...we call a belief an illusion when a wish-fulfillment is a prominent factor in its motivation, and in doing so we disregard its relations to reality, just as the illusion itself sets no store by verification."[365] An illusion then is not necessarily an error, unlike a delusion—that is, illusions "need not necessarily be false... unrealizable or in contradiction to reality." What is characteristic of illusions is that: 1) they are derived from deep human wishes, and 2) the belief is held (or would be held) in the absence of any compelling evidence, or good rational grounds, in its behalf.

It is impossible to deny that both Israelis and Palestinians are in the grip of very powerful illusions which only serve to prolong the conflict and prevent any mutual understanding. What are some of these illusions, or pipe-dreams, as the great American playwright Eugene O'Neill would call them? Following O'Neill, we can distinguish between pipe-dreams of yesterday and pipe-dreams of tomorrow. For example, the belief shared by many Israelis that they have a biblical right to the land (the ancient biblical lands of Judea and Samaria) and that God gave it to the Jews for all time is undoubtedly an illusion or a pipe-dream of yesterday. It is not affirmed because there is any real evidence for it, but because it satisfies a deep-seated psychological need for a God-given Jewish homeland. The belief that by expanding the settlements Israel will augment its national security is a pipe-dream

---

365 Sigmund Freud, *The Future of an Illusion* (New York: W.W. Norton & Company Ltd., 1961), 40.

of tomorrow. It is important to note how these illusions sustain and reinforce one another, and constitute a psychological barrier which is that much more impervious to critical reflection. Israel's illusions have served to create the logic for occupation, ultimately perpetuating the dehumanization of the Palestinians.

The Palestinians, for their part, are not without their own illusions. They believe, for example, that God has reserved the land for them, and appeal to the fact that they had inhabited the land for centuries. The presence of the al-Aqsa Mosque and the Dome of the Rock in Jerusalem attest to their unmitigated historical and religious affinity to the Holy City. They also cling to the idea that they will someday return to the land of their forbearers, as they have and continue to insist on the right of return of the Palestinian refugees, even though this has become a virtual impossibility. The Palestinians cling to their pipe-dreams of yesterday and tomorrow just as blindly and desperately as the Israelis, which leads to resistance to and fear of change.

This has contributed to making the Israeli-Palestinian conflict both chronic and intractable, as the various illusions are continuously and consciously nurtured by daily encounters between the two sides. It would thus appear that the psychological concept of resistance to change is extremely relevant as well. First, a distinction is needed between resistance to persuasion, which is conscious and deliberate, and inner unconscious resistance to change. In his essay "The Psychological Dimensions of the Israeli-Palestinian Conflict: the Role of Psychological Resistance," David Rabinowitz, one of Israel's leading psychiatrists, observes that an important function of unconscious resistance is that it is protective in nature.[366] In seeking bridging concepts that could link between the domains of psychology and politics in the Israeli-Palestinian conflict, it could be proposed that a collective mutual resistance to change protects a vulnerable identity. Compared to the stable and mature political identities of the American, British, and French nations, the political identities of both the Israeli and Palestinian peoples are, in a way, in their adolescence. Identities in this setting are more vulnerable, and the protagonists are

---

366 David Rabinowitz, "The Psychological Dimensions of the Israeli-Palestinian Conflict: The Role of Psychological Resistance" (in correspondence with the author, Haifa, Israel, 2012), 1.

naturally more defensive and resistant to change. By its very nature, the players must find it difficult (if not impossible) to articulate this publicly, as to do so is to admit to this vulnerability.

The concept of psychological resistance to change may well affect the political setting in general and the Israeli-Palestinian conflict in particular; it is closely connected to perceptions at many levels. Indeed, psychological resistance provides protection for vulnerable identity formation in the Israeli-Palestinian conflict. It is this mindset, strengthened by historical experiences, which transcends the more than nine decades since the Israeli-Palestinian conflict began. Individuals and groups, Israelis and Palestinians alike, have and continue to interpret the nature of the discord between them as "you versus me" in a prejudiced and selective way. In turn, this has stifled any new information and enabled the continuing resistance to change, which could shed new light on the nature and the substance of the conflict and help advance the peace process.

The concept of unconscious resistance to change in this setting links well to the view of perceptions driving the polarization in the conflict. Historical experience, which formulates perceptions, serves among other things to enhance the sense of identity of "who we really are," a formative collective assumption that sits at the bedrock of both key players and drives functional and dysfunctional behavior. As Rabinowitz puts it, "the central benefit of this powerful unconscious resistance to change provides is the protection of a relatively vulnerable core identity [primary gains]…Secondary gains, however, are essentially the side-effects of the chronic polarization of this conflict: powerful allies offering material support [the US' support of Israel and moderate Palestinians verses Iran's support for Palestinian militants such as Hamas], alluring narratives, public attention, useful alliances etc."[367] In principle, such a mindset prevents either side from entertaining new ideas that might lead to compromises for a peaceful solution. The paradox here is that majorities on both sides do want and seek peace, knowing full well that this would require significant concessions, but are unable to reconcile the required concessions with imbedded perceptions that have precluded these compromises as a result of resistance to change.

---

367 Rabinowitz, "The Psychological Dimensions of the Israeli-Palestinian Conflict: The Role of Psychological Resistance," 2.

Thus, to mitigate the Israeli-Palestinian conflict, we must first carefully look into the various elements that inform the psychological dimension of the conflict, and discuss how they impact the relationship between the two sides and what it would take to alleviate these psychological impediments as prerequisites to finding a solution.

HISTORICAL EXPERIENCES
AND PERCEPTION

FEBRUARY 11, 2013

Underlying the Israeli-Palestinian conflict are the scars that each side carries from their respective traumatic pasts. Their perceptions of each other were engendered by their independent religious traditions as well as their historical experiences as they related to one another. Unfolding events—violence, mutual recrimination, etc.—between Israelis and Palestinians over the past seven decades, however, have made it virtually impossible for them to settle their differences. Maintaining an adversarial mindset toward each other has thus provided the justification and rationale to perpetuate their historical grievances through constant rancorous public narratives, placing the blame for the continuing discord on the other.

The Jewish experience throughout the Diaspora was one filled with discrimination, persecution, anti-Semitism, and expulsion culminating in the Holocaust. The genocide perpetrated during the Holocaust was surely something new in history: never before had a powerful state turned its immense resources to the industrialized manufacturing of corpses; never before had the extermination of an entire people been carried out with the swiftness of an assembly line. The fact that many Jews were prevented from avoiding death camps by immigrating to Palestine added yet another layer to the horrific experiences of the Jewish people. The Jews have carried the scars of this past with them and still hold to the view that it can happen again unless they remain vigilant and relentless in protecting themselves at any cost. With this past in mind, the establishment of the state of Israel was seen not only as the last refuge to provide protection for the Jewish people but also the realization and hope of both secular Zionism and biblical prophecy (i.e., the return of the Jews to their ancient homeland). Thus, religious and nonobservant Jews believe this trust must be guarded with absolute and unwavering zeal.

Yet, this historical sense of victimization and injustice has served to nurture the allegiance that each Israeli feels toward the state and each other with naturally-engendered, negative emotional sentiments toward the enemy. From the Israeli perspective, the establishment of Israel on the heels of the Holocaust was seen (and continues to be viewed) as the last chance to create a refuge; they must therefore remain on guard to protect Jews' welfare and wellbeing wherever they may live and at whatever cost. This sense of victimization resulted from an intentional infliction of harm in the past, universally viewed as utterly unjust and immoral. Yet, it has led to a lack of empathy toward perceived enemies; for example, it manifested itself in Israel shirking responsibility for the Palestinian refugee problem and violating human rights, all the while promoting self-righteousness.

Compounded, these conditions inherently endure, particularly when accompanied by extensive and continuing violence against Israel and growing concerns over national security. They are further strengthened by the Palestinians' public narrative, which openly promotes the rejection of the very existence of the state. The Palestinians, for their part, have hardly made any serious effort to comprehend and appreciate the psychological implications of the Jews' historical experience of religious persecution. Instead of understanding the Israeli mindset that was formed by the horrific past, the Palestinians have either denied the Holocaust altogether, or bemoaned that it did happen. It is not that the Palestinians should be held responsible for the Jews' historic tragedy, but that they failed at a minimum to appreciate the Israelis' mindset in effectively dealing with the conflict.

For the Palestinians, the experience of the Nakba (the "catastrophe"), precipitated by the 1948 war, was no less calamitous. From their perspective, they were living in their own land, albeit for centuries under Ottoman rule and then under the British Mandate. They are absolutely convinced that during the 1948 war they were forced out of their homes by Israelis (in fact, many were encouraged to leave by their Arab brethren and return 'following the defeat of Israel' for the spoil.)

Either way, over 700,000 Palestinians found themselves as refugees, an experience that has lasted for decades and continues to endure, leaving an indelible impression on their psyche; currently, nearly five million Palestinian are refugees.[368] This traumatic experience served to bind Palestinians together in the same way that the Jews coalesced following the Holocaust, with each side believing their tragic historical experiences are unparalleled in scope and magnitude. The fact that the Arab states manipulated the Palestinian refugee problem over many decades to their advantage does not change the reality on the ground; it did not alter the Palestinians' mindset, their perception of what the Israelis have done, or their sentiment and disposition about their plight.

Subsequent and frequent violent encounters between the two sides, especially after the 1967 war, further aggravated the Palestinian refugee problem. This war not only created another wave of refugees, but also set the stage for a bloody confrontation, during which many thousands lost their lives on both sides. The Israeli settlement project provided daily blows to Palestinian pride while demonstrating the futility of their efforts to stem Israeli encroachment on their territory, especially in the West Bank. The occupation and the repeated humiliation of the Palestinians further deepened their resolve to oppose the Israelis at whatever cost, but all was to no avail. The Israelis have proven to be a formidable foe and the Palestinians' resentment, hatred, and animosity have naturally only increased.

Israelis have never fully understood the significance of what the Palestinians have been enduring, how this has impacted their psychological dispositions, and why they have shown no desire to reconcile their differences with Israel. Israelis often argue that since nearly 800,000 Jews left their homes[369] (or, as many believe, were forced out)

---

368 See Takkenberg, "UNRWA and the Palestinian Refugees After Sixty Years: Some Reflections;" and Josh Rogin, "Did the State Department Just Create 5 Million Palestinian Refugees?," *Foreign Policy*, May 25, 2012, http://thecable.foreignpolicy.com/posts/2012/05/25/did_the_state_department_just_create_5_million_palestinian_refugees.

369 Ed West, "The Forgotten Refugees: Jews Forced Out of Arab Countries. What About Their Right of Return?," *The Telegraph*, May 16, 2011, http://blogs.telegraph.co.uk/news/edwest/100088159/the-forgotten-refugees-jews-forced-out-of-arab-countries-what-about-their-right-of-return/.

across the Arab Middle East and North Africa and largely settled in Israel, the Palestinian refugees must be considered as a de facto swap with the Jewish refugees. This view not only dismisses the historic trauma experienced by the Palestinians, but also disregards their national aspirations to establish a homeland of their own, especially in light of the 1947 UN Resolution 181 (known as the Partition Plan), which called for separate Jewish and Palestinian states. This psychological fixation, reinforced by public narratives and education in schools, has prevented either side from coming to grips with the inevitability of peaceful coexistence.

Understanding the Israeli and Palestinian mindsets from the historical perspective is central to appreciating their respective resistances to change, especially if they continue to harbor political agendas that overshoot what they can realistically attain. That is, will their historical experiences, bequeathing a sense of mutual victimhood, be mitigated by the changing reality, or will they hold onto them until they achieve their objectives, however illusionary they may be? Indeed, do the Jews' and the Palestinians' unprecedented historical suffering—although they do not fall into the same category—somehow ontologically elevate them from "victims" to "Victims," guaranteeing them, and by extension contemporary Israelis and Palestinians, an unconditional status of moral untouchability?

The French philosopher Alain Badiou is right to suggest that we need to question the presumption "that, like an inverted original sin, the grace of having been an incomparable victim can be passed down not only to descendants and to the descendants of descendants but to all who come under the predicate in question, be they heads of state or armies engaging in the severe oppression of those whose lands they have confiscated."[370] Indeed, victim mentality has become a political tool in the hands of those who seek to promote their interests at the expense of the opposing political parties, not to mention the enemy.

The Palestinian culture of victimhood, on the other hand, was equally divisive in that it perpetuates the refugee problem by promoting popular refusal of permanent resettlement. Palestinian

---

370 Badiou, *Polemics*, 160.

leaders have also used it as a tool for public indoctrination, ensuring that the Palestinian plight remains central to any political and social discourse. Palestinians and their leaders have carefully and systematically ingrained their victim mentality in the minds of one generation after another through the media, schools, and places of worship.

Israelis and Palestinians alike (especially those who, like Hamas, seek the destruction of Israel) must become more self-critical in their use of victimhood; both sides need to realize that neither has a monopoly on the position of "the victim" and neither is granted a morally unimpeachable status as a consequence of their historical experiences or the shifting realities on the ground. The effect of adverse historical interaction, however, can be mitigated over time or reconciled through dialogue, eventually leading to changes in perception.

Notwithstanding their traumatic historical experiences, neither the Israelis nor the Palestinians can or should use history to foreshadow the present requirements to make peace. Historical experiences can be both instructive and destructive; a student of history must learn from past experiences but not emulate them and thus obscure a contemporary reality that can no longer be mitigated short of a catastrophe, in particular Israeli-Palestinian coexistence. The Palestinians have every right to demand the immediate end to the occupation and live with dignity; Israel has an equal right to satisfy its legitimate national security concerns. These two requirements are absolutely compatible and provide the only basis on which to build a structure of peaceful coexistence.

Without denying the Jews' and Palestinians' sense of victimhood, perpetuating their conflict ironically creates new generations of victims, robbing them of their future only because their elders want to cling to the past.

RELIGIOUS CONVICTION AND REALITY

FEBRUARY 14, 2013

The Arab-Israeli conflict is generally viewed as a political and territorial conflict, yet the underlying religious component has created a certain mindset that further complicates the struggle and adds to its intransigence. Both Jews and Muslims alike have mystified the struggle, projecting cosmic significance and introducing national and religious pride into the equation.

The Israelis' own religious narrative is one that is based on the biblical connection of the Jewish people to the land of their forefathers. As Prime Minister Netanyahu reminded the U.S. Congress in his May 24, 2011, address, "This is the land of our forefathers, the Land of Israel, to which Abraham brought the idea of one God, where David set out to confront Goliath, and where Isaiah saw a vision of eternal peace."[371]

Most Israelis believe that no distortion of history can deny the religious component that has created a bond, spanning thousands of years, between the Jewish people and the biblical Jewish land. Since the ancient Hebrews are not historically the same thing as Jews—not culturally and not even religiously—the Hebraic tradition of 3000 years ago, having little similarity to modern Jewry, hardly means an inheritance in land for Jews. That said, and with religious faith requiring no evidence, for many Israelis it is simply unacceptable to completely relinquish control of the West Bank, known in biblical times as Judea and Samaria.

From that perspective, it is inconceivable for them to surrender their holiest shrines, especially the Wailing Wall (the outer wall of

---

371 Benjamin Netanyahu, "Speech to the US Congress" (Washington, DC, May 24, 2011), http://www.jpost.com/Diplomacy-and-Politics/Text-of-PM-Binyamin-Netanyahus-speech-to-the-US-Congress.

the Second Temple), allowing Jerusalem to be governed by any other peoples or an international governing body. As a result, despite all Israelis happily accepting the 1947 UN Partition Plan, they have always held onto the dream of eventually repossessing all of Jerusalem, particularly the Old City.

The affinity to the holy city, which has for millennia symbolized the Jewish sense of redemption, created a powerful motivation to capture the city when it came within their grasp during the Six Day War in 1967. The fall of Jerusalem in the wake of the war remains an unmatched event and came to symbolize Jewish absolution. This historic development created a renewed awakening that vindicated the religious premise which was embedded in the Jewish psyche for centuries. The realization of what was believed to be a far-fetched dream under the most difficult of circumstances was now seen as the work of the Almighty. Considered in this light, we can understand or at least provide a framework for the zeal of those who are committed to keeping all of Jerusalem and much, if not all, of the West Bank under Israeli jurisdiction—they see that as the fulfillment not only of God's promise but God's very will.

What further explains the mindset of these believers is that no man can reason to the contrary of God's plan. Regardless of the facts on the ground (the existence of the Palestinians and their claim to East Jerusalem), the Jews in and outside Israel consider it their obligation to do everything in their power to fulfill God's will, which transcends humanity's narrow perception of reality. This explains the position of many Israeli Jews who see no wrongdoing in building new and expanding existing settlements in the West Bank, particularly in East Jerusalem.

From the settlers' perspective, they are merely fulfilling what God has ordained; for the Jews to earn the right to hold onto Jerusalem they must prove that they are worthy to repossess it, even if this includes suppressing the Palestinians and defying the international community. For these reasons, regardless of how powerful the resistance of Palestinians, other Arab and Muslim states, and much of the international community to the Israeli position, the religious mandate trumps any and all opposition: the settlers view themselves as pursuing God's mission and must demonstrate unshakable resolve, tenacity, and willingness to make any sacrifice necessary before He once again grants them the Promised Land.

With the recapture of Jerusalem and control asserted over the West Bank, what seemed to be destined to remain only a pipe-dream was suddenly transformed into a reality. This development was then strengthened by concerted efforts toward creating permanent anchors on the ground through building settlements and infrastructure needed to augment continuity. These efforts led to the gradual galvanization of intergroup factions, especially the settlement movement, which has gained tremendous political sway and uses it effectively to block any policy or action on the ground that could compromise the settlement enterprise. Indeed, successive Israeli governments, regardless of their ideological leaning, have bent to the settlers' whims.

The expansion of the settlements, along with the prospect of building the young Jewish state on the entire mythological ancient homeland, has created this particular and most powerful psychological disposition. As this religious mindset has become even further embedded in the Israeli psyche, the nearly decisive power of the settlement movement has made it increasingly difficult to contemplate a return to the 1967 borders, with or without some land swaps.

Due to religious convictions tied to Islam's third holiest shrines in Jerusalem—the Al-Aqsa Mosque and the Dome of the Rock (Haram al-Sharif)—Muslim leaders, like their Jewish counterparts, will not compromise on Jerusalem or on recovering much of the West Bank's land. Many Muslim scholars believe that Muhammad made his Journey from Mecca to Masjid Al-Aqsa (literally, "furthest mosque") in Jerusalem before he ascended to heaven. Although the Al-Aqsa Mosque was built long after the death of the prophet, Surah 17:1 states that Mohammad visited the site where the Al-Aqsa Mosque was subsequently erected. This belief is certainly not limited to the Palestinians but shared by all Muslims, further complicating any solution to the future of Jerusalem. Like the Israelis, the Palestinians too have shown absolutely no flexibility in this regard.

One other difficulty that adds to the psychological impediment in relation to Jerusalem is the Palestinians' sense of ownership, which has been uninterrupted for centuries. Although Arabs have lived with Jews in relative peace, Jews were treated as second-class citizens, who in turn largely accepted subordination in order to maintain peaceful relations. Centuries of Arab perception of Jews as a subordinated minority make it nearly impossible for them to accept Jews as equals, not to mention as a superior power forcefully usurping land they consider their own. The Palestinians' position in connection with Jerusalem and the entire West Bank must therefore be seen in this context as well.

Further consideration of the Arab view of Islam as the final revelation of the three largest monotheistic religions (including Judaism and Christianity) and of Muhammad as the last prophet accentuate Palestinian and Muslim unwillingness to compromise in what they believe to be their inherent religious duty to obey God's final revelation. Here again, the psychological barrier embedded in religious precepts creates a mindset willing to defy reality. Yet, no one is permitted to challenge God's decree and Muhammad's edict.

In The Future of an Illusion, Freud made the claim that religious beliefs should be viewed as wish-fulfillments, or beliefs chiefly motivated by deep-seated human wishes; i.e., illusions. When we look without bias at the beliefs held by so many on both sides of the Israeli-Palestinian conflagration, who could not help but agree with his assessment? Of course, an illusion could turn out to be true: the belief that the Jewish people would someday establish a mighty state on the very same land where their ancient ancestors once lived was certainly illusory only a hundred years ago. Even if we agree with Freud that religious beliefs are illusions, we cannot agree with his prediction that such illusions are likely to wither away any time soon.

In the final analysis, religion has been and will most likely continue to be the repository of our most deeply held wishes and beliefs, as it is for many Israelis and Palestinians alike. For believers on both sides, religion constitutes nothing less than the very substance of their lives, the core of their existence and world-view. The question is: can both parties be brought to reconcile their beliefs to the changed reality on the ground? Neither Israelis nor Palestinians can be expected to undermine their most cherished religious convictions, but if disappointments are unavoidable, the convictions recognized and honored by the other side and by the global community must be adapted and reinterpreted in light of new and undeniable conditions. To take a crucial example, while neither side can forsake Jerusalem without compromising their religion, they can begin to accommodate their aspirations to the prospect of Jerusalem as the capital of two sovereign and independent states.

Perhaps then the historical and religious commitments of both sides can be respected. It is only through mutual realization of spiritual hopes and ideals that Israelis and Palestinians will reconcile and see the fulfillment of God's promise of peace—and that is surely no mere pipe-dream.

THE PERIL OF MUTUAL DELEGITIMIZATION

FEBRUARY 20, 2013

Although a majority of Israelis and Palestinians realize that co-existence based on a two-state solution may well be inevitable, intractable voices on both sides simply refuse to accept this reality.

In Israel, a powerful right-of-center constituency rejects the notion that Palestinians constitute a nation with the right to establish an independent state of their own. Among Palestinians, powerful groups like Hamas likewise reject the premise that Jews comprise a nation with the right to have an independent state; even those Palestinians who concede this issue certainly do not feel the Jewish state should be erected on Palestinian land. To further propagate their respective positions, both Israeli and Palestinian rejectionists are engaged in mutual and systematic delegitimization of the other, including the denial of each other's basic human rights. Although the 1993–1994 Oslo Accords presumably changed (at least to a certain degree) the nature of the relationship between the two sides through mutual recognition, they did not fundamentally mitigate the doubt each side held, or altered their predisposed perception of the other. That is, the mutually embedded rejectionist sentiment in their respective psyches creates insurmountable resistance to change, especially by inciting deliberate actions that further reinforce rejection of the other.

In probing the psychological barriers to change, we must also pay close attention to the manner in which helplessness and radical vulnerability inhibit the positive transformation of the status quo. Helplessness arises when one's relation to the self or to the world is systematically undone at the hands of another; coordinated with this...is something worse, a loss of trust in the world."[372] While the

---

372 J.M. Bernstein, "Torture," *Political Concepts: A Critical Lexicon* (1) (2011), http://www.politicalconcepts.org/issue1/torture/.

sense of being exposed and constitutively vulnerable is doubtless more severe among Palestinians, we should not hastily assume that because Israel is an immensely powerful state, its citizens do not also share in this experience; constant concerns over personal security and chronic fear of change are more than enough to foster vulnerability of the self among Israelis.

The leadership on both sides have too often sought to instill public resentment by maligning public narratives and denying the rights and humanity of the other. Palestinians, for example, blame Israel for the suffering caused by the refugee problem while Israel blames the Palestinians for the never-ending terrorism and violence, especially the second Intifada that stunned Israelis and shattered any remaining residue of trust.

Refutations of the other's public narratives, however, are not limited to statements or announcements made by officials. For example, Israelis view the Palestinian insistence on the refugees' right of return as an effort to obliterate the Jewish identity of the state. Similarly, Palestinians consider Israel's settlement building throughout the West Bank a gross encroachment on their land for the express purpose of denying them the opportunity to establish their own state. By insisting publicly only on their respective rights, both sides view the other's actions merely as efforts to delegitimize and undermine the other.

The campaign of mutual delegitimization, not limited to the po-litical and public domain, has developed into a culture that permeates all social strata, particularly education and the media. This aspect of delegitimization is more troubling than any other in that it not only denies each other's rights in the eyes of the contemporary general public but also poisons the next generation of adults, who are indoc-trinated in childhood to reject the other. Palestinian textbooks have and continue to distort the factual historical account of what actually happened between Israelis and Palestinians and how the current situ-ation came to pass. Palestinian geography books fail to delineate Israel on maps, and teachers that express hostility plant in the minds of young students a deep-rooted hatred for Jews, perpetuating the delegitimization of Israel and making it extremely difficult to mitigate the damage when Palestinian children come of age.

In Israel, new history textbooks were, in fact, published and introduced into Israeli junior and senior high schools in 1999 after the Oslo peace agreement was signed. While these new textbooks attempted to offer a more balanced account of the Israeli-Arab conflict than previous publications, they still presented a typical nationalistic narrative, which left little room for recognizing the legitimacy of the Palestinians. Thus, instead of using the classroom to promote each other's rights and plights, schools on both sides of the border have become laboratories manufacturing perceptions useful in the delegitimization of the other. Of course, these perceptions are further and frequently reinforced by violent events, perpetuating cultures of hatred at home, at temple, and in the mosque.

In Israel, where a largely free press is a given and both print and electronic media run the gamut from extreme-right to extreme-left, many news outlets openly criticize the government for its treatment of and policy toward the Palestinians. The same cannot at all be said about Palestinian media. This is particularly problematic because as a result the criticism and condemnation of Israel, regardless of how justified it may be, becomes institutionalized, leading to the formation of a popular mindset that makes reconciliation with Israel all the more difficult. To be sure, conscious efforts toward delegitimizing the other not only cause suffering and harm to both sides but also permits and justifies continuing moral infractions against the opposing faction. Delegitimization sustains conflict, minimizes concessions made by both sides, and inadvertently leads to heightened resistance to change and renewed violence.

In weighing the psychological impediments to change, the significance of the process of socialization cannot be ignored, especially if we want to understand how both sides are able to justify moral infractions against the other. That is, we need to explore not only the forces that push people into performing violent and oppressive acts but also the psychological forces that contribute to the weakening of moral restraints that routinely check individuals against performing acts they would normally find reprehensible.

The recent documentary The Gatekeepers (2012), about the Shin Bet (Israel's General Internal Security Service), is to be commended for raising precisely this issue, among others. Herbert Kelman categorizes at least three processes involved in socialization, which deserve to be mentioned. The first process is authorization. Rather than recognizing oneself as an independent moral agent, the individual feels that they are participating in a "transcendent mission," one that relinquishes them of the responsibility to make their own moral choices. The second is routinization, the process through which an action is organized and divided among numerous individuals such that "there is no opportunity for raising moral questions and making moral decisions…Each individual carries out routine tasks without having to think of the overall product created by these tasks."[373] What should be emphasized here is that the aura of professionalism permits the insider to perceive the process not as the brutal treatment of other human beings "but as the routine application of specialized knowledge and skills."[374] Finally is dehumanization, whereby the other is systematically excluded from the moral community to which one belongs; it becomes unnecessary for agents to regard their relationship to the other as ethically significant. In short, the victim of dehumanization is denied any moral consideration.

Ignoring grievances and suffering: Although a majority of Israelis seek a resolution to the conflict based on a two-state solution (supported by many think tanks and a wide range of media outlets), a demeaning attitude toward the Palestinians signifying they do not deserve to, or cannot, be treated as equals pervades the culture. In this way, Israelis have become complacent toward the occupation, and content to ignore the urgency to create a Palestinian state. Israeli indifference toward the Palestinians' plight has become second nature, creating a mindset among Israelis that blames the Palestinians for their problems.

I believe that the category of "social death" (originally proposed as a way of thinking about the social-psychological impact of slavery) is entirely relevant to understanding the suffering of the Palestinians.

---

373 Herbert C. Kelman, "The Social Context of Torture: Policy Process and Authority Structure," in *The politics of pain: Torturers and their masters*, eds. R.D. Crelinsten and A.P. Schmid (Boulder, Colorado: Westview Press, 1995), 29.

374 Kelman, "The Social Context of Torture: Policy Process and Authority Structure," 31.

Applying this concept means coming to grips with the real and awful impact of being utterly overpowered by another, of having one's home ransacked and one's village arbitrarily divided by the building of fences (presumably to prevent terrorism), of having one's house raided in the middle of the night, terrifying women and children, and of losing the sense of having any control over one's life. Not unlike African-Americans under Jim Crow or South Africans under apartheid, Palestinians have seen their humanity systematically denied by the forces of occupation. Yet, Israel continues to ignore the grievances and suffering of those whose lands it confiscated, the consequence of this state-sanctioned delegitimization being little short of soul death for Palestinians.

The ever-present possibility of terrible and unpredictable violence not only destroys the hope that the situation will someday be resolved but also increases the sense of shame, despondency, and the will to retaliate to make the other suffer. The trauma suffered by the victim of deliberate violence lingers on in its aftermath as a part of the victim's very sense of self, and "existential helplessness is categorical for the being of humans."[375] The point here is that this sense of existential helplessness has and will continue to grow among the Palestinians (and Israelis) if the conflict is allowed to continue indefinitely.

Whether we are talking about the settler who will stop at nothing to maintain control of the land or the militant Palestinian who is sworn to the destruction of Israel, both see themselves as pursuing a divinely authorized mission, the fulfillment of which absolves them of any moral culpability. Categories of zealotry consistently and accurately apply to both Israelis and Palestinians, while blind refusal of reality by influential voices on both sides obscures the voices of those on the fringes seeking a solution. This will only result in further alienation and perilous delegitimization of the other, and is certainly the recipe for Mutually Assured Destruction.

---

375 Bernstein, "Torture."

NATIONAL SECURITY AND THREAT MISPERCEPTION

FEBRUARY 27, 2013

Israel's historical experiences, coupled with decades of violent confrontations with Arab states and the Palestinians, have created a major psychological barrier that places Israel's legitimate national security concerns at the front and center of its domestic and foreign policy. Regardless of how exaggerated Israel's sense of vulnerability may seem to its detractors, the Palestinians cannot afford to dismiss Israel's concerns which are deeply embedded in the psyche of every Israeli. That said, nothing, including military might or even the expropriation of the entire West Bank, will guarantee Israel's national security, short of comprehensive peace.

What was once Israel's legitimate national security concern has now become a tool by which to oppress the Palestinians, expropriate their land, and prevent them from establishing a Palestinian state. In fact, Israel's fixation on "security" and the harsh measures it employs, presumably to achieve an impregnable national security condition, is making the Palestinians increasingly vulnerable. As Henry Kissinger observed in his book, A World Restored: "...the desire of one power for absolute security means absolute insecurity for all the others."[376]

The relative quiet that has prevailed in the past few years only obscures the gathering storm that will hit Israeli shores with devastating velocity. Israel's continued intoxication with seizing Palestinian territories is akin to an addict who keeps injecting himself with a deadly substance to make him feel euphoric, never mind that it is only temporary and could end with his demise.

Unfortunately, those Israelis supporting the notion of a "Greater Israel" satisfy their lust for more Palestinian land under the guise of

---

376 Kissinger, *A World Restored*, 2.

enhancing Israel's national security. Yet the Israelis' national and personal security cannot be ensured by expropriating more land to establish so-called "defensible borders." After all, the distance between the Jordan River and the Mediterranean Sea hardly exceeds 42 kilometers (26 miles). In the age of rockets and precision missile technology, territorial depths can no longer guarantee Israel's security. This was glaringly demonstrated during Operation Pillar of Defense in November 2012 when Hamas was able to rain hundreds of rockets on Israel, some of which reached the outskirts of Jerusalem and Tel Aviv.

National security is becoming an obsession in Israel, a kind of idée fixe- as Joseph Conrad observed, "A man haunted by a fixed idea is insane."[377] For sure, there is a certain madness involved in Israel's compulsive pursuit of absolute security, evident in a number of ways that have produced the precise opposite effect. Israel's national security now serves as the means of justifying every conceivable abuse that one people can inflict upon another, including the confiscation of Palestinian land, the destruction of homes and property, torture, and targeted killings, which so often lead to the death of innocents as well. Yaakov Peri, former head of the Shin Bet was quoted in an AP interview, February 2012, saying "Just force, just battle, just deception won't bring peace between the nations."[378]

The expansion of settlements in the name of national security is another manifestation of Israel's utter disregard for the Palestinians' aspiration to establish their state on the same land, making them a security liability rather than an asset. The continuous construction of fences and walls, which will soon surround the entire country, are the physical manifestation and the most ready symbol of the madness- Israel is effectively building a prison for itself. What we are witnessing is the formation of a garrison state, as Israel becomes progressively more isolated, politically and physically, from its neighbors and the international community.

---

377 Joseph Conrad, *Nostromo: A Tale of the Seaboard* (New York: Harper & Brothers, 1904), 319.

378 Aron Heller, "Israeli Ex-Security Officials Largely Favor Peace," *Associated Press*, February 20, 2013, http://bigstory.ap.org/article/israeli-ex-security-officials-largely-favor-peace.

Israeli officials are quite explicit about the way they give no
thought or consideration to what lies ahead for the country ten or
twenty years down the line. In an interview with the New York Times
on December 26, Naftali Bennett, the leader of the newly formed
party HaBayit Hayehudi (Jewish Home), posed to himself a rhetorical
question: "What do we do in the long term? I do not know."[379] This is
a guy who seeks to expropriate Area C, which represents 60 percent
of the entire landmass of the West Bank, and who aspires to become
prime minister. I am certain that Prime Minister Netanyahu does not
know either what havoc is in store for Israel 15–20 years down the
line. Imagine, Israel's future and perhaps the future of world Jewry
rests in the hands of reckless leaders who have no strategy, no vision
or even a clue about Israel's fate should they continue to pursue the
policy of territorial expansion.

In her book On Violence, Hannah Arendt makes a fundamental
point which Israelis and militant-minded Palestinians would do well
to remind themselves of. She writes, "Violence can always destroy
power; out of the barrel of a gun grows the most effective command,
resulting in the most instant and perfect obedience. What never can
grow out of it is power."[380] Far from being the same, violence and
power are antithetical, precisely in the sense that violence diminishes
the power of those who employ it, necessitating the use of more
violence in the effort to maintain control. This is what we see happening in the case of Israel, inasmuch as it must continue to use
the machinery of violence, by other means, as a way of maintaining
control over the territories.

Israel's ultimate national security requirements rest only on a
comprehensive peace constructed on multiple security measures over
which every politically nonbiased Israeli defense and security expert
agrees upon. During a conference in Tel Aviv in December 2012,
Gabi Ashkenazi, the former Chief of Staff of the Israeli army, reconfirmed the sentiments of many of his colleagues when he said:

379 Rudoren, "Dynamic Former Netanyahu Aide Shifts Israeli Campaign
Rightward."

380 Hannah Arendt, *On Violence* (New York: Harcourt Brace & Company,
1970), 53.

"Israel must recognize the limits of its power and cooperate with forces that support Israeli interests."[381] This was aptly expressed by another top Israeli military commander, Shaul Arieli, who said, "We believe that peace will provide better security than anything else."[382] Otherwise, all security measures, however coercive, elaborate, and sophisticated, cannot guarantee Israel's national security.

A Comprehensive Peace

Every effort must first focus on achieving a negotiated peace agreement to accommodate Israel's legitimate national security concerns and respect the Palestinians' right to live freely on a contiguous land mass in an independent state alongside Israel. To ensure and further enhance their mutual security, any peace agreement must be based on certain provisions, mechanisms, logistics, and a timeline designed to ensure compliance based on reciprocity. This would allow for mutual mitigation of biases and selective perceptions over each other's intentions and willingness to deliver and foster trust, which is sine qua non to a lasting peace.

To prevent a repeat of the withdrawal from Gaza in 2005, which was precipitous, unilateral, and ended up with Hamas' taking over and using Gaza as a launching ground for rockets, the pullout from the West Bank must entail a number of critical measures, including full logistical coordination with the PA, tight security arrangements, a phased withdrawal, an established timeframe between each phase, and specific reciprocal measures by the Palestinians. It can be argued that had then-Prime Minister Sharon followed such a framework in Gaza, the result would have been entirely different today.

Israel's security is inextricably linked to its ability to forge people-to-people relations that can mitigate the psychological security

---

381 Philip Podolsky, "Former IDF Chief Indicates Israel Should Withdraw From West Bank Unilaterally," *The Times of Israel*, December 9, 2012, http://www.timesofisrael.com/former-idf-chief-says-israel-should-withdraw-from-west-bank-unilaterally/.

382 Aron Heller, "Israel's Former Security Chiefs Largely Favor Peace," *Associated Press*, February 20, 2013, http://news.msn.com/world/israels-former-security-chiefs-largely-favor-peace.

hang-ups between the two sides. Imagine the effect of allowing tens of thousands of Palestinians and Israelis to visit each other, sharing stories and experiences and intermingling in restaurants and places of entertainment. Nothing can change perceptions about each other more than these casual encounters, the result of which were shocking for those few on both sides who have had this experience. It is time to change the image of an Israeli in the eyes of a Palestinian youth from a soldier with a gun to a normal and friendly face.

The development of trade and commercial ties between the two sides is fundamental to fostering a mutually vested interest in beneficial relationships that reveal and enhance the humanity of both sides and allow them to resolve any arising problem peacefully. The psychological effect of peaceful conflict resolution becomes central to the development of nonviolent culture. This requirement, more than anything else, provides a point of departure that affects all other aspects of coexistence.

Preserving Credible Deterrence

Since there is lingering distrust between the two sides, Israel will insist on a credible military deterrent that will dissuade current and future enemies from threatening it, lest they do so at their own peril. For Israelis, the "Never Again" mindset (in reference to the Holocaust) is not a slogan; they are bent on doing whatever necessary to prevent history from repeating itself.

In this regard, Israel and the United States can ensure that no single state or a combination of states is able to overwhelm Israel militarily by maintaining a qualitative military edge along with America's continued guarantee of Israel's security. Psychologically, these security measures provide Israel the comfort it needs and reduces the urge to go on the offensive when provoked.

Maintaining Full Security Cooperation

By virtue of the Israelis' and the Palestinians' past experiences, full security cooperation between the two sides remains a prerequisite. Progress made between Israel and the PA demonstrates that effective security cooperation is possible, even in an atmosphere of tension. The success of this cooperation was made possible by the PA's commitment to peace as well as Israel's willingness to fully collaborate by easing Palestinian mobility, coordinating with their internal security, and improving intelligence cooperation.

Borders and National Security

Every American administration since President Carter has supported the idea that the 1967 borders provide the baseline for negotiations, to which every Israeli government since then has concurred. Even if Israel were to draw its own final borders, the contours of these borders would not enhance Israel's national security. The annexation of more land two or three kilometers deep into the West Bank will make little difference from a security perspective.

Those who promote the notion of a "Greater Israel" under the guise of national security seek to surround the Palestinians from the east, west, north, and south, isolating them completely and denying them contiguity. This would doubtless be rejected by the Palestinians, denying Israel even a semblance of peace as the Palestinians are psychologically, emotionally, and physically committed to rid themselves of the occupation.

An International Peacekeeping Force

Israel's demand to keep residual forces along the Jordan River to prevent the smuggling of weapons and the infiltration of terrorists from the Jordan Valley is not likely to be accepted by the Palestinians as they would view that as a continuation of occupation, only in a different form. Instead, an international peacekeeping force (perhaps with symbolic Israeli and Palestinian participation) will have to be stationed there. The force should be assembled from specific countries that recognize Israel and have a vested interest in maintaining peace, including Jordan, Egypt, Saudi Arabia, and EU nations like Britain, France, and Germany, operating under the military command of the United States. Such a robust force should be empowered by the United Nations Security Council (UNSC) to act to maintain calm and prevent the smuggling of weapons and the infiltration of terrorists. This force cannot be removed without an explicit UNSC resolution, where the United States enjoys veto power.

A Demilitarized Palestinian State

The newly-established Palestinian state should be demilitarized, with its security assured by the United States. Regardless of their military prowess, the Palestinians will never be in a position to challenge Israel militarily and no country, including Israel, would threaten a Palestinian state at peace with its neighbors. There are several countries that do not have any military forces including Costa Rica, Andorra, and Liechtenstein, who continue to live in peace.

The idea here is that the lesser Israel's national security concerns are, the greater political and territorial concessions it will make. Instead of wasting hundreds of millions of dollars on military hardware, future Palestinian governments should respond to the yearning of the people by investing in economic development, education, health care, infrastructure, and democratic institutions that will enable them to take pride in their achievements.

A Regional Security Umbrella

Once a peace agreement is achieved and all security measures are in place, the United States could offer a security umbrella along the lines of what former Secretary of State Hillary Clinton proposed in June 2009, under which all nations in the region who are at peace with Israel (and each other) could belong.[383] Such a regional security umbrella would also deter outside adversaries such as Iran and prevent it from intimidating or threatening any state in the area.

Reviving the Arab Peace Initiative

In the context of Israeli-Palestinian peace negotiations, Israel should accept the principles of the Arab Peace Initiative (API), **which was proposed in 2002 and reintroduced in 2007**, and agree to

---

383 Landler and Sanger, "Clinton Speaks of Shielding Mideast From Iran."

convene with representatives of the Arab League to discuss its merits. This would open the door for negotiating a comprehensive Arab-Israeli peace agreement, beginning normal relations with the Arab states and by extension with all Muslim states. Those who claim that this would be the wrong time for Israel to make such a move given the Middle East's sweeping turmoil are wrong. This is precisely the right time, when diffusing the conflict with the Palestinians becomes even more urgent. Israel does not need a fire in its backyard or a fifth column at a time when it must focus on the Iranian threat and the potential disintegration of Syria—both of which will have major regional repercussions that will directly affect Israel's national security.

In this regard, the revival of the API cannot be over emphasized. As the former head of the Mossad, Meir Dagan, stated in June 2011 at Tel Aviv University, "We must adopt the Saudi Initiative, we have no other way, and not because the Palestinians are my top priority but because I am concerned about Israel's wellbeing and I want to do what I can to ensure Israel's existence."[384] The revival of the API would strengthen United States and Israeli relations with the Arab world while advancing their shared regional strategic interests. True, not every Arab state in the region will jump on the peace bandwagon, but the Arab countries who wield significant influence, especially in the Gulf and North Africa, will be the most eager to establish full diplomatic relations with Israel—that in and of itself will be a game changer.

The real threat to Israel's national security from militant Islamic groups is not misperceived; it can be quantified and dealt with effectively as Israel has demonstrated time and again. To manufacture a threat, however, and try to remedy it with extra-territoriality is undermining not only Israel's security but its very future. The time has come for the Israelis to be awakened to this harsh reality.

---

384 Koutsoukis, "Former Mossad Head Advocates Saudi Peace Plan."

ALON BEN-MEIR

THE SELF-IMPOSED IDEOLOGICAL SIEGE

MARCH 13, 2013

Even a cursory review of the core ideologies of right-of-center Israelis and extremist Palestinians strongly suggests that regardless of the dramatic changes of the political landscape since 1948, they remained ideologically besieged, making the conflict ever more intractable. Since Israelis and Palestinians know that coexistence under any scenario is inescapable, the question is what it would take to modify their ideological bent to achieve a political solution to satisfy their mutual claims to the same land.

The contradiction between Israel and the Palestinians, in connection with "the land of Israel" as defined by right-of-center Israelis or "Palestine" as classified by Palestinian Islamists, is starkly evident in Likud's and Hamas' political platforms. The Likud platform states, "The Jewish communities in Judea, Samaria and Gaza are the realization of Zionist values…Settlement of the land is a clear expression of the unassailable right of the Jewish people to *the Land of Israel* [emphasis added] and constitutes an important asset in the defense of the vital interests of the State of Israel. The Likud will continue to strengthen and develop these communities and will prevent their uprooting."[385]

Hamas' platform affirms that "Palestine is Arab and Muslim Land; Palestinians are one nation regardless of location; the Palestinian People are still in the process of National Liberation and have the right to use all means including armed struggle to achieve this goal."[386]

Insisting on these principles amounts to a political dead-end as neither can force the other by any means to relinquish their claim to the

385 "Likud Party Platform from the 15th Knesset," Jewish Virtual Library, http://www.jewishvirtuallibrary.org/jsource/Politics/likudplatform15.html.

386 "The Covenant of the Islamic Resistance Movement," The Avalon Project, August 18, 1988, http://avalon.law.yale.edu/20th_century/hamas.asp.

same land, short of catastrophe. The question is, can they modify their ideological stances without abandoning their core ideological positions? Ideology is often understood to be "the process whereby social life is converted to a natural reality" or "the indispensable medium in which individuals live out their relations to a social structure."[387]

In either case, there are consistent efforts by Israeli zealots and Palestinian extremists to legitimize their respective ideologies by adopting a different strategy. As Terry Eagleton points out, "A dominant power may legitimate itself by *promoting* beliefs and values [ideology] congenial to it; *naturalizing* and *universalizing* such beliefs so as to render them self-evident and apparently inevitable; *denigrating* ideas which might challenge it; *excluding* rival forms of thought...and *obscuring* social reality in ways convenient to itself."[388]

Thus, to understand the depth of the Israeli and Palestinian contradictory positions, we must look briefly at the evolutionary development of the conflict from its inception. The Jewish community sought to establish a state of its own early in the twentieth century, which was subsequently granted by the UN partition plan in 1947, thereby legitimizing the Zionist ideology to establish a Jewish Home in the ancient biblical land.[389] The Palestinians refused the partition plan along with the rest of the Arab states, who waged a war on the nascent state resulting in the loss of more territory and the mass exodus of Palestinian refugees. Although the Palestinian Liberation Organization (PLO), which led the Palestinian revolutionary movement, and Israel recognized each other at the Oslo Accords in 1993, Hamas (established in 1987, likely as a result of 20 years of occupation) continues to object to Israel's existence altogether.

Immediately following the 1967 war, Israel offered to return all the captured territories except East Jerusalem; the offer was rebuffed by the Arab League (AL). Convening in Khartoum, Sudan in the same

387 Terry Eagleton, *Ideology* (New York: Verso, 2007), 2.

388 Ibid, 5.

389 "UN Partition Plan," *BBC News*, November 29, 2001, http://news.bbc.co.uk/2/hi/in_depth/middle_east/israel_and_the_palestinians/key_documents/1681322.stm.

year, the AL submitted their three infamous NO's: no peace, no recognition, and no negotiations with Israel.[390] That response was seen by the Israelis as an outright rejection by the Arab states of Israel's very existence, despite the Israelis' willingness to relinquish the captured territories, which continues to resonate in the minds of many Israelis.

In the process, both sides moved to act to enforce their ideological beliefs. The Israelis consistently pursued settlement policies, and the Palestinians, especially Hamas, held onto their militant resistance. The continuing violent confrontations, in particular the second intifada and the Israeli crackdown on Palestinian terror attacks, further deepened the gulf between them while intensifying mutual distrust.

Ideological and political factionalism in both camps has made the conflict increasingly intractable. Since the creation of Israel political parties have mushroomed, reaching at one time more than 20 parties. As a result, all governments have been coalition-based, consisting of several deeply conflicted parties with little consensus on how to address the Palestinian problem and the disposition of the occupied territories. In the last election, 12 parties passed the threshold (receiving at least two percent of the electoral vote to qualify) and are currently represented in the Israeli Knesset.

Although weakened in the last election, the right-of-center parties still represent nearly half of the Israeli electorate and hold significant sway over settlement policy. What started with the building of a few settlements to protect Jerusalem has now become a major enterprise embedded in the ideology that "the land of Israel" is the Jews' inherent historical land. The settlers' movement became a powerhouse and now enjoys tremendous influence on any government, regardless of its ideological makeup.

Factionalism within the Palestinians has made it also impossible to speak in one voice. Following the 1993 Oslo Accords, however, a growing majority of Palestinians began to realize that they must find a way to co-exist with Israel, which subsequently became the

---

390 "Khartoum Resolution," League of Arab States, September 1, 1967, http://www.cfr.org/world/khartoum-resolution/p14841?breadcru mb=%2Fpublication%2Fpublication_list%3Ftype%3Dessential_ document%26page%3D69.

official policy of the Palestinian Authority (PA) in the West Bank. Hamas, which controls Gaza, continues to struggle to find a way to reconcile with the reality of Israel. Yet, despite the growing pragmatic view, a significant constituency of Israelis and Palestinians continues to reject one another on ideological, religious, and political grounds.

The question is how to reconcile ideological ethos with certain irreversible realities on the ground—Israeli-Palestinian coexistence—and their mutual claim to the same territory. History and experiences suggest that regardless of how deep an ideological conviction may be, it cannot be sustained if it does not enshrine justice, fairness, and human rights at its very core. An ideological shift will become inevitable due to:

Inevitable failure: Notwithstanding the success of right-of-center parties in Israel and Hamas' continued resistance, both will realize that **failure is imminent**. The falsity of the Israeli position to help to legitimate a dominant political order and the socially useful (or necessary) illusion will backfire. Indeed, there are certain conditions on the ground which neither can change, in particular **their coexistence**. Ideological divergence notwithstanding, their fate is intertwined and they must choose between reconciliation or mutual self-destruction.

Changing political wind: The changing political landscape among Israelis and Palestinians suggests that both camps are undergoing a gradual ideological shift. Fatah came to the conclusion that violence as a means by which to achieve political objectives has failed and began to focus on a solution by peaceful means. Hamas, however, has adopted a two track approach. They began to signal their readiness to establish a Palestinian state based on the 1967 borders under conditions of no war and no peace (*hudna*), while maintaining a military approach (armed struggle) as an option, primarily for domestic consumption.

Arresting shift to the right: The recent election in Israel indicated that there has not been a further shift to the right and, in fact, a significant segment of the population moved to the left-of-center, which calls for an end to the conflict with the Palestinians. While hardcore ideological positions continue and systematic distortions of communications (for example in connection with national security and its linkage to the final borders) do exist, the new political map may well slow the settlements' incursion due to the growing strength of the constituency that rejects the status quo.

The demographic factor: As a result of the rapidly changing demographic ratios between Israelis and Palestinians, Israel is in imminent danger of losing its Jewish majority. Sooner than later Israel must choose between a true democracy with a sustainable Jewish majority or a democracy in name only, as discrimination against the Palestinians becomes a tool of necessity to maintain its Jewish dominance. If Israel refuses to relinquish much of the West Bank, it will have little choice but to resort to an apartheid state, inviting international censure, condemnation, and sanctions.

The failure of armed struggle: Unless a negotiated agreement with Israel is reached, no armed struggle will dislodge Israel from its current position. The peace process, however, has evolved to a point where the PA has given up on armed struggle and instead resorted to unilateral actions, guided by the belief that it is the only way to advance its goal and force Israel's hand. The Palestinians were successful in their efforts to upgrade their diplomatic status to nonmember observer state at the UN General Assembly, and Hamas, though it occasionally challenges Israel by the use of force, also recognizes that armed struggle has outlived its usefulness.

No gains but increased vulnerability: In the clash of ideologies, however, there comes a point where neither side is making any gains but is actually becoming increasingly vulnerable. Israel is becoming ever more isolated and the Palestinians are watching the territory of their future state be usurped to make room for more settlements. The forecast for both sides appears to be bleak and further worsening. In the long term, however, Israel will end up on the losing side as the Palestinian cause will continue to garner overwhelming international support.

The potential for massive violent explosion: Given the simmering situation and the frustration over the stalemate, a violent eruption may well become inevitable. Ideology aside, the average Palestinian is edging ever closer to challenging the occupation. They understand that Israel has the capacity to quell such a violent challenge but they are now prepared to emulate their counterparts in Syria and other Arab countries, who have sacrificed themselves for their freedom. For Israel, this would represent a major dilemma as cracking down on Palestinian demonstrators will evoke international outrage, as the majority of the world views the Palestinians as the victims of immoral occupation.

Israelis and Palestinians can certainly introduce a modified version of their ideological bent, as the reality allows for a gradual shift without sacrificing their ideological principles or losing face. The Palestinians can establish a state on a part of their homeland and Hamas will also recognize the inevitable and may well follow the PLO and come to terms with Israel's existence. The Israelis must accept the fact that Israel will be limited to the 1967 borders with some land swaps. This is not to suggest that all issues will readily be resolved, but the realization that coexistence is not negotiable will trump the ideological ethos of both sides.

The alternative is the continuation of this self-imposed ideological siege, which is bound to fail the test of time at a price that neither side can afford to pay.

CONCLUSION

LOOKING BACK IN DISMAY AND
FORWARD TO DELIVERANCE

The Israeli-Palestinian conflict is the longest in modern times and sadly it does not appear to be any closer to a resolution, even after seven decades of continuing struggle. A score of interim agreements meant to lead to a peace accord were overshadowed by as many acts of major violent confrontations and thousands of bloody incidents and acts of terrorism. Many Israelis and Palestinians have come to accept the notion that the conflict cannot be resolved and can only be managed to minimize the destruction and loss of lives.

Only a mad man could subscribe to this view. The idea that the conflict can indeed be managed indefinitely is flawed because it is based on the assumption that both sides have an intrinsic interest in maintaining the status quo of no major war and no peace.

The failure to reach a negotiated peace agreement, coupled with the many violent episodes and shifting geopolitical conditions that occurred since the 1993 Oslo Accords, which was supposed to usher in a comprehensive peace, strongly suggest that the status quo is not sustainable and is dangerously deteriorating.

The following brief summary of events and policies glaringly demonstrates that the responsibility for the worsening relations falls squarely on both sides' shoulders:

The disregard of the psychological dimension of the conflict

The psychological dimension of the conflict, which has impacted every conflicting issue between the two sides, has hardly been paid any heed to, especially from historic, religious, and security perspectives.

Few efforts have been made to understand and appreciate the other's legitimate grievances, fears, concerns, aspirations, and convictions. Ignoring the psychological divide has made it impossible to mitigate their differences and prevents them from negotiating in good faith.

The continuing occupation

The occupation was and still is the single most reviled ailment from which the Palestinians have suffered psychologically, emotionally, and physically. It has rendered the Palestinians hopeless and despairing, and contributes ever more to the deepening hatred and hostility toward Israel.

The Israeli practices in the occupied territories—from arbitrary arrests, night raids, restrictions on mobility, expropriation of land, control over natural resources, and repeated brutal acts—have profoundly alienated three generations of Palestinians, to whom the occupation is the mother of all evil.

The terrible consequences of the occupation can be understood in terms of social death (a concept developed by Orlando Patterson in his book Slavery and Social Death), referring to the condition of a people not viewed, accepted or treated as fully human by the rest of society.

The total powerlessness that marks this condition may appear most starkly under slavery and apartheid, but one could argue that the longest occupation in modern history has made social death a painful reality for millions of Palestinians as well.

All other conflicting issues are directly and indirectly related to the occupation and thus its continuation has chipped away at any residue of good-will. Ending it is sine qua non to reaching an agreement; absent that, the Palestinians' hostility will never recede.

Rancorous public narrative

They have mutually and continuously engaged in acrimonious public narratives, maligning and delegitimizing each other, creating the perception among their respective publics that the other has no sovereign rights.

Successive prominent Israeli politicians have openly dismissed the prospect of the two-state solution and keep insisting that Israel is not an occupying power. The Palestinians remain trapped in their own vitriolic narrative, with widespread anti-Israeli indoctrination in schools, media, and public and private institutions.

While a persistent majority of Israelis and Palestinians have yearned for peace for the past two decades, their leaders have shown no commitment to that end, as manifested daily by their rancorous charges and counter charges even during peace negotiations.

The settlements enterprise

The settlements have grown exponentially since the 1993 Oslo Accords. The total settler population in the West Bank and East Jerusalem has more than doubled from 257,700 to 582,031, an increase of 125%.[1] From the time Netanyahu came to power in 2009, the growth in the West Bank alone was nearly 25%.[2]

While the total land mass of Israeli settlements in the West Bank is less than 3%, the real issue is that the settlements are dispersed throughout the territory. There are 157 settlements and outposts strategically designed to prevent the Palestinians from controlling a contiguous land-mass in the West Bank. These occupy 593,009 acres,

---

1   "By Hook and by Crook: Israeli Settlement Policy in the West Bank," B'Tselem (Jerusalem, July 2010), p. 9-10, http://www.btselem.org/download/201007_by_hook_and_by_crook_eng.pdf.

2   Ishaan Tharoor, "Map: The spread of Israeli settlements in the West Bank," *The Washington Post*, December 22, 2014, http://www.washingtonpost.com/blogs/worldviews/wp/2014/12/22/map-the-spread-of-israeli-settlements-in-the-west-bank/.

which is 4.5 times larger than what is stated by Israeli officials.[3]

Nothing has provoked and antagonized the Palestinians more than the settlements and their continuing expansion, which they view as a direct assault on their aspiration to build a viable state on the same land.

The use of force

Both sides are guilty of using force first to seek remedy or retribution for violent acts of the other. The frequency of major conflicts demonstrates how their relationship has deteriorated even further.

The Second Intifada, which erupted in 2000 and saw scores of suicide attacks killing more than 1,000 Israelis, was a turning point for Israelis from which they have yet to recover.

Since 2008, there were 3 major conflagrations between Israel and Hamas. Operation Cast Lead (December 2008 to January 2009) began as an escalation of rocket attacks following Israeli incursions into Gaza to destroy Hamas' tunnels.

Operation Pillar of Defense, in November 2012, ratcheted up following the assassination by Israel of Ahmed Jabari, chief of Hamas's military wing. The most recent conflict, Operation Protective Edge (July-August 2014), was a response to the escalation of tensions following the kidnapping and murder of three Israeli teenagers and the revenge killing of a Palestinian youth.

These repeated conflagrations only deepen the mutual hatred and distrust between the two sides, setting the peace process back and making the prospect of reconciliation ever more remote.

---

3   As reported by *Haaretz* (Chaim Levinson, "Israel's West Bank settlements grew by twice the size of New York's Central Park in 2012," *Haaretz*, May 27, 2013), Civil Administration data lists settlement-controlled land as 538,303 dunams (133,018 acres), whereas B'Tselem ("By Hook and by Crook: Israeli Settlement Policy in the West Bank," B'Tselem (Jerusalem, July 2010) reports that the total land area controlled by the settlements is 2,399,824 dunams (593,009 acres).

The failure of peace negotiations

Since 1993 there have been numerous peace negotiations which have ended in failure, including the Camp David Summit (2000), Taba Summit (2001), peace talks between Olmert and Abbas (2007-2008), direct talks between Israel and the Palestinians in 2009-2010 brokered by George Mitchell, and John Kerry's 2013-2014 initiative.

Although the "usual suspects"—including the Palestinian refugees, the right of return, the status of Jerusalem and the Temple Mount, national security, borders, and the future of the settlements—were front and center in these negotiations, it is fundamentally a lack of commitment that has prevented them from reaching their presumed objective.

This dismal state of affairs finally forced the Palestinian Authority to turn to the United Nations for recognition and restitution. Tired of the unending conflict and blaming Israel for the lack of progress, the international community has largely sided with the Palestinians.

To be sure, many elements have contributed to the alarming deterioration in the peace process, which has now reached its lowest point since 1993. By placing the Israeli-Palestinian conflict front and center on the global stage, the PA has been able to change the political discourse of the conflict and create an irreversible political fact, putting Israel on the defensive.

Israel can fight back, but it will only lose further political ground and suffer from the far-reaching implications should it continue to defy the international community (especially its European allies and the US) and refuse to end the occupation.

Conversely, the Palestinians will make a terrible mistake if they simply rely on the international community to do their bidding. They must demonstrate, in words and deeds, that they are ready to make an unshakable commitment and the necessary concessions to reach an agreement.

Both sides must remember that while the past 22 years were dismaying at best, the changing political environment holds the promise of deliverance—if they only will it.

APPENDIX

Appendix 1

United Nations General Assembly Resolution 181
November 29, 1947

The General Assembly,

Having met in special session at the request of the mandatory Power to constitute and instruct a Special Committee to prepare for the consideration of the question of the future Government of Palestine at the second regular session;

Having constituted a Special Committee and instructed it to investigate all questions and issues relevant to the problem of Palestine, and to prepare proposals for the solution of the problem, and

Having received and examined the report of the Special Committee (document A/364) including a number of unanimous recommendations and a plan of partition with economic union approved by the majority of the Special Committee,

Considers that the present situation in Palestine is one which is likely to impair the general welfare and friendly relations among nations;

Takes note of the declaration by the mandatory Power that it plans to complete its evacuation of Palestine by 1 August 1948;

Recommends to the United Kingdom, as the mandatory Power for Palestine, and to all other Members of the United Nations the adoption and implementation, with regard to the future Government of Palestine, of the Plan of Partition with Economic Union set out below;

Requests that

The Security Council take the necessary measures as provided for in the plan for its implementation;

The Security Council consider, if circumstances during the transitional period require such consideration, whether the situation in Palestine constitutes a threat to the peace. If it decides that such a threat exists, and in order to maintain international peace and security, the Security Council should supplement the authorization of the General Assembly by taking measures, under Articles 39 and 41 of the Charter, to empower the United Nations Commission, as provided in this resolution, to exercise in Palestine the functions which are assigned to it by this resolution;

The Security Council determine as a threat to the peace, breach of the peace or act of aggression, in accordance with Article 39 of the Charter, any attempt to alter by force the settlement envisaged by this resolution;

The Trusteeship Council be informed of the responsibilities envisaged for it in this plan;

Calls upon the inhabitants of Palestine to take such steps as may be necessary on their part to put this plan into effect;

Appeals to all Governments and all peoples to refrain from taking any action which might hamper or delay the carrying out of these recommendations, and

Authorizes the Secretary-General to reimburse travel and subsistence expenses of the members of the Commission referred to in Part 1, Section B, Paragraph I below, on such basis and in such form as he may determine most appropriate in the circumstances, and to provide the Commission with the necessary staff to assist in carrying out the functions assigned to the Commission by the General Assembly.

The General Assembly,

Authorizes the Secretary-General to draw from the Working Capital Fund a sum not to exceed 2,000,000 dollars for the purposes set forth in the last paragraph of the resolution on the future government of Palestine.

PLAN OF PARTITION WITH ECONOMIC UNION

Part I.—Future Constitution and Government of Palestine

A. TERMINATION OF MANDATE, PARTITION AND INDEPENDENCE

The Mandate for Palestine shall terminate as soon as possible but in any case not later than 1 August 1948.

The armed forces of the mandatory Power shall be progressively withdrawn from Palestine, the withdrawal to be completed as soon as possible but in any case not later than 1 August 1948.

The mandatory Power shall advise the Commission, as far in advance as possible, of its intention to terminate the mandate and to evacuate each area. The mandatory Power shall use its best endeavours to ensure that an area situated in the territory of the Jewish State, including a seaport and hinterland adequate to provide facilities for a substantial immigration, shall be evacuated at the earliest possible date and in any event not later than 1 February 1948.

Independent Arab and Jewish States and the Special International Regime for the City of Jerusalem, set forth in Part III of this Plan, shall come into existence in Palestine two months after the evacuation of the armed forces of the mandatory Power has been completed but in any case not later than 1 October 1948. The boundaries of the Arab State, the Jewish State, and the City of Jerusalem shall be as described in Parts II and III below.

The period between the adoption by the General Assembly of its recommendation on the question of Palestine and the establishment of the independence of the Arab and Jewish States shall be a transitional period.

B. STEPS PREPARATORY TO INDEPENDENCE

A Commission shall be set up consisting of one representative of each of five Member States. The Members represented on the

Commission shall be elected by the General Assembly on as broad a basis, geographically and otherwise, as possible.

The administration of Palestine shall, as the mandatory Power withdraws its armed forces, be progressively turned over to the Commission, which shall act in conformity with the recommendations of the General Assembly, under the guidance of the Security Council. The mandatory Power shall to the fullest possible extent coordinate its plans for withdrawal with the plans of the Commission to take over and administer areas which have been evacuated.

In the discharge of this administrative responsibility the Commission shall have authority to issue necessary regulations and take other measures as required.

The mandatory Power shall not take any action to prevent, obstruct or delay the implementation by the Commission of the measures recommended by the General Assembly.

On its arrival in Palestine the Commission shall proceed to carry out measures for the establishment of the frontiers of the Arab and Jewish States and the City of Jerusalem in accordance with the general lines of the recommendations of the General Assembly on the partition of Palestine. Nevertheless, the boundaries as described in Part II of this Plan are to be modified in such a way that village areas as a rule will not be divided by state boundaries unless pressing reasons make that necessary.

The Commission, after consultation with the democratic parties and other public organizations of the Arab and Jewish States, shall select and establish in each State as rapidly as possible a Provisional Council of Government. The activities of both the Arab and Jewish Provisional Councils of Government shall be carried out under the general direction of the Commission.

If by 1 April 1948 a Provisional Council of Government cannot be selected for either of the States, or, if selected, cannot carry out its functions, the Commission shall communicate that fact to the Security Council for such action with respect to that State as the Security Council may deem proper, and to the Secretary-General for communication to the Members of the United Nations.

Subject to the provisions of these recommendations, during the transitional period the Provisional Councils of Government, acting under the Commission, shall have full authority in the areas under their control including authority over matters of immigration and land regulation.

The Provisional Council of Government of each State, acting under the Commission, shall progressively receive from the Commission full responsibility for the administration of that State in the period between the termination of the Mandate and the establishment of the State's independence.

The Commission shall instruct the Provisional Councils of Government of both the Arab and Jewish States, after their formation, to proceed to the establishment of administrative organs of government, central and local.

The Provisional Council of Government of each State shall, within the shortest time possible, recruit an armed militia from the residents of that State, sufficient in number to maintain internal order and to prevent frontier clashes.

This armed militia in each State shall, for operational purposes, be under the command of Jewish or Arab officers resident in that State, but general political and military control, including the choice of the militia's High Command, shall be exercised by the Commission.

The Provisional Council of Government of each State shall, not later than two months after the withdrawal of the armed forces of the mandatory Power, hold elections to the Constituent Assembly which shall be conducted on democratic lines.

The election regulations in each State shall be drawn up by the Provisional Council of Government and approved by the Commission. Qualified voters for each State for this election shall be persons over eighteen years of age who are (a) Palestinian citizens residing in that State; and (b) Arabs and Jews residing in the State, although not Palestinian citizens, who, before voting, have signed a notice of intention to become citizens of such State.

Arabs and Jews residing in the City of Jerusalem who have signed a notice of intention to become citizens, the Arabs of the Arab State

613

and the Jews of the Jewish State, shall be entitled to vote in the Arab and Jewish States respectively.

Women may vote and be elected to the Constituent Assemblies.

During the transitional period no Jew shall be permitted to establish residence in the area of the proposed Arab State, and no Arab shall be permitted to establish residence in the area of the proposed Jewish State, except by special leave of the Commission.

The Constituent Assembly of each State shall draft a democratic constitution for its State and choose a provisional government to succeed the Provisional Council of Government appointed by the Commission. The Constitutions of the States shall embody Chapters 1 and 2 of the Declaration provided for in section C below and include, inter alia, provisions for:

Establishing in each State a legislative body elected by universal suffrage and by secret ballot on the basis of proportional representation, and an executive body responsible to the legislature;

Settling all international disputes in which the State may be involved by peaceful means in such a manner that international peace and security, and justice, are not endangered;

Accepting the obligation of the State to refrain in its international relations from the threat or use of force against the territorial integrity or political independence of any State, or in any other manner inconsistent with the purpose of the United Nations;

Guaranteeing to all persons equal and non-discriminatory rights in civil, political, economic and religious matters and the enjoyment of human rights and fundamental freedoms, including freedom of religion, language, speech and publication, education, assembly and association;

Preserving freedom of transit and visit for all residents and citizens of the other State in Palestine and the City of Jerusalem, subject to considerations of national security, provided that each State shall control residence within its borders.

The Commission shall appoint a preparatory economic commission of three members to make whatever arrangements are possible for economic co-operation, with a view to establishing, as soon as practicable, the Economic Union and the Joint Economic Board, as provided in section D below.

During the period between the adoption of the recommendations on the question of Palestine by the General Assembly and the termination of the Mandate, the mandatory Power in Palestine shall maintain full responsibility for administration in areas from which it has not withdrawn its armed forces. The Commission shall assist the mandatory Power in the carrying out of these functions. Similarly the mandatory Power shall co-operate with the Commission in the execution of its functions.

With a view to ensuring that there shall be continuity in the functioning of administrative services and that, on the withdrawal of the armed forces of the mandatory Power, the whole administration shall be in the charge of the Provisional Councils and the Joint Economic Board, respectively, acting under the Commission, there shall be a progressive transfer, from the mandatory Power to the Commission, of responsibility for all the functions of government, including that of maintaining law and order in the areas from which the forces of the mandatory Power have been withdrawn.

The Commission shall be guided in its activities by the recommendations of the General Assembly and by such instructions as the Security Council may consider necessary to issue.

The measures taken by the Commission, within the recommendations of the General Assembly, shall become immediately effective unless the Commission has previously received contrary instructions from the Security Council.

The Commission shall render periodic monthly progress reports, or more frequently if desirable, to the Security Council.

The Commission shall make its final report to the next regular session of the General Assembly and to the Security Council simultaneously.

C. DECLARATION

A declaration shall be made to the United Nations by the Provisional Government of each proposed State before independence. It shall contain, inter alia, the following clauses:

General Provision

The stipulations contained in the Declaration are recognized as fundamental laws of the State and no law, regulation or official action shall conflict or interfere with these stipulations, nor shall any law, regulation or official action prevail over them.

Chapter 1: Holy Places, Religious Buildings and Sites

Existing rights in respect of Holy Places and religious buildings or sites shall not be denied or impaired.

In so far as Holy Places are concerned, the liberty of access, visit, and transit shall be guaranteed, in conformity with existing rights, to all residents and citizen of the other State and of the City of Jerusalem, as well as to aliens, without distinction as to nationality, subject to requirements of national security, public order and decorum.

Similarly, freedom of worship shall be guaranteed in conformity with existing rights, subject to the maintenance of public order and decorum.

Holy Places and religious buildings or sites shall be preserved. No act shall be permitted which may in any way impair their sacred character. If at any time it appears to the Government that any particular Holy Place, religious, building or site is in need of urgent repair, the Government may call upon the community or communities concerned to carry out such repair. The Government may carry it out itself at the expense of the community or community concerned if no action is taken within a reasonable time.

No taxation shall be levied in respect of any Holy Place, religious building or site which was exempt from taxation on the date of the creation of the State.

No change in the incidence of such taxation shall be made which would either discriminate between the owners or occupiers of Holy Places, religious buildings or sites, or would place such owners or occupiers in a position less favourable in relation to the general incidence of taxation than existed at the time of the adoption of the Assembly's recommendations.

616

The Governor of the City of Jerusalem shall have the right to determine whether the provisions of the Constitution of the State in relation to Holy Places, religious buildings and sites within the borders of the State and the religious rights appertaining thereto, are being properly applied and respected, and to make decisions on the basis of existing rights in cases of disputes which may arise between the different religious communities or the rites of a religious community with respect to such places, buildings and sites. He shall receive full co-operation and such privileges and immunities as are necessary for the exercise of his functions in the State.

Chapter 2: Religious and Minority Rights

Freedom of conscience and the free exercise of all forms of worship, subject only to the maintenance of public order and morals, shall be ensured to all.

No discrimination of any kind shall be made between the inhabitants on the ground of race, religion, language or sex.

All persons within the jurisdiction of the State shall be entitled to equal protection of the laws.

The family law and personal status of the various minorities and their religious interests, including endowments, shall be respected.

Except as may be required for the maintenance of public order and good government, no measure shall be taken to obstruct or interfere with the enterprise of religious or charitable bodies of all faiths or to discriminate against any representative or member of these bodies on the ground of his religion or nationality.

The State shall ensure adequate primary and secondary education for the Arab and Jewish minority, respectively, in its own language and its cultural traditions.

The right of each community to maintain its own schools for the education of its own members in its own language, while conforming to such educational requirements of a general nature as the State may impose, shall not be denied or impaired. Foreign educational establishments shall continue their activity on the basis of their existing rights.

No restriction shall be imposed on the free use by any citizen of the State of any language in private intercourse, in commerce, in religion, in the Press or in publications of any kind, or at public meetings.

No expropriation of land owned by an Arab in the Jewish State (by a Jew in the Arab State) shall be allowed except for public purposes. In all cases of expropriation full compensation as fixed by the Supreme Court shall be said previous to dispossession.

Chapter 3: Citizenship, International Conventions and Financial Obligations

1. Citizenship

Palestinian citizens residing in Palestine outside the City of Jerusalem, as well as Arabs and Jews who, not holding Palestinian citizenship, reside in Palestine outside the City of Jerusalem shall, upon the recognition of independence, become citizens of the State in which they are resident and enjoy full civil and political rights. Persons over the age of eighteen years may opt, within one year from the date of recognition of independence of the State in which they reside, for citizenship of the other State, providing that no Arab residing in the area of the proposed Arab State shall have the right to opt for citizenship in the proposed Jewish State and no Jew residing in the proposed Jewish State shall have the right to opt for citizenship in the proposed Arab State. The exercise of this right of option will be taken to include the wives and children under eighteen years of age of persons so opting.

Arabs residing in the area of the proposed Jewish State and Jews residing in the area of the proposed Arab State who have signed a notice of intention to opt for citizenship of the other State shall be eligible to vote in the elections to the Constituent Assembly of that State, but not in the elections to the Constituent Assembly of the State in which they reside.

2. International conventions

The State shall be bound by all the international agreements and conventions, both general and special, to which Palestine has become a party. Subject to any right of denunciation provided for therein, such agreements and conventions shall be respected by the State throughout the period for which they were concluded.

Any dispute about the applicability and continued validity of international conventions or treaties signed or adhered to by the mandatory Power on behalf of Palestine shall be referred to the International Court of Justice in accordance with the provisions of the Statute of the Court.

3. Financial obligations

The State shall respect and fulfil all financial obligations of whatever nature assumed on behalf of Palestine by the mandatory Power during the exercise of the Mandate and recognized by the State. This provision includes the right of public servants to pensions, compensation or gratuities.

These obligations shall be fulfilled through participation in the Joint Economic Board in respect of those obligations applicable to Palestine as a whole, and individually in respect of those applicable to, and fairly apportionable between, the States.

A Court of Claims, affiliated with the Joint Economic Board, and composed of one member appointed by the United Nations, one representative of the United Kingdom and one representative of the State concerned, should be established. Any dispute between the United Kingdom and the State respecting claims not recognized by the latter should be referred to that Court.

Commercial concessions granted in respect of any part of Palestine prior to the adoption of the resolution by the General Assembly shall continue to be valid according to their terms, unless modified by agreement between the concession-holders and the State.

Chapter 4: Miscellaneous Provisions

The provisions of chapters 1 and 2 of the declaration shall be under the guarantee of the United Nations, and no modifications shall be made in them without the assent of the General Assembly of the United Nations. Any Member of the United Nations shall have the right to bring to the attention of the General Assembly any infraction or danger of infraction of any of these stipulations, and the General Assembly may thereupon make such recommendations as it may deem proper in the circumstances.

Any dispute relating to the application or interpretation of this declaration shall be referred, at the request of either party, to the International Court of Justice, unless the parties agree to another mode of settlement.

D. ECONOMIC UNION AND TRANSIT

The Provisional Council of Government of each State shall enter into an undertaking with respect to Economic Union and Transit. This undertaking shall be drafted by the Commission provided for in section B, paragraph 1, utilizing to the greatest possible extent the advice and cooperation of representative organizations and bodies from each of the proposed States. It shall contain provisions to establish the Economic Union of Palestine and provide for other matters of common interest. If by 1 April 1948 the Provisional Councils of Government have not entered into the undertaking, the undertaking shall be put into force by the Commission.

The Economic Union of Palestine

The objectives of the Economic Union of Palestine shall be:

A customs union;

A joint currency system providing for a single foreign exchange rate;

Operation in the common interest on a non-discriminatory basis of railways inter-State highways; postal, telephone and telegraphic services and ports and airports involved in international trade and commerce;

Joint economic development, especially in respect of irrigation, land reclamation and soil conservation;

Access for both States and for the City of Jerusalem on a

non-discriminatory basis to water and power facilities.

There shall be established a Joint Economic Board, which shall consist of three representatives of each of the two States and three foreign members appointed by the Economic and Social Council of the United Nations. The foreign members shall be appointed in the first instance for a term of three years; they shall serve as individuals and not as representatives of States.

The functions of the Joint Economic Board shall be to implement either directly or by delegation the measures necessary to realize the objectives of the Economic Union. It shall have all powers of organization and administration necessary to fulfil its functions.

The States shall bind themselves to put into effect the decisions of the Joint Economic Board. The Board's decisions shall be taken by a majority vote.

In the event of failure of a State to take the necessary action the Board may, by a vote of six members, decide to withhold an appropriate portion of the part of the customs revenue to which the State in question is entitled under the Economic Union. Should the State persist in its failure to cooperate, the Board may decide by a simple majority vote upon such further sanctions, including disposition of funds which it has withheld, as it may deem appropriate.

In relation to economic development, the functions of the Board shall be planning, investigation and encouragement of joint development projects, but it shall not undertake such projects except with the assent of both States and the City of Jerusalem, in the event that Jerusalem is directly involved in the development project.

In regard to the joint currency system, the currencies circulating in the two States and the City of Jerusalem shall be issued under the authority of the Joint Economic Board, which shall be the sole issuing authority and which shall determine the reserves to be held against such currencies.

So far as is consistent with paragraph 2(b) above, each State may operate its own central bank, control its own fiscal and credit policy, its foreign exchange receipts and expenditures, the grant of import licences, and may conduct international financial operations on its own faith and credit. During the first two years after the termination of the Mandate, the Joint Economic Board shall have the authority to take such measures as may be necessary to ensure that—to the extent that the total foreign exchange revenues of the two States from the export of goods and services permit, and provided that each State takes appropriate measures to conserve its own foreign exchange resources—each State shall have available, in any twelve months' period, foreign exchange sufficient to assure the supply of quantities of imported goods and services for consumption in its territory equivalent to the quantities of such goods and services consumed in that territory in the twelve months' period ending 31 December 1947.

All economic authority not specifically vested in the Joint Economic Board is reserved to each State.

There shall be a common customs tariff with complete freedom of trade between the States, and between the States and the City of Jerusalem.

The tariff schedules shall be drawn up by a Tariff Commission, consisting of representatives of each of the States in equal numbers, and shall be submitted to the Joint Economic Board for approval by a majority vote. In case of disagreement in the Tariff Commission, the Joint Economic Board shall arbitrate the points of difference. In the event that the Tariff Commission fails to draw up any schedule by a date to be fixed, the Joint Economic Board shall determine the tariff schedule.

The following items shall be a first charge on the customs and other common revenue of the Joint Economic Board:

The expenses of the customs service and of the operation of the joint services;

The administrative expenses of the Joint Economic Board;

The financial obligations of the Administration of Palestine, consisting of:

The service of the outstanding public debt;

The cost of superannuation benefits, now being paid or falling due in the future, in accordance with the rules and to the extent established by paragraph 3 of chapter 3 above.

After these obligations have been met in full, the surplus revenue from the customs and other common services shall be divided in the following manner: not less than 5 per cent and not more than 10 per cent to the City of Jerusalem; the residue shall be allocated to each State by the Joint Economic Board equitably, with the objective of maintaining a sufficient and suitable level of government and social services in each State, except that the share of either State shall not exceed the amount of that State's contribution to the revenues of the Economic Union by more than approximately four million pounds in any year. The amount granted may be adjusted by the Board according to the price level in relation to the prices prevailing at the time of the establishment of the Union. After five years, the principles of the distribution of the joint revenue may be revised by the Joint Economic Board on a basis of equity.

All international conventions and treaties affecting customs tariff rates, and those communications services under the jurisdiction of the Joint Economic Board, shall be entered into by both States. In these matters, the two States shall be bound to act in accordance with the majority of the Joint Economic Board.

The Joint Economic Board shall endeavour to secure for Palestine's exports fair and equal access to world markets.

All enterprises operated by the Joint Economic Board shall pay fair wages on a uniform basis.

Freedom of Transit and Visit

The undertaking shall contain provisions preserving freedom of transit and visit for all residents or citizens of both States and of the City of Jerusalem, subject to security considerations; provided that each State and the City shall control residence within its borders.

Termination, Modification and Interpretation of the Undertaking

The undertaking and any treaty issuing therefrom shall remain in force for a period of ten years. It shall continue in force until notice of termination, to take effect two years thereafter, is given by either of the parties.

During the initial ten-year period, the undertaking and any treaty issuing therefrom may not be modified except by consent of both parties and with the approval of the General Assembly.

Any dispute relating to the application or the interpretation of the undertaking and any treaty issuing therefrom shall be referred, at the request of either party, to the International Court Of Justice, unless the parties agree to another mode of settlement.

E. ASSETS

The movable assets of the Administration of Palestine shall be allocated to the Arab and Jewish States and the City of Jerusalem on an equitable basis. Allocations should be made by the United Nations Commission referred to iii section B, paragraph 1, above. Immovable assets shall become the property of the government of the territory in which they are situated.

During the period between the appointment of the United Nations Commission and the termination of the Mandate, the mandatory Power shall, except in respect of ordinary operations, consult with the Commission on any measure which it may contemplate involving the liquidation, disposal or encumbering of the assets of the Palestine Government, such as the accumulated treasury surplus, the proceeds of Government bond issues, State lands or any other asset.

F. ADMISSION TO MEMBERSHIP IN THE UNITED NATIONS

When the independence of either the Arab or the Jewish State as envisaged in this plan has become effective and the declaration and undertaking, as envisaged in this plan, have been signed by either of them, sympathetic consideration should be given to its application for admission to membership in the United Nations in accordance with article 4 of the Charter of the United Nations.

Part II.—Boundaries

A. THE ARAB STATE

The area of the Arab State in Western Galilee is bounded on the west by the Mediterranean and on the north by the frontier of the Lebanon from Ras en Naqura to a point north of Saliha. From there the boundary proceeds southwards, leaving the built-up area of Saliha in the Arab State, to join the southernmost point of this village. There it follows the western boundary line of the villages of 'Alma, Rihaniya and Teitaba, thence following the northern boundary line of Meirun village to join the Acre-Safad Sub-District boundary line. It follows this line to a point west of Es Sammu'i village and joins it again at the northernmost point of Farradiya. Thence it follows the sub-district boundary line to the Acre-Safad main road. From here it follows the western boundary of Kafr-I'nan village until it reaches the Tiberias-Acre Sub-District boundary line, passing to the west of the junction of the Acre-Safad and Lubiya-Kafr-I'nan roads. From the south-west corner of Kafr-I'nan village the boundary line follows the western boundary of the Tiberias Sub-District to a point close to the boundary line between the villages of Maghar and 'Eilabun, thence bulging out to the west to include as much of the eastern part of the plain of Battuf as is necessary for the reservoir proposed by the Jewish Agency for the irrigation of lands to the south and east.

The boundary rejoins the Tiberias Sub-District boundary at a point on the Nazareth-Tiberias road south-east of the built-up area of Tur'an; thence it runs southwards, at first following the sub-district boundary and then passing between the Kadoorie Agricultural School and Mount Tabor, to a point due south at the base of Mount Tabor. From here it runs due west, parallel to the horizontal grid line 230, to the north-east corner of the village lands of Tel Adashim. It then runs to the northwest corner of these lands, whence it turns south and west so as to include in the Arab State the sources of the Nazareth water supply in Yafa village. On reaching Ginneiger it follows the eastern, northern and western boundaries of the lands of this village to their south-west comer, whence it proceeds in a straight line to a point on the Haifa-Afula railway on the boundary between the villages of Sarid and El-Mujeidil. This is the point of intersection. The south-western boundary of the area of the Arab State in Galilee takes a line from this point, passing northwards along the eastern boundaries of Sarid and Gevat to the north-eastern corner of Nahalal, proceeding thence across the land of Kefar ha Horesh to a central point on the southern boundary of the village of 'Ilut, thence westwards along that village boundary to the eastern boundary of Beit Lahm, thence northwards and north-eastwards along its western boundary to the north-eastern corner of Waldheim and thence north-westwards across the village lands of Shafa 'Amr to the southeastern corner of Ramat Yohanan. From here it runs due north-north-east to a point on the Shafa 'Amr-Haifa road, west of its junction with the road of I'billin. From there it proceeds north-east to a point on the southern boundary of I'billin situated to the west of the I'billin-Birwa road. Thence along that boundary to its westernmost point, whence it turns to the north, follows across the village land of Tamra to the north-westernmost corner and along the western boundary of Julis until it reaches the Acre-Safad road. It then runs westwards along the southern side of the Safad-Acre road to the Galilee-Haifa District boundary, from which point it follows that boundary to the sea.

The boundary of the hill country of Samaria and Judea starts on the Jordan River at the Wadi Malih south-east of Beisan and runs due west to meet the Beisan-Jericho road and then follows the western side of that road in a north-westerly direction to the junction of the boundaries of the Sub-Districts of Beisan, Nablus, and Jenin. From that point it follows the Nablus-Jenin sub-District boundary westwards for a distance of about three kilometres and then turns north-westwards, passing to the east of the built-up areas of the villages of Jalbun and Faqqu'a, to the boundary of the Sub-Districts of Jenin and Beisan at a point northeast of Nuris. Thence it proceeds first northwestwards to a point due north of the built-up area of Zie'in and then westwards to the Afula-Jenin railway, thence north-westwards along the District boundary line to the point of intersection on the Hejaz railway. From here the boundary runs southwestwards, including the built-up area and some of the land of the village of Kh.

Lid in the Arab State to cross the Haifa-Jenin road at a point on the district boundary between Haifa and Samaria west of El- Mansi. It follows this boundary to the southernmost point of the village of El-Buteimat. From here it follows the northern and eastern boundaries of the village of Ar'ara rejoining the Haifa-Samaria district boundary at Wadi 'Ara, and thence proceeding south-south-westwards in an approximately straight line joining up with the western boundary of Qaqun to a point east of the railway line on the eastern boundary of Qaqun village. From here it runs along the railway line some distance to the east of it to a point just east of the Tulkarm railway station. Thence the boundary follows a line half-way between the railway and the Tulkarm-Qalqiliya-Jaljuliya and Ras El-Ein road to a point just east of Ras El-Ein station, whence it proceeds along the railway some distance to the east of it to the point on the railway line south of the junction of the Haifa-Lydda and Beit Nabala lines, whence it proceeds along the southern border of Lydda airport to its south-west corner, thence in a south-westerly direction to a point just west of the built-up area of Sarafand El 'Amar, whence it turns south, passing just to the west of the built-up area of Abu El-Fadil to the north-east corner of the lands of Beer Ya'aqov. (The boundary line should be so demarcated as to allow direct access from the Arab State to the airport.) Thence the boundary line follows the western and southern boundaries of Ramle village, to the north-east corner of El Na'ana village, thence in a straight line to the southernmost point of El Barriya, along the eastern boundary of that village and the southern boundary of 'Innaba village. Thence it turns north to follow the southern side of the Jaffa-Jerusalem road until El-Qubab, whence it follows the road to the boundary of Abu-Shusha. It runs along the eastern boundaries of Abu Shusha, Seidun, Hulda to the southernmost point of Hulda, thence westwards in a straight line to the north-eastern corner of Umm Kalkha, thence following the northern boundaries of Umm Kalkha, Qazaza and the northern and western boundaries of Mukhezin to the Gaza District boundary and thence runs across the village lands of El-Mismiya El-Kabira, and Yasur to the southern point of intersection, which is midway between the built-up areas of Yasur and Batani Sharqi.

From the southern point of intersection the boundary lines run north-westwards between the villages of Gan Yavne and Barqa to the sea at a point half way between Nabi Yunis and Minat El-Qila, and south-eastwards to a point west of Qastina, whence it turns in a south-westerly direction, passing to the east of the built-up areas of Es Sawafir Esh Sharqiya and 'Ibdis. From the south-east corner of 'Ibdis village it runs to a point southwest of the built-up area of Beit 'Affa, crossing the Hebron-El-Majdal road just to the west of the built-up area of 'Iraq Suweidan. Thence it proceeds southward along the western village boundary of El-Faluja to the Beersheba Sub-District boundary. It then runs across the tribal lands of 'Arab El-Jubarat to a point on the boundary between the Sub-Districts of Beersheba and Hebron north of Kh. Khuweilifa, whence it proceeds in a south-westerly direction to a point on the Beersheba-Gaza main road two kilometres to the north-west of the town. It then turns south-eastwards to reach Wadi Sab' at a point situated one kilometer to the west of it. From here it turns north-eastwards and proceeds along Wadi Sab' and along the Beersheba-Hebron road for a distance of one kilometer, whence it turns eastwards and runs in a straight line to Kh. Kuseifa to join the Beersheba-Hebron Sub-District boundary. It then follows the Beersheba-Hebron boundary eastwards to a point north of Ras Ez-Zuweira, only departing from it so as to cut across the base of the indentation between vertical grid lines 150 and 160.

About five kilometres north-east of Ras Ez-Zuweira it turns north, excluding from the Arab State a strip along the coast of the Dead Sea not more than seven kilometres in depth, as far as 'Ein Geddi, whence it turns due east to join the Transjordan frontier in the Dead Sea.

The northern boundary of the Arab section of the coastal plain runs from a point between Minat El-Qila and Nabi Yunis, passing between the built-up areas of Gan Yavne and Barqa to the point of intersection. From here it turns south-westwards, running across the lands of Batani Sharqi, along the eastern boundary of the lands of Beit Daras and across the lands of Julis, leaving the built-up areas of Batani Sharqi and Julis to the westwards, as far as the north-west corner of the lands of Beit-Tima. Thence it runs east of El-Jiya across the village lands of El-Barbara along the eastern boundaries of the villages of Beit Jirja, Deir Suneid and Dimra. From the south-east corner of Dimra the boundary passes across the lands of Beit

Hanun, leaving the Jewish lands of Nir-Am to the eastwards. From the south-east corner of Beit Hanun the line runs south-west to a point south of the parallel grid line 100, then turns north-west for two kilometres, turning again in a southwesterly direction and continuing in an almost straight line to the north-west corner of the village lands of Kirbet Ikhza'a. From there it follows the boundary line of this village to its southernmost point. It then runs in a southerly direction along the vertical grid line 90 to its junction with the horizontal grid line 70. It then turns south-eastwards to Kh. El-Ruheiba and then proceeds in a southerly direction to a point known as El-Baha, beyond which it crosses the Beersheba-EI 'Auja main road to the west of Kh. El-Mushrifa. From there it joins Wadi El-Zaiyatin just to the west of El-Subeita. From there it turns to the north-east and then to the south-east following this Wadi and passes to the east of 'Abda to join Wadi Nafkh. It then bulges to the south-west along Wadi Nafkh, Wadi 'Ajrim and Wadi Lassan to the point where Wadi Lassan crosses the Egyptian frontier.

The area of the Arab enclave of Jaffa consists of that part of the town-planning area of Jaffa which lies to the west of the Jewish quarters lying south of Tel-Aviv, to the west of the continuation of Herzl street up to its junction with the Jaffa-Jerusalem road, to the south-west of the section of the Jaffa-Jerusalem road lying south-east of that junction, to the west of Miqve Yisrael lands, to the northwest of Holon local council area, to the north of the line linking up the north-west corner of Holon with the northeast corner of Bat Yam local council area and to the north of Bat Yam local council area. The question of Karton quarter will be decided by the Boundary Commission, bearing in mind among other considerations the desirability of including the smallest possible number of its Arab inhabitants and the largest possible number of its Jewish inhabitants in the Jewish State.

B. THE JEWISH STATE

The north-eastern sector of the Jewish State (Eastern Galilee) is bounded on the north and west by the Lebanese frontier and on the east by the frontiers of Syria and Trans-jordan. It includes the whole of the Huleh Basin, Lake Tiberias, the whole of the Beisan

Sub-District, the boundary line being extended to the crest of the Gilboa mountains and the Wadi Malih. From there the Jewish State extends north-west, following the boundary described in respect of the Arab State. The Jewish section of the coastal plain extends from a point between Minat El-Qila and Nabi Yunis in the Gaza Sub-District and includes the towns of Haifa and Tel-Aviv, leaving Jaffa as an enclave of the Arab State. The eastern frontier of the Jewish State follows the boundary described in respect of the Arab State.

The Beersheba area comprises the whole of the Beersheba Sub-District, including the Negeb and the eastern part of the Gaza Sub-District, but excluding the town of Beersheba and those areas described in respect of the Arab State. It includes also a strip of land along the Dead Sea stretching from the Beersheba-Hebron Sub-District boundary line to 'Ein Geddi, as described in respect of the Arab State.

C. THE CITY OF JERUSALEM

The boundaries of the City of Jerusalem are as defined in the recommendations on the City of Jerusalem. (See Part III, section B, below).

Part III.—City of Jerusalem

A. SPECIAL REGIME

The City of Jerusalem shall be established as a corpus separatum under a special international regime and shall be administered by the United Nations. The Trusteeship Council shall be designated to discharge the responsibilities of the Administering Authority on behalf of the United Nations.

B. BOUNDARIES OF THE CITY

The City of Jerusalem shall include the present municipality of Jerusalem plus the surrounding villages and towns, the most eastern of which shall be Abu Dis; the most southern, Bethlehem; the most western, 'Ein

Karim (including also the built-up area of Motsa); and the most northern Shu'fat, as indicated on the attached sketch-map (annex B).

C. STATUTE OF THE CITY

The Trusteeship Council shall, within five months of the approval of the present plan, elaborate and approve a detailed statute of the City which shall contain, inter alia, the substance of the following provisions:

Government machinery; special objectives. The Administering Authority in discharging its administrative obligations shall pursue the following special objectives:

To protect and to preserve the unique spiritual and religious interests located in the city of the three great monotheistic faiths throughout the world, Christian, Jewish and Moslem; to this end to ensure that order and peace, and especially religious peace, reign in Jerusalem;

To foster cooperation among all the inhabitants of the city in their own interests as well as in order to encourage and support the peaceful development of the mutual relations between the two Palestinian peoples throughout the Holy Land; to promote the security, well-being and any constructive measures of development of the residents having regard to the special circumstances and customs of the various peoples and communities.

Governor and Administrative staff. A Governor of the City of Jerusalem shall be appointed by the Trusteeship Council and shall be responsible to it. He shall be selected on the basis of special qualifications and without regard to nationality. He shall not, however, be a citizen of either State in Palestine.

The Governor shall represent the United Nations in the City and shall exercise on their behalf all powers of administration, including the conduct of external affairs. He shall be assisted by an administrative staff classed as international officers in the meaning of Article 100 of the Charter and chosen whenever practicable from the residents of the city and of the rest of Palestine on a non-discriminatory basis. A detailed plan for the organization of the administration of the city shall be submitted by the Governor to the Trusteeship Council and duly approved by it.

3. Local autonomy

The existing local autonomous units in the territory of the city (villages, townships and municipalities) shall enjoy wide powers of local government and administration.

The Governor shall study and submit for the consideration and decision of the Trusteeship Council a plan for the establishment of special town units consisting, respectively, of the Jewish and Arab sections of new Jerusalem. The new town units shall continue to form part the present municipality of Jerusalem.

Security measures

The City of Jerusalem shall be demilitarized; neutrality shall be declared and preserved, and no para-military formations, exercises or activities shall be permitted within its borders.

Should the administration of the City of Jerusalem be seriously obstructed or prevented by the non-cooperation or interference of one or more sections of the population the Governor shall have authority to take such measures as may be necessary to restore the effective functioning of administration.

To assist in the maintenance of internal law and order, especially for the protection of the Holy Places and religious buildings and sites in the city, the Governor shall organize a special police force of adequate strength, the members of which shall be recruited outside of Palestine. The Governor shall be empowered to direct such budgetary provision as may be necessary for the maintenance of this force.

Legislative Organization.

A Legislative Council, elected by adult residents of the city irrespective of nationality on the basis of universal and secret suffrage and proportional representation, shall have powers of legislation and taxation. No legislative measures shall, however, conflict or interfere with the provisions which will be set forth in the Statute of the City, nor shall any law, regulation, or official action prevail over them.

The Statute shall grant to the Governor a right of vetoing bills inconsistent with the provisions referred to in the preceding sentence. It shall also empower him to promulgate temporary ordinances in case the Council fails to adopt in time a bill deemed essential to the normal functioning of the administration.

Administration of Justice.

The Statute shall provide for the establishment of an independent judiciary system, including a court of appeal. All the inhabitants of the city shall be subject to it.

Economic Union and Economic Regime.

The City of Jerusalem shall be included in the Economic Union of Palestine and be bound by all stipulations of the undertaking and of any treaties issued therefrom, as well as by the decisions of the Joint Economic Board. The headquarters of the Economic Board shall be established in the territory City. The Statute shall provide for the regulation of economic matters not falling within the regime of the Economic Union, on the basis of equal treatment and non-discrimination for all members of the United Nations and their nationals.

Freedom of Transit and Visit: Control of residents.

Subject to considerations of security, and of economic welfare as determined by the Governor under the directions of the Trusteeship Council, freedom of entry into, and residence within the borders of the City shall be guaranteed for the residents or citizens of the Arab and Jewish States. Immigration into, and residence within, the borders of the city for nationals of other States shall be controlled by the Governor under the directions of the Trusteeship Council.

Relations with Arab and Jewish States. Representatives of the Arab and Jewish States shall be accredited to the Governor of the City and charged with the protection of the interests of their States and nationals in connection with the international administration of the City.

Official languages.

Arabic and Hebrew shall be the official languages of the city. This will not preclude the adoption of one or more additional working languages, as may be required.

Citizenship.

All the residents shall become ipso facto citizens of the City of Jerusalem unless they opt for citizenship of the State of which they have been citizens or, if Arabs or Jews, have filed notice of intention to become citizens of the Arab or Jewish State respectively, according to Part 1, section B, paragraph 9, of this Plan.

The Trusteeship Council shall make arrangements for consular protection of the citizens of the City outside its territory.

Freedoms of citizens

Subject only to the requirements of public order and morals, the inhabitants of the City shall be ensured the enjoyment of human rights and fundamental freedoms, including freedom of conscience, religion and worship, language, education, speech and press, assembly and association, and petition.

No discrimination of any kind shall be made between the inhabitants on the grounds of race, religion, language or sex.

All persons within the City shall be entitled to equal protection of the laws.

The family law and personal status of the various persons and communities and their religious interests, including endowments, shall be respected.

Except as may be required for the maintenance of public order and good government, no measure shall be taken to obstruct or interfere with the enterprise of religious or charitable bodies of all faiths or to discriminate against any representative or member of these bodies on the ground of his religion or nationality.

The City shall ensure adequate primary and secondary education for the Arab and Jewish communities respectively, in their own languages and in accordance with their cultural traditions.

The right of each community to maintain its own schools for the education of its own members in its own language, while conforming to such educational requirements of a general nature as the City may impose, shall not be denied or impaired. Foreign educational establishments shall continue their activity on the basis of their existing rights.

No restriction shall be imposed on the free use by any inhabitant of the City of any language in private intercourse, in commerce, in religion, in the Press or in publications of any kind, or at public meetings.

Holy Places Existing rights in respect of Holy Places and religious buildings or sites shall not be denied or impaired.

Free access to the Holy Places and religious buildings or sites and the free exercise of worship shall be secured in conformity with existing rights and subject to the requirements of public order and decorum.

Holy Places and religious buildings or sites shall be preserved. No act shall be permitted which may in any way impair their sacred character. If at any time it appears to the Governor that any particular Holy Place, religious building or site is in need of urgent repair, the Governor may call upon the community or communities concerned to carry out such repair. The Governor may carry it out himself at the expense of the community or communities concerned if no action is taken within a reasonable time.

No taxation shall be levied in respect of any Holy Place, religious building or site which was exempt from taxation on the date of the creation of the City. No change in the incidence of such taxation shall be made which would either discriminate between the owners or occupiers of Holy Places, religious buildings or sites or would place such owners or occupiers in a position less favourable in relation to the general incidence of taxation than existed at the time of the adoption of the Assembly's recommendations.

Special powers of the Governor in respect of the Holy Places, religious buildings and sites in the City and in any part of Palestine.

The protection of the Holy Places, religious buildings and sites located in the City of Jerusalem shall be a special concern of the Governor. With relation to such places, buildings and sites in Palestine outside the city, the Governor shall determine, on the ground of powers granted to him by the Constitution of both States, whether the provisions of the Constitution of the Arab and Jewish States in Palestine dealing therewith and the religious rights appertaining thereto are being properly applied and respected.

The Governor shall also be empowered to make decisions on the basis of existing rights in cases of disputes which may arise between the different religious communities or the rites of a religious community in respect of the Holy Places, religious buildings and sites in any part of Palestine.

In this task he may be assisted by a consultative council of representatives of different denominations acting in an advisory capacity.

D. DURATION OF THE SPECIAL REGIME

The Statute elaborated by the Trusteeship Council the aforementioned principles shall come into force not later than 1 October 1948. It shall remain in force in the first instance for a period of ten years, unless the Trusteeship Council finds it necessary to undertake a re-examination of these provisions at an earlier date. After the expiration of this period the whole scheme shall be subject to examination by the Trusteeship Council in the light of experience acquired with its functioning. The residents the City shall be then free to express by means of a referendum their wishes as to possible modifications of regime of the City.

Part IV. Capitulations

States whose nationals have in the past enjoyed in Palestine the privileges and immunities of foreigners, including the benefits of consular jurisdiction and protection, as formerly enjoyed by capitulation or usage in the Ottoman Empire, are invited to renounce any right pertaining to them to the re-establishment of such privileges and immunities in the proposed Arab and Jewish States and the City of Jerusalem.

Adopted at the 128th plenary meeting:

In favour: 33

Australia, Belgium, Bolivia, Brazil, Byelorussian S.S.R., Canada, Costa Rica, Czechoslovakia, Denmark, Dominican Republic, Ecuador, France, Guatemala,

Haiti, Iceland, Liberia, Luxemburg, Netherlands, New Zealand, Nicaragua, Norway, Panama, Paraguay, Peru, Philippines, Poland, Sweden, Ukrainian S.S.R., Union of South Africa, U.S.A., U.S.S.R., Uruguay, Venezuela.

Against: 13

Afghanistan, Cuba, Egypt, Greece, India, Iran, Iraq, Lebanon, Pakistan, Saudi Arabia, Syria, Turkey, Yemen.

Abstained: 10

Argentina, Chile, China, Colombia, El Salvador, Ethiopia, Honduras, Mexico, United Kingdom, Yugoslavia.

Appendix 2

United Nations Security Council Resolution 194 (1948)
December 11, 1948

The General Assembly,

Having considered further the situation in Palestine,

1. Expresses its deep appreciation of the progress achieved through the good offices of the late United Nations Mediator in promoting a peaceful adjustment of the future situation of Palestine, for which cause he sacrificed his life; and

Extends its thanks to the Acting Mediator and his staff for their continued efforts and devotion to duty in Palestine;

2. Establishes a Conciliation Commission consisting of three States Members of the United Nations which shall have the following functions:

(a) To assume, in so far as it considers necessary in existing circumstances, the functions given to the United Nations Mediator on Palestine by the resolution of the General Assembly of 14 May 1948;

(b) To carry out the specific functions and directives given to it by the present resolution and such additional functions and directives as may be given to it by the General Assembly or by the Security Council;

(c) To undertake, upon the request of the Security Council, any of the functions now assigned to the United Nations Mediator on Palestine or to the United Nations Truce Commission by resolutions of the Security Council; upon such request to the Conciliation Commission by the Security Council with respect to all the remaining functions of the United Nations Mediator on Palestine under Security Council resolutions, the office of the Mediator shall be terminated;

3. Decides that a Committee of the Assembly, consisting of China, France, the Union of Soviet Socialist Republics, the United Kingdom and the United States of America, shall present, before the end of the first part of the present session of the General Assembly, for the approval of the Assembly, a proposal concerning the names of the three States which will constitute the Conciliation Commission;

4. Requests the Commission to begin its functions at once, with a view to the establishment of contact between the parties themselves and the Commission at the earliest possible date;

5. Calls upon the Governments and authorities concerned to extend the scope of the negotiations provided for in the Security Council's resolution of 16 November 1948 and to seek agreement by negotiations conducted either with the Conciliation Commission or directly with a view to the final settlement of all questions outstanding between them;

6. Instructs the Conciliation Commission to take steps to assist the Government and authorities concerned to achieve a final settlement of all questions outstanding between them;

7. Resolves that the Holy Places—including Nazareth—religious buildings and sites in Palestine should be protected and free access to them assured, in accordance with existing rights and historical practice that arrangements to this end should be under effective United Nations supervision; that the United Nations Conciliation Commission, in presenting to the fourth regular session of the General Assembly its detailed proposal for a

permanent international regime for the territory of Jerusalem, should include recommendations concerning the Holy Places in that territory; that with regard to the Holy Places in the rest of Palestine the Commission should call upon the political authorities of the areas concerned to give appropriate formal guarantees as to the protection of the Holy Places and access to them; and that these undertakings should be presented to the General Assembly for approval;

8. Resolves that, in view of its association with three world religions, the Jerusalem area, including the present municipality of Jerusalem plus the surrounding villages and towns, the most Eastern of which shall be Abu Dis; the most Southern, Bethlehem; the most Western, Ein Karim (including also the built-up area of Motsa); and the most Northern, Shu'fat, should be accorded special and separate treatment from the rest of Palestine and should be placed under effective United Nations control;

Requests the Security Council to take further steps to ensure the demilitarization of Jerusalem at the earliest possible date;

Instructs the Conciliation Commission to present to the fourth regular session of the General Assembly detailed proposals for a permanent international regime for the Jerusalem area which will provide for the maximum local autonomy for distinctive groups consistent with the special international status of the Jerusalem area;

The Conciliation Commission is authorized to appoint a United Nations representative who shall cooperate with the local authorities with respect to the interim administration of the Jerusalem area;

9. Resolves that, pending agreement on more detailed arrangements among the Governments and authorities concerned, the

freest possible access to Jerusalem by road, rail or air should be accorded to all inhabitants of Palestine;

Instructs the Conciliation Commission to report immediately to the Security Council, for appropriate action by that organ, any attempt by any party to impede such access;

10. Instructs the Conciliation Commission to seek arrangements among the Governments and authorities concerned which will facilitate the economic development of the area, including arrangements for access to ports and airfields and the use of transportation and communication facilities;

11. Resolves that the refugees wishing to return to their homes and live at peace with their neighbors should be permitted to do so at the earliest practicable date, and that compensation should be paid for the property of those choosing not to return and for loss of or damage to property which, under principles of international law or in equity, should be made good by the Governments or authorities responsible;

Instructs the Conciliation Commission to facilitate the repatriation, resettlement and economic and social rehabilitation of the refugees and the payment of compensation, and to maintain close relations with the Director of the United Nations Relief for Palestine Refugees and, through him, with the appropriate organs and agencies of the United Nations;

12. Authorizes the Conciliation Commission to appoint such subsidiary bodies and to employ such technical experts, acting under its authority, as it may find necessary for the effective discharge of its functions and responsibilities under the present resolution;

The Conciliation Commission will have its official headquarters at Jerusalem. The authorities responsible for maintaining order in Jerusalem will be responsible for taking all measures necessary to ensure the security of the Commission. The Secretary-General will provide a limited number of guards for the protection of the staff and premises of the Commission;

13. Instructs the Conciliation Commission to render progress reports periodically to the Secretary-General for transmission to the Security Council and to the Members of the United Nations; 14. Calls upon all Governments and authorities concerned to cooperate with the Conciliation Commission and to take all possible steps to assist in the implementation of the present resolution;

15. Requests the Secretary-General to provide the necessary staff and facilities and to make appropriate arrangements to provide the necessary funds required in carrying out the terms of the present resolution.

Appendix 3

United Nations Security Council Resolution 242 (1967)
November 22, 1967

The Security Council,

Expressing its continuing concern with the grave situation in the Middle East,

Emphasizing the inadmissibility of the acquisition of territory by war and the need to work for a just and lasting peace in which every State in the area can live in security,

Emphasizing further that all Member States in their acceptance of the Charter of the United Nations have undertaken a commitment to act in accordance with Article 2 of the Charter,

1. *Affirms* that the fulfilment of Charter principles requires the establishment of a just and lasting peace in the Middle East which should include the application of both the following principles:

(i) Withdrawal of Israel armed forces from territories occupied in the recent conflict;

(ii) Termination of all claims or states of belligerency and respect for and acknowledgment of the sovereignty, territorial integrity and political independence of every State in the area and their right to live in peace within secure and recognized boundaries free from threats or acts of force;

2. *Affirms further* the necessity

(a) For guaranteeing freedom of navigation through international waterways in the area;

(b) For achieving a just settlement of the refugee problem;

(c) For guaranteeing the territorial inviolability and political independence of every State in the area, through measures including the establishment of demilitarized zones;

3. *Requests* the Secretary-General to designate a <u>Special Representative</u> to proceed to the Middle East to establish and maintain contacts with the States concerned in order to promote agreement and assist efforts to achieve a peaceful and accepted settlement in accordance with the provisions and principles in this resolution;

4. *Requests* the Secretary-General to report to the Security Council on the progress of the efforts of the Special Representative as soon as possible.

Adopted unanimously at the 1382nd meeting.

Appendix 4

Beirut Declaration on Saudi Peace Initiative
March 28, 2002

Following is an official translation of the full text of a Saudi-inspired peace plan adopted by an Arab summit in Beirut on Thursday:

The Arab Peace Initiative

The Council of Arab States at the Summit Level at its 14th Ordinary Session, reaffirming the resolution taken in June 1996 at the Cairo Extra-Ordinary Arab Summit that a just and comprehensive peace in the Middle East is the strategic option of the Arab countries, to be achieved in accordance with international legality, and which would require a comparable commitment on the part of the Israeli government.

Having listened to the statement made by his royal highness Prince Abdullah bin Abdul Aziz, crown prince of the Kingdom of Saudi Arabia, in which his highness presented his initiative calling for full Israeli withdrawal from all the Arab territories occupied since June 1967, in implementation of Security Council Resolutions 242 and 338, reaffirmed by the Madrid Conference of 1991 and the land-for-peace principle, and Israel's acceptance of an independent Palestinian state with East Jerusalem as its capital, in return for the establishment of normal relations in the context of a comprehensive peace with Israel.

Emanating from the conviction of the Arab countries that a military solution to the conflict will not achieve peace or provide security for the parties, the council:

1.   Requests Israel to reconsider its policies and declare that a just peace is its strategic option as well.

2.   Further calls upon Israel to affirm:

644